D1546309

Olaf Stapledon

Utopianism and Communitarianism

Lyman Tower Sargent and Gregory Claeys
Series Editors

W. Olaf Stapledon.

OLAF STAPLEDON

Speaking for the Future

ROBERT CROSSLEY

With a Foreword by BRIAN W. ALDISS

Syracuse University Press

First Edition 1994
94 95 96 97 98 99   6 5 4 3 2 1

This book has been supported by a grant from the National Endowment for the Humanities, an independent federal agency.

Frontispiece: Portrait of Olaf Stapledon, by Howard Coster, 1938. *Courtesy National Portrait Gallery, London.*

The paper used in this publication meets the minimum requirements of American National Standard for Information Sciences—Permanence of Paper for Printed Library Materials, ANSI Z39.48-1984. ∞™

Designed by Victoria M. Lane

Library of Congress Cataloging-in-Publication Data
Crossley, Robert.
    Olaf Stapledon : speaking for the future / Robert Crossley.
        p.   cm. — (Utopianism and communitarianism)
    Includes bibliographical references and index.
    ISBN 0-8156-0281-2
    1. Stapledon, Olaf, 1886–1950.   2. Authors, English—20th century—
Biography.   3. Science fiction—Authorship.   I. Title.
II. Series.
PR6037.T18Z6   1994
823'.912—dc20
[B]   93-38221

MANUFACTURED IN THE UNITED STATES OF AMERICA

To Monica McAlpine

ROBERT CROSSLEY is a Professor of English, University of Massachusetts—Boston. He is the author of *H. G. Wells* (1985) and *Talking Across the World: The Love Letters of Olaf Stapledon and Agnes Miller, 1913–1919* (1987).

CONTENTS

Contents

ILLUSTRATIONS

FOREWORD

Brian W. Aldiss

THE HISTORY OF MANKIND'S COMPLAINTS against its own shortcomings is a long one. Complaint is perhaps not the worst of occupations, and is made more enjoyable when gods or a god can be blamed for various perceived shortcomings.

The high-minded subject of this biography spent a lifetime railing against humanity's shortcomings, in which he surely included his own. Though happily married, as happiness goes, Olaf Stapledon suffered from an existential loneliness. His books echo with loneliness: it occupies the vast spaces between galaxies. This is the isolation experienced by intellectuals; Stapledon's contemporary, Bertrand Russell, forever complained of it, while surrounded by friends, colleagues, and lovers.

Stapledon's greatest creation, the Star Maker, that compassionless molder of cosmos after cosmos, becomes impatient with our cosmos and is about to relegate it with all its imperfections to a back shelf in a search for something better. Many of Stapledon's novels—*Sirius* is an instance—represent what the poet Theodore Roethke calls "the long journey out of the self." That Stapledon's scientific knowledge is allied with this spiritual impulse gives his fiction its intense visionary distance.

Robert Crossley brings out well Stapledon's sense of division within himself. Even the Star Maker, emblem of his philosophical cogitations, is given, like Shiva, a dual nature, mild and terrible. "This book has two authors" is the opening sentence of *Last and First Men*. Stapledon's last book, published only a few months before his death in 1950, is entitled *A Man Divided*. In a posthumously published story, "The Peak and the Town," one of the characters speaks of "the double life" as "a marvellous duplicity." That duality went unhealed.

This curious but far from unique condition was with Stapledon all his life. We are already indebted to Crossley for *Talking Across the World*, his edition of Stapledon's love letters to Agnes Miller, the woman he married. Even in his first letter, dated 30 March 1913, Stapledon speaks of accepting something outwardly but inwardly doing quite the opposite.

Serving as an ambulance driver in the First World War, Stapledon was forced to observe at first hand the divided nature of his fellows: remorseless in enmity, yet at other times compassionate to friend and foe alike.

> O wearisome condition of humanity!
> Born under one law, to another bound;
> Vainly begot, and yet forbidden vanity;
> Created sick, commanded to be sound

Thus Fulke Greville, in the early seventeenth century. Poets were often aware of the dichotomy of which he speaks. In the nineteenth century, Matthew Arnold, in his splendid poem "The Buried Life," talks of how

> There rises an unspeakable desire
> After the knowledge of our buried life

This element in Stapledon drove him to seek to expand the boundaries of human sensibility. A pleasant moral purpose is always in evidence. In this, as Crossley points out, he is practically unique among science-fiction writers. If, indeed, he is a science-fiction writer.

If he is not, then this must be said, that the attention paid to him, beyond the first reception of his books, has come from within the science fiction field, to use that term broadly. Stapledon does not earn an entry to himself in the *Oxford Companion to English Literature*. Crossley relates the touching scene when Stapledon visits the United States towards the end of his life. He becomes embarrassingly involved in the debacle of an international peace meeting in New York. Stapledon is then all that an intellectual should be—brave, outspoken, and going against the common grain. He is also ineffectual and derided: there are times when it is almost impossible to speak truth; this is one of them. Neither the American nor the British press seem to know who he is. A second-rate philosopher? Only the Hydra Club, a gathering of New York science fiction writers, recognizes him as the genius who wrote *Last and First Men*.

To their lasting credit, Frederik Pohl and other members offer Stapledon financial assistance. The youthful Theodore Sturgeon pays him tribute. It was a pleasant moment for Stapledon in an otherwise pretty disastrous occasion.

If it is difficult to see why full recognition of Stapledon's genius is still delayed, it is not hard to see why Stapledon has had few disciples, even among those who read and admire him. He defies emulation. His imagination is a Niagara. His discussion of "strange forms of time" encouraged me towards my *Galaxies Like Grains of Sand.* Arthur C. Clarke also evinces a Stapledonian influence. But we are English writers and naturally gravitate towards his laden idiolect.

Stapledon is very much an English writer, both thought and cadence showing the influence of Milton's *Paradise Lost,* just as C. S. Lewis owes much to him. It's the more impressive that the best scholarly work being done on him takes place on the western shores of the Atlantic.

Crossley brings out the engagement, courage, and—well, *niceness* of Stapledon's life. I confess it does not absorb me perennially, as do the lives of Mary Shelley and H. G. Wells—to both of whom Stapledon seems to owe something of a literary debt; perhaps his insistence on his buried life removes him from us. He is not hail-fellow-well-met. Of course, in our day his reticent version of a love life is absorbing. How period is his quarrel with monogamy, his agonizing over an extramarital affair, consummated at last with his wife Agnes's acquiescence! During the same decade, Aldous Huxley—something of a kindred spirit, one might imagine—took the ladies he fancied, or who fancied him, casually to his bed; and his wife remembered to send them a bunch of flowers afterwards if her husband forgot. But the Huxleys were a part of the Bloomsbury group, which Stapledon affected to despise.

Many of Stapledon's philosophical preoccupations remain live issues. On them I am scarcely qualified to comment. But I appreciate the force of Crossley's perception that Stapledon wrestled all his life with that basic contradiction: the emotional sterility of atheism set against the intellectual unacceptability of theism. So the Star Maker stands aloof from his own creation. So, too, Stapledon is forced to a belief in the future—that thin soup on which we must all sooner or later nourish ourselves.

Even those writers today, who believe that space can somehow be "conquered" in metal ships and fleets, make similar obeisances towards tomorrow. Few can achieve the mastery of prose which became Stapledon's, or that indwelling and compassionate spirit which Crossley describes so touchingly.

It's a great joy to have such a well-informed biography. It would prove the ticket, in an ideal world, for Olaf Stapledon's ascent to Olympus, to assemble there with the other gods in whom he did not believe.

ACKNOWLEDGMENTS

THE PERSON MOST INSTRUMENTAL to this project and who most deserved to see it come to fruition is no longer alive. Agnes Stapledon, whose preservation of her husband's papers made a circumstantial account of his life possible, gave me unrestricted access both to manuscripts she had donated to the University of Liverpool and to the great wealth of materials she retained in her possession. Although we had only corresponded, never met, when I first talked with her in a nursing home in 1982, she handed over the keys to her house and invited me to move in and read whatever I found. This was the single most generous offer I have received in my career as a scholar, and now many years later I remain moved by her extraordinary gesture of trust. Agnes Stapledon died in the Spring of 1984, three days before her ninetieth birthday.

Generosity is a Stapledon trait, and in the past ten years I have depended on the hospitality and assistance of the Stapledon family, who in naming me Olaf Stapledon's literary executor have granted me unconditional use of both public and private papers. I thank particularly Mary Stapledon Shenai, John David Stapledon, and Sarina Tetto Stapledon—daughter, son, and daughter-in-law of Olaf and Agnes Stapledon—who have fed me, housed me, introduced me to friends of the family, plied me with documents and memories and good talk. And trusted me. Although they have corrected errors of fact in my work, they have never tried to withhold information or alter my interpretation of events, even when they disagreed with my judgments. I count them as my friends. And there are others: Benjamin and Jason Shenai; Thomas Stapledon; Richard and Jean Stapledon; Susan Stapledon; Mariel Stapledon. I am indebted to all of them, but none can be blamed for anything that appears in these pages.

A great many people contributed to this reconstruction of Stapledon's life, but I must single out those who shared letters or agreed to extended interviews: Geoffrey Ashe, Gwynneth Alban-Davis, the late Wolfgang Brueck, Arthur C. Clarke, Margaret and Norman Cullen, George Eustance, the late Ruth Fletcher, Holda Fowler, Gwenda Hollander, Frank Kermode, Lady Naomi Mitchison, Fay Pomerance, Winifred Primrose, Mona Scholefield-Allen, and Geoffrey Wood. I offer special thanks to the person known in this book as "N." who, while unhappy about its publication, has been both dignified and candid in dealing with a biographer she had reason to detest.

I have benefited from exchanges of information with scholars working on related projects, including Peter Mills, Daphne Patai, Stephen R. L. Clark, and, especially, Patrick A. McCarthy who started all this in 1980 when he asked me if I knew Agnes Stapledon was alive (I didn't), gave me her address, and convinced me to write to her. As the project grew, my research was greatly aided by diskettes sent by Curtis C. Smith containing work-in-progress toward a secondary bibliography on Stapledon done with his collaborator Harvey Satty. Harvey himself gave unsparingly from his immense knowledge of my subject, and he commented on most chapters in draft, saving me from many an embarrassment. The complete manuscript was read by four people who offered practical, perceptive, often wonderful advice; anyone who reads this book to the end with some pleasure should give credit to Laurence Davies, John Huntington, Patrick McCarthy, and my dear friend and longtime mentor, Francis R. Hart.

I worked with the staffs of many institutions, and nearly all responded with patience and resourcefulness. My greatest thanks go to personnel at the Sydney Jones Library, University of Liverpool—and in particular to two now-retired curators of the Special Collections Department which houses the Stapledon Archive: M. R. Perkin and John Clegg. I am also grateful to Friends' House, London; Abbotsholme School; Manchester Grammar School; the British Library; the Bodleian Library; Balliol College Library; City Libraries of Liverpool; Liverpool University Archives; National Library of Scotland; University of Sussex Library; Abbot Hall Art Gallery, Kendal; University of Reading Library; Bristol University Library; King's College Archives, London; University College Library, University of London; National Portrait Gallery Archives, London; and the BBC Archives, Reading.

In the United States, I have enjoyed the support of curators and librarians at the Harry Ransom Humanities Research Center, University of Texas; Woodson Research Center, Rice University; Rare Book Room, University of Illinois Library; Special Collections, Boston University Library; Queens Library, New York; the Widener, Pusey, and Gutman Libraries at Harvard

University; and the Library of Congress. At the University of Massachusetts–Boston, Reference librarian Janet Stewart was a constant help, and the diligent work of Hildegarde von Laue and Sylvena Clarke at Interlibrary Loan Services kept books flowing steadily toward me for nearly ten years. In the final years of work I depended increasingly on the generosity and practical help of Joyce Carbone in the Core Curriculum Office.

With the legal tool of the Freedom of Information Act, I was able, after long delays, to examine some expurgated and often poorly copied documents from the U.S. Department of Justice, the Department of Immigration and Naturalization, and the F.B.I. By contrast, the staff at the National Archives in Washington was remarkably efficient and helpful in delivering and declassifying many government documents relevant to Stapledon's work as a peace activist.

Permission to quote from published and unpublished sources by the following individuals and institutions is gratefully acknowledged: Geoffrey Ashe; Quentin Bell; Arthur C. Clarke; Frank Kermode; Naomi Mitchison; Richard Rieu; John David Stapledon; Peters Fraser & Dunlop, Ltd.; Robert Hale, Ltd.; Trustees of the National Library of Scotland; Curator, Julian Huxley Papers; P.E.N. Archive, HRHRC, University of Texas; R.I.B. Library, Reed Book Services; Bell Archives, University of Reading; A. P. Watt, Ltd., on behalf of the Literary Executors of the Estate of H. G. Wells; Science Fiction Research Association; and Sussex University Library.

I began my research with several faculty development grants from the College of Arts and Sciences, University of Massachusetts–Boston, which helped me spend parts of summers in London and Liverpool between 1982 and 1986. The National Endowment for the Humanities granted a fellowship for 1989–1990 during which most of the book was drafted; without that crucial period of unbroken time my work would not yet be done. I am most grateful to my College and to the NEH for their indispensable aid.

The editors at Syracuse University Press, especially Cynthia Maude-Gembler, have been warmly supportive and diligent in shepherding a complex and sometimes messy manuscript through the processes of approval and production. Bettie McDavid Mason, my copy editor, scrutinized the manuscript as minutely and relentlessly as if the world's fate depended on it—an author's dream. To Charles Backus, who has twice appeared as if by magic at critical moments in my projects on Stapledon and godfathered them, I offer my gratitude for his willingness to gamble on Stapledon and me.

It would be presumptuous of me to thank Brian W. Aldiss for the foreword he has contributed to this biography; many imaginative writers have felt the impulse to acknowledge Stapledon's genius, and this foreword allows a glimpse of one great speculative artist taking the measure of another. I press my nose against the glass and admire the spectacle.

Finally I sing the praises of those closest to me. My son, Andrew McAlpine Crossley, has grown up with this project in one of the very few homes in which the name Olaf Stapledon *was* a household word. He has even had the temerity to speak of him, as I do, as "Olaf." As this book is finally about to leave my care, so too, alas, is Andy. I thank him for sharing his youth with Olaf and with me.

I dedicate this biography to my wife, Monica McAlpine, because she has been its most precious supporter and bravest critic, because she too believes in speaking for the future, and because I love her.

ROBERT CROSSLEY

Boston, Massachusetts
October 1993

OLAF STAPLEDON

BOILING THE BONES

Biography and the "Minor" Writer

*"I am keeping a Shakespeare book. I like this best: I could
be bounded in a nutshell, and count myself a king of infinite
space." 1896*

"I am the jackdaw, free, but uncertain." 1934

"I am just me." 1949

EARLY IN THE TASK of researching my subject, I decided to stop worrying about
intimations of a fool's errand in the often-repeated question, "Olaf who?" There
is, I told myself, an honorable tradition of biographical writing about "minor"
figures, from Johnson's *Life of Savage* through Holroyd's *Lytton Strachey*. A
Life of Stapledon might not find a place in such select company, but aspiration is a necessity for writing. All the same, there were times when the utter
lack of recognition of Stapledon's name tested my morale. Once, when I applied at the National Portrait Gallery in London for photographs, I was told to
do my homework. "No, we wouldn't have anything like that here," a curator
reproved me. "We keep only pictures of English people here." I protested (in
unimpressive American tones), "Olaf Stapledon *was* English, as English as you
are." He wouldn't hear of it. Not until I begged him to consult an old *Who's
Who* did he concede the point and go off to search the files. A few weeks later
fresh prints were struck from the fifty-year-old negatives.

The nine studio poses taken for Penguin books in 1938 by the celebrity
photographer Howard Coster show several sides of William Olaf Stapledon at

fifty-two, the high point of his literary career. There is a beatific Olaf, a big
notebook open on his knees and an earnest smile tentatively forming on his
lips. There is a spooky close-up, garishly lit, of a puffy-faced Olaf staring
unnervingly out of the darkness into the camera eye. A more urbane Olaf sits
at a rakish angle, eyebrow arched, right leg over left knee, fist planted on hip.
But the pose Penguin used for the dust jacket of *Philosophy and Living* epito-
mizes the public image of the author in his heyday. A large, sober face, scarcely
lined and topped by a wave of hair, is turned slightly away. Eyes, wide and
sad, are fixed on a distant point. This Olaf is cerebral, aloof, solitary,
otherworldly. Each of the poses tells some of the truth about Olaf Stapledon.
They sit now newly printed in their box at the National Portrait Gallery,
uncalled-for save by the insatiable biographer memorializing a vanished fame,
a buried life.[1]

The farce at the gallery's inquiry desk was not without its lesson for the
biographer. If a curator trained to know the public and artistic figures of his
country could be so sure that Olaf Stapledon was a Scandinavian, what would
the common reader make of his name? About the time I began asking questions about Stapledon and reading his papers, Brian Aldiss wrote a lead article in the *Times Literary Supplement* championing a revival of interest in
Stapledon's fiction. Regretting the uneventfulness of Stapledon's life, he did
not call for a biography.[2] The *TLS* essay, recognizing that Stapledon was again
being read, at least on the North American side of the Atlantic, was a momentous event. But there could be no illusion that the author's name was yet a
household word with any but a tiny minority of readers.

Aldiss had issued a challenge: *Was* Stapledon's life really so lacking in
incident? Two centuries ago Wordsworth founded modern autobiography by
insisting in *The Prelude* that "there's not a man / That lives who hath not had
his godlike hours." The forty-four years before 1930, when Stapledon had virtually no public life, provide ample demonstrations of Wordsworth's principle.
Consider one divine hour never forgotten. In Egypt in 1890 a young boy sat
in the darkness and saw through his father's telescope the stunning contours
of the mountains of the moon. For many years that sight "would flash myste-
riously upon him with bewildering and even devastating effect," he later wrote,
evoking a universe that would never fully be rationalized.[3] If he had not written a line about other worlds in his adult life, the epiphany on an Egyptian
rooftop would have remained one of those "spots of time" that define a life.

Like all lives, Olaf Stapledon's had plenty of drama in it; we have only
to recognize it as dramatic. But it was not a democratic impulse to compose a
Wordsworthian hymn to the plain man that prompted me to write this book.
Under the night skies of Egypt and of England's Wirral peninsula, in the lecture halls of Balliol College and on the streets of Liverpool, in a Red Cross

ambulance in the Great War, among dockers and artisans in adult education classes, and on windy seacliffs in North Wales, an extraordinary imagination took shape, no less impressive for its long gestation period. The fiction Stapledon published in the 1930s and 1940s first drew me to him because, in their mixture of cosmic scope, utopian passion, and skeptical inquiry, they seemed a repository of still-urgent questions about the relationships among spiritual longing, scientific knowledge, and political responsibility. His biography is an index of the modern era, and it glosses the excitement, anxieties, and uncertainties of an improbable era that began before Victoria was declared Empress of India and ended after the incineration of two Asian cities, the era that embraced the death of God, the birth of a new physics, the shrinking of the planet, and the threat of human extinction. Late in life Stapledon himself justified a biography in a set of unfinished letters to the future: "It is just possible that my very obscurity may fit me to speak more faithfully for my period than any of its great unique personalities."[4]

In 1930, without advance fanfare, Stapledon produced a history of the future he called *Last and First Men,* and the Shakespearean scholar John Dover Wilson hailed its unknown author as the literary voice for the age of Einstein. In 1936, H. G. Wells sat him down in London to "settle the Whole Damn Silly Universe."[5] Bertrand Russell praised the austerity of his imagination, and Virginia Woolf envied his 1937 *Star Maker* as the kind of book she aimed at. Throughout the thirties reviewers regularly attached the word "masterpiece" to his strange, speculative, nearly plotless fictions, but by 1945 the fountain of critical acclaim had gone dry. A career launched in middle age was punctuated by short-lived vindications and poignant failures, and Stapledon came to lament the "texture of good luck and bad management" that had governed his literary life.[6] A literary biography focused on 1930–1950 is never at a loss for incident and anecdote, for thrilling success and the age-old fascination of watching Fortune impassively turn her wheel.

But what of the life as a whole, including the years before *Last and First Men?* Olaf Stapledon played a role, rarely at center stage and often as a kind of invisible man, at some of the formative events of the last hundred years. His earliest years were lived in the small English colony at Port Said, at the entrance to the Suez Canal. From a childhood at the crossroads of the British economic empire, he took away images of a multi-ethnic world and of imperialist arrogance he never forgot. As one of the first tutors in the Workers' Educational Association, he was a pioneer in the effort to democratize education. During the Great War he evolved a pacifism that led him to ambulance work for the Quakers and was later reconstituted in the disarmament movement of the thirties and antiwar activism at the outset of the Cold War. His politics were always on the Left but always fell short of an unqualified endorsement of

Marxism. He aligned himself with the Russian revolution, the Republican side of the Spanish Civil War, the cultural initiatives of the Progressive League, demonstrations against government censorship, and, in the year of his death, the first phase of antiapartheid protest.

Yet, when he died in 1950, nearly everything he had written and everything he had stood for was fading from popular memory. A few people recalled vaguely *Last and First Men,* but the oblivion that settled over Stapledon's name was so pervasive that the effort to recover his life has meant confronting a great emptiness: memories dimmed in people who hadn't been asked about him in four decades; caches of letters long since chucked out; publishers' records removed and vanished; BBC recordings of his broadcasts disintegrated. Only his widow was confident that someone would sometime call for the primary materials that document his life and career. When I met Agnes Stapledon in 1982, ill and frail, I found that she had kept her husband's study intact, nearly as he left it thirty-two years earlier. She had been patiently waiting for me.

A biographer's pleasure is in tracing people, hunting documents, and discovering meaning in the relics and recollections that time and chance preserve, all the while trying to penetrate the evasions of those who actively dislike biography. Stapledon himself designed one of his best novels as a sham biography and poked fun at the anxious figure of the researcher: in the 1935 *Odd John,* the biographer is repeatedly nicknamed by his subject "Fido." But even Boswell had to put up with that innuendo, and the biographer as dogsbody is at least a little less unflattering than the image proffered by a friend of Stapledon's whom I approached some years ago for reminiscences. "Poor dear Olaf with all the vultures descending, however kindly, on his corpse," Naomi Mitchison wrote to me in what I took to be a rebuke (however kindly) to biographical curiosity.

Some people whom I descended upon were eager to pass on gossip treasured up for decades; others were emphatically loath to stir up the past. "I am not just archaeological evidence," one person who wishes not to be named in this book quietly scolded me. "Archaeological evidence doesn't have feelings." Another friend took care of that problem a long time ago. The novelist Leo Myers asked Stapledon in 1943 to burn all his letters and discourage the ghouls. "When one sees what is done now-a-days in the way of boiling up the bones of the second-rate dead, *no one* can feel safe," Myers worried. I can quote this grisly indictment of biographers only because Stapledon could not bring himself to carry out the burning. But Myers, shortly before he committed suicide, destroyed all but four of Stapledon's hundreds of letters to him. Unable to outwit his own biographer, Myers got his revenge against somebody else's.[7]

The brutal phrase "second-rate dead" questions the need for books like this one. As writer, educator, philosopher, and activist, Stapledon, while he was alive, remained just barely within the peripheral vision of the larger public. Preferring Liverpool to London, he sacrificed celebrity, and he always found it congenial to slip back into the comfortable obscurity of the North whenever he felt the pressure of too much attention. Given that two-thirds of his life was an excruciatingly protracted apprenticeship to a brief period of small fame, skepticism is inevitable: Why bother to boil up this particular set of bones?

A long-postponed or erratic career is a familiar feature in the lives of literary women, and readers have come to expect that their biographies will tell a story in which accomplishment is firmly embedded in difficulty and distraction, in the small pleasures and disabling frustrations of ordinary living. The works of "minor" literary figures like Charlotte Perkins Gilman or Zora Neale Hurston or Katharine Burdekin are celebrated, appropriately, as triumphs of the persistent assertion of talent in the face of adverse circumstances. Stapledon's struggle to establish himself as a writer, lacking such compensatory models, felt to him like, and may look like, failure.

Although he might have taken comfort in Milton's confession of procrastination over *Paradise Lost* ("long choosing and beginning late"), nearly every other male modernist artist—Eliot, Stravinsky, Ernst, Lawrence, Prokofiev, Hemingway, Eisenstein, Moore—made an impact in early manhood. By the time they were twenty-seven, Eliot had published *Prufrock,* Stravinsky had composed *The Firebird,* Lawrence had finished *Sons and Lovers,* and Eisenstein had shot *Potemkin.* At the same age, just before the First World War, Stapledon had yet to define a vocation as he worked doggedly over shipping ledgers in his father's office and wrote limping, old-fashioned verses. When he finally emerged seventeen years later with *Last and First Men,* he projected a fantastic version of his late-blooming, preternaturally youthful self in the figure of an ageless prophet in the far future. "Not till he was forty, and still physically in earliest prime," he wrote of the Divine Boy of Patagonia, "did he gather his strength and deliver himself of his mature gospel."[8]

Once his audacious visions began appearing, some readers spoke of him in the same breath with Swift and Milton, Bosch and Michelangelo and Beethoven. They discovered a Stapledon who inverted Gibbon by telling of the rises and falls of humanity over the next two billion years in *Last and First Men;* who led a spiritual pilgrimage for the modern agnostic, modeled after Dante's *Divine Comedy,* in *Star Maker;* who resuscitated Utopia in *Odd John* with an unlikely collection of children, physical freaks, and outcasts; who interrogated scientific ethics and the definition of humanity in a sequel to Mary Shelley's *Frankenstein,* the "fantasy of love and discord" he called *Sirius;* who turned the Cassandra of Attic legend into a symbol of the nuclear age in *The Flames;* and who wrote an idiosyncratic version of *Pilgrim's Progress* in the delicate allegorical memoir "The Peak and the Town."

Although Stapledon's innovations were always responsive to the inherited literary tradition, the sheer, dumbfoundingly original quality of his books prompted readers to a *je ne sais quoi* as often as it evoked a comparison. Journalists likened him to H. G. Wells, but the shrewdest critics recognized that the similarities were only superficial. Stapledon was never enough in the mainstream to command sustained attention and so distant from the coterie of authorized modernists that he got only sporadic, abbreviated publicity. Opining that *Sirius* was "almost a great book," Arthur Koestler may have captured exactly the sense of conditional fame that hung over Stapledon during his lifetime and curtailed his reputation after his death.[9]

When Wells wrote his autobiography, he called himself a "sample brain." Stapledon's intelligence was too offbeat and his place in the cultural pantheon too insecure for him to make such a claim, but the passage of nearly fifty years since his death lets us see that what might have appeared most peculiar in his life, as in his fiction, was in actuality symptomatic of the times—his and, still to a large degree, ours. Those who read his fiction may feel that he speaks most powerfully in the chastising voice of a prophet who worried about an increasingly Americanized planet and who foresaw the tyranny of specialization in the "Great Brains" of *Last and First Men,* the horrors of a vulgarized mass media in *Star Maker,* the warehousing of the poor and the unemployed in *Darkness and the Light,* and the madness of the atomic age in *The Flames.*

Distance, of course, can produce its own distortions. The detached perspective is limited by the angle of vision, a point brought home to me by one of Stapledon's nephews who, when I asked for his clearest memories of my subject, told me that Uncle Olaf had the ugliest feet he had ever seen. He saw Stapledon with the eyes of a five-year-old sitting on a grassy lawn and looking straight up at the horny calluses on the soles of his barefooted, almost elderly, mountain-climbing uncle, whose legs were cocked up over a garden chair.[10] My kind of detachment may produce images just as narrow in range and focus, may end up evoking a Stapledon who is more a character than a person.

Stapledon's friend Iris Origo, author of several biographies of Renaissance Italians, knew that life writing and truth telling were not easy to reconcile: "Every life is at once so complex and so simple, so perplexing and so clear, so superficial and so profound, that any attempt to present it as a unified, consistent whole, to enclose it within a rigid frame, inevitably tempts one to cheat or to falsify."[11] No biographer can be inoculated against such temptations, can always know when he has fallen into the trap of inventing rather than recovering a life. If it is dangerous, however, to seek a skeleton key that will unlock a whole personality or a vanishing cream that erases blemishes, there is another potential failure of life-writing. A biography without pattern or insight is mere chronology and muddle. There are themes and plots, foreshadowings

1. "I Am the Jackdaw": caricaturing H. G. Wells.
Courtesy H. G. Wells Papers, University of Illinois.

and recapitulations, recurrent images and concealed ironies and some red herrings in lives as in novels. Stapledon himself habitually referred to turning points in his life as new "chapters." Lives are constructed as well as lived. Looking for the patterns in Olaf Stapledon's life and work, I have taken a few hints from the author himself.

In his earliest recorded literary response, in a childhood commonplace book assembled when he was ten years old, young Olaf identified himself with Hamlet—the brilliant, isolated, contemplative, perpetual youth. "I could be bounded in a nutshell, and count myself a king of infinite space." The boy eagerly asserted a defiant spiritual freedom, in spite of all constraints, that the adult Stapledon never repudiated or outgrew. In youth and age, he had more than a touch of Hamlet, including a large measure of self-doubt, the talent (and the curse) of an analytic temperament, and something of the tragedy of unfulfilled promise.[12] Olaf Stapledon knew the melancholy and gaiety, ambition and modesty, skepticism and saintliness, brash impulse and cautious self-scrutiny, loyalty to tradition and hostility to empty convention that coexist precariously in Shakespeare's philosophical idealist.

In his maturity Stapledon tried out another self-image. He humbled himself in mock-idolatry before the encyclopedic and dogmatic mind of H. G. Wells, a generation older than himself. In a splendid cartoon he depicted Wells on the road to Utopia but sketched himself as an observant bird perched atop an ideological prison. Inside were the representatives of "Homo Proletariensis" looking anxiously across the road at a cage full of prisoners labeled "Homo Religiosus." Setting himself apart from both saints and revolutionaries, Stapledon adopted the pose of the skeptic. He glossed his self-image: "I am the jackdaw, free, but uncertain."[13] Neither melodious nor pretty, the jackdaw is a dark scavenger, fit emblem of a writer less remarkable for original ideas or fluid style than for quirky independence, sharp eyes, satirical laughter, and a knack for rummaging the stray anxieties and absurdities of his age.

The jackdaw Stapledon situated himself, typically, on the margin, and, just as typically, he displayed a wry humor at his self-imposed marginalization. "Free, but uncertain" may be a more telling self-advertisement than the phrase chosen by Leslie Fiedler, who picked up the title of Stapledon's last novel and pronounced him "a man divided."[14]. There is enough truth to that designation to make it a plausible point of departure for understanding Stapledon. But it also flattens a life into a thesis, reduces multiplicity to mere self-contradiction. A thesis that serves the literary critic well enough may be much less useful for the biographer. When I first interviewed the author's son, he was uncomfortable with some of the labels and boxes, the pigeonholing and institutionalizing my questions seemed to require. "To me he was just a father," John Stapledon reminded me. The son's protest, I realized later, echoed the father's.

On 29 March 1949 my only biographical predecessor, Sam Moskowitz, saw Stapledon on a stage at a peace rally in Newark, New Jersey, in his single brief moment of international notoriety. The Cold War was in progress. He had just crossed the Atlantic for the first time in his life and encountered the new American witch-hunt in its first virulent outbreak. Political thought was under siege and single vision tyrannized over all complex, multiple perspectives. Outsiders were suspect. "Free, but uncertain" was a paradox the American stomach could not digest.

On that March night Moskowitz may have been the only person in the Mosque Theater who had read any of Stapledon's fiction, the only one who hadn't come to hear political oratory but to see a legend. The name of Olaf Stapledon had passed by word of mouth through a small group of American science fiction readers who had discovered his out-of-print fantasies and fables of the 1930s. Now he was sixty-three, gray-haired but still plump-cheeked as an adolescent. A newsman's camera that night captured the impression of youth, and the next day's papers showed a figure who looked no older than the man Howard Coster had photographed eleven years earlier. When he stood up awkwardly on the stage in Newark and attempted to calm the storm over his supposed political loyalties, he spoke wearily, with the ghost of a smile, and pronounced his concise anti-autobiography: "I am not a Communist. I am not a Christian. I am just me."[15]

It is this Olaf Stapledon, a legendary name to a few, an enigma to most, just a plain man by his own reckoning, who arrives at La Guardia Field in 1949, the year before his death, in chapter 1.

I

LAST THINGS FIRST

La Guardia Field, 24 March 1949

AFTER A NINETEEN-HOUR FLIGHT through the night and into the day, pausing to refuel in Shannon and Gander as the clock drifted backwards, the 7 P.M. Pan American *Bald Eagle* out of London taxied to La Guardia Field's terminal on an unseasonably warm Thursday morning. The passengers prepared for the rituals of immigration and customs, but one of them was due for more than routine interrogation. He had been interviewed repeatedly at the American embassy in London, uncertain whether he would be allowed to enter the United States. His fate had preoccupied the English press. On 18 March the American ambassador advised the secretary of state that W. Olaf Stapledon was a "type of woolly and confused intellectual who makes a very docile fellow traveller," but nevertheless authorized a visa, to be collected in Liverpool on the twenty-first, that would let him attend an international peace conference in New York.[1] The next day the visa was abruptly withdrawn but then, within twenty-four hours and without explanation, just as abruptly reissued. All day long on 23 March, as reporters scrambled after him, the journey remained in doubt.

The "fellow traveller" who arrived at La Guardia on 24 March ended up traveling by himself. On the eighteenth the other members of the British peace delegation, all better known than Stapledon, had also been approved for entry to New York and then had the decision reversed on the twenty-second by Lewis Douglas, U.S. ambassador to the Court of St. James. But visas were never reissued for the physicist J. D. Bernal, the actress Patricia Burke, the novelist Louis Golding, and the historian of science J. G. Crowther. Each of them, when summoned to the embassy to surrender the visas, was told that the reason was confidential.[2] In fact, the decision was made by Secretary of State Dean

2. Arriving at La Guardia Airport, 1949.
Courtesy Queens Library, New York: Herald Tribune *morgue.*

Acheson with the written approval of Harry Truman. Similar last-minute recalls of visas occurred in other countries. "From a propaganda point of view,"
Acheson secretly advised the President to approve visas only for official gov-
ernmental delegates from Communist countries. By isolating the Soviets and
Eastern Europeans, the State Department could promote the impression that

the Cultural and Scientific Congress for World Peace, being hosted by the
American Council for the Arts, Sciences and Professions, was a Communist-
front meeting. Private individuals who applied for visas were to be refused,
unless an individual's attendance was in the interest of U.S. policy. Acheson
anticipated no exceptions. He did not want to risk the spectacle of a credible
noncommunist Western European attacking the United States government as
an obstacle to peace.[3]

But an exception finally was made in England. A little-known lecturer and
writer from the suburbs of Liverpool survived the purge. On Wednesday, 23
March, he telephoned his wife in the North of England to say that he had his
visa again and a plane seat booked for that night, but he had been warned that
he still might be turned back when he landed in New York. At the London
airport he was seen off by three of the companions who were to have gone
with him. Then, swathed in a heavy topcoat and looking vulnerable, almost
infantile beneath a wide-brimmed hat, Olaf Stapledon smiled hesitantly and
boarded the airliner alone.

In New York neither Stapledon's name nor face was familiar, but a host
of photographers at La Guardia saw to it that his earnest profile appeared the
next day under agitated headlines on the front pages of American newspapers.
His picture was upstaged by photographs of the star of the conference, the owl-
ish and unsmiling Dmitri Shostakovich, and of scores of anti-Stalin demon-
strators, heckling the delegates and calling for the release of the Hungarian
cardinal Josef Mindszenty. The open and benign face identified by the *New
York Times* as belonging to "William Olaf Stapledon, the British philosopher
and psychologist" seemed out of place. The *Times* description was at least
roughly accurate, if somewhat unhelpful. Other newspapers misidentified him
altogether as a natural scientist, a professor, and a Londoner.

American journalists didn't know Stapledon, didn't know, for instance,
that nobody called him "William." They simply repeated the formal name
printed on the passport and the ill-fitting description of him in press releases
prepared by the conference organizers. Sometimes they inferred what wasn't
there at all. The passenger was British, certainly, and a philosopher of sorts.
More active as a teacher of philosophy than as a researcher, he had no academic appointment and no graduate student disciples to spread his reputation.
Since 1911 he had tutored philosophy to railwaymen, dockworkers, housewives, and artisans under the auspices of the Workers' Educational Association. He had published both popular and scholarly philosophical books, starting
with *A Modern Theory of Ethics* in 1929. His seldom-noticed articles had been
appearing for over twenty years in journals, but most professional philosophers
in the United States drew a blank at his name. Psychologist? His Ph.D. came
from the days when psychology was taught out of philosophy departments,

but he didn't work in a lab and had no consulting office. Far fewer psychologists than philosophers knew his work. For years friends had been urging him to move from Liverpool to London, where he would be more visible and better connected, but stubbornly he clung to his roots on Merseyside.

News reports during his eleven days in the U.S. rarely identified him as a novelist, although some young science-fiction collectors realized with amazement that, of all people, Olaf Stapledon (*they* knew the "William" didn't really count) was the sole Western European attending a controversial meeting in Manhattan. They knew little of his politics or of his commitment to peacemaking. They admired an incomparable writer of speculative and utopian fiction, only a little of which had seen print in the United States. Since the late 1920s, Stapledon had been writing the most breathtakingly original scientific and philosophical romances of the century. That was the achievement he preferred to emphasize. "I am the author of works of fantastic fiction, meant to be symbolical of contemporary human problems, and of sundry books bordering on philosophy." In 1936, Alfred Kazin had heaped praise on one of those books, *Odd John,* and compared its title character with Prometheus and Coriolanus as a tragic misfit.[4] But that was the last of Stapledon's fictions to be published in the U.S. For most Americans on 24 March 1949, the name of Stapledon was one they had heard for the first time just a few days before, and the name would fade again in another week when the newspapers were bundled up for rubbish.

Olaf Stapledon was almost sixty-three when he first came to North America. A few years earlier he had written a long story called "Old Man in New World." In a sense, that is what he was, even though he was still trim and agile, with a swimmer's build and a rock-climber's hard calves and horny feet. He had a full head of once-blond, now steel-colored hair, a schoolboy's smooth, ruddy, puffed-out cheeks, a disarming smile, and a swinging gait. From most angles he looked younger than his years, except when a camera flash-froze the wrinkled, heavily-tendoned neck that told his real age. Neither he nor those who knew him well guessed he would be dead the next year, but his arteries were steadily hardening and he had begun to admit to feeling older than he looked.

Today he was just wobbly from the transatlantic journey, and anxious to get to his hotel. His first view of the United States was, however, not the fancy suite that had been reserved for him at the Waldorf-Astoria but the inside of a small, bare room at the airport where Joseph McHugh, an inspector from the Immigration and Naturalization Service, sat in front of a typewriter. The "Alien," according to Justice Department records, stood with his right hand raised and swore under penalty of perjury and imprisonment to be truthful. Then for over two hours the philosopher-psychologist-writer-alien-peacemaker

sat at a table and calmly recited his answers to Officer McHugh's questions
while the typewriter keys clicked.[5]

The next morning English newspapers extended the two hours in the
immigration office to three or even four, described it as a grilling, and imagined he had been "dictating the story of his life."[6] The truncated autobiography produced under the circumstances was as laconic and unilluminating
as might be expected from the prosaic, sometimes ludicrous questions put
to Stapledon.

He was born on 10 May 1886, in Wallasey, in the English county of
Cheshire. He admitted to using a name other than his "full and correct name"
of William Olaf Stapledon: "I am known as Olaf Stapledon for literary purposes." Unsure where his father, William Clibbett Stapledon, had been born,
he thought the event might have occurred "on the high seas." Of his mother,
Emmeline Miller Stapledon, he could only shrug, "I have no idea where she
was born." Asked why he was in New York, he said that Harlow Shapley, the
Harvard astronomer, had invited him to address a World Peace Conference and
to lecture at other locations. Further questioning determined that he had not
been to the United States before, expected to stay ten days, had eighty dollars
in his pocket, and owned a return ticket. The Alien's political allegiances were
of special interest:

Q. By whom was your passage paid?
A. By the Conference. That is it was sent to me from the Conference.
Q. Of what societies, associations, clubs or organizations are you now or have
you ever been a member?
A. The Mind Association; The Authors' Club, London; The University Club,
Liverpool; Sandon Studios Society, Liverpool; The Aristotelians Association;
The Royal Institute of Philosophy; The Society for Psychical Research; The
United Nations Association; The Federal Union; The Crusade for World
Government; The Fabian Society; The Dasca Club, Liverpool; I belong to
some others of the same kind that I cannot now remember.
Q. Are you a member of any political organization?
A. I am a member of "Common Wealth" a very small political party in
England but I am not active in it and being [sic] a member of the Fabian
Society which is affiliated with the Labor Party. I am also a member of the
British Soviet Society, a society for friendly relations.

And then began the cycle of questions permanently identified with the
American liturgy of inquisition in the Cold War era.

Q. Are you or have you ever been a member of the Communist Party?
A. No.

Q. Are you now or have you ever been an anarchist?
A. No.
Q. Are you now or have you ever been a person who advises, advocates, or teaches, or are you now or have you ever been a member of or affiliated with any organization, society, association or group which advises, advocates or teaches opposition to all organized government?
A. No.

These were succeeded by even lengthier, more syntactically tortured multiple queries about his interests in vandalism, sabotage, assassination, and the overthrow of the American government, to which the Alien kept repeating a simple negative. Only once did he reply with a "yes," when he acknowledged giving money to the International Brigade during the Spanish Civil War. The examination ended with an inquiry into ideological convictions that elicited some prudent but revealing self-portraiture.

Q. Do you believe in the doctrine of Karl Marx and Lenin?
A. I think that Karl Marx made a lot of very sensible remarks and some very foolish ones. I am not a Marxist. I consider him a very important contributor to social thought but in many ways I think that he was profoundly mistaken.
Q. Do you believe in the form of government that now exists in the USSR?
A. I believe in the form of government that now exists in the Soviet Union *for the Soviet Union.*
Q. Do you advocate such form of government?
A. Not for anything but the Soviet Union.
Q. Are you a member of, affiliated with, or active in, or on behalf of, a political organization associated with or carrying out policies of any foreign government?
A. No.
Q. What is your field of writing?
A. Fiction and philosophy and psychology.
Q. What are your political connections?
A. I am a Socialist.

Abruptly the interview was over. Joseph McHugh had reached the end of his questionnaire; he filled up his fourth sheet of paper and gave the typewriter platen a roll. The Alien proofread the document, penned in a correction, neatly initialed each page "WOS," and signed a sworn declaration of its accuracy. After so much bureaucratic formality, the ending was anticlimactic and colloquially American. "Okay, you can come in."

Outside the little room, sweating in 75 degree heat, the press was waiting for Olaf Stapledon. Despite the ordeal of the flight and an apparently pointless biographical exercise, he was in good humor and curious to see the New World. He grinned in response to pleas for a comment and said diplomatically, "The interrogation was all very friendly, and my own feeling is that I was sorry to have been such a nuisance."[7] Over the succeeding days he tried out both whimsical and serious answers to the commonly asked question of why he had been allowed into the country. The next morning, at a press conference at the Waldorf, he joked about his unique status: "I suppose they let me come in because they think I'm harmless." Later he called the revocation of so many visas "fantastic" and "foolish," and he guessed that he had been admitted only because he "sometimes criticised Russia."[8]

Undoubtedly, both hypotheses were true. When he defended contemporary English and American literature against a vituperative attack by the secretary of the Soviet Writers' Union in Poland the previous summer, American diplomats in Poland summarized his speech in a secret memo to Secretary Acheson. An FBI report, prepared for J. Edgar Hoover in mid-March 1949, confirmed that Stapledon told Soviet delegates to the Polish conference that no ideology had a monopoly on the truth.[9] He had also roundly criticized U.S. foreign policy when he was in Poland, and the State Department must have realized that he was not a reliable mouthpiece for American policy. He may, nevertheless, have been judged harmless and ineffectual—a political nobody who might be of some use but who could do little damage. If Olaf Stapledon the philosopher had had the status of, say, Bertrand Russell he would probably not have been granted a visa—but Russell had already pleased the State Department by cabling a public denunciation of the conference as "Stalinist-inspired."[10]

Finally escaping the reporters at La Guardia, who would describe him in their dispatches as "slight," "birdlike," "wispy," and "elfin," Stapledon was greeted by Martha Dodd Stern, novelist and daughter of the former American ambassador to Germany. They collected his bag and got into a taxi for the Waldorf. There American and foreign delegates were assembling and there too, unknown to Stapledon, agents of the FBI were assigned to begin surveillance of the speeches, activities, and personal contacts of the delegates. On the ride into the city he fell into conversation with the cab driver. The day before, on the way to the London airport, his English taxi driver had groused, "Tell those Yanks to stop putting it over us and dragging us into war." Now his New York driver, not to be outdone for bluntness, boasted that the U.S.A. was "the greatest of all countries" and "ought to smash Russia at once and take charge of the world."[11] The peace delegate was taken aback and wondered if the whole country was in a war-fever. In a novel written fifteen years earlier, he had had a character say, "A nation, after all, is just a society for hating foreigners, a sort of super-hate club."[12] That caustic definition was about to get a fresh application.

When the taxi pulled up to the elegant twin towers on Park Avenue, Stapledon got his first view of the picket lines and police guards he had to negotiate throughout his stay. He heard members of the American Legion chanting: "Down with the reds! Down with the pinks! Down with the lefties! Down with the UN!" As he made his way into the Waldorf, Eastern European women in native costume dropped to their knees to recite the Hail Mary. A grim-faced man held a sign reading, "Shostakovich! Jump Thru the Window." It was the overture to what *Life* magazine would call the "comic opera" of the peace conference, but few people except the smuggest onlookers laughed.[13]

"How I hate all political work," Stapledon had confided a few years earlier to his friend, the Scottish novelist and social activist Naomi Mitchison.[14] For most of his life he had dutifully but uncomfortably carried out what he accepted as his political responsibilities, while eluding the spotlight. He craved literary celebrity and political anonymity. But his days of notoriety in the United States put him in the unaccustomed role of spokesman for an entire continent.

On 24 March that role was still largely ceremonial. He delivered quips to reporters, exchanged pleasantries over cocktails with his hosts, and sampled the style of American high society. That night he wrote to his wife Agnes about "the poor man" from Immigration who had cross-examined him and the "vast document" that had to be typed. In Olaf's version the interview with Officer McHugh became the story of a bureaucrat charmed by a mischievous philosopher into conspiratorial irreverence over the absurd paper-shuffling process of conducting a witch-hunt. "At first he was very formal, but soon I began to laugh at the whole business, and so did he, and finally we were bosom friends. All rather funny." As midnight approached on the end of his first day in America, he betrayed a lifelong penchant for political naïveté. He spread out the New York papers in front of him and predicted a triumph for the peace movement:

> The Conference is causing a terrific sensation here. 2000 people are coming to the dinner tomorrow, and 700 have been told there's no more room. The press gives it "banner headlines", and is violently hostile. The State Department has obviously made a fool of itself and ensured that the Conference shall be a huge success.[15]

The confidence wouldn't last. If Olaf Stapledon had another weakness, apart from wishful thinking, it was for debilitating second thoughts. Before the conference was over he was, characteristically, doubting that it had made any difference, uncertain whether in coming to his second world peace meeting in six months he had overreached his modest talent for practical politics.

Whatever the public outcome, the trip to New York had a place in the pattern of his life and his work. He always scorned the ivory tower and, though he loved solitude, whether writing a lecture or climbing the North Welsh hills or surveying the night sky with his telescope, he believed that the intellectual and the artist were obliged to come out of the study and down from the clouds into the world. When others urged him to a career in shipping or in academic philosophy, he chose instead to teach working people and air force officers and to write utopian fiction because he envisaged an educated democracy in which all men and women were citizens of the world. Despite a temperamental distaste for politics, Stapledon forced himself to make speeches, chair committees, and distribute leaflets anyway when he felt that human survival or human decency was at stake.

In literature as in politics, he combined moral outrage with a dogged optimism. Despite an often bleakly cosmic view of the smallness of human achievement, he had not grown misanthropic as H. G. Wells did in his old age. His earliest work of fiction killed off the human species eighteen times in a dazzling variety of plausible ways. He imagined the world destroyed by an atomic chain reaction, smashed by its own aging moon, frozen in an ice age, and scalded by the sun's explosive death throes, and always humanity displayed a remarkable resiliency in remaking itself and its habitat. Stapledon called the book *Last and First Men*. In New York, in the infancy of the Nuclear Age and the Cold War, he feared reality catching up with his imagined apocalypses. I am here, he would tell audiences during his tour of the East Coast, because I don't want to be the last man on earth.[16]

In *Last and First Men*, written in 1928 and 1929, Stapledon predicted accurately enough some of the features of American life he would observe for himself in 1949. A long satiric section of his history of the future was devoted to the Americanization of the planet over the next several centuries. The fanaticism, acquisitiveness, racism, prudery, and arrogance of "the tapeworms of the planet," as Stapledon's imagined Chinese call the Americans, are treated in *Last and First Men* with relentless scorn. Their belligerence, disproportionate consumption of the world's goods, and solipsistic belief in America as "the guardian of the world's morals" were sins that the novelist catalogued and that the peace delegate saw practiced with undiminished gusto.[17]

Yet Stapledon also came to New York as a tourist, and like every tourist, he gaped. With boyish pleasure he wrote to his wife on Waldorf-Astoria stationery, "Well, here I am. My address is as above, in fact in the world's most prodigious luxury hotel. The whole city is a prodigy, especially at night, with all the neon lights."[18] He marveled at the appointments in his suite and the shocking cost of coffee and a fruit salad in the hotel café. He had seen the city in all its splendor before—in his mind's eye—with its tawdriness concealed by distance. In the spectacular closing panorama of the 1937 *Star Maker*, his narrator orbits the earth at the conclusion of a visionary journey through time and space. Surveying from the stratosphere the varying landscapes and cities of the planet, he ends not, as one might expect or as H. G. Wells might have done, with London, but with the New World and the transoceanic travelers arriving there:

New York, dark against the afternoon sun, was a cluster of tall crystals, a Stonehenge of modern megaliths. Round these, like fishes nibbling at the feet of waders, the great liners crowded. Out at sea also I saw them, and the plunging freighters, forging through the sunset, port holes and decks aglow. Stokers sweated at furnaces, look-out men in crow's-nests shivered, dance music, issuing from opened doors, was drowned by the wind."[19]

Stapledon in Manhattan enacted the two most durable, and most deeply interwoven, themes of his life: the ordeal of politics and the thrill of strange visions. He didn't fit in the New World landscape, even though he had been able to visualize it long before. He was, more deeply and inevitably than the Justice Department could have known, an alien in America. He made this journey, alone and uncertain, to play a role, however quixotic, in the infant peace movement that became a vital counterforce in the terrible new world born in Hiroshima in 1945. Stapledon approached political activity as an uneasy outsider, registering powerfully those senses of discovery and anguish, of cultural estrangement and remoteness of viewpoint, that formed the distinctive ambience of books like *Odd John, Star Maker,* and *Sirius*. The view of New York as seen by a shivering look-out man in the crow's-nest is as good a dramatic image as any of the combination of detachment, excitement, and discomfort he brought to all his political as to his literary adventures.

The visit to the United States that began on 24 March 1949 was the last major public event of Stapledon's life. Its details will acquire more meaning later, after the first sixty-two years of his life have unfolded. For now, it is enough to say that how he behaved in New York was as much a matter of psychological inheritance as of literary disposition and political allegiance, for there is one last dimension to Olaf Stapledon's American venture, an autobiographical loop not evident to the inquisitive Immigration Service nor to most readers of his fiction.

Stapledon told Joseph McHugh that he didn't know where his parents were born, though he suspected the "high seas" for one of them. It was a reasonable guess. Many of his Victorian relations had started life at sea and remained on the sea or nearby for most of their lives. The scientific romancer's obstacle-ridden trip across the Atlantic in 1949 gave him a modern taste of the risky living of his world-circling, nineteenth-century seafaring ancestors. If traveling to America by air was only a pale shadow of the rougher and far longer experiences of the Captains Stapledon and Miller, his paternal and maternal grandfathers, on their ships of sail in the previous century, the loneliness of this 1949 voyage, and the burden of responsibility the traveler bore, existed in strange symmetry with a perilous transoceanic journey made by his mother, a sea captain's daughter, eighty-five years earlier. And in his earliest youth, Olaf Stapledon with his mother Emmeline had known what it meant to be a stranger in a strange land. The land was Egypt.

2

BONDAGE IN EGYPT

1886–1901

IN EQUATORIAL WATERS on the Indian Ocean, twelve days out from Bombay in February of 1864, Captain John Miller of Liverpool became a father again. The circumstances were harrowing, even for people inured to the rigors of life at sea. Like many wives of the masters of long-distance sailing ships, Maria Burgess Hayward Miller joined her husband on Far Eastern trading voyages that might last a year or more. She was experienced at conducting family life on the ocean and took the precaution of hiring a nurse to accompany her in her third pregnancy. But a calamity occurred. Some weeks into the voyage Nurse Brown unexpectedly died; after the sea burial Maria's only female companion on the ship was her twelve-year-old daughter, Emmeline, who tried to reassure her. "Don't be too troubled, Mama. I'll help you."

When Maria went into labor, her sole attendants were her husband and daughter. After delivering the baby, John Miller put him into the arms of young Emmeline to wash and dress. Between illness and stress the baby's mother lost her milk, and with no prospect of a wet-nurse until they made landfall the family resorted to invention and luck. Captain Miller found a teapot, scoured and boiled it, filled it with diluted rice water, and rigged up a cotton glove finger over the spout. With this makeshift suckling device, Emmeline nursed her infant brother Frank for almost two weeks as he became thinner day by day. "Any self-respecting twentieth-century baby would have died, but the Victorian baby, like its generation, made shift to live without properly organized assistance," wrote Emmeline's cousin, Edith Hope Scott, in an informal family history.[1]

But this is not just a story about the unsung heroisms of a Victorian baby, a plucky girl, and an unflappable old salt. There are loops and twists worthy of the plot of a Victorian three-decker novel. Twenty-two years later, in 1886, a grown-up Emmeline Miller, having married another sea captain's son, set out from Egypt for her lying-in. After a sea journey better timed than her mother's, Emmeline Miller Stapledon gave birth to her only child, Olaf, in a suburb of Liverpool. And then in the next generation, at the close of the First World War, Olaf became engaged to his Australian cousin, Agnes Miller, daughter of the same brother Frank whom young Emmeline had nursed all the way to Bombay. From Sydney, Agnes Miller sailed to Liverpool in the spring of 1919 for her wedding, stopping over in Bombay, where fifty-five years earlier her grandfather John Miller and her aunt Em, now about to be her mother-in-law, had registered the birth of her father. Thus family history wound itself into a complex symmetry in which births and weddings and transoceanic voyages were intricately knotted across time. Having kept her brother alive for a crucial fortnight in 1864, Emmeline Stapledon, the heroine of Edith Hope Scott's narrative of Victorian seafaring life, ensured her own line of descent.

While the Miller family drama was being played out off the coast of India, in Liverpool the end of the era of sail was growing inevitable because of a gifted engineer with a classical education. Alfred Holt was building the first three experimental ships—*Agamemnon, Achilles, Ajax*—of the Blue Funnel Line of the Ocean Steam Ship Company. In the mid-1860s Holt developed a highly efficient steam engine that would make the Far Eastern trade profitable for a new breed of coal-fired liners; the fleet he built in the last third of the century, all named for Homeric heroes, revolutionized British shipping.[2] It made Captain John Miller's barkentine obsolete, and by 1870 it caused another merchant-mariner, Captain William Stapledon of North Devon, to change jobs in response to the new commercial realities.

Since the fourteenth century North Devon shipbuilders had kept busy, supplying vessels for the siege of Calais, for the fleet that routed Spain's armada, and for the fishing trade with Newfoundland. By 1800, however, orders for the royal navy were flowing to the big dockyards at Plymouth in South Devon, and the smaller yards on the north coast at Barnstaple, Bideford, and Appledore were reduced to building fishing boats for the local trade.[3] But the economic decline of North Devon did not diminish the allure of the sea. In the late eighteenth century, the Devonshire Stapledons, remnant of a renowned ecclesiastical and political family in the Middle Ages, gave up working the family farm in Buckland Brewer to become sailors.

The Stapledons settled in picturesque Appledore, a collection of whitewashed fishermen's cottages on narrow, hilly, cobbled streets overlooking an estuary at the confluence of the rivers Taw and Torridge. William Stapledon, born in 1829 the son of master mariner James Stapledon of Bude Street, Appledore, went to sea at the age of sixteen. By the time he was twenty-three, he was master of the trading bark *John Patchett* and kept a journal of his first voyage from Glasgow to Australia and the East Indies—a journal studded with drawings, verses, edifying morals, and outbursts of sexual hunger and home-sickness that was later closely studied by his grandson. "A ship-master in those days," Olaf Stapledon wrote, "was not only a navigator, a magistrate, a house-keeper, a doctor, a priest to perform the last rites over the dead, but also a re-cluse with ample time for meditation. My young grandfather had to keep the peace between the quarreling members of his crew, to cope with a rebellious chief officer, to deal as best he could with diseases, with no aid but a medical book and a medicine chest."[4] William Stapledon's versatility also included a shrewd head for business.

From 1856 to the late 1860s, Captain Stapledon commanded sailing ships for the merchant houses of the North of England and made five voyages to the Orient. He married Elizabeth Clibbett, daughter of the principal shipbuilder in Appledore, and after the birth of his first two children, William Clibbett and Thomazena (known as Zena), was prosperous enough to plan a grand hillside house in Northam, just south of Appledore, overlooking the thousand-acre pas-turage called the Burrows, the Pebble Ridge beach, and the grim, flat slash of Lundy Island several miles out to sea. Elizabeth Stapledon never lived to in-habit the house called Lakenham (she died in 1867 after giving birth—at sea— to her third child), but her grandson Olaf, in a leap from the age of sail to the atomic age, used the views from the house in Northam to stage an apocalypse in his first work of prophetic fiction in 1930. The landscape that Kipling made famous in *Stalky and Co.* Olaf Stapledon devastated with a tidal wave in *Last and First Men,* after the world's first atomic test blew Lundy to pieces.[5]

Captain Stapledon was not yet forty when his wife died, and he was not resigned to being a widower. He asked Elizabeth's sister, Mary Clibbett, to marry him, but the Church of England considered vows between a man and his sister-in-law invalid, and the wedding took place in France. Anglican law designated the eight children born to William and Mary illegitimate. The Captain's fury at this church policy turned him into an agnostic—a habit of thought he passed down to his son Willie and his grandson Olaf.[6] By the time of his second marriage, Captain Stapledon knew that the future of seafaring was not going to lie in North Devon or with sail. In 1869, in a stroke of great enterprise, he went to the Mediterranean end of the newly finished Suez Ca-nal and set up a shipping agency to represent Alfred Holt; there he oversaw the refueling and repairing of Holt's Blue Funnels passing through the Canal, procured stevedores for loading and unloading cargoes, and looked after the general interests of the absentee owner.

When William and Mary Stapledon arrived at the frontier settlement of Port Said, leaving the three children of his first marriage in Appledore to be

3. Captain William Stapledon of North Devon and Port Said.
Courtesy John D. Stapledon.

educated, Mrs. Stapledon discovered that she and Madame de Lesseps, wife
of the Canal's engineer, were the only two European women in the town. But
she devoted herself to making her husband comfortable while he made the family fortune. Mary Stapledon focused her energies on the new family she was
raising in Egypt, and her stepchildren at Lakenham knew her as a chilly figure
who expected quiet submission whenever they saw her. For Willie, oldest of

the Captain's first set of children, his aunt-stepmother's insistence on her rights of approval and disapproval over his conduct proved exasperating, especially after he fell in love with the daughter of one of his father's sea-captain colleagues. She was Emmeline Miller.

Captains John Miller of Liverpool and William Stapledon of Appledore had met in various ports when both were engaged in transporting English troops to China in the period of exploitation that followed the Opium War of 1839–1842.[7] When he was working for Liverpool merchants, Captain Stapledon liked to bring his family to visit the Millers. Later the visits were reciprocated, and various Millers took the train from Liverpool for extended stays in North Devon. It was during one such visit to Lakenham, in October 1878, that the twenty-seven-year old Emmeline Miller dazzled Willie Stapledon, an impressionable nineteen. The gallant twelve-year-old shipboard nurse of 1864 had grown into a sophisticated, well-read, coolly handsome brunette who prided herself on independence of mind and on her elegant, tight-waisted dresses. That she was already engaged to a Liverpool man and that Willie was booked for Port Said to work at his father's shipping agency did not stop him from declaring himself. "I was only a wild boy lover, who wanted you as he might want the moon," he remembered, and Emmeline caught the mood: "I was drawn to you resistlessly though at first quite unconsciously from the first few weeks we were together."[8] She was conscious enough to travel to Liverpool and dissolve her engagement, even though Willie was about to leave England for four and a half years. But in love as in childbirth, a Victorian could be more resourceful than a modern. Willie courted Emmeline assiduously by letter until they were reunited and announced their engagement in 1883.

Emmeline was not easy to win—both on her own account and because Willie's stepmother tried to block the marriage. Early in 1883, Willie went from Port Said to Liverpool to ask Emmeline to marry him, without first stopping in North Devon to consult Mary Stapledon. She angrily complained of his rudeness and announced her opposition to the marriage on the grounds of disparity in age. Willie was dumbfounded. He thought it "absurd" of her to make a fuss over a mere matter of form (her official consent) and what was none of her business anyway (his fiancée's age). He tore up her letter. His married sister Zena sided with him, but his father felt he had "made a nice mess of it with Mamma."[9] Willie did not back down. He wrote sharply to "Mamma" that he had put in "over four years not too easy or agreeable work" in Egypt, giving up "everything I cared about most" for the sake of the family business, and had earned the right to marry as he pleased. Besides, he told his stepmother, he and Emmeline were old enough to know their own minds. "Do you think that I could suppose that anyone had a right to forbid us and spoil our whole lives?"[10] It was the most rebellious act of Willie's life.

Emmeline had her own doubts about marrying Willie, but parental permission wasn't the problem. Her mother urged her to accept, but Emmeline was torn between love and service. She had been reading extensively in the literature of social reform and had founded with her brother Ernest a Liverpool Ruskin Society for discussion of the ideas of Carlyle and Ruskin. Willie was uneasy about her zealous attachment to Ruskin's Guild of St. George and its injunctions to practice economy and simplicity in life, but under prodding agreed not to call her a "Ruskinite," though she had taught him the term.[11] According to Emmeline's convictions, married life must be unsullied by lucre and pledged to good works; but, she found herself attracted to a young man who embodied the very ethos of commerce that Ruskin said was to be scorned. As a "Companion" of his Guild, she had twice visited and dined with Ruskin at "Brantwood," his home in the Lake District, and she decided to consult "the Master" about her suitor with his quite unacceptable job in an outpost of the Empire.

In a pair of letters, Ruskin urged her to cling to the utopian vision "Carlyle and I have been all our lives trying to show people,—the folly—vanity—and sometimes even direct mischief of palliative and patchwork, when the entire soul and body of a thing is false and rotten." But to her surprise he told her just what young Englishwomen had been hearing for generations: that she should cheerfully bend her own will to her mother's wisdom. Her commitment to social reconstruction should be pursued (though how?) in the familiar context of woman's duty to home and family:

> All you can do is to keep patiently and steadily fixed in your attention on the roots and first causes of evil—till you can see your way to attack them: in the meantime of course pulling whom you can out of ditches or feeding whom you can who are hungry, but not in the least supposing *that* to be your appointed work. Women's work is to make their own households happy, and to keep everything in order round them—not in the least to be army-nurses or public almoners.

In a second letter, Ruskin told her that her spouse's occupation need not concern her and that marital domesticity would be a useful "trial" of the depths of her love of neighbor. "Howbeit," he added mournfully, "the only thing I am really sorry for you in—or for myself in fear of losing you—is the going out to Port Said (wherever that may be)."[12]

With the Master's approval, Emmeline agreed to be engaged. Willie deluged her with grateful letters and pledged devotion to her ideals. He filled his commonplace book with high-minded flourishes, resolving to "overcome all feeling whatever of shyness or fear, remembering I am a man and hers—her knight."[13] In October of 1884 he came back again from Egypt to marry

Emmeline at Wallasey, across the River Mersey from Liverpool, and to honeymoon in Ruskin country, in the heart of the Lake District. For Emmeline, if the arrival of a chivalric lover from the Orient seemed to herald a fairy-tale marriage, the departure for Port Said and a household in its small British enclave took off the bloom. Emmeline Stapledon could never, as Mary Stapledon did, submerge all her own tastes and interests to further her husband's profession, and practically from the moment she landed in Port Said she found the place dismal and comfortless and looked for escape hatches.

For his part, despite inclinations toward conventional domesticity (he brought Coventry Patmore's "Angel in the House" to read to her on their honeymoon), Willie struggled to respect Emmeline's individuality. On Christmas Eve of 1884 he outlined a regimen for learning how to talk to a spouse:

I am determined:
1. In all intercourse with her to say only what I feel in my soul to be true, and seek always to understand her full meaning, answering her in all calmness and love and so avoiding all excitement in talk.
2. To speak with her of all my concerns, keeping no secrets hidden from her, yet with all rightful reserve, and to have trust in her gentle guidance always.
3. Not to interfere in her department in any way except at her request, but then to give her all help.
4. To bear with her in all things and to forbear ever to blame her or find fault with her.
5. To show her all respect & honour always: both when alone and especially before others.
6. To "honour her with arduous life": to joyfully show myself "the servant of her rule"—thinking nothing too much trouble, or too great, or too small, that she bids me do.[14]

As a sample of self-conscious, middle-class, neo-Arthurian civility, the memorandum is both touching and ominous; all its patience and solicitude would be required.

For seventeen years the Stapledons had to weather tensions caused or aggravated by physical illness and emotional stress, by Willie's overwork at the shipping agency and Emmeline's longing for Liverpool society, and by an endless succession of packings and unpackings, farewells and reunions that stunted and warped their relationship. Shuttling back and forth between the Middle East and the North of England, sometimes together but more often separately, they endured a kind of "commuter marriage," when commuting meant several weeks' roundtrip journey by sea and rail, undertaken only once or twice a year. Emmeline movingly assessed the toll this arrangement took on their marriage:

Dear dear our life is rushed through in temporary snatches. There is no
stability about it, when we are together things are always going to be put
right during our next separation, during the separation the time is rushed along
to drag its weary feet till our next meeting & in two years we are where we
were before! And so the fruitless round goes on till we shall come to the end
of the reel & there is nothing more left to unwind![15]

Sixty years after Willie and Emmeline were married, their son Olaf marveled that his parents had not only negotiated the geographical constraints on
their life but somehow tolerated the cultural straitjacket that handicapped a
whole generation of bourgeois husbands and wives teetering on the brink of a
new century. Despite minimal education, rigid divisions into male and female
spheres of activity, sexual ignorance, and general "wrongheadedness," he wrote,
the marriages of his parents' circle and era were resilient: "Genuine personal
love, which is perhaps commoner than the cynics believe, is able to triumph
over a good deal of hostile convention, though not without suffering."[16]

The Victorian Stapledons suffered, in and out of Egypt, for many years.
Early in their marriage, quiet nights at Port Said were spent in evening dress
when, after a meal prepared by Egyptian servants, husband and wife retired
to read Shakespeare aloud together, with the aid of a primer. But the romance
of such intimate evenings without the stimulation of other people or of recre-
ations other than books soon wore off. Business might interrupt Willie at any
moment if an angry ship's master came complaining in the middle of the night
about the size of his fuel allotment, and Emmeline soon realized that she had
married a man consecrated to work. The young marriage began in an atmosphere of strain and disappointment and finally entailed a ten-year separation.
Long after she gave up living in Port Said, Emmeline retained a lively sense
of its unsatisfactoriness: "One's whole life is invaded & swallowed up by ships
& all their chances & mischances. The mind is never for an hour free from
them so there can be no tranquillity."[17]

A Frenchman in 1891 found Port Said full of transients, with no distinctive character of its own: "There is nothing here but a little European scum
jettisoned upon the edge of the desert, in which all the streets come so strangely
to an end."[18] Another visitor wrote, "There are no sights, no amusements, no
society. Everybody is saving his money for a summer somewhere else."[19]
Ruskin claimed not to know where Port Said was, but Kipling discovered "that
sand-bordered hell" in *The Light That Failed* (1890): "There is iniquity in many
parts of the world, and vice in all, but the concentrated essence of all the iniq-
uities and all the vices in all the continents finds itself at Port Said."[20] Whether
Emmeline saw much iniquity at first hand is doubtful, but she felt quarantined
in a tiny zone where activity was constrained and intellectual gratification
thwarted. If Willie knew much about Port Said vice, he was discreet about it.

With a population of 20,000 in 1885, Port Said was an artificial creation of European commerce. Shops were run by Italians, Jews, and Greeks—rarely by Arabs. Most of the native Egyptians, who were employed as coal haulers, lived near the fishing grounds of Lake Manzaleh at the western end of the town, well apart from the foreign quarter. Such social life as the Stapledons had was determinedly English, and in the latter 1880s the anglicization of Port Said accelerated with the building of a hospital, a Protestant church, a new European hotel, a sporting club, and even a British prison. When Emmeline became pregnant late in the summer of 1885, however, Port Said was still raw and unfinished, and her chief pastime was reading. For Emmeline that meant, above all, the writings of Ruskin and Carlyle.

During her pregnancy Emmeline read *The Early Kings of Norway*, a fantasia on the thirteenth-century *Heimskringla* of Snorri Sturluson, in which Carlyle drolly rehearses the bloody exploits of the first Norwegian monarchs, three of whom were named Olaf: Olaf Tryggveson, the first to accept Christian baptism, Olaf the Thickset (later Saint Olaf), and Olaf the Tranquil, elegant and refined and apparently therefore the dullest of the Olafs. The first two King Olafs, both sea captains who attempted commerce with England, resonated with the Stapledon family history—and Emmeline would have been specially drawn to the devout and self-sacrificing Saint Olaf. But it is Olaf the Tranquil, dismissed by Carlyle in two quick paragraphs as a "fantastic" creature, who sounds most like the Olaf Stapledon who came to be. Gentle in manner, more talented at art than at warfare, the third Olaf was a "slim-built, witty-talking, popular and pretty man, with uncommonly bright eyes, and hair like floss silk."[21] When their son was born a month prematurely on 10 May 1886, at the Miller house in Wallasey, Emmeline and Willie (who hurried in from Egypt just two days before she went into labor) named him William Olaf, but he was always called simply Olaf.[22] In deference to Willie's agnosticism, the baby was not baptized, but when he was eight years old Olaf got a letter from his father telling him, "If it had not been for Carlyle I don't expect we should ever have called you 'Olaf', so you must always regard him as a sort of god-father of yours."[23]

The name is uncommon in England. As far as Emmeline was concerned, it probably mattered less that it didn't sound English than that it was as far from suggesting Egypt as possible. Given her wide reading in Carlyle, she must have known, besides his history of Norway, his most famous account of a King Olaf, the opening lecture in *On Heroes, Hero-Worship and the Heroic in History*. There Carlyle finds in Saint Olaf a transitional figure between the old world of fable and the new world of science; the saint's legendary meeting with Thor—said to be the last sighting of one of the ancient gods—defines the spiritual and aesthetic losses suffered in the making of the modern world.

The name Emmeline gave her baby did not serve badly as a portent of the future author's concerns to marry literature and science, assert the interdependence of tradition and change, and map an authentic, nondoctrinal spirituality for a post-Christian era.

Most of all, however, the name Olaf is associated with the North, and throughout his life, in his art as in his thought, by psychological chemistry and habit, Olaf Stapledon was always more powerfully drawn to the lucid, crisp, chilly, and bleak contours of northern landscape and imagination than to the sunnier paganism and easeful pleasures of the Mediterranean or even to the metropolitan charms of the South of England. As an adult he liked to say that he always remained a child of Egypt.[24] But he lived like a Scandinavian.

Shortly after the birth Willie returned to Egypt, but Emmeline stayed behind until November, when she and her six-month-old baby sailed to rejoin him. Emmeline minded nearly everything about Port Said—its climate, its polluted harbor, the heavy smell of coal, the noisy ships refueling day and night, the lack of cultural institutions, the periodic outbreaks of cholera, and an ambience of muscular capitalism alien to her Ruskinian ideals. Although she could hear the Arabs chanting as they worked in teams of fifty loading coal onto ships at anchor, Emmeline knew few Egyptians other than household servants and the water carriers who hauled in supplies daily in the days before a freshwater canal was opened in 1895. In more congenial circumstances, she might have used Port Said as a laboratory for implementing her reformist principles. But when she once enlisted Willie's support for replacing the wretched housing of the Arabs employed by the agency, the idea was immediately rebuffed by his father.[25]

Until 1891, when severe depression drove Emmeline to leave Egypt with Olaf, the family managed to stay together most of the time, save for summers in Wales when mother and son fled the heat of the Canal zone. Olaf's earliest childhood memories were of the barren but hypnotic Egyptian landscape. He had a small hoard of images and narrative fragments from the first five years of his life, his "very ancient days when Port Said was the whole world and England was a fairy place where they said there were green fields": the thrilling sight of a black Sudanese soldier in a sentry box with "a splendid bayonet that shone in the sun"; the high ceilings of the Port Said house and its un-English balcony; flamingos drifting in elongated formation over Lake Manzaleh; the bars of scrap iron scaled with rust that he would dig out of the sand and carry, staggering, to the foundry for a penny.[26] Photos show a toddler with shoulder-length blond curls in a white suit and brass-buckled shoes, and in sailor's costume and sunhat sitting pensively in an Egyptian replica of an English garden. In one picture, a fat-cheeked, straight-backed boy is having tea with his mother and his pet terrier, Rip, on the balcony; in another,

4. Young Olaf with Rip in Egypt, ca. 1891.
Courtesy Mary S. Shenai.

naked and skinny as a salamander, he is leaping from a rowboat into the Canal.

Young Olaf loved to be taken to the docks and aboard the great variety of ships passing through the Canal, developing, he later said, "a romantic fascination" with ships and an addiction to drawing them. Watching the constant traffic of commercial vessels, most flying the colors of the British empire, and conscious of the English warship on permanent guard in the harbor, he got a child's-eye view of imperialism.[27] And in his Egyptian days he had his first, terrifying experience of philosophical doubt, what he called in a radio broadcast in the 1940s "my earliest encounter with 'the problem of appearance and reality' ":

> When I was a child in Egypt, my mother used to put me to bed, kiss me good night, and take away the candle. In the dark, a horrible idea sometimes seized me. Perhaps God had wiped out the whole world beyond my room, including my parents. True, there was still a crack of light under the door; but God might have painted a sham crack there to cheat me. Sometimes I grew so frightened that I screamed, till my mother came. But how could I be sure that it was my *real mother,* the very same one that had kissed me good night? Perhaps this was only an imitation mother, a phantom, that God had hurriedly made to stop my screaming.[28]

Although Willie had not gone to a university and had had only a modest systematic education before going out to Port Said to work for his father, he had an amateur's passion for the classics and for science. Alongside the volumes of Carlyle, Ruskin and Emerson, Bunyan, Elizabeth Barrett Browning, and George Macdonald that represented Emmeline's tastes, were Willie's set of Greek and Roman translations, a complete Shakespeare, and works by Darwin, Huxley, Lockyer, and Tyndall. He kept fastidious notebooks for copying out long extracts from his scientific reading, and in the early years of his marriage he set problems for Emmeline to solve—and she dutifully wrote out answers.

As his son became old enough to learn lessons, Willie took his scientific education in hand. "The formulae, the diagrams, the experiments! How I remember them!" Olaf later wrote. In the kitchen Willie illustrated suction by holding a plate of hot porridge upside down over the boy's head. On one occasion, his father threw a lump of sodium into water, and the molten sphere fizzed helter-skelter around the basin until it exploded and a hot drop hit Olaf in the eye—an accident that may have caused or accentuated a slight discrepancy in size between his eyes.[29]

Olaf's training in history and philosophy, two of the three disciplines central to his fictional masterpieces, belonged to his formal education at Oxford and Liverpool universities. But his love for natural science went back to his youngest days in Egypt and on holidays in North Wales, when his father would come visiting during the decade of separation in the 1890s. At Port Said, Willie set up a telescope on the iron balcony, and the clear, wide-horizoned desert sky gave his child a starstruck wonder at the "appalling contrast between the cosmos and our minute home-lives" that he never outgrew.[30] In middle age Olaf traced his knowledge of physics to a day in the Welsh mountains when Willie used the crisscrossing ripples in a lake to anticipate in a crude way the insights of wave mechanics. That dramatic illustration became for his son "the paradigm of all physical sciences, and at the same time an epitome of the mystery of life."[31]

Emmeline had a more conventional piety toward life's mysteries, and Olaf resented her efforts to repress his scientific curiosity. Once when Willie came to his wife's lodgings in Festiniog in North Wales for the Christmas holidays, he offered his son a first lesson in embryology:

> About fifty years ago, when I was a child, my father started a collection of birds' eggs for me. On one occasion a thrush's egg that he was blowing turned out to be partly hatched. Bits of a recognisable chick were forced into the saucer. I remember a tiny leg appearing and some disordered strands of blood vessels. This was for me a rather momentous experience, for I had been brought up to be kind to animals, and here was my father destroying what was obviously the beginning of a baby bird. I was torn between horror and curiosity. My father had done his best to fire me with a passion for knowledge; and so when he pointed out the various disintegrated organs, I was fascinated. In the middle of this little science lesson my mother appeared. She was thoroughly shocked. It was not right, she said, that a child should see such things. My father ought not to encourage me to pry into the sacred mysteries of life. In this matter her attitude was typical of the time, and my father's was rather in advance of it.[32]

The parents' struggle over lessons—and over whose views of appropriate knowledge would prevail—limned a larger competition over possession of their son that was intensified by geographical distance. When Willie wrote to his wife on their fourth wedding anniversary, he estimated that they had already spent about one of their four married years separated and prayed that they might "have less time apart in the next four years."[33] In fact, the proportion of time together got smaller. Emmeline's seasonal retreats to England with her son in 1886 and 1888 soon became year-round residence while Willie remained in bondage to his father's firm in Egypt. In June 1891, Emmeline and Olaf left for Liverpool aboard the Blue Funnel *Cyclops* for what would be an eleven-month parting and the first phase of a ten-year sundering of the family, relieved only by annual visits. Willie wrote of his sadness at losing his child: "It is not that he will be changed I think of so much, it is that I am missing all this happiest time in his little life—no, he does not understand how long the parting is for, and it is better so—but really there is only quite a small bit of the time gone yet—it is dreadful to think of the whole length of it."[34]

That summer when he wrote a sonnet for his wife's birthday, as he did every year, Willie emphasized in the sestet that, having Olaf with her, she had

both a heavy responsibility and a possible cure for the depression that had
prompted her departure:

> Bright Hope is with thee, rosy, golden-haired,
> And thy salvation, with sweet duty, rests
> In guiding his young soul, which being prepared
> By thee for valiant battle, victory wrests.
> Having this dear gift, traitrous cravens we
> Despond to stray in: let it our Star be.[35]

To Olaf, Willie began sending a weekly typed letter, telling him of doings at
the Canal and expressing his anxiety lest his son forget him. "I wonder will
you think of Father today," or "Think of Fa a bit sometimes and of the happy
times we had together here," he wrote plaintively.[36]

Those happy times resurfaced decades later in Stapledon's late-blooming
literary career. Although he lived in Port Said for only five years (excluding a
few visits in the mid-1890s and a four-month nostalgic return at the age of
twenty-six), the stream of letters from his father between 1891 and 1901 not
only kept his impressions vivid but mythologized those young years when all
three members of his little family were together. The boy's telescopic visions
"of a universe that teemed with suns and inhabited worlds" bore fruit four decades later in the great cosmic inquiries of the 1930s, *Last and First Men* and
Star Maker. The international assortment of characters in his 1935 utopia *Odd
John* is explicitly linked to Port Said, "the most cosmopolitan spot in all the
world."[37] But the novel closest to Olaf's Egyptian memories is an extraordinary fantasy, overtly based on genetic experiments performed in the early 1940s
by C. H. Waddington. *Sirius* is the story of a dog chemically and surgically
altered with a large brain of human dimensions. When Naomi Mitchison asked
him in 1944 why he had written such a book, at once bizarre and improbably
moving, he replied, "I was brought up with a rather intelligent fox-terrier in
Egypt, and this book profited by that quite a lot. In fact it now seems to me a
sort of distorted act of piety toward that former but never quite forgotten beloved."[38] The author's explanation did not tell the whole truth about *Sirius* and
the "beloved" that inspired it, but he traced the wellsprings of imagination all
the way back to a five-year-old's first visionary gleams.

His pet dog Rip, with whom he was frequently photographed in Egypt
and to whom he sent numerous childish notes enclosed in his own letters to
his father, was often named by the adult Stapledon when he talked about *Sirius*.
He told an audience in Manchester in 1947 that his novel had been inspired
by an early "vision," and he sketched that insight into "the aliveness of all
living things" in his partly autobiographical *Last Men in London* (1932):

His boon companion of early days had been a terrier, with whom he used surreptitiously to share his bread and butter, bite by bite. Of course he believed that this creature had a mind much more like his own mind than was actually the case; but also, by long experience of this animal, he learned to enter into imaginative sympathy with a mind that was not human. This canine friendship drove deep into his own mind and heart both a sense of the kinship of all living things and a sense of their differences. . . . In short, during this phase of his growth he was overwhelmed with what some would call a mystical apprehension of the inner being of all living things, and shocked by their insensitivity to one another, their essential harmfulness to one another.[39]

Set exclusively in Wales and England, *Sirius* nonetheless has the deepest Egyptian roots of all Stapledon's books. The young boy photographed with his terrier sitting upright at the table is father to the man who imagined a sheep dog raised as a human child in a Welsh family.

In 1891, Olaf's loneliness, a product of the two thousand miles between himself in Liverpool and Willie and Rip in Egypt, was heightened by the fact that on her return to England his mother became increasingly withdrawn. "I have been a poor unsatisfactory troublesome wife for you my poor Willie," Emmeline lamented in 1891, hoping her husband could understand how little control she had over periods of depression when "nothing was left but the blackness of darkness," when she felt "hounded by all the Furies through a waste howling wilderness forsaken by God & men."[40] Willie alternated between fear for her emotional stability ("You threaten unspeakable things," he wrote in alarm when she raised the specter of taking herself "off the scene altogether"[41]) and bitterness over her refusal to live with him:

With regard to what you say about my life here, you are right in the main but spoil it all by tirades against Port Said. Perhaps the people here are not men & women—perhaps they are no further developed than apes—perhaps they are contemptible—only your wonderful Liverpool society seems to an outsider not so infinitely better after all. You may perhaps have got to the ourangatang [*sic*] stage but that is about all. It is all very well to talk, but the difference between Liverpool high tea and Port Said dinner is much greater in your imagination than in reality.

He made a point of declaring he would not be a hermit but would plunge into whatever social life Port Said offered: tennis, swimming parties, dances, theatricals, and other "frivolities." If she disliked thinking about the mischief he might get into, she must accept that "this is the effect of too much living apart."[42]

Almost certainly Emmeline's depression had a physical basis. Although she tended to hypochondria about both her own health and Olaf's, her letters allude to very difficult menstrual periods, to debility caused, one doctor told her, by a deficiency in the mucous membrane that left her womb "raw," and to an "ulceration" of the ovaries that caused excruciating pain and for which she found little medical relief.[43] How well Emmeline managed to conceal her distress from her young son during these years is hard to tell, but she tried to "keep away from him when a bad fit is on."[44] Olaf was aware of some of her obsessive behavior, since he recalled how as a small boy he made tiny paper windmills to try to locate drafts in their lodgings and how relentlessly Emmeline pursued each fluttering to its source until she was sure she had blocked the air passage.[45] But his absent father absorbed the boy's imagination more than his jittery mother.

After he had visited Port Said in 1894 for his eighth birthday and could write well enough, Olaf began sending monthly letters to his "Dear Fa." But in 1891 he had no direct way of communicating with Willie, and his mother's influence was paramount. In England, reinforced by Millers, who were more religious than Stapledons, Emmeline taught her son to say bedtime prayers, and always he included a fervent wish that God would send his father home from Egypt. Once when old Captain Stapledon, Willie's father, was on a business visit to Liverpool, he proposed calling on Emmeline (a prospect that terrified her because she knew her father-in-law disapproved of her self-imposed exile). Olaf misunderstood and thought it was *his* father who was coming. "He was greatly uplifted & then dashed down when I put him right. He doubled up on my knee and wept for a few silent moments."[46] When a temporary reunion was imminent in the summer of 1892, Emmeline reacted strangely: "My heart is sick with hope deferred—I feel nervous & almost frightened at meeting you again." But a greater fear was that, after seeing her, Willie might conclude she was not fit to be trusted with Olaf: "My blessed boy! no shadow of a doubt ever crosses his serene anticipation of the future—I try to share his faith, but Willie you mustn't divide him from me—he is *all* I have, remember, at least so it often seems to me in my dark times."[47]

When he visited Liverpool in 1892, Willie brought news of what sounded like a momentous change. Captain Stapledon, now sixty-three, was about to retire as head of the Port Said firm. The name was to be altered to Stapledon and Sons Shipping Agency, and Willie and his brother James would be partners, with Willie as senior officer. The Articles of Partnership specified that the captain was to be guaranteed £1,400 per annum from the profits of the business and that during his lifetime no "fundamental changes" in the agency would be made without his consent. Willie would get an annual salary of £700, with an extra £500 for upkeep of the house at Port Said.[48] What the paper contract does not make plain is that this represented a loss of income for Willie.

5. William Clibbett Stapledon, Olaf's father.
Courtesy John D. Stapledon.

If Emmeline harbored a hope that the promotion would make a more normal family life possible, it quickly evaporated. She wanted Willie to delegate
most of the daily work to subordinates and spend more time in England. Instead, he threw himself into the job even more singlemindedly, taking on a
larger share of the drudgery than his brother Jamie. Emmeline was again

pressed to return to Port Said to support her husband. When she dared complain to her father-in-law that Willie was doing too much, he was immovable and told her that his son was "on the high road to making a large fortune" and she ought to be thankful. Such "beautiful theories," Emmeline told Willie, did not impress her. "I have to grapple with the facts & find them very different." Her tenth wedding anniversary just past, Emmeline resented the prospect of another ten or twenty years of long-distance marriage: "It has already cost me my youth & health & I have nothing else left to pay."[49]

When Willie made a brief Christmas visit to Liverpool in 1894, Emmeline was left "quivering with disappointment." Jamie, she found out, was taking a three-months' holiday, and her anger at Willie's constant pleading of obligations to the firm spilled over into icy sarcasm about what had happened since he and his brother had been "raised to the dignity of being partners." The partnership was nothing but a "wretched farce" of his father's devising. Willie should admit he was nothing more than a clerk and "let the world know that that is your position & not the horrible make-believe which we have been forced into all the time at Port Said & which I have all along hated from my very soul."[50]

Emmeline's protest had no effect. Willie felt guilty and trapped, but he neither changed jobs nor altered his work habits. He once offered to come home and "break stones on the highway" if there were no other way to support his family, but the hyperbole showed how unprepared he was to make a serious economic or filial break.[51] Meanwhile, Emmeline, with her sister Louisa Kirkus and her cousin Edith Scott, purchased a house, "Bryn Hyfryd," in the isolated mountain village of Festiniog in North Wales, to release herself from hired lodgings and long stays with relations. On Willie's trips to England the reunions took place at Bryn Hyfryd, but most of the time Emmeline and Olaf had no company there except for an occasional visit from her sisters Sophia and Louisa. By 1897, six years after her flight to England, Emmeline was calling herself a "a poor forlorn widowed creature." If the phrasing was characteristically self-dramatizing and morbid, it also captured the paradox of her married life.[52]

Emmeline loved Willie. Her sense of deprivation was acute: "Dear husband—oh so far away—what would I not give to have your arms to enfold me when I get into bed—but it is all cold & lonely."[53] Some of her relations saw her as a spoiled, nervy, self-pitying weight on Willie, lacking the toughness of spirit and the wifely impulses of her seagoing forebears. Her sister Sophia, for one, grew sick of her woeful saga and told her "what a helpless contemptible creature" she had always been.[54] But a more sympathetic reading of Emmeline's story reveals, intertwined with the symptoms of nervous breakdown, an uncertain struggle to break away from a life in which obedience and resignation were cardinal virtues. Olaf himself heard from his mother a story that explained her distaste for self-effacing domesticity. As a child in the 1860s, she saw her father, home from a long sea voyage, sit all evening silently reading by the light of the household's one candle held between his face and an outstretched newspaper "while his sons and daughters, and his wife also, sat in outer darkness."[55] The boys could look forward to acquiring the choice place in their own homes, but women's deference was never outgrown: Captain Miller's wife sat as much outside the light as his daughter. In her maturity Emmeline was articulate about her needs. As a wife she asked "why I should always pretend to be cheerful & perfectly contented with everything."[56] Refusing an assigned place in the shadow of her husband's advancement, she yearned for emancipation from the social "ulcerations" which took as heavy a toll on her as gynecological ailments. After she died in 1935 Olaf praised her for being among the first women to take up cycling "in a long dress, the edge of which was surrounded with lead discs to keep it down decently over her ankles."[57] Emmeline Stapledon's inchoate feminism may have been more substantial—and more costly to her—than her son's jolly image of a lady bicyclist suggests.

Olaf always had a deeper sympathy for and a more generous appreciation of his father's accomplishments, partly no doubt because his mother's low spirits had an immediate impact on him, and because, seeing his father mostly on holidays, he was less directly exposed than Emmeline had been to the effects of Willie's obsession with work. Both early and late in life, Olaf was strongly conscious of the psychological links between his father and himself. One scene from his youth captures the persistence of his affectionate scrutiny of Willie.

When he was ten, Olaf visited Port Said. Something in the house was different from his younger days there. In the dining room his father, not his grandfather, now sat at the head of the table under a dominating oil portrait of Captain Stapledon, his glittering eyes and firmly compressed mouth, just verging on a smile, set in a shaven face fringed with a Krüger beard. This was not the crusty patriarch and businessman from whom the boy could confidently expect a half sovereign whenever they met, but the immaculate young sea captain in vigorous manhood, dressed in resplendent black and gold, painted in China during one of his early voyages. The portrait collapsed time, making the father in the picture look contemporary with the son seated under it. Little William Olaf, looking down the table at these two other William Stapledons, one looming behind the other, saw the continuities and contrasts in three generations of family faces and temperaments. Within a few years the romantic image of his powerful young grandfather would be canceled by the teenaged Olaf's last glimpse of a bedridden, "wildly muttering old man" slowly dying from the effects of a stroke, unable to recognize his grandson's face. In his fifties, with his father dead and his grandfather's portrait then hanging in his own house, Olaf put into words what the ten-year-old could only vaguely sense:

Comparing that face with my memory of my father's face in his prime and with my own in the shaving mirror, I see the unmistakable but subtle family likeness behind the idiosyncrasies. All have the same strong hair, though the colour is different, and my grandfather's is oiled and waved, my father's close-cropped, and mine like grass that has been badly scythed. Our noses are similar, but mine the most uptilted. And so on. My father's prevailing expression I remember as definitely different from that of my grandfather in the portrait and his photographs. My father's is gentler, kindlier, more humorous, but also sadder. There is more humility in it, and perhaps a deeper-flowing consciousness. I wonder how far this difference was due to differences of individual temperament and individual experience and how far to prevision of the great change from Victorian optimism to latter-day self-doubt and disillusionment.[58]

Apart from intermittent visits, the father Olaf knew best, from ages five to fifteen, was the author of graceful, solicitous letters, full of colorful ship-talk, retellings of Kipling stories, curious tidbits of science and classical lore, reports on the much-loved Rip, inked sketches of the liners and ships of sail passing through the Canal, and exotic postage stamps and dried flower speci-mens. Corresponding with his father, Olaf could achieve a friendly intimacy that helped abolish distance. A letter was a private space in which he had to himself all of his father that he could have. He made up secret languages whose codes were known only to Willie, and he wrote up installments of a long-run-ning fantasy about dog-and-tiger wars, described his boyish inventions (a min-iature leather canoe, a ship made from a biscuit tin, a game of skill combining—inexplicably—marbles, croquet, football, billiards, and golf), and copied out treasures from his commonplace book. He designed coats of arms and mottoes for himself—one of the longest lasting being a dog's head with the legend, "Find Out." In his earliest letters, printed in block capitals and with little punctuation, Olaf added his childish refrain to Emmeline's constant theme of homecoming:

MY DEAR FATHER

I AM LEARNING TO SING AND TO SEW I AND MOTHER WANT YOU TO COME HOME AND MOTHER WANTS HER BRASS TRAY MOTHER TOOK ME TO THE PICTURES ON YOUR BIRTHDAY AND IN THE BUS I GOT A POCKET FULL OF TICKETS. THIS IS A CHRISTMAS LETTER AND I SEND YOU A CARD. WE ARE ALL GOING IN A CAB TO COUSIN EDITHS HOUSE TO HAVE TEA ON CHRISTMAS DAY. LAST CHRISTMAS YOU REMEMBER YOU AND MOTHER AND AUNTIE AND MR RIP ALL CAME TO TEA IN THE BREAKFAST ROOM AND WE HAD STRAWBERRIES AND RIP SAT ON THE TABLE AND HAD SOME ON HIS PLATE AND TWO LUMPS OF SUGAR GIVE RIP MY LOVE

YOUR LOVING OLAF[59]

No such loving notes to his mother survive. Olaf's proximity to Emmeline made them unnecessary, but other forces thwarted the close relationship that Emmeline both craved and consistently undermined. Well-meant commands in Willie's letters to young Olaf sowed resentment: "Be a good boy and do all you can to please Mum." "Be brave and learn to obey Mother always." "Mum thinks it makes you spell badly to write to me by yourself. I want you to show her that it will not do so."[60] Not only was "Mum" a burden and a duty to be faced bravely by the little boy, but very likely he learned to blame Emmeline for his separation from this invariably genial and thoughtful correspondent. And there was the question of Olaf's health and Emmeline's worried and exhaustive efforts to protect him from English winters, recurrent chest colds, high spirits that resisted confinement, and the usual run of childhood diseases. In a moment of clearsightedness she reflected how her preoccupation with her child's temperatures and cough may have done neither of them good:

> I have always been very much absorbed in him I fear & being thrown so much alone with him & his delicacy making him such a constant charge & tie, I have simply no chance of drawing in outside interests so that now I really feel no life or soul myself, only within the limits of his wellbeing & interest, which is not healthy for me, nor at all advisable for him either.[61]

Throughout the years of separation, Olaf had repeated attacks of bronchitis along with scarlet fever, diphtheria, and pneumonia. For months at a time between 1892 and 1899 he was, or was treated as, a virtual invalid. Emmeline was vexed by the constant care her son seemed to require. "He is a tiresome child," she wrote when his chest filled up with fluid one spring; Olaf and the weather are "two very uncertain qualities."[62] Given his robust constitution, strenuous exercise, and addiction to cold baths at all seasons in his adult years, Emmeline's accounts of Olaf's delicacy as a child are remarkable. Her sister Louisa thought she exaggerated his weakness when he was actually "strong as a horse."[63] The seriousness of his illnesses cannot be gauged from the compulsive cataloguing of symptoms that was inseparable from Emmeline's own neurosis about health and an effort to make maternal devotion compensate for her supposed failures as a wife.

Her opinion that Olaf was psychologically underdeveloped is more credible, since she may have helped keep him immature. She told Willie that at age twelve their son was "very little in advance of what he was at four years old." He lacked dexterity, she claimed, because of "very pretty hands with delicately shaped fingers, more fit for a girl I often think but sadly useless either for others or himself." But Emmeline thought his will too well developed, and as he entered adolescence and began arguing about her health policies, she

6. Olaf and Emmeline Stapledon in Liverpool, ca. 1894.
Courtesy John D. Stapledon.

alluded to "exceptional restrictions & safeguards I am compelled to lay upon
him." She repeated this theme so often that Willie wondered if she was im-
plying that Olaf was "abnormal," a suggestion at which she promptly bristled:
"He is very much the same as other boys in every way, perhaps a shade dirtier
but that's only a detail."[64] Whenever her husband appropriated one of her interpretations of Olaf and tried to explore it with her, she turned it into an out-
rageous charge that *Willie* was making and peremptorily rejected it. This
contentiousness became dramatic in a struggle over Olaf's education.

The combination of frequent illnesses and interruptions caused by visits
either from or to Egypt made Olaf's formal schooling erratic for much of the
decade of the nineties. Willie and Emmeline did some home teaching: he continued instruction in science, arithmetic, and classical myth by letter when they
were apart; Emmeline considered Olaf's moral education her province. She
read him expurgated Bible stories and *Pilgrim's Progress,* made him memorize psalms, taught cleanly habits, and disciplined naughtiness. She also trained
him to copy out edifying proverbs for practice in handwriting as well as in
virtue. Each parent had an influence on Olaf's reading. Willie had catholic tastes

and encouraged him to sample everything from Homer to the Romantic poets, from Lyell's *Principles* to Kingsley's *Water Babies*. From his mother he inherited a lifelong interest in the literature of social reform, but she was blind to the pleasures of novels. Once when Olaf was deep into *Rob Roy,* she handed him Nansen's arctic journals as an antidote to "the empty excitement of fiction which is such a temptation to gobbling."[65]

As Olaf grew old enough to go to school, the house in Festiniog became unsatisfactory as a permanent residence. Willie rented a house for Emmeline at 17 Arundel Avenue in Liverpool, close to the little school her cousin Edith Hope Scott ran out of her Cressington Park house. Miss Scott had her charges read poetry aloud every day, and Emmeline felt sure that under her tutelage Olaf would be safe from any "abuse of scientific teaching" that promoted materialistic views of nature.[66] Ironically, the only memory Olaf recorded from Miss Scott's school was a boy's "malicious pleasure" in loudly shouting "hell" during recitations of Tennyson's "Charge of the Light Brigade."[67]

In 1895 he enrolled at the best day school on Merseyside, Liverpool College Upper School, in the fashionable Sefton Park district. Liverpool College moved Olaf out of the orbit of Emmeline's circle of women friends and relatives, but it did not provide a complete escape from the hothouse environment at 17 Arundel Avenue. When Willie asked if he ever brought friends home from school, Emmeline replied that Olaf was not sociable. "As far as I can tell he 'holds his own' all right amongst the boys," she wrote, "but of course he does not mix with them much as he does not play cricket or join in their games outside school." The "of course" was her doing, for she kept such "watch & guard over him" that he had few opportunities for friendship:

> I dare not let him go out a walk alone as it is a case of putting on his coat or taking it off according to the wind & direction we are going in. He must not go on wet grass—he must not stand still in a cold wind—he must be all buttoned up if rain comes on etc etc. To go out with a schoolfellow would be fraught at present with many risks, which would one or other most probably result in fresh cold, temperature & cough so of course I dare not risk it on any account.

Although she criticized Olaf's dawdling, "endless arguing," lack of concentration, inability to do anything for himself, and mind that "wanders vaguely all over the Universe," she encouraged and even required a complete dependency.[68] His hermetically sealed isolation frustrated Olaf and prompted his father to intervene.

In 1899, when Willie mentioned the risk of Olaf's lacking "any manliness or self-reliance, the so frequent result of a boy's being brought up under a woman's rule," Emmeline took "very great exception" to the inference that she was incompetent to manage a male teenager. She pointed out that Olaf was the third boy she had raised, having cared for her brothers Ernest and Frank after her father's early death, "& the first two were quite a success."[69] Nevertheless, Willie persuaded her to moderate Olaf's regimen. That winter he was writing excitedly to his father about football matches and ice-skating. Being, as he once said, "a vile little snob," he proudly marched off to Liverpool College with new friends in his starched Eton collar, black blazer trimmed in red, gray gloves, and bowler hat that comprised the standard uniform of the "Liverpool Gentlemen," as the self-assured sons of businessmen at the school called themselves.[70]

The Upper School's principal, Frank Dyson, was a progressive classicist from Cambridge who had his staff slow the pace of lessons in order to get a higher standard of work. But Emmeline, who took Olaf's intellectual slowness as an article of faith, believed the school coddled her son, moved him up in the forms too rapidly, and let him get away with too many errors.[71] His spelling did rank next to the bottom of his class and his mathematical attainments were—and would always be—shaky, but he was among the best students in history and Latin, for which he got top marks in 1900 from the hard-drinking Thomas Nicklin. He won awards for bookplate designs and watercolors under the guidance of the art master, William Webster (for whom he felt a warm affection).[72]

Long afterward, Stapledon called the teaching at Liverpool College "uninspired" and the emphasis on competition a mere "echo of commercialism," but at fourteen he was happy there.[73] Just how happy became apparent when the issue of boarding school arose. His parents began exchanging thoughts on this subject at the end of 1899; typically, Emmeline, though in favor of sending him away, questioned whether Olaf might be too immature to succeed. She reminded Willie that she considered their son young for his age and no match for his contemporaries: "Now whether this is misfortune or not it is a *fact* & has to be taken into account in our plans."[74] When Olaf learned what was afoot, he became morose. He overheard his mother and cousin Edith discussing the question and jumped to the conclusion that his parents wanted to get rid of him so that they could be together in Egypt. As Emmeline reported the event, Olaf turned to her and said, " 'Look here if you two want to go to Port Said let me board with Mr. Webster' & turned his face to the wall & quite broke down."[75]

As touching as Emmeline found this moment (such vignettes, including an effort to quote Olaf's exact words, are rare in her correspondence), it did not alter her belief—shared to a lesser degree by Willie—that a child's feelings were irrelevant to decisions about education. In fact, she realized when Olaf broke down and cried how "very firmly rooted" he felt in Liverpool, and she resorted to emotional extortion. When he sulked over being sent away she threatened to do it sooner than anticipated:

> I pointed out to him that our decision must be guided by various considerations all of which we must take into account & that one of these at any rate he had in his own power viz. his *present* conduct at home—that if we saw he was not doing well we should be forced to conclude that something either in the house or in the College surroundings was not suiting his particular nature & that then, as with a plant that was not doing well we should be obliged to try transplanting. He said nothing in answer to this, but he has certainly taken it in.[76]

Boarding school could be manipulated as a punishment, but if Emmeline thought Olaf's failure to talk back to her was a token of submission, she misjudged the depths of a teenager's silence. That he was effectively and pointedly shut out of a decision affecting his own welfare left him deeply angered. In one of the most unforgiving recollections of his youth, he acknowledged that his father did not require the unquestioned deference typical of Victorian fathers and encouraged "man-to-man" conversation. But in the sentences that follow, both parents are indicted:

> However, in spite of this happy relationship there were many things in my childhood which underlined my inferiority. For instance, I was frequently sent out of the room so that the adults could talk freely, particularly when they wanted to discuss me, and what was to be done about me. This practice used to fill me with rage, fright and distrust.[77]

For a time the fractious issue of boarding school receded into the background while the three Stapledons celebrated the most momentous event in their family history since Olaf's birth: the long-hoped-for permanent return of Willie to Liverpool. How William Stapledon came to have a post in 1901 as one of the managers of the Ocean Steam Ship Company's Blue Funnel Line, alongside Alfred, Richard, and George Holt, is a mystery. He replaced the retiring Albert Crompton, the company's fiscal watchdog, during a period of phenomenal expansion for the Blue Funnel Line that began in the 1890s and accelerated until 1914.[78] Olaf believed that Crompton chose his successor and that Willie's frugality at Stapledon and Sons, where he did well by the Blue Funnel's interests, recommended him as a man who would protect the financial position of the Holts.[79]

Whatever lay behind Willie's ascension to the board of managers, its effect on his family was immediate. In January and February of 1901, Olaf solemnly recorded the stages of Queen Victoria's final illness, her death and funeral, and the memorial service in Liverpool. The next month he and Emmeline headed for Port Said to help Willie pack up the family possessions; the passage from the Victorian to the Edwardian age coincided exactly with the new era in the Stapledon microcosm. Slipping out of the shackles of his dying father's Egyptian agency (which he turned over to his brother Jamie), Willie saw a dramatic increase in his salary. He and Emmeline had devoted much of their correspondence during the years they were apart to reviewing their accounts, carefully calculating Olaf's school costs and the expenses of travel back and forth across the Mediterranean. From 1901 forward the Stapledons lived in ever-increasing comfort.

Within a year of his return, Willie could afford to buy a house in the desirable seaside town of West Kirby on the Wirral peninsula, which flourished as a bedroom community for Liverpool businessmen as public transport improved at the century's end. Emmeline's spirits soared. With her husband back she was no longer beholden to her sisters, who had come to see her as a perpetual problem on their hands. Now Emmeline picked up her old interests with renewed enthusiasm: the Ruskin Society, the National Home Reading Union, exhibitions at Liverpool's Walker Gallery, evening poetry readings with Willie. And when applications for her son's boarding school were filled out, the space for "Father's occupation" would no longer say "shipping agent" (or "clerk," as she once bitterly put it), but "steamship owner."

Olaf turned fifteen. So exhilarated was he by his father's restoration that he did not dwell on his own departure for boarding school, ten months away. He and Willie set up the telescope that had been shipped back from Egypt and a smaller one recently purchased for Olaf. He acquired a planisphere in order to learn the constellations, and he settled into prolonged, contented readings in astronomy and geology: *The Story of the Heavens, The Story of the Planets, The Romance of Geology, The Universe, Recent Advances in Astronomy, The Cause of an Ice Age, Astronomical Myths*.[80] The litany of titles is a clear intimation of the imaginative contours of the literary career that lay ahead.

3

AN EDUCATIONAL LABORATORY

1902–1905

IN THE SUMMER OF 1889, Edith Hope Scott was sitting in Mulberry Cottage in Liverpool, home of the Ruskin Society, reading a proposal for a new boarding school in Derbyshire promising to "add to scholarship not only the conventional practicalness of games, but also the pleasure and discipline and skill of good workmanship." The school would be called Abbotsholme. Childless herself, Edith knew that her cousin Emmeline Stapledon would realize "how near to Ruskin's idea it was." Although Olaf was just three years old, his mother had been primed by Willie to start compiling a dossier for their son's education: "My idea is this—that we should make the subject of Education our Study, reading what we read carefully, word for word, without any haste whatsoever— making extracts of all that appears to us valuable; carefully summarising, indexing & classifying these extracts—and in every way giving the subject all the patient thought we are capable of." [1]

When more than a decade later Willie and Emmeline decided that Olaf should leave Liverpool College's day school and live away from home, Emmeline activated her files and seized the chance to put a Ruskinian stamp on her son's education. The Abbotsholme School was at the top of her list. Willie would have preferred Olaf to have the classical schooling he had been denied, and a decision was not reached easily or without reservations on Willie's side. (Edith said they "argued the skin off their minds.") Nevertheless, he accompanied his wife on an inspection of Abbotsholme and must have liked what he saw, or at least agreed to try it for Emmeline's sake. [2]

"There are *no towns near,* and the district is one of the healthiest in England," boasted the school prospectus. [3] Overlooking the river Dove and

47

occupying 133 acres of hayfields, orchards, shady dells, and wooded hills on
a country road out of the old Roman town of Rocester, Abbotsholme was a
world apart from the crowded streets of commercial Liverpool. On 1 May 1902
when Olaf, in a new suit of Harris tweeds, got off the train in Rocester, the educational experiment was in its second decade. New buildings had gone up at the
century's end, and the site was a busy assortment of classrooms, workshops, laboratories, and farm buildings, presided over by a light-filled chapel in which the
carved heads of Dante, Shakespeare, Cromwell, Goethe, Nelson, and Ruskin
peered down from the corbels and where the liturgical staples were Blake,
Carlyle, Mazzini, and psalms in the headmaster's unorthodox translations.

Abbotsholme was designed to be edifying. "There are crowds of casts of
Greek & Roman statues about the place," Olaf wrote shortly after he arrived.[4]
Over the fireplace in the dining hall, a beaten copper hood proclaimed (and
still does) in beautiful engraving, "Men May Rise on Stepping Stones of Their
Dead Selves to Higher Things." Visitors to the headmaster's study sat on cus-
tom-built chairs from the workshops of C. R. Ashbee's Guild of Handicraft;
each chair was inlaid with the Abbotsholme pentangle, the name of a virtue to
be cultivated (Purity, Love, Fidelity, Reverence, Wisdom), and a Blakean aphorism running along its arms and back: "The Imagination Realises All That It
Invents" or "Religion Is the Harmony of Reason and Love."[5] At once iconoclastic and quaintly idealistic, Abbotsholme in 1902 had attained some stability and public recognition after the pioneering 1890s when Stanley Unwin and
Lytton Strachey had been among its early and disgruntled residents.

The school's founder, headmaster, and spiritual battery was Cecil R.
Reddie. He had studied chemistry and medicine at Edinburgh and Göttingen,
but the deepest influences on his educational enterprise were Ruskin as social
critic, Carlyle as celebrator of German culture, and Edward Carpenter, the Scottish champion of Whitman, democratic primitivism, and sexual liberation, with
whom Reddie maintained a long acquaintance.[6] A loud, nonstop talker, Reddie
taught briefly in established English public schools, but found the curricula
anemic, the masters lacking in pedagogical training, and the boys' daily lives
repressed and spiritually empty. He wanted a utopian alternative. Carpenter
and the Glasgow socialist Robert Muirhead persuaded William Cassels—a
farmer and, like Carpenter, an associate of the Fellowship of the New Life,
the parent organization of the Fabian Society—to lend Reddie £2,000 to reno-
vate an Elizabethan manor house that opened in 1889 as the center for a combined boarding school and working farm.[7]

From its opening Abbotsholme was an expression of Reddie's personality. Striding through the hallways with his black gown billowing over gray
knee breeches, wool stockings rolled down over work boots, and his customary bowl of milk to serve for morning tea on the run, he always provoked com-

ment. A visiting French sociologist, attracted by the experiment, was flummoxed by Reddie's manner, so unlike a sacerdotal Parisian schoolmaster's, so much more like that of a Wild West frontiersman.[8] The founder of Abbotsholme wanted a school both Germanic and American in method, emphasizing self-discipline and practicality, that would train the sons of what he called "the directing classes" in civic responsibility. Calling the school an "Educational Laboratory" in which new ideas about the psychology of learning could operate free from a rigid classical curriculum, he aimed to refurbish the idea of a public education. In his typically feisty way, Reddie worried the word "public":

> Most of these "Public" Schools are *endowed,* that is, receive an income out of the national earnings. In this sense they are public, in that they receive what might justly be called public aid, although there is no proper public control of those endowments. The children of the Ruling Class in this way receive an education largely at the public expense. Their first endeavour should be, therefore, to consider the claims of the masses. But their education is not sufficiently inspired by the right motive—the wish to serve the public.[9]

That sort of proclamation was tailor-made to appeal to the genteel progressivism of someone like Emmeline Stapledon.

A typical class of Abbotsholmians in 1902 consisted in part of the sons of Liberal parents seeking an alternative to the snobbery of Eton or Merchant Taylors and the sons of newly prosperous families with no entrée to more prestigious boarding schools. Reddie had to scramble to employ and retain assistant masters sound enough in scholarship to satisfy outside inspectors, experimental enough in pedagogy to satisfy Reddie, and self-assured enough to withstand the headmaster's assault on their egos. The questions on the application form for prospective masters reflected Reddie's habitual brusqueness as much as his educational commitments:

> "Are you English, Scotch, Irish, Welsh, or what?"
> "Are you a non-smoker?"
> "Have you ever suffered from mental overwork, brain-fever, or any brain disorder (in what years)?"
> "Are you fond of boys?"
> "Have you received systematic *practical* training in the art of Teaching?"[10]

An Abbotsholme teacher was expected to be inventive: the German master had a boy pantomime taking off his shoes or making a bow while others narrated the action in German; a history class learned the dynamics of power politics by enacting the conspiracy against Julius Caesar; one of Olaf's teachers assigned an essay on "the Qualities of an Ideal King" and joined with his pupils in writing the exercise. Not all the staff were happy about surrendering their accustomed authority, and the rate of turnover was high. Some grumbled that Abbotsholme boys knew less than an average public school student, but Reddie thought that scope and habits of mind mattered more than examination knowledge.[11] He demanded of his staff a precise sequencing of lessons in which students moved from things to ideas, from experiences to concepts. Each master kept a red notebook for daily records of the weather, his duties, his own moods, and the moods of his students; each had a separate pink book for summary and analysis of every lesson he gave.[12] The headmaster's dogmatism made staff meetings a trial of endurance, and his chastisements drove a wedge between pupils and teachers. Reddie prompted many an Abbotsholmian, including Olaf, to identify with the head against the masters, to feel that Reddie was one of them while the masters—many of them restless, demoralized, and irritable—seemed prigs and spoilsports.[13]

Abbotsholme took its keynote from neither the Dickensian learning factory of Mr. Gradgrind nor Eton's competitive playing fields but from the communal ideal of the Arthurian court. The ceremony marking a boy's ascent to the senior ranks featured a pledge from the chivalric code ("Honour all men; fear God; honour the King; defend the weak; champion the truth, and love the Brotherhood").[14] Reddie's principles and the rituals that supported them had impact: the boys worked in teams, professed no rivalries, cherished an old-fashioned spiritual idealism, took pride in the trust their headmaster lodged in them, and acquired a cheerful, exhilarating, seldom systematic education. In his maturity Olaf saw the "fallacies & hidden horrors" in Reddie's "exaltation of boyhood" and the "Youth Movement atmosphere" of Abbotsholme, but he also traced his later philosophical formula for the good life, "personality-in-community"—the interdependence of self-cultivation and social responsibility—to his boarding school days.[15]

At Abbotsholme textbooks were regarded as instrumental rather than essential, a relic of medieval monasticism, and masters were ordered to teach their pupils *how* to use the books in their fields. It was Reddie's trademark to question the value of words and to subordinate books and lectures to solid things, examined with hand and eye and reasoned about in the company of peers and a skilled leader. Despite his fierce misogyny he could sound like an acolyte of Maria Montessori: "A book is merely a multiplication of words. If the word is a ghost, the book is an army of ghosts, and the education through books, wholly or mainly, must be a phantom education. . . . To sit with books, studying the ghosts of things, is not wholesome for anyone, least of all for boys between twelve and twenty, when the blood craves for activity and hard muscular work."[16]

By all accounts, Reddie's own classes were enlivening and unpredictable. His method was interrogative, and the slate at the front of the classroom was dusty with blue chalk queries in his precise and clipped style: "How does the Blood move? How shall we try to discover this?" CR, as his students called him, disdained memorization, hectored any boy he suspected of glibness, and relentlessly demanded a "concrete case" to illustrate abstractions and principles. He taught a little of everything, and there was no telling what startling connection might be drawn between apparently unrelated topics. A session on hygiene could deal as much in economics as in physiology, a class on Tudor history would digress into an evaluation of the English character (with invidious comparisons to the Germanic), and an economics lesson might conclude outdoors with a tour of Abbotsholme's sewage system. CR never worried about covering the fine points of a subject as long as he had his boys working intensely, and he ignored anything that smacked of mere accumulation of data.

His teaching of chemistry swept away the imparting of formulas and authoritative demonstrations of experiments by the master. An American visitor watched how a recitation worked:[17]

"What are we to do today?" inquired Dr. Reddie.
"To make some matches, sir."
"What constitutes a match, such as you are about to make?"
"A piece of wood tipped with sulphur and phosphorus."
"Why will you tip the wood with sulphur and phosphorus?"
"To ignite the wood."
"Are both sulphur and phosphorus necessary to ignite the wood?"

At this point the students' stock of knowledge was depleted, and Reddie illustrated the problem. Placing some sulphur on a block of wood and a sliver of phosphorus on a sheet of paper, he told the boys to be ready to describe their observations. The sulphur sat inertly on its wood, but after a short time thin strands of vapor began rising from the phosphorus. The inquiry proceeded:

"What change is taking place in the sulphur?"
"None whatever."
"What in the phosphorus?"
"It is passing off in the form of vapor. It is oxidizing."
"What is oxidation?"
"It is slow combustion."
"Can any of you now see the necessity for using both of these chemicals in the making of a match?"

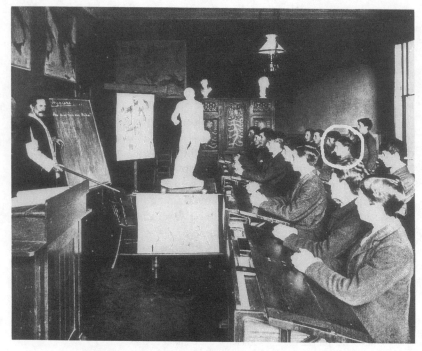

7. C. R. Reddie conducts a hygiene class at Abbotsholme;
Olaf Stapledon *circled.*
Courtesy the Librarian, Abbotsholme School, Rocester.

Getting no response, Reddie gently brushed the phosphorus with a wood shaving and it burst into flame and vaporized. He touched wood to the sulphur; nothing happened. Finally he applied a hot wire to the sulphur and it burned. Lifting up the paper on which the phosphorus had rested, he invited the boys to inspect it. They saw only a light scorch mark, but the wood underneath the sulphur was visibly burnt. At once a pupil stood up and reasoned the conclusions: burning sulphur could easily ignite wood, but sulphur itself was hard to ignite, while phosphorus ignited readily but burned at too low a temperature to have much effect on the paper. A match therefore required phosphorus to stimulate the sulphur sufficiently to burn the wood. The gratified chemistry master then permitted the class to manufacture some matches, and no attentive boy ever forgot the properties of the two chemicals he carried in his pockets for the rest of his life.

CR's pedagogy was a legend. His pupils either hated his methodical interrogations or they became disciples, and parents were impressed by the passion of his teaching. He was "both a genius and a crank," according to the publisher Stanley Unwin, recalling his days at Abbotsholme. He found Reddie's teaching astonishing for its energy and its eccentricity; he had the charm and perhaps the chicanery of a hypnotist.[18] But when his methods collided with the conservative admissions standards of universities, the Abbotsholmian could discover himself at a disadvantage. Like all educational innovators, the founder of a new school (and his students) still had to answer to the mandarins of the old school. Though Olaf had extra chemistry tutorials in Reddie's study along with the formal course, chemistry was the only section of the University of London matriculation exam he failed, to Reddie's chagrin, since all his theories told him that London was preferable to stodgy Oxford or Cambridge.

The headmaster's regular forum for exhorting, scolding, and uplifting his one hundred students was the chapel's pulpit. Twice a day the boys gathered for readings and music. Reddie included as many literary and historical readings as scriptural texts, with special emphasis on Britain's native visionaries and prophets. During Holy Week adolescent voices filled the chapel with the words of the Passion and the Beatitudes, Reddie's translation of "The Serene Death of Sokrates," Gilchrist's *Life of Blake,* Carlyle on the death of Cromwell, Wordsworth's "Immortality Ode," and the chapter on symbols from *Sartor Resartus.* In its ideal form, morning and evening chapel exemplified the collegial spirit of Reddie's utopian vision:

> Boys who *can* read are privileged to read the Lessons; and, moreover, may select their own material; and seldom fail in matter or manner. They often suggest the subject for a talk (or sermon), are encouraged to criticize it; and sometimes frankly do so. This is surely better for the preacher, who too seldom has any idea what boredom he has caused, or what mystification, or what edification.[19]

Not every chapel service matched the ideal. Many boys found the routines predictable; some resisted doing the readings; and Reddie himself was seldom the sweetly reasonable figure portrayed in his publicity. He could be terrifying to younger students and ludicrous to older ones during one of his public rages. One evening, Olaf recalled, "CR got in a huge wax" over the singing and "cursed the school for a few minutes, then stalked out."[20] Less colorfully, Reddie had the fanatic's talent for dullness when, in Olaf's term, he "gassed" interminably on a favorite topic. An Abbotsholme boy heard many variations on the themes of the sinfulness of shoddy work, the noble cultivators of the soil, and the unhealthfulness of linen collars. Disputatious and glint-eyed, Reddie identified himself wholly with Abbotsholme, and if the school functioned, as he liked to say, as "an ideal miniature kingdom" in which the boys could practice at citizenship, then CR could also play-act at being Cecil Rex.[21]

A day at Abbotsholme was packed with things to do indoors and out, and Olaf protested to his parents three days after arriving, "You do not seem to get any free time at all here."[22] Rising at 6:55, he washed in cold water, dressed, attended chapel, and made his bed before breakfasting and starting morning classes. Lunch was followed by fifteen minutes of quiet reflection and then two hours of Reddie's celebrated "Afternoon School," manual labor that might encompass anything from fence mending to pulling rhubarb to sheep dipping to collecting honey from the school's hives to repairing the farm tools. If the weather made outdoor work impossible, the boys learned sewing or carpentry. Afterwards came more conventional recreation—cricket, tennis, ice-skating, or canoeing—before classes resumed from four until six. A large dinner, with little meat and plenty of cooked vegetables, salads, and fruits, was followed by an evening recital or lecture in the chapel. Immediately after dismissal, Olaf went to the dormitory room he shared with six other boys to wash his head, chest, and feet in cold water, brush his teeth, and, according to Reddie's rules of order, "so go to Bed clean inside and out."[23]

One inspector commented discreetly that the rules governing life at Abbotsholme were "elaborate." Another was openly skeptical: "There are rules posted," Colin Scott noted drily, "which are not too formal or simple, some of them, indeed, being esoteric, if not occult." In a 1905 sermon Reddie told his boys that the rules for the proper chewing of food were of more practical and spiritual benefit than the Thirty-Nine Articles.[24] But Reddie's omnipresent broadsheets, crisply printed up by the boys on Abbotsholme's own press and hung in every building, were even goofier than his sermons. "Good ventilation," CR admonished his boys from the wall above their chilly beds, "promotes the oxygenation and the healthy circulation of the blood, which warms the body." In a subsection of this poster, hung in every dormitory, the headmaster's voice grew still fussier: "The sleeper should lie on the side, right or left (perhaps alternately for the sake of resting all the muscles); and turn over upwards. He should never sleep on his back or face; both postures, particularly the former, induce bad dreams, and the latter interferes with proper breathing. The legs should be slightly bent to keep the body steady." Reddie's patented earth cabinets, which composted the vegetable garden and fascinated Lytton Strachey, gave rise to a whole paragraph of rules on the use of toilets after bedtime. Here cross-referencing of one set of posted regulations against others generated delirious comedy:

VISITING CABINETS AT NIGHT. If a Boy has been used at home to go to Cabinets late, until he overcomes the habit (see *When should we visit the Earth Cabinets* and *How are the Earth Cabinets to be used?*), he must go before Evening Chapel so that after Chapel he can go straight to Bed. If, after reaching his Dormitory, he be forced to go to Cabinets, before going to Bed or during the night or on getting up, he will use the one appointed, and report the matter at the earliest opportunity to his Captain who will report it to the 'Medical Officer' in the Dispensary after Dormitory Parade. (See *How is the Sick Department Organised?*)[25]

Another poster, headed "What Are the Educative Merits of Bathing?", outlined his ideas on swimming as the best of all exercises, on the aesthetic and moral value of nudity, on the intimate contact of the human body with water as "worship of Nature."[26] Like all his pamphlets, it was an obsessive catalogue of first principles, but the practical results were undeniable: every Abbotsholmian learned to swim under the tutelage of his peers without adult intervention. A committee, run by a captain and vice-captain, gave lessons and tests to inexperienced students to bring them through seven stages of proficiency culminating in underwater swimming and lifesaving. Cold-water bathing became Olaf's lifelong habit; in his fifties he used to flabbergast his neighbors, who watched him crack the ice on the Dee estuary in West Kirby for a January dip.

Reddie also designed the boys' clothes. In revulsion from "the artificial livery of modern civilization," Reddie cultivated a rigorous functionalism. Gray Norfolk jackets were to be all wool, without lining (which collected dust), belted, lapelled, and arrayed with patch pockets with button flaps, each designed to hold specific items: notebook, tickets, watch, stylograph, and toothpick. Clothing was subjected to medical analysis and political speculation. Reddie forbade starched shirts as a weakener of healthy lungs, linen collars as a source of sore throats, bowler hats as emblems of urban idleness, and leather belts because they caused ruptures; pointed shoes were proscribed from fear of bunions ("How many battles have been lost through *corns?*")[27] Intrusive as these injunctions seem, many a student coming to Abbotsholme from another school found to his relief that this headmaster prized comfort above mere good grooming. A boy might not feel stylish in Reddie-made woolens, but no one was going to call him out for failing to brush his hair.

Olaf, nearly sixteen when he began at Abbotsholme, was conscious of entering boarding school at an advanced age. Some of his tastes and habits were still juvenile, and as an only child he had always been indulged. He expected to continue his favorite pastimes, and he made a list of toys and treasures to take from West Kirby to Rocester, among them a "son of a gun" water pistol and, holding pride of place in the inventory, his telescope and star maps.[28] As it turned out, the duties a new boy owed his senior students, the demands of his studies, and the extensive farm work in the daily routine left little time for stargazing in Olaf's first term. Reddie thought that most of his charges were coddled at home. Too little physical work and too much profitless spare time left them ignorant and complacent about the production of the food they consumed and the conveniences they enjoyed.[29]

By the end of his first term at Abbotsholme, Olaf was into the swing of the place and enjoying himself. He did his share of potato digging and haymaking; learned biology and woodcarving; and with several accomplices even risked CR's wrath in a raid on the fruit cellars. His health seemed to improve dramatically once his temperature was no longer being monitored every day by his mother. She had nervously packed an umbrella for him, but he was the only student at the school who had one—and he made a point of going bareheaded in the rain for the rest of his life.[30] In his first summer term, Olaf joined the list of injured neophytes who had not yet learned to handle farm tools. Having slashed his foot on a great double-pronged rake so heavy it had to be drawn by two boys, he wound up in the sickroom, where first aid was given by a student prefect who was trained to disinfect and stitch up even deep cuts without calling for help.[31]

A year later Olaf was an old hand. In July 1903, William and Emmeline received an engraved invitation printed on the Abbotsholme Press to attend the rites of the annual Harvest Home Festival. In the moonlight they watched their son march up to the barn on the hilltop as the last haystacks were ceremoniously transported by wagon to the accompaniment of bugles, fifes, concertinas, and violins. Then all gathered round a huge bonfire of weeds intended to recall the morning's liturgical lesson on the Parable of the Tares before returning to the chapel for a concert, including this year Schubert's "March Militaire" and a quartet that allowed Olaf to display his new skills on the violin. Afterwards came the harvest supper, some recited psalms, and CR's annual talk on the moral value of productive labor. A few days later term examinations began, and when the results were posted Olaf was ranked second in the school.

Life at Abbotsholme allowed for a large measure of the independent, the unexpected, and the offbeat. Early in his career Olaf encountered one of the school's curricular innovations designed to foster independent study: "We each have to get a 'term book'. It must be Ruskin or Carlisle [sic] or something like that. It must be your very own, and you must buy it now. I have ordered [Ruskin's] 'Elements of Drawing'. It is supposed to be the 'nucleus of a future library!' "[32] Guest speakers brought in new ideas. When Edwin Abbott, the Shakespearean scholar, amateur mathematician, and author of the geometrical fantasy Flatland, lectured on a new system of shorthand he had invented, Olaf wrote in his journal that all the boys were going to learn "Swiftograph."[33] They were always encouraged to make a laboratory of their daily activities. Every Thursday was vegetarian day in the dining room when plates were heaped with lentils and artichokes, and Olaf joined a group of students who proposed to give up meat altogether, the sort of nutritional exercise CR boisterously approved. The experiment lasted six weeks, and Olaf recorded its end with mixed feelings: "We stopped the vegetarian diet by having tough chicken for dinner (8 year old I should think)."[34] He joined the Natural Science Society for regular Saturday night slide lectures, and the Abbotsholme Dramatical Society gave him a part in an open-air production of *Alcestis* in Greek. He tried brewing and drinking dark "nettle beer," signed on to a forestry project, became a member of the cycling club, and did a course in "Physiography, or Geography of the Universe, which includes Astronomy, light, heat, sound, geology, biology, electricity, etc."[35] In theory, an Abbotsholme education aimed at unity; in fact, the school offered a splendid chaos of ideas and experiences, unified only by CR's sweeping, know-it-all syntheses, regularly propounded in the school chapel.

In little more than three years in Reddie's educational laboratory, Olaf's impressionable mind absorbed the headmaster's passions and prejudices. In 1904 he became a dormitory prefect, and with that job came a privileged chair in Reddie's study for late-night conversations with the German educationists who frequently visited. During his last two terms in 1905, Olaf held the post of "head boy" and met daily with CR to discuss school issues both academic and disciplinary. Abbotsholme gave him his first taste of responsibility and his first real circle of friends, including an Italian from Bergamo named G. C. Baldini and N. J. Skottowe, to whom Olaf had to give one of the "lickings" Reddie expected his prefects to administer for impudence, foul language, or abusive treatment of others. Olaf dispatched his authority efficiently. "I licked Colpoys after chapel for disobedience. Gave him 11," reads one brisk journal entry. But he responded to his disciplinarian's duties most keenly when he could be inventive, especially if the penalty were athletic: "I took Colpoys, Townsend, Tebbutt and Skottowe for a run to Marston Church 2–2.30. It was punishment for them & exercise for me."[36]

Olaf became an apologist for the Abbotsholmian idea of education and, though he resisted discipleship, he valued the tokens of CR's approval, which he received more frequently the longer he stayed. One of Reddie's happiest accomplishments was the setting up in 1902 of the Abbotsholme Press. Under the direction of a master printer, students learned typesetting, printing, and book design, while the school acquired a supply of durable, attractive songbooks, calendars, school magazines, chapel liturgies, and, of course, Reddie's indispensable monographs of school rules. Olaf edited one of the Press's earliest books, a strikingly candid photographic record of the school, the 1904 *Book of Illustrations of Abbotsholme*.[37] Aesthetically the books and brochures issued by the Press were superb. The paper was smooth and tough, the printing bright, sometimes multicolored and in ornate type fonts, the page edges sharp and gilded, and the covers beautifully embossed with the school seal of two naked boys and a sunrise representing the school motto "Glad Day, Love and Duty."

"Glad Day—Love and Duty" was also the title given to one of the school's three prominent iconographic emblems of Reddie's idealization of male youth. Executed as a bas-relief by W. C. Pilsbury, the art master in the 1890s, "Glad Day" grafted an image of innocence derived from William Blake onto Reddie's own design for the intertwined ideals of personal friendship and social responsibility. The second, a garish French painting called "L'Ange des Splendeurs," showed a boy being rescued from serpentine temptations and lifted up to higher things under the outstretched wings of angelic protection. The most dramatic of the three icons was installed after Olaf's time at Abbotsholme, but the ethos it commemorated was already well established in the first years of the century. Commissioned as a memorial to Abbotsholmians killed in the Great War and overlooking the chapel altar, it is known as "The Radiant Lover." A triple-life-size frieze of a transfigured adolescent nude based on Blake's *Glad Day* painting, the piece was executed from a photograph of an anonymous Abbotsholme boy who adopted the Blakean pose. Each of these reverential images reflected the care with which Reddie celebrated but also disguised, as much from himself perhaps as from anyone else, a fascination with the beauty of his students. He almost certainly was a repressed pederast who sublimated physical desire in an intellectualized passion for serving boys and shielding them from corruption.[38]

Olaf recognized that Reddie was odd without grasping the sources of the headmaster's obsessions. While CR's dramatic presence was inescapable in the small confines of Abbotsholme, the school was not just a one-man show. Olaf's loyalties to Abbotsholme went deeper than Reddie's personal magnetism and certainly deeper than admiration for the quality of instruction, which was uneven at best; he thought most of the masters "appallingly idiotic."[39] Having lived most of his life in virtual quarantine, he savored the intimate, unanxious sense of community that Abbotsholme fostered. In this respect he enacted one of Reddie's dearest educational beliefs. Unlike other headmasters panicked by Oscar Wilde's trial, Reddie continued to say that hero worship was a natural stage of growing up and that boys' affections for each other should not be thwarted. His creed was posted in the dormitory: "The too common attempt to eliminate from a Boy's life all affection, on the ground that it breeds sentimentality or creates risks, ends in producing both impurity and brutality. The exaggeration of Competition is the source of Lust, which can only be conquered by Love."[40]

The "miniature kingdom" at Abbotsholme was a singlemindedly Platonic society; masters were dismissed if they married, and Reddie would splutter at any suggestion of coeducation. With "camaraderie" as its cardinal virtue, Abbotsholme was to remake the Englishman so that he could stand confidently alongside the courtly Spaniard, the polite Frenchman, and the charming Italian as a warmhearted global citizen who would no longer "offend the world by a want of sympathy and feeling, or, in a word, affection, in both public and private conduct."[41] That aspiration resided in the school anthem, "The Love of Comrades," distilled from Whitman's poem of the same name and laced with a jigger of British imperialism:

> Come! We will make the Continents inseparable;
> We will make the most splendid race the sun ever shone upon;
> We will make divine magnetic Lands:
>   With the love, the love of Comrades;
>   With the life-long love of Comrades;
>   With the love, the life-long love of Comrades.[42]

Having enrolled him at Abbotsholme when he was just two years short of the usual leaving age, Olaf's parents were unsure how long to let him stay. Olaf expected to leave in the summer of 1904 to begin university work, but the plan was dashed when he failed to matriculate at the University of London. His eighteenth birthday came in May 1904, and he needed intensive work to gain a university place the following year. William Stapledon felt that he had gotten enough or too much of Abbotsholme, and he inquired among friends for a suitable tutor to coach his son at home. But Emmeline worried that if Olaf left school he would "fritter away his time" in West Kirby. She wanted him to stay at Abbotsholme while taking extra work for the entrance exams. Another year under Reddie at 120 guineas could be subtracted from the time to be spent at Oxford, she proposed in a startlingly cool assessment of her son's intellect and her ideas about his future:

> It is no use thinking that Olaf is going to be a scholar, he has not the least bit the making of one & you can't go against Nature. Give him of books & study as much as will be useful to his temperament but not more or it will hinder & not assist his development. . . . We have to judge for the boy entirely in this matter and let our judgment be guided by a consideration of the boy himself. He has no student's thirst for knowledge or he would be keen about going to College himself which he is not & our real object in sending him there is really for other purposes than the actual learning & passing the exams which will be equally well accomplished in a three years as in a full four years stay—possibly better so. Nor does it essentially matter to us, or to himself as he is going into business, in what estimation the exams he takes are held by the world. That he should work for them thoroughly & pass them creditably is the point.[43]

Olaf did not know much about such behind-the-scenes parental analysis. His intellectual interests, though not yet highly disciplined or specialized, were deeper than his mother credited them, and nothing in his diaries or letters suggests an overmastering desire to be a businessman. He loved ships but wanted to draw them, not manage them. Like Emmeline, Reddie foresaw Olaf in a commercial career because it fit his grand design of having Abbotsholmians infiltrate the economic centers of the nation, but Olaf's horizons were altering. He had discovered poetry, and while his mother read *Unto This Last* aloud during the August holidays in 1904, his tastes were moving beyond domestic Ruskinism towards Blake and Spenser. He ended that summer at the top of the school in English and had fantasies of a venturesome future as a writer. A note in the spring of 1905 records a first step toward literary apprenticeship in a form that served him well in later years: "I wrote a letter to an imaginary person in Midway Island, as an experiment." Four days later another cryptic journal entry perhaps points to more writing experiments: "I see now, though not clearly, my future course. An indefinable change has come over me."[44] Whatever the exact nature of the change, it is unlikely to have been a sudden craving for a managerial post with the Ocean Steam Ship Company.

Another premonition of his future during the Abbotsholme years occurred during the Easter vacation of 1903. In March and April of that year, Emmeline's Australian brother Frank Miller brought his family to visit Liverpool. On 30 March, Olaf called on the Millers and met their oldest child, his cousin Agnes. The event did not seem important enough to Olaf for him to enter it in his diary for that year, but its meaning grew in his imagination as time passed and it recurred in both private and published writings for the rest of his life. On the fifth anniversary of that meeting he recalled its details precisely: "Five years ago in the Garsdale drawing room I sat and saw Agnes come into the room in a green silk frock. She warmed her hands at the fire, and I fell in love with her." By the time he wrote that diary entry, he was an Oxford undergraduate, newly acquainted with Dante's *Vita Nuova,* and ready to impart a literary and magical significance to the event: "I had thought of love before, but this was new, and love at first sight. She was nine and I was seventeen."[45] Dante, as Olaf knew by then, claimed to have had his first view of Beatrice Portinari when she was nine years old. But the teenager of 1903 was not yet ready for so portentous an interpretation. When nine-year-old Agnes went back to Australia, Olaf wrote simply, "I am particularly lonely without Agnes. I am very fond of her."[46] That childish affection then entered a long period of dormancy until Agnes's return to England in 1908.

Through all the normal fluctuations of interest and desire in an adolescent, one passion remained constant in the four years at Abbotsholme: studying the stars. Once he adjusted himself to the busy school schedule, he always made time for his telescope and planisphere. When his father sent information about entrance exams for Oxford and urged him to prepare seriously, Olaf responded that he needn't worry about passing some sections: "Science will always be a recreation subject for me, especially astronomy."[47] The books he read between 1903 and 1905 are weighted heavily towards that interest, leavened with scientific romance and preternatural fantasy: *The Telescope,* the *Popular Atlas of Astronomy, Other Worlds Than Ours* ("It makes one want to take a trip to each of the planets"), the *Inferno,* and—a lasting influence—*Dr. Jekyll and Mr. Hyde.*[48] When he took the train to Oxford in mid-1905 for the Responsions and Smalls exams, a French edition of *20,000 Leagues Under the Sea* came with him for light reading. ("It is a thrilling book.") Ten days before the exams, when he should have been preoccupied with study, he wrote, "I did not get to sleep till midnight owing to contemplation of the stars."[49] Though he could not yet guess it, the unusual conjunction of poetry and astrophysics, of voyages through seas and through galactic space, of telescopic and theological visions, was shaping his unique contributions to fiction twenty-five years on.

Olaf was first drawn to Oxford in August of 1903. He spent part of a holiday visiting Exeter Cathedral and examining the funeral monuments to his fourteenth-century ancestors Sir Richard de Stapeldon and Bishop Walter de Stapeldon. The two of them had endowed a building at Oxford called Stapeldon Hall, later Exeter College, and reserved twelve free places for poor scholars.[50] His imagination lit by images from his distant family past, Olaf returned to school the next month where it happened that an Oxford don (a rare creature at Abbotsholme) was visiting. Olaf questioned him about Exeter's entrance standards, and he learned he would need more work in the ancient languages. But when he asked for help he got a good look into the headmaster's darker side. Reddie refused, as Olaf explained to his father:

> You know he very much disapproves of the Universities, & of course does not want me to go. He advised me to go to London or Birmingham, & nearly got angry when I said I *wanted* to go to Oxford. He read me an address by Norman Lockyer [astronomer and founding editor of *Nature*] against Universities, and several other things by Huxley etc. He thinks it is an absolute waist [*sic*] of time to go to the University, & that I certainly ought to go somewhere where I can "learn commerce." He does not seem to think there is any good in Oxford. I wish you would write to him, it is no good my trying to have it out with him. I should only put my foot in it somehow, & get into disfavour. He thinks he knows a lot about ships & says it is no earthly good learning Latin or Greek in order to go in for ships.[51]

The battle with Reddie over the universities clouded Olaf's final two years at Abbotsholme, though ironically it was the University of London, favored by CR, that refused in the end to admit him while Oxford took him despite a jerrybuilt classical education. Only firm intervention by William Stapledon prevented Reddie from dictating Olaf's career along his own lines. So vulnerable was Olaf to the headmaster's influence that William had to write several times asking him not to discourage his son and to give him a chance to meet the requirements for either Exeter (if he chose English literature) or Balliol (for modern history). William also had Emmeline's prejudices to contend with, and she shared Reddie's doubts about Oxford after Olaf failed the London examination. While recovering from an illness in North Wales, she pressed her husband to call on Reddie, who "is in much the better position for judging, being Olaf's teacher." But having agreed against his instinct to send Olaf to Abbotsholme in the first place, William would not give Reddie carte blanche. Nor would he accept Emmeline's estimate of Olaf's incapacity. Even if their son were not naturally gifted, Oxford might yet make a scholar of him. "It is by giving him a chance of aiming high that this may be accomplished, not by saying it is good enough to go to any college that has an easy entrance."[52]

Throughout the autumn and winter of 1904, what William called "this Olaf business" tried everyone's patience. To end the strain of trilateral negotiations with Olaf, Reddie, and Emmeline by letter, Willie asked his wife at the end of September if she felt well enough to come home and talk over their differing views before he visited Abbotsholme. "My opinion is quite clear that it would be best for Olaf if possible to go to Balliol—he is much influenced by his surroundings & Balliol is distinctly a scholarly college." Studying history would provide "a proper training for the mind," which William doubted could be accomplished by Olaf's alternative choice of English literature. With Emmeline he made his case directly, but to avoid offending the volatile Reddie, he decided that if he were assured that Olaf would get extra time on his Greek, he would not press anything more definite on either his son or Reddie.[53] William's prudence triumphed. Within a month Olaf reported that CR had "more or less consented that I should go" to Balliol and had "written to the 'boss' of the Col" with all the particulars.[54]

In December of 1904, Olaf went to Oxford for four days of examining in history and oral trials in French. Further exams had to be passed the next summer, and his preparations would have to compete with greatly expanded duties at Abbotsholme after Christmas when Reddie named him "head boy"—in effect, the school's chief administrative assistant. The head boy had to supervise the other prefects, oversee the school's discipline, and appear regularly in the chapel pulpit. "I have to get up & gas to the whole school nearly every day," Olaf remarked wearily to his father. In fact, the school was a veritable storm of crimes and punishments, and the masters were exacerbating the situation by insisting on frequent lickings for insolence and swearing. By early

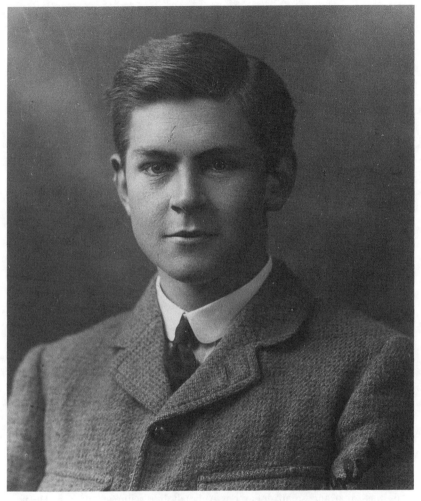

8. "Head Boy" at Abbotsholme, 1905.
Courtesy John D. Stapledon.

spring the nineteen-year-old Olaf was worn out, tugged between fear of the
forthcoming exams and pride in demonstrating his competence at adult responsibilities. "CR is pleased with me," he boasted in his journal, but he was earn-
ing the headmaster's respect at the expense of his own interests.[55]

Olaf struggled to manage everything being asked of him, and on the back
of a postcard he drew a pen-and-ink cartoon of "my new patent nightmare"—

a self-portrait as a pop-eyed horse branded with the five-pointed Abbotsholme
star and juggling with its forefeet a whirling mass of objects representing competing obligations: a text of Euripides, a prefect's rulebook, a violin, a spilled
inkpot, a rugby ball.[56] When William learned what was going on, he sent Reddie
a stiff note objecting to the amount of prefectorial work. Only then did Olaf
get any breathing space. As the date of the exams approached, he worried about
repeating his failure to get into London: "Awfully lugubrious about Smalls in
three weeks. I fear I have not a great chance."[57]

In July, however, there was rejoicing in CR's study and relief in the drawing room at 2 Marine Park, West Kirby, when the telegram arrived at
Abbotsholme inviting Olaf to take up residence at Balliol in October. The most
difficult aspect of Oxford for Olaf was over. He had got in. Two years later he
wrote what reads like an I-told-you-so letter to Reddie:

> I think the ordinary Abbotsholmian is well adapted to University life. This
> may sound strange, but I am sure it is true. The Abbotsholmian, as a rule,
> takes life more seriously than most other boys. This may be in itself good or
> bad, but in conjunction with a University career it is certainly good. . . . It is
> probably harder for an Old Abbotsholmian to do brilliantly at Oxford, but he
> can get great benefit and little harm from three or four years' residence.[58]

Abbotsholme permanently marked Olaf's character and his distinctive way
of looking at the world. Many of his later thoughts about the social obligations of citizenship are modeled on Abbotsholmian practice. The revulsion from
"herd-mindedness" that led him to work for the Society of Friends during the
Great War, his campaign for reform of the English educational system, his
knack for woodworking and handicrafts, the genre of his first book—*Latter-
Day Psalms*—in 1914, his habits of nude sunbathing and cold baths, his commitment to global unity, his disdain for intellectuals who didn't like to soil
their hands, his depiction of utopian experiments (and their failures) in his
fiction, his enrollment of his own son at the school in the 1930s—all these
activities great and small document Abbotsholme's impact on him. He was
lucky enough to be there during Reddie's healthiest years, before the emotional
collapse that made life miserable for later students and threatened the school's
existence.[59] A decade after leaving Abbotsholme, writing to his father from
the war zone in France and not aware of the severity of Reddie's problem,
Olaf weighed the virtues and limitations of his boarding school and its temperamental founder: "I wish Abbotsholme was not so stuck up about itself. It
is based on a glorious idea, and it did ever so much for me. But I wish Dr R
was more modest."[60]

In a rush of activity, Olaf finished up his final weeks at Abbotsholme in
the summer of 1905: correcting examination papers for CR, receiving the purple

and red colors of the school's "First XI" on the soccer field, being photographed clothed and naked for Reddie's records of his athletic teams, and attending his final service in the chapel on 26 July.[61] The liturgy for departing students was one Reddie strove to perfect. Its centerpiece was a Lesson drawn from the Gospel of John: Jesus' washing of his disciples' feet. In its printed version Reddie interpolated his own allegorical interpretations of major characters (Simon Peter is "Concrete Fact, Material Facts" and Judas Iscariot "Applause of Cities; Conventionality"), but the transparent psychological identification of the headmaster with Jesus is unspecified, save by the capital letters in which the text of the Lesson concludes: "DO YE KNOW WHAT I HAVE DONE TO YOU? YE CALL ME 'TEACHER' AND 'MASTER,' AND YE SAY WELL, FOR SO I AM. IF I, THEN, YOUR MASTER AND TEACHER HAVE WASHED YOUR FEET, YE ALSO OUGHT TO WASH ONE ANOTHER'S FEET; FOR I HAVE GIVEN YOU AN EXAMPLE, THAT YE ALSO MIGHT DO AS I HAVE DONE TO YOU."[62]

At the request of Olaf and the other young men who were leaving Abbotsholme that July, Reddie made no special mention of them in his parting sermon. At the end, the entire school joined in singing "The Love of Comrades," and the younger boys filed off to bed. Olaf did not spend his final night at Abbotsholme in the dormitory. He chatted until dawn with his friends and in the morning, "after many sad fare-wells and with a heavy heart," he dispatched his trunk to the railroad station and climbed on his bicycle to ride the seventy-five miles to his parents' house.[63] August would be spent in furious exercise, climbing Mt. Snowdon, sailing and fishing off the Welsh coast, sleeping outdoors in the mountain landscapes of Wales that always drew him to them. September was a time to pack for Balliol and visit the tailor for garments different from the loose-fitting woolens of Abbotsholme. And for the first time Olaf's love life was getting complicated.

4

Mediocria Firma

1905–1909

STAPLEDON'S ADOLESCENCE was not as scandalous as that of his fictional juvenile delinquent Odd John, but it seemed almost as prolonged as that of the perpetually youthful Divine Boy in *Last and First Men*. When James Barrie's *Peter Pan* received its first staging in 1904, Olaf was already an avatar of the boy who would never grow up, and well into his fifties people still nicknamed him "Peter Pan." At nineteen, as he left Abbotsholme, he was conscious of looking fourteen, and emotionally he was far younger than his years. Without playmates in Egypt, then sheltered for years from contagion, and finally immured in the intensely male world of Abbotsholme, he had had few opportunities to meet girls in any setting other than family parties at "Garsdale," the fashionable Liverpool home of his maternal aunt and uncle Louisa and William Kirkus. The most intriguing of the relatives of his own age he encountered at Garsdale were the daughters of the Australian and New Zealand branches of his mother's family: Elizabeth Miller and her younger sister Dorothy—two of the seven daughters of Zena and Ernest Miller, manager of the Auckland Colonial Sugar Refinery—and, most fatefully, Agnes Zena Miller, oldest child of Frank and Margaret Miller of Sydney.

Olaf's eventual marriage to his first cousin Agnes has been the subject of gossipy speculation. In fact, there is both more and less than meets the eye of the amateur psychoanalyst. Three of Olaf's early crushes were on cousins. This is not coincidence but pattern, though the pattern has nothing to do with incestuous inclinations.[1] Other first cousins were on hand with whom Olaf never fell in love—notably Enid and Ruby Kirkus, who lived in Liverpool. But the cousins from the South Pacific, who visited England only rarely, had the special charm of familiarity combined with romantic distance. In the cases of Elizabeth and Dorothy Miller, with whom he kept up voluminous correspondences for many years, puppy love was transformed fairly rapidly into brother-sister relationships that permitted the kind of intimate confidences not available to the only child of a straitlaced mother and an often-absent father. His growing affection for Agnes, however, tapped something deep and was different from the schoolboy infatuations with his two other cousins. It was, at once, literary, passionate, willful, and mysterious. But in 1905, when Agnes was only eleven years old and 12,000 miles away, another of the Miller girls appeared in Liverpool and Olaf suddenly found himself in the full bloom of desires that had had no outlets under the boarding school regime.

The Auckland Millers had made a summer visit, and the beautiful, dark-haired, seventeen-year-old Elizabeth Miller was staying on with her Aunt Louisa's family for the autumn term at Liverpool College for Girls. Everyone made a fuss over Libbie. As her parents' oldest daughter she got the favored treatment that might have been reserved for a son had she not been lucky enough to have her only brother seventh in line behind six girls. She was a mischievous, energetic stimulant to the stuffy dinners and evening entertainments at Garsdale, and when she joined the Kirkuses and the Stapledons on their annual joint August holiday to North Wales, Olaf had the pleasant task of giving her a tour of Conwy Castle and leading her up Mount Snowdon. Self-conscious that he was in a transitional period between Abbotsholme and Balliol, Olaf believed he was opening a new chapter in his life.

When he was back at West Kirby in September, packing up for Oxford, the feelings aroused in Wales persisted, and they took the epistolary form that defined his erotic life over the next two decades. In early October a new note came into his journal that had not appeared before: "I stayed up till 1 o'clock writing a letter to Elizabeth, a love letter."[2] For two weeks he moped on the beach, took long, solitary bicycle rides, and escaped into Jane Austen's *Emma* while recording Elizabeth's kind but definite refusals to be drawn into his fantasy. Throughout these weeks facades were maintained: he pretended illness to explain why he kept to his room so much; at an unsuspecting aunt's request he indulged in the "sad pleasure" of designing a bookplate for Libbie; the annual excursion to the autumn exhibition at the Walker Art Gallery brought the Liverpool and West Kirby contingents together to the teenagers' discomfiture; and a family outing to a performance of *The Tempest* tested Olaf's powers of disguise. Elizabeth "looked lovely in a blue silk dress," he wrote in his diary. "Of course I was feeling awful all the time, and did not conceal it over well."[3] On the eve of his departure for Oxford, he wrote her once more, pressing his affections on her, but she did not reply.

Elizabeth remained a weight on Olaf's heart and a running footnote in his diary until she finally boarded a ship for New Zealand on 23 December, but the brave new world of Oxford compensated for, or provided a distraction from, unrequited love. Late in the afternoon of 13 October, he walked through the front gate in the yellowed walls of Balliol College and found his name stenciled in fresh black paint at the foot of No. 3 staircase in Brackenbury building. He was shown to his rooms by the legendary head porter, Ezra Hancock, who would take Olaf's name at 8 A.M. roll call for the next four years and try to ensure that he observed the 10 P.M. curfew that Balliol undergraduates devoted their ingenuity to evading. He surveyed the sitting room, outfitted with electric light, and the small adjoining bedroom with its tin tub for cold-water morning bathing (privacy being the only advance in luxury over Abbotsholme's ascetic regime), and then he set off to purchase a gown and mortarboard. That afternoon he made his first new friend, Robert Darbishire.[4]

Before more than a few days had gone by, he had collected most of the Balliol friends that would matter to him—Charles May, with whom he often shared lodgings; Walter Lyon, a distant relation of Sir Walter Scott; Keimin Matsudaira, son of an official in the Japanese royal household; and William Kermack of Edinburgh. Although Darbishire, a Manchester aesthete with weak eyes and bad teeth, was the friend whose literary advice Olaf came to value most, the friendship with Willie Kermack—who shared Olaf's father's nickname—became the most formative, intense, and troubling of all his Oxford associations. The two of them often hiked through Wales together on holidays, attended Wagner operas, golfed, and argued theology and politics. "What an awful mug!" Olaf later recalled as his first impression of Kermack, remembering how "his orthodox toryism and my general radical extravagance clashed every day" and how exhilarating were "the talks we used to have, & the fights about all things under the sun."

Retiring, painstaking, and full of self-doubt, Kermack developed a platonic crush on Olaf who, slow at first to realize the strength of his friend's feelings, later regretted the cruelty with which he turned aside the unwanted displays of affection. Kermack "feels these things more than I do," Olaf wrote to himself. "But I *won't* be undeservedly admired by him, or anyone else."[5] An early poem captures both his fondness for Kermack and his awkward discomfort with intimate male bonds:

> A little dreaming; sometimes a sigh;
> A real endeavour to love him ever;
> And that is I.
> A world of loving,—of loving me;
> A constant warring against fate's marring;
> And that is he.

A little praying to light me by;
An endless grieving at my deceiving;
And that is I.
A heart that knows not perplexity;
A man's own blindness, but no unkindness;
And that is he.
Poor gallant comrade! I pray to die,
Lest he discover how poor a lover,
Alas, am I.[6]

None of Olaf's close friends belonged either to the smartest social set at Oxford or among the intellectual stars. Most came from Scotland or the North of England. All were politically more conservative than he. Not a single one, including Olaf, achieved a "First" in his degree examinations. Among the later luminaries at Balliol with him but never mentioned in his letters or diaries were Julian Huxley, Harold Nicolson, and the Biblical scholar Ronald Knox. The Etonians at Balliol whose premature deaths in World War I would make them popular icons—Julian Grenfell and Charles Lister—had little to do with the déclassé scholar from Liverpool and Abbotsholme. E. V. Rieu, later Olaf's editor at Methuen, was also at Balliol in these years, but their contacts were limited to their common membership in the Arnold Society, a debating club. Early in his adult life, as later in his literary and philosophical career, Stapledon was more comfortable, if not entirely happy, inhabiting the fringes. Resistant to the snobbery of old money and often feeling out of his depth in elite intellectual circles, Olaf at Oxford manifested the provincialism that he later proudly claimed as a badge of honor.[7]

In 1905 the Etonians still dictated the social life of the college, but there was a counterforce at work. In Olaf's years Balliol was at the height of its reputation as the Oxford college that most persistently linked intellectual culture with public service. The study of ancient literature and history had flourished under Benjamin Jowett's mastership, but it was also Jowett who made the first professorial appointment in Modern History in 1872. Jowett built a Balliol faculty that by 1900, a decade after his death, was firmly committed to energetic teaching and social reformation. Edward Caird, the master of Balliol when Olaf arrived, explained the college's philosophy to undergraduates in this way: "While you are at the University, your first duty is self-culture, not politics or philanthropy. And when you have learned that duty, and learned all that Oxford can teach you, then one thing that needs doing by some of you is to go and discover why, with so much wealth in Britain, there continues to be so much poverty and how poverty can be cured."[8]

In his first year at Balliol, after the "insane and cumbersome ceremony" of Matriculation,[9] Olaf kept busy with Tacitus and Darwin, lectures and debates, and essays prepared for dons with the irreverent Oxonian nicknames the

boy from Abbotsholme quickly adopted: Smug (A. L. Smith), Fluffy (H. W.
C. Davis), and Sligger (Francis Urquhart). Stapledon began attending the lectures of Arthur Lionel Smith, not the historian with the most distinguished publications at Balliol, but widely known as the most generous tutor on the faculty
and a powerful advocate of social and educational progressivism. His series
of twelve lectures on such questions as the Poor Laws, Socialism, Local Government, and the Land System drew a full house at Balliol Hall every year.
Hands jammed into his pockets and his forehead tightly contracted, Smith never
stopped moving as he lectured. His style was epigrammatic, his historical interpretations emphasized the moral impact of events, and he invited students
to connect past and present, to find the common ground between the issues of
history and the lives they were leading.[10]

Smith seldom led students to read original sources or provoked them to
break new ground in basic research; his talents were in synthesizing, organizing, and generalizing. A disciple of the modernist methods of F. W. Maitland,
he preferred social to political history; as one of Stapledon's contemporaries
recalled: "He could persuade us that the village muck-heap was of greater moment to our ancestors than the quarrels of kings."[11] Had Smith been alive in
1930 to read *Last and First Men,* he would have recognized in his former
student's chronicle of the future a familiar combination of grand historical gen-
eralization and microscopic analysis of supposedly minor events. Like Smith,
Stapledon distrusted the view of history as a procession of "great men." The
construction of history in *Last and First Men* as a complex interweaving of
human will and natural accident, of evolutionary progress and crippling moral
error took Smith's sociological and anthropological methods of interpreting
cultural change in the past and projected them forward.

When he finished his first term at Balliol and returned for the holidays to
West Kirby, Olaf's personal and political feelings were churning. Just before
Christmas 1905 he saw Elizabeth Miller to her tiny cabin on the ship that would
take her across the world. He wandered melancholically around the deck until
the final bell sounded and then left in tears; on Christmas Eve he "got up and
was sick of life," indulging the theatrical lovesickness that would govern his
diary entries for the next two weeks.

In mid-January there was jubilation among the Stapledons over the news
of the Liberal victory in the national elections. "All our conversation is politics now," Olaf wrote with an excitement he was unable to match until the end
of the Second World War, when socialism was in flower in national politics.[12]
As soon as he left West Kirby for Oxford, he plunged back into the opposition, relishing debate with his Tory friends: "We talked politics the whole time,"
he wrote on the night he returned to Balliol. "I was the only Liberal, so it got
hot."[13] Night after night, instead of pining over Elizabeth, he would sit and

argue over cocoa or join the Arnold Society's debates on social questions, where he was fined sixpence in March "for waving the cake about" during an outburst over international peace prospects.[14] The first year's binge of modern history, contemporary politics, twice-weekly sessions at the Ruskin Drawing School, Bible classes undertaken with Willie Kermack, and bouts of Shelley and Dante kept his mind off Australian cousins but did not solve the dilemma of what to make of his life.

In the summer of 1906, he was tramping through the Wirral peninsula with his father, confessing to the same vague ambitions and uncertainties he had felt the year before at Abbotsholme: "I do not want to go into an office. I want to write some day, but not too soon. I don't know what to do."[15] Increasingly he felt the strain between his academic work and his enjoyment of sports, between his eagerness to speak on every subject at the Arnold Society from armaments to vivisection and the tedium of the formal study of history, between the kind of writing he had to do and the kind he thought he wanted to do. Throughout his Oxford years he struggled with failures of confidence ("I wish I had a more imposing personality," he lamented[16]); he worried about the frustrations of insistent sexuality (his diary records repeated efforts to "be strong" and "shun disgrace"); and he doggedly practiced verses that invariably slumped under the weight of self-indulgence and rhetorical bombast. Later, the loss of some of his sexual inhibitions was accompanied by a growth in his powers as a writer, as if erotic and poetic liberation were interdependent. During World War I, in another period of terrible isolation, he wrote one of his boldest poems, "Sin," that attempted to absolve himself from feeling shamed by the secretive pleasures of his university days:

> I have touched filth.
> Only with the finger tip I touched it,
> inquisitive of the taste of it.
> But it creeps.
> It has spread over my body a slime,
> and into my soul a stupor.
> It is a film over the eyes,
> blurring the delicate figuring and ethereal hue of things.
> It clogs the ears;
> The finer tones of truth are muffled from me.
> Beauty has turned her back on me.
> I have hurt her; I am desolate.
> There is no escape from myself.
> And in my loneliness,—
> it was because of mad loneliness,—
> I touched again.
> I dabbled a moment in the sweet filth,

and fled back shuddering in the silence.
Presently I shall slink down again and wallow,
for solace in my mad loneliness.

When the poem appeared in the partly autobiographical novel *Last Men in London*, it was attributed to Olaf's fictional alter ego Paul and glossed by the narrator as a token of the "abject guilt and disgust in respect of bodily appetites" suffered by a whole generation laboring under "the prudery of its predecessors."[17]

At Balliol, Olaf produced such earnestly unimaginative essays for his tutors as an analysis of the difference between the society governed by etiquette, neglecting realities for show, and the mannerly society founded on a real respect for others.[18] He had the advantage of working with Balliol's finest history tutor, but somehow A. L. Smith could not light a fire under him. "I don't seem to get on at all well with Smug," Olaf remarked sadly, "though I like him personally."[19] The self-inventory compiled in his second year at Balliol, when his work in history took second place behind his athletic conditioning for the college boat races, is a ragtag collection of disappointments, indefinite pleasures, and truncated ambitions:

> I am not progressing very brilliantly. Reading is at present confined to the French Revolution. The time at the barge is my principal opportunity. I have not yet spoken at the Union, training debars it, nor am I sorry. I speak regularly at the Arnold. I have written something this term, more successfully than before, I think. My ideas are slowly becoming more ordered, I hope. But I have not decided what to live by, & it is high time. My eye is turned towards Garden Cities & Social Work. My drawing is sadly neglected.

Inspired by the utopian "garden suburb" of the workers' village built by W. H. Lever for employees of his soap factory in Port Sunlight, not far from the Stapledon house in West Kirby, Olaf thought he might combine a socially useful architectural career with a literary vocation: "It is an honest trade to design men's dwellings & their public buildings."[20] Emmeline, however, became impatient with her son's fickleness and insisted that learning architecture would take too long after so much time in history.

Intellectual and vocational uncertainties did not keep Olaf from savoring the one uncomplicated delight of his Oxford years. Before he had been at Balliol a week, he was drawn into the other activity besides modern history for which the college was then renowned: competitive rowing. The dominant personality was Laurence Jones, secretary of the Oxford University Boat Club, who organized a systematic visitation of the freshmen by senior oarsmen to persuade them of the "manliness" of rowing and their duty to sacrifice study for the good of the college. Stapledon was probably the Northerner whom Jones recalled plying with his standard pitch: "When a freshman from the North told me that, for recreation, he intended to 'do some cycling', I read him what was almost a religious homily. He had to be convinced of the shame and sin of solitary rides about the Oxfordshire lanes when his College needed him in the second Togger."[21]

Any proselytizer would have found in Olaf a subject on whom appeals based on public obligation and the spirit of the school worked like magic. He picked up the collegiate rowing slang as quickly as he had the dons' sobriquets, and his diary grew thick with references to "tubbing" (daily training races on the river), "toggers" (eight-oared boats rowed in the "Torpids" competition), "Torpids" (the spring interuniversity race named when Christ Church in 1827 left the other colleges in stunned inactivity by launching an unprecedented second crew), and "bump suppers" (celebrations after a team's boat "bumped" the lead boat to take over first place). Soon Olaf was thriving on the rituals of a conditioning run every morning, tubbing in the afternoon, and "cocoaing" at night with his teammate Charles May.

His diary for his first term at Oxford tells far more about rowing than about modern history. When his team, "by some marvelous fluke," won the Morrisons Fours race, Stapledon imagined he had arrived on the Oxford scene.[22] At the elaborate Morrisons dinner, complete with champagne, cigars, hearty speeches, and heartier toasts, coach Laurence Jones eulogized each of the four men on the winning crew, initiating an evening of giddy dissipation. "Then to the *dance* in hall, sundry people were drunk especially [Gerald] Dixon. The rest were v. jolly & even t.t.'s [teetotalers] were merry. I danced with Lyon. Must learn to dance! Only had one dance, though I was asked a lot. At 12 Auld Lang Syne. Then to Lyon's rooms where we talked. May was somewhat drunk & very wrecked."[23] A transition from the sober regimen of health food, puritan labor, and early bedtimes at Abbotsholme had been accomplished.

In February 1907 his eight-man crew, in cream jerseys with magenta crosses, beat Trinity College, Cambridge, in the Torpids race. Laurence Jones trained Olaf and his crewmates to use oars with specially shaved handles, so slender that the thumb and fingers could encircle them and take pressure off the forearm and wrist. Short, swift strokes moved the heavy boat sleekly, with apparent effortlessness, to the head of the river Isis to the rapturous praises of boat-mad Oxford students and dons, including A. L. Smith himself. Captained by Kenneth Bell and with Olaf at 135 pounds in the number 2 "Stroke" position and the Byronically handsome aristocrat Julian Grenfell at number 3, the 1907 Balliol I team was, according to the once-standard textbook on rowing, "the best fixed-seat crew" of its era.[24] Stapledon was more a determined than a powerful oarsman. His coach's notes described him as "light but pretty"; at Stroke he

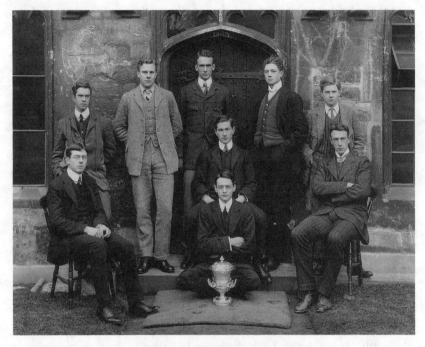

9. The 1907 Balliol I Rowing Team:
Stapledon, *rear right*; Julian Grenfell, *second right*.
Courtesy Stapledon Archive, Sydney Jones Library,
University of Liverpool.

showed "extraordinary gameness & grit" in driving his crew forward.[25] After the Torpids victory telegrams poured in from old Balliol men in the House of Commons and around the country. The bump supper was even more lavish than the Morrisons bash, and Olaf and his mates guzzled champagne out of the challenge cup and toasted, speechified, and danced till midnight.

Jones and Grenfell never really welcomed Stapledon into their crowd apart from these special occasions. For his part, Olaf found Grenfell "a nuisance because he insists on going off to ride his horse" instead of socializing with the rest of the crew. He also had a low opinion of Grenfell's mind ("dense in the extreme").[26] Much later he recalled his amazement when he read Grenfell's most famous poem, "Into Battle," printed in newspapers after his death in Asia Minor in 1915: "I rowed in several boats with him, and never knew he was a poet. In fact I thought he was a philistine."[27] Ronald Knox admitted that the seventeen Etonians who came to Balliol in 1905 (who included both Grenfell and himself) formed an intimate and exclusive clique. An unfriendly memoirist called the Grenfell crowd, many of whom died in the Great War, "not so much the flower of England's manhood, as good material spoiled."[28] In his last novel, *A Man Divided* (1950), full of autobiographical shadows, Stapledon took his own potshot at the Edwardian "bloods" he had known at Oxford in the person of the blond, athletic James Victor Cadogan-Smith and "the ideal of complacent gentility which he and his set embodied."[29] Olaf of Merseyside was always more at ease with the less flamboyant, less privileged group of Darbishire, May, Lyon, and Kermack. Among the oarsmen he preferred the Rhodes Scholars from Canada and Australia to the Etonians. But the training for college races every year gave him a gratifying taste of the sporting life of Balliol, and his selection to the Henley Regatta teams in 1907 and 1908 (when he stayed at the memento-laden home of the Antarctic explorer Captain Robert Scott) took his mind off what was turning out to be an undistinguished academic record.

As his concerns over a career mounted and as he confronted degree examinations in the spring of 1908, Eros intervened again. His cousin Agnes Miller came visiting from Australia with her family. She was now fourteen, and Olaf had created a highly romanticized memory of her last visit, when she was nine years old, to the home of his aunt Louisa Kirkus in Liverpool. Then she was a little, thin-limbed girl in green who enjoyed being taken to the zoo and playing parlor games, but by 1908 Olaf had thoroughly mythologized their first meeting on 30 March 1903. "The old spell rose again," he wrote on the fifth anniversary of that meeting. "Love has paralysed me."[30] The old spell, deliberately induced throughout his life, and often in the springtime, involved replaying the events of 1903. Writing from the front during World War I, he recreated the night at Garsdale when at bedtime Agnes leaned suddenly over the banister and shyly murmured, "Good night Mr O! Your hair bobbed all over your face and you gave me a kiss, at which of course I was wildly overjoyed inside, and quite phlegmatic outside."[31] The passage of time turned a child's kiss into a harbinger of things to come.

He saw her for just a week in 1903 but imagined her as the "guiding spirit" of his next five years. During the spring of 1908, Olaf and Agnes saw much more of each other. She stayed at his parents' house for a fortnight in March, and Olaf read to her in the evenings and rushed to his diary afterwards to record his excitement and despair. In April he watched her as the Fairy Blackstick in an amateur production of Thackeray's *Rose and the Ring* in Liverpool and was dazzled by her fey appearance in a white gown trimmed in gold, with a pink scarf and a rose in her hair: "I seemed to see in her something new, and yet that I remember from ages and ages ago as it were in another world. A strange trick of the brain, I suppose. Her fascination passes all words."[32] His usually terse diary entries blossomed into lush recitatives as he struggled to say what he felt. But how much reality lay hidden beneath the rhetorical flights of his diary prose is hard to guess. The chivalric poses of undying devotion suggest a wish to be in love more than a credible passion in a young man nearing twenty-two: "Someday may I have the opportunity of doing her a great and difficult service even if I never gain her love."[33] But such language was still commonly and authentically used to express erotic feeling, until rhetorical tastes underwent a sea change in the aftermath of World War I.

Unsure how to act, and with no one to confide in at home, Olaf wrote a long "confessio amantis" to Willie Kermack. Kermack's "sympathizing, but amused" reply scared him. When he returned to Balliol in mid-April, not wanting his lofty raptures to become a college joke, he kept quiet.[34] He composed sonnets and used his journal to articulate his fantasies and to write his way through his confusions. Innocent of her son's tender passions, Emmeline proposed bringing Agnes and her sister Rosie to Oxford in late May during "Eights Week" when Olaf was rowing and just before the Millers were due to return to Australia. The prospect gave Olaf a nervous thrill. "I must create a good impression on the 28th & not be a fool."[35]

Agnes's arrival generated paroxysms of alarm, anticipation, and neo-Arthurian sentiment in Olaf's diary. She and Rosie stood on the banks of the Isis to watch the races, and afterwards Olaf showed them around Oxford; for three nights he wrote expansively in his journal of the tricks of Agnes's voice, of her hair brushing against his face as they looked at photos, of soulful gazes, but he also suspected that she shared little of his infatuation. "I wonder if she has any idea how things are. God help me to be strong & brave, chaste & generous, devoted to duty, that I may grow worthy of her."[36]

He was afraid to be direct with her, but they spent one enchanted morning in a tradition of Oxford courtliness, floating down the river Cher in a punt. As he poled the boat past the crowds on the bank, Olaf was struck by the contrast between Agnes, in a plain, unprepossessing frock with her flyaway honey-blond hair floating unpinned around her face, and "the amazingly dressed-up sister of one of my fellow oars," Julian Grenfell.[37] The day ended in London with a tête-à-tête over Keats's "La Belle Dame sans Merci" and a wistful evening parting. He kissed her at the door of her hotel and said, "I am so glad you came to Oxford." She said, "So am I" with a seriousness in her voice that Olaf wanted to interpret as recognition of his love.[38]

The next day Agnes and her family sailed for Australia. Olaf and Emmeline saw the Millers off, and Olaf found enough privacy to kiss Agnes twice and to hold hands. Then he journeyed glumly back to Oxford and worried to his journal:

10. Agnes Miller, age fourteen, 1908.
Courtesy John D. Stapledon.

These have been blessed days, but bitter. I have dared to think sometimes what cannot be true; but things make as if it was partly true. It is almost too much to bear. I think this writing is foolish, but it cannot be helped just now. Shall we ever meet again? What use is it if we do? I will do everything that is not wrong to see her again soon. Circumstances *must* be moulded. But what good is it, even if difficulties are overcome? I am too common for such a one. Anyhow she would never have me. My child, my love; not mine, soon no more a child, and someone else's love. Hell.[39]

Five years passed before this trembly lovesickness became something more than a one-way indulgence in imagination, but in the meantime Olaf undertook some scientific reading by J. A. Thompson that eased his mind on one score: "In the evening I read Heredity, about the Heritability of Disease & Consanguinity. 'The idea that two healthy cousins who happen to fall in love with each other should not marry, is simply preposterous.' "[40]

Oxford in the Edwardian era still expected most of its tutors and all of its undergraduates to be bachelors, and the university provided a haven for the romantic celibacy Olaf was determined to maintain until Agnes was ready for him. There was little pressure to acquire sexual experience with women—and indeed there was little pressure of any kind on the young men of Oxford. Olaf could drift. But if his intellect was never deeply engaged and if his social development remained on hold, Balliol nevertheless mattered in his long struggle to define a vocation.[41]

In the autumn of 1906, A. L. Smith convened a special meeting of the members of Balliol College to discuss how they could apply the principles of an activist Christianity to the social welfare of their poor neighbors. Students packed the hall on two successive Sundays to identify the most urgent social, racial, and economic problems. Discussion was heated but abstract, and at the close of the second session Smith implored his audience: "Do not let this enthusiasm wane for lack of a practical outcome. Let us have a committee of the whole College to investigate in what direction the corporate influence of the College may be brought to bear upon the problem presented."[42] The thirty elected members drew up a modest recommendation to open a club for boys in the Oxford slums, to be staffed and managed by undergraduates. There were misgivings about the proposal: that turnover of participating students would make continuity difficult, that the club would languish during the long summer vacation, and that so large an investment of time might endanger academic work. Despite these reservations, money was pledged, and in February 1907 the college opened the Balliol Boys' Club in rooms rented from a candy factory in Littlegate Street in "The Friars," a damp, poorly paved working-class neighborhood near the city gas works.

A sizable crowd of townies showed up on the club's opening night when the Balliol men donned an ill-fitting piety to lead the Balliol boys in prayer and read the regulations governing conduct at the club. Sampling life in the slums turned out to require more patience and generate less glamor than many Balliol men anticipated. Although no strangers to collegiate rowdiness, they found the noise and hostility to discipline hard to manage in the boys; at the same time, they worried that if they kicked an unruly boy out of the club, they might be repaid by a gang eager to dust up the university toffs. Whatever notions the undergraduates might have harbored about creating a classless utopian oasis in the middle of the Friars was tempered by the discovery that the boys did not prefer to play rugby rather than gamble and did not instinctively look up to the gentlemen who had stepped down to meet them. "That reading a book could be work was a matter for laughter," recalled one volunteer who learned the gulf between his conception of labor and that of the local errand boys who visited the club.[43]

The Balliol elite who powered the rowing teams took little interest in the project. Laurence Jones admitted in his memoirs that few of his crowd even noticed that the servants who looked after their every domestic and sartorial need lived in basements or cramped attics and were dressed shabbily even on Sundays. "Although there was a Balliol Boys' Club in the Oxford slums to exercise us in practical compassion," he wrote, "most of us were content with admiring the unselfish few who ran it."[44] During his last two years at Oxford, Stapledon was one of those few, though he often made his trek to the club out of a joyless sense of moral duty. He was at Littlegate Street regularly on Saturdays to play soccer, to box in the club's "bashing room," or to talk with boys in the tiny library. Occasionally his spirits would be lifted by conversations like the one he had with a crippled young man about Jules Verne and adventure stories, but Olaf was bored by snooker and cards.

In the fall of 1908, Stapledon was elected an officer of the club when it began an expansion of its services by holding evening classes "in subjects which will be of practical use to the boys," a trial run for the long years he later spent teaching working adults. Every Wednesday he also showed up to manage the refreshments and to lead the boys in prayer, a duty he liked to think of as "shocking" for "a heathen like me."[45] Though his diary has few details about his work at the club, hinting in the vaguest terms at disappointments and failure, an episode in his 1932 *Last Men in London* is more revealing. Here the club has been displaced from an Oxford to a London slum and is run by a priest known as "the Archangel":

> Paul found great satisfaction in doing odd jobs for the Archangel. He took up work at the boys' club. Unfortunately he soon found that he was not much good with boys, having few of the attributes which they admired. He was useless at boxing and billiards, useless at back-chat. And he had no authority, for in his heart he was frightened of the boys. But for the Archangel's sake, and also for self-discipline, he stuck to the club. Finally he took charge of the canteen. He was cheated over halfpence, and at the end of the evening he basely made up the losses out of his own pocket. In intervals of selling coffee and buns he sat behind the counter reading. But this furtive practice caused him much heart-searching; and when the Archangel was about, he put his book away and tried to be genial with the boys.[46]

Olaf's discomfort at the Boys' Club was not a good portent for the year he would put in at schoolmastering after he left Balliol. But Oxford did influence him in a more lasting and favorable way, and once again the decisive force was A. L. Smith. More than any other Oxford don, Smith was visibly and vocally engaged in educating the proletariat and opening up the university to working people. As Smith was responsible for inducing Stapledon to go out to the Other Oxford at the Boys' Club, so too he planted the seed for his later decision to become a tutor for the Workers' Educational Association.

As the leader of a committee that in 1908 issued the pathbreaking report *Oxford and Working Class Education,* Smith advocated small tutorial classes for workers, along the lines recommended by the WEA, in preference to the nineteenth-century system of large and impersonal "university extension" lectures. Smith himself taught in the Oxford branch of the WEA and in 1910 started the first Oxford summer school for working people. He freely asserted his conviction that many of the workers he tutored were the intellectual peers of Oxford undergraduates; reading a random sample of essays written by WEA students in 1909, he declared that "at least one third of them reached the level of a first class in the Modern History School."[47] While other dons feared the influx of the town into the sheltered precincts of the university, Smith reveled in the ferment, the iconoclastic questions, the leavening of the Oxonian lump that a new constituency might promote. With humor and sympathy he soothed the bitterness some workers brought to a place they had come to resent. When one WEA student sneered at Oxford's venerable buildings and said, "This is the sort of place my mates and I are going to smash," Smith supposedly replied, "Look, let me show you round and tell you its history. You'll be able to smash it so much better, once you know."[48]

Little of this revolutionary educational thinking affected Olaf immediately. He was too busy agonizing over his own tutorial essays and examinations to pay close attention to what Smith and some of his colleagues were doing in their spare time. But in the atmosphere of 1908 at Balliol, he could hardly be ignorant of the WEA and the constant stream of outside speakers Smith invited to the college to discuss higher education for workers. After one such speech Olaf made a resolution: "The Varsity & the Workers are each only half educated, in opposite ways. Cooperation is necessary! I have applied for information." A few days later he acquired pamphlets issued by the WEA and decided to subscribe to the Association, reflecting, "I only wish I could do actual work for it."[49] The wish lay fallow for several years, but he was beginning to move beyond the kid-gloved liberalism of his parents' generation.

At Smith's behest, Stapledon began writing something every day during his last year at Balliol, and the more he wrote the less sure he was about his attraction to social work of the kind exemplified by the Balliol Boys' Club. Every time he tried to think seriously about vocation, he found himself torn between his social conscience and his desire to write, and it would take him twenty years before he got those competing claims to work in harness. At the same time he was not drawn, as his mother hoped he would be, to the idea of working alongside his father at the Holt Shipping Company and learning how to be a manager in Liverpool or, perhaps, in Port Said. His fantasies turned irresistibly to the impractical and even socially questionable study of literature, though now it was too late to take an English degree:

> Surely anyone who has not very much time for reading should not go into technical subjects otherwise than for business. Is it not better to spend time on the great literary works of the world, while perhaps having one 'special subject' somewhat connected with work, say Egypt? My ambition at present is to have more than a nodding acquaintance with Homer, Dante, and Shakespeare. . . . My other ambition is to learn German sufficiently well to read Goethe. But in these days one feels one ought to plunge into Karl Marx, J S Mill and kindred matters. While one is reading Dante one thinks of the attitude of the Ruskin College men, who are refusing to study both sides of the question of socialism, and one thinks that rightly or wrongly the three great poets and all mere literature are like to be put on the shelf out of reach as unpractical when socialism has the upper hand.[50]

Three revealing pieces of writing survive from the Oxford years. "I stand as yet only knee-deep in the river of life," Stapledon wrote in 1907 in his first published work, an essay printed in the *Old Abbotsholmian,* but he had the callow reformer's readiness to identify the "retrograde forces" impeding the development of a higher stage of civilization: industrial pollution, alcoholism, sensual depravity, and overpopulation—the first of these defined as the most serious, the last blamed on the second and third.[51]

A year later he wrote again for the same magazine, this time without the pursed-lipped moralizing of his earlier piece, on a theme that would be central to his first major work of fiction more than twenty years later. "To the ancient the human type was a rock, created fixed for evermore. To the man of the last century it was a cloud, ever changing but unalterable. To us it must be a virgin continent, to be cultivated and civilised."[52] He had been reading Mendel and arguing with Willie Kermack that within a few years "Mendelism will be as commonly accepted as 'Darwinism' is now."[53] Olaf's exploration in 1908 of the plasticity of the human form, a notion suggested by new advances in genetics and their implications for an "art of eugenics," foreshadows the anatomical inventiveness in *Last and First Men,* his history of the human species over the next two billion years. His 1908 futurist vision of "The Splendid Race" is a fair sample of an emerging preoccupation of his thinking, although the fictional masterpieces of the 1930s and 1940s took a far more critical view of the risks of genetic engineering:

> It is considered almost sacrilegious to breed men in the way we breed cattle. We must not meddle with the divinely directed course of evolution. We must not try to confine the fires of love, and if we do try we shall fail. Love is a divine spirit, too powerful and too fleeting to be controlled by human devices. Such are the objections raised.
>
> But why is it sacrilegious to use direct means for the improvement of the human breed? We have been given wherewithal to climb a little nearer to divinity. Are we to stand mesmerised within the chalk circle of convention? No doubt we must act with caution. Our knowledge being still incomplete, we must not attempt very much at first. But let us at least have the will to progress.[54]

The longest and most suggestive of his early writings is the only essay of Stapledon's preserved in the archives of Balliol College. Delivered before the Balliol History Club on 23 October 1908 and "pretty successful," according to the author, "Jeanne d'Arc" is an account of the dramatic heroism of "the last and greatest of the Mediaeval saints." Olaf proposed that Joan was a true visionary whose celebrated "voices" were the product neither of hallucination nor hysteria but of "natural causes."[55] His effort to find the mean between sympathy and skepticism was dutifully academic and unexceptional. The plodding summaries of historical documents and modern biographies were uninspired (though the author complimented himself on being "quite fluent in making a winding up speech"[56]), but the choice of subject is intriguing. The essay on Joan is the earliest surviving exhibit of a lifelong interest in telepathy and mystical experience, and of the visionary politics of such later fictions as *Odd John, Star Maker, Darkness and the Light,* and *The Flames.* The undergraduate's psychological examination of Joan is a first step toward the unprecedented science-fictional strategies created decades later. The unlikely peasant girl fired to heroic action by disembodied voices impressed Olaf deeply enough that his first works of mythic fiction, *Last and First Men* and *Last Men in London,* would be cast as the work of a twentieth-century amanuensis taking dictation from human voices projected from Neptune in the far future.

But Olaf in 1908 and 1909 in his final terms at Oxford could neither predict that triumph nor even guess that such a line might be traced. He was too busy fretting over the kind of degree he was going to get. He would have liked first-class honors, if only to show his mother that he could do it. Under the tutelage of H. W. C. Davis, the strictest taskmaster among the Balliol history dons, he worked harder than ever at economic history, colonial history, and literary history in his final year. He cut his hours at the Boys' Club and labored over his essays. By the end of 1908, he felt he was doing his most successful work since coming to Oxford, but he was still discouraged: "I see I am not good enough for a first, by long chaulks."[57] He resigned himself to working hard enough for a second-class degree, deciding not to give up his rowing and stake everything on a probably unobtainable first. The motto of his medieval ancestors, "Mediocria firma," which he regularly imprinted on his homemade bookplates, meant "steadfast in the middle course," but the joking mistranslation he liked to give it—"a firm mediocrity"—comes close to naming his sense of himself in 1909.

When spring came, he was restless and uneager to spend all his evening hours on history. He began sketching a set of magical legends based on Welsh myths; reading one of these, "The Tale of Rhosawel," to his parents, he hoped they would not guess that the story was an allegory of his own idealized passion for Agnes Miller.[58] At Balliol, spring fever took a variety of forms. After victorious rowing matches there were riotous celebrations on the Quad: Julian Grenfell raced around barechested hurling bowls, Olaf tried taking snuff "with disastrous consequences," and rounds of champagne led to roof-prowling escapades conducted out of sight of the college wardens and the town police.[59] Defying curfews, Olaf slipped out one night with Robert Darbishire for a midnight scramble over the college wall, dashing through moonlit streets for a 2 A.M. naked swim in the river. Afterwards, running barefoot through a sheep park to get warm, they were spotted by "an ever accelerating bobby" whom they finally eluded as they sprinted back over the college rooftops and through a window to Robert's room, where they ate fruit and cake before falling asleep to the music of early morning thrushes.[60] In the 1930s, when Stapledon wrote about the rubber-limbed Odd John clambering up drainpipes and over roofs to elude capture, he was inventing a murder mystery but also remembering his own college exploits.

In the summer of 1909, he wrote his exam papers in history and passed tests in French and Italian, and his journals record a dispirited sense of the mediocrity of his performances. The next month, after undergoing the only formal military regime of his life in a two-week camp with the Oxford Officers' Training Corps, came the news that he had received second-class honors. "I am satisfied, but of course not excited. Father & Mother are pleased. At least it will be all right for my being a schoolmaster."[61] He had by then lined up a tentative appointment as an assistant master in history at a distinguished and progressive school, the Manchester Grammar School, then under the headmastership of one of the country's most innovative educators, John Lewis Paton. If a move into teaching represented something of a falling off from loftier or more lucrative ambitions, Olaf had at least secured a desirable post in an institution full of tradition and under a mentor of vision and ripe intelligence. What remained uncertain was how much talent he had for instructing young children and whether he had really found work that could gratify a mind un-eager, as he wrote in "The Splendid Race," "to stand mesmerised within the chalk circle of convention."[62]

5

LIFTING THE CURTAIN

1909–1912

AS IT WAS IN 1909, sandwiched between the square and charmless Manchester Cathedral and the gray sprawl of the train yards at Victoria Station, the four-centuries-old Manchester Grammar School on Long Millgate stood in the center of the life and gloom of a proud, progressive industrial city. Manchester had excellent art galleries, the new John Rylands Library, and venturesome theaters, and nestling alongside the famous Grammar School were the dark corridors of Chetham's, the nation's oldest public library, in whose tiny reading alcove Marx and Engels first conversed. But the city was also noisy and filthy. The air was thick with pollutants. Manchester stank.

When the novice schoolmaster Olaf Stapledon first walked into the assembly hall of the Grammar School, its enormous thirty-foot-high windows looked out on nothing, dark as they were with the crusted smoke of coal fires. Windows were kept tightly shut to insulate the teaching from the whistling and screeching at the station and the clattering iron ferrules on horse-drawn lorries jouncing baled cotton over cobblestones. The building was suffocating, especially in the cramped attic classroom assigned to the new assistant master. Olaf, craving the sea breezes of Wirral, felt claustrophobic. He could not enter into the spirit of the schoolboys' anthem:

> Round us are factory, forge and store,
> Market and cattle pen,
> But here in our factory 'mid the roar
> Work we at making men.[1]

Two days into the autumn term, struggling with anxieties over his work and repelled by his surroundings, Olaf groaned, "Oh it is all hateful, & this beastly town is ghastly."[2]

Although apprehensive about his first term of school teaching, Stapledon did little systematic preparation. "I have not made any real notes," he regretted as he left Liverpool. "I feel fearfully unequipped, & dread the whole thing."[3] He had signed on for only a year at Manchester, and no sooner had he arrived than he began anticipating his resignation. After four years at Oxford, where mental work was leavened by punting, cocoa parties, barefoot jogs in the meadow, and the proximity of friends, the daily round of reading, notetaking, working up lectures, conducting classes, and correcting essays left him peeved and exhausted. "I have to spend the whole evening till 11 working for the next day, which is loathsome," he complained after the first week. By the second week he was panicky: "I cannot manage small kids a bit, & I am pretty bad with the rest. I fear this job will not do. I am not cut out for it a bit. I fear I have made a mistake. Things are going badly. The prospect of a whole year of it is awful."[4] In cheap digs on Egerton Road, he shared a sitting room with two other young men, one of whom was "garrulously tipsy every night," but neither roommates nor the company of the assistant masters on the school staff relieved his sense of alienation from Manchester.[5]

In his mid-forties Stapledon ransacked his life for episodes of *Last Men in London;* there he told of an unhappy period in his character Paul's life at a London school. Paul took teaching "very seriously" but was "always behindhand, and therefore in class always uncertain." Slow to discipline unruliness, he was baited by his students until the classroom descended into chaos. One afternoon when classes had ended, "Paul, seated upon his dais, dropped his head forward on his chalk-dusty hands." Tears coursed through his fingers, and he uttered a desperate prayer. " 'Oh God, oh God,' he cried, 'make me different from what I am.' "[6] The episode was drawn from an actual day at Manchester Grammar School, for Olaf told the same story in a letter to his fiancée during World War I:

> This cousin of yours was once a schoolmaster, a very juvenile and unskilled one. He bit off more than he could chew. Once I remember he made a fearful muddle of a class, and at last when the bell had gone and all the boys had left the room, he, sitting in his black gown at his desk, dropped his face on his arm and despaired. He made up his mind that he was utterly good for nothing in this world and would gladly have slid out of it. He won't forget that incident ever.[7]

Olaf's muddle had little to do with Manchester Grammar School itself. The High Master, John Lewis Paton, embraced educational ideals and tactics geared to Stapledon's temperament and his experience at Abbotsholme, but he applied them in more rational and subtle ways than Cecil Reddie had been able to manage. MGS sought an economically diverse body of students, reserving by statute fifteen percent of its seats for those unable to pay the fees. Paton brought the number of free places closer to a quarter, and he actively recruited poor boys from Manchester's large Jewish community. Because of the inner-city location there were no playing fields, but Paton scourged the cult of sport for its antidemocratic tendencies. "The reason that our utilitarian reformers of curricula say nothing about the uselessness of games is at bottom social," he wrote caustically. "To play cricket is *genteel,* to dig potatoes isn't. Dirty play, such as football and steeplechasing, is held in esteem, 'dirty work' must be left to the lower orders."[8] Scorning authoritarianism, he used to say that a study of Shakespeare's schoolmasters would make one of the darkest chapters in literary criticism. He told his colleagues, "Go read your Shakespeare and see if Caliban did not learn more in one hour from two drunken rascally butlers than he learned in twelve years from the dignified and unbending Prospero."[9]

John Stuart Mill's autobiographical account of the affective deficiencies in his education made a powerful impression on Paton, and he told new teachers at the school to remember that children always have feelings even when they may not have reasons.[10] At MGS, as at Abbotsholme, lessons were built up from foundations in observation and experience. Science masters used inflatable bladders to teach the lung's operation, had students grow beans in herbaria, and taught animal physiology with a live cat rather than a stuffed bird. Knowing that the pedagogy he endorsed might seem too leisurely for "these pushful days," Paton spoke for the value of trial and error and of student-centered learning. Knowledge attained "as the outcome of need consciously realized, and practical effort consciously directed, is part and parcel of the child's own mind and does not fall away like the knowledge plastered on by the proficient syllabus-teacher."[11]

Olaf took all this to heart and worked at making his lessons dramatic and participatory. To the annoyance of masters in adjoining rooms, his students loudly reenacted the wrangling of the barons and King John at the signing of Magna Carta and produced vivid sound effects for a French ship sinking during the Battle of Sluys.[12] In poetry lessons he trained his boys to read Tennyson with unsentimental expressiveness, though their naïve responses to the moral and psychological issues in *Idylls of the King* dismayed him. He never felt easy with his preadolescent charges, although they often enjoyed him more than he realized. An economist and Labour party leader who had become Stapledon's most famous former pupil recalled himself as "a precocious and rather bumptious school-boy" who was "awestruck" by the young master from Balliol. The boy was one of Paton's Jewish scholarship students, Harold Laski.[13]

Olaf admired Paton's commitment to inventive, fully engaged teaching and wanted to emulate it; yet, however much the principles spoke to his idealism, the work left him feeling burdened and ungratified. Before the year was out, he composed a brief memoir of a young schoolmaster who could not square pedagogical theory with his own limitations:

> If the novice has five classes a day, and takes at least an hour and a half in preparing one in [the] orthodox manner, what time is there for reports, or for those out-of-class school interests which we are told are so vital? As for private activity—clearly that is impossible. Consequently reports of lessons never see the light, plans become rapidly fainter and fewer, and are nonexistent at the end of the first fortnight, and preparation becomes an attempt to acquire as much knowledge with the aid of the book as the average boy will have without it. Again, we are told that the form master should be a kind of spiritual father to his form; he will train their souls no less than their minds; he will see that the tone of his form is irreproachable, that public spirit is abundant, and he will give kindly advice to individuals. But when the novice is confronted with twenty-five or thirty unknown faces, each concealing a self as shy and reserved as his own, and divided from him in each case by a distinct gulf, the ideal of intimacy fades into an indiscriminate and rather fatuous geniality.[14]

There were few compensatory pleasures in Manchester.. Olaf enjoyed the jewel of Manchester art museums, the Whitworth Gallery, where he studied pictures that made a lasting impression: George Frederick Watts's massive allegory in oils, *Love and Death,* and the gorgeous Blake watercolor, *The Ancient of Days.* Both spoke to his imaginative attraction to grand, superhuman flourishes and to the ultimate mysteries of human and cosmic design. His Balliol friend Robert Darbishire, grandson of the Robert Darbishire who endowed the Whitworth, now lived in the city, and Olaf depended on him for conversation and advice. When teaching depressed him, he turned to writing for consolation. At the De Quincey Club, the literary society at MGS, he read a paper on Browning, and at home he labored over his own verses, copying all his short poems into "a rather scanty & rough collection."[15] He began planning bigger projects, many connected with his seafaring heritage. No drafts survive of his most ambitious poem, if it ever got beyond the dreaming stage: "I have a very workable scheme for a big epic, Drake, if ever I have the worthy skill. Meanwhile plod."[16] A reader of the dutifully uplifting rhymes drafted in his journals from these years will not feel much sense of loss for the vanished manuscripts of other "epics" he showed Darbishire in the summer of 1910.

One formative experience of 1909–1910 occurred away from Manchester altogether. For years Olaf had been reading Dante in both English and Italian, and an offer from his mother to accompany her to Florence during the Christmas holidays was quickly accepted. After Christmas mass at Notre Dame in Paris, Emmeline and her son took the train into the Alps and through the Simplon tunnel to Milan. There a day of organized museum walks left him grumpy. "Sightseeing is trying. I like to see things accidentally, & to think," he wrote in his diary. But when he arrived in Florence his spirits lifted: "We came suddenly on the Duomo, Baptistry & Campanile all shining with their black & white marble. Weird & all hung with history and tale."[17]

Emmeline was inclined to rely on her Baedeker and her Ruskin and to sign up for all the standard tours, and Olaf's patience held for a few days. The city exhilarated him. "I read Dante all the time," he recorded as he made daytime visits to the landmarks—Dante's house, the Uffizi and Pitti galleries, the Medici chapel—and wrote poems in the evenings. He was overpowered by the unfinished Michelangelo statues, "fell in love with" the Botticelli Venus, and bought a colored photograph of his favorite piece of all, Raphael's *Madonna della Seggiola*. His mother's company was less satisfying, and at last he broke off for a day's lone crosscountry hike; he swam a stream, climbed for a prospect of the city from Mount Morello, and finally made his own self-guided tour through Florence's slums.[18] But Olaf's mind was not exclusively on art or sociology or landscapes: Florence inevitably brought to mind his Australian cousin Agnes Miller, whom he had first glimpsed when she, like Dante's Beatrice, was nine. He rang out 1909 and rang in 1910 in his room overlooking the Arno by writing her an illustrated letter, the earliest of his letters in their long correspondence to have survived.[19]

The Italian journey did not reconcile him to a return to the Grammar School, and as the new term began Olaf looked forward to some less taxing employment that would allow him time for writing poetry. The obvious solution was to take a junior position in his father's firm, Alfred Holt's Ocean Steam Ship Company, though his mother—who had argued for a managerial career when he was at Abbotsholme—was now unaccountably stressing "the soul destroying and wearing nature of business."[20] But Emmeline was not the only inconsistent player in the tragicomedy of Olaf's venture into schoolmastering. He worried about getting "fossilized" and falling "into the grip of luxury" at the Holt offices. Shipping was a respectable industry, but he could not boast that the industrialist was a nobler being than the pedagogue: "I am keenly mourning the prospect of office instead of school," he wrote as he planned his letter of resignation. "This is so much more human; it is *the* only grand profession." When he finally completed his last day at MGS, Olaf made a squelchy departure: "Away, away, very chokey & woebegone. Alas, it is the end of all things. Je suis desolé."[21] In more measured public oratory, he explained how someone drawn to the ideal but lacking the gift for teaching might have to admit that he was "in the wrong place":

> Let him bow before the genius of the true schoolmaster for whom these things are very truth indeed; but let him not consent to join the crowded throng of false schoolmasters who have neither the genius nor the desire. Let him bow with an enlightened respect for the good schoolmasters he has known as masters or colleagues; and let him quietly withdraw.[22]

Olaf had a convenient retreat available. His father, whose responsibilities as a manager of the Ocean Steam Ship Company had been increasingly well rewarded, at last had a house befitting his position in Liverpool's commercial and philanthropic circles. In June 1910, William and Emmeline moved into a spacious new building at the top of Caldy Hill, two miles from the center of West Kirby. Called "Annery" after the fourteenth-century home of Bishop Walter de Stapeldon in North Devon, the house was adorned inside and out with bas-reliefs of classical figures commissioned by William. Extensive grounds commanded sweeping views over West Kirby north to the Irish Sea and west to the mud flats and estuary of the Dee River and the Welsh mountains. Annery, quiet and elegant, would be Olaf's home base for the next ten years, but in the summer of 1910 he wanted a rougher life. As respite from or penance for his disastrous year in Manchester, he put in a month of strenuous farmwork at the old family estate of "Galsworthy" in North Devon.

There the Stapledons' tenants set Olaf to chopping wood, cutting nettles, pitching oats, churning butter, harvesting wheat by sunlight and moonlight, and cleaning out the cow houses. "The dung was v[ery] tight," the old Abbotsholme boy wrote with satisfaction, "& I sweated & strained with a fork."[23] He daydreamed about Cousin Agnes, collected images for his poems, ate hungrily morning, noon, and night, and enjoyed the conviviality of a plain kitchen democracy. "We all lived in a great tiled kitchen, with a *huge* open fireplace & no grate," he wrote to Agnes. "Family & labourers all fed at one table, but there was no cloth at the lower end."[24] The working holiday put a buffer between the humiliating memories of his first paying job and the sedentary deskwork ahead of him in Liverpool. North Devon was rich in powerful and contradictory family associations, and Olaf's visits always added something to the growing compost of memories that later fed his literary work.

Willie Stapledon's brother James always spent the late summer at their father's old house at Northam, not far from Galsworthy, to escape the Egyptian heat, and the Liverpool Stapledons timed their trips to North Devon to coincide with James's holidays. Ever since Olaf had learned to shoot a gun when he was seventeen, a visit to Devon meant an invitation to go stag hunting on Exmoor. As he got older, he anticipated the yearly hunting party with more loathing than fascination. The 1911 hunt was worse than most. On the first day, he shot a calf by mistake, and a few days later, as he wrote in his diary, disgust passed into a resolve not to participate again: "I fired, wounded, reloaded, fired at wrong one, wounded. I had to finish off both & did it badly. Horrible business."[25] This bloody deerstalking was his last, but the experience stuck with him for a long time. Exmoor became a frequent point of reference in his World War I letters to Agnes Miller when he wanted to describe the random and clumsy butchery of the war. His 1935 *Odd John* describes a rite of passage in the wilderness in which John kills a stag in the Scottish highlands. The novel's account of gruesome experimentation with primitive, handmade weapons and John's clinical dismemberment of the deer's corpse recaptures not what the young Stapledon actually did but how he came to feel about the stag hunts on Exmoor. When John calls the doomed deer "a symbol" of human vulnerability, when he laughs aloud at the realization that "life is brief and wild, and death too is in the picture," and when he bursts into tears as the stag bleeds to death, the author was enriching old experiences with later insights.[26]

In September 1910, Stapledon made a pilgrimage to a Devon site that helped define his personal mythology. Exeter Cathedral houses Walter de Stapeldon's massive episcopal throne of carved oak and his ornate funeral monument with an image of the risen Christ looking down promisingly on the sculpted effigy of the bishop. Olaf took self-conscious inspiration from his medieval ancestor's devotion to public-spiritedness and moral principle. Bishop Stapeldon, professor of canon law, founder of Exeter College, chaplain to Pope Clement V, and Edward II's Lord High Treasurer, was the most illustrious figure in the Stapledon family tree. In 1932 when Stapledon told Naomi Mitchison that he was descended from a bishop killed for trying to educate people, he distorted the historical facts of Walter de Stapeldon's ambush by a London mob in 1326 protesting his loyalty to the unpopular Edward, but he was constructing a credible pedigree for his career as philosopher, teacher, and prophet.[27]

On October 31, he took the ferry from Birkenhead to Liverpool and walked to Alfred Holt's India Buildings to join the Inward Freight Department of the Ocean Steam Ship Company. For two and a half years he handled manifests, cash accounts, customs reports, and lists of numbers that would repeatedly bedevil him. Although his fascination with ships and the people who worked on them remained constant from his earliest youth, he had no talent for the business of shipping. But, he persuaded himself, "it is not as hard work as school teaching!"[28] In fact, the Manchester laments about poor lectures, recalcitrant students, and dreary nights preparing lessons were soon replaced in his diary by a litany of scribal moans over accounting blunders: "Bills bills bills of lading. Oh lord"; "I am making stacks of mistakes at the office"; "I am making an awful mess of this freight cash"; "I am £200 out in my cash balance."[29] As long as he worked for Holt's, he contrived to spend as much time as possible walking along Liverpool's extraordinary seven miles of docks, climbing aboard the company's Blue Funnel liners, and engaging their captains in talk. But at his desk his mathematical ineptitude was exceeded only by an accelerating desperation. After less than a year on the job, he told his Australian cousin, "I am sure I shall be sixty after another three months at the office."[30]

Throughout 1911, Olaf searched out distractions. He filled up weekends and evening hours with projects, joining Liverpool's Philomathic Society to debate contemporary social issues and talking on nineteenth-century writers to one of Emmeline's favorite organizations, the National Home Reading Union. With his uncle Ernest Miller he discussed (not for the last time) psychic research and pondered his aunt Louisa's advice to try hypnotism as a cure for the blues. He drew sketches for a children's book by his godmother Edith Hope Scott; made careful studies of Blake's biblical illustrations and Keats's "Hyperion"[31]; edited his old boardingschool magazine; dug the new garden at Annery; taught boy scouts to swim; signed on for amateur theatricals in West Kirby; tried the latest fashion in dancing, the Boston, and was delighted with it. "I am living a very full life, but doing everything rather dilettantely," he told himself at year's end. Temporary escapes did not resolve the central issue. Outwardly busy and bright, the boy who refused to grow up sounded a note of desperation in his diary: "The office continues unsatisfying. What in God's name is one to do?"[32]

Literary efforts provided relief, but there were no artistic breakthroughs. He continued to write verses for criticism by his parents, but one unfledged poem not shown to William or Emmeline was a ninety-four-line metrical history of his decade-long obsession with Agnes Miller. "I saw her first in green," Olaf opens his freighted memory of the nine-year-old visitor from Sydney rubbing her hands before the fire in 1903. Linking her characteristic dress to the seasonal timing of the Miller family's visits to England, he recalls how "again she came in green" during the spring of 1908. Certain that Agnes has not guessed the depth or persistence of his feeling, the poet, like Dante in the *Vita Nuova*, finds a sign of destined union in the eyes of his young Beatrice.[33] The poem has only personal, not artistic, value, but it introduced a motif to be repeated in Stapledon's mature fiction. At the opening of the 1937 *Star Maker* he recalled his first intimation of a "predestinate" union when he looked into the eyes of a mythologized Childe Agnes and as late as 1946 in *Death Into Life* he continued to elaborate the memory: "It was as though your eyes were

11. The boy who refused to grow up: Olaf at Annery, 1912.
Courtesy John D. Stapledon.

for me windows, and as though curtains were drawn aside, revealing momentarily a wide, an unexpected and unexplored prospect, a view obscure with distance, but none the less an unmistakable prevision of our common destiny."[34]

Among the frivolous prose sketches of 1911 is a charming fantasy about himself as a dancer swaying to the homely music of a Liverpool dinner party. Abruptly his toes leave the floor and he floats out from Merseyside to the Sahara to the Indian Ocean, acquiring a lengthening string of partners while the music of fiddles and fifes drifts in from the constellation of Orion. At last he joins Agnes Miller in Australia in a universal waltz that, he fancies, with many feet would smooth and buff the earth's surface, making the planet gleam in the eye of a cosmic beholder. Twenty-five years would pass before he returned to extend that image in the glorious fourth chapter on interstellar exploration in *Star Maker,* but for now he was tentatively identifying the mysteries that would claim his most mature speculations: "I wonder what glories are beyond. One would like to lift up the corner of the curtain at the sunset some evening, where the glory comes underneath it. But I suppose curtains are not meant to be lifted—or only by some people."[35]

More mundane curtains began lifting for Olaf in 1911, and behind them were sights that awakened a social conscience slumbering since his days at the Balliol Boys' Club. Throughout his life he alternated between two competing impulses, the products of his Stapledon and his Miller inheritances. Olaf the cosmic philosopher, drawn to abstract reasoning, titanic visions, metaphysical doubt, the language of the night sky, the expansive imaginings of scientific romance, took his cues from the cerebral and unworldly pastimes of William Stapledon who, despite a shrewd business sense, remained as much a psychological isolationist as his own sea-captain father. From the Millers, Olaf inherited a commitment to immediate political realities, to the moral obligations of the privileged to the unprivileged, to an equitable society. His mother's Christian progressivism emphasized social improvement, the amelioration of suffering, and the moral imperative of good works; his father, though an upright Liberal philanthropist, stood for an agnostic intellectual integrity that assumed no divine order in the universe and no guarantees for the success of merely human enterprises. As Olaf grew older, he brought the two halves of his inheritance into closer harmony and insisted on their necessity to each other; the practical and the speculative, the local and the planetary, the political and the astronomical, the material and the spiritual perspectives were reliable guides to conduct only when they worked in intricate symbiosis. The two sides slowly began to mesh in 1911.

Reading Wells's *New Worlds for Old,* Olaf boldly declared, "I am a socialist," even as he totaled accounts for the capitalists at Holt.[36] By midsummer his bookish socialism received an added stimulation. A transport strike, a foretaste of the massive general strike that would paralyze Merseyside in 1926, briefly closed down much of Liverpool. Cycling across Wirral toward the office, Olaf saw armed encampments in the suburbs and soldiers patrolling the city. On the "Bloody Sunday" of 13 August, after several days of unrest, what has been called a "police riot" erupted during a demonstration on the plaza in front of St. George's Hall near Liverpool's Lime Street Station. The crowd was charged, many people were beaten with batons, and there was angry looting in central Liverpool. Before the strike collapsed a few days later, shots were fired and several workers killed.[37]

The strike jolted Olaf into comparing his relatively trivial problems over work with those of the carters in Birkenhead and the tram drivers in Liverpool. His head was in the clouds and his eyes on the stars, "all the while down below the very insides of the earth are rumbling as if to erupt."[38] Looking for something to do in solidarity with those who had struck, he sought out the Workers' Educational Association, just getting established on Merseyside. In October he started attending weekly meetings. By year's end he was giving occasional talks to large groups and running a weekly WEA tutorial class in modern history. In tones of noblesse oblige it took him several years to eradicate from his habits of speech, he told Agnes of a talk on Carlyle's "Hero Worship" he gave to forty-two Birkenhead workers: "If they enjoyed it as much as I did, their applause must have been sincere. It is the subsequent discussion that is so fascinating. I can't tell you how weighty their remarks are (nor how idiotic at times). Most of them have suffered enough misery (of one sort & another) to make the ordinary person like me a permanent blackguard. Yet mostly they are splendid, misguided men."[39]

He read a paper to the National Home Reading Union describing one of his tutorials and left behind one of the few circumstantial accounts of his teaching. He told his audience, in part:

> I have the privilege of reading "Past & Present" with a class of some dozen working men, all of them to some extent hostile to Carlyle, yet all of them, I think, under his spell. When I expound the meaning of words a considerable interest is shown, and they care for some exactness. When I tell them about the classical or other allusions the interest displayed is merely polite. But every now and then one or other will read out some striking sentence, and either ask for the meaning of it, or begin to criticize it, or vehemently to agree with it. The metaphors and similes and allusions are to them a foolish tissue-paper wrapping to be torn from the meaning as quickly as possible. In fact they often declare that Carlyle really "keeps a lot back, and doesn't say anything clearly, so that he can change his mind later if he wants to."[40]

Throughout the winter of 1911–1912 he met with his WEA class and continued discussing Carlyle, Darwinian evolution, and heredity, and when the course ended in early February he resolved to return the next winter and take on a larger share of teaching.

The abortive strike of 1911 brought to the surface questions that eventually drove Olaf out of the employ of Holt and shaped the rest of his life. Working for one of the relatively progressive shipping families in Liverpool's

Steam Ship Owners' Association, he became acutely aware of the contrast between the complacency of even the most benevolent firms and the dire straits
of the unemployed who flooded the docks looking for a day's work. The contrast had personal, as well as ideological, force for Olaf as the son of one of
his firm's directors. His love for William Stapledon was seasoned by the long
decade of separation from 1891 to 1901, when his father seemed a godlike
figure. Now as his own political sensibilities matured, the son's distrust of a
system that conferred economic privilege not only on his father but, by inheritance, on himself disturbed his universe. Olaf knew that William had risen
slowly through the ranks of the Ocean Steam Ship Company, and the handsome salary he commanded in 1911 was purchased with many years of faithful labor, strained family ties, and heavy responsibility. He did not love his
father less for the money he brought home from Holt's; and William Stapledon,
in the Holt tradition, was always generous to the city of Liverpool and its poor.[41]

But Olaf neither worked as hard as his father nor believed as unwaveringly
in the goodwill of the owners nor trusted the sufficiency of charitable sentiments that predated Marxian analysis. He dreaded living parasitically off
William's capital. By an accident of birth, he enjoyed a materially easy life
that let him indulge his ambitions, and the "flagrant discrepancy" between effort and comfort that produced in him a "boringly familiar guilt and shame,
like an old corn" bothered him all his life.[42] In a fragment of family biography
he wrote in 1942, ten years after his father's death, Olaf worried over his
"money-power, passively acquired" from inherited stocks and securities, from
the accumulated labor of several generations of Stapledons in North Devon,
Liverpool and Egypt, and from the invisible sufferings of the anonymous many
who had lived and died in the service of the ships that produced Liverpool's
wealth:

> My father bought those stocks and shares. He won the power to buy them by
> hard work, intelligence and responsibility in service of his shipping company.
> He was nothing of a drone. He was a worker, but a human worker, not a
> worker-ant; for he knew what he was working *for,* however indirectly, namely
> for the well-being of human individuals and the clarification of human culture.
> He knew about ships and he cared painstakingly for the men in them. And
> they loved him, because he understood them and respected them, and because
> he did not spare himself. But the seamen and stokers worked in their manner
> no less hard than he worked. Their homes, which they so seldom visited, were
> cramped and mean, and not at all like his home. Their children were taught
> in over-crowded schools, and not in the best way yet devized [*sic*]. And while
> they still were children they were cast into the economic cauldron, not sent
> to the university to be assiduously tended. My father was a good man in a
> bad system. He had ability and he was loyal, but also he had luck. The system,

through the person of his father, gave him a good start, which it denied to others no less able. And I was given an even better start; unless, indeed, in all this careful cultivation of the young there is some hidden error, some emasculating poison.[43]

At age twenty-five Olaf was still too callow to be able to put fully into thought and language the nature of this lasting anguish, but petty frustrations at the office drove him to frantic protest. In January 1912 he was totaling accounts of a million pounds and couldn't locate a three-shilling error; in mock horror he wrote, "All my insides are turning to figures. My heart beats in additions; the hair on my head stands up & tries to count itself; I digest by long division."[44] By then, though, the joke was forced. Desperate for a change, in the spring of 1912 he took up a standing offer from his father's brother James to come to Port Said and work for a while in the family agency, Holt's representative at the Suez Canal. The work at Stapledon and Sons, where Olaf would do bookkeeping, board ships for inspections, translate telegrams, and negotiate with captains for their coal allotments, offered little challenge beyond what the Liverpool office provided. But while Willie hoped that Port Said might stimulate his son's interests in shipping, the salvage of a career in business was not the motive for Olaf's flight into Egypt. He wanted a respite from familiarity, an opportunity to work on his poetry, and not least a nostalgic return to the scene of his ancient memories of troops of flamingos "flying high up with long necks straight out in front and long legs straight out behind, and the sunset adding to the pink of their wings, and below them the sand, and Lake Menzaleh, and a few pointed felucca sails."[45]

Determined not to arrive in Egypt like a spoiled junior executive on holiday, he bypassed the Blue Funnel passenger liners for a well-worn cargo boat whose only entertainments were the dinner conversations in the captain's quarters. During the thirteen-day voyage to Port Said, the ship's doctor, Olaf, and the one other paying passenger were invited by the veteran captain to argue everything from free will and determinism to whether flooding the Sahara would alter the balance of the earth. Captain James Walker—staunchly tory, pessimistic on principle, abstractly devoted to a family he seldom saw, the quintessential male loner—so intrigued Olaf that he became one of the men of action and character whose portraits Olaf began writing in Egypt. A year later in a lecture called "Culture, True and False," he again used Captain Walker as a prime example of the detachment necessary for true culture, and he planned a central role for him in a six-chapter, never-written book called *Being and Doing*.[46] Dining with Walker on the *Calchas* provided a coarser version of the postprandial debates Olaf had enjoyed at Oxford's Arnold Society and had Liverpool's Philomathic:

As we became more intimate the topics of conversation grew more serious
and more interesting. The seriousness of the subject did not, however, deter
him from keeping us in a constant laughter. "Here," thought I, "is the cynicism
of the man. He respects nothing." Yet his merriment was always directed
against some abuse or inconsistency, save when it was of the nature of a rough
caress. . . . Once, indeed, seriously cornered, he declared that all human action
was based on selfishness, and easily proved that this is so, in a certain sense.
He then affirmed, rather to our surprise, that all pleasure, no matter how
refined, is at bottom sensual. Here too he scored a clear victory. "Pleasure,"
he said, almost devouring me with his serious eyes, "isn't worth that much."
He snapped his fingers, and glowered. We agreed, and added that generous
action is the only way to content. He laughed, and said, "If everyone thought
less of themselves than of other people the world would stop."[47]

Behind Captain Walker's hearty pessimism lay a personal history of failure. For many years he had piloted ships for Holt's freight service to the
Far East; when Blue Funnel passenger service to Asia began early in the twentieth century, Walker became the first captain in the new fleet. But he was a
disaster. He was unable to tailor his gruff sociability to the urbane manners
the new clientele expected of a captain. Worse, passengers reported that, although a recent widower, he flirted with a young woman he was charged to
escort to her fiancé in Australia; soon afterward he was sent back to running
cargo boats. When Olaf met him in 1912, he had become a "character," a company outlaw. James Walker was as irreverent as the adult WEA students who
refreshed Olaf after a day among managers and their acolytes in the mahogany
chambers of India Buildings. In addition, Walker was a philosopher manqué
with "a sneaking appreciation for the sublime,"[48] the hook that caught at Olaf's
fascination:

> The same man, standing on the bridge at sunset would speak solemnly of
> the stars, and of the littleness of man; of man's will as an instrument in the
> hands of God, and of the mysterious order of the universe as an overpowering
> argument that there is a personal god. Once he turned suddenly upon me and
> said in a low voice, "What is it they say? 'To him a million years are but a
> day.' No! Good Lord, they're less." The essence of the Walkerian philosophy,
> as we called it, was the infinite power of God overshadowing not only the
> power but the will of man.[49]

Stripped of any vestiges of the personal, anthropomorphized God of orthodox
Christianity, Walker's philosophy can be seen as a rough draft for the Stapledonian
theological speculations of *Star Maker* and *The Opening of the Eyes*.

Olaf reached Port Said on 22 March 1912. He saw on the jetty a land-
mark that hadn't been there in his boyhood (and that survived until Gamal

Abdul Nasser's soldiers smashed it in the anticolonialist fervor of 1956). It was a bronze statue of Ferdinand de Lesseps, one hand gripping an engineer's map and the other outstretched to the canal, promising "Aperire Terram Gentibus": to open the earth to all nations. Much had changed since the 1890s: Port Said had more European hotels and clubs; a tramway had been built; the canal's pollution had been reduced and the old fears of cholera allayed by deepening the channel to allow in cleansing tidal waters; and the town (though not yet the Canal itself) had electric light. Port Said was less a rough-hewn frontier outpost of the empire than it had been twenty years earlier; by segregating themselves from the poor Arab quarters, the British civil servants and commercial residents had fashioned a hothouse facsimile of genteel English society on the scrubby pink sands along the harbor. But as he surveyed the town Olaf seemed oblivious to the changes; still exotic by comparison with Liverpool, Port Said matched enough of his childhood memories for him to pronounce "All as before, in the essentials."[50]

Before settling into work at the agency, he became a tourist, spending five days in Cairo and Memphis with his cousin Norah Stapledon. Mostly, the antiquities left him unmoved; he told his mother, in a show of republicanism, that "the ordinary seated majesties are wearisome."[51] The only monument that charmed him was the Sphinx as seen after dark, when the moonlight and artificial illumination with magnesium smoothed the statue's battered features and made it seem "alive, haughty, sneering." He was put off by the noisy crowds of Europeans clambering over the Sphinx and stayed long into the night waiting for the other tourists to return to their hotels: "The silence of the desert is a mighty silence. We left her still gazing out ahead, very much awake. Behind her were the pyramids & Sirius. That was by far the most impressive thing we have done yet, & not to be forgotten."[52]

The motley faces, languages, and costumes fascinated Olaf in the crowded bazaars of Cairo, and back in Port Said he found himself in what was then, in the words of the narrator of *Odd John*—Stapledon's only novel to use an Egyptian landscape—"the most cosmopolitan spot in all the world. Levantines, Greeks, Russians, Lascars, Chinese firemen, Europeans on their way to the East, Asiatics on their way to London and Paris, Moslem pilgrims on their way to Mecca,—all passed through Port Said. Scores of races, scores of languages, scores of religions and cultures jostled one another in that most flagrantly mongrel town."[53] On the veranda outside his bedroom at dusk, Olaf drank in the unfamiliar sights and sounds: mandolins thrumming while Maltese girls giggled and shrieked; a Turk and a woman from his harem smoking languorously on the balcony of the Turkish embassy; the rusty rattle of ships dropping anchor in the harbor; bats coasting in and out of rooms; braying donkeys competing with brass bands and gramophones in the night air; a sudden blaze of search-

lights as a ship began a night transit of the darkened Canal; carriages gallop-
ing from the station after the arrival of the day's last train; chanting lines of
Arab coal heavers carrying fuel to a mail boat.

In such surroundings his interest in an office job in Liverpool took a steeper
plunge. As his birthday approached, he wrote to his parents in some embarrassment, but with a new eloquence, of his inability to commit himself either to the
business or to the well-defined life his father's success had made possible:

> Twenty six years is a long time to spend purely in learning. The raw produce
> has been coming into the factory for twenty six years, and the finished article
> does not seem to be going out yet. . . . As you know I feel that my lot has been
> cast almost too much in a bed of roses, or rather that having done so well for
> roses, I ought to get a little of the rocks for experience, being of an
> unenterprising & lazy disposition. I ought to be thankful that the rocks never
> come my way, & indeed I am. Unexpected rocks are undesirable; but to seek
> out the rough ground is sometimes good. However that does not seem possible,
> so I am thankful for a new variety of roses for a bit![54]

Although he wished it otherwise, Olaf could not get around the fact that
in many ways his sojourn in Egypt really was an extended holiday. His duties
at the agency occasionally got him up in the middle of the night for an arriving freighter, but the work was not arduous. He learned to type, he developed
the distinctive shorthand he would later use for first drafts and revisions of his
literary works,[55] and he appreciated the variety of human types passing through
the Canal. Most days left him time for horseback riding, tennis, roller-skat-
ing, or swimming, and in the evenings there were moonlit picnics by motor
launch and dancing beneath the palms and tamarisks.

He found friends in the diplomatic community, including two unattached
young women nearly his own age—Marjory Strange, an Englishwoman "with
cat's eyes and the figure of Artemis," and Basilikiki Psalti, a lively French-
speaking Greek known to everyone as Kiki, "the belle of Port Said." Olaf told
his mother that he tended to "fall in love with quite 25% of the girls I see,"
including both Marjory and Kiki.[56] But this blanket boast screened the fact that
he was actually drawn to a single person—the eldest daughter of the British
consul, fifteen-year-old Helen Blech, half-Syrian but fair-haired and blue-eyed
(like his cousin Agnes, as he remembered her at fourteen in 1908). He danced
at the Sporting Club and the Casino Palace Hotel, often partnered with Kiki
but yearning for the girl too young to attend ("It is all Helen, Helen for me").
His journal records the exquisite discomforts of tumbling with Helen as they
roller-skated together and the sexual tingle of their afternoon swims in the
warm, salty canal water: "Helen & I played together wildly & recklessly. The
touch of her is maddening."[57]

It had happened before. Olaf was infatuated by someone too young to reciprocate and too distant for a simple courtship. Just as he pursued Elizabeth Miller in 1906 as he was leaving for Balliol and she was about to return to New Zealand, and just as he would later court Agnes Miller in 1913 on the verge of her departure for a year in France and Germany, so in 1912 he chose an oddly unpromising moment to tell Helen Blech, who had assumed for weeks that he was in love with Marjory Strange, " 'It is you, my dear,' at which she was surprised in the extreme."[58] The extremity of her astonishment must have been related to the fact that Olaf declared himself only three days before he was to go home to Liverpool on 11 July. Always the timing and the object of his declarations of love seem to have guaranteed frustration and rejection. He left Egypt after a stay of less than four months with little to show except a deep tan, a wounded heart, a thin collection of unimpressive verses, an abandoned epic poem, and a firm decision, supported now by Uncle James, who was convinced Olaf was not happy, to change jobs at the first chance.[59]

For two years he had sampled the shipping business in two of the most extraordinary ports in the world. Liverpool was at the height of its prestige and economic power in 1912, and Port Said, in the era before air transport, was the crossroads between East and West. No other seaports under British control saw such comings and goings of freighters and liners, of cargoes and passengers on a daily basis. Both places attracted Olaf, but neither could seduce him into the bourgeois securities of a management post. Back in Birkenhead in August and faced with work he hated, he made several resolves. One, a result of reading Thoreau's *Walden* and William James's "Energies of Men," was to adopt "a kind of Yoga" to get him through the dull days.[60] Another was to get away from his desk whenever possible and talk with workers who crowded the Mersey waterfront. He began roaming the docks to find out why the men were contemplating another strike and why they rejected management efforts to "decasualize" dock labor and offer regular, weekly work.

His third resolution was to find audiences for his own thoughts and words. In a burst of activity over the last five months of 1912, he wrote a series of personal essays ("Office Life," "A Study Circle," "Chewing the Cud," and "The Plunge") and revised his poems for submission to newspapers; he took on a new six-month course in history for the Workers' Educational Association, spent seven weeks researching eugenics for a debate at the Philomathic Society, and wrote a speech on proletarian education for the Liverpool Ruskin Society.[61] A final resolution was to leave Annery and pursue the social work he had been dabbling in after hours. Over his mother's objections he took a room at the Liverpool University Settlement, at the edge of one of the city's slums, and began visiting the flats of destitute Irish immigrants, counseling mothers on free meals and medical services for their children.

Olaf's relations with his mother, now sixty-one, were in perpetual tension during the autumn of 1912, exacerbated by the arrival of yet another of his antipodal cousins, Dorothy Miller of New Zealand, to study nursing and physical culture at the YMCA Gymnasium in Liverpool. After his Egyptian interlude Olaf chafed more than ever under Emmeline's old-fashioned proprieties, and she in turn felt increasingly shut out of conversations; with his new commitments to social work in the city, he was, or claimed to be, too tired for long evening talks with her. But when Dot Miller showed up for an occasional weekend at Annery, Olaf's taciturnity melted and the gaiety of the two of them (Dot was then twenty-one) aroused Emmeline's jealousy.

Olaf sought Dot's advice about his feelings for their cousin Agnes, always a sore point with Olaf's mother. She began to transfer her distaste for his romantic fantasies about Agnes to a suspicion that another cousinly infatuation was brewing between Olaf and Dot. While he was living at the Settlement, these tensions simmered but were contained. But when he returned to Annery for a long Christmas holiday and Olaf, Dot, and Emmeline found themselves in frequent close and tense company, the pot boiled over. In mid-January, abruptly and without explanation, Emmeline fled the house and spent several days with her cousin and confidante, Edith Hope Scott. Olaf and Dot concluded correctly that their pointed exclusiveness was to blame. In a snippy letter, however, Olaf played at ignorance: "I cannot imagine what made you fly off so suddenly to Cressington, and have been trying to see if I had a guilty conscience in any way, but find less trace of one than usual."[62]

Emmeline must have replied at once and in unambiguous detail of her concerns that her son and niece were flaunting an unseemly intimacy in their conversations, because Olaf then wrote her a longer, more defiant letter:

> I quite understand it is useless to hope to desuade [*sic*] you from your view, & yet I feel I must say a word or two more, for the honour of human nature in general. For, you know, you practically affirm that no intimate relations other than sexual are possible between a man & a woman. . . . *Please* do not prevent me from having a real reliable work-a-day sister! It will be so good for me! I have never had one before, except Elizabeth, and she is so far away, & otherwise employed. I am the brother of the whole family of them, whether you like it or not. I am sorry, but I was long ago constituted so. Until Dot came I was never as intimate with any girl as with Elizabeth. She did me no end of good, & perhaps I repayed her. She may not need it in the future. But Dot does just now. It is good for her. The curious part of it all is that it is only your disapproval that has made me talk in this eloquent & excited way about a thing which in other households would have come as a matter of

12. Dorothy Miller in nurse's attire, 1914.
Courtesy John D. Stapledon.

course, and through its very use & wont would never have been so earnestly desired! In fact you make me laugh at myself for having to act the part of a clandestine adorer, which I am not! It is no use talking. But there is just one other point. Dorothy, do believe me, does not in the least take my attention off other girls; rather the reverse, since I began to know what a girl is like. I insist that you believe that, because otherwise it merely means that you do not at all understand me. If anyone were to hold my attention in that way, I assure you it would not be Dot, but another, with regard to whom also I fear you do not understand. . . . But *surely* you see the difference between a close blood relation and an outsider. I like Dot because we are so much the same, & all that. But the whole fun of the thing would be gone if somehow we were to cease to be such near blood relations. All our relations are the same except our parents. She is the nearest relation I have (here) of my own generation. We are looking, not *into* each other's eyes with a sense of excitement, but *out* of each other's eyes with a sense of kinship. However, the longer I talk, the worse I shall make it seem.

Olaf concluded with a stinging rebuke to Emmeline's other stated concern; namely, that preoccupation with Dot had taken his mind from his work. He reminded her that she used to grumble that he worked too much and neglected her. But perhaps his mother was the problem: "You did not like it when I was busy. I 'slack' because I keep hoping for some interesting talk. That stimulates one's brain a little. Also I slack because I get tired in the evening, having generally been at it in the early morning. I will take care to be busy in future, since now you desire it. I think you are a little hard to please."[63]

This remarkable letter is a tissue of evasions, partial truths, perceptive family psychology, youthful cruelty, and astoundingly shallow self-scrutiny. If Emmeline overreacted to the playful behavior of Dorothy and Olaf, her son surely protested too much the uncomplicated nature of his attachment, as he nearly admitted when he noticed how his letter was belaboring the subject. He knew he was on shaky ground. According to his diary, eleven days before he excoriated Emmeline for her suspicions, Olaf wrote Dot to tell her he might be falling in love with her. A few days later he took her for a long walk down the Dee estuary to Heswall and Parkgate; afterwards they strolled back along the water, took out their cigarettes, and lay down in a combe close enough that "I could hear Dot's heart beating." He read Browning aloud to her and then, he writes, "I confess to myself I was in a very peaceful heaven. Because we lay so very close together she said, 'Is it all right?' I said 'Quite all right, Dot.'" After running back to Annery they had tea, went dancing, and slowly walked home, arms entwined, by moonlight. "A day of days!" the diary entry concludes.[64] What he was saying out loud to his mother about his brotherly feelings toward Dot on 23 January is belied by what he was saying to himself on the eighteenth. The sarcastic tone taken to Emmeline masked his own anxiety and confusion over precisely what he was feeling.

For a long time Olaf simply didn't know whether he wanted a lover or a sibling. When he urged Emmeline a few weeks after the blowup to let Dot "be the daughter you ought to have had," the phrasing leaves in doubt whether he was trying to console her for an absence in her life or accuse her of failing to provide him with a sister.[65] The recurrent comings and departures of his cousins from the South Pacific tended to blur the issue. Their status as family members encouraged innocent and brotherly intimacies; their distance made them seem like exotic beings from another world; and Olaf, seeming at times a permanent adolescent, enjoyed these flirtations and rebelled against what he took to be—and perhaps was—excessive maternal solicitude over a passing stage of loneliness and hormonal energy.

The deeper issue for Olaf was not really Dot but Emmeline. Long afterwards he was still trying to figure out why his mother always infuriated him. During World War II, when Emmeline had been dead for ten years and he was nearing sixty, Olaf wrote a never-finished set of imaginary letters to a militiaman, full of feelings about the gulf between himself and his own grown children and their generation. There at last he came to terms with Emmeline. In a passage transparently about his mother and father, he wrote about two people who taught him a lesson in love:

One of them preached love, often with real cogency, but love was in practice vitiated by sheer possessiveness and lack of imaginative sympathy. The same person preached reason also, but in the act of reasoning was often led astray by some irrelevant desire or pre-conceived opinion. There was another, who loved without advertising the fact, who had insight into my nature and my needs, and respected them; who reasoned also, not wholly without prejudice, for we are all prejudiced, but with an earnest desire to think honestly. By one of these two I was treated with endless devotion of the conventional sort, but I was not allowed to be myself. I was expected to conform to a particular pattern. I was owned. By the other I was respected as a fellow human being of distinctive character and capacity. I might, of course, be severely criticized when I behaved foolishly or fell short of generosity, but I was never owned.[66]

The words are unforgiving and set father against mother in harsh contrast. Only after she was dead could Olaf clearly see and state the grievances that lay behind the mockery and deceit in his fight with Emmeline over Dot Miller over thirty years before.

Complicating the furor over Dot in the first months of 1913 was Olaf's knowledge that another cousin, whose spell he had been under for a decade and whom he was determined *not* to think of as a sister, was already on a liner from Australia and headed for Liverpool. Once Agnes Miller came to Annery, Dot's role slipped back to that of sisterly advisor. Agnes, too, would be a problem for the possessive Emmeline, who would have as her ally this time her brother Frank, Agnes's father. But unfazed by parental reservations on either side of the family, Olaf singlemindedly pursued Agnes's affections from March

1913 forward, without distraction or doubt. As he prepared to make his definitive break with the Ocean Steam Ship Company and to enact a six-year epistolary courtship, his "childhood, which lasted some twenty-five years," finally came to an end.[67]

6

POETRY AND THE WORKER

1913–1914

CHILDHOOD PORTRAITS of Agnes Miller suggest a fairy-tale creature, all gauzy dresses and winsome innocence, with a steady gaze that hints at a wisdom beyond her years. But to an unbiased eye the photographs of her as a young woman have little magic in them. With her wispy blond hair, full cheeks, and shyly vulnerable smile, Agnes looks inelegant and (an old-fashioned word is needed) sweet. The gravity that looked ageless at nine and even at fourteen suggested matronliness at nineteen. Plain dresses and domestic poses reinforce the impression. Her large, pale eyes were her most arresting feature, but there was no unearthly beauty in her face, little to suggest a femme fatale or a painter's goddess, none of the free-spirited sensuality of Rupert Brooke's circle of "neo-pagan" women. Yet for Olaf, Agnes was Keats' Belle Dame sans Merci. She was Dante's and Dante Gabriel Rossetti's Beatrice. She became, in various flights of fancy, Artemis and Athena, the Sleeping Beauty and an undine. Five years' worth of fantasies created a richly embroidered version of the short, diffident, sunbrowned teenager who came to Annery in 1913. On a late-February night, two months into the Miller family's quinquennial English visit, Olaf unpacked his imagination in a rush of pent-up feeling. He told Agnes he had loved her for ten years. She was "troubled, & said she could not understand."[1]

Since returning to Australia from her previous trip in 1908, Agnes had kept up a desultory correspondence with her cousin. He dispatched samples of his verses, jaunty accounts of his city adventures, and mock-jeremiads on the drudgery of office life. What he didn't directly reveal in his monthly letters was his unshakable faith that he was meant to marry her. He celebrated romantic fate when he described the marriage of another cousin, Enid Kirkus:

13. Agnes Miller in Australia, age nineteen.
Courtesy John D. Stapledon.

"There are weddings & weddings but a very few seem to have been predestined from the beginning of time."[2] His whimsical project of inventing an "ideograph"—a gramophone of the mind that could transmit thoughts unambiguously—was a coded effort to let Agnes know he had something to say to her.[3] But she could not read his mind. He had made indirection such a habit that, sitting on her veranda in Sydney and enjoying the boyish, scatterbrained letters from England, she did not guess, any more than Helen Blech had guessed in Port Said, the message he was trying to send. Now suddenly, almost exactly ten years from the day the little girl in green first caught his eye as she warmed herself by the fire at Garsdale, Olaf was saying that she was the "star" to whom he pledged "love and worship."[4]

About to be separated from her parents for a year's study of piano in Europe while they returned to Sydney, Agnes was flustered by Olaf's proposal. Before she left for the Continent he undertook a springtime pursuit, following the Miller family and their hosts Louisa and Willie Kirkus from Liverpool to Wales. Agnes's baby sister Ruth was not quite five years old, and her earliest memory of Olaf was as part of a troupe of gorgeous young people—her sisters Agnes and Rosie, Dot Miller, and the Kirkuses of Liverpool (Cuthbert, Ruby, Enid, and Cecil)—laughing and wandering, arms linked, through fields of wildflowers on the Welsh hills. The boys were dressed in white and the girls in bright colors, and to a five-year-old's eye they all seemed carefree and Olaf the most high-spirited of all.[5] His journals tell a different story. He felt clumsy and demoralized. Whenever he was alone with Agnes, he made a mess of his courtship. "I am a poor wooer," he concluded after his Welsh offensive.[6]

He courted more effectively in writing. Even when Agnes disliked a letter's contents, she still replied to it, and her rejections were coy enough to encourage another installment. "It is strange, every word of it & I can't realise it at all, none of it. You see when I was made I think there was a certain part of me left out or else mine is a very poor specimen—that part called the heart," she wrote teasingly of one of his outpourings. "So what is one to do with a being like me."[7] Olaf figured out exactly what to do with Agnes: inundate her with letters. If he lacked the physical aura and presence of mind to sweep her off her feet, the pen gave his courtship just enough distance and self-conscious control to let him be charming and irresistible, although the sister-brother duo of Olaf's mother Emmeline and Agnes's father Frank were far from happy about the affair.[8]

As Agnes left for Rouen in May 1913, the first tentative love letters blossomed into an epistolary campaign that would last the length of the entire First World War—a million and a half words on his side and another million on hers. He saw her several times in the next fifteen months: on a Swiss holiday, surrounded by aunts and uncles; at Christmas in Liverpool and Caldy when she returned briefly from Dresden; during a private four-week visit Olaf made in Paris to celebrate their birthdays in May 1914; and in Liverpool and Surrey, in the weird atmosphere of the summer of 1914 when the war abruptly rearranged private lives. None of these interludes was very satisfying to either party—save the trip to Paris, which Olaf savored for the hint of scandal it breathed to his more prudish relatives. Each of his pleas for marriage ended with a negative, leaving Olaf in a state of nervous irritability. Face-to-face meet-ings seemed merely to roil the smoothly flowing current of their correspondence.

In October 1914, two months after the declaration of war, Agnes boarded a Blue Funnel liner for Sydney. Letters could sustain them, she and Olaf be-lieved, for a little while. In fact, once they were dependent on the written word, the courtship acquired a new and regular and far more satisfying rhythm for both of them. Perhaps, Olaf thought, if the war ended as quickly as many people anticipated, he would go to Australia in the summer of 1915 and finally win Agnes's love and her father's approval. But neither saw the other again until the spring of 1919.

The full story of this long-distance romance is told elsewhere in the voices of the two lovers in their selected letters called *Talking Across the World.* The weekly letters Olaf wrote in 1913 and 1914 became nearly daily in the years thereafter—a ritual and a solace during the war's loneliness. The regular com-position of his courtship letters marked the true beginning of his literary ca-reer. He once jokingly exclaimed in mid-sentence, "By Jove, why didn't I make my living by writing love letters!" and in a soberer vein asked Agnes, "You won't mind if some of my letters to you are rather like essays on literary sub-jects will you?"[9] The correspondence provided ideal conditions for a writer's workout: an admiring audience and a regular forum for storytelling, stylistic experiment, and literary posing. As the separation stretched to more than four years, Olaf's letters became a repository of deepening philosophical thought, of decisive shifts in political awareness, and of sensitive, first-hand observa-tions on the Great War.

One change was already in progress during Agnes's 1913 visit to England. Late in 1912, Olaf was offered a promotion as an assistant to Lawrence Holt (like William Stapledon, one of the five managers of the Ocean Steam Ship Company). In a junior managerial post, he would have to start taking the work far more seriously—indeed, would become bound in a new way to the com-pany. He decided to be candid with his father, who was anticipating the pleas-ant prospect of father and son working side by side. But Olaf feared a loss of self-respect if he stayed on at Holt's only out of filial piety. William urged all the reasons why he should not give up a secure future, but Olaf, his sights on a different future, explained why he did not expect to stay on much longer:

> Perhaps I realize the financial difficulty more than you imagine. I think I know exactly how foolish it is to give up a goodly place in the sun. I realize also that life is a poor thing if you can't do it purely off your own bat. On the other hand I would rather not have wealth and "power," for this very reason. For I never should have got that wealth and power entirely off my own bat. I feel that I have no particular right to it, & if I had it I should not make good use of it, either of the wealth or of the power. It is no use doing a thing because

it is the obvious thing to do, & because others would be glad of it. It is no use funking something else because it is horribly uncertain. Believe me, I have got to do the other thing somehow, whatever happens. If I thought that the job I am to have in the Liverpool Office would make me change my mind I would fight shy of it. I am very glad to be of use for a winter, but if there is any chance of its making me decide to do what I never can do as well as others, I had better not go. It is just this way. If I take to business permanently it will be for no other reason than that I can't get at something else. It will be a confession of defeat, & I shall be ashamed of myself for ever.[10]

His resolve to leave Holt's hardened during the early months of 1913. He was running a study circle on Carlyle for fifteen workingmen that winter and had just seen his first poems into print; he wanted more time for social work and writing, the first of which would pay little and the second much less.[11] He knew he could not support himself from these activities, but a tutor for the Workers' Educational Association would earn £60 for each class of thirty workers who enrolled for a 24-week course. That would enable him to give up his salary at Holt's without the humiliation of an allowance from his father. While Agnes was studying in Dresden and Berlin, he sent her upbeat letters about his new roles as educator and social worker and his prospects for a modest income sufficient to support a family. To Agnes's mother (more approachable than her father) he wrote that he was "fearfully and wonderfully in love" with her daughter, who was the catalyst that "wakened" him out of "dreaming in the office" and propelled him into the "great movement" of adult education.[12]

Although Olaf's last official day at Holt's was 7 June 1913, his allegiances were transferred months before. He had taken up residence during weekdays at the Liverpool University Settlement (an imitation of the original English Settlement, London's Toynbee Hall). From the Settlement, at the edge of the university precinct on Nile Street, he made his weekly round of visits to poor immigrants in the slums of Toxteth. Some evenings he went next door to the David Lewis Club, a recreational institution within sight of the docks, where 650 working-class members could for twopence (the price of a beer) get a week's admission to the club's billiard and reading rooms, lecture hall, and lively theater, where laborers could (and in numbers did) enjoy productions of Ibsen, Shaw, and Wilde. Occasionally Olaf walked down Princes Road into the genteeler environs of the Sefton Park branch of the National Home Reading Union, a network of reading circles modeled on the American Chautauqua and intended to nurture middle-class impulses to self-cultivation.[13]

At the David Lewis and the NHRU, Olaf spoke on a wide range of subjects, political (women's suffrage, proletarian education), literary (the Lake Poets, Robert Louis Stevenson), and whimsical (ghosts). In the spring of 1913, while tutoring for the WEA, he organized more study circles on history and literature by contacting workers' cooperatives, trade unions, and adult schools around Liverpool.[14] By midsummer he was at full steam: he had a large set of "case papers" for his regular visitations in Toxteth; he had joined the executive committee of the Liverpool WEA; he was booked to tutor at a new workers' summer school in Bangor, North Wales; and he had lined up three classes on the Industrial Revolution for the winter term in the towns of Preston, Southport, and his birthplace, Wallasey. In the autumn he added commitments to a weekly poetry circle, Monday night debates at the David Lewis Club, inspections of factories and gas works to assess working conditions, a regular column on adult education for the Warrington *Examiner,* and a series of freelance lectures designed as trial runs for a six-chapter book he wanted to call *Being and Doing.* "I have got more than I can do," he told Agnes.[15] But Stapledon was brimful of energy, and the work did not keep him from the exercise he craved and exulted in. People later called him "England's original jogger," and on brisk winter evenings in the year before the Great War a slim, baby-faced twenty-seven-year-old could be observed huffing up and down the roads of the Wirral peninsula: "Ran in storm & hail to Oxton & back, being paced part way back by a cyclist. It was about 13 miles. All the while I could have shouted for joy."[16]

When Olaf first applied for a room at the Liverpool Settlement in 1912, a new residence hall had just opened. By October of the next year, the interest of young, university-educated men in Settlement work was so strong that all the available places were quickly taken.[17] In 1913, Olaf was one of fourteen residents, each with his bed-sitter, his committee assignments, and an appetite for urban social work. The new warden of the Settlement was the ambitious, red-tied Fabian, Frederick J. Marquis (later Lord Woolton), who came from Manchester at the age of twenty-five to study Liverpool's huge problem of immigrant poverty. Marquis scorned the pieties and charities of the Liberal rich; he proposed to investigate the causes of poverty and help residents of the slums take fuller charge of their own lives. Living next door to some of Liverpool's neediest citizens, Olaf and his colleagues were to move beyond what Marquis called "dreams without insight, theories without substance" and view Toxteth both as a laboratory for the new science of sociology and as their neighborhood.[18]

Thrice-weekly WEA classes in outlying towns competed with Settlement projects for Olaf's time. Headachy and "tired as a thawing snow man" after riding the late train from his Friday class in Lancashire, he often arrived at the darkened Settlement to find a midnight cold supper left for him by the warden.[19] The gesture was typical of Marquis's solicitude, but Olaf kept his distance. To his mother he confided that Marquis sat up well into the morning and "hatched Machiavellian schemes" to be pursued by the residents, whether they were interested in them or not, and he told Agnes that Marquis was "over-

working and nerve-strained." The sociological imagination, Olaf believed,
lacked a spiritual factor, and Marquis and his wife didn't take a long enough
view of what was needed to improve poor people's lives: "They have not the
poetry of life. They are absorbed in statistics and institutions and facts. They
are doing good work of course. Material conditions must be altered before any
wide culture can come. But there is the good seed to sow, to come up in due
season."[20] When he once observed the warden preside at a "court of appeals"
to which parents charged with keeping their children out of school had been
summoned, he was surprised at how he bullied the parents and tended to favor the inspectors. The warm advocacy of the poor that Olaf was accustomed
to in Marquis's study seemed to evaporate when he had to assume an official
role.[21]

At the Liverpool Settlement the future author of *Last and First Men* lived
and worked with the future Cambridge biochemist V. H. Mottram, the future
psychologist Cyril Burt (later discredited for fraudulent research), and a skinny,
long-haired bohemian, Eric Patterson, "the most kindred to me."[22] Here, for
the first time since he left Oxford, Stapledon found a society of like-minded
men who gave him a sense of belonging; they stayed up late arguing and planning and having raucous pillow fights, which the warden was seldom inclined
to break up. It is easy to scoff at well-to-do Oxonians having a last fling at
collegiate life and referring blithely to "slumming" (Olaf often used the term
in his letters), but they worked hard and had genuine accomplishments. "The
place," according to Marquis, "was pulsating with ideas" and almost immediately began having an impact on the standard of living of its neighbors.[23] The
Settlement men created a "poor man's lawyer"; advised families on how to
use city services and public institutions for their own welfare; got the Liverpool
City Council to fund a long-sought dental clinic; monitored nutrition and health
at local schools; gave vocational counseling to teenagers who left school; prosecuted parents who abused their children; gave dinner to sixty noisy children
in the Settlement Hall each evening; and opened a boys' after-school club.

Choosing to live at Nile Street was one of Stapledon's most productive
breaks with his family. His father, characteristically, endorsed the decision by
becoming a benefactor of the Settlement, and on one occasion bailed Marquis
out when debts threatened to close the building.[24] Emmeline, however, still a
keen Ruskinian and Unitarian, was drawn to more pastoral retreats and genteel good works. She always favored Olaf's periods of rustication when he
went off to work on the family's Devonshire farm or to chop wood and mend
fences in solitary bliss at Edith Hope Scott's cottage in the forest of Wyre.
She found it hard to accept her son's voluntary urban exile in Liverpool. He,
in turn, was embarrassed by her old-fashioned almsgiving and wanted a taste
of reality that the house on Caldy Hill could not offer:

She was far ahead of the average in her will for social reform (not, of course, social revolution), but in personal charity she always held that even the most "deserving" poor ought to be grateful for cheap and nasty gifts. When poor relations or retired servants seemed insufficiently pleased with the harsh and ugly but durable clothing which she gave them, she complained that they ought to be thankful to have things that would last, and not bother about looks.[25]

At the Settlement, Olaf could meet the poor on more nearly their own terms, offering the means of self-help and expecting no gratitude. To Agnes he spoke bluntly of his decision to give up Annery for the city: "It makes all the difference to one's work to be here, all the difference between being in a back water & being in a strong stream of thought & action."[26]

He continued to visit Annery on weekends and holidays, but the city attracted him irresistibly. In March 1914 he drafted the poem that opened his first book, *Latter-Day Psalms:*

I went into a city to see if there be God.
The sun was hidden from my sight; the city roared in my ears.
The people hurried to and fro all the day long; their eyes were unquiet.
The half of them starved, and saw death daily before them. The half of them
     were surfeited, and stirred up strange desires.

Surveying the disease, vices, and ignorance of the very people he visited as a Settlement case worker, the poet put theology in the witness box: "If there be God, has he made them so? What part had God in the founding of this city?" The recognition that slums are a human institution did not inhibit spiritual protest: "If there be God, he shall be no God of mine."[27] The rebelliousness of the poem is largely adolescent, but it looks forward to the finer-tuned agnostic questioning of the 1937 theological romance *Star Maker.* Three other psalms composed in the spring of 1914—"Spirit," "Omnipotence," and "The Heavens Declare"—picture the meditative poet on a hillside comparing the distant, icy stars with the teeming populace of the city spread out beneath him, a prospect vision that also anticipates the epiphany on Caldy Hill that Stapledon used as the narrative frame for *Star Maker.*

The best of the poems collected in *Latter-Day Psalms* have more to them than chip-on-the-shoulder theological posing. If the poet went to Liverpool to seek God, he also had less rarefied motives. In one poem, reprinted in its entirety as the cover of an issue of the WEA journal the *Highway,* Stapledon wrote what sounds like a sanitized transcript of his daily encounters with the working poor at the David Lewis Club and in the tenements:

I went into the city to be with men, and to learn their hearts.
I met them in the streets and in the public places, and the Spirit greeted me
through their eyes, even from behind their hardness of heart.
I was with them in their homes, and their hearts opened to me like roses, so
that I am filled with the fragrance that is in men's hearts.[28]

After years of toying with ineffectual rhymes on artificial themes, life in working-class Liverpool gave Stapledon the material for his first authentic (if not distinguished) poetry. He visited a docker's basement flat to ask why the children weren't in school. Once inside, he found a woman who had been beaten by her husband; six filthy children, some with visible boils and sores and one wheezing from whooping cough; and a baby wrapped tightly in a gray shawl to keep its hands from scratching its blistered face. The sight awoke Olaf's sense of the cruelty of the cosmos: "They were not an *extremely* poor family as things go," he wrote to Agnes. "But they are an extremely miserable family,—the gods of pain again." Social work brought to a head a long-standing conflict between his commitment to economic justice and his spiritual convictions that human tragedy called for vision as well as relief. He said he wanted to write a poem that would address this family's plight, that would "express one's feelings besides merely recommending free meals for the kids."[29]

Late in March 1914 he sent Agnes samples of his new poetic mode, "a cheap modern imitation of the Psalms of David." Within a month he was telling her, "Psalmistry is like a fever, it runs in the veins."[30] The new form let him interrogate social and religious complacency as he mapped his own autobiography. Several of the psalms contrast the view from Nile Street with the view from Caldy Hill, the desperate lives of the slum-dwellers with the privileged intellectual torments of the suburban poet. In "My Cup Runneth Over" the speaker denounces himself:

I have no merit beyond my brother. Have I stolen my brother's blessing?
He has no respite from labouring all the day long, and the fruit of his
labour he shall not use.
The fruit of his labour is my beatitude. Because of him I have leisure to seek
beauty.
His eyes are blinded with toil. He is cursed because of me.[31]

Throughout the spring he built up his stock of psalms, mailing them to Agnes for comment and bundling the whole lot off to Paris in May when he visited her. From Paris he wrote to his father, who had been reading some of his earlier rhymed verse:

You offered to publish a book of verses for me. I don't think they are worth publishing, so there is an end of that. But hope you will transfer the offer to publishing something else, of which those "psalms" shall be the neuclius [sic]. Those I firmly believe are worth publishing when they are made a complete series. I felt on a more solid foundation in doing those. The verses, I fear, sprang originally from the desire to write verses. These things spring from the necessity of saying something.[32]

In Paris work on the psalms alternated with lovers' strolls in the Luxembourg gardens, discussions of modern sculpture, picnic expeditions to St. Cloud and Fontainebleau, and, with Agnes on his arm "resplendent in a light blue cloak, apricot veil & no hat," an evening at the Opéra, where Diaghilev's Ballets Russes danced to Schumann's "Papillons" and Richard Strauss's brand-new *Josefslegende.* Diaghilev's 1914 season was not his most memorable, not to be compared with the premiere of Stravinsky's *Le Sacre du Printemps* the previous year. But Olaf, whose pleasure in ballet was lifelong and enshrined in his fictional history of the Seventh Men in *Last and First Men,* thought the company's dancing "wonderfully graceful & expressive" and had Agnes play "Papillons" on the piano and "explain" it to him.[33]

On his return to England, he spent June at Annery and at the family farm in North Devon, revising the psalms he had done so far and composing new ones in order to have enough by October for "a little book." Most of the new poems, notably a series of mythological studies of Artemis, Jaweh, Buddha, Christ, Satan, and Our Lady of Heaven (inspired by his visit to Notre Dame cathedral in May), were written quickly but read like bookish exercises. What he composed in June ended up being the weakest part of the published collection.[34]

There are two exceptions. "Strife," drafted at Annery on 10 June and the longest of all the psalms, is a prescient forecast of the emotional revolution to occur in just a few months, after the guns of August drew millions of European men into uniform. "I fairly racked my brains and fought it out word by word," the author said of "Strife," but in the end he was unhappy with it—a "literary spasm," "woolly, obscure and ineffective," "too Carlylese," "a poor shadow of what I meant."[35] Yet certain lines are so vividly cast that, were it not for the date on the manuscript and a critique of the poem in a letter from Agnes on 20 June, one would guess that this vision of mass destruction and spiritual violation could not have been written before autumn:

Warriors go forth from their homes, fresh with kisses. They go to destroy
    one another, made glad with the prayer of nations.
Each host calls the sun friend, and the stars give heart to each on the night marches.
They rush together in battle, calling on God for victory. Each cries, "God is
    on our side."[36]

The other intriguing poem from this period is "Salvation," written at Galsworthy, the farm in Devon. It is the only psalm for which there is a detailed record of the event that prompted it. On 22 June the tenant farmers at Galsworthy, Mr. and Mrs. Fishleigh, invited their landlord's son to join them for worship at a local Methodist chapel, a squat, almost windowless building lit by oil lamps— very different from the graceful Anglican parish church on a hilltop at Northam a few miles away where the seafaring generations of Stapledons were buried. The minister, using a text from the Epistle to the Ephesians, began what Olaf thought at first an eloquent sermon on peace: "The people listened and sometimes murmured approval, and some sighed at the first mention of peace." But then the preaching shifted to the priority of saving one's own soul before all else, and Olaf became annoyed, for the sermon contradicted both his Liverpool-fired social sense and his own visionary theological politics:

There's more for a man to do than the saving of his own little speck of a soul. Soulsaving is a means, not an end. If every one "saves" his own soul the greater end, the "saving" of all souls & all soul, will be done. A man's first duty is to save his own soul only because his own soul is the bit of soul that has been entrusted to him to save, not because if he doesn't save his soul he'll go to hell and be burnt, nor because if he doesn't save it he won't get that peace. . . . Why always this insistence on heaven? As if a few years spent down here were to earn eternal peace or damnation! Rubbish. If we go on living as personalities after death we go on striving and stumbling and climbing.[37]

Immediately (the manuscript bears the same date of 22 June) Olaf turned this experience into a poetic dialogue that begins:

"Save thy soul," saith the preacher. "Be that thy one care."
Is there then nothing more urgent for thee than to save thy soul? Was it for
  that only that spirit was entrusted to thee?

This psalm, "Salvation," ends with an admonition to abandon spiritual narcissism. "Come out from it, and enter into the hope and fear that is greater than thou."[38] An inescapable observation from a comparison of these two accounts of the Methodist sermon is that Olaf's greater gift was for prose. Although the poem has one vigorous phrase ("If indeed thou hast a soul, forget it"), for the most part the narrative version has more grit, immediacy, and verbal energy, but that was a conclusion Olaf himself wouldn't draw about his poetry for another fifteen years.

One biblical imitation, a "wondrous rhapsody" drafted early in June just after his Parisian holiday, did not make it into *Latter-Day Psalms*. Olaf described the untitled poem as "of the nature of a psalm, but rather more like the Song of Songs." "It is from me to you," he told Agnes, and perhaps his ignorance of psychoanalysis prevented him from being embarrassed at sending her a poem freighted with yearning images of repressed passion.[39] On the other hand, he surely knew what sort of text the Song of Songs was; under cover of scriptural conventions, he could safely charge his poem with the sexual tension left over from his four weeks of celibacy with Agnes in Paris. The poem begins:

> Open to me, my beloved, open to me thy very soul; where no other has entered!
> Open to me the door of thy holy place, for God calls me in to thee!
> I will fill thee as a rushing wind that cometh in from the sea in summer and
> maketh glad the city; as the west wind that taketh possession of the forest.

The psalmist goes on to replay, with erotic suggestions more wishful than actual, the weeks in Paris when he "dwelt beside thee in the city where all manner of peoples are gathered together," when he was "alone with thee in the night." The unpublished psalm, with reminiscence eliding into a longed-for epithalamion, was part of his mail-order campaign to secure Agnes as his wife: "Open to me, my beloved, my bride!"[40]

Stapledon suspended work on *Latter-Day Psalms* at the end of June. Agnes's return to England in early July, his departure for a WEA summer school in North Wales later that month, the August declaration of war, urgent wooing in September, followed by cold shoulders and tearful farewells before Agnes sailed for Australia in October, all conspired to push the book of poems to the back of Olaf's mind. Once Agnes, still unpledged to marriage, was on her way to Sydney, the emotional vacuum was filled again by the project of the psalms. Olaf showed the poems to his WEA students for reactions; one footsore worker was so taken with them that he had his wife read psalms aloud at night while he soaked his feet in mustard and hot water.[41] William Stapledon agreed to underwrite an edition of five hundred gilt-edged and five hundred cheaper copies from the Liverpool publisher Henry Young and Sons in time for Christmas, but Olaf worried that the volume would be "so slim as to be practically only a pamphlet."[42] On the verge of his publisher's mid-November deadline, he quickly wrote five new poems to give the collection more bulk, and several ("The Rebel," "War," "Apollo") belong to the book's best work.

Of these last psalms, "Apollo" and "Athena" are the most personal. Whether or not he grasped it at this stage, Olaf's own career was bound up in the figure of Apollo, the creative solar spirit whom the poet identifies with the music of the universe and cosmic tragedy; the second line of "Apollo" reads like a motto for the Stapledon of the 1930s: "Thou hast taken stars and space to be thy language. Life and death is the music of thy lyre."[43] "Athena"—

written at Emmeline's request to gloss a passage in Ruskin's *Queen of the Air*
but privately designed by the author as a homage to Agnes—was said by Olaf
to be the central piece of the whole book.[44] A dispassionate reader will hesitate to take a lover's compliment for reliable literary criticism, but Agnes's
influence on *Latter-Day Psalms* was real.

Before he began the psalms, Olaf had trouble getting useful responses to
his work: his friend Willie Kermack had "less poetry than a pen wiper," Robert
Darbishire had "different canons of art," and only William Stapledon ever offered criticism both shrewd and sympathetic.[45] In 1914, Agnes supplanted them
all as his chief reader and critic. In Paris in May and for the fortnight they spent
in Wales in July, they worked on the poems together. In August she read them
all aloud to see how they sounded.[46] Olaf wanted her name in the printed text,
but by autumn their courtship had moved into a very uncertain phase:

> Now my dear, this book, which may or may not prove a success, should by
> rights be dedicated to A.Z.M. since she inspired it so, and helped directly
> not a little also. But how can I dedicate it when I am not sure if you would
> like it so? Well, there is a tacit dedication to you in most of the pieces, very
> clearly to be seen in some. And the whole thing strives to be full of the best
> of you. . . . Someday something bigger and better shall openly bear your mark,
> if you will allow.[47]

Tacit dedications to Agnes continued in nearly every book he published in the
1930s and 1940s, but only the last to appear in his lifetime—*A Man Divided*—
was inscribed, almost openly, to "A."

Olaf chose to conclude *Latter-Day Psalms* with an asymmetrical diptych
comprising two of the last psalms he wrote: the long poem "War"—a fierce
dialogue on militarism and pacifism—and the brief, elegiac "Peace." Unlike
his earlier "Strife," these poems were directly influenced by news from the
Western Front and stand as Stapledon's first public pronouncements on the
Great War. "War" reverberated powerfully with his own deepest anxieties in
late 1914; with Agnes on her way to the Pacific, he felt at one with the poem's
young men "parted from our beloved, whom we thought to wed," and he was
both repulsed by and drawn to the patriotic fervor for enlistment that swept
the country:

> Mothers shall give up their sons. Fathers shall be alone in their old age.
> The dead shall be a mighty host; and there shall be agony, and horror, and
>   grief immeasurable.
> The innocent shall be trampled under foot, and the victor shall be debased
>   with blood-thirstiness.
> But the peoples shall rise up, and the oppressor shall fall.

War music is in the air like a summons, and the heart beats to the drum.
Therefore let us go forth gladly even into the place that is Hell. Surely we
will go singing even down into the pit.[48]

The language of this poem, like that of all the pieces in *Latter-Day Psalms,*
slips too often into archaism and bombast to achieve more than occasional rhetorical power. The volume is less notable for its rare flashes of elegance than
for political and theological iconoclasm. It is full of intimations of the work
to come, but the chasm separating the *Psalms* from *Star Maker* is formidable.
Stapledon thought he was attempting something new and unorthodox, but one
has only to read Hardy's "Channel Firing" (composed during British naval
maneuvers in April 1914) or Eliot's "Love Song of J. Alfred Prufrock" (published a few months after the *Psalms*) to see how far removed his was from
the pioneering voices of modernist poetry. A few weeks after publication, Olaf
deprecated his psalms as "poor things after all," but "a very small and doubtful beginning of a message."[49] Nearly two decades later, in the history of his
alter ego Paul in *Last Men in London,* he made an oblique literary judgment
on his first book. The narrator finds Paul's "quasi-biblical" poems mere "literary exercises," imitative in technique, deficient in real spirituality, and seldom
vitalized by imagination."[50]

In style *Latter-Day Psalms* derives as much from Cecil Reddie's eccentric translations of the Psalms of David used at Abbotsholme as from the familiar King James version Olaf was required by Emmeline to memorize in
his youth.[51] The mood of theological inquiry, especially in the first ten poems,
owes something to Olaf's favorite Victorian poet, Robert Browning—especially
to "Caliban upon Setebos." The sensibility of the overtly political psalms recalls Blake's *Songs of Experience,* as in the bitter working-class voice of "The
Rebel" who, echoing Blake's chimney sweep, protests: "Mighty is your God,
for he made the stars and enslaved the peoples. Loving he is not, for he made
me."[52] Of the few critics who have paid attention to *Latter-Day Psalms,* one
describes the cadences as "vaguely Whitmanian," another deprecates the poetry as "a sort of free verse" lacking in distinction. Even Agnes sniffed the
odor of Longfellow in one of the mustier images in "Strife."[53]

The poems' debt to Carlyle is signaled in the collection's title, which, Olaf
said, "flashed on me" during a conversation with his father.[54] When *Latter-
Day Psalms* appeared three days before Christmas (a delay at the bindery causing it to miss most of the holiday trade), it flaunted its pedigree with an extract
from Carlyle's *Latter-Day Pamphlets* on the title page. The passage both glosses
the shattered complacency of Europeans in the early months of the Great War
and broadcasts the crossing of apocalypse with Utopia that came to define
Stapledon's career:

There must be a new world if there is to be any world at all! That human things in our Europe can ever return to the old sorry routine, and proceed with any steadiness or continuance there; this small hope is not now a tenable one. These days of universal death must be days of universal new birth, if the ruin is not to be total and final! It is a Time to make the dullest man consider; and ask himself, Whence *he* came? Whither he is bound?—A veritable "New Era," to the foolish as well as to the wise.

When *Latter-Day Psalms* was issued, the author wrote brightly to Nina Barnard, Agnes's aunt and chaperone during her year in Europe, that it "is apparently beginning to sell already, which is comforting." His optimism was unfounded. The press was small and the timing was bad; there were virtually no reviews, and sales were very modest.[55] In 1914, Olaf Stapledon was a literary nobody and his unsophisticated verse-record of metaphysical doubts and mythic icons, ideological commitments and visionary aspirations meant nothing to the reading public outside a small circle of family friends and WEA colleagues. During the Second World War, the unsold stock of *Latter-Day Psalms,* warehoused by Henry Young and Sons, was incinerated in the German bombardment of Liverpool. Today it is the rarest of Stapledon's books.

As life in Liverpool gave new direction to Olaf's poetry, it also stimulated his ambitions as an essayist for "the ordinary public." To Margaret Miller, Agnes's mother, he wrote with studied casualness, "The editor of 'Public Opinion' has offered me two golden guineas if I will give him a suitable article for his paper. That has given me the idea that a little judicious journalism might be amusing and profitable, besides being good practice in managing the English language." His journalism in 1913 and 1914 was mostly limited to articles about workers' education, usually printed anonymously.[56] He also tried turning some of his public lectures into articles.

One such essay, "The People, Self Educator," originally an address to the Liverpool Ruskin Society, proposes that those whom the upper classes call "uneducated" are self-educated, and that teachers of working people succeed only when they see themselves not as authorities handing down wisdom but as inspiriting catalysts who motivate workers to seize their own education. This progressive view of education is disfigured, however, by ideas about race the author would later outgrow: "No parental care on the part of a conquering nation will turn Bushmen into Britons. On the other hand no lack of schools and colleges can make of the New Zealanders anything other than a civilized race."[57] During World War I, Stapledon's Anglo-Saxon prejudices dissolved into a more generous view of global community, and while he long remained curious about eugenics (at least until the revelations of Nazi experiments several decades later) he distanced himself from the notions of cultural homogenization on white European terms found in his earliest prose writings.

A more impressive effort in prose was signaled by a plan Olaf divulged in a letter to Agnes. He wanted to bring a group of workers from his WEA classes to Annery to "show them nature, and watch the results" in their reading of poetry. Then he would begin a series of essays on poetry from workingmen's viewpoints.[58] The first part of this self-conscious experiment in uplift never occurred, whether because Olaf had the good sense to see its condescension, or because he could not solve the practical problem of transporting his Lancashire and Cumbrian students to Caldy village, or because Emmeline Stapledon was uneager to offer her home as a workers' educational outpost. But one stage of his literary apprenticeship grew out of the abortive idea of reading poetry with workers in Annery's gardens. In the October 1913 issue of the *Highway,* the official magazine of the WEA, W. O. Stapledon, as he signed himself, indicted the educational establishment: "Those who once would not admit that the worker could grasp any education at all are holding as their last impregnable citadel that poetry at least is beyond him."[59]

This opening sentence of "Poetry and the Worker" stated the premise he would try to dismantle in a series of five articles, published over a year and a half, including separate analyses of Wordsworth, Tennyson, Browning, and Shakespeare from a workers' perspective. Literature, he argued, was not inaccessible to workers nor should it be viewed as a luxury in their lives. He granted that no one will find "in Wordsworth's poems a pocket guide to life," but the experience of poetry deepens feeling, excites the imagination, and connects individuals to the world more effectively than any other intellectual study.[60] The best of these articles is on Stapledon's idol, Browning.

"The beauty of the world is less than the beauty of men and women. Their lives are more wonderful than the obedient march of the stars." In arguing for the dual perspectives of the cosmos and the human person, Stapledon claimed Browning as a pioneer in territory largely ceded by other poets to the novelists: the psychology of individual growth in the context of social evolution.[61] Browning's poetry would encourage working-class readers to resist the notion that their lot is fated and fixed. The essay tapped into a reservoir of some of the author's most deeply held beliefs. ("It's hard to squash a book into three pages," he told Agnes as he was writing it within severe space restrictions.[62]) This essay also prompted his first fan letter, from a reader grateful for his avoidance of technical analysis in favor of connecting poetry to ordinary experience; having heard that "we are to have Mr. Stapledon at Barrow next year" for a WEA course, the correspondent deduced the pedagogy of the tutor from the literary criticism of the essayist.[63]

When Olaf argued the relevance of poetry to working people, he was not only advancing a literary or a sociological idea but was furthering a personal agenda. By the summer of 1914, he had been teaching WEA classes for a year and a half. An inspector wrote favorable reports on his classes at Preston and Southport, praising Stapledon's management of the diversity of ages (two students at Southport were over seventy) and the care of his comments on student essays.[64] The latter could not be taken for granted. Albert Mansbridge, the WEA's founder, had just published a manual that scolded tutors who failed to mark essays fully and "contented themselves with making some comment such as 'very good' or 'excellent.' "[65] Olaf first met Mansbridge at a lunch in Birkenhead in 1914—a "tall, pale, and slightly flabby" man who disconcerted him by "staring at me in an enquiring sort of way after each remark he made to everyone in the room, as if all his remarks were a psychological experiment on me." Mansbridge took him aside, told him he had heard good things about his work, and offered to send him to Australia in 1915 to drum up WEA business—a prospect Olaf had his own reason to welcome.[66]

For all his success, Olaf grew unhappy with his lectures on industrial history and was sure that WEA students needed a richer diet than economics and history. In his diary and letters, he reiterated his frustration, and the informal poetry circles he started up in Preston and Birkenhead in 1913 were efforts to find a new teaching direction. Flush from his first *Highway* article, he complained to a WEA inspector who visited his class on the enclosure movement that "I can't teach this subject, that I have bored my students, that I *must* have literature next winter." He had to be more patient than that. He had one more year of history classes before war interrupted his teaching, and only in the winter of 1920 did he get his first WEA classes in poetry.[67]

Olaf's one chance before the war at a different kind of workers' course was the annual WEA summer school at Bangor in North Wales. The summer schools were designed as educational holidays for working people to give them a taste of residential life at a university. Sam Whittall, an artisan from Barrow who came to be Olaf's favorite WEA student, wrote glowingly of the 1913 session, "The Bangor summer school shines out of the gloom of workaday life like a meteor on a moonless night. Here were gathered men and women from the mill and the mine, and men and women from the schools. One section with the desire 'to know' burning like an unquenchable fire, the other with a zealot's ardour to teach." But he was not so besotted with the romance of Bangor that he failed to mention the bittersweetness of the beautiful setting: "There is perhaps a little too much. It hurts the visitor from the wretched industrial towns. He is conscious all the time that he has 'to go back.' "[68]

In his first stint as a tutor at Bangor in 1913 Olaf banked the fires of zeal and tried to fade into the scenery: "I see such a lot of new things that I generally sit and watch and listen," he told Agnes. "I am as quiet as a mouse except when I am tutoring. It is so absorbing to watch and listen that one forgets that one ought to talk. I puff away at my pipe in a corner and occasionally come out with a huge scream of laughter."[69] He soon found himself excited and moved by the experience of living in a classless democracy, however temporary and artificial. The mix of lectures and mountain excursions, poetry readings and Welsh musical concerts, unhurried discussion of student essays and fierce political debate exhilarated him. Able to enjoy more extensive and intimate conversation with his students than the weekly meetings on Merseyside allowed, he found his conviction of the value of working for the WEA richly confirmed:

> This really is a wonderful new thing to me—crowds of illiterate people all ravenous for knowledge, all on fire with a new ideal, all ready to make a tin god of you or metaphorically to "spit in your face," as they would put it, according to your deeds, & the way you happen to strike them. Here also is a thing, affecting some five million people, trying to educate without bias a population that is split into ever so many rabid sects. Here also are men who have been driven from employment for their views, & persecuted by all kinds of secret means. It is a real live thing, is it not, however incomplete. And yet most people have never even heard of the WEA.[70]

After this initiation in 1913, the next year's summer school ought to have been even more gratifying. Former students had spread the word and enrollments were larger; Olaf had become fast friends with the summer director, Evan Hughes; and just before he set out for North Wales, Agnes had agreed to marry him (though by mid-August she had changed her mind).[71] On the night of 1 August, he wrote lightheartedly of his climbs up and down the Welsh hills, sketching a map for Agnes of his walking route to Bangor. Only near the end of the letter is there a terse allusion to the wider world: a note of relief that Agnes got out of Paris before "all this war scare."[72] On the second of August, 160 working men and women arrived by train for their holiday of study and writing, and a few hundred miles away throngs in front of the Kaiser's palace cheered as the German army moved swiftly toward Luxembourg. Sitting in his room that evening in a cul-de-sac of the United Kingdom as declarations of belligerency issued from European capitals, Olaf wrote: "We are in the midst of the European crisis & the beginnings of war. It is unimaginable."[73]

For a few days the tutors and students tried to conduct education as usual. On 3 August, Olaf declared the war news to be "like a fairy tale" and "unrealisable" in his remote Welsh fastness. But by the sixth, some students had already left, called home to shipyards, or police work, or emergency duty at their offices. As Olaf lay in bed, he heard troop trains shrieking in the night every five minutes, and he surrendered his desire for, or affectation of, insulation from the conflict: "I shall be glad to get away from this secluded corner into touch with things."[74] When he finally returned to Liverpool by steamer via the Irish Sea on the night of the fifteenth, he came upon an alien world: guard boats patrolling the mouth of the river Mersey; the river seething with ships entering and leaving the port; blue funnels painted black to denote their appropriation for government service; and searchlights sweeping the darkened docks of Liverpool and Birkenhead. He had come home to the Great War. Slightly later than most other Englishmen, Olaf Stapledon made an abrupt end to the summer of 1914 and slipped into the new age.

7

THOROUGHLY BEWILDERED

1914–1918

STAPLEDON'S CAREER IN THE GREAT WAR defies simple definition. By temperament neither a soldier nor a resister, he tried to adopt a stance that would suit his predilection for the middle course, but the war did not cooperate. From 1914 to 1918 he brooded and agonized over his role, often driven by frustration into revising his views and sometimes exploding into anger. He hated the war and the nationalist rivalries and slurs that motivated its participants and its apologists on the home fronts. But with a conscience as fine-tuned to self-doubt as Hamlet's, he could never be an unwavering C.O. Exactly how an initial plan to enlist in the British army evolved into a troubled allegiance to the pacifist movement must remain, in part, a mystery. The rich lode of information and reflection in his journal, begun in 1900, abruptly thins out in midsummer 1914. "I have given up keeping a diary methodically," he wrote ten days before the war started. "Notes & occasional general surveys suffice."[1] Here and there a patch of journalizing surfaces in a sea of wide blue expanses, but from 1914 until his death the slim, blue vest-pocket books labeled "diary" dwindled to mere appointment calendars,

In semiautobiographical fables—notably, *Last Men in London* (1932) and, to a slighter degree, *A Man Divided* (1950)—there are glimpses of Olaf from young manhood to age thirty-five that help fill out the picture, although the transition from remembrance to fiction was seldom uncomplicated. Only once in his life did he publish a memoir not wrapped in parable or philosophical argument. In the mid-1930s, Julian Bell assembled the reminiscences of World War I resisters, and Stapledon gave a modest account of his decision to stand apart, not on grounds of conscience but in hesitant fidelity to a still undefined utopian vision. At the same time he felt the pull of a contrary loyalty to his fighting contemporaries:

> The story that I have to tell is not one of heroic war resistance for the sake of a clearly apprehended ideal. It is a story of long and inconclusive heart-searching, of a deeply felt conflict of loyalties, and of a compromise which, though perhaps inglorious, was, I believe, at least an honest attempt to do justice to both claims as they were felt at that time by a thoroughly bewildered young man.[2]

In the war's first year, he agonized over how and when to join in the great national and Pan-European ordeal. Until the Military Service Act took effect in January 1916, Britain relied on a voluntary army. All during the autumn of 1914, Olaf expected to take a commission from Oxford, where he had had officers' training in 1909; the only impediment was the completion of his four contracted winter term courses for the WEA. In November, with instructions from Oxford in hand, he nearly gave up his classes to join the army summarily because, he told Agnes Miller, "drum-beating fills one with a wild desire to go off and be one of a great army, and live the grand foolish life of a soldier, & be universally (not quite) approved, and share in the deed of the age."[3] What held him back must be guessed from his later fiction. In *Last Men in London* Paul, inspired by children dressed as soldiers and marching to the music of homemade instruments, follows a beckoning poster to the very threshold of a recruiting office only to turn guiltily aside at the last moment, not grasping (as, presumably, Stapledon did not grasp in 1914) that his "obscure intuition" was not the rationalization of cowardice but a token of a higher loyalty "to the enterprise of Life."[4]

As late as 30 December, Olaf visited his oculist to be sure he could pass the army's eye test, and his New Year's resolutions for 1915 ("most inauspicious of years" with "the clock set back who knows how long") spoke his confusions: "I don't want to join the war, but I must enlist or do something in the Spring at latest." He was stuck in a paradox: "I am simply *longing* to do what I don't want to do."[5] Yet, within a month he posted an application for work in a pacifist organization. What prompted the sudden change of heart? How did he, not himself a Quaker, end up driving an ambulance for the Society of Friends from 1915 to 1919? What sort of pacifist was he? His alternative service has been labeled a "three years' holiday from responsibility," an ungenerous characterization of work Stapledon himself unhappily realized others would call "shirking." In Julian Bell's anthology he wrote: "Conclude, if you will, that the wielders of white feathers drove me to take up the best imitation of military service that conscience (or sheer funk) would tolerate. To myself the situation presented itself otherwise. Somehow I *must* bear my share of the great common agony."[6] Temperament as much as ideology did motivate his attraction to the Friends' Ambulance Unit, but he was not on holiday. His forty-two months with the Quakers entailed continuous and arduous service, physical privation, and equal measures of mental anguish and bravery.

The career of the FAU began on the last day of October 1914. A contingent of forty-three young Quakers, having completed six weeks' drill and certification in first aid, crossed the Channel with eight cars under the flag of the British Red Cross. Calling themselves the "First Anglo-Belgian Ambulance Unit" while the Society of Friends discussed whether to lend its name to the work, this vanguard intended to set up a base on the coast and proceed directly to Flanders.[7] But the volunteers arrived in France to an unimaginable sight: thousands of wounded soldiers, many gangrenous, weeping, and long unattended, lay on straw piles in dirty freight sheds outside Dunkirk Station, where they were unloaded in batches of six hundred at a time from trains moving down slowly from the front. In their first five days, the Quakers exhausted themselves dressing wounds, administering medication, and consoling the dying. The correspondent covering the event for the weekly newspaper the *Friend* put out an urgent call for more relief workers. The British consul in Dunkirk, officers of the French armed forces, and others who watched the Friends coping with a situation that engulfed their small numbers praised the efficiency of men whose anti-war convictions they deplored.

Within a few weeks the French authorities asked the Quakers to take a position just behind the front lines and assist in evacuating the wounded. By the end of November, the Unit had two functioning hospitals, several aid stations near the front, and an administrative headquarters and supply depot. The motto of this "knight-errant" corps was, in the words of a member: "Find work that wants doing; take it; regularise it later if you can." The methodical, low-key heroism of the Friends' Ambulance Unit became legendary in France, but it was ignored in the English popular press. Apart from subscribers to the *Friend*, which issued regular summaries of the Unit's activities throughout the war, few Britons in 1914 knew of its work.[8] Not surprisingly, Stapledon was totally ignorant of the FAU until January 1915.

The impetus for his application came from the sister of Agnes's mother, Hannah Maria Barnard, known to everyone as Auntie Nina. Just before Christmas 1914, Olaf sent her a note with a copy of *Latter-Day Psalms*. He told her, as he had others, that he would enlist in April after completing his WEA obligation. "I don't want to, but it must be done." At the same time, fortuitously, he asked for news of Agnes's cousins in Rouen, Alfred and Beatrice Fryer.[9] Like all the Barnards—including Agnes's mother—Auntie Nina was a Quaker, and she followed news of the FAU in the *Friend*. Seizing on Olaf's intimation of reluctance to enlist, she told him to write to Alfred Fryer. In Rouen, where many Quakers worked at the Red Cross Hospital, the Friends' Corps was known and respected. Alfred, by then in the French army, sent Olaf a full report on what the English Friends were doing and recommended that he join them.

Within a few weeks, with Nina Barnard as a sponsor, he was being interviewed in London by the physician Sir Henry Newman, chairman of the Ambulance Unit Committee, to whom he conveyed his father's offer to purchase an ambulance if the committee were inclined to look favorably on a non-Quaker driver. Olaf finished his WEA term, enrolled in a first aid course, and awaited the committee's decision. Meanwhile reports from Flanders in the *Friend* described a growing workload for the Unit. The pioneers needed fresh volunteers and more cars desperately. Early in 1915, with just a dozen new applications pending and the Red Cross withdrawing its financial support, Newman struggled to supply men and equipment; Olaf's offer of himself and William Stapledon's vehicle was gratefully accepted.[10] On 15 April he signed the papers that made him a driver for the FAU

Stapledon's about-face was abrupt and prophetic, but not untypical. He leaped forward to an understanding of the war that would eventually be shared by large numbers of Englishmen, especially those in khaki. The trench experience induced in many a soldier a sardonic view of home-front patriotism. As the holocaust on the Western Front grew, the fervor that swept the young into the war diminished. The bitter lines of "Recruiting" by E. A. Mackintosh, wounded and gassed at the Somme in 1916, dead the following year at age twenty-four, registered the change:

> "Lads, you're wanted, go and help,"
> On the railway carriage wall
> Stuck the poster, and I thought
> Of the hands that penned the call.
>
> Fat civilians wishing they
> "Could go and fight the Hun."
> Can't you see them thanking God
> That they're over forty-one?[11]

Stapledon's change of heart had little to do with recruiting posters or pacifist theory or religious scruples about killing. The crucial influence came from his WEA students. Before conscription, the war was championed more eagerly by university-educated gentlemen than by the sort of working man—inquiring, skeptical of political leaders, hardened by experience—who enrolled in WEA courses. During and after autumn classes in 1914, Olaf's students kept deflecting discussion towards the war and their tutor's possible enlistment. To

Agnes he confided his belief that the Germans must be driven from France, but reported that most of his students were antiwar.[12] In a pub after one class, he heard horror stories about the British retreat at Mons and foresaw "such an international hatred as never was before" after the war. Further discussions made him "more and more sceptical of Britain's self-righteousness." His nationalist sentiments undermined, he arrived at "a miserable state of doubt & vacillation." He admitted, "I never thought I was so shaky."[13]

Patriotism, especially in the first months of the war, was augmented by appeals to cults of friendship and neighborliness, to which Abbotsholmian and Ruskinian doctrine made Stapledon susceptible. When Lord Derby, in a famous speech at St. George's Hall in Liverpool, proposed "Pals" battalions in which friends and co-workers could be assured of serving in the war together, platoons began forming throughout the North of England.[14] In later years Stapledon castigated such "herd-mindedness," but in 1914 the call of the herd was powerful. During a heated argument in the streets of Workington, one of his students berated his utopian tutor for not defying public opinion, insisting that "it's morally wrong of anyone with [your] views to enlist." Retelling the story both to Agnes and to his mother, Olaf struggled to maintain his belief that he should still go: "the community has a burden to bear & it's everyone's business to take their share," but, he concluded, it is "a poor cause to fight for."[15] Just as his pro-war views were weakening, his old Balliol friend, the "very well-bred-orthodox-conservative-imperialist" William Kermack visited Annery before Christmas and urged him to join the other Oxford men in uniform.[16] Swayed by the appeal to solidarity, he determined to enlist when the holidays ended.

Looking back on this period a year later, Olaf interpreted his indecisiveness as a flaw of character: "I always want to agree with everybody and do what everybody expects me to do. That is a most insidious sin, and needs fighting always. It was a marvel that it did not lead me to get a commission, for instance, just because 'everybody was doing it.'" Two decades later his narrator in Last Men in London recreated "the heart-searching bewilderment of minds which could not find harmony either with the great mass of their warring fellows or with the more relentless pacifists." And in 1950 he published the story of an alter-Olaf who lives the cushy life of an Oxford "blood" and enlists in the army without really caring which side won. This "man divided," Victor Smith, so opposite Olaf in experience and yet deeply akin to him in temperament, turned the wisdom of Ecclesiastes into paradox: "There is a time for protest, and a time for acceptance. But best is to do both at once, always."[17] In such a frame of mind in January 1915, Olaf found what looked like a solution in a long typewritten letter from Alfred Fryer describing the unique work of an ambulance unit, which combined pacifist principle with dangerous work near the line of fire.

The Friends' Ambulance Unit was, as many Friends recognized, some of them scornfully, a compromise between conscientious objection and enlistment. A member could be in the war but not of it, wear semimilitary garb but not carry a weapon, work alongside an army but be exempt from military orders. The FAU was, in the words of the narrator of *Last Men in London*, a "fantastic organization," an "anomalous organization, whose spirit was an amazing blend of the religious, the military, the pacific, the purely adventurous, and the cynical."[18] The balancing act that membership in such a dizzyingly paradoxical society required was often imperiled by a variety of external threats to the Unit's existence throughout the war, by the reservations of Agnes and her father over the pacifist cause, and by Olaf's own vulnerability to second thoughts. More than once he asked Agnes some version of the question, "Do you think I am a coward to seek after noncombatancy?"[19] But he never seriously believed he was a coward; he worried only that others might think so.

More difficult than naming Stapledon's motive for joining the FAU is fixing the nature and degree of his antiwar feelings. His son has insisted, "My father wasn't a pacifist at all," and Quaker historians would concur. In the 1940s, Stapledon would support the war against Hitler in carefully chosen words: "My (qualified) pacifism has been put in cold storage."[20] In fact, the qualifications to his pacifism were of long standing. Unlike his Quaker colleagues, he was not categorically opposed to the taking of life; when Woodrow Wilson proposed a League of Nations, Olaf said he would fight for it. "I had no belief that killing, simply as such, must in all circumstances be wrong," he wrote for Julian Bell. "It was war, modern war, that was wrong, and foolish, and likely to undermine civilisation. It was nationalism that was wrong; and militarism, and the glib surrender of one's responsibility to an authority that was not really fit to bear it."[21]

Nor were *all* modern wars invariably wrong in his view. Wars of liberation, wars of social revolution might exercise a moral imperative; when he got word at the front of the October revolution in Russia, he applauded the Bolsheviks "in spite of their oppression of their enemies."[22] In a startling episode from *Last Men in London*—based on an actual luncheon at Euston Station where Olaf unexpectedly met his former Balliol classmate Herbert Sharpe, an army chaplain in the war—Paul, on leave from the FAU, dines with a patriotic chaplain nicknamed "the Archangel" and confronts him on the European political situation:

> Over coffee Paul suddenly asked, not without malice, "What would Jesus have done?" While the priest was looking at the tablecloth for an answer, Paul, to his own horror, said in a loud clear voice, "Jesus would have shot the politicians and the war lords and started a European revolution." There was

a silence in the restaurant. The pained Archangel murmured, "Strange talk from a pacifist, isn't it?" Then at last quite suddenly Paul's pacifism defined itself in his mind, assumed a precise and limiting outline. To the Archangel he said, not too loud, but with conviction, "To fight for one's nation against other nations in a world insane with nationalism, is an offence against the spirit, like fighting for a religious sect in a world insane with sectarianism. But to fight for revolution and a new world-order *might* become necessary." Paul was surprised at himself for making this statement. How it would grieve his pacifist friends![23]

Because the Great War was being fought to preserve an exhausted and pharisaical status quo, refusal to fight was the honorable course. So Olaf believed in what he felt were his best moments. As the war ground on, his antiwar sentiment fluctuated with events: angry and frustrated by the introduction of conscription, he declared himself in 1916 an "out & out pacifist," but as late as September 1918 he still toyed with the thought of joining the infantry out of a "gregarious instinct" to help end the war.[24] Often tempted to return home either to enlist or to go to prison, he never abandoned the Ambulance Unit as the only compromise available to meet his own divided allegiances.

In mid-February 1915, seizing Stravinsky's metaphors of springtime and performance that were emblems of the era, Olaf felt at last a sense of belonging: "We are in the dawn of a new age, a new truth; don't you feel it in the air, like the spring? Isn't it good to play a little part, however small, in such a spring?"[25] He wanted to be at Ypres within six weeks, but the route to the war zone was full of detours. It took a lengthy search of automakers, heavily booked with government requisitions, before he came upon a roomy, gray Lanchester that could be refitted as an ambulance. Then he had to learn how to drive the cumbersome thing along the narrow lanes of Wirral and how to repair its insides. He observed surgery on victims of traumatic accidents at a Liverpool hospital "to get one used to the sight of things, & [it] is rather necessary in my case."[26] Then, just as he finished his WEA classes and was ready to go to Dunkirk, he had an emergency appendectomy at the end of April. It was three months before he was fit to crank up the Lanchester again.

Finally on 1 August 1915, with passport and Red Cross badge and a new short haircut, Olaf took his ambulance to France. By then Agnes had at last agreed to marry him—although the war made theirs a marathon engagement—and he was eager to prove his courage, because, under her conservative father's influence, she was expressing doubts about whether relief work was a sufficient response to German aggression. If Olaf had fantasies, however, of breaking in his car with a dramatic assignment to dangerous front-line operations he was quickly introduced to the mundane realities of FAU life. He pulled on heavy blue overalls and spent all of August doing unromantic mechanic's work at the Unit's garages in Dunkirk, learning the censorship rules that governed outgoing mail, and discovering how heavily time could hang on one's hands through long periods of the war.[27]

The initiation into actual ambulance work came in September, in soaking weather, as he wove along narrow, crater-pocked roads by night without artificial light. Traffic was heavy and constant, with columns of marching troops and an occasional startled horse and rider brushing alongside the ambulance; there were quagmires in place of shoulders at the roadside, barricades manned by sentries, and ritual exchanges of passwords. The injured men Olaf collected had already been given triage at an aid post, to which they had walked or been carried by stretcher from the far western end of the front, near the coastal town of Nieuport, where the barbed wire straggled down to the ocean. The driver then loaded the men into the double-tiered stretchers in the rear of the Lanchester, protected only by canvas from the elements and shells, and relayed them to a hospital. Stapledon learned to moderate his driving—going fast enough to get the severely wounded to treatment without delay but not so recklessly as, in a car without shock absorbers, to reinjure them. But under fire he sometimes raced the ambulance over bad paving no matter how much his patients screamed nor how piteously they cried out to him, "Doucement! doucement!"[28]

That September a colleague, the nineteen-year-old Frederic Taylor, and the patient he had just helped into an ambulance were killed instantly when a shell landed next to the aid post. Olaf reported the death to Agnes with a matter-of-fact terseness that shocked her more than anatomical explicitness: "You tell of it in so few words, just as if it were nothing."[29] It was a deliberate, a learned response—or anesthetizing of response. By the end of September, he could concentrate on driving and keep up casual patter with his orderly without being undone by the cries of his "couchés" in the back of the ambulance. The famous "detachment" in the face of individual suffering and dying worlds recommended by the narrator of the 1937 *Star Maker* as the necessary attitude toward an indifferent universe got its dress rehearsal in the front seat of an ambulance on the roads of wartime Flanders.

Meanwhile in Sydney, Agnes, dependent on Olaf's letters and on what she could deduce from months-old issues of the *Friend*, got few details of her fiancé's work in the war zone. The FAU censor inhibited Stapledon to some degree, but an internal censor was at work too. When John Masefield went to France with the Red Cross, he spared his wife no image of amputation, disfigurement, vomit, and excrement, but Olaf alluded only vaguely to bloody episodes, rarely expatiating on "those gruesome sights that drop one through one's crust of accustomed levity and callousness and make one realise things." He was still Edwardian enough to draw a veil over most of the horrors he witnessed. Later, his son and daughter could not recall his telling a single war story.[30] Only in *Last Men in London*, when he confronted his past within the disinhibiting freedom of a complex fiction narrated by a telepath from the far future who used "the colourless but useful creature" Olaf Stapledon as mouthpiece, did some of the impacted memories of his ministry to dying Frenchmen emerge into expression:

> He was in the courtyard that served the Convoy as a parking-ground. A score of blue figures tramped past the gateway singing, exchanging pleasantries with the English. They marched on, and disappeared behind the wall. Then there was a shattering explosion, followed by dead silence. The English rushed out into the road. There lay the twenty blue figures, one of them slowly moving the stump of an arm. Blood trickled down the camber of the road, licking up the dust. It flowed along the gutters. Paul and his mates got stretchers and carried away those who were not dead, shouting instructions to one another, for the shelling continued. During this operation Paul had one of those strange fits of heightened percipience which my influence sometimes brought upon him. Everything seemed to be stamped upon his senses with a novel and exquisite sharpness, the limpness of the unconscious bodies that he lifted, a blood-stained letter protruding from a torn pocket, a steel helmet lying in the road, with a fragment of someone's scalp in it, bloody and lousy. Paul's legs were trembling with fright and nausea, while the compassionate part of him insisted that these unhappy fellow mortals must be succoured.[31]

What Stapledon did record from 1915 to 1918 in the daily installments of his correspondence with Agnes was the intimate life of the men of Section Sanitaire Anglaise 13, his group of fifty or so FAU drivers, mechanics, and medical orderlies attached to a French infantry division. Out of meals, walks, and books shared with colleagues; rugby matches with French soldiers and souvenir hunting among the ruins of front-line towns; petty rivalries, frivolous mischiefmaking, and heart-to-heart talks about girlfriends and pacifism and psychology, the convoy created a microcosm of community within the larger world of warfare. As the fighters in the trenches formed their own societies— grimly comic facsimiles of the social world they had left behind—so the relief workers did the same. SSA. 13 became an extension of the male societies Olaf enjoyed at Abbotsholme, at Balliol, at Liverpool University Settlement; on nights when they weren't on emergency duty, the drivers would "chuck things at one another like school boys or hold subdued and eager conversations in corners, all about books or art or God & his creation."[32]

The governance of the FAU was founded on the Quaker traditions of meeting and consensus. Unlike soldiers under an unquestioned discipline, Unit members demanded, and usually got, open discussions with their officers over any proposed change in procedures. Despite the hideous context of the war that created and maintained it, the convoy worked, as its official historians said, like "a small republic, autonomous within its own boundaries."[33] But as his idealism was worn down by the alternation of deadening routine and deadly sights, Olaf saw the fragility and artificiality of this utopian world within a world. He was in love with someone twelve thousand miles away, his careers as teacher and writer felt hopelessly stagnant, and the nervewracking monotony of the war drove him to distraction. "I am tired to misery with all things motor and mechanical," he wrote after six months in the Unit; after thirty-eight months, complaining evolved into a grief essentially cosmic: "Oh heavens, but I am sick of dealing with shattered human beings. Always noise and blood and agonies, & each single little tragedy is such a mere atom of the whole."[34]

In *Last Men in London,* Paul identified the conversations, both within the convoy and between the pacifists and the French infantrymen whom they saw every day, as the basic human connection in the midst of the war's shattering of norms and bonds:

The weeks and months passed, weeks made up of sultry day-driving and pitch-black night-driving, of blood-stained blankets, packs, overcoats, of occasional alarms, of letters written and received, of bathes in the sea, not far from the steel entanglements which crossed the beach at the end of the line. Then there were talks, talks with those who shared the dilemma of Paul himself, and talks with the utterly different beings who accepted the war with a shrug; laborious, joking conversations with innumerable *poilus*, and still more laborious smutty jests, sometimes with Algerians and Moroccans.[35]

The fifty men of SSA 13 were various enough to make a diverse, classless society. The replication of upstairs-downstairs distinctions in the trenches between officers and "other ranks," subaltern and scout, had no counterpart in the FAU. The convoy's work—whether ambulance runs, train evacuations, garage duty, dugout building, or civilian inoculation—threw its members into chance combinations, but when he was free to choose his own associates, Olaf tried to match his colleagues to particular activities or specialized topics of conversation. He did not always seek like-mindedness. Relishing intellectual argument, he emerged from the war with broader horizons and more catholic tastes than he took away from Oxford.

With the Yorkshire metalworker and trade unionist Harry Locke and the flippant schoolmaster Denis Goodall, Olaf talked socialism; with the Cambridge student Teddy Wilson, the only one of his colleagues who could pace him on his six-mile morning jog, he tended the convoy garden and hashed over the latest articles in the *Nation;* with Julian Fox, son of a famous Quaker family, and the freethinking Irish rationalist and head mechanic Francis Wetherall he debated religion. Routh Smeal, a big, muscular, bulldog-faced, twenty-year-old cynic, liked to walk in the woods with Olaf, discussing sex and evolution. Alan Sokell, who shared Stapledon's pleasure in birdwatching, and the sober convoy feminist Thomas Anderson, who never spoke a dirty word except when he talked in his sleep, joined a WEA-style study circle Olaf set up for the convoy.

When Charles Marshall, the convoy's oldest member, took over the command of SSA 13, he made Olaf his chauffeur and as they drove to and from the front consulted him (though he considered Stapledon "a lurid radical") on the Unit's policy toward the French army. Lewis Richardson, a meteorologist whom some thought Olaf's only intellectual peer, absorbed him in technical discussion of astronomy and physics. And the "alternately sweet and viperish" Scottish painter Eric Robertson initiated a skeptical Stapledon into new developments in art theory.[36] At times Olaf felt cramped by the enforced intimacy of the convoy or infuriated by the intolerant group of fundamentalist Christians in the Unit. Then he would go for solo walks in the old royal forest, during the months when SSA 13 was stationed at Compiègne, or take refuge in his ambulance to be by himself. And to write.

Talk was public and communal, but the other great solace of the war years was the private, even secretive, occupation of composing. To Agnes he described a place of "inner light" to which he retreated to nourish a war-numbed brain on fantasies of his distant lover: "There is a secret room in the midst of me lit entirely by that imagination of you. In order to do any serious thinking it is necessary to go into that room." He knew that even these private acts were at least partially public in the enclosed world of the FAU. "I sit for hours in my car, writing, writing. And everyone wonders at me." A surviving caricature of the man the convoy artists called "Stap" or "the Stymie" shows a diminutive, pipe-smoking Olaf bundled in his voluminous, much-mended sheepskin coat in a bare wooden hut, earnestly writing, no one knew what, "in his little book."[37] The little book has disappeared, but except in the last months of the war, when he felt beaten down by constant ambulance runs and the dreariness of his fourth year in uniform, he did not slacken his drive to discover whether he had a literary vocation. Much of his wartime writing (probably the best of it) was correspondence, including the vast series of love letters, but there were other efforts—in prose and verse—often mailed to Agnes but seldom, as the cartoonist intimated, shared with other members of the convoy.

In the strange limbo he occupied between the departure of Agnes for Australia in October 1914 and his crossing to France in August 1915, Olaf had tried to finish a book. Reconceived and redrafted again and again during the war, this earliest, untitled incarnation of his ambition to produce a secular bible

14. Stapledon as "The Stymie":
caricatures from *The Little Grey Book* of the Friends' Ambulance Unit.
Author's copy.

for a re-born modern world was, by his own account, "chaotic."[38] Mixing prose
treatise and psalms, philosophical speculation and personal dogma, the manuscript is both jejune and overwrought. A potted survey of human civilizations
from ancient Egypt to the rise of modern Germany suggests later Stapledonian
sweeping panoramas, but there isn't a scrap of originality here. Only a few
passages break out of schoolboy simplicities.

A section of the manuscript dated 3 November 1914, when people were just realizing the massacre of European youth that was upon them, calmly assesses the promiscuity and the wastefulness of Nature: "Of the dandelion's seeds one shall take root. Life is prodigal of giving birth, and breathes into every young thing expectations of long joy; but the world makes war upon all the children of Life and sweeps them away."[39] Evoking a Bergsonian *élan vital* indifferent to individual suffering and political culpability, Stapledon presages the cosmic perspectives of his most mature imaginative work. The manuscript also reveals a fascination with scientific models for community. When he analyzes how individual cells first "fended for themselves alone, until for protection they clung together" to form complexly interdependent organisms, Stapledon links biological to political science in a progression from the stage of human individualism to a higher stage of social symbiosis. The life sciences were crucial to a utopianism in which politics recapitulated phylogeny. It was not a new idea; in *The Time Machine* and a host of utopian writings, H. G. Wells had been connecting biology and political vision for twenty years. But where Wellsian utopias had a direct line to the researches of Darwin and Huxley, Stapledon was drawn to the philosophers of science—at this time to Bergson, William James, and Winwood Reade, and later on to Whitehead, Arthur Eddington, and J. B. S. Haldane.

Olaf worked conscientiously to shed the "horridly over decorated" style of his prewar writings and his propensity for grand, hollow abstractions. He experimented with new voices and genres.[40] His daily letter to Agnes gave repeated practice in a more intimate style of writing, and some of the most striking prose he produced between 1915 and 1918 was in the form of unpremeditated descriptions written for her. From his ambulance window he once watched a troop of Siamese soldiers en route to the front and reached back to a ghastly memory of stag hunting with his uncle James on Exmoor in North Devon to fashion a splendid simile: "Yellow, crumpled faces they had, and fierce mustaches. Some were dead tired with marching and had the strange loose jerkless walk that is like nothing but the last gallop of a hunted stag, so supple and well lubricated and dead tired."[41] Listening to the convoy pianist playing Schumann on an out-of-tune, borrowed piano, he imagined (and anticipated his own later fiction of) an alternative world in which the music had a life of its own: "Schumann is so characteristic of himself, so full of hints of his own other pieces. And some of his most characteristic turns and phrases seem suddenly to open a window into that other world; and if you are ready you jump right through, & the window shuts—behind you; and the rest of the piece is all 'other world.'"[42]

What his letters to Agnes lack in conventional but censorable war stories is amply compensated by the unexpected and the fresh: a cameo of an aged

French peasant calmly laboring under her load of firewood; the sight of a plump hibernating rodent uncovered in the straw, sleeping its way through winter and war; the hilarious juxtaposition of a pompous French general, gorgeous in blue and red and gold, and the ruddy, bare-kneed, raggedy-shirted English joggers saluting breathlessly as they pump past him on their morning run; the inept memorial to a Quaker colleague "in a certain church-yard under a little wooden cross that bears a little British rosette and the curious inscription, 'Mort pour sa patrie.'"[43] At their unstudied best the letters to Agnes constituted an ongoing writer's workshop.

Olaf also worked more deliberately for literary effect in what he called "snapshots," some in aphoristic verse reminiscent of Blake's proverbs in *The Marriage of Heaven and Hell,* some in prose fables drawn from his war observations or his memories of the Liverpool slums.[44] He took a try at *vers libre,* sending samples to Agnes for criticism; a number of these poems, revised in the 1920s, appeared in journals and anthologies and in *Last Men in London.* After reading Wells's *Ann Veronica,* he made preliminary sketches for a discussion novel in which his favorite ideas would be distributed among a large cast of characters, including a pair of letter writers modeled on Agnes and himself. On a more modest scale, he summarized his social vision in "a clear, business-like way" in a booklet addressed to the men and women of England, but despite "an awful grunt and sweat," the product disappointed him. And always he returned to his fixation with a definitive philosophical guide to the questions of the modern age. "Quite unsaleable madness," he called the third draft of his philosophical manuscript in 1916.[45]

Of this major project, by then titled "In a Glass Darkly," he wrote near the end of 1917: "I am finishing for the *fifth* time the writing of a book that was first tried four years ago. This last is far better than the fourth that was finished in the summer; but still it is hopelessly inadequate, pedestrian, prosy, muddled."[46] Throughout 1918, through gas and shellfire, he carried in his pocket the twenty-five thousand words of the "much bescribbled manuscript of the world's greatest and still unpublished flight of imagination." Of the many versions of this often-mentioned book, only an early draft of 1914–1915 and an incomplete and radically altered postwar typescript remain.[47] Although Stapledon did not finally abandon the project until the early 1920s, he had already summed up its history and pronounced its epitaph by 1918:

Was there ever a book that took so much re-writing? Indeed it has not been written, it has grown of its own accord & very spasmodically. I don't know if I am doing right or wrong in giving so much time & thought to this one effort. I don't know that I even care whether it is right or wrong. All I care is that the book when it is completed shall be sound. If in years to come the world (!) asks me, "What did you do in the great war?" and I have to say, "I wrote a book," I don't care for the world's condemnation, nor for anybody's; for if the book be the true and beautiful thing that I am trying to make it, it will justify me.[48]

The desire to produce a self-justifying book was thwarted until 1930, when *Last and First Men*, a revolutionary amalgam of fiction, cultural anthropology, philosophical myth, and future history, changed his life. In 1918, at thirty-two, Stapledon was too parochial, inexperienced, ill-read, and word-clumsy to be up to that task, but "In a Glass Darkly" was his most important apprentice piece.

During his four-year stint in the ambulance corps, he published just three pieces of prose, all in 1916. Of the three, the last printed was the first written. Titled by an editor "The Seed and the Flower," it had been known to Agnes simply as "the war & peace stories."[49] A sequence of five vignettes, "The Seed and the Flower" is a didactic parable with an intricate structure of interlocking parts: the first story follows an old farmer who goes to war to avenge his daughter's rape, turns pacifist under combat, and is executed by his superior officer; in the next story that officer, distressed by the execution, commits suicide after being chastised by a charismatic youth arrested as an enemy spy; in the third the young man is revealed to be not a spy but a visionary peacemaker who, in disillusionment, ends up as a happy warrior. And so forth. The cunning design is vitiated by melodramatic narration, by the tendentious ladling out of moral dilemmas, and by the author's fondness for *thee*'s and *ye*'s, which lend a pseudobiblical gravity and a too-genuine archaism to what might have been a distinctly modern fable. Written while he was convalescing from his appendectomy in 1915, "The Seed and the Flower" betrays an easy optimism about the effectiveness of martyrdom and mass protest for ending the war. The miraculous armistice that concludes the narrative is not the sort of event Stapledon ever put to paper once he had seen war at first hand—although the spectacle of pacifist martyrdom in the service of utopian ideals came to be an important motif in his later fantasies, *Star Maker* (1937) and *Darkness and the Light* (1942).

While on home leave in November 1915, he began a less ambitious but more successful piece for a new monthly magazine being edited by FAU writers. "The Road to the Aide Post" recounts the questions that haunt an ambulance driver in Flanders as he transports two wounded men from a clearing station to a hospital. Is he doing the saner thing in rescuing wounded rather than fighting? Should he go home and enlist? Does pacifism ever work as a strategy against human wickedness? Or is the war the necessary "red dawn of a new age"?[50] Although the central character in "The Road" is the son of Quakers, as Olaf was not, the questions are emphatically his. The crucial issue is reserved for the story's final sentence, when the narrator proposes that the driver is not an exception or a freak but a representative of the age's doubts and hopes: "He is a type, is he not?"[51] In the desire to portray his mouthpiece character as typical and a harbinger of days to come, Olaf pushed fiction simultaneously toward parable and autobiography.

His third publication in 1916 was the anonymous "Reflections of an Ambulance Orderly." Even if his authorship hadn't been confirmed by Agnes, the Stapledon imprint would be evident in its astronomical details: warfare enacted under the "bright spheres" of Venus and Jupiter; a vision of the reddened moon rising over the German lines; and the distinctive notion that "under the light of the stars, war itself may help a man to a new knowledge of the communion of all men." This was not primarily an essay on the stars, however, but journalism written to a specific occasion: the passage of the Military Service Act and its impact on the members of the FAU. Once conscription became law, government tribunals determined who was and who was not a legitimate conscientious objector; a tribunal could also require a man to apply to the FAU as a form of alternative service. Because the Unit had always been a strictly voluntary operation, the possibility that new members might join under state coercion challenged its fundamental integrity and raison d'être.

In the early months of 1916, the issue polarized the Society of Friends and FAU members, who debated whether the Unit was so badly compromised that they might have to choose to disband and join either the army or the absolutists in prison. Stapledon's article, printed in the *Friend* and directed principally to the Ambulance Unit Committee in London, which was considering the Unit's future, made the case for the continuing viability of the FAU:

> Some say that peace can be established only by a passion of goodwill. But may it not be that some are called to that work here and some there? While there is the chance of serving those who nobly suffer through humanity's error we cannot stay at home. Toward these patient, courageous, cheerful, and no doubt misguided fellow-men we extend our "passion of goodwill." Because of our oneness with humanity we dare not hold ourselves apart from the calamity.[52]

It was the familiar Stapledonian position of "mediocria firma"—steadfast in the middle course.

Olaf's reflections in the *Friend* contributed to the campaign to keep the Unit alive during the riskiest months of its career. The then-commander of the FAU, Leslie Maxwell, had crafted an agreement whereby the ambulance convoys, unwanted by the British army, were attached to a division of the French army. The French provided food and a small stipend to each Unit member, and the FAU commander had to accept an honorary commission in the army, sharing authority with a French lieutenant assigned as liaison. This restructuring ensured that, in the altered circumstances of conscription, war resisters would still be allowed to do some form of relief work. Many Friends found the scheme unpalatable. For an ambulance unit to be independent on sufferance, to be an adjunct to a military entity, went beyond paradox. The FAU, as its official historians stated the dilemma, "remained in France in order to do something; there were some who felt that it should remain there chiefly in order to be something. The two ideals were in a sense incompatible."[53]

The committee in London finally agreed to maintain its support, but by May of 1916 a minority of FAU members felt they had to leave—most for prison, a few for the armed forces. Those who stayed to endure the terrible winters of 1916–1917 and 1917–1918, the diminishing rations, and the peril of the offensives of 1917 and 1918 continued to suffer periodic doubts about their choice. "I don't want to be quit of the war till we have had a taste of its worst," Olaf wrote Agnes at the beginning of 1917.[54] He got several tastes.

After endless rounds of puncture mending, lubricating, and button polishing in the vacant, freezing early months of 1917, in April, Stapledon, in a "strange blend of exaltation and fright," drove into the valley beneath the heights of Reims where the French were opening a big assault against the German line. He warned Agnes that he might die. The attack was bloodier than anything he had yet witnessed; one ambulance was bombed into scrap iron, and two drivers were seriously injured. Olaf himself, his ambulance stuck on a one-lane road behind a huge horse-drawn limber pulling a field gun to the front, watched a shell fall directly on the vehicle. Smashed wood and the bodies of two drivers and six horses blocked the road until Olaf and a team from SSA 13 got out tow ropes and pulled the debris and the dead horses into a ditch.

With little time for sleeping or eating, the convoy worked twenty-four-hour shifts of ambulance duty and emergency road repairs. Olaf remembered an entire night spent squatting in a ditch waiting for the next call for a driver while shells flew overhead in both directions. By the middle of the month, the drivers could not keep up with the multitude of wounded at the aid posts and in the shelled villages of Wez and Thuizy, let alone the two-mile-long procession of wounded Frenchmen and German prisoners limping down the road from the front. Finally, when soldiers in the French division for which SSA 13 was working mutinied to protest the botched attack and massive loss of life, the division was withdrawn from the front and the ambulance men returned to another long spell of boredom.[55]

For the rest of 1917, the infantry of the French sixteenth division remained unruly and the command treated them gingerly, keeping them largely out of action. As a result SSA 13 found itself with little to do besides occasional ambulance runs during gas attacks. Restless, Stapledon and several colleagues pressed a long-pending request to form a corps of stretcher-bearers to carry casualties directly from the first-line trenches to the aid posts, but the effort was rebuffed by authorities unwilling to let anyone not under military orders so close to the front.[56] In the winter of 1917–1918, Olaf was reduced to refurbishing the convoy library, organizing poetry readings, waiting for the motorcyclist to bring the mail, and tending the chilblains on his feet. The FAU, billeted at a farm in Maffrécourt, took out its frustrations in rugby matches with the idled French soldiers. Olaf, playing fullback, got his only "war injury" there, a kick to the head that hospitalized him for five days.[57]

From what the English called "Toothbrush Hill," the steep bluff overlooking the Maffrécourt plain, the drivers had an unobstructed view of the lines of trenches stretching east through Champagne as far as the Argonne forest. At night they could hear the guns thundering and see the distant starburst of shells in the wide sky. Almost at times the war, glimpsed from this prospect, seemed a thing of beauty. One of Olaf's closest friends on the convoy, the painter Eric Robertson, wrote in his 1917 diary of explosions, dust, and smoke against the evening sky as "a perfect expression of art." Under the veil of distant smoke, there was horror, Robertson wrote, but "I found my eyes gazing with a look of wonder and exhilaration at the beauty of the reality."[58] A similar bifocal vision, mingling repulsion and acceptance before a vast, inhuman, and awesome reality, made an indelible impression on Olaf's sensibilities.

When the frost broke in March 1918, heavy German bombardments resumed. The roads were peppered with shells, several ambulances were wrecked, and Olaf's dugout was hit. Frequent attacks of mustard gas compelled him to sleep behind a gas curtain and to wear a suffocating respirator that fogged up his vision when he drove.[59] During momentary lulls he inhabited a loft whose door opened from ceiling to floor; there he would prop up his head on a straw pillow and a pair of bricks to stargaze at night and by day to observe swallows, "gracefullest of birds" that settled trustingly alongside him. In this period of suspense as the German armies slowly pushed forward at many points along the Western Front, Olaf thought about that "almost inexpressible thing— the supremacy of nature over the horror of war"; as soon as the war ended he returned to this theme in "Swallows at Maffrécourt" and several other experiments in sprung rhythm.[60]

Although SSA 13 was busy in the spring and early summer of 1918, Maffrécourt did not receive the full brunt of the huge German offensives. Despite continuing casualties there was social life in the town, and the noncombatant drivers mixed easily with the soldiers. The diversity of troops on this part of the front fascinated Olaf: Moroccans with whom he practiced his long-unused Arabic; a large contingent from the segregated black American army whose "flashy band" and unmilitary ease he admired; Bretons with whom he attempted to speak in halting Welsh; an Angevin royalist and playboy whose amatory boasts he treated with wonder and envy; a Russian driver assigned to a French army staff car; and various Italian, Senegalese, and Indochinese soldiers.[61] Here he could revel in a provisional society in which, as he always wished, national and ethnic barriers were down: "If I am English first of all, I am European deepest of all. Why Europe—rather the world. I am *man* before being Englishman."[62] In these cosmopolitan circumstances he recalled the "fearfully bellicose" speeches in Liverpool on his last leave made by his xenophobic cousins Edith, Lily, and Daisy Scott, who sang the splendors of war: "The only hope is that the people who have been *in* the furnace may not be so mad and venomous and blind as the people who sit round the furnace and talk politics. Men are blind angels that cannot recognize one another."[63]

In the last four months before the armistice, Olaf felt the hottest blasts from the war furnace. The last, desperate German strike began in mid-July, succeeded by a French counteroffensive that began pushing the Germans back across the line they had clung to for four years. Like the other ambulance drivers, Olaf slept in his car fully clothed and booted, with gas mask at hand, ready to move at once. A rare journal entry for this period crushes the terror, confusion, and emotional devastation of this last stage of the war into telegraphic notes: "All my windows blown in. Left a man in the ditch for dead & he was only wounded. Ashamed *ashamed*. Should have stopped, but he seemed too smashed for not dead."[64]

As the ambulance corps followed the French infantry through no-man's-land and into what had been German-occupied France, they entered a landscape of nightmare. Roads were chewed up into pieces and were under fire from German planes; swarms of flies hovered over rotting corpses of men and horses; the smell of decay and of Yperite gas assailed nostrils, stomachs, and nerves; any cellar not already blown up might conceal a mine; towns were sinks of pestilence. There were few habitable billets, and when Olaf with a few companions crawled into an abandoned pigsty to sleep in its debris, they were nearly buried alive the next morning by French engineers on a cleanup operation, who took them for corpses. Aside from a mild dose of gas, Olaf came through the final phase of the war unharmed, and his car was the only one not damaged by shells. But for a small group, SSA 13's casualties were significant: "3 dead, 4 wounded, 2 shell-shocked, and a whole crowd gassed."[65]

Olaf's last scene in the war was anticlimactic and marked with a weary humor that masked or replaced deeper feeling. The convoy received two divisional citations for bravery and several individual decorations by the French army, although the Quakers downplayed such doubtful tokens of military glory.

In a previous batch of decorations Olaf had been passed over. On 8 November word came that he was one of four Englishmen being cited for heroism during "les plus violents bombardements" of September and October. He was amused that the citation called him "careless of danger," since he "often had to refrain from speaking for fear of my voice going all of a dither." A week after the armistice, while walking out for a cup of tea, he happened to pass Henry Brown, second-in-command of the Unit. "Oh, glad I've met you: I can get rid of this." Brown reached into his pocket and handed over a small packet wrapped in tissue. Inside was a bronze cross backed by crossed swords with a tiny head representing the French Republic in the center, all hanging from a blue-and-gold ribbon with a bronze star. This was the formal ceremony at which Olaf was invested with his Croix de Guerre.[66] When he got home, he treated the medal as casually as it had been proffered to him. He tossed it into a drawer and never bothered to mention it either in his own voice as memoirist in *We Did Not Fight* or in the autobiographical fiction of *Last Men in London*.[67] Once the armistice was signed, his attention shifted from the dubious rewards of war to anticipation of his long-postponed marriage. As 1918 ended he wrote to Agnes: "Come quickly! It is no use talking to you any longer about the dull little affairs of SSA 13. All those are of the past, and it is the future that concerns us."[68]

8

THE SLEEPER AWAKES

1919–1924

FOR OVER FOUR YEARS Agnes Miller's life had revolved around the Australian postman who brought the daily installments of her literary, her disembodied courtship. When the war ended and she sailed for England to be married, she panicked: "We had never been together at all & been wholeheartedly in love. When we got engaged I thought I was in love with Olaf—the whole man, mind & body & all—but really I only knew his mind. It was his letters I was in love with."[1] Olaf so strongly trusted the power of his love to abolish distance and time that he never disturbed the myth by voicing the sort of anxiety Agnes expressed. But a vivid dream recorded during the war suggests that, beneath outward confidence, he feared a devastating estrangement after so prolonged a separation. He dreamed he had promised to marry "a woman I had never seen." Introduced at last, he found "a sick spectre of womanhood" dressed in black crepe with black "disheveled hair" like water weeds. She was tall and angular with "huge" eyes like "muddy wells of sentimentality and spookishness." Her features were a nightmare of Rossetti and Burne-Jones."[2]

The dream-woman, Olaf naïvely believed, was an anti-Agnes obviously different from the actual person (short, blond, full-faced, and robust). But two features of Agnes Miller on which he always doted were present, though transformed, in the dream: the large eyes dominating her face and the loose, tangled hair he loved to watch blowing in the wind. His nightmare conjured up an Agnes who had grown into a stranger during the years of war, and the prospect of unguessable differences haunted him with a terrifying sense of bereavement. As the day of reunion, 30 April 1919, drew near, Olaf warned his fiancée that *he* had changed: she might not recognize the "purple-faced middle-aged man with a wrinkled forehead" who would greet her at Liverpool. But the joke about his face (which Agnes thought "ridiculously juvenile" when she met him on the dock) masked a nagging uncertainty whether he and his cousin would really still know each other.[3]

Olaf would have happily built a marriage on his cherished myth of destined love, but Agnes insisted on being courted all over again in 1919. She wanted to know the man behind the letters. "I am stubborn in love," he boasted, and with an ardor that convinced her he was no phantom, Olaf took her on moonlit walks in Wirral, on swimming parties on the River Dee, on mountain hikes in North Wales; he read Jane Austen to her and drove her in the touring car in which he had chauffeured the SSA 13 commander; he rang her on the telephone (a new resource since 1914) and still wrote the occasional letter. Within a month Agnes decided she had fallen in love with a "new Olaf."[4] In Wales he renamed her Taffy, a Kipling-inspired endearment for the new Agnes he discovered that spring; never used in public, "Taffy" was his salutation in every letter to her until he died.[5]

The second courtship of Agnes Miller and Olaf Stapledon lasted from 30 April until mid-July of 1919. It lacked the drama and quotability of the six-year romance by letter begun in March 1913, but its very ordinariness was a dose of reality. By putting the wedding date back two months, Agnes not only got what she wanted but helped Olaf realize that he too needed to exorcise spectral illusions. Their marriage at Friends' Meeting House in Reigate, Surrey, from the home of Agnes's Auntie Nina was uncomplicated and happy, unlike the wedding fiasco Olaf imagined in his final novel, *A Man Divided*. There Victor Cadogan-Smith, a decorated Great War veteran and junior partner in a shipping firm, refuses his bride at the altar. "'Edith,' he said, 'we mustn't go on with this. I've—I've just waked up, and I see quite clearly that I am not the one for you, nor you for me.'"[6] Inverting the fairy tale of the sleeping beauty, Victor wakes into a clear-eyed rejection of romantic delusion. In fashioning this alternative version of himself, curiously like and unlike his actual self in 1919, Olaf made a final purgation of his World War I nightmare. *A Man Divided,* the only book he dedicated to Agnes, was a private homage to the woman he saw with newly opened eyes in 1919. "To A[gnes]," the cryptically initialed dedication reads, "In Gratitude To Her For Being T[affy]."

His long-postponed marriage accomplished by midsummer 1919, Stapledon faced a still-longer-postponed dilemma over a career. In France a couple of days before the armistice, Eric Robertson asked why he didn't just decide to be a full-time writer. "The sort of writing I want to do must be meagre in bulk," Olaf told him, "and the result of active experience amongst people. I don't at all want to be a 'litterateur.'"[7] He also knew he would have to earn a living in the only way for which he had talent, inclination, and experience. He must teach. He had already tried and eliminated teaching children, and he did not have the credential for a lectureship; besides, as he had said in 1915, "universities are not to my liking."[8] There remained the prospect of tutoring for the Workers' Educational Association, if he could avoid the long train journeys and overnight hotels he had tolerated as a young bachelor before the war. Then, in what have been called "the heroic days" of the adult education movement, Olaf had been one of just seventy-six WEA tutors in Britain—one of only twenty who taught three or more classes at a time—but now he wanted stability and time at home more than a hero's laurels.[9]

During the war he had kept up his contacts with Frederick Marquis at the Liverpool University Settlement and John Dover Wilson, who had visited his classes as a WEA inspector, and as the war moved toward a resolution, he realized he must make an energetic job hunt, "for I have two serious disqualifications—the fact that I am mixed up with pacifism, & the fact that I have no academic connexions nor standing."[10] He wrote to an old acquaintance, the Birkenhead shoemaker-turned-educator Horace Fleming, who had supplied the boots Olaf wore at the front—and made them so tight that he had to forgo socks except in the bitterest cold. In 1915 he had converted an old Georgian mansion in working-class Birkenhead into Beechcroft Settlement, and he now invited Stapledon to become a tutor there. Fleming intended to make Beechcroft the center of adult education on Merseyside and a workers' residential college. "The common criticism that is brought against such places," Olaf knew, "is that they take the man out of his social class so effectively that he never goes back, & consequently the class does not benefit from his education." He hoped Fleming might be better at running a school than at bootmaking, but his biggest worry about becoming a residential tutor was directed inward: "My general history I have mostly forgotten. Literature, the thing I really want to do, I have never really worked at. Consequently I shall be in a hole."[11]

When the Friends' Ambulance Unit disbanded in January 1919 Olaf was too late for the 1918–1919 season of adult-education classes, but he began lining up possibilities for the following autumn. Fleming, it turned out, had so little money that teaching at Beechcroft came close to being volunteer work. He could, however, give Olaf and Agnes the use of a small house in Heswall— a tempting offer since housing was in short supply—but Olaf feared being drawn into uncongenial administrative work at Beechcroft. He went to the WEA to look for something more to his liking and was disappointed to learn that the stipend for a WEA course had gone up from £60 in 1914 to only £70 five years later; a full slate of four courses taught over six months would produce a "very paltry figure," given the steep rise in the cost of living. He could add £30 a year in unearned money—interest from stocks his father had given him— but he would need additional work in the summers to support himself and his wife.[12] William Stapledon's assets in 1919 amounted to £150,000, but he and Emmeline lived on just £1,500 a year, reserving a substantial portion of their wealth for "the support of movements we believe in," "charities which we think sound," and "the amelioration of the lives of people we know." The contrast between father's and son's financial worth always pricked at Olaf's pride. He did not want his life "ameliorated" by paternal charity; nevertheless, he and Agnes gratefully accepted William's wedding gift of an eight-room, semidetached house on Grosvenor Avenue in West Kirby, which they began occupying in April 1920.[13]

Olaf temporarily solved the problem of money by profiting from changes in the institutional relationship between the WEA and the universities. After the war the Ministry of Reconstruction pressed the universities to enhance the pay scale of extramural tutors and to give them the status of university staff members.[14] The Extension program at Liverpool, under the joint control of Liverpool University and the Merseyside WEA, established several staff positions designated for extramural work. Accepting one of these posts, which made the tutor simultaneously an insider and an outsider at the university, Olaf took on four WEA courses per year, some lectures at Beechcroft under university auspices, and minor duties at the university at an annual salary of £500. In the 1919-1920 season only one of his courses—at Blackpool—was far enough from Liverpool to require lengthy travel and an overnight stay. The arrangement was as close to ideal as he could expect and his active association with Liverpool University Extension lasted more than fifteen years.[15]

In 1920, Olaf was clearer than he had been a decade earlier about his political commitments to education. He had sloughed off some of his romanticism for a more practical (and less condescending) attitude toward teaching workers; his years in the classless world of the FAU had gone a long way to taming down the snobbery of Oxford and stoking up the reformist impulses of his inheritance. But while surer of his utopian-socialist principles than ever before, in some ways he enjoyed the WEA less than he had in 1914. The war had unsettled him as a teacher, "not merely in making one forget one's subject, but in upsetting all one's faith in one's own personality and 'call' to teach."[16] His 1919-1920 classes, as he had hoped, were in literature rather than industrial history but, feeling deficient in the nineteenth-century novel, he put in long days at the library reading Dickens and George Eliot—hours subtracted from time for his old book manuscript and his poetry. He fretted over the lack of space for a study in the cramped lodgings in Carpenter's Lane, West Kirby, which he and Agnes took in autumn 1919 despite Emmeline Stapledon's tearful urging that they share Annery with her.[17]

As he began his courses in October, he had another reason to worry about balancing teaching with writing while making ends meet on a WEA salary.

Three months after their marriage, Agnes wrote her mother to say that she was in the second month of pregnancy: "Olaf & I are very glad that it is going to be—but we are rather sorry it is quite so soon."[18] On the last day of May 1920, Mary Sydney Stapledon was born at 7 Grosvenor Avenue, and Olaf, in his mid-thirties and a creature of his own routines, found himself having to adjust, not always gracefully, to having his day ruled by Mary and the pram.

Circumstances did not allow him to recover his vocation without inner conflict, and the larger world failed to cooperate with his utopian dreams. Throughout the war Stapledon expected a great cultural reordering—spiritual and ethical as well as political and economic—once the world extricated itself from the catastrophe of 1914–1918. Woodrow Wilson's League of Nations and the October revolution in Russia seemed tangible signs of change, but as Olaf tried to start up a new life, the Allies worked strenuously to undermine the Bolshevik regime, the United States turned its back on the League, the Treaty of Versailles was used to legitimize vindictiveness, and Cosmopolis was nowhere on the horizon. A reunion with a figure from his past reinforced Stapledon's disenchantment.

The headmaster of Abbotsholme School paid a visit to Liverpool. Sixty-five, white-haired, and as irascible and opinionated as ever, Cecil Reddie was making a final effort to rebuild the school before his forced ouster in 1927. Joining Olaf for dinner with Frederick Marquis, Reddie launched a brisk defense of his familiar notions of Teutonic cultural superiority. Olaf was angry that the war had not dislodged any of his old teacher's views on nationalism and German manifest destiny. "We had a furious fight," he told Agnes, "and I told 'CR' the truth about his prejudices."[19] Reddie's views might be dismissed as those of an old crank on the verge of emotional collapse, as he was, but Olaf sensed that CR was also representative of a pervasive resistance to the idea of a world community. Far too few people had begun the 1920s with the cosmopolitan perspectives he had assumed would be the chief positive effect of the war.

The exciting political context in which Stapledon had imagined himself engaging the cause of democratic education had evaporated. Like the protagonist in H. G. Wells's turn-of-the-century dystopian romance *When the Sleeper Wakes,* he arose from a long hibernation to find himself a displaced person in a society that did not offer the comfort of things as they used to be and did not endorse the gratifying challenges of things as they might be. The Great War had flayed the world and exposed both its hidden cancers and its unexploited capacities for healthful regeneration. As Olaf continued the metaphor in the years just after the war: "It was good that this civilized skin should be stripped from us, for it was diseased. But alas, the new skin now forming is much as the old."[20] When he returned to full-time teaching in 1919, he did so with energy and a gritty determination to do it right, but the fire of his old idealism was cooled.

As he had changed during the war, so had the WEA. One notable change was a sharp rise in the number of women students. From the movement's beginning, working women had been active and articulate, objecting to the term "working men" (and substituting "workpeople") in public discussions and insisting on the name *Workers'* Educational Association. Before 1914, Albert Mansbridge found that only 15 percent of a workers' class were women, although they attended more regularly than the men and were eager publicists for the classes. During the war women's enrollment kept climbing until by 1919 they comprised nearly 45 percent of WEA students in England and Wales.[21] Olaf's courses in the 1919-1920 season included one class composed entirely of women—a third-year literature course for Birkenhead schoolteachers. When his other classes disappointed him by lax attendance or "stodgy" attitudes, the women teachers always perked him up.[22]

But, if Victor Smith's acerbic views in *A Man Divided* were drawn from Olaf's memories of WEA work, the Birkenhead teachers (who were professionally motivated to take the work seriously) were exceptional. As Victor, a WEA tutor, tells it, the women who enrolled in courses were "the inevitable spinsters who have nothing else to do, and are apt to take the line that if only people would be kind to each other, we shouldn't have any social problems."[23] *A Man Divided* contains the author's fullest commentary on the WEA, although neither Victor's misogyny nor the vinegary flavor of a novel of 1950 (when the Association's day had passed) should necessarily be identified with the Olaf of 1920. The novel's criticism of the adult education movement, however, does reflect an ambivalence that grew in Stapledon throughout the 1920s and 1930s.

In a 1923 lecture whose title he admitted had a personal relevance, he put the question to a group of Merseyside schoolmasters: "Why Teach?" Knowing that his audience might consider his question "impertinent," he emphasized, "I ask *for information*. Please help. Why do *you* teach?" He told his own educational history, recalling himself as a dull pupil who got sleepy during lessons and as an ineffectual schoolmaster whose year at Manchester was pure torment. Tutoring for the WEA, he feared, was also mostly a failure for the simple reason that "no one ever *learnt* anything." He spoke feelingly of the paradoxes of education: when he was taught *Hamlet* as a child, it was ruined for him, and he never learned to enjoy it until he had to teach it—and ruin it for others. At home his three-year-old daughter was learning to talk very well without any teaching, but learning to draw and count badly despite—or because of—his efforts to instruct her.[24]

Few occupations provoke as many vocational crises as teaching does, and Stapledon was gifted at self-doubt. Irregular diary entries in 1920 and 1921 record occasional delight in a successful lecture but more often dismay at students' wrangling and carping, their failures of attention and focus, their lack of readiness for literary study. He told his father that his students were bored with Blake and found Browning "too stiff on the whole." "I find that what they really want is rather English Composition and practice in speaking."[25] His impatience had not yet sunk to the burned-out cynicism of Victor Smith's verdict (the narrator calls it a "tirade") on the limitations of the WEA's noble purpose of achieving democracy through a weekly tutorial:

> We are supposed to be giving something like a university education to the working population of this country. But of course we can't possibly do anything of the sort, except in a few cases. A univerity education involves all sorts of things that the members of extra-mural classes can't possibly bring. It involves young and supple minds full of vigour and curiosity. It involves access to plenty of books. It involves intensive tuition, and heaps of time for reading and writing. But our students are mostly far from young; their minds are already set; they come to the job after a hard day's work; they're not capable of serious study, because they have never learnt what serious study means; they can't read heavy books; they find great difficulty in expressing themselves in writing; they mostly mistake asseveration for genuine discussion . . . The good souls we do get hold of don't really want the life of the mind at all. They want either a little easy entertainment after the serious part of the day is over, or the *cachet* of being an educated person. Or else they come in search of data and propaganda to use against their political opponents. Mind you, I don't *blame* them for these motives. In their circumstances they are bound to want these things. But you can't create an educated democracy on that basis. We are supposed to be building Jerusalem in England's green and pleasant minds (and, God, they're green all right); but we are not going about it in the right way. Mind you, we are doing something well worth doing, in its own little way. But we are not doing what we pretend we are doing.[26]

It took Stapledon many more years as a tutor to reach the point of abandoning the WEA If he never fully endorsed Victor Smith's scathing critique, he revealed something close to despair in a letter he later wrote to his daughter when, at the age of twenty-two, she stunned him by suggesting that she might go into WEA work. By then, in the midst of a second world war, Olaf felt it was clearly not the route either to Utopia or to professional gratification for the teacher:

> Long ago it used to be a very fine pioneering social service, but today it's very different. You don't often get real working class people—mostly lower middle. That doesn't matter really, but the trouble is that the vast majority

are much too tired or too lazy to [do] any serious work. The whole thing is far more dilettante than it was even when *I* began tutoring. The standard of work is generally very low, though there are some few brilliant classes and one or two really keen individuals in most classes. As a job, WEA tutoring gets a bit depressing, unless you are one of the really keen and brilliant tutors, who make a great thing of it. The ordinary tutor (i.e. me) is always struggling against his own ignorance and the amiable sluggishness of the class. . . . Certainly one gains a vast amount of experience of social conditions and of human nature. It certainly educates the tutor. It also allows you most of the summer to work on your own. In spite of these advantages it really is rather heartbreaking unless you feel you have a special gift for it. Extra mural work leads nowhere unless sooner or later you get out of it, into academic or social work of some other kind.[27]

Thus the disenchanted voice of 1942, but even at the start of 1921, Olaf was tempted to strike out for something new. His life was accommodating marriage and parenthood better than teaching and writing: "This New Year finds us well-accustomed to domestic life, well content with each other & with Mary, financially very rotten, in health very well. My work is unsatisfactory. I am not pulling my weight, either as a tutor of tutorial classes or as a writer of books (*a* book) that are never finished." When his birthday came around, he repeated the theme more concisely: "35, alas! blessed with the best of wives & daughters, & cursed with futility."[28] Nevertheless, 1921 was a year of decisive change, if he recalled chronology accurately in a note he composed for the dust jacket of the 1939 Pelican *Philosophy and Living:* "As a married adolescent of thirty-five, I woke. My mind painfully emerged from a larval into a kind of retarded and deformed imago state."[29]

He began stealing time from classwork to recast the book he had been writing throughout the war, now going by the title "The Sleeping Beauty." When he finished the winter term of 1920-1921, he decided, "I must chuck staff tutoring as it is too amateurish, leads nowhere, & does not keep us," but by then he had chucked jobs so often that self-respect kept him from simply walking out on the WEA.[30] The combination of straitened finances, unfulfilled ambitions, and a new baby made him tense and irritable, and Agnes, enduring a steady diet of his "grousing & grumbling & criticising," agreed that something had to be done.[31] William Stapledon, ever generous and uncomplaining, provided the necessary monetary support.

Olaf felt ready to set aside his bias against universities in order to find intellectual companionship and stimulation and perhaps sponsorship of his writing. Unwilling to live entirely on a subsidy from his father, he would continue to work half-time for the WEA if he could be admitted to a Ph.D. program in psychology. With that credential he might at last become a full-fledged insider,

securing a lectureship and gaining more control over his career. The amphibi-
ous creature known as an extramural staff tutor had small opportunity for
growth or advancement, and despite improvements in salary for WEA tutors,
their prestige was still minimal. The great lights among the WEA teachers—
Olaf's old tutor A. L. Smith at Balliol, the historian R. H. Tawney in London,
the social theorist G. D. H. Cole—as well as such local Merseyside luminaries as the literary historian Oliver Elton and the sociologist A. M. Carr-Saunders
were not staff tutors confined to extension classes but university professors who
freely chose to teach workers as part of their professional self-definition. Olaf
hungered for such freedom. But since he would be nearly forty by the time he
completed a Ph.D. thesis, a professorial appointment was far from assured.

In the spring of 1921 he went to see Alexander Mair, head of Liverpool
University's philosophy department (which at that time encompassed the study
of psychology). Mair was "cautious but encouraging" about his prospects and
asked Olaf to let him see the manuscript he had labored over for so many years.
Olaf shut himself up in West Kirby and for nearly two months worked as best
he could, against the background of a neighbor noisily going mad night and
day, to complete, shorten, polish, and type what would be the last version of
"The Sleeping Beauty." On 29 June he called again on Professor Mair, gave
him the typescript, and spent the summer nervously awaiting a verdict.[32]

What Mair read that summer would have revealed a good deal about its
author's still-raw but prodigal mind. The title suggested a fairy tale, but, like
William Blake, Stapledon wanted to cleanse the doors of perception: "All our
effort seeks to awaken in the world the mind that shall see, by no mere act of
faith but by irrefutable sense, that all that ever happened is beauty exquisite as
the rose," he announced, deploying his favorite metaphor of sleeping and waking. Stapledon's visionary auguries include Wordsworth's rainbow, the blue-
ness of a speedwell blending into the blue sky, the "elegance of diatoms," the
flashing of Sirius in the night sky, a smoothly running engine, the roar of gun-
fire, Othello's remorse, the patience of Tess, the bold thighs of a naked diver,
a girl with sunlit hair and sunbrowned face. The miscellany, compounded out
of the common stock of romantic poetry and the figures of tragic literature,
out of the Great War, new technology, microscopic and telescopic observation,
Victorianism undraped, and the countenance of his Australian wife, crisply defies expectation as cliché bumps up against new-minted image. Familiar cultural tokens are given iconoclastic analysis, as in a shrewd comment on
Shakespearean psychology:

> Iago saw beauty in skilfully poisoning a spirit that trusted him. If ever there
> was false beauty this was it. But the things that pleased him were the exercise
> of his psychological skill, the sense of his power to turn the current of events,

and a deep vendetta instinct. And of these the first two are in themselves beautiful, though he turned them to evil uses, and the last sprung in mankind's early days from a crude sense of justice. But the root of justice is the herd-instinct that finds the noblest of beauties in society. Thus it seems that Iago's devilry was due less to the presence of something essentially evil than to the absence of something good. He lacked love.[33]

The truncated typescript of "The Sleeping Beauty" maps characteristic Stapledonian themes and formal experiments. Its genre is the manifesto—which makes it the precursor of the later "book of dogmas" called *Waking World* (1934); the idea of God as a great musician whose notes are alien to humanity is a sketch for the infinitely complex and chilling deity in *Star Maker* (1937); and the old tale of the Sleeping Beauty, with the beloved's sleeping and waking used as figures for states of spiritual consciousness, underlies all his later utopian thinking. In the fairy story, when Beauty opens her eyes, her whole court reawakens. "But the World is a sleeping beauty of another kind. Not until all her court has been roused can she, the Soul of the World, be wakened. And her sleep, not of a hundred years but of a hundred thousand aeons, is a sleep of no ripe beauty but of a mind unborn."[34]

The eleventh and final chapter of "The Sleeping Beauty" is a labored effort at an alpha-and-omega myth of cosmic origins and ultimate destiny; its chief adornment is a climactic fantasia on human history from the paleolithic "first men" through the civilizing of the planet and its later wreckage in a future war to a recuperation of the earth when human nature is remade in preparation for outward movement to other planets and stars before the final cosmic dissolution. Here was Stapledon's first uncertain foray into science fiction, using a clumsy imitation of Wells's method in the 1920 *Outline of History;* in a few years he would outgrow the model with his own imaginative scenarios for the future in *Last and First Men.*[35] If Alexander Mair urged Olaf to forget "The Sleeping Beauty," it was probably the right advice, since he was still a long way from achieving a usable form, an authoritative voice, and skill at linking abstract ideas to narrative design and detail. Rhetorically, "The Sleeping Beauty" shows little advance over the preachments of *Latter-Day Psalms* and the crude allegorizing in "The Seed and the Flower," but the philosophical discourse was far richer than in the version of "In a Glass Darkly" he had written at the beginning of the war.

No account survives of what Mair said about the typescript, but Olaf never again mentioned "The Sleeping Beauty," and he must have been persuaded to put that nearly ten-years' project behind him and make a fresh start. Mair advised him to take an M.A. in philosophy first, before doing his Ph.D., because it was all too evident, as Stapledon himself once acknowledged, that he had "not read a serious philosophical book until he was over 30."[36] When he matriculated for the 1921-1922 session, he chose as the subject of his course of study "the use and significance of the symbol in psychology"—a topic closely tied to the interests he had been following in "The Sleeping Beauty."[37]

In age and temperament Olaf was not a conventional graduate student. He planned his course of study while working up his German and preparing his syllabus for two extension courses in Shakespeare for the WEA. With evening lectures to prepare and a wife and child at home, he had little time to socialize with other students; he became friendly only with another man in his late thirties, J. E. Turner, and an exchange student, Kuo Chieh Chang (on whom the young Chinese physicist in *Last and First Men* may be based).[38] At first, Olaf found the M.A. program intimidating: "I am technically deficient," he thought after listening to another student's seminar paper on the relativity of knowledge. Following another meeting he wrote, "I get rather lost in the discussion."[39] The war had left him out of touch with new trends in philosophy and psychology, and he determined to repair his deficiencies. Early in 1922 he immured himself for days in the British Museum Reading Room from opening to closing time, devouring Freud: *The Interpretation of Dreams, Leonardo da Vinci, Delusion and Dream, Theory of Sex, Totem and Taboo, Wit and Its Relation to the Unconscious*. "Ever so much to read."[40]

He seized every chance to explore Freud's understanding of the symbol. When the psychoanalyst R. E. Wilkinson visited Liverpool, Olaf had two long talks with him about the therapeutic uses of dream symbolism and made detailed records of the dreams Wilkinson helped his patients interpret. He had nearly missed his chance of meeting Wilkinson by protesting the University Club's policy of banishing the Frankfürter *Zeitung* from its newspaper holdings, thereby alienating the club member who had promised to introduce him. "Damn! But it is so foolish to exclude what Germans say even if you do regard them as enemies. I want to know what even the Devil has to say."[41] A more prudent reserve might have served his professional advancement better, but throughout this crucial decade, a desire for academic respectability was at war with irrepressible questioning of habitual modes and avenues of thought.

Stapledon found seminar papers hard to write because they required compressing ideas into a neat thirty-minute presentation when he wanted to arrive at "epoch-making conclusions." He would work night and day to produce 10,000-word essays that he then had to cut by two-thirds, often feeling that the result looked like "a most wildly speculative effort." Mair urged Olaf not to trim the venturesome and speculative ideas from his papers but to let them "be tried on the dog" (as he liked to describe the process of reading a paper to the seminar); making a respectable thesis of them would come later.[42] By the term's end Stapledon felt intellectually secure enough to declare for a Ph.D. Dissatisfied with what he saw as the rationalist excesses of orthodox Freudianism, he altered his topic from the psychological study of symbols to a philosophical analysis of the problem of meaning.

The topic was a gamble, Mair thought, but a courageous choice, and his student frequently needed to have his confidence pumped up. "He thinks the awful quagmire I have got in is quite promising," Olaf told Agnes. "He says most people would never have got into the quagmire, never have bothered to go near it."[43] At Liverpool, Stapledon worked harder than he had ever done before, and he held at bay his fear that a lectureship was a fairly bleak prospect for a fortyish man with a penchant for philosophical extravagance. The effort seemed to uncork fresh reserves of energy, and his pace nearly matched the hectic level of 1913 and 1914. In addition to the demands of his research and of ongoing tutoring at Beechcroft and outlying towns for the WEA, he studied Esperanto, joined the League of Nations Union, and worked for the Labour party with other university colleagues who were, according to the Reverend Stanley Mellor, "frazzling away our souls" trying to push Liverpool to the left.[44] In "The Sleeping Beauty," Olaf asked himself, "Is it not clear that the labour movement, even with all its folly and treason and prejudice, is the birth throes of a new Mankind?"[45]

In his microcosmic world there was also another birth—of his son John David in November 1923. In a slant-rhyme poem about the new baby, Olaf revealed some anxiety about his age, the fact of parenthood, and the future:

> Baby hand
> clung to mine:
> the man
> leaves me behind.
>
> He's expert,
> I wool-gather.
> We live together—
> apart.[46]

Poetry became Stapledon's literary preoccupation once he decided to let go of "The Sleeping Beauty." He had been writing verse all through the war and into the early years of his marriage, but he had as yet little reason for optimism about his future as a poet. He doggedly revised poems he had written in France and composed new ones. He started gathering what he had written since 1920, along with twenty-six poems culled from those done between 1912 and 1919, into a handwritten, leather-covered octavo labeled "Verse by WOS," but until 1923 he did not succeed in placing anything in journals or anthologies.[47] Like the poem on the birth of his son, many of his verses played on the philosophical meaning of some intimate event in his life.

Some poems, including one he flattered himself to think of as "shocking," were shown to friends but not sent out to journals:

> We lie together, the girl and I,
>   late, in a meadow.
> The world swings round, and after day—
>   night, the great shadow.
> I cannot see, so feel my dear.
> Hand, venturing, creeps in her breast, and oh—
>   soft as feathers!
> The grass is warm. Why suffer clothes?
> I loosen her smock and steal it away,
>   like sheath from lily.
> Oh throbbing flank and smooth pale thigh!
> Oh sacred region bared for me!
> The stars kiss all, and so kiss I.
> Then—the deed in rhythm.[48]

The eroticism is breathlessly adolescent, tinged with the sexual celebration he was just discovering in D. H. Lawrence—another reminder of what a late bloomer Olaf, at thirty-seven, was. The identity of "the girl" is not an interesting mystery—she is either Agnes or, more likely, a fantasy creature. He had a languorous fascination with beautiful and unattainable women, particularly with film and stage stars, as Agnes recalled, but his flirtations, at this stage of his life, remained Platonic.[49]

His old FAU colleague Eric Robertson introduced him to a young woman named Primrose Morgan, a member of the Liverpool Repertory Theatre, where she took the ingenue's roles, and Olaf dashed off a *jeu d'esprit* on the occasion, telling Agnes to take particular note of these middle lines: "I seek no part in you, my dear. / I have a mate. My treasure's there." "Because I love you just the way I do," Olaf wrote to Agnes of this poem, "I can fall in love with any sweet child (of 24) and not love you the less for it, can sort of laugh at myself for being in love, and tell you all about it and be quite sure you'll laugh too. (If you didn't I should find my delight in this little person collapse like a pricked bubble.)"[50]

Whether Olaf fully understood his need to "confess" his infatuations is a matter for wonder, but there is no doubt that his innocence was in marked contrast to Robertson's experience in extramarital love. To Stapledon he seemed enviably sophisticated but also thoroughly and intriguingly debauched; whenever they got together they talked long into the night about the "things that naturally would be talked about by the combination Robertson-Stapledon, namely women, dress, women, art, women, my poems, women, philosophy, women, conflicting loyalties, women etc etc." Robertson's bright and iconoclastic play of ideas compensated for what made his provincial friend from Liverpool feel uneasy: an unblushing egotism and elastic moral standards. When Robertson's luck turned, Olaf persuaded William Stapledon to lend him money, but had to overcome his father's disapproval of the artist's being "mixed up with lots of other people," as Olaf delicately described a busy sexual life. Especially after his divorce from his wife Cecile, Robertson's reputation for being "inhuman and a satyr" grew, according to Olaf. "And there's no doubt he is both in a way. Art and sex seem to make up his whole universe."[51]

Olaf's universe was roomier, and in the early 1920s most of his poems were launched into a void. "The Athenaeum has duly returned my poetic opus," he reported at the beginning of the decade, the first in a long series of refusals. "I must try to get in touch with a prominent man."[52] The effort to find a patron resulted, over the course of seven years, in unproductive brief contacts with Lascelles Abercrombie and T. S. Eliot. A minor and highly reclusive poet, A. S. J. Tessimond, became friendly with Olaf and appreciated his work, but was of no practical help to him. Only Sydney Fowler Wright, an accountant-turned-writer, a founder of the Empire Poetry League, and editor of the League's Merton Press and of the journal *Poetry*, helped Olaf break into print. Nine years after *Latter-Day Psalms*, Olaf's poems began appearing in the pages of *Poetry*, in the June 1923 issue, and in two anthologies edited by Fowler Wright.[53]

Of the sixteen authors featured in the 1923 *Poets of Merseyside*, Stapledon had the largest group of poems (eight) and was singled out in Fowler Wright's introduction as practicing a "new and very beautiful art."[54] Unlike all the other contributors, he shunned rhyme and iambic pentameter and worked in loose, open rhythms reminiscent of his earlier psalms and of the mixed prose and verse of Blake's *Marriage of Heaven and Hell*. His poems centered on spiritual conflict and the design of the universe, and the cleverest ones offered some of the elliptical and brain-teasing pleasures of Browning's dramatic monologues. The poem that got the most attention (Fowler Wright reprinted it the following year, and it was broadcast in the summer of 1924) was a hyperplastic fable called "A Prophet's Tragedy." It opens:

> I have set up my God over the God of my enemy.
> I have broken down his image and fouled his holy place. I have
> assigned the name of his God for the droppings of cattle.
> But I have written on the sky in stars the name of the real God, who is
> mine. I have written his name on the sun's eye and branded the earth his slave.[55]

"A Prophet's Tragedy" is not a great leap forward from *Latter-Day Psalms*.
Like most of the Stapledon poems Fowler Wright selected for publication, its
theme is mildly unorthodox, but in idiom and attitude it is a regression to late-
Victorian earnestness.

There are a few hints of Stapledon's poetics from this period. In a letter
to Fowler Wright, he explained one of the first two poems he published in 1923,
"Timber," originally written at Compiègne in 1916:

> Stroke of the axe! The trunk shivers and gapes.
> Stroke on stroke! The chips fly.
> "Oh year upon year upon year I grew, since I woke in the seed."
> Stroke on stroke! Raw wounded wood, and the heart laid bare.
> "Oh sun and wind and rain. Oh leafing and the fall of leaves.
> Oh flower, love, and love's fruit."
> Strong bite of the axe! Staggering, crying timber.
> Down!
> And the little branches and the twigs are shattered on the ground.
> And the woodman stands measuring.
> Man of what timber art thou?

In his gloss Olaf described a sequence of intended sound effects: "the reiterant
heavy stroke of the axe, a kind of shuddering complaint by the tree, the heavy
fall (which breaks in upon the previous rhythms), followed by the crumbling
of branches crushed on the ground." With alliteration and assonance interlocking the lines, he thought he created an unintrusive pattern and an effect like
"the richness of heavy wine, or Hardy's *Egdon Heath*."[56]

In a brief essay on prosody from 1924, Stapledon sided with those who
were "tired of orthodox rhyme and metre." He urged the development of new
meters only after study of traditional forms. "The beauty that we seek presupposes a familiarity with rhyme, just as the modern musician's delight in 'dis-
cords' presupposes a familiarity with an older and simpler music." He
championed *vers libre* but maintained a "reverence" for the achievements of
older poetry. As in many later pronouncements on political and social as well
as aesthetic issues, he wanted to straddle the claims of tradition and innovation. He tried to subvert lilting formulas by inventing what he called "atro-
ciously bad" rhymes ("pleasure," "thither," and "caterpillar" in one poem), but
his rhythmic and sonic ingenuities were usually canceled by crudities of diction and a fatal attraction to gaseous generalities.[57]

Stapledon's most extensive comments on poetic issues came in two lectures given to the Beechcroft Poetry Circle. In the first he asked whether older
poetic traditions could still speak to the present—to a starving Germany, a bored
England, a revolutionary Russia. Although on rare occasions a poet might lead

the way out of social darkness into the light—he cited the maker of "La Marseillaise"—he thought few poems capable of directing change, despite the claims of poets themselves and the automatic pairing of the adjective "inspiring" with the noun "poetry." A poem he had held up to WEA students before the war as a shining example of the power of literature he now invited his Beechcroft audience to consider much more skeptically:

> We are the music makers,
>   And we are the dreamers of dreams,
> Wandering by lone sea breakers,
>   And sitting by desolate streams;
> World-losers and world-forsakers,
>   On whom the pale moon gleams:
> Yet we are the movers and shakers
>   Of the world forever, it seems.[58]

The falsity of the sentiment lay in the exaggeration of a poem's ability to reach deeply into the way either kings or workers actually think. "Poets may see far ahead, but cannot take people with them *unless people have seen something for themselves.*"[59]

Two years later at Beechcroft, he assembled a revisionist catalogue of his once-favorite poems and poets: Keats's "Hyperion" was too "aloof" from the world; the "Immortality Ode" of Wordsworth was "wrongheaded"; Browning uttered "mere wish fulfillment"; and Tennyson's love poetry, save *In Memoriam,* consisted of a "polished surface only." People craved poetry but most of the canonical texts were "soporific." Science demanded new subjects, and political change required a new poetics. A revolution in knowledge had established a new relation between the human species and the universe, which few poets had yet caught up with. And in a democratic culture poetry would have to speak in a new voice, with less reliance on the accents of the past.[60] If poets could not create revolutions, they should at least reflect the revolutionary spirit.

Stapledon valued spontaneous feeling, freshness of image, absence of intellectual clutter in poetry, but few of his own verses are free from the premeditation and tendentiousness he imagined himself shedding. Whenever he tried too hard to be original, he lapsed into embarrassing errors of judgment. A dreadful poem depicting God as a young architect creating nebulae and stars out of the smoke drifting up from a cosmic cigarette may represent the nadir of his published work.[61] On the other hand, if he followed his actual tastes as a reader, he was likely to imitate the no longer fashionable work of an earlier generation. The poets of his youth—Browning, Tennyson, Meredith—exercised more influence over his writing than the newer theories of poetry he wanted to endorse but hadn't the heart or perhaps the talent to put into practice.

Revealingly, the only editor who relished Stapledon the poet was Fowler Wright, who repeatedly denounced modernism in the pages of *Poetry*. Scorning the "nonsense" of "T. S. Eliot and others of the same fraternity," Fowler Wright used his regular editorial column and the prefaces to his many anthologies to condemn the literary "abortions" of the avant-garde and "morbid elements in contemporary poetry."[62] He was a nasty reviewer, but he grew defensive when other journals castigated the stale canons of taste that governed his editorial selections. He repeatedly brandished one example of his tolerance for experiment: "I am tired of trying to make either its advocates or detractors understand that I am not hostile to Free Verse in the least, but to Bad Verse only. I gave instant recognition to the Free Verse of Mr. Olaf Stapledon." For five years he made the unknown Stapledon his chief exhibit in noisily proclaiming his receptiveness to new forms.[63] Had Olaf been a better poet than he was, he still could not have benefited much from Fowler Wright's publicity. Being huzzaed by so notoriously self-aggrandizing an antimodernist could only have made him suspect in the tight London world of coterie poetry. The search for a "prominent man" to boost his work resulted in Stapledon's yoking his rickety wagon to an ill-tempered mule pulling him in the wrong direction.

Stapledon's ideas about poetry were not notably advanced or well informed, but they were neither as philistine nor as self-serving as Fowler Wright's. The most intriguing statement of Olaf's theory of verse—one that marks his difference from his patron—is an unpublished piece, in some ways more modernist than most of his published ones, called "Of Poems":

> Poems, believe me, are not made,
>   but found.
> They are not ghostly radiances
> projected by the creative mind
> to deck the gray reality
>   with a phantom gold.
>
> A poem is a brute fact
>   in the world,
> an intricate feature for discovery,
> to be known where it lies, fixed
> in the nude and swift loveliness
>   of the exact real.[64]

A few of his poems of the twenties put this imagist principle to work (although imagism was a movement whose time had already come and gone when Olaf took up the cause). "Two Chinese Poems" suggests the modest kind of success he was capable of in this mode:

I

Noon on the moor.
A curlew is calling.
The hill's feet are cooling
in the mere.

II

Evening on the moor.
The lone bird is wailing.
Mists are welling
from the mere.

This may have been both his best "found" poem as well as one of his subtler uses of slant rhyme; it is also one of the few poems he published in a venue not controlled by Fowler Wright.[65]

After years of trying to peddle his verses to periodicals in Great Britain and North America and with little to show for it apart from Fowler Wright's imprimatur, Olaf was starting to guess that he would not make his mark as a poet. There was one more significant poetic experiment ahead of him—only partly finished and never published in its intended form—but his career as a poet was essentially ended by 1927. After that year he published only two poems—in 1939 and 1940—except for the recycling of nine earlier pieces in the 1932 *Last Men in London*. In the first half of the 1920s, the sleeping writer in Stapledon began to stir. In the next five years, moving from poetry to prose and raising his sights beyond little magazines, he found his voice and tapped powers of thought and eloquence that no one, perhaps including himself, could have extrapolated from his protracted struggle for a literary identity.

9

PHILOSOPHER AND PROVINCIAL

1925–1929

"IN THE MIDST OF LIFE we are in philosophy," Stapledon wrote at the opening of a new Liverpool branch of the British Institute of Philosophical Studies, created in 1925 as a civic forum for philosophical debate.[1] For him speculation was as essential to humanity as economic justice; that was why he had steadily shifted his teaching toward philosophy, psychology, and poetry. He felt no contradiction between skeptical inquiry and practical ethics, between the life of the mind and life itself. In "Auguries of Innocence" Blake rhymed against the metaphysical mood: "If the sun and moon should doubt, / They'd immediately go out." On this point Olaf reversed the verdict of one of his favorite poets:

> Who dares to doubt
> while the sun is out
> is a man.[2]

Shuttling back and forth between elementary WEA classes and the rarefied atmosphere of the Philosophy Seminar at Liverpool University, between political canvassing for Labour causes and library research, Stapledon, in words he used to title an article in the year of his death, was living the life of "a plain man talking about values." And writing about them. Late in 1924 he submitted his doctoral thesis in the area of inquiry now called semiotics.[3] He was two months shy of his thirty-ninth birthday when he presented himself on 5 March 1925 to the vice-chancellor of Liverpool University for his degree. His mind was less on ceremony (which he always hated) than on a lecture he was writing on "Democracy as an Ideal," on the recent thrill of hearing a scratchy performance of Schumann and a clear reading of the news on a neighbor's radio, and on an exhibition and sale he and Agnes were planning at their house the following week for his old Ambulance Unit friend, the nearly destitute Eric Robertson.[4] At the high moment of his investiture as a philosopher, Dr. Stapledon was, typically, in the midst of an energetic, many-sided life.

The one-word title of his thesis, "Meaning," was concise, cryptic, and brazenly inclusive, for the author saw himself working "at the point where psychology, physical science, logic, and epistemology are united."[5] The topic was lively and controversial among philosophers of the period, perhaps most visibly in C. K. Ogden and I. A. Richards's 1923 *The Meaning of Meaning,* with which Stapledon sustains a running argument in his thesis. An admirer of his later fiction and philosophy, looking for traces of the work to come, can discern a familiar intellectual style in the 433 pages of critical summary and technical analysis of competing views of how (and whether) we make sense of the world: "So called 'false' meanings are always true meanings, within a certain system, but no meanings at all in the system in which they are falsely taken to be meanings," or "The only fully intelligible universe is a monistic universe. It does not, however, follow that the universe really is fully intelligible." At such moments the thesis writer prefigures the creator of alternate universes in *Darkness and the Light* and the agnostic narrator of *Star Maker.* On the very problem of change and continuity, Olaf admitted a rare self-conscious joke: "I, who as a child nibbled a jam tart and said I didn't, am in some sense the same I who now nibble at philosophy."[6]

In another sense, though, the author of "Meaning" is neither that child nor the later philosophical romancer. It is Stapledon the graduate student who is on display, and his thesis is no less opaque, prolix, and dull than most theses in any field. The writing exhibits the limitations of its genre—a genre directed to a tinier, more enclosed audience than would read even his most difficult fiction. Those who are not experts in epistemology must take on faith Alexander Mair's judgment that the author produced "one of the freshest and most suggestive treatments of this difficult subject," worthy of publication; insiders might be more skeptical of hyperbole. In any case, Mair's assertion that his student would "make a place for himself, both for matter and manner, among the younger philosophical writers" is a heartbreakingly mistaken prophecy of Stapledon's academic reputation but an inadvertently accurate estimate of the special niche he would carve out in modern literature. On the basis of his speculative fiction, he would become Merseyside's most influential philosopher without ever holding a university chair.[7]

The postwar philosophical protagonist of the 1932 *Last Men in London,* whose experiences parallel many of Olaf's own, engages in what he calls intellectual touring on a second-class ticket.[8] The phrasing was an embarrassed

shorthand for both Stapledon's second-class B.A. from Oxford and his Ph.D
from a university of the second rank. Nevertheless, the Philosophy Seminar
on Brownlow Hill was accessible and welcoming to an older, married, paci-
fist-veteran of the war who was working as an extramural tutor. Had Liverpool
University not been there, it is unlikely that Stapledon would ever have gone
beyond being an amateur philosopher. Once suspicious of the academy, he
found that his graduate studies led him to hanker after a lectureship; when he
botched a pronoun reference and seemed to identify himself with the Liverpool
historian Professor Charles Webster, he half-seriously interpreted the slip as a
"Freudian symbolic act meaning 'I wish I was a Prof!'"[9]

To turn his Ph.D. into the makings of an academic post was no laughing
matter. Olaf knew what was required. In the prewar days a Balliol don had no
need to worry about compiling a fat dossier of articles, and someone like
Mair—a gentlemanly classicist who seldom joined the debates in philosophical journals—could secure a professorship with little published research. "I
have to get a background" and "get known" and "dish up bits of thesis as articles," Olaf explained to his father. He dispatched a chapter to a Chicago journal and had plans for several more articles, but little of "Meaning" ever saw
print.[10] Mair, in failing health and lacking the influence of a great scholar, was
not able to help much. At the cost of a great upheaval for his young family,
Stapledon might have had an appointment abroad, but he decided to look for
an opening at a British university. Mair told him that he'd better start writing
a book.

At first Olaf was optimistic about his chances. He set to work on a critique of Bertrand Russell's *What I Believe,* hoping that the powerful G. E.
Moore would print it in his journal *Mind,* where it would command the attention of leading philosophers. His manner was ingratiating ("Mr. Russell's moral
criticism is always as wholesome as the drawing up of blinds after a funeral"),
but he was not afraid to play the callow upstart: "Mr. Russell's confident judgment that the rest of the universe has no bearing on values seems only one
degree less naïve than the contrary view that there is a God who is necessarily
our well-wisher."[11] The interrogation of Russell's beliefs established the pattern of what became Stapledon's trademark inquiry into the relationship between moral choice in the human sphere and the design of the cosmos. That
issue, already present in *Latter-Day Psalms,* governed the major works of his
career from its first mature presentation in the essays that led to *A Modern
Theory of Ethics* in 1929, through the dazzlingly baroque theological speculations of *Star Maker* in the next decade, to the fragmented meditations on God
and evil in the posthumous *Opening of the Eyes* of 1954.

Meanwhile Olaf took Mair's advice and began his first book, on a topic
few English philosophers were inclined to pursue: the impact of psychology

on ethics in the disenchanted aftermath of the Great War. In a burst of energy, he drafted almost half of *A Modern Theory of Ethics* by midsummer 1925. Then, on a visit to Oxford, he awoke to the realities of academic employment in a faltering economy for an older candidate working on an unfashionable topic:

> There are so many people, with far more experience and mental agility than mine, who are shelved. One of my troubles is that I am much more advanced in essential philosophical insight than in the scholarly and historical side of the thing. And while, for writing, the former is all that really matters, for university teaching one must have the latter. But somehow it's harder for me to be a scholar than for "a snowball to get out of hell.' Clearly my only hope is to get known a bit by writing. . . . But altogether the prospects are not bright. If I do ever succeeed in contributing a little bit to modern thought I shall sing a Nunc Dimittis and drink champaign [*sic*].[12]

Olaf's intuition that his philosophical gifts might not suit a scholarly forum proved right. He still hadn't found his medium. Later that summer Moore rejected his essay on "Bertrand Russell's Ethical Beliefs," and it ended up in the less prestigious and visible Philadelphia publication, the *International Journal of Ethics,* where he also got a preliminary hearing for two chapters of *A Modern Theory of Ethics.*[13]

Stapledon was dutifully piling up his credentials (mostly in North America), but the effort did not translate into a successful campaign for a lectureship. When he applied for vacancies in 1926 at the University of Swansea and Queen's University in Belfast, he came up empty-handed. The next year Swansea had a temporary opening, and a former Liverpool extramural tutor there tried to recruit his old friend for the job, but by then Olaf's ardor for university life was cooling again. He told his father that although the "obvious thing to do is to say yes," he wasn't sure it was worth the trouble to seek a post that had no future "when very possibly my real work lies elsewhere."[14]

Discouraged as he was by the academy's indifference to him, Olaf continued to find outlets for his philosophical ideas and to experiment with new modes of expression. As a postgraduate in the Liverpool Extension but with no other department to call his home, he still participated in Mair's Philosophy Seminar, where he had first worked out the issues for his doctoral thesis. The Seminar—a biweekly, yearlong symposium on a single topic attended by the staff and graduate students in the department—now became the proving ground for the chapters of *A Modern Theory of Ethics* and for the bold speculations of the work that would define Stapledon's career, *Last and First Men.* In 1927–1928 the seminar studied Whitehead's *Science and the Modern World* and addressed the question: "What is the bearing of scientific discovery upon the problems of philosophy?" It was an issue tailor-made for Olaf who, while working on his thesis, had become deeply fascinated by the intersections between philosophy and the physical and behavioral sciences.

One of his presentations to the Seminar in 1927, "The Idea of Simple Location," caused a sensation. Examining the links between Heisenberg's uncertainty principle and Whitehead's "fallacy of misplaced concreteness," he proposed that the relationships between space and time were such that no object could be simply located. What is most concrete about an event, he argued, is its influence, which may be spread out over vast reaches of space and time. His paper provoked so much comment that a second week of discussion was scheduled and copies were circulated to all the members to review. When the Seminar reconvened, there were so many questions that Olaf had to be asked to prepare responses at yet another session. Departmental records show that the Seminar devoted a month to Stapledon's paper—an unparalleled event in the surviving Minute Books of the Seminar.[15]

Not ordinarily the most active discussant, Olaf sat through Seminar meetings with a nearly expressionless face, seldom giving away his position unless provoked. At forty, slim and pink-cheeked, with an unruly mop of blond hair and alert pale blue eyes, he looked ageless and a little inhuman. When he spoke up—especially if his own work was under discussion—he slipped into the funereal tones and exaggerated politeness he adopted whenever he felt self-conscious. Neither flamboyant nor aggressive, Stapledon's measured arguments suggested a mind operating on an entirely different frequency from anyone else's. His mind was absorbent and generous enough to take in viewpoints very different from his own, but he came at topics from an angle that often led to controversy. One day, he told Agnes, it was "mostly me against the rest, about the religious sense." Rejecting anthropocentric assumptions, he would ask how any decision should be judged in relation to the nature and purposes of the universe. Determined to make terrestrial acts confront ultimate reality, to set the human microcosm against the backdrop of an unfathomable macrocosm, he took a philosophical stance that seemed visionary—or cockeyed. On days when he held the floor and argued issues that were close to him, he came home exhilarated and exhausted.[16]

Mair took ill in 1927 and his successor as Professor of Philosophy, Alan Dorward, took over the Seminar. Although he felt more at ease with the fatherly Mair than with the stodgier Dorward, Olaf remained a loyal participant. During the last years of the 1920s, before he broke into public view with *A Modern Theory of Ethics* and *Last and First Men,* the Seminar was his main intellectual lifeline. "Not till he was forty, and still physically in earliest prime, did he gather his strength and deliver himself of his mature gospel." The words describe the fictional "Divine Boy" of Patagonia, "the Boy who Refused to

Grow Up" in *Last and First Men,* but they also sound like a self-portrait of the eerie Peter Pan–like figure in the Philosophy Seminar, quietly assembling, sorting, articulating, and previewing the elements of the two books he delivered, after he had turned forty, in 1929 and 1930.[17] Many of the people he credits for advice and inspiration in those two volumes—Mair, J. E. Turner, the aesthetician L. A. Reid, the oceanographer James Johnstone—were regular attendants or guests at the Seminar.

Friendships made in the Philosophy Seminar gave Stapledon access to other professors at the university on whom he relied for technical advice as he began creating a distinctively interdisciplinary oeuvre. He wrote "a rather casual little letter on eugenics" to A. M. Carr-Saunders, Professor of Sociology and later Director of the London School of Economics, and was elated to be taken to lunch. "I think I stood the ordeal remarkably well. It was amusing to find oneself talking to a eugenics expert just as though one knew all about it," he said.[18] For the latest on relativity theory, he turned to the physicist James Rice, who twice chaperoned Einstein's visits to the university; from P. G. H. Boswell, Liverpool's first Professor of Geology, he learned much about the remaking of the earth's surface that went into *Last and First Men;* and Leonard Martin, Professor of English, editor of the standard texts of several seventeenth-century metaphysical poets, and Olaf's West Kirby neighbor, became a lifelong friend to whom he invariably turned for stylistic criticism of work-in-progress.[19]

As the decade advanced, an idea for an extravagant piece of prophetic fiction, provisionally titled "The Future Speaks," began germinating in Stapledon's imagination, but for a time this prototype for *Last and First Men* yielded to the book on ethics that he hurried to finish. Many files of the publishing firm of Methuen were destroyed during World War II, and it is now unclear just when and under what circumstances Olaf got his contract for *A Modern Theory of Ethics.* The bare first mention of the book is in his diary during a summer holiday in 1928: "Work on Ethics (for publishers)." By late autumn he was finishing the proofs, feeling crowded by his WEA classes, and regretting the lack of time, he wrote in an apparent reference to *Last and First Men,* "to do anything on the next book."[20]

The editor with whom Stapledon worked on *A Modern Theory of Ethics,* as he did for all his later books with Methuen, was the classicist E. V. Rieu. It is not surprising that his editor should turn out to be one of his classmates from Balliol in the century's first decade. Although Rieu was not a close friend at Oxford, in the small world of Englishmen educated at the two ancient universities, old boys' connections must have counted for something in Methuen's decision to publish Stapledon's first philosophical book. But if a string were pulled on his behalf, after fifteen years of struggle and obscurity since *Latter-*

Day Psalms, who could begrudge it? When the *Ethics* appeared on 31 January 1929, followed by an American edition in July, Agnes's ten years of faith in her husband's much-heralded message was justified, and, in Annery, Willie and Emmeline embraced Olaf as if he were the prodigal son. He had earned his champagne and the right to sing a tipsy "Nunc dimittis."

The book was not widely read, but its few reviews—mostly in professional journals—were respectable. The *Times Literary Supplement* saw it as an important contribution to idealist theory, and for C. D. Burns it was "almost a shock" to read a book on ethics that did not limit itself to platitudes or mere uplift and earned its billing as a *modern* account of classical philosophical dilemmas. The lengthiest and harshest review, by the American Laurence Sears, found the approach so alien to the daily concerns of life that ethics became "impotent."[21] The book led Stapledon into a flattering exchange of papers with C. Lloyd Morgan, a leader in the philosophical movement of "emergent evolution," and to invitations to review new books on ethics for the *Journal of Philosophical Studies.*[22] But *A Modern Theory of Ethics* did not fit smoothly into the groove of academic philosophy in 1929 nor did it produce any offers of a lectureship.

The linking of ethics to cosmology and the climactic discussion of the relation of moral theory to ecstasy puzzled and irritated professional readers accustomed to philosophical argument that was minute, critical, and carefully delimited rather than speculative or, in Olaf's own word, "wild."[23] At the same time, the style was sufficiently technical and ingrown to ensure that the book would remain "intellectual caviar" for the common reader, as an American reviewer put it.[24] A layperson has to push through two hundred pages of colorless disputation before coming upon passages in the final chapters on admiration, zeal, disillusion, and ecstasy that are suddenly lit by the fire of Stapledon's most passionately held beliefs, passages in which philosophy shades into something like religion and in which autobiography spills over into the argument.

In illustrating the ecstatic mood, he revealed how deeply his wartime experience of being simultaneously a participant and a noncombatant penetrated his spiritual outlook and nourished an almost frightening capacity for accepting the unacceptable:

> It is possible, for instance, to be on the verge of panic, to be reduced to quivering incapacity and terror, and yet all the while to be an exultant onlooker, rapt in observation of the spectacle, yet in a queer way aloof. It is possible even in the compulsive reaction to pain in one's own flesh, and even while helplessly watching a beloved's pain, to be, precisely, in the very act of frantic revulsion, coldly, brilliantly, enlightened, not as to the excellence of pain, but as to the excellence of the universe.[25]

The agnostic piety Stapledon embraced in his mature years, his attraction to the mood of eighteenth-century deism as expressed in Alexander Pope's famous epigram "Whatever is, is right," is both an intricately reasoned proposition and a psychological war wound. And whether considered as philosophy or as autobiography, this calm resignation to, and exultation in, suffering is the single most troubling, and for some readers offensive, motif in his philosophy and fiction.[26]

A Modern Theory of Ethics has had its champions. The first serious appraisal of Stapledon as a philosopher, a 1947 essay by E. W. Martin, recognized how his first book, seeking a way out of the moral dead end of the Great War, remained pertinent in the aftermath of the second war because it strayed beyond the customary boundaries of academic philosophy into terrain where only such audacious explorers as Spinoza and Blake had gone before. Ten years after the author's death, the historian Crane Brinton anthologized part of A Modern Theory of Ethics and praised the genuine modernism of its linking of ethics to psychology. In the 1980s, when Stapledon's fiction received fresh readings, critics saw the forgotten book on ethics as the springboard from which he made the leap to fictive myths.[27]

The publication of A Modern Theory of Ethics caused no immediate change in Olaf's fortunes or habits of work. He continued to divide his time between Liverpool and the Wirral peninsula, between extramural teaching and philosophical research. About his next book—a work of fiction—he was so secretive that barely a mention of it survives until he began reading proofs a few months before publication. His ambition—to chronicle the next two billion years of human history—and his fantastic premise of telepathic narration by a man from the far future were so outlandish that he prudently kept the project to himself until it was clear what would come of it. In the university precinct he drew from a rich brew of ideas and provocative questions that flavored the speculations of Last and First Men, but its composition took place invisibly at home in West Kirby.

There he sought orderliness, a refuge from teaching, and a quiet place to write. In the back garden at 7 Grosvenor Avenue, he groomed paths through the neat rows of peas and beans and then went inside to draw elaborate colored charts that mapped the history and future of the solar system. He cleared a space for himself in the attic, insulated from his children's play in the garden and the clouds of steam rising from the boiled laundry in the kitchen. The bare study at the top of the house was off limits until eleven in the morning when Agnes and Mary were invited to come up for tea and sometimes hear him describe his morning's work. Visitors at afternoon tea heard nothing about the writing of Last and First Men. Only Agnes, with her "devastating sanity," followed Olaf draft by draft through the writing with "pettifogging" suggestions for cutting and rearranging and simplifying. "That seems a bit far-fetched," she would remark with careful understatement about some bizarre cultural arrangement or anatomical grotesquerie in her husband's chronicle of *homo sapiens* in millennia to come.[28]

Olaf kept work in the study separate from life in the rest of the house. He did not enjoy lingering over food, but at mid-day, after a quick meal, he sat at the dining-room table carving sleek wooden ships, motor-powered for launching in the saltwater pool in West Kirby. When the miracle glue "Duro-Fix" came on the market, the smell of acetone would drift through the house as he kept his hands busy cutting and pasting scraps of leather into wallets, cases, and book covers as gifts for friends and family. His leatherwork was practically a cottage industry, and everyone who knew him accumulated samples of his handicraft. He even used the glue to patch up his disreputable garden shorts, a collection of strips and rags so full of Duro-Fix that they could be stood up on their legs in the hall like a fantastic sculpture or a joke out of *The Invisible Man*. "The whole of my childhood," his daughter Mary remembered, "seems to have been held together with Duro-Fix." At bedtime, in David's little room at the front of the house, Olaf made up fairy tales, concoctions of old sea stories from the Stapledon family lore and the adventures of a wonder-boy named John, illustrated with hand-drawn maps.[29]

Music was the irreplaceable evening pastime at Grosvenor Avenue. The gramophone would be wound up for Beethoven or for the Paul Robeson recordings Olaf began collecting. Much of the family entertainment, however, was provided by Agnes at the piano, playing Scottish airs, Brahms lieder, or an occasional popular song that Olaf liked to sing in duet with her. The odd scene in *Last Men in London* in which a man and woman on Neptune face the end of the solar system by trying to master the archaic sounds of their favorite twentieth-century terrestrial artifact, "Old Man River," was, Mary Stapledon thought, based on her parents' makeshift concerts and inspired by Robeson's performance. As the children grew, everyone in the family acquired a recorder for homemade quartets in the sitting room. Late in the twenties Agnes and some West Kirby friends drew Olaf into the Liverpool Nonesuch Folk Dancing Society at Sandon Studios. There every Wednesday evening the philosopher threw himself into dancing with a good-natured will and boyish verve but little skill, according to his partners. "He was very jerky in his movements, uncoordinated," recalled a "conspirator" who enjoyed setting Olaf up for the group's amusement. "We were so wicked. We used to send him down the wrong line so that he was jigging all by himself."[30]

Agnes's father, retired from his import firm in Sydney, had moved his wife and youngest daughter Ruth, known as "Pete," back to England. After Frank Miller died in 1925, Pete, by then seventeen and eager for lively company, spent as much time as she could enjoying the high spirits at Grosvenor Avenue. She brought her jazz records, which she couldn't play at home, to try out on her brother-in-law. Sometimes she joined the Stapledons on the two-mile hike up to Annery for the regular Sunday afternoon teas with Emmeline and Willie, and she noticed the glum resignation Olaf, in contrast to the rest of the party, assumed for the occasion. Agnes took Sunday tea in stride, knowing she would invariably be asked to sing at the piano but not having to haul the same emotional baggage as her husband up Caldy Hill. "The inevitability of Sundays was terrible for Olaf; he had no way to get round it," Pete said of those visits to Annery.

Mary and David enjoyed being taken by their grandfather into the Annery garden for peaches and figs and a look at his prized beehives; around him in old age there was a mystique of heavy veiling and the odors of smoking cardboard and beeswax. At seventy-five Emmeline was more demanding, fussing over the children's sticky fingers and complaining of drafts. She tried everyone's nerves, and her son's most sharply. She kept the furnace at full blast and Olaf spent many afternoons pacing through the enclosed house like a caged lion, chafing at the dull conversation and nearly suffocated by the heat. "Olaf, dear, do sit down," his mother often said in the sweetly impatient tone that charmed no one. To her annoyance he seized every opportunity to get people into the garden or to organize walking parties to nearby Stapledon Wood. As a young man he had loved Annery and retreated there from the unhappy days at Alfred Holt and Manchester Grammar School, from the social work in the Liverpool slums and the dreariness of war service. By the time he was forty, however, the Sunday expeditions to his parents' house were an obligation whose tedium he could barely disguise. His course in life now emphatically parted from Willie's, he knew he would not ever feel comfortable in Annery's genteel elegance again. "Thresholds are restless places," he had observed as he waited to go to the Belgian Front in 1915; the last years of the 1920s, when he was on the verge of his breakthrough as a writer, provoked a similar restlessness.[31]

He was growing almost as unhappy with Liverpool as with Annery. A 1923 article on Merseyside poets described London as "a literary vampire" and lamented the young writers from the provinces who are "sooner or later absorbed by the metropolis."[32] But for most of his career, Olaf, loyal to the North Country and not gregarious enough to thrive in the capital, preferred a train ticket to London and a Wirral address. When in London he had no entrée to Bloomsbury, and he would have been as uneasy in that circle as he had been with the Etonians at Oxford. He liked Liverpool's more comfortable cultural institutions. The Philharmonic, the Repertory Playhouse, the Merseyside Film Institute, the Picton Library, the University Club, the Pre-Raphaelite splendors of the Walker Art Gallery, and the contemporary arts at the Bluecoat Chambers provided solid urban amenities, and Olaf frequented them all. At the Film Institute he saw pictures that shaped his imagination: Lang's *Metropolis* and Eisenstein's *Fall of St. Petersburg,* a documentary on the Antarctic expeditions, and most of Greta Garbo's films. The venturesome Repertory, jewel of the North of England, provided rich doses of O'Casey and Shaw, Coward and Galsworthy, as well as more unusual offerings: Elmer Rice and Susan Glaspell and English premieres of several of O'Neill's plays.[33] Olaf contributed to Merseyside life with talks in a variety of settings—from classes on *Kidnapped* for boys in the dockland to introductions to psychology for inmates of Walton prison.[34] And when he had enough of the soft pleasures and grimy sights of Liverpool, the chance to walk barefoot on the nearly deserted beaches of Anglesey or to clamber up the sheer face of some still-unspoiled Cumbrian peak renewed his spirits.

But in the mid-twenties his loyalty to Liverpool wavered. Working as hard as he ever had at making a name as a philosophical writer and feeling constrained by young children, aging parents, dull students, and Tory neighbors, Olaf thought about moving his family to London. His trips to the British Museum always seemed hurried, and anything less than a fortnight in the Reading Room left him frustrated. "Liverpool streets are dull after London ones," he grumbled.[35]

What was wrong with Liverpool streets can be guessed from a family friend, a young physician who arrived in the city on New Year's Day of 1928 to take up her first appointment, at Liverpool Stanley Hospital in Bootle. Two days after her arrival, Joan Walker called on the Stapledons in West Kirby and described her shock. She had worked in London's East End, but it had not prepared her for the sight of Liverpool's shoeless children walking through the dirty snow and the ubiquitous impoverished Irish women wandering like zombies (or like the darkly draped proletarians in Lang's *Metropolis*) with black shawls over their lowered heads.[36] As Olaf surveyed his surroundings, it must have seemed that little had changed since his crusading days with Frederick Marquis and the Liverpool University Settlement. One could pour all one's energies into the city and still be swallowed up by it. To save himself from despair, he had to lift his sights beyond Liverpool, beyond the seaside province of West Kirby, and beyond the receding prospect of an academic career.

But he did not finally find the solution to Liverpool's shabbiness in London. As a boy Olaf quoted Hamlet, "I could be bounded in a nutshell and yet count myself a king of infinite space." The adult could still echo that childish bravado. For Stapledon the provincial and the cosmic were no antinomy; he inhabited, in Northrop Frye's phrase, "a city of which the stars are suburbs."[37] His imagination thrived in sunlight and starlight, and to get a taste of the freedom of infinite space, he permitted himself a single luxury in his cramped study.

15. Children's holiday: Olaf with Mary and David
in the Lake District, ca. 1928.
Courtesy John D. Stapledon.

Recalling the childish pleasures of the broad iron balcony at Port Said and the
open ceiling of the barn in wartime Maffrécourt through which he viewed birds
and constellations, he brought a carpenter to the attic. He had a large hole made
in the roof and an ingenious door built that could be slid up on rollers to create an open skylight. On bright days he stripped down to his shorts and basked

in the sunshine as he wrote or read, and he encouraged his children to do the same. "Such blissful ease also follows the act of love," he told them of sunbathing. He brought Mary and David to the study in the hope of recreating the thrillingly informal scientific instruction his father gave him. But he didn't have Willie's light touch. Once, as his children sat in a patch of brilliance coming through the roof, he explained photosynthesis as "potted sunlight" in green plants. "We were embarrassed by being placed in a strange pupil-relationship instead of the familiar daddy-child relationship," Mary recalled. "We were silly and giggly—the lesson was a failure."[38] The special mood that contact with the heavens always called out in Olaf was too private and serious to survive tutoring and the giggles.

It was after dark that the attic skylight assumed its real importance. Ever since the days in Egypt when he and Willie and Emmeline used to scan the night sky from the telescope set up on their balcony, the sight of the stars had enthralled him. When he built Annery in 1910, Willie installed an unwieldy, 300-power telescope on the roof, where his son spent many a night. Now that Olaf had a room with a view of his own—though it was just a little crow's nest down in the suburban darkness of West Kirby, not the rooftop eyrie up on Caldy Hill—he could indulge his oldest pleasure, the closest thing in his life to a religious rite. He carried his own small telescope up to the attic, and when there were no clouds he, and sometimes Agnes with him, practiced what he called in a 1926 poem "Star Worship." "Admiring what is most far from us," he wrote, "we escape our mean selves"; in the chapel of his attic-observatory he would "tell over the rosary of the stars."[39] The nightly viewings from the top of 7 Grosvenor Avenue produced in him, as in the protagonist of *Last Men in London,* "that tremor of recognition, of unreasoning expectation" which "the stars had ever given him."[40] At the end of 1926, against the backdrop of that familiar and yet persistently mysterious and chilling skyscape, Olaf gave close attention to a scholarly paper in *Nature* by the astronomer James Jeans.

No scientific periodical has made a greater impact on the literary world than *Nature,* the venerable British journal started in 1869. During the first four decades of the twentieth century, under the guidance of its most famous editor, Richard Gregory, the journal grew famous for the intellectual vigor of articles that explained the broad significance of the latest scientific research. The *New York Times* called the style of a *Nature* article "as sparing in words as a sonnet and as impersonal as a brick."[41] A scientist could respect its professional standards, and a humanist could follow the prose. For someone like Stapledon, eager to unite the discoveries of natural science with the insights of philosophy and the literary imagination, a subscription to *Nature* was an intellectual necessity.

Like Arthur Eddington and Julian Huxley, James Jeans belonged to a generation of writers who moved comfortably between what would later be called the two cultures of scientific and humanistic thought. If not a golden, this was at least a gilded age of scientific writing when J. B. S. Haldane could boast, "In my last book on genetics, there are seven quotations from Dante's *Divine Comedy*."[42] Although Jeans's exposition in "Recent Developments of Cosmical Physics" was technical—the measurement of stellar size and mass, the chemical components of stars, atomic annihilation and the generation of stellar radiation—he placed his data in a broad philosophical context as he surveyed a shift from astronomers' provincial interest in our solar system to a new concern with the universe as a whole. In vivid metaphors he assigned new horizons to scientific inquiry: "Like the animalculae [*sic*] of the raindrop looking out on to Niagara, we discern that our physics and chemistry are only the fringes of far-reaching sciences; beyond the seashore we have explored in our laboratories lies the ocean the existence of which we are only just beginning to suspect."[43] Jeans's account of the philosophical implications of the inhuman distances between us and the stars, the vast disproportion between human and cosmic interests, excited Olaf's imagination. He began writing his most accomplished sequence of poems.

At first he called the poems "Astronomical Posters." Then, conceiving a more elaborate cycle, he made them the first installment of "Metaphysical Posters"; on the title page of a typed set of twenty-three, labeled "First Volley, Astronomical," he noted that they were "inspired by Professor J. H. Jeans's paper on Recent Developments of Cosmical Physics."[44] The "first volley" of "Metaphysical Posters" directly took up the challenge of Jeans's final paragraph, in which, having summarized how physics had been transformed in the first quarter of the twentieth century, he posed the most radical of questions: "What, then, is life?" Jeans sampled four kinds of responses: that life is "the final climax towards which the whole of creation moves" at the extravagant expense of eons of nebular and stellar radiation into the wastelands of space; that life is an accidental by-product of Nature, of little significance to cosmic processes; that life is "a disease which affects matter in its old age" after stars have passed their vigorous prime; that life is the only reality, the creative force behind the stars rather than the product of the stars' colossal energy. Physicists could offer a magnificent multiplicity of possible interpretations of the new data of existence, Jeans said in sum. "I do not, however, think there is any one way of evading them."[45]

That humanity might just be emerging from its childhood, groping for a first mature understanding of the universe and its own physical and metaphysical status, was the implication of Jeans's survey and the argument of Stapledon's poetic sequence. The second poem in "Metaphysical Posters" describes the unmooring of the modern world from a stabilizing but now-disproved faith in an intimate cosmos:

Children suppose that chairs and tables
are an audience to their play;
and we, children always,
must still pretend
that the stars
care.
And yet we know them globes of gas,
immense and fervid,
but vapid.

We call them fixed,
and ancient.
And yet they fly like dust on the wind;
and each in its phases
is a cloud changing,
and like a man
must end.
Not always was the heaven this wide
fire-pricked void.
Once was a closer, glimmering darkness,
whence the stars
crystalised.
In that beginning the sun was not,
life was not spawned,
nor anywhere
looked mind.

Nor Russell, Wells, nor Freud, nor Bernard Shaw
gospelled as yet through dark suburbia.

Other poems in the sequence represent the stars as accusers of self-impor-
tant human beings or as foliage on the cosmic tree, as senile onlookers to the
spreading "disease" of mind in the universe or as the old lamps from which a
human master may yet summon the jinn, as gems to be gathered by a future
humanity voyaging to other constellations or as continually evaporating and re-
condensing energies that are virtually immortal. The final poem in the volley—
one of six that in slightly revised form eventually found their way into *Last Men
in London*—refuses the mood of disenchantment that the new understanding of
the universe might seem inevitably to impose. In a reaffirmation of subjectivity,
the sexual union of two lovers becomes more important than anything else in
time or space. From erotic ecstasy come the rhythms that make the music of the
spheres. Like Dante before him and T. S. Eliot just after him, Stapledon celebrates the still point at the center of an elegantly rotating universe:

For then we knew
quite surely
that all the pother of the universe
was but a prelude to that summer night
and our uniting,
and all the ages to come
but a cadence
after our loving.[46]

When he finished the twenty-three poems inspired by Jeans, Olaf started a "second volley," called alternatively "The Seven Spheres" or "The Nether Worlds." As the first volley had been motivated by telescopic vision of superhuman realities, this round of "Metaphysical Posters" would peer microscopically into "the world of cells, / the world of atoms." Spying on the dance of protons and electrons, the osmotic nourishing of the body's cells, the spermatozoon sculling through dark liquid passages, the poet searches "down the precipice from mind's ledge" and enters the miniature worlds out of which life and mind emerge.

Stapledon drafted six poems for the second volley of "Metaphysical Posters" before giving up the sequence. There is an unusually formal announcement of the project's abandonment at the back of the handwritten manuscript: "The aim of this series was to depict the sphere of human affairs as hung between nether and upper worlds. Below lie the worlds of organic matter and of inorganic matter; above lie, in ascending order, the terrestrial sphere in which is enacted the drama of mind's evolution on this planet, the sphere of the stars, the sphere of the remote universes, and the sphere of eternity. But by the time the sphere of common sense was reached the enterprize [sic] was seen to be a failure."[47]

What had failed him was form; the idea behind "Metaphysical Posters" persisted. A poetic sequence may not have provided the maneuvering room he needed for a visionary myth, growing in his mind, of the human place within the inhuman reaches of space and time. For years he had treasured up an image of human brevity and the outer darkness from the eighth-century history of the Venerable Bede. "The earliest example of 'English' thought," Olaf wrote in 1915, "is the description of life by that old Saxon fellow as like the passage of a bird from the darkness through a lighted room and out into the darkness again. In modern English literature you have such things as Carlyle's passage about the quickly succeeding life of humanity on the earth—'hasting like a train of heaven's artillery across the astonished earth. . . . oh heavens whither?'"[48]

By the 1920s he no longer thought of Carlyle as a "modern," as he did when he made him patron saint of *Latter-Day Psalms*. Having outgrown his parents' tastes, Olaf acknowledged Carlyle only as "a poet, a psychologist, but no philosopher." But he never surrendered the conviction of 1915 that "there is a very big thing to be said by me" after the war in the form of a changeful vision, "now vague and to be doubted, now brilliant and all-absorbing."[49] He decided to put the poetic intuition of Carlyle on a firmer base by writing a prophetic account of the future of the human species, rigorously observant of the discoveries of contemporary science. He believed he could produce an extended and ultramodern gloss on the haunting Anglo-Saxon image of the mortality of life on earth. To do so meant working on a scale that would dwarf not only Bede's *Ecclesiastical History* but Gibbon's *Decline and Fall of the Roman Empire* and even Wells's best-selling work of the decade, *An Outline of History*.

Stapledon needed to invent a genre that combined features of the chronicle-history, the satirical voyage, the scientific romance, and the philosophical conte. The story he wanted to tell in *Last and First Men* would make unusual demands on its readers. They would be asked to see themselves as others in the distant future might see them, to whom they would appear not moderns but ancients. Readers must forego anything like a familiar narrative plot, would have to tolerate abrupt transitions and great gaps in the story, would encounter more telling and less showing than they were accustomed to in novels. With two billion years to cover, the pace would be so fast and the passages of time so huge that the reading experience could be likened only to a distinctly modern form of travel. The narrator, speaking from the remote future, must issue special reading protocols:

> I have to present in one book the essence not of centuries but of aeons. Clearly we cannot walk at leisure through such a tract, in which a million terrestrial years are but as a year is to your historians. We must fly. We must travel as you do in your aeroplanes, observing only the broad features of the continent. But since the flier sees nothing of the minute inhabitants below him, and since it is they who make history, we must also punctuate our flight with many descents, skimming as it were over the house-tops, and even alighting at critical points to speak face to face with individuals.[50]

If our species was still in gestation—as Jeans had claimed in *Nature*—if we in the twentieth century were just emerging into humanity, what would we look like, Stapledon wondered, to a more fully developed human being of the future? Which would be the "critical points" in the evolution of the species? If we could face individuals in our future, would their faces—not to mention hands and torsos and brains—still resemble ours? And if we could imagine the perspective of ultimate humanity, how might it guide the choices of the fledgling human beings of the "modern" era? The questions were bound to produce surprises. If, as J. B. S. Haldane said in a widely quoted aphorism very much on Stapledon's mind, "the universe is not only queerer than we suppose, but queerer than we *can* suppose," why shouldn't the future history of humanity be equally fantastic?[51] Sometime late in the 1920s, in time somehow rescued from a schedule crammed with teaching and scholarly writing, Olaf finally wrote the big book he had dreamed of for fifteen years.

10

THE FUTURE SPEAKS

1930–1932

GREAT VISIONARY FANTASIES can be triggered by the least likely occasions for vision. *Paradise Lost* took shape while Milton was a blind outlaw in hiding from the restored monarchist government. Mary Shelley wrote her best novel in postpartum trauma after a dream in which she rubbed her dead baby back to life. The underworld of the Morlocks in H. G. Wells's *Time Machine* recreates the ventilated tunnels through which his mother and her fellow servants carried platters of meat from a kitchen outbuilding to their employers' table. Out of the misery and terror at the Somme in the Great War grew J. R. R. Tolkien's voluminous history of the elves. Ursula LeGuin's ambiguous Utopia, *The Dispossessed,* emerged from a youthful memory of the face of J. Robert Oppenheimer. Stapledon's most famous book, *Last and First Men,* had equally well-hidden roots.

On spring and summer holidays, Olaf and Agnes enjoyed nothing better than to pack a few necessities into their rundown Sunbeam, relic of the FAU years, and motor down the Wirral peninsula towards Chester, turning west for the Welsh mountains and the sea. On mountain holidays they boarded at a farmhouse, but near the coast they liked to pitch a tent in a field and wander the beaches and cliffs, exploring tidal pools along the rocky shore. In July 1926 near St. David's Head, where the far western tip of Wales pokes out into St. George's Channel, they bathed and strolled day after day in sun and rain along the Pencaer peninsula. The holiday was restorative for Olaf, who had been working steadily for over a year on philosophical papers and his book on ethics. He had just learned of his failure to get a position at the University of Swansea. Near the end of their stay, he recorded in his naturalist's diary for

28 July: "Saw 19 *Seals,* 15 on one rock together." Two days later he returned to the spot for another view of the seals. On the thirty-first, when Agnes was resting, he wrote with evident excitement: "I ran to the seal haunt." In the midst of mostly blank pages and occasional colorless jottings, these exhilarated notes stand out in bold relief.[1]

Nothing else like them appears in his diaries of this period until two summers later when Olaf took his whole family to Anglesey, the big, flat island at the northwest extremity of Wales across the Menai Strait. This time he brought the page proofs of *A Modern Theory of Ethics.* Most mornings he corrected proofs and then set off with a picnic lunch to range along the rugged coves of Anglesey's north coast. At Cemaes Bay there is a sheltered, crescent-shaped sandy beach where the children could play and bathe under Agnes's supervision. Just east of the beach, rising abruptly out of deep water, the gorse-dotted cliffs of Llanbadrig peninsula, topped with pasturage, run for several miles along the shore overlooking the gray-green Irish Sea. Olaf seldom saw a cliff he could resist climbing. Each day he scrambled up, sometimes with Mary or David, but more often alone. The cliff path, meandering perilously close to sheer precipices, offers dizzying perspectives; a lone walker along those cliffs is buffeted by the stiff, cold Welsh wind that often scours the path. All along Llanbadrig slim gorges slice deeply into the high grazing land and expose layers of purple and dun rock in a geological time line that stretches down a hundred feet or more to clumps of fallen boulders in the water. More than six decades after Olaf's holiday at Cemaes Bay, a traveler can, at least at some seasons of the year, still have the cliffs to himself, with only the occasional sheep for a companion. On clear days the huge green facade of the Wylfa nuclear power plant on a distant promontory west of the bay is the single obtrusive reminder of the passage of time.

For a fortnight in August and September 1928, Olaf's diary has the repeated refrain of "WOS on cliffs," with reports of seals sighted or failures to find seals.[2] The interest borders on obsession, as if seals were the holiday's chief objective. What exactly was he looking for? What did he end up seeing on the cliffs of Llanbadrig? One thing he must have seen in this scarcely human landscape, just over a high rise of pasture about a mile from Cemaes Bay, is a startling incongruity. In a deep hollow, invisible from the bay approach until one is suddenly standing above it, there is a tiny stone church and an acre of churchyard ringed by a low wall. Tilting tombstones stretch nearly to the lip of the cliff. It is hard to imagine how anyone digs six feet down into this stony terrain, but the churchyard is crowded. Climbing further east to the next high point a quarter of a mile away and looking back, a walker gets a different view of the graveyard and its irregularly shaped stone wall, like a tarnished necklace laid out carelessly on the green turf, an emblem of human occupation and human mortality. The walker who peers down the sheer cliff at that point might see, as Olaf did on his lucky days, seals stretched out on huge rocks far below, with cold waves churning around them. It is a grand site. Standing there, one believes it could conjure visions.

In the mid-thirties Stapledon told an interviewer that the plan of *Last and First Men* came to him "in a flash" while he was watching seals. "Afterwards I simply pumped my scientific friends for all the information I needed and settled down to write the story from the viewpoint of a man living in the distant future."[3] Ten years later, speaking in Manchester to promote his 1947 novella *The Flames,* he embellished the account of what he named his "Anglesey vision" by comparing himself on the cliffs facing the Irish Sea with "stout Cortez" in Keats's sonnet "On First Looking into Chapman's Homer":

> Then felt I like some watcher of the skies
> When a new planet swims into his ken;
> Or like stout Cortez when with eagle eyes
> He star'd at the Pacific—and all his men
> Look'd at each other with a wild surmise—
> Silent, upon a peak in Darien.

He had had, he told his Manchester audience, an unbidden imaginative experience; later came a secondary stage in which "the artificer gets to work" creating "extravagances" to flesh out and rationalize the vision.[4]

But something in these legendary accounts doesn't sound quite right. If the interviewer recorded the conversation accurately and if the author remembered the exact sequence of events, the moment on Anglesey in August or September 1928 led directly on to the research and writing. He "simply" consulted some scientists, invented practically on the spot a strikingly unusual narrative viewpoint, and, although he had never before produced a piece of fiction more than a dozen pages long, rattled off in just over a year a densely textured imaginary chronicle of the evolution of *homo sapiens* over the next two billion years. It is not an impossible timetable, even though *Last and First Men* is a very big book (and had been bigger still in draft). In fact, given the other substantial projects he had in hand through the summer of 1928, Stapledon could not easily have begun writing a new book much before the autumn of that year. But he must have severely cut back the time he gave his four WEA classes and have put all other writing on hold to give *Last and First Men* nearly singleminded attention in late 1928 and throughout 1929.

This timing might account for a composing process executed at white heat while the writer was in possession of a fully formed conception of the book, but it strains belief that the idea for *Last and First Men* didn't come to him until the waning days of the summer of 1928. Such a schedule does not allow for a germinating period when the initial "flash" of vision could work its way through his mind, according to his usual creative procedure as he once described it to Agnes:

> The process of producing such things with me consists of (a) a sudden idea (b) a period of desultory & occasional thought, or toying with the idea (c) a mighty struggle with a pencil and a piece of paper, by which a few disjointed lines are made with no success, then often (d) a spell of disgust and 'chuck it you ass", (e) then perhaps another and more successful & fluent effort with a pencil followed by (f) a series of improved copies one upon another in quick succession, each supposing itself the final version (much waste of the nation's paper supply) (g) sometimes, alas seldom, a sudden cessation of hostilities, and sense of complete victory. Even after that a few small touches may be added months afterwards. But you see what a labour goes to produce so small a result.[5]

Long afterwards, writing to a visionary painter who filled her canvases with untransmuted private myths, Olaf said, "Visions, in your sense, do not come to me. I have to imagine everything laboriously, and criticize it step by step. These two powers, creative imagination and critical intelligence, are always opposed to one another; and yet it is only in their clash that great art or great intellectual achievement can occur."[6]

   Last and First Men was in every respect a breakthrough for Olaf, and perhaps it was characterized by an extremely short incubation period when imagination and intellect wrestled each other. A passage deleted from his preface to the book, however, describes a fallow period before the narrative took shape: "I have worked, as any writer must work, by keeping certain ideas and appreciations 'warm' in my mind, and watching their self-elaboration into a coherent theme. The main outline of that theme came to me rather suddenly, and for some weeks the secondary features continued to unfold themselves. Only when I began the task of writing was I conscious of active manipulation and criticism."[7] But when was there time for his usual "period of desultory & occasional thought" when the ideas for *Last and First Men* could warm and grow?

   The simplest solution is to assume that in public statements about *Last and First Men* Stapledon conflated the Welsh holidays of 1926 and 1928. His "Anglesey vision" of 1928 may not have been a distinct event but a recapitulation of a vision he first had at St. David's Head in 1926. Agnes, the only witness to her husband's epiphany on the Welsh coast, in later years spoke of the occasion as a holiday shared by the two of them; that would fit the 1926 visit, but not the 1928 trip to Anglesey, when Mary and David were also present.[8] Olaf's hectic search for seals on Anglesey recorded in his 1928 diary may have been an effort to relive an experience he had had two years before when he was too busy to follow it up. If visionary ideas generated in 1926 were kept simmering, he had had frequent chances at the Liverpool University Club to question his scientific colleagues and to mull over their answers, letting them seep into his imagination. Then, we may suppose, in 1928, with the *Ethics* completed, he returned to the vision of 1926 and the notion he had of a new direction for his writing. By September 1928 he was free at last to devise the "main outline" of *Last and First Men* and begin the arduous process of constructing the future history of the human race. But it remains to ask exactly what Olaf saw in Wales, whether in 1926 or 1928, and what seals have to do with *Last and First Men*.

The seals he observed were sunning themselves on the rocks, squirming and squealing with almost human vulnerability as the waves hit and drenched their warmed skin with cold spray. This much Agnes Stapledon, nearly fifty years after the event, could say for sure.[9] Olaf himself never revealed exactly why the seals he saw from the cliffs of St. David's Head or Llanbadrig mattered so much. In a lush passage from his final book, he erased all specificity about the occasion, not mentioning Anglesey or Wales or seals or even *Last and First Men,* but as he tells it in *The Opening of the Eyes,* an ecstasy on the beach inspired not simply one book but a life's work. "Long ago (it was while I was scrambling on a rugged coast, where great waves broke in blossom on the rocks) I had a sudden fantasy of man's whole future, aeon upon aeon of strange vicissitudes and gallant endeavours in world after world, seeking a glory never clearly conceived, often betrayed, but little by little revealed. . . . Since then, year after year, I have tried to create in words symbols of that vision."[10] From the literary products of that vision, we can guess what passed through Stapledon's imagination as he watched the seals and the ceaselessly moving tidal waters orchestrated by the invisible moon: the original emergence of terrestrial life from the ocean; the huge spectacle of geological time imprinted on the rocky coastline; a sense of wonder at the biological forms that intelligence might take in other environments, in other times; the alternative pageant of evolution and civilization that might have occurred had the first humans been an aquatic species; the splendor, the oddity, and the fragility of all mind and life.

All these themes figure in the fictional details of *Last and First Men* as finally written, and seals themselves make a notable appearance in the far future when the "fifth men," a mutation of the original human stock in exile on Venus from a shattered earth, slowly adapt to life on a watery alien planet:

> After some millions of years of variation and selection there appeared a very
> successful species of seal-like submen. The whole body was moulded to
> stream-lines. The lung capacity was greatly developed. The spine had

elongated, and increased in flexibility. The legs were shrunken, grown together, and flattened into a horizontal rudder. The arms also were diminutive and fin-like, though they still retained the manipulative forefinger and thumb. The head had sunk into the body and looked forward in the direction of swimming. Strong carnivorous teeth, emphatic gregariousness, and a new, almost human, cunning in the chase, combined to make these seal-men lords of the ocean. And so they remained for many million years, until a more human race, annoyed at their piscatorial success, harpooned them out of existence.[11]

This startling metamorphosis, typical of the method of *Last and First Men* in its intellectual compression and casually brutal conclusion, almost certainly owes less to literary models in Ovid or Milton than to the author's peculiar seaside vision. It was one of the first episodes he set down in a raggedy eighty-six-page first draft, using the scrawled shorthand in which he customarily roughed out ideas at high speed.[12]

Olaf kept no record of the stages of composition of *Last and First Men;* what evidence survives is piecemeal and teasing. An occasional visitor to the Stapledons in 1929 remembered that he emerged from the upper part of the house late in the afternoons for tea but was invisible for the rest of the day. His sister-in-law said his attic-study was sacrosanct: "When Olaf was up there we'd shout for him to come down to get his lunch."[13] A few friends got inklings of the strange narrative taking shape. Two scientist-colleagues, P. G. H. Boswell and James Johnstone, used to lunch with Stapledon at the University Club, where he plied them with queries about evolution and sketched out fantasies about future human physiology. Sidney Scholefield-Allen, president of the Merseyside Fabian Society, listened to trial ideas for the social arrangements of a future humanity, and Leonard Martin, Professor of English at Liverpool University, heard the general plan of the book while out walking with Agnes and Olaf.[14]

Hints of three distinct phases in the composition of *Last and First Men* can be detected in fragmentary manuscript material. "Random Notes," a "General Plan," and pages of sometimes indecipherable draft survive for an early version, titled "The Future Speaks." Stapledon imagined a human descendant from the remote future outlining the history of our species from the twenty-first century until extinction. The planet enjoys a precarious peace after a Wellsian "open conspiracy" to replace nationalism with a global government; the cosmopolitan movement, however, lacking any spiritual base, succumbs to American cultural values.[15] A cataclysmic Sino-Antarctic atomic war in the third millennium is followed by slow progress toward Utopia before the exhaustion of natural resources and solar changes threaten the planet with unbearable cold. The new ice age requires emigration to Venus and the genetic engineering of a second human species adaptable to the new environment. After a golden age on Venus, another flight—this time to Mercury—necessitates the manufacture of a third human species who become a race of philosophers. At last, as the sun chills still more and an icy climate from which there is to be no reprieve settles on Mercury, one of these "last men" makes telepathic contact with the twentieth century before silence descends on the solar system. Although the scheme of "The Future Speaks" would be greatly modified and elaborated, the basic framework for Stapledon's history of the future was in place.

A second phase in the development of *Last and First Men* can be deduced from two enormous, intricate, and beautiful multi-columned time charts, done with colored pencils on sheets of graph paper taped together and keyed to an eleven-chapter version. This text, now lost, came between the early drafts of "The Future Speaks" and the final draft of *Last and First Men* that went to the typist. In this intermediate state the three human species were enlarged to eight; there was increased emphasis on alterations in human biology; the sojourn on Mercury was abandoned for a migration to Neptune; and, most tellingly, the future contained more and lengthier "dark ages" when no human culture flourished. A single page of memorandum from autumn 1929 gives a glimpse of the author worrying over the book's vast time scales: a series of dates ranging from the earth's formation two billion years ago to the collapse of the moon four hundred million years hence precedes the titles of three works of geology and archaeology to be consulted.[16]

By early 1930 a third form of the narrative, based on eighteen successive human species stretched out over the next two billion years, was nearly finished and frantic alterations had begun. "The book ought to be handed in next week," Olaf told his father in January, "but won't be ready for many weeks yet, as it needs a lot of revision. In fact it looks as though it would miss the spring publishing season, which is a nuisence [*sic*]. The real difficulty is going to be to cut it down drastically without spoiling it."[17] Throughout the spring he made excisions to get the manuscript down to a length that Methuen was willing to print; the contents page of the final holograph copy is filled with columns of figures representing calculations and recalculations of numbers of words and pages to be cut, with desperate queries about entire episodes he might have to sacrifice. He had a final conference with his editor in London on 20 June, completed the preface shortly thereafter, departed for Germany on 7 July, and came back to work on the proofs in August.[18] At the very most, it would appear, Stapledon spent twenty-one months writing *Last and First Men*—from its first sentence to the last revision.

In his preface he characterized it not as a novel but as "an essay in myth creation." Not wanting "to resuscitate the fossilised remains of myths that once were alive and potent," he sought a myth compatible with science and oriented to the future, free from nostalgia for the sentiments of outworn creeds but also skeptical of the new myth of progress.[19] Although he later spoke wincingly of his failure to foresee Hitler in the near future, in many respects *Last and First Men* has proved a remarkably prescient guidebook to the anxieties of the late twentieth century. The account of the "Americanization" of the planet, the possibility of atomic annihilation by accident or political madness, the cultural disaster of "the end of oil," the scientific challenge and ethical risks of genetic engineering, the spiritual folly of the obsession with youth among the Patagonians of the hundredth millennium, the development of artificial intelligence in his chilling Fourth Men, known as "the Great Brains"—each of these episodes has grown more pertinent in the decades following the book's appearance.

Last and First Men's first reader—and first teacher—was specially suited to the book's mythic ambitions. Leonard Martin was a specialist in the religious poetry of the seventeenth century, and Olaf asked him to criticize the entire manuscript before he sent it to Methuen. Martin may have been the ideal critic for a book of Miltonic proportions.[20] As *Paradise Lost* defined cosmic history by drawing a line backwards into uncharted time to a cataclysmic revolt in the heavens and a microscopic act of disobedience on earth, *Last and First Men* sketched humanity's forward history, through eighteen major mutations of the species in three planetary habitats over a period equal to the amount of time that had elapsed between the formation of the planets and the twentieth century. Milton put the original pair of arcadian human beings at the center of his action, and Stapledon made his focal point our last descendants living in a crumbling utopia on a dying world. Like Milton, Stapledon dealt in moral rises and falls, in global catastrophe and recovery, and strove to reconcile the perspectives of philosophy and natural science, the claims of tradition and innovation. But the richest foretaste of *Last and First Men* is in books 11 and 12 of Milton's epic. There Adam sees and hears the history of the future from an angel's point of view and, learning of the world's ultimate redemption, ponders the influence that the future may have on his own present. Exactly that possibility motivates the far-future Neptunian last man to narrate the full story of humanity to the "first men" of the twentieth century. With its cyclical structure and emphasis on loss and consolation, *Last and First Men* is a renovated *Paradise Lost:* a story of human paradise repeatedly lost and regained and ultimately lost for good, but with Miltonic theology edited out. Although not strictly a secular vision, Stapledon's history neither assumes humanity as the crown of creation nor depicts a Creator; the cosmos often assaults the eighteen human races, but it is always impersonal and silent.[21]

Milton aside, the genre of the future history was virtually without precedent. Many analogues can be found for aspects of Stapledon's chronicle, but none fully anticipates its form. In his early WEA years, Stapledon read Winwood Reade's nineteenth-century treatise on human suffering, *The Martyrdom of Man,* and, while finding it "horribly cocksure," he admired it as "a sort of popular & graphic history of the universe from the non-religious point of view." Even farther back in the network of influences is a book Olaf read with rapture as a teenager at Abbotsholme, Richard Proctor's *Other Worlds Than Ours.* Its last chapter, on "Supervision and Control" of the universe, imagines "an intelligent Neptunian observing and interpreting events on earth."[22]

Of far more consequence was the most famous of Bertrand Russell's early essays, "A Free Man's Worship," written in 1903 and reprinted in the 1917 collection *Mysticism and Logic.* Russell proposed to define the appropriate human response to the godless and hostile cosmos disclosed by science. That "the whole temple of Man's achievement must inevitably be buried beneath the débris of a universe in ruins" was a fact not to be doubted. But human beings still must confront the dread of extinction. One could choose Promethean revolt against a repugnant universe or, as Russell preferred, a disciplined resignation to fate. "Only on the firm foundation of unyielding despair," he wrote, "can the soul's habitation henceforth be safely built." In his margin Olaf penciled a query, "Why therefore despair? Beauty, not immortality, is the ideal." His copy of the essay is larded with marginal notes, questions, and disagreements; there is a big red *X* alongside Russell's views on tragedy, and against a passage on the submission of desire to intellectual integrity there is the complaint, "He always confuses desires for the self & desires for the world."[23] Because Stapledon rarely marked up his books (usually limiting himself to a few strokes in the margin and some chaste notes in green pencil on the back flyleaf), the heavy annotation of "A Free Man's Worship" tells a tale. *Last and First Men* is both an extended variation on Russell's theme and, in certain psychological and metaphysical respects, a retort.

More recent works also made an impact. In 1923, Stapledon read Wells's *Outline of History* and in 1927 J. W. Dunne's *Experiment in Time,* the first a model of synoptic and generalizing history and the second an investigation of telepathy that challenged the commonsense metaphor of time's arrow. He also read Gerald Heard's *Ascent of Humanity,* but found its notions of psychological evolution unreliable. An essay acquired in 1928, during the early phase of *Last and First Men*'s composition, had a far greater impact on the decision to extend the book beyond the relatively modest confines of the outline in "The Future Speaks": J. B. S. Haldane's "The Last Judgment." Haldane's speculative apocalypse is a cornucopia of unelaborated but provocative guesses and fancies about the future, around many of which Olaf built entire episodes—the depletion of fossil fuels and the destruction of the earth by its disintegrating moon, the development of new human senses and the abolition of pain through eugenic manipulation, the terraforming of Venus and the fashioning of a stumpy dwarf humanity to colonize Jupiter.[24]

The models that guided Stapledon's thinking and planning were mostly scientific, historical, and philosophical. Despite the appreciation of his work by science fiction writers and readers, literary sources for *Last and First Men* are scanty. Unlike earlier utopias and scientific romances like Bellamy's *Looking Backward* or Wells's *First Men in the Moon, Last and First Men* cared less to tell a story or dictate a social program than to imagine a plausible scenario of change. Such later experiments as Wells's *Shape of Things to Come* (1933) and its 1935 film adaptation and Katharine Burdekin's *Proud Man* (1934) and *Swastika Night* (1937) come closer to Stapledon's purposes, as does Warren Wagar's recent *Short History of the Future* (1989).[25] As befits someone trained in history and philosophy, Stapledon had his speaker from the future pose two central questions: What does it mean to be human? To what extent can human beings control and adapt to change? The reader of such fictions is not invited to gawk at a fantastic future but to pay attention to the political, scientific, and moral processes by which the future emerges from the present.

If its epic and historical claims and its status as myth were uppermost in the author's mind, it was the scientific boldness of *Last and First Men* that captivated its stunned first readers, many of whom did not recognize the author's name. From London the poet A. S. J. Tessimond wrote, "You've made time, man, mind thrilling, and damned few people have done that." John Dover Wilson, the WEA inspector turned Shakespearean editor, was distracted from all other work for four days: "You have invented a new kind of book & the world of Einstein & Jeans is ready for it." Haldane the geneticist found the science of *Last and First Men* "unimpeachable," assumed incorrectly that Stapledon worked in a research laboratory, guessed that his own essay "The Last Judgment" had been an influence, and offered free consultations on the author's next myth. Haldane's sister Naomi Mitchison was "entranced" and "didn't read anything else, even the daily paper, till I'd finished it." The astronomer Arthur Eddington "appreciated equally the wisdom of its sense and the subtlety of its nonsense." Julian Huxley, just having collaborated with Wells on the massive *Science of Life,* sent an effusive message: "The blend of imagination and scientific plausibility is more than Wellsian!" Three readings convinced the novelist L. H. Myers that no one "deals with the immensities with such judgment." Gerald Heard, thrilled to find a book that treated his pet interests in telepathy and group consciousness with scientific rigor, wrote four times to Stapledon within a month and used his connections in London newspaper circles to turn himself into a one-man publicity machine for the book.[26]

The unsolicited fan mail had a directness of comment often absent in the lavish, though sometimes uneasy, reviews that began appearing in England in

October 1930, and a few months later in North America. The journalistic superlatives that garnished nearly every notice ("tremendous," "audacious," "entirely original," "gargantuan," "unique," "Michelangelisque" [sic]) suggest the climate of excitement around the book but in themselves reveal little about *what* reviewers were recommending aside from the scope and novelty of *Last and First Men*. One commentator, assessing the book's reception eight months after publication, even suggested that it may have lost potential readers because of blurbs that indulged in rhetorical overkill.[27] A common denominator of the reviews—both the many that believed in the book and the few that doubted—was uncertainty about an appropriate standard for measuring the book's achievement.

In both England and North America, *Last and First Men* was noticed in an extraordinary range of journals, from the British *Good Housekeeping* to New York's *Chemical and Metallurgical Engineering*. Some themes recur in review after review: that the author was utterly unknown; that the book's genre was a puzzle; that its nearest relations were the satiric fables of Samuel Butler and the scientific romances of Wells; that summaries made it sound ridiculous. Its novelties required close reading, and, the *Times Literary Supplement* remarked in frustration, the dense narrative texture was such as to "defy abridgment." "If you skim it, you may find it dull," Arnold Bennett warned readers. *Last and First Men* is the season's "outstanding odd book," J. B. Priestley wrote, one that resists "any recognised category."[28]

Reviews from across the Atlantic picked up the chorus. The *Saturday Review* called it the most remarkable account of the future ever written—neither a Verne romance nor a Butler satire nor a Wellsian prophecy but "a mad myth, soberly written." The *New York Times* detected a biblical grandeur in the writing and the *New York Herald Tribune* found the book too forceful "to deserve any such colorless label as Utopian."[29] The frequent allusions to Butler, Verne, and Wells were the effect of Methuen's publicity effort, which tried to hitch an unknown author to literary stars, but discriminating reviewers, especially in Britain, were quick to discount the comparisons. The *Observer* noted superficial resemblances, but insisted that *Last and First Men* "stands alone" in scope, style, imagination, and quality of thought; *Oxford Magazine* thought the "boldest imaginings of Mr. Wells pale before the dreams of Mr. Stapledon"; and several reviewers found Stapledon's submicroscopic Martians cleverer and more credible than the monsters in *The War of the Worlds*.[30]

Negative criticism was rare, save in religious periodicals that chastised the book's godlessness and, ironically, in a cool reception from the Liverpool press. A columnist at the *Liverpool Post* got an advance copy and wrote archly, "I have not read it, but certainly it looks a very unusual book. I have not detected a scrap of dialogue in it from beginning to end." When the *Post*'s official review came out, it became clear that Stapledon was to be a prophet without honor in his own city. The narrative was found overblown and wearying. "Curiosity cannot reach out across so vast a span. Sixteen [*sic*] different races of men populating half the planets in the solar system in turn, seem in a work of fiction almost as excessive as sixteen different heroines. One loses interest in some, and then in all of them."[31]

But for some readers the hold of *Last and First Men* on the imagination was so powerful that they mythologized how they came to read it. J. B. Priestley read it on the overnight train from London to Scotland. "It was the perfect setting. The rush of the train was the rush of centuries. The loneliness and darkness of the journey were the counterpart of the loneliness and darkness of Man's journey, as revealed in this extraordinary book." As a young man Arthur C. Clarke selected it from an exactly remembered shelf at knee-level in a public library in Somerset and it determined his career. In a medical officer's quarters in India during World War II, Brian Aldiss glanced through a copy of the Pelican edition while he was awaiting an inoculation and was so captivated that for the only time in his life he stole a book. Doris Lessing was given it as a girl by an eccentric neighbor in Southern Rhodesia who told her, "You must read this if you never read anything else!"[32]

Stapledon did not let the hometown press dampen his elation. *Last and First Men* vindicated him. His father had heard him speak endlessly of his literary ambitions. He had read his son's verses since he was a teenager, watched the vicissitudes of an unpromising career for twenty years, and frequently dug into his pockets to bail him out. Willie, who would live only two more years, must have wondered whether his only child would ever find his way without him. In his turn, Olaf was torn between filial affection and an ache to throw off the yoke of a father's kindly disappointment. The very last poem he had published in the 1920s, "Squire to Knight," was desperately autobiographical:

> You are old,
> Your work is done,
> And you may rest
> Henceforward.
>
> But I am young,
> My task not shown.
> Your counsels rust
> My sword.[33]

Three years later he had proof that his talent was for real. At a celebratory party Olaf reveled in the applause of his friends, one of whom asked what Willie thought of his success. Ordinarily a light drinker, Olaf was stimulated by the warmth of the alcohol and the occasion to brandish a copy of his book with Oedipal glee: "This will finally show him!"[34] It was a supremely youthful gesture. But Olaf was almost too old for it. One of the ironies of his success was that he was touted as a leading candidate for the prestigious Hawthornden Prize, and one newspaper even announced prematurely that *Last and First Men* had won. Actually, he was disqualified when it was discovered that he did not meet one condition of the award. At forty-four he was three years too old, and it went instead to Geoffrey Dennis's *End of the World*—a more conventional book of forecasts that had often been reviewed alongside Stapledon's.[35]

Even without a prize, Olaf's life changed dramatically as a result of *Last and First Men*. He entered long correspondences with several people who stimulated his work—especially L. H. Myers and Naomi Mitchison, the Danish art historian Aage Marcus, and the great panjandrum himself, Wells. Trips to London and contacts with the intellectual world became more frequent, though he never got any closer than the outer fringe of Bloomsbury, "being myself at heart a barbarian," he remarked offhandedly.[36] But Jack Haldane invited Olaf to his lab at London University, and in 1931 he was welcomed into a small, comfortable circle presided over by Mitchison and Gerald Heard, which gathered in the upper room of the Café Royal on Regent Street. There, reclining on the plush red banquettes and ordering off the cheap menu, they had long lunches discussing each other's work, arguing politics and aesthetics, and eyeing the moving feast of celebrities who made the Café Royal the place to go for literary contacts and gossip in the years between the world wars.

Back on Merseyside, Olaf's national attention brought new speaking engagements outside the adult-education circles that had been his bread and butter as a lecturer. He found himself addressing conservative audiences who wouldn't have dreamed of inviting a socialist WEA tutor but were glad to have a speech by a well-known local writer. The marriage of lecturer and listeners was not always happy. Speaking on "Selfishness—Its True Place in Business" at a Liverpool Rotary Club luncheon, he deplored competition as the symptom of an archaic individualism and left his audience baffled by what one Rotarian lamented as "an abstruse ethical subject" not well-suited to a hotel meal.[37] Before long, Olaf resigned from the Philosophy Seminar at the university and reduced his WEA classes to one per term to make room for other paid talks and to give himself time to write. The sales of *Last and First Men* were good enough to tempt him to the thought that he might be able to replace at least some of his teaching income with royalties from popular writing. At Methuen, E. V. Rieu was already asking for a sequel.

Olaf had a golden opportunity to capitalize on the interest in *Last and First Men* and help create an audience for his next book. Early in 1931 a producer at the BBC scheduled him to talk on a topic of his choosing related to his book.

16. Cosmic provincial: the author of *Last and First Men,* ca. 1931.
Courtesy City Librarian, Liverpool Central Libraries.

On 2 April he made his first national broadcast. As a neophyte he had been told to rely on short sentences and simple words, use the first person, pause often, and have a picturesque opening and a challenging final sentence.[38] Dutifully, he began his twenty-minute talk on "The Remaking of Man" by announcing that "Human nature is like our English climate" and ended with a panorama of the utopian splendors that await the remade man "before the

ultimate frost destroys him." Without the insulation of the fictional apparatus of
Last and First Men, he speculated freely on the wonders that could be anticipated once eugenicists, within a century or two, began constructing a healthier,
long-lived human specimen with enhanced sensory powers and a more finely
calibrated moral sense. On air the romancer became once again the teacher, and
not all listeners liked what they heard; a Catholic journalist thought Stapledon
"entitled to indulge in these flights of fancy" in fiction, but was shocked to learn
"the pagan, God-denying philosophy that underlies all this."[39]

The radio brought Stapledon's ideas to far more people than ever heard
his WEA lectures or read his books. Olaf was excited by the educational potential of broadcasting, and he took other occasions to speak on philosophical
and political topics. He also wrote a clever radio script based on *Last and First
Men,* but it was never produced, presumably because the dialogue, never his
strongest suit as a writer, was too flat-footed to make effective drama.[40]

His love affair with radio, however, was not uncritical. He despised the
BBC's director Sir John Reith as a tool of Tory interests, and from his brother-
in-law Lynton Fletcher, a staff member at Broadcasting House in London, he
learned about Reith's policy of firing any employee adjudged the guilty party
in a divorce.[41] In various forums Stapledon excoriated the mass media for distorting public debate or lulling people into intellectual torpor. Even before his
first BBC talk he had wondered mischievously whether people were masters
of their radios or vice versa. One of the delights of *Last and First Men* is an
episode in which invading Martians, viral organisms in the form of greenish
clouds, are injured in their search for intelligent life on earth when they unwittingly pass through radio beams:

> Presently the Martians discovered the sources of terrestrial radiation in the
> innumerable wireless transmitting stations. Here at last was the physical basis
> of the terrestrial intelligence! But what a lowly creature! What a caricature
> of life! Obviously in respect of complexity and delicacy of organization these
> wretched immobile systems of glass, metal and vegetable compounds were
> not to be compared with the Martian cloud. Their only feat seemed to be that
> they had managed to get control of the unconscious bipeds who tended them.[42]

The parody, Olaf came to see, was not far from the truth. "The B.B.C. is
making citizens," he wrote a short time later. "It has contrived to wake up quite
a large minority of ordinary men and women to care about the life of their
community and to be interested in current problems." But the ordinary bipeds
would remain only semiconscious unless radio ceased being an organ of national culture and became an international medium of communication, education, and liberation. The risk was that radio—and later television—would

become a leveler of opinion and an incitement to emotionalism, disseminating propaganda for official views. Nevertheless, in a utopian sentiment that anticipated by half a century political movements profoundly affected by broadcasting, Stapledon wondered in 1932:

> What would have happened if, throughout the present Far-Eastern crisis, the Japanese public had heard every day on the wireless what the rest of the world was saying about their Government's dealings with China? What if, decades before the crisis, the youth of the Eastern and Western peoples could have been in constant radio intercourse, exchanging ideas, modifying each other's opinions? In this case, of course, the linguistic difficulty would have been very great; but, as time advances, English will increasingly serve as an international language, unless Esperanto or some other artificial speech takes its place.[43]

In the afterglow of *Last and First Men,* as Stapledon sought to put his vision of world citizenship before a larger public, he overcame his shyness and wrote to the best-known agitator for a new global order. So many reviewers had instinctively invoked the name of H. G. Wells that Olaf felt he had better introduce himself. Almost exactly one year from the day *Last and First Men* was published he wrote a letter of such modesty and charm that Wells, who found flattery irresistible, was bound to reply:

16th October 1931

Dear Sir,

A book of mine, *Last and First Men,* has received a certain amount of attention, and nearly every review has contained some reference to yourself. Recently I have come to feel that if you happened to notice the book, a copy of which the publishers must have sent you, you might wonder why I had not the grace to make some acknowledgment of your influence. Of course it cannot matter to you whether a new writer admits his debt or not; and anyhow you may not have seen the book or the reviews. All the same I should like to explain. Your works have certainly influenced me very greatly, perhaps even more than I supposed when I was writing my own book. But curiously enough I have only read two of your scientific romances, *The War of the Worlds,* and *The Star.* If I seem to have plagiarized from any others, it was in ignorance. Your later works I greatly admire. There would be somethng very wrong with me if I did not. They have helped very many of us to see things more clearly. Then why, I wonder, did I not acknowledge my huge debt? Probably because it was so huge and obvious that I was not properly

aware of it. A man does not record his debt to the air he breathes in
common with everyone else.

Yours very truly

W. Olaf Stapledon[44]

Literary historians have been so eager to trace a lineage from Wells through
Stapledon to later practitioners of science fiction that they have quoted the homage of the final sentence out of context. But it was Wells the utopian and the
public educator, not the romancer, whose forgiveness Olaf asked for whole-
sale borrowing. The letter was forwarded to Wells on tour in the United States;
from Boston he sent back a gruff, vulgar, typically Wellsian absolution (in
which, like many other readers, he got Stapledon's title wrong): "It is all balls
to suggest *First & Last Men* (which I found a very exciting book) owes anything to my writings. I wish it did." He told Stapledon he was endorsing the
book in his new encyclopedia of economics, *The Work, Wealth and Happiness
of Mankind,* and, always on the lookout for a disciple, invited him to visit his
London flat or his French villa.[45] Their first meeting did not occur until five
years later, but they began exchanging books, reviewing each other's work,
and debating philosophy and politics by letter.

By mid-1931 Stapledon was deep into a second work of fiction and a big
fifty-page essay on the future for what would turn out to be a highly controversial children's outline of modern knowledge. The new fiction was developing oddly. When Methuen suggested a sequel to *Last and First Men,* Olaf went
back to some material cut from that book—a circumstantial account of life in
the year 2,000,000,000. The first pages of the new book contain some of his
purest science-fictional imaginings: five-mile-long space ships from the colonies of Jupiter and Uranus landing in the oceans of Neptune, close-ups of physi-
ologically remarkable extraterrestrials at work, at play, and in love, hauntingly
alien landscapes, architecture, and ecologies. But in proportions and emphasis the new work had only a tangential connection to its predecessor and has
never been popular with readers of science fiction. The title he finally settled
on, *Last Men in London,* was meant to chime with the earlier work but was
hopelessly mismatched with the book he actually produced.[46]

Last Men in London and *Last and First Men* shared just one narrative
premise. In each the future speaks to the present through an apparent fiction
generated by telepathic contact between a last man and one of the first men.
The second book extended that premise by having a Neptunian actually possess the mind of a first man to study it and to alter it. The result was a book
far more introspective and openly personal than the first. In *Last Men in London,* Stapledon began composing a version of his own intellectual and emotional history transferred to a young man whom he initially called Henry

Firstman. This protagonist, whose name he changed in a later draft to Paul, undergoes experiences that duplicate or gloss events from Olaf's childhood and early adult years. But the self-study was filtered through a complex narrative membrane. Under the Neptunian narrator's influence, Paul joins the same ambulance unit as Olaf Stapledon, "the colourless but useful creature" who thinks he is the author of *Last Men in London* but is only a "mouthpiece" of the far-future man inhabiting his imagination. Later, after the war, when Paul looks up his old FAU colleague Stapledon, "that timid and comfort-loving creature" lets him read *Last and First Men* while it is still in manuscript.[47] At once neatly severed from his autobiographical counterpart and brought into close proximity with him, Paul both is and is not Olaf. Stapledon remembers his own past but observes it as if it happened to someone else. All autobiography mixes memory and invention, self-vivisection and self-effacement, but the narrative tactics of *Last Men in London* explicitly dramatize the philosophical and practical problems of life-writing.

Last Men in London is cunningly organized as a biographical study of a first man (a young Olaf) told through the unwitting instrumentality of the historical Olaf (reduced to a comic nonentity) by a detached and manipulative last man, who turns out to be himself another Olaf. In the opening chapter the last man takes us on holiday in the remote future with his mate, a Neptunian named Panther who has a primitive "mass of hair, flame-like, smoke-like," atypical of the women of Neptune, and eyes that are mysterious, potent, and hypnotic. Floating hair and enchanting eyes always meant one person for Olaf. It is a futuristic Beatrice-Agnes we see reclining with her ultimate Olaf on the beach of a Neptunian fjord, a little "corner where the land juts out into the sea as a confusion of spilt rocks." Together they watch the life in a tidal pool, including small humanoid sea creatures who represent a devolutionary offshoot from the human species. "What a world this pond is!" the last woman exclaims.[48] It is the most astonishing of Stapledon's several versions of his great epiphany on the Welsh beach in the 1920s, as the last man himself is one of Stapledon's most revealing self-incarnations: the displaced artist-philosopher, a disembodied mind poised outside time and simple location.

Stapledon the writer, presiding over the three Olafs of *Last Men in London,* orchestrated a remarkable experiment in form. The extraterrestrial narrator's repeated formula in the next-to-last section of the novel, "I recall myself to myself," provides the final clue to the genre of this strange if not wholly satisfying book. "I shall smile when I remember this book," the last man says, "this strange hybrid sprung from the intercourse of a purely Terrestrial mind and a Neptunian mind, earth-infected."[49] Often neglected because it seemed a failed scientific romance lacking the mythic resonance of *Last and First Men, Last Men in London* deserves to be read as a daring literary mutation. A telepathic *Bildungsroman,* a science-fictional portrait of the artist as a young man, it is Stapledon's *mémoire fantastique.*

Nor is *Last Men in London* simply private and idiosyncratic, of interest only as coded self-disclosure. Just as H. G. Wells two years later in his *Experiment in Autobiography* presented himself as a "sample brain" with both a personal story to tell and "a history of my sort and my time," so Stapledon studied himself as a representative of the early twentieth century, coming of age as a citizen of the world.[50] In naming his specimen Henry Firstman, he crudely underlined the effort to enlarge autobiography into cultural history. The reduction to Paul made the gesture subtler. Stapledon may have been drawn to the biblical name of Paul because of its association with a profound conversion in which an old identity (Saul's) was shed and a new one awakened in its place.[51] There may also have been a more contemporary stimulus to change the name. The protagonist of one of the period's most widely read novels, Erich Maria Remarque's *All Quiet on the Western Front,* was called Paul and had been acclaimed as a type for the generation that survived the Great War. In the mental history of his Paul, seen through the distorting lenses of several partial versions of himself, Stapledon offered a revisionist account of the experience and the consequences of the war.

Comment on World War I in *Last and First Men* as published was limited to two paragraphs early in the book, but much had been eliminated in the early months of 1930 when Stapledon was making ruthless cuts. He had surveyed the "genuine foretaste of Armageddon" on the Western Front: "Human organisms in thousands were dismembered, disembowelled, crumpled up and trampled into the mud like unconsidered insects. Human minds were twisted and shattered by the long mental conflict between terror and pride, insurgent brutality and refinement, self-seeking and comradeship, the insane sentiments of nationalism and the sentiment of human loyalty."[52] An uncut *Last and First Men* would have shown a movement to abolish war being swallowed up in the 1920s by a resurgent patriotism that buried the lessons the war should have taught. This analysis of war and of the failure of postwar cosmopolitanism, intended for the first chapter of *Last and First Men,* became the thematic focus of *Last Men in London.* Placing his Paul in the shadow of Remarque's Paul, Stapledon wanted not only to reinforce *All Quiet*'s visceral revulsion from the killings but to teach the still-unlearned lesson of the war: the need for a fundamental change of heart, an imaginative commitment to a new order. *Last Men in London,* only a footnote in the history of the scientific romance, remains an original and worthy contribution to the memoir literature of the Great War.

Later readers, coming at the book with other expectations, have been irritated by it, but in the last months of 1932 reviewers saw what Stapledon was up to. Alternately "enthralled and repelled," a Birmingham critic considered it required reading: "There is a lesson in it that should be crammed down the throats of the war-mongers who are still with us." The London *Guardian* found the book sagacious and beautiful, though its genre was uncertain—"a satire, a sermon, or what you will on the breakdown of civilization in Europe"—and doubted only whether the "romantic envelope" of the Neptunian frame story was really necessary. Even the Liverpool press, typically acerbic about the "cumbrous" and "nauseating" romance elements in Stapledon's work, recognized a value in the "social criticism of England before, during and after the War."[53] And although Olaf's private life was unpublicized, reviewers intuited the personal dimension of the book. The preface to *Last Men in London* claimed that it had neither hero nor "distinct personalities." But the *Times Literary Supplement* observed that "few persons have ever been more vividly and completely characterized than Paul." A New Zealand reader shrewdly guessed that the book owed most not to literary models but to "the earlier years of Mr. Stapledon."[54]

The achievement of *Last Men in London* was to some degree overshadowed by the controversy over an anthology called *An Outline for Boys and Girls and Their Parents,* published just four weeks earlier. Victor Gollancz, the most prominent publisher on the Left, hoping to exploit the current rage for "outlines," asked a rising young socialist writer to edit a guide to the modern world for children. Naomi Mitchison was thirty-four years old, one of the Scottish Haldanes, a mother of five, and already author of a dozen books. Short, pale, and stocky, a bundle of energetic impulses, she had a reputation as an iconoclast, a feminist, and a peppery intellectual combatant. She appreciated good manners but never wasted time on mere pleasantries. Naomi could make withering comments on ideas and people she disapproved of, and she held grudges against those who snubbed her. Sometimes she got as good as she gave. When she and a young niece arrived for lunch once at her favorite London haunt, the Café Royal, they were refused entry by the doorman because they were not escorted by a man. Naomi was enraged. "Do you take me for a tart?" The attendant answered smoothly, "I'm sure I couldn't say, Miss."[55]

There was another, more vulnerable side of Naomi, who often worked herself to the point of physical and emotional exhaustion. Olaf wrote of one afternoon at the Café Royal: "It was an odd lunch because Naomi, chewing turbot the while, kept flooding her face with tears, ostensibly through a sort of maternal feeling for the Revolution, but really I think because she is in a nervy state and in the doctor's hands all the time."[56] Her motherliness also took the form of generous championing of other writers, to whom she wrote detailed letters as each of their books came out, as she did for Olaf. She enjoyed collecting interesting people—W. H. Auden and Margaret Cole and Stevie Smith

and Harold Laski—and mingling them at the huge parties she and her husband Dick, a Labour party activist, gave at their London house, "River Court,"
in Hammersmith. Naomi was a gregarious hostess and an indefatigable talker;
she had no trouble coming up in 1931 with an impressive group of writers for
the Gollancz children's *Outline*. Both of her regular lunch companions from
the Café Royal, Gerald Heard and Olaf, joined Auden, Cole, Dick Mitchison,
and others on the contributors' list.

When the *Outline* appeared in September 1932, there was warm appreciation for Naomi's editorial work in Scottish newspapers and in leading English periodicals—notably the *New Statesman, Times Literary Supplement,* and
London Mercury. But the right-wing press was aghast at the many essays, including Olaf's, that took the Russian revolution as a signpost for the future.
Clerics, led by the Archbishop of York, launched a holy war against the book
for its indifference to institutional Christianity, to which Naomi made a typically uncompromising reply: "If this is the way the Churches treat it, I think
the worse of them. I have deliberately asked my contributors to leave out all
comment on Church Christianity, as this seems to me to have gone so far from
what the Founder meant that it has become valueless, especially to those who
really believe that Jesus meant what he said, and not what St. Paul, or any
other Pope, or any bishop, put in His mouth."[57] Newspaper letter columns were
rife with denunciations, and in the *English Review* Arnold Lunn conducted a
freewheeling fourteen-page tirade against the *Outline*'s anti-Christian ethos.
Naomi, whose chatty style in the introductory sections of the book was sav-
aged by Lunn, later blamed the book's commercial failure on his ferocious
attack.[58]

Olaf's chapter of the *Outline,* called "Problems and Solutions, Or The Future," attracted comment on both sides of the debate—far more than Auden's
slender essay on literature, which most reviews ignored. Stapledon asked children to imagine a new world, free from a "blind and mean loyalty to nations,"
for which they should be prepared to die. Preoccupied with his own rehearsal
of the Great War as he drafted *Last Men in London,* he emphasized that those
born after 1918 must consult the memories of witnesses to an event already
receding into history. "Those who did not see the war cannot possibly imagine what it was like," he warned. With an eye to the Land of the Young he was
imagining on Neptune, he proposed strenuous, dangerous, but nonmartial challenges to exercise youthful vigor and competition. Knowing the temptation of
war as adventure for young men, he begged them to find other outlets for
gallantry: "Rather than preserve war, we had better allow duels again, and
tournaments."

The chapter is full of Stapledonian themes becoming familiar to his adult
readers: the British empire's obsolescence; the ideal of an effectively cosmo-

politan league of nations; the shrinking of the globe by improved communication and transport; the prospect of unimaginable wars to come; the urgency of disarmament; the redistribution of the earth's wealth; our coming ability to remake nature and the human race itself. Sounding like a jolly pied piper, he declared most parents psychologically incapable of change and invited the young, in a repeated conspiratorial phrase, to follow him toward "the world we are going to make."[59] The refrain echoes across thirty years to his boarding school song:

> Come! We will make the Continents inseparable;
> We will make the most splendid race the sun ever shone upon;
> We will make divine magnetic Lands:
> With the love, the love of Comrades.[60]

At forty-six, identifying himself with his preadolescent audience, he still had a touch of the Boy Who Refused to Grow Up.

But this was nearly his last enactment of that theme. "I have had rather a heavy time lately," he told Naomi in the summer of 1932. "And the book I am trying to finish has become rather a nightmare."[61] In fact, as Olaf wrote *Last Men in London* and his piece for the *Outline,* William Stapledon was slowly dying at Annery of progressive heart failure. *Last Men* contains a striking image of Paul's father, "an imaginative amateur" scientist modeled on Willie, giving his young son a first lesson in wave mechanics, stirring the waters of a lake on the Welsh moors. In a late interpolation in the manuscript, that physics lesson is expanded into a parable about being and dying. "The father said, 'That is what you are yourself, a stirring up of the water, so that waves spread across the world. When the stirring stops, there will be no more ripples.'"[62]

All through the spring of 1932, as he prepared for Willie's death, the burden of his father's financial affairs and the care of his mother, "an insoluble problem," grew.[63] Walking up Caldy Hill to visit his father in his final illness, Olaf thought about the autobiographical events he was reshaping in *Last Men,* thought about what he wanted to say to the next generation in the *Outline,* thought about his inheritance from Willie. His father had introduced him to astronomy, the study more essential than anything else to all his later work. And yet the cosmos Olaf came to see was different from the one his father saw, though they used the same telescope. Down on Grosvenor Avenue, drafting his *mémoire fantastique,* Olaf wrote Willie's epitaph in Paul's account of the difference between father and son:

> Even his father, who had helped him to discover the new world, did not seem to appreciate it as it deserved. To the father it did indeed seem wonderful.

He called it "sublime." But for him it remained merely a sublime irrelevance. It compelled his attention, and in a manner his admiration also; but the tone of his voice, when he was talking of it, suggested a veiled reluctance, almost resentment. He seemed, in spite of all his scientific interest, to be happier and more at home in the world of the Iliad or of the "Faerie Queene." The son, on the other hand, though he did his best to appreciate these dream worlds, was never moved by them.[64]

The description of the father, in carefully measured words that adjust praise to an assertion of the son's difference, fits the gentle businessman who had once called himself Emmeline's knight and who spent his life among ships named for Homeric heroes. If Olaf could never fully share Willie's pleasure in chivalry and classicism, he knew he had profited from the rippling effect of his father's scientific amateurism. On 29 June, Olaf sent off the manuscript of *Last Men in London* to Methuen. William Stapledon's heart stopped on 12 July, and he was cremated the next day.

II

MAPPING UTOPIA

1933–1935

TUCKED INTO OLAF'S SCHOOL TEXT of Thomas More is an inked map headed "Utopia. W. O. Stapledon." Topographically precise, drawn carefully to scale, his utopian island is just off the coast of Macaria (the blessed place) and Achoria (the melancholy place). Pubescent eros has designed a landscape in which geography overlays anatomy: lines mark the route past the tiny Petrina Island guarding the narrow entrance to Utopia and through a slender strait into an enormous enclosed harbor, Megakolpo (the great womb). The main island, a long crescent two hundred miles wide at its thickest point, is dotted with towns scattered along a 1,500-mile arc that embraces Megakolpo. A second drawing, of an enlarged Petrina, shows buildings just visible on its rocky central summit and on promontories stretching into the sea.[1]

It is a schoolboy's daydream, compounded of the pleasure of seascapes, the mysteries of sexuality, a knack for draftsmanship, and an urge to put his own stamp on More's utopian fantasy. Three decades later Olaf began mapping, in words rather than pictures, more ambitious no-places that could house the enlightened societies and awakened individuals of his maturer speculations. His utopian schemes of the thirties emphasized political and spiritual regeneration, but erotic liberation was not neglected. When Bertrand Russell suggested that university students of the opposite sex be encouraged to live together, a newspaper correspondent interviewed officials at Liverpool University for their reactions. In conservative Liverpool nearly everyone, including the president of the Guild of Undergraduates, denounced the idea. The head of the School of Architecture, asked whether the proposal didn't hark back to an ancient Greek practice, responded caustically, "I should rather describe it

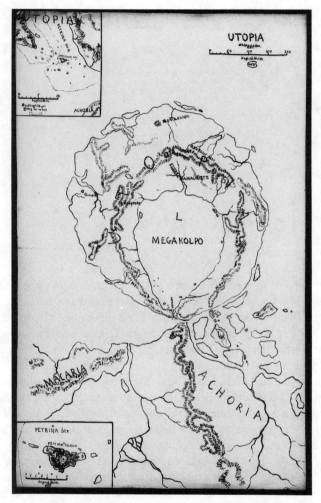

17. Erotic geography: young Olaf's map of Utopia.
Courtesy Stapledon Archive, Sydney Jones Library,
University of Liverpool.

as a harking across to a modern American one." Only Stapledon was ready to
defend Russell's proposal as desirable and necessary, "but in the present state
of public opinion it is quite impossible."[2]

Being a spokesperson for the university was a new role for Stapledon. His
literary fame had brought the lectureship denied him five years earlier on the
basis of his philosophical research. Liverpool's philosophy department gave

him a one-year contract for 1932–1933, and Olaf took up his new duties while
retaining one WEA class in Birkenhead on Tuesday nights. At the end of 1932,
he was mulling over an offer to make the appointment permanent. Against the
advantage of putting his finances on a firm basis he weighed the infringements
on his freedom. He sought guidance from Leo Myers—the wealthy, opinionated novelist who, himself suspicious of academics, nevertheless lived on the
fringes of Cambridge and had friends among the professorial staff. The two
of them had been corresponding ever since *Last and First Men* appeared, and
the sophisticated and prickly Myers had become Stapledon's somewhat unlikely confidant and intellectual sparring partner. "I think I enjoy giving advice almost more than most people," Myers wrote, warning of the risks of living
solely off the resources of William Stapledon's estate:

> The security of an *earned* income, however small, is not a thing to be despised.
> Still less to be despised is the sense of stability afforded by a definite place in
> the world; to say nothing of the human contacts which it gives rise to. The
> danger threatening a person who is working imaginatively and in isolation is
> that he will lose contact with the actual world. My advice would be to accept
> the permanent post at the University, provided that it will not occupy too much
> of your time. In your position I should cynically decide to give as little time
> and thought to my academic work as possible. This, however, is not really
> cynicism; for you can feel sure that as a teacher you will be infinitely superior
> to 90% of the other teachers. You have only to thrust Last & First Men into the
> hands of your pupils, and you will have done far more good than anybody else.[3]

However much he tried to palliate it, Myers's advice *was* cynical, as Olaf
immediately recognized. It had the opposite effect from what Myers intended.
Asked to choose between writing without the security of an academic position and embracing a literary career subsidized by halfhearted teaching, Olaf
found that he believed in good teaching too much to accept the compromise.
In his temporary lectureship, he had classes every Monday, Tuesday, and
Wednesday morning and filled up the afternoons with student conferences.
There would be "a vast amount of work," he told Leo, if he joined the staff
permanently. In the end he declined the appointment, resuming full-time university lecturing only once again, during World War II, as a substitute when
the head of the philosophy department could not complete his courses.[4]

Deciding against the imaginative writer's common practice of accepting
university employment (and conferring the luster of his name on the institution) in exchange for time to write at his students' expense, Stapledon showed
that his utopian ethics was more than an allegiance to an abstraction. In the
years just after *Last Men in London,* he offered provocative glimpses of
Utopia in platform speeches with panoramic titles like "Man's Prospects,"

"Ourselves and the Future," and "Living on Other Planets." Although he discounted the value of his fictions as prophecies, listeners in the pinched circumstances of the 1930s drank in his images of a prosperous future global community. "Properly applied," Olaf told one group, "science can turn the world into an aristocratic society, in which all the dirty work will be done by machinery, and all will have ample leisure." These talks, often to young audiences, were not Disneyfied tours of the technological marvels that awaited the next generation. Cautioning against escapist fantasies, he typically concluded a speech by exhorting his listeners to consider the practical requirements for making a more humane future. The most practical first step, he liked to tell them, was taken with the imagination. We must learn to think of society in human terms, not in national or racial stereotypes, he said, and must "familiarise ourselves with the idea 'Man.'" Only on that foundation could planning for a diverse, harmonious, and free new order commence.[5]

In 1934 he broadcast a speech to the country's Unemployed Clubs on machinery and labor in the future. Stapledon was unsure, as he told a foreign correspondent, whether the producer would allow him to read his text as written:

> They invited me, and then when I submitted a sketch of what I had to say, they hesitated a long time before accepting. However it is fixed now, though of course they may find the actual typed talk too subversive after all, in which case, no doubt they will suppress it. The subject is the Future of Mechanization, which obviously has a black as well as a bright side.[6]

A partially disintegrated recording of this address, rescued by the Stapledon family from the BBC archives, contains the only known transcription of Olaf's voice. When Agnes once asked him what he thought about the importance of "nice" accents, he replied, "Certainly in the days when I used to live among people who always spoke so, namely at Oxford, I used to think anything else was at best flat and undistinguished and at worst very painful. But that was long ago. My own talk for instance is now very undistingushied, largely owing to the F.A.U. and W.E.A."[7]

On the radio Olaf spoke in a clear, slightly lilting tenor, in soft North Country tones—neither Oxonian nor Liverpudlian nor BBC-didactic—of the risks and promise of a world in which machinery would increasingly determine the pace and quality of life. His manner was confidential and colloquial, with some mild pulpit-pounding: "We are all more or less machine-mad. Our minds stink with machinery, and the lust of mechanization. Our gods are speed, mechanical invention, and mass production. We are like children that are crazy over some new mechanical toy. We are becoming insensitive to all the really interesting things in the world. And we are going dead inside." The rhythms and rhetoric of the broadcast give a more reliable clue to Olaf's attractiveness as a tutor of working people than the abstruse language of his philosophical fiction. The "subversive" design of the talk is apparent in the way in which he framed a Wellsian forecast of a future in which machines served a liberated and healthy humanity. Anticipating by a year the imagery of the film *Things to Come,* Olaf sketched a seductive picture of soaring buildings, pedestrian skywalks, fully automated households, and personal flying machines floating in the smokeless air. All this, he told his audience, would come to pass if there were fundamental economic and political changes:

> If control remains in the hands of a class which is devoted to private enterprise, this dream will never be realised. Instead the future will be far blacker than the present. For as the existing economic system becomes more insecure (and it is daily doing so) those who believe in it will sincerely feel that *every* means must be used to preserve it. And in a not very remote future increased mechanization will give them immensely increased power to crush opposition. The plain man's freedom, such as it is, will vanish. He will become a helpless cog in a rickety machine. If he rebels or criticizes, all sorts of grim mechanized dodges will be used to suppress him. But indeed few persons will have the imagination to criticize authority, for by means of highly mechanized propaganda, the government will mould every man's mind to suit its own purposes. The press, the cinema, and above all the radio, will be used in such a manner as to give voice only to officially approved ideas and moral principles. Ordinary human beings will become mere mindless robots. And sooner or later, slowly or swiftly, the whole system will break down, and civilization will be lost.

On that dispiriting note, Olaf yielded the microphone to the BBC announcer, who brightly reassured the audience that succeeding commentators would take a rosier view of the future.

Not content simply to be a lecture-and-radio pundit, Olaf set to work on a "book of dogmas" that would lay out a comprehensive prescription for building a global Utopia.[8] That book he ultimately called, in his favorite metaphor, *Waking World.* The most challenging, ambiguous, and artful of his utopian writings, however, was a work of fiction written nearly in tandem with *Waking World* in 1933 and 1934. Fleshed out from a discarded chapter of *Last Men in London* and given a teasing subtitle ("A Story Between Jest and Earnest") reminiscent of More's skepticism about Utopia, the book's title underwent several alterations. From awkward suggestions of a tract ("Disportment" or "The Career of a Sport") the title evolved to emphasize a personality rather than a thesis—"John Alive" and finally, at a very late stage, *Odd John.* With *Odd John,* Stapledon for once did not have to warn readers that this fiction was "not a novel." Inventing his first truly rounded character, a physical and mental freak who rejects the prevailing ethical and cultural norms, he also conducted his most troubling excursion into Utopia, one that epitomized the decade's dwindling hopes, in the era of Mussolini, Hitler, Stalin, and Franco, for achieving the good society.

Utopia in the 1930s was in a fragile condition. Its credibility had been weakened by the worldwide economic depression as well as by lingering postwar disenchantment with idealism, by dictatorships on the Right and Left that curdled enthusiasm for centralized social planning, and by the literary assaults of dystopias like Yevgeny Zamyatin's *We, Proud Man* and *Swastika Night* by "Murray Constantine" (pseudonym of the feminist Katharine Burdekin), and, most widely read of all, Aldous Huxley's *Brave New World.* Going against the tide, James Hilton's wistful *Lost Horizon* depicted an exotic Shangri-La, more a Utopia Lost than a model to be emulated. One of the most original utopian romances of the century, Burdekin's *The End of This Day's Business,* failed to find a publisher in the 1930s and remained buried for fifty-five years after she had written it.[9]

The one name that remained unwaveringly, passionately identified with Utopia as an achievable ideal was that of H. G. Wells. Two organizations committed to creating Utopia sprang up under Wells's banner, and Stapledon became a charter member of both. The portentously named Federation of Progressive Societies and Individuals late in 1932 and the H. G. Wells Society in 1934 attempted to mobilize Britons into the "open conspiracy" for a bloodless global revolution that Wells had been urging since the mid-twenties. Olaf's own dogmas in *Waking World* and the tragic failure of Utopia in *Odd John* cannot fully be understood apart from the history of these societies.

Under its first president, the popular philosopher and broadcaster Cyril Joad, the FPSI was pledged to world government; it aimed to educate children as global citizens, to secure fundamental rights and economic justice for all people, to eliminate the baleful influence of churches on individual freedom, and to safeguard the planetary environment. The program attracted writers, social workers, students, sexual libertarians, agnostic rationalists, and middle-aged liberals to its meetings in London. In 1934, Joad edited a *Manifesto,* with essays by leading members of the federation on topics ranging from disarmament to reform of the abortion laws, from central economic planning to the politics of psychoanalysis. Predictably, the *Manifesto* was derided by the Right, but even the *Daily Worker* found it a dull assortment of "idle daydreams" by intellectuals "completely adrift." Another riposte from the Left scorned the *Manifesto*'s authors as "an insulated minority" innocent of the tactics of a mass movement.[10] Even after the FPSI changed its name to the more manageable Progressive League, it failed to muster the political nerve to turn utopian sentiments into practice. The League remained a collection of well-meaning theoreticians who for twenty years talked mostly to themselves. Olaf began his association with the FPSI in the spring of 1933 with a talk on "The Aims of World Planning."[11] His *Manifesto* essay on "Education and World Citizenship" was the product of his WEA teaching and an extended application of Wells's famous aphorism in *The Outline of History* that humanity was in a race between education and catastrophe. Economic revolution and educational reform were inseparable, Stapledon wrote, and the reforms needed were curricular, administrative, pedagogical, and psychological. Students had to learn to be critical of their own knowledge, and teachers needed rigorous training and better rewards for their work. Olaf's recommendations on the qualifications for teachers reflected both the FPSI's commitment to sexual freedom and the fantasies of the boy who drew an eroticized map of Utopia:

> The future citizens should not be formed under the influence of adults who are to a greater or less extent crippled through lack of sexual experience. Today there are no doubt many in the profession who do work of a high order in spite of their virginity. But if they had managed to lose their virginity, their work would have been even better. The spinster mentality, female or male, is disastrous in teachers. Headmasters and headmistresses especially should either be married or have temporary sexual relations.[12]

F. R. Leavis, generally dismissive of the *Manifesto,* singled out Stapledon's essay—for its proposals on the literary curriculum rather than its paean to sex for teachers—as the most valuable because the author was unafraid to "de-Wellsianize" educational theory by promoting aesthetic judgment in the global citizen.[13]

The Progressive League published a small journal, *Plan,* to which Olaf infrequently contributed; it held panels on topics like press censorship and telepathy, and it sponsored nudist weekends for members. The League helped Olaf widen his horizons beyond the Merseyside Fabians and WEA. But as an effort to institutionalize utopian agitation, it was virtually useless. Wells, who drafted most of the platform printed in the *Manifesto,* kept his distance once he suspected the League to be made up mostly of political chatterboxes. Olaf, more patient with ineffectual organizations, stayed on friendly terms with its members but limited the energy he invested in it. When he was offered the League's presidency he accepted conditionally—the condition being a set of proposals for making the League "a crusading organisation which were so radical as to be quite beyond its resources."[14] The offer, to Olaf's relief, was withdrawn.

The history of the H. G. Wells Society is briefer but just as unedifying. With Wells's blessing, the Society proclaimed that its members were open conspirators who would change minds and institutions. Vernon Porter, its young chairman, foresaw a cultural evolution with a fairy-tale ending: "The work of the Society would go on quietly, enthusiastically, continually, with ever-widening range, until one day mankind would wake up to find the World State no longer an inspiring vision but a living reality."[15] Three speakers were advertised for the Society's first public meeting on 15 May 1934 at Caxton Hall in London: the suffragist Sylvia Pankhurst, the dilettante journalist Gerald Heard, and Stapledon. The hall was crowded by a youthful, racially diverse audience. In a lengthy address Olaf, described by an observer (perhaps only by contrast to Pankhurst and Heard) as "a forceful he-man," asked the Society to keep a distinction between education and propaganda, realizing that any utopian community must foster critical intelligence in its citizens, starting with its children.[16] At the same time, he said, an effective movement had to make emotional appeals because the opposition would not hesitate to use sentiment, propaganda, and theatrics to maintain the old order. Utopians needed fresh symbols, and "we should beat our opponents on their own ground and make use of even flags, banners, and slogans." Finally, previewing a theme in his *Waking World,* he hedged on Wells's social vision that neglected art and religion and overprized science; a reconstructed society must be wary of "scientists going the way of priests and becoming a hard and dogmatic caste."

By the end of 1934, Olaf was saying of the Society, "I do not feel sure it is going to be an effective force"; over the next two years he wrote an occasional note for the newsletter, but the Society's aloofness from politics and its refusal of Marxist analysis led him to drop quietly away.[17] Wells's dissociation was noisier. Utopian thinkers inevitably get irritated with the imperfect structures built from their blueprints, and Wells, nearing his seventieth birthday, was reluctant to stake the implementation of his vision on amateurs. He had met with Wilson and Stalin and Roosevelt, retained a loyal following of readers, and commanded the attention of the press throughout the English-speaking world. He was also working on a screenplay he expected to convey an irresistible cinematic vision of Utopia. He could get his message across to masses of people more capably, he believed, than the sincere but inept members of a utopian club. "The H. G. Wells Socy is none of my doing," he told an inquirer. "But they asked to use the name & as they took their programme whole out of my books I thought it was graceless to refuse. (But I have got their promise to change it next year.)"[18] The Society was renamed The Open Conspiracy and then Cosmopolis before being absorbed by the Federation of Progressive Societies and Individuals in 1936. Wells did not mourn its passing. When someone asked in 1943 how to join, H. G. told his secretary to reply, "He is happy to say the HGW Society is as dead as mutton."[19]

Stapledon's link to Wells was firmest in the years from the founding of the FPSI to the outbreak of World War II. His letters are full of genial flattery. "The fertility of Wellsian minds is astounding to slow persons like me," he gushed on one occasion, and on another, "What it is to be H. G.!" After their first actual meeting in 1935 when they talked about the making of the film *Things to Come,* Olaf wrote, "I had always regarded you as one of those famous mythical beasts, like the Lion and the Unicorn, that no one actually meets." The old beast was charmed. A few days later came a copy of his screenplay, inscribed, "Olaf Stapledon, Bless him. H. G. Wells."[20] As fiction writers they had little to say to each other. H. G.'s pathbreaking scientific romances were thirty years behind him when he met Stapledon, and the younger man's philosophical myths were in conception, pace, and texture foreign to Wells's gift for story. It was as utopists that they were drawn together, even though they quickly discovered crucial differences in their aims and tactics.

Waking World is a record of Stapledon's loyalty to the utopian idea in the face of the dystopian 1930s and of his heretical departures from Wellsianism. Its composition is traceable to a meeting with Victor Gollancz in the summer of 1932 after Olaf had finished his essay on the future for Naomi Mitchison's *Outline for Boys and Girls.*[21] Impressed by the enormous commercial success of Wells's *Outline of History,* which continued a full decade after its first edition, Gollancz decided that his firm should follow up the Mitchison anthology with more "outlines." He proposed that Olaf write a book for older teenagers on what they could do to create the world their children would inhabit. Gollancz advertised it as "It Is Up to You: An Appeal to the Young" for his spring list of 1933. But he never actually wrote a contract, and he declined to publish what Stapledon submitted. The rejected manuscript has disappeared, but a few traces of the episode remain: a synopsis of "It Is Up to You" printed in Gollancz's advertisement; an aside by Naomi Mitchison in a letter to Olaf ("Make Victor give you a contract; he is a wretch"); and a cryptic acknowledgment in the preface to *Waking World: "*To Mr. Victor Gollancz's shattering comments on an earlier and abortive experiment I owe much."[22]

No longer addressed specifically to the young, *Waking World* retained the conceptual framework of an "outline" and dramatically asserted the author's debts to and disagreements with Wells. Stapledon deplored the fashion of Wells-bashing from the Left and the Right, while granting some truth both to the Marxist critique of Wells's deafness to economic interpretations of history and to Tory criticisms of his anti-intellectualism. Wells established the genre of the "outline" and set the standards by which later cultural syntheses should be judged, but the author of *Waking World* announced, "I refuse to be blinded by gratitude."[23] Two years earlier he had made a similar gesture. Wells's praise of *Last and First Men* in the final pages of *The Work, Wealth, and Happiness of*

Mankind did not inhibit Stapledon, in a review of the book, from scolding Wells for scamping the humanities and for not seeing "that education is more than the business of teaching people to use encyclopaedias." Playing on the title of Wells's romance of the future, *When the Sleeper Wakes,* and on his own metaphor for advanced consciousness, he concluded, "If the sleeper is to come fully awake, he must see more than his own body."[24]

Waking World set out to correct an exclusively biological definition of human nature. Properly understood, Stapledon argued, the scientific revolution encouraged a "spiritualizing" process fundamentally different from the complacency of religious doctrines that assigned human beings a unique role in Creation. By dethroning humanity, scientific research can purify religion, restoring the meaning of "religare" (to tie back): "In giving man a sense of his indissoluble unity with the rest of the cosmos; and persuading him to be glad of it, the influence of science has been almost literally *religious,* binding, harmonizing."[25] By yoking religion and science, in however unorthodox a way, *Waking World* subverted a central tenet of Wellsianism. A modern, secular Utopia of the sort Wells had been boosting since the century began did not fulfill all human needs. The old gods of Greece and Judea, of the Vatican and Canterbury might be dead, but the religious sense had not atrophied.

Olaf sent Wells a copy of the book, alerting him to its criticism. H. G.'s rebuttal has been lost, but its content can be guessed from a splendidly colored cartoon Stapledon sent back. It shows an inaccurately tall and skinny Wells (whom Olaf had not yet met) striding between two cages and heading up an open road toward a utopian sunrise. His back is turned to the caged representatives of "Homo Proletariensis," but he is superciliously waggling a finger at a bishop, a top-hatted aristocrat, and a neo-primitive in animal skins in the cage labeled "Homo Religiosus." Wells may have complained (as he did later) that Olaf's "religion" played into the hands of regressive churchmen, social elites, and crackpots, because the cartoonist includes a self-defense against such charges. At the upper right a large black bird perches on the workers' prison. "I am not *really* in either of the cages, believe me!" Olaf wrote on the drawing. "I am the jackdaw, free, but uncertain."[26] It was a fresh emblem of his characteristic pose of the outsider who can see both sides of an argument, but the placement of the image suggested less waffling than might be expected of one who was "mediocria firma." In his uncertainty the jackdaw nevertheless still aligns himself with the Left; it is Wells who treads the middle way, so busy disputing and so self-assured that he doesn't look where he is going or perhaps notice that he is going there alone.

Although Stapledon and Wells had real ideological and temperamental differences, a reviewer of *Waking World* noticed one remarkable similarity: "Mr. Stapledon is developing just as Mr. Wells did. He began by producing a first-rate scientific romance, 'Last and First Men,' corresponding to 'The Time Machine.' Now he has produced a non-fictional account of the world to which he hopes we are waking, just as Mr. Wells did in 'Anticipations.' "[27] Scientists, however, were as unenthusiastic about *Waking World* as was Wells. The physicist J. D. Bernal, whose work Olaf admired, thought it hopelessly, piously old-fashioned. He accused the author of demanding from science a mystical "beatific vision" without realizing that science did not pronounce on ultimate values. Stapledon was merely revisiting the Stoicism of the later Roman Empire, which blindly worshiped anything that exists simply because it exists: "No other religion may be possible to an intelligent and honest man in these days, but we may well ask whether religion which has lost so much of its content is worth preserving at all." The criticism wounded Olaf because he relished the praise scientific readers had heaped on *Last and First Men.* "I'm afraid *Waking World* has damned me in the eyes of the scientists. It's sad, because I have usually a dog-like respect for them. And yet—they're so *sure* of themselves."[28]

His shift from fiction to social prophecy divided readers. Some, like the Marxist Amabel Williams-Ellis, regretted the change of genre, believing that a subtler, more convincing case for the same ideas had been made in *Last and First Men.* Those hostile to fantasy, like Lyon Blease of Liverpool University, found *Waking World* more agreeable "because in it he speaks in his own person, and not through the mouths of any post-historic monsters." Blease's review, the first generous notice his work got from a Liverpool paper, regretted that "Stapledon's best book so far" would appeal only to a "select audience" until the universities learned how to "multiply Stapledons." The most astute assessment of *Waking World* appeared in a minor educational journal that found the book "curiously unmoving." The author was too resolutely reasonable; he was an idealist whose fire was edited out of his prose; instead of a rousing call to wake up, his book offered readers only "an encyclopaedia without tears."[29]

Although Stapledon himself thought *Waking World* "not really a satisfactory book," it typified the decade in its devotion to sweeping change and its concurrent instinct that the time wasn't right.[30] The book ends in melancholy: "As things stand in Europe to-day, with the capitalists in control both of arms and propaganda, and Fascism on the increase, the hope of a world-wide and thorough revolution is indeed forlorn." Both those who liked and those who disliked *Waking World* saw its conclusions as "symptomatic," "a sign of the times, and an example to the times."[31] Ironically, while he was chided for diluting utopian aspiration in stoic pessimism, in retrospect one part of Stapledon's prescription for change was far too sanguine. Appealing for pacifist noncooperation with the extreme Right, he overestimated in 1934 the power of moral example to affect the course of Nazism. Ten years later he was unable to repeat the proposition in *Waking World* that "you cannot in cold blood shoot a whole people."[32] Even ten months later, in *Odd John,* he wasn't so sure.

Waking World, like any utopian document, was the product of both disinterested speculation and a private agenda. The desire to emulate and challenge Wells as a social visionary is the most evident but not the only personal motive behind the book. Olaf was still coming to terms with his father's death; as his own children entered their teenaged years, he concerned himself with freedom of thought in education; and, having made a name as a writer, he was working out an aesthetics by which he could situate himself in relation to the modernist movement. Each of these preoccupations was reflected in *Waking World.*

Olaf's uneasy sense of filial debt did not vanish but grew after William Stapledon's death in 1932. When the will was probated, he inherited over £50,000 in cash, stocks, and property.[33] Free for the first time in his adult life from financial worry, he could further curtail his teaching and spend as much time as he liked writing. He had the money to send his children to boarding school and to acquire a larger house. But coming into such good fortune in the middle of the Great Depression when he was regularly proclaiming the sins of capitalism, Stapledon suffered over the apparent contradiction between his convictions and his bank account. Some of his friends on the Left were so used to a life of economic privilege that they felt no need to apologize for any discrepancies, but he squirmed. Rather than hide the issue, he put it out to air. In a speech called "Why I Am a Socialist," he voiced the paradox in direct, personal terms: "I feel the Class War in myself. I live largely by dividends; therefore I dread financial decline. I want order, security, comfort, luxury, and another part of me espouses the Workers' cause and sees it as mine in the long run."[34]

In *Waking World,* envisioning a society that supported philosophers and teachers on a scale commensurate with their labor, he undertook an equally forthright self-scrutiny:

> Now I am no highbrow, or only a very imperfect one. But bourgeois I certainly am, in up-bringing and in present circumstances. I live chiefly on dividends and other ill-gotten gains, even while I proclaim that the system on which I live must go. . . . Having failed to earn enough by honest toil (toil there has been, but of a sort that society does not see fit to recompense adequately), I fall back with due thankfulness on dividends, until such time as the community has the sense to take to itself ownership of the means of production, and to afford me some less disreputable source of income.[35]

In private, Olaf and Agnes went on as frugally as they always had, spending little on food and clothing, using their new margin to travel more frequently and to pay the expenses for educating Mary and David. The glamorous parties at River Court in Hammersmith, where Naomi Mitchison would appear gowned in cream silk and her hair banded with embroidered fillets, were a luxurious treat for the Stapledons. "I love beautiful stuffs and dresses," the well-born Naomi once confided to the shopkeeper's son Wells. When Olaf called on H. G. at his Regent's Park flat, he took in the elegant appointments. "He said he was determined to make himself comfortable for the 'last ten years' of his life," Olaf, wrote in provincial bemusement, "and he has certainly succeeded."[36]

While he was writing *Waking World,* Olaf was looking over schools for his children. He had first gone to a boarding school at the advanced age of sixteen, and he believed that prolonged home life was a stunting influence. Remembering his long years in the company of Emmeline Stapledon and her friends, he wrote bitterly in *Waking World,* "In childhood we are marred by parents and other adults who have neither talent nor experience to fit them for their work. They do as well by us as they have it in them to do . . . but our very minds they patiently, stupidly, lovingly, or with unconscious hate, bind and distort."[37] For Mary, Olaf chose the liberal and venturesome Badminton School, where Iris Murdoch and Indira Nehru were among her classmates. He sent David, just before his thirteenth birthday, to his own old Derbyshire school, Abbotsholme. Neither of his children wanted to leave home, but their wishes were not consulted any more than Willie and Emmeline had consulted their son's back in 1901. Mary came to enjoy Badminton. David, "a very shy creature" according to his father, was unhappy. His passions were for music and the outdoors, both available in plenty at Abbotsholme, but he hated having his life organized for him by schools.[38]

As his children grew older, Olaf's long-standing interest in education widened to include the teaching of adolescents, and he was often invited to speak at secondary schools. Freedom of thought was so crucial, he said (with mischievous self-citation), that "all manner of cranks and disreputable people should be asked into the schools, to advocate, passionately, their particular recipes for society." If that meant that children heard justifications of treason, incest, or sacrilege, it was better that their minds be exercised than pacified. A young man who heard Stapledon speak to an assembly of students in the late thirties recalled how his bleakly scientific picture of universal destruction at the end of the world contrasted with the uplifting pieties of other visiting speakers.[39] In *Waking World* Olaf emphasized provoking youthful minds rather than training them in social obedience. Too much time got spent on Anglocentric culture, nationalist-biased accounts of history, and canonical literature of the past, "sacred texts to be saluted by insincere gestures of veneration."[40]

In addition to exhibiting his thinking on economics and education, *Waking World* illuminates Stapledon's dilemma about the Modernist movement.

In an unpublished essay of the early 1930s, "Thoughts on the Modern Spirit," he labored to appreciate the aesthetic revolution. He valued T. S. Eliot's poetry for its "music of facts" generated from the dissonances of modern life, but of modernism in general he wrote more primly: "In much contemporary work nausea seems an end in itself. And it is often difficult to say of any writer whether his vomiting is spontaneous or artificially induced for fashion's sake. Witness much that has appeared in certain 'modernist' periodicals, often of transatlantic origin."[41]

The bibliography to *Waking World* indicates he was not ignorant of the landmarks of literary modernism—*Ulysses* and *The Wasteland*, the works of Woolf and Lawrence—although little in the text suggests a detailed or specific appreciation of any single work. More revealingly, his chapter on art celebrates the "difficult beauty" of work that stretches the limits of our aesthetic capacities and "outrages our normal dispositions with a sense of discord or perversion or sheer ugliness." Difficult beauty is a feature of works of art that force us to entertain new possibilities or to see what hasn't before been seen.[42] The category of "difficult beauty" is relevant to Stapledon's own experimental fiction—especially *Odd John* and *Star Maker,* even more than *Last and First Men*—but his explicit application of the principle outside the pages of *Waking World* was to the visual and plastic arts.

Britain had lagged behind the rest of Europe in accepting the new schools of painting, sculpture, and architecture in the postwar years. A major exhibition in 1934, designed to break through crusted resistance to modernist trends, was mounted by a group of eleven artists calling themselves Unit One. Barbara Hepworth, Henry Moore, Paul Nash, Ben Nicholson, and the other members of Unit One, with Herbert Read as chief interpreter and advocate, displayed their work in April at the Mayor Gallery in London. Many journalists reporting on the exhibition were unable to get beyond philistine jokes about "modern art," but the show was nevertheless historic—and *Unit 1,* Read's edited assemblage of statements by the participating artists, had the force of a manifesto. Unit One, Paul Nash announced, hoped for the kind of impact that the Pre-Raphaelite Brotherhood had managed in the previous century; it stood for "the expression of a truly contemporary spirit, for that thing which is recognised as peculiarly *of today* in painting, sculpture and architecture."[43]

After a month's residence in London, the show was to begin a six-city provincial tour in Liverpool. As its arrival at the Walker Gallery was being anticipated, a columnist for the *Liverpool Post* broke the news that Stapledon had been invited to open the exhibition—"a graceful gesture from one branch of modernist art to another."[44] If Olaf was unsure of his relation to modernism, some people never questioned it.

The Liverpool opening of Unit One was lively. It provoked a sermon from the pulpit of the Anglican cathedral, and a bowler-hatted man who blundered unwittingly into the ceremonies at the gallery glared at the works on display, muttering, "More like a lunatic asylum."[45] With his old artist friend Eric Robertson in attendance, Olaf tried to put the crowd into an accepting mood: a work of imagination should encourage its beholders to be experimental, "to bring out the tentative beginnings of new ways of experience." Acknowledging that he himself did not yet have the language for naming or analyzing his responses to the Unit One pieces, he urged everyone to feel the works first and worry about articulating their meaning later. In particular, he exhorted spectators not to impose an inappropriate aesthetic on new forms: "Away with mere representation; that is the business of the camera. Away with the telling of a story; that is the business of the story." Pointing to a sculpted nude, one wag in the audience asked the speaker if he wanted to marry it. "What one wanted in a statue was not the same as what one wanted in a wife," Olaf drily replied.[46]

When somebody wrote to the *Liverpool Post* to complain that Stapledon's address had failed to explain what the Unit One artists were up to, Olaf sent in a lengthy letter. "The aesthetic experience itself must come before theoretical explanations of it," he wrote, unrepentant about his difficulty in making a reasoned commentary on the exhibition. As someone who pursued a "constructive interest" in his spare time, he enjoyed the play of color and shape in many of the pieces. Artists were discovering the capacities of stone, paint, wool, wood; deftly manipulating and transmuting forms to create a deeper pleasure than "simple decorative patterns"; appeasing "unconscious cravings" for liberation from convention. His account of the aims of Moore or Hepworth might be naïve or imperfect, Olaf granted, but the artists themselves were not working in words. What he felt—and his feelings, he insisted, were unassailable— was that Unit One freshened the imagination and opened "new vistas of reality."[47] For three weeks, the letters page of the *Post* crackled with the pros and cons of the exhibit and Stapledon's defense of it.

His championing of Unit One was not purely aesthetic. The artist's effort to open people's eyes was inseparable from a political awakening. A month after the Unit One opening at the Walker Gallery, Stapledon joined three thousand protestors at Liverpool Stadium to denounce the government's "Incitement to Disaffection Bill." The bill, making it a criminal offense for civilians to distribute subversive writings to members of the armed forces or for soldiers to possess such materials, gave police special powers to enter premises for search and seizure without a warrant on a mere suspicion of the presence of seditious literature. The star speaker at the rally was the radical scientist and ex-soldier J. B. S. Haldane, who dared the police to seize not only his copy of the *Communist Manifesto* but also "the life of St. George, the patron saint of England, who was a soldier and was executed for disobeying orders. He was ordered to sacrifice to an idol and would not do it." Stapledon could not match Haldane's biting wit, but he warned of a new barbarism in conflict with a new civilization: "Both were born during the war, but unfortunately the new civilization was born with its eyes shut, and the barbarians wanted to drown the kitten before its eyes opened."[48] Haldane was more eloquent than Stapledon in Liverpool Stadium, but the importance of vision as a political issue and the extinction of a nascent Utopia by fearful government agencies were two of the core ideas around which his new work of fiction was forming.

Odd John was more modest in scope than Last and First Men—with which reviewers itched to compare it—but its very accessibility lent it a greater capacity to disturb and scandalize. Many readers found their experience of the book, starting with the fetus-like, androgynous, Negroid portrait of John in garish colors on the book's jacket, intensely disagreeable. Not only in its packaging but in its narrative mischief Odd John came closer to being modernist in the mode of Unit One than anything Olaf had written thus far. With the irreverence of a Dadaist applying a goatee and mustache to the Mona Lisa, Stapledon rewrote Peter Pan to give Barrie's eternal boy a fearsome intellectual precocity, the talent for robbery and cold-blooded murder, a mean laugh, and the strangest menagerie of lost children imaginable. Odd John Wainwright's cohorts, every bit as grotesque as the figures in Edward Burra's Unit One paintings, include Jelli, a bowlegged Hungarian girl with a harelip and an overdeveloped head shaped like a hammer; Ng Gunko, the red-haired Abyssinian with one huge dark eye and a small blue one; the neckless Tibetan Tsomotre, whose head grows straight out of his shoulders; and a young Chinese called Hwan Tê with two thumbs on each hand. Lo, John's lover, resembled "a piece of sculpture come to life, something in which the artist had stylized the human in terms of the feline." John describes her body as if it were a surrealist's dream vision, "all steel springs covered with loose velvet."[49]

The story of a prodigy with extraordinary mental powers, the leader of a freakish group of supermen and superwomen who would constitute homo superior, originated in the nursery at Grosvenor Avenue. In the late 1920s, Olaf began entertaining his children with what they called the "John Stories," serial adventures of an amazing boy who captained a ship and outwitted all his enemies. "The great pleasure of the John Stories was the maps," his daughter recalled. "These were drawn at the beginning of the story, usually of a fantastic island with cliffs, peaks, ravines, rivers, gullies, estuaries, sand banks, reefs and so on. We watched them being drawn in detailed contour and a mysterious cross would be marked here and there, which would become of significance in the story later."[50] The stories were not written down, the maps no longer exist, but a colored drawing of John (the basis for the artist's spooky

18. Stapledon's painting of Odd John.
Courtesy John D. Stapledon.

version on the book's jacket) shows the strange being Olaf envisaged—a dark-
skinned boy with enormous black pupils in gray-green eyes set beneath a
macrocephalic skull capped with woolly white hair. As he appears in
Stapledon's novel, John Wainwright is a more satirical and chilling figure than
the hero of his children's bedtime stories; his role is far more political, and
his fate is a utopian tragedy.

The transformation of John the boy-wonder into John the utopian oddity was under way by early 1932. The later chapters of *Last Men in London* introduced the idea of "abortive supermen"—"unfulfilled approximations to a new species" among twentieth-century *homo sapiens*. Most of these creatures, like "Humpty," who shows up in Paul's classroom, are reviled as physical monsters or treated as if retarded. The miserable Humpty, whom neither ordinary kindness nor therapeutic psychoanalysis can help out of his loneliness, kills himself in despair over his inability to find anyone else like himself. At the end of the Humpty episode, the narrator of *Last Men in London* writes of another freak, destined to a greater achievement than Humpty's. "Of this other, of the utopian colony which he founded, and of its destruction by a jealous world, I may tell on another occasion."[51] That character was odd John Wainwright.

An extremely compressed version of what became *Odd John* exists as a rejected appendix in the manuscript of *Last Men in London,* an eleven-page handwritten draft headed "John's Story." While lacking the circumstantial and psychological detail of the later novel, "John's Story" outlines the political and ethical strands of *Odd John*'s plot with astonishing completeness: John's early life as a philosophical toddler and autodidact; his "diabolic" teenage years of deception, larceny, and terror in a single-minded quest for others like himself; the refusal of John and his companions to observe conventional sexual mores; the establishment of a utopian island in the South Pacific; the hostility of nation-states (in this instance Great Britain and the Soviet Union) to any alternative social forms; the decision of British military forces to destroy the children in order to save them; the colony's choice of mass suicide rather than surrender to their "inferiors."[52]

Olaf told Aage Marcus that *Odd John* was a "a novel which is not meant to be taken very seriously, though it has a serious side." His "story between jest and earnest" can indeed be read as a lark, full of private jokes. Agnes saw a version of herself in John's steadfastly patient mother Pax, and a reviewer thought he recognized "a Liverpool personage of some importance" in the devastating caricature of James Magnate, the executive whose ego young John unravels in the novel's most extended dialogue.[53] The famous modern poet to whom John writes an unctuous fan letter in chapter 9 sounds suspiciously like Eliot as Stapledon described him in "Thoughts on the Modern Spirit." John's workshop of gadgets (he takes credit for inventing, among other things, the zipper, the potato peeler, and detachable pockets) recalls Olaf's behavior during the Great War when he would "gadgetise solidly for a couple of days," making custom toolboxes for the ambulances, leather hangers for shrapnel helmets, and other home-made conveniences.[54] The harrowing rite of passage in the wilderness when John kills a stag with his bare hands comes out of bloody memories of stag hunts with Uncle James Stapledon on Exmoor from the time

19. Climbing the "Innominate Crack," Cumbria.
Courtesy the late Mrs. Ruth Fletcher.

Olaf was seventeen. The sight of John as "a sort of wild boy" scaling impossibly sheer cliffs in northern Scotland prompts an observer in the novel to exclaim, " 'God! The lad could climb! He *oozed* from hold to hold.' "[55] A photograph of Olaf at the Innominate Crack in the Lake District, taken by his brother-in-law in the mid-thirties, might evoke similar amazement, though by then he was a "lad" of fifty.

The character of John is not the only magnet in the novel to attract filings from Olaf's own life. The narrator—John's biographer, whom his subject wickedly nicknames "Fido"—also sometimes stands in for Olaf. When he accompanies John to Port Said, the narrator says of his Egyptian days what Olaf could have said about his five months in Port Said in 1912: "There was nothing for me to do but to play tennis, bathe and indulge in mild flirtations." When John lampoons the Bloomsbury literati as buzzing flies caught in the web of their own superficiality, the narrator starts feeling insecure in his own literary pretensions. But John's mock-reassurance neatly ricochets off Stapledon's slender literary reputation: "Strikes home, old thing, doesn't it? Never mind, you're not *in* the web. You're an outsider. Fate has kept you safely fluttering in the backward North."[56] Just before John's utopian island blows apart, "Fido" carts off cases full of records detailing the research conducted during the colony's short life. Among them Stapledon planted a preview of his next work of fiction—*Star Maker*—already in progress as he was finishing *Odd John:* "There was also an amazing document, written by John himself, and purporting to give an account of the whole story of the Cosmos. Whether it should be taken as a plain statement of fact or a poetic fantasy I do not know."[57]

Although Olaf deprecated the serious side of *Odd John,* its jesting has the edgy particularity of *Gulliver's Travels.* The priggish responses of Liverpool University to Russell's proposals on students' living arrangements are darkened in *Odd John.* The twenty-two young utopians on John's island engage in a variety of amatory diversions as they sort themselves out into couples; English proprieties are so outraged by "boys and girls on the loose" that the political authorities hire thugs to exterminate them, as much for their offense against sexual custom as for anything else.[58] What dooms the utopian experiment in *Odd John* is lack of tolerance for difference of any kind and a fundamental insecurity—political, moral, and psychological—on the part of the ironically named "Pacific Powers" (Britain, Japan, Russia, France, Holland, the United States) who descend on the island. The new world is throttled by the old, children are sacrificed to soothe their elders' anxieties, and *homo superior* is extinguished in infancy by the recalcitrant ape-men who outnumber him. John, usually cool and clinical in judging the defects of *homo sapiens,* bursts out at one point with Swiftian ferocity: "Cattle! Cattle! A whole world of cattle! My God, how they stink!"[59]

With utopian hopes collapsing under the pressure of Japan's invasion of China, Mussolini's manic imperialism, and the growing shadow of the Third Reich, Stapledon permitted his anger and his worst fears indirect expression in the odd career of John Wainwright. The novel's nihilistic last sentence, recording the atomic detonation that ends the colony, is an obituary for Utopia in the thirties: "Suddenly there was blinding light and noise and pain, then nothing."[60]

Odd John has a pivotal place in the history of fictions that imagine the difficult emergence, by natural process or artificial intervention, of a higher form of humanity. Of the notable "superman" novels that preceded it—Mary Shelley's *Frankenstein,* Wells's *Food of the Gods,* and J. D. Beresford's *Hampdenshire Wonder*—Stapledon indicated the express influence of the last of these on his book.[61] Several later contributions to the type, all by authors who read Stapledon carefully, have the mark of *Odd John* on them. John's *homo superior* in search of a community becomes Wells's *homo sideralis* in *Star-Begotten* (1937) and Theodore Sturgeon's *homo gestalt* in *More Than Human* (1953). Arthur Clarke's metamorphosed children in *Childhood's End* (also 1953) are nearly as weird as John's companions. Our last glimpse of Ben Lovatt in Doris Lessing's *Fifth Child* (1988), of all the analogues the one most nearly like *Odd John,* is an image of him on the television screen "standing rather apart from the crowd, staring at the camera with his goblin eyes, or searching the faces in the crowd for another of his own kind."[62]

Recent commentaries on *Odd John* assume Nietzsche as a presiding philosophical influence. Actually, when Olaf read *Also Sprach Zarathustra* he thought it "pompous" and "ludicrously egotistical," declaring himself "hostile" to its central ideas.[63] Nevertheless, what he objected to in *Zarathustra* others might find all too evident in the career of John. One friendly reader of the novel dissented sharply from the tradition of utopian "supermen" the author had joined. Jack Haldane told Olaf the idea of an evolutionary sport was "perfectly possible" scientifically, but he deplored a regressive ideology that premised Utopia on a charismatic leader with telepathic powers:

> I totally and radically disagree with your general attitude to social problems. As a (not too thorough-going) Marxist I believe that man progresses to a better state of society by developing the internal contradictions latent in the existing state, and *not* by the godlike activity of great men (the fascist theory). . . . It seems to me that your attitude is the kind which leads people to fascism.[64]

A number of readers who had thrilled to Stapledon's cosmic fictions were unenthusiastic about his utopian novel. Some, like Haldane, had political reservations and others found *Odd John* morally objectionable. In attempting the intimacy of a novel, he achieved, one reviewer said, only a "ghastly inhumanity" and, according to V. S. Pritchett, demonstrated that he was after all "primarily a maker of sociological, ethical, and political arguments." Peter Quennell, like others who thought *Odd John* fell between the stools of existing genres, found it "unconvincing as only a semi-realistic, semi-philosophical book can be."[65]

While *Odd John* did not garner the nearly unanimous praise given *Last and First Men,* Olaf still found much to gratify him, sometimes from unexpected quarters. The *Evening Standard,* hardly one of London's highbrow papers, named it the Book of the Month for October 1935, claiming the author had "one of the deepest and strangest imaginations of our times" and was "a great prophet-propagandist, the most stimulating or the most dangerous according to the creases inside your skull." L. A. G. Strong thought *Odd John* triumphed brilliantly over the usual limitations of the novel of ideas. "Like Sir James Jeans, Mr. Stapledon has the happy knack of being able to clothe even his most abstruse ideas in words that everybody can understand." The critic for *World Jewry* valued the depiction of "the infinite longings which are at once the hope and the despair of our finite selves." Cyril Joad wrote two extravagant reviews, commending Stapledon's combination of mind and fancy: "Some of us can think, but we have not the imaginative power to clothe the bare bones of our thought; more of us can imagine, but lack the intellectual backbone upon which to hang the creatures of our imagination. Mr. Stapledon can do both. He is at once philosopher and literary artist."[66]

In the United States, where Dutton brought out an edition nine months later, *Odd John* received more attention than had *Last and First Men.* Many of the North American notices emphasized jest over earnest and downplayed any intellectual demands the book might make on readers. "On a warm summer night there is nothing more refreshing than a flight thru a realm of fantastic and fascinating imaginations and weird ideas," a Midwestern reviewer wrote airily. "This book surely will take your mind off the heat." More squeamish than their English counterparts, American critics worried the "odd" qualities of the book and seemed puzzled by the point of it all. "In England, they are saying that Mr. Stapledon has a wonderful imagination," a syndicated columnist wrote. "Yes, he has; but does he use it to the best purpose?" More sophisticated reviewers threw up their hands at the task of explaining the kind of novel under review; as the *Saturday Review*'s reporter put it with Yankee succinctness, "Sounds phoney when described, but is genuinely impressive."[67]

Unsure how to define *Odd John*'s "fugitive" value, Alfred Kazin was impressed by it as a tragedy of genius, recalling Shakespeare's *Coriolanus* and Shelley's *Prometheus Unbound.* The *New York Times* found it a "seductive" fable although lacking any charms of style. Another New York critic made a request of the author: "Please supply more books for American consumption. But not fiction. 'Odd John,' as a story, is interesting enough, but somewhat awkward and unbalanced. We should prefer the medicine straight from the herb, without the dubious coating of narrative sugar."[68] *Odd John,* however, was the last of Stapledon's books in any genre to be published in a separate American edition in his lifetime.[69]

Although his career as author and public figure in England was barely five years old at the end of 1935 and some commentators were still misdescribing, him as "quite a young man," Olaf was turning fifty.[70] Some of his best work still lay ahead in the next fifteen years, and the book many people consider his masterpiece was in early stages of composition in 1935. But his reputation as a writer of fiction was already at a peak he would not rise to again before his death, and he was starting to suspect that his professional life was not going to have the brilliant finish he wanted. For the American publicity campaign for *Odd John,* he produced a miscellany of comic self-assessments that sum up an imperfect life at midcentury:

> Fortunately, I have independent means, for I am no good at making money. I do a good deal of public speaking in the Liverpool area, chiefly for peace and internationalism. I outrage my respectable neighbors by cutting my grass naked to the waist. In theory I am emancipated from 'Victorian' morality, but in practice thoroughly respectable and domesticated. I spent five years trying to learn to crawl and cannot do it decently yet. I am almost a vegetarian, by taste, not principle. My hair won't lie down and is a constant source of ribaldry in my family. I am a Socialist living largely on dividends. Left Wing people regard me as an old-fashioned liberal, and liberals consider me a dangerous revolutionary. I find writing autobiographical notes extremely difficult and cannot think of anything more to say.[71]

Despite the effort at cheeriness, he cast himself largely in negatives, as a collection of deficits and disabilities, a well-intentioned irrelevance, a nice man if not quite an effectual one, destined to remain harmless, slightly eccentric, disappointed, and misunderstood. It is almost as if he were drafting a brief for the neglect that lay ahead.

12

But Today the Struggle

1936–1937

THE BIGGEST LITERARY PROJECT of his career, one that went to the roots of his intellectual and imaginative life, taxed Stapledon's energies in the middle years of the decade. He began writing as early as 1933, while still at work on *Waking World* and *Odd John,* but *Star Maker* was a book he had been rehearsing all his life. In the Egyptian days of his childhood, Willie's telescope opened his eyes to the glories of the night sky. "He had already seen a ship disappearing below the horizon, and had been told that the earth and the moon were round. But actually to see the rotund moon, no longer as a flat white shilling, but as a distant world covered with mountains, was an experience whose fascination he never outgrew."[1]

Only one thing had changed since he was five years old. In Olaf's imagination the borrowed light of the moon yielded to the remoter, more mysterious light of the stars, seen in their splendid thousands in the unpolluted skies of Wirral. "I believe that the way people behave in the presence of the stars is one of the best guides to the understanding of their characters," he told his seventeen-year-old cousin Agnes in 1912:

> There are those that are struck dumb, & forget that you are talking to them. They stand gazing, and making imaginary voyages of discovery among distant suns. They are not oppressed by the smallness of the earth. They forget the earth all together [*sic*]. And there are those who, standing under the stars, keep looking at the earth in the light of the stars. Again there are those that are peevish when you remind them that the stars are suns. They rhapsodize over the "lamps of heaven," and their mystic beauty, but they will not in their

hearts accept that the stars are any more than ornaments of the sky, lit to inspire poets and lovers. . . . I think perhaps the greatest change that has come to the human mind since the middle ages is the conception of the infinite heavens, wherein the earth is a point, not the all important centre. And as (in my view at least) the second beauty of the world is the beauty of the stars on a clear night, this change of conception is very important to the growth of humanity. The first beauty of the world is that of the human face, either man, or more often woman. And as the true understanding of the beauty of a face depends on the understanding of the type of character which it expresses, so also is an understanding of the nature of the stars necessary to a full appreciation of their beauty.[2]

Almost from the time he learned to use pen and paper, Olaf could not help writing about the stars—in youthful diary passages and in the poems of *Latter-Day Psalms,* in reports from his ambulance post during the war and in his verses of the twenties. In *Star Maker* he aimed to be comprehensive and definitive, to settle the human place in the universe, "to swallow the Whole," as Wells said in a mixture of admiration and distaste when he saw the finished product.[3] If *Waking World* was Olaf's "book of dogmas," *Star Maker* was to be his confession of faith as a pious agnostic.

The Danish art historian Aage Marcus first met Stapledon on an English visit in 1934 and heard about "the Cosmos-book," Olaf's vague designation of his work-in-progress. Over the next three years, Marcus got periodic reports on how the project was faring. After *Odd John* appeared, Olaf wrote, "I am now engaged on my book about the stars, a more serious undertaking. Indeed I have started afresh on it several times and been dissatisfied." Marcus was thrilled: "I was *very* glad to learn that the Cosmos-book is now proceeding well; that book has haunted me as no other since you told me about it that April night 1934. . . . You may believe that I long for it!!"[4]

A preview of *Star Maker* slyly inserted into the final chapter of *Odd John,* when the narrator discovers a manuscript on the history of the universe, is a sign of Stapledon's determination to complete his most audacious myth. Unlike *Last and First Men,* which he wrote as a virtual recluse, the cosmos-book was widely circulated in manuscript. The first person to get an extensive look was Naomi Mitchison. The draft of a cosmic history, from the first nebulae to the extinction of all life, accompanied Naomi late in the summer of 1933 on a difficult visit to her aging father in Perthshire. "I am in the bloody middle of patriarchy here," she wrote. Her commentary, affected by father-daughter struggles and "bottlesfull" of antirheumatic analgesic that left her head and her prose spinning, is one of the shrewdest assessments ever made of

Stapledon's powers and limitations as a writer. She felt that the Cosmos-book needed a lot more work:

> The thing that worries me about it is this God business (and possibly the he and she symbolism). You may be able to pull it off, but the difficulty is that God has got such frightful connotations—he *is* an old man with a beard, he's patriarchal anyhow, and you of all people mustn't encourage the idea of the patriarchy. Still, as I say, you may be able to get round it. The thing that I believe you are so immensely good at is convincing detail—almost mechanical detail—about something one knows nothing about and hasn't even imagined, but which yet you can make absolutely clear. The parts of Last and First Men that I think I have re-read most are the middle parts with all the detail about people who aren't impossibly remote. I'm so afraid you may be carried by remoteness beyond this convincing matter of detail. . . . But do put in lots and lots of "facts" about the middle part, the wars and so on. If you do that you can make people believe all the mythology. You are a funny fish really, you believe it yourself or something as near believing as makes no odds. And yet you pretend to be a great practical he-man! You are very young in some ways, you are still telling yourself stories, but you do it so well that you convince yourself (that's rather what I do, so I know): blessed are the pure in heart for they shall see God. But don't make him so MALE all the time—it's that which annoys me!

What she had read, labeled "Discarded MS. of Star-Maker," was found forty years later in Stapledon's desk and published under the title *Nebula Maker*.[5]

As work progressed, Olaf consulted other friends. Jack Haldane sent titles on astrophysics for "your cosmogonic story," and Marcus bought him a copy of J. D. Bernal's *The World, the Flesh, and the Devil*.[6] Leo Myers, the Cambridge novelist who was Olaf's most faithful correspondent from 1931 until he took his life in 1944, doubted whether a suitable style could be found for the book. "If you can bring it off, it will be colossal." Myers read the whole book in installments in 1936, making trenchant criticisms of both its conceptual framework and its language. Echoing Naomi, he found the Star Maker "too *anthropomorphized*" but implored Olaf not to cut any of the detail that gave mythic weight to the narrative. After reading the first two chapters, the Anglo-Italian writer Iris Origo, a friend of Myers, wrote, "It is as if you had suddenly presented me with some new kind of eyesight."[7]

Despite such encouragements, he could not concentrate on the book. It was not just that the writing proved difficult or that he had been absorbed in *Odd John* until the middle of 1935. *Star Maker* posed problems different from those of his other big but human-centered book, *Last and First Men*. The two-billion-year history of the human race—the subject of the earlier book—gets just half a paragraph in *Star Maker*. Never before had humanity been so definitively marginalized in a work of fiction. In 1935, with the danger to human civilization from the fascist powers rising, a philosophical myth composed of arabesque speculations about the nature and purpose of the universe seemed hard to justify. How could a history of the cosmos speak to a world beginning to go mad as war seemed thinkable again not twenty years after Versailles? And for Olaf it was not only the planet that was under siege. His personal microcosm—the intimate community of Agnes and himself—so long taken as a given, was in its most fragile condition since their separation during the war. As *Star Maker* slowly took shape on paper, the cosmic fantasy absorbed the personal and political anxieties that haunted him.

Stapledon kept interrupting work on *Star Maker* because he could not turn his eyes from the growing disaster in Europe, Africa, and Asia. Just when the completion of *Odd John* freed him to concentrate on the cosmos-book, the world situation darkened. Ominous as was Hitler's takeover of Germany, it was Italy's brutal subjection of the Ethiopian empire, Africa's last remaining uncolonized nation, that galvanized Olaf into political activism. In October 1935 he joined the No More War movement's three-day national conference in Liverpool, where the chief topics were the Abyssinian invasion and the newly issued brochures of the Home Office on civil defense against air raids or poison gas attacks. For the first time since 1918, the government acknowledged the specter of a second war. Mussolini's relentless bombing and use of chemicals in Abyssinia dramatized how vulnerable civilian populations were to a science of war more deadly than had been known in the 1914–1918 era. The new pathology, fed by increasingly efficient weapons of mass murder and terrorism, was brilliantly captured in a cartoon by David Low depicting Il Duce, rockets of poison gas strapped around his waist, saluting a tableful of grinning Borgias, each with a flask of poison and a raised cup, toasting the latest refinement of their methods. The imagery of the cinema augmented the nightmare. The film of H. G. Wells's *Things to Come* premiered early in 1936 and vividly prophesied the destruction of London from the air and the gassing of its inhabitants in a new world war begun on Christmas Eve, 1940.[8]

After the No More War conference, Olaf took on speaking engagements with missionary ardor. The prospect of global war pushed him headlong into the peace movement and into a long, unproductive effort for a worldwide referendum on disarmament. While a national rally to save Abyssinia was in progress at the Albert Hall in London on 8 May 1936, he campaigned on Merseyside for economic reprisals against Italy. Mussolini, he said, was "drunk with success," and English indifference to the massacre of Africans had left what remained of the country's reputation for fair-mindedness in ruins. With other writers he repeatedly pressed Stanley Baldwin's government for more sanctions. Through the League of Nations Union and the International Peace Campaign, he worked on a last-ditch effort to strengthen the League, a deeply flawed institution, he knew, but the only existing mechanism of international order. He spent the tenth of May, his fiftieth birthday, at an antifascist rally in Liverpool, and the following week he spoke to youth groups in Wirral on the dangers of the herd mentality among young Germans and Italians.[9] By then, with Francisco Franco preparing the attempted coup that precipitated civil war in Spain, fascism was metastasizing throughout Europe.

Temperamentally, Olaf both dreaded and vibrated to this kind of work. Although he longed to retreat to his study and write, the crisis activated his instinct for teaching, and he drew on whatever local status he had to rally people to protest. Lacking the ready access to the national press of prominent government critics like Wells, Eleanor Rathbone, and Sir Stafford Cripps, Stapledon was inevitably relegated to the margins of the peace movement. Nevertheless, throughout the North of England he was to be found on the platform at many city and small-town peace meetings. Often recruited by youth groups and Labour clubs, he took on a burden of political organizing, writing, and speechmaking that added nearly a year to his planned schedule for completing *Star Maker.* "The winter months have been particularly rushed," he wrote in spring 1937 when he finally reached the stage of correcting proofs, "as I keep getting myself let in for semi-political activities locally, though I have no gift for them at all, and I don't really like speaking in public."[10]

Apart from work on *Star Maker,* most of Stapledon's writing in these hectic years was of the sort that could be accomplished in a sitting or two. He reviewed regularly for *The London Mercury,* despite Leo Myers' anxiety that it was hurting his imaginative work.[11] But after he stopped weekly tutoring for the WEA in the mid-thirties, fees for free-lance lecturing and reviewing, along with royalties, were his sole sources of earned income. Stapledon's reviews were seldom eloquent, though in his critiques of Russell's atheism, Aldous Huxley's pacifism, and Wells's faith in positivist science, the reviewer was recording his own intellectual history.[12] Another experiment in income-producing writing was less successful. He tried his hand at short fiction, producing a dream story about a musical universe, "A World of Sound," which he ended up donating to a fundraising anthology for the Royal Liverpool Children's Hospital, and a fantasy of cultural reversals set in West Kirby and called "East Is West." The latter, written in 1934, he was unable to interest anyone in publishing.[13] But his letters to editors of newspapers in this period, though they earned no money, aroused real interest.

Adult-education circles on Merseyside had for many years served Olaf as a left-wing intellectual oasis, but Liverpool as a whole—and his middle-class town of West Kirby—did not share his politics. Now, as a local celebrity, his opinions were more public and audible; for the first time he became the object of scornful, sometimes ad hominem, criticism. In the autumn of 1935, an antagonist who refused to disclose his identity and signed himself "Ignotus" (the pseudonym may have disguised the fact that he *was* personally known to Olaf) began ridiculing the "pathetic" utopian politics of "men of Dr. Stapledon's intellectual calibre." In frequent letters to the *Liverpool Post*, "Ignotus" professed astonishment at the logical failures of a trained philosopher, and his use of the title "Dr." whenever he referred to Stapledon reinforced the leaden sarcasm of his attacks.[14]

Explaining why *Star Maker* was now "definitely postponed" till the next year, Olaf told Aage Marcus in 1936, "Lately I have been extremely busy, chiefly with speaking at peace meetings and carrying out an interminable correspondence in the local press."[15] His replies to "Ignotus" and to other correspondents who joined the fray (including a representative of the British Union of Fascists and Alan Graham, the Conservative M.P. for Wirral) were at first temperate restatements of his views, then gymnastic explanations of the consistency of his call for disarmament with support for a League of Nations peace-keeping police, and finally impatient dismissals of the red-baiting, logic-chopping tactics of his opponents. Before and after he addressed a youth rally in Birkenhead in June 1936, he was admonished that his participation lent support to the Young Communists' League, one of the rally's sponsoring organizations. Olaf was fed up:

> What does it matter whether the peace rally was inspired by the Communists or not? I see no reason to believe that they played the chief part in it, but if they were responsible, I am proud to have cooperated with them in carrying out their very sensible idea.
>
> Some people are so herd-minded that they see every situation solely in relation to their own group-obsessions. Anything coming to them from their group must be good; anything coming from a group regarded as the enemy must be bad. This is a simple way of behaving, but it is not the way to deal with the complex problems of our world.
>
> The hypnotic influence of group-ideologies is one of the most damaging plagues of our age. It kills the power of spontaneous thought and feeling, and reduces us all to blurred and mindless echoes of one another.[16]

Through much of 1936 "Ignotus" dogged Stapledon's steps, at first chiding his defense of pacifism in an era of bullying dictators and in later months accusing him of hypocrisy for supporting the International Brigade's mission to Spain. When Olaf chaired a crowded protest meeting at Picton Hall in September 1936 and castigated the British government's policy of nonintervention in Spain, "Ignotus" gloated that he had revealed himself as a "per-fectly-trained Jesuit":

> Once again we are confronted with the very unedifying spectacle of Dr. Stapledon trying to balance himself on the rickety fence that stands between pacifism and military preparation. His balance is precarious; in fact, he seems to topple off altogether at some points of his performance. Not long ago this ardent pacifist was trying to inveigle us into a war with Italy; now he appears to be spoiling for a fight with Spain. . . . Are we to understand that Dr. Stapledon has abandoned his position as a pacifist? It is no use his trying to persuade us (or his cronies) that he is a pacifist if he is willing and even anxious to make war to ensure the triumph of his own principles. If that is the quality of his pacifism, then he is no better than the rest of us.

At this point a defender of Stapledon entered the debate under the pen name "Radix," attacking the smugness of "Ignotus" in exposing an opponent's de-fects without ever risking an argument of his own.[17] "Ignotus," however, was not so easily put off.

Throughout October 1936 and into early November, in the wake of Olaf's leading role in a Liverpool "Peace Week" from 28 September to 4 October, "Ignotus" behaved with irrepressible glee, firing off letters to the *Post* every few days and chortling over what he took to be his opponent's concession that pacifism had failed in the face of Hitler and Franco. Dr. Stapledon, "Ignotus" claimed, was abandoning disarmament because he had come to see that his own political agenda required the use of force. The doctor had at last revealed himself as an armchair theorist out of touch with political reality, and sensible citizens need no longer be distracted by naïve philosophers.[18]

In his final contribution to the debate, the usually serene Stapledon lost his temper. He would not retract his conviction that disarmament was the best strategy, though a heroic and risky one, for achieving peace; indeed, Stanley Baldwin's "National" government of Britain (a Tory-dominated rul-ing coalition) was "not fit to be trusted with an airgun, let alone an air force." But even Labour might be equally untrustworthy, because military arms of-fer too powerful a temptation to use force for jingoist motives. That, he said in reply to "Ignotus," was the view of a *real* realist. He had proposed com-promises from the strict position of unilateral disarmament only because in the present national debate there was no consensus to disarm, but he contin-ued to hope that British disarmament, accompanied by an international con-ference on arms and the dissolution of Imperial possessions, would start a chain reaction that could cause fascism to "crumble and vanish" and usher in a new, more mature age:

Is this clear enough for "Ignotus"? I say, disarm, disarm, disarm! But if Britain won't, we must make the best of a very bad job and at least work for international control of armaments. Pacifism alone cannot save the world from impending disaster. So long as only a minute proportion of the world's population is pacifist, pacifists should be ready to compromise. Personal pacifism is not incompatible with urging people to manage armaments in the less rather than the more harmful way. I, at least, have no use for a pacifism that is too pure, too self-righteous, to compromise and to undertake a lot of hard thinking in order to set up a more effective system of international law and order.[19]

After this letter the *Post*'s editor closed correspondence on the topic and "Ignotus," never identified, was not heard from again.

One candidate for "Ignotus" is Alan Dorward, Alexander Mair's successor as chair of philosophy at Liverpool University. Olaf had participated with Dorward in the Philosophy Seminar until 1932, but never really warmed up to him. In early 1936, Dorward in his own name contested Stapledon's views on the League of Nations, though with only a hint of Ignotian sarcasm in the observation that his politics betrayed the "creative imagination" of *Last and First Men*. Olaf cheerfully noted that Dorward's letter to the *Liverpool Post* did not represent "the first time that his diabolical intelligence has triumphed over my (approximately) divine innocence."[20] Presumably, he meant philosophical disagreements in the Seminar, unless he suspected Dorward to be the diabolical intelligence behind the triumphant "Ignotus" of the previous autumn. If Dorward himself was not "Ignotus," most likely someone whom Olaf saw at the University Club was. Whoever hid behind the nom de plume was well versed in Stapledon's career, had followed his public appearances and pronouncements with some care, and attacked him with zealous malice.

Olaf's major political initiative in the turmoil of the mid-thirties was an ill-fated "Peace Letter" designed to launch a mass movement for disarmament. Its inspiration was twofold. In a highly publicized "Peace Ballot" of 1934-1935, sponsored by the League of Nations Union, eleven million Britons cast votes in favor of continued British membership in the League, reduction of armaments, and the use of economic sanctions to restrain aggressive nations. The Peace Ballot, a model of skilled and well-financed political organizing, had a modest success in legitimizing the rhetoric of peace and disarmament, although its impact on foreign policy was simply to reinforce the Baldwin government's timidity. The other influence on Olaf's scheme was the Peace Pledge Union, brainchild of Canon R. L. "Dick" Sheppard, vicar of St. Martin-in-the-Fields Church in London. He asked men to sign postcards pledging, "I renounce War and never again will I support or sanction another, and I will do all in my power to persuade others to do the same." By mid-1936, 100,000 men of military age had signed.[21]

Olaf imagined a similar popular initiative, begun in his own country and then transmitted as a Letter from the citizens of Great Britain to "All the Peoples of the Earth." He wanted millions of signatories to endorse the dismantling of colonial empires, a global economic plan, a world court to adjudge international disputes, and "the complete abolition of national armaments."[22] He asked Viscount Cecil if the network created for the Peace Ballot could be appropriated for his Letter, and Cecil was mildly encouraging. But reactions from experienced political activists and literary figures were mixed, with lukewarm endorsements most common. Lord Allen of Hurtwood, chairman of the Independent Labour party, kept promising his support, but no practical help followed. The Marxist John Strachey told Olaf he liked the idea but somewhat disingenuously declined to endorse it in the *Daily Worker:* "I think the reaction of many League of Nations Union people would be that this was a Communist stunt. It would be much better if the idea came from you." Aldous Huxley dismissed the Letter out of hand.[23]

In the earliest draft of his "Open Letter to All the Peoples of the Earth," sent to H. G. Wells in March 1936 for comment, Olaf made support for the League the linchpin of the campaign. "I feel so hopelessly ineffective in comparison with you that as soon as I think of sending you these documents they begin to look damned silly," he wrote. In reply Wells minced no words:

> I wish I saw more of you. You would do me good & I should do you good.
> Do for God's sake forget about the League of Nations—get round it, get
> behind it, enlarge your basis, escape from the nationalist & diplomatic
> conventions that fester at Geneva..... And blast "*Peoples*". They are really
> only people with a tendency to clot.

Olaf took H. G.'s hint and called on him in London in April, but he was rubbed sore by the implication that his Letter was naïve:

> Naturally *I* don't care a damn about nationalism or peoples, but most people
> still do, and my little scheme was to catch as many million signatures as
> possible by stating the essentials in the way most likely to seem sound to
> most people. A People with a big "P" is only a crowd of ordinary persons,
> but those crowds are distinct from one another, just as London & Glasgow
> are. However, to hell with the big P. It was only put in for clarity's sake. And
> to hell with the League,—if there is any other available concrete symbol and
> focus of cosmopolitanism. But there's not.[24]

Later in 1936, before the International Writers Association, Stapledon emphasized that he had no gift for public affairs, but in the dangerous circumstances of 1936 everyone needed to "make an uproar." He had readied a third draft of his Peace Letter, whose aim, he said, was to steer between platitudes and ideological dogma and "yet also mean something." By then Haile Selassie had fled Addis Ababa, the Italian king Victor Emmanuel III had been proclaimed emperor of Ethiopia, and the occupation of the Rhineland by the Nazis had begun. Barely a murmur was heard from the League of Nations because the major powers feared offending Mussolini or Hitler. In disgust Olaf began removing from his Letter all references to the League—the "mausoleum" at Geneva, as he came to call it.[25] The League had been exposed as a weak reed ever since the Japanese invasion of Manchuria at the beginning of the decade, but by the close of 1936 it was thoroughly rotten.

Olaf grew desperate to bring his work on the Peace Letter to some kind of conclusion. In June 1936 he had begun a drive to finish *Star Maker*, rapidly producing chapters for Leo Myers to criticize. "Methuens want it by December," he wrote to Aage Marcus in early September, "but I doubt if I can finish it so soon."[26] Meanwhile, he dispatched his fourth and last draft of the Peace Letter to thirty newspapers. The ten-point Letter began appearing in papers at the end of September. Its seventh and eighth articles, calling on Britain to "surrender for the good of humanity any privileges, imperial or economic" acquired through commercial exploitation and to grant its colonies "self-government speedily and without restriction," generated a flurry of correspondence in *John O'London's Weekly*. When a reader objected to such "emotional blather" since he could not imagine what privileges Englishmen had at the expense of other people, Olaf was moved to wonder whether the reader, ignorant of the unrest in India, Kenya, and Egypt, was under the illusion that "the British Empire is a purely philanthropic institution."[27]

But it was not only cranks who took a dislike to the draft. The International Peace Campaign, whose sponsorship he had counted on, turned out to be, in Stapledon's words, "terrified of being captured by the left," and the only sort of Peace Letter it would endorse would have to be so tamed down as to be utterly toothless.[28] In any case, the events of the latter part of 1936 soon made the project obsolete. The collapse of the League and, still more important, the outbreak of fascism near at hand in Spain threw the Left into disarray and brought this phase of Olaf's pacifism to an abrupt end.

The change was evident during the Liverpool Peace Week, for which Olaf gave the keynote speech on 28 September at the Bluecoat Chambers in central Liverpool. The night before, he had chaired a protest meeting sponsored by the Relief Committee for the Victims of Spanish Fascism. With characteristic frankness he told his audience of his discomfort opening a peace week the day after helping pass a resolution to send munitions to the Spanish loyalists. He was still sure that fighting for any nation was the tactic of an obsolete geopolitics, but armaments existed and were being used by the enemies of cosmopolitanism. He would not proscribe the use of force under all circumstances, and, as a newspaper correspondent reported his speech, he prompted laughter when he said he "refused to be bound down by any principle as a pacifist, but gloried in being 'completely unprincipled.'"[29]

This was more than a platform joke for Olaf. In the First World War, he had not been an absolute pacifist; as a creative writer he resisted absolute canons of taste in literature; and as a philosopher his ethics were pragmatic and situational. His old personal motto, "mediocria firma," was still pertinent to an antiabsolutist temperament. Typically, he stated his own dogmas unequivocally and then adjusted and compromised, regretfully and painfully, as circumstances required. Although "Ignotus" seized on the Peace Week speech as evidence of muddled and opportunistic thinking, Olaf was far from alone. The war in Spain—which the Left designated an invasion rather than a "civil war"—caused many political realignments in England, with the pacifist Left mobilizing to aid republican Spain and the Right taking up the pacifists' "no war" slogan to justify not intervening against Franco.[30] To the sneers of "Ignotus" ("What should I, what would Liverpool do without him?") Olaf responded without embarrassment:

> I set little store by the label "pacifist." I am very sure that in the personal sphere non-violence is practically always more effective than violence. I am even more sure that war between national States is a huge and laughable mistake. I do not feel so certain that when an established government, backed by a great majority of its people, is attacked by military rebels with foreign aid, such a Government should be prevented from buying arms in our country.[31]

As the war intensified, Olaf used the local press to present a historical and economic context for events in Spain "in order to counter in some degree the terrible ignorance and misrepresentation which exists on Merseyside." He helped organize medical relief and food shipments from Liverpool to Madrid; he served on a defense committee for seventeen Liverpool sailors arrested in Boston for refusing to accept a cargo of nitrates destined for the Franco forces in Seville; he attended a screening of a documentary film on the siege of Madrid; he sat on the platform at Liverpool Stadium in March 1937 at a memorial for five Merseyside workers killed in action with the International Brigade, and the following month, at a formal ceremony in Picton Hall before five empty chairs draped in red and black, he delivered a eulogy. "I myself am

at heart a pacifist. I have seen too much blood," he told the audience. He wished
he could follow his own "inner light" and never take a life, but in an emergency he did not know whether he might kill. "Anyhow I salute these young
men."[32]

That summer he and Agnes worked on the evacuation of Basque children after the bombing of Guernica, finding homes for a hundred refugees in Birkenhead.
Asked his views on the Spanish war for an anthology of writers' responses, Olaf
indicted England's do-nothing stance, linking the government's reluctance to dismantle its own empire to tacit acceptance of fascist imperialism:

I support the Spanish Government because, whatever its failings, it is
defending the oppressed and preserving culture. I believe that a British
Government sincerely sympathetic to Spain, or sincerely neutral, could end
Fascist aggression by firm diplomacy without causing a general war. But
firmness over Spain must be combined with readiness to internationalize our
own ill-gotten gains.[33]

A year and a half later, reviewing *Studies in a Dying Culture,* the celebrated
posthumous collection of Marxist essays by a young literary critic who died
with the International Brigade, Olaf explored the dilemma of the pacifist in
the thirties. In Christopher Caudwell's scathing denunciation of the "ignoble
place" of pacifists in contemporary culture, he found evidence of "the blindness and ruthlessness of the young man who is so dazzled by one truth that he
neglects all others." Stapledon argued that the ideal of nonviolence needed to
be preserved, even if it could not be successfully applied in the current crisis,
"lest the Revolution be poisoned at its source." Honoring Caudwell's passion
and his sacrifice, he clung to his own belief that civilization also needed those
voices of detachment, critical individualism, and anti-ideological restraint for
which the youthful fighter had such contempt. He realized, and respected the
fact, that Caudwell's response to such admonitions would be the impatient disclaimer, "But to-day the struggle."[34]

The reviewer understood the sentiment, because dedication to the daily
political struggle had governed his own life as a creative artist in these years.
Drafts of theological speculation and intergalactic fantasy for chapters of *Star
Maker* were often put aside to chair meetings or raise funds for refugees. He
was passionate on behalf of disarmament and in protest against the bombings
in Abyssinia and Spain. But while taking the Spanish loyalists' part, he resisted the psychology of the partisan, and his appeals to readers and listeners
were framed by his profoundest beliefs in freedom and uncertainty. In a speech
at Port Sunlight in January 1937, he summarized two versions of the war in
Spain. By one account the Franco-led rebels were engaged in the noble task

of crushing the atheism and communism being fostered in Spain by Russian saboteurs; by the other, the republican government was heroically struggling to preserve liberty against a fascist insurrection supported by German and Italian money and weapons. Olaf was unambiguous in endorsing the latter interpretation, but a reporter covering the speech was struck by his remark that "people should be a little careful in swallowing everything they were told," whether they were listening to a government minister or a local author.[35]

As serious as he was about presenting the facts of the war, he never forgot the difference between propaganda and education and wanted his listeners to be skeptical of everything they heard. That loyalty to self-conscious detachment overrode all other loyalties, especially when Olaf was in his study. He had worked so intensively in the last months of 1936 on *Star Maker* that his critical faculties were numbed. He finished the last chapter just before Christmas and needed to produce a typed copy almost at once for his editor. Weary and in doubt, he asked Leo Myers to advise him on cuts. The letters Myers wrote on Christmas Eve and Christmas Day did not ease his mind. All through the year Leo had been rallying Olaf's spirits about *Star Maker*. On 21 November, before he saw the last few chapters, he wrote, "I don't see how—at this stage in human knowledge—a better book on such lines could be written." Suddenly at Christmas his praises grew bland and he carped at the representation of the Star Maker in the climactic visions. The conclusion "trivialized" the myth and revealed a Creator with no ethical sense. Myers thought Olaf had better recast the entire framework of the book as a dream rather than a vision.[36]

From the time Myers first read a synopsis of *Star Maker* in the summer of 1934, he wanted it "primarily to be *a work of art*." He was enthralled by it as a theological romance and cautioned against political allusions that might soon render episodes obsolete. He wanted Stapledon to develop "language almost Biblical."[37] Despite Olaf's insistence that *Star Maker* was "not a novel," Myers criticized it as if it were one, demanding high seriousness and stylistic elegance of the sort he attempted in his own trilogy of the 1930s, *The Root and the Flower*.[38]

To the degree that *Star Maker* belongs to the literature of spiritual quest, Myers was an ideal reader (although, happily, Stapledon took little of his advice about altering the theological vision of the final chapters). Few twentieth-century works of fiction take theological inquiry as far as *Star Maker* does, and the work it has most often been compared to is the *Divine Comedy*. What Dante built, Stapledon dismantled. Where Dante invested a stable cosmos with a supremely authoritative, managerially efficient, and just but loving God, Stapledon found radical instability in multiple cosmoses, launched and discarded by a force inaccessible to human understanding. As for the Star Maker's relationship to his creation, love has nothing to do with it. But as original a work of theological romancing as *Star Maker* is, it is not merely idiosyncratic. In 1934, Olaf read one of the landmarks of modern theology, Rudolf Otto's *Idea of the Holy,* and found a kindred spirit. He was soon recommending Otto's concept of the "numinous" or radically "other" nature of divinity and telling people that awe was the central religious emotion, "a corrective to the much commoner idea that the essence of religion is the conviction of the deity's friendliness."[39]

The image of the Star Maker as a failed artist, eternally discontent with his work, may have been a projection of Olaf's own persistent sense of artistic shortcoming. But the Star Maker is more than just a fantastic portrait of the human artificer; he defines the problem of God in the modern world. Like much of what Stapledon had written since *Latter-Day Psalms, Star Maker* aspired to be modern in its thinking while still using the traditional apparatus and language of devotional literature. It enacts a search for meaning in a demythologized universe, for a reconciliation of spiritual need with scientific plausibility and philosophical rigor. The quest for the Star Maker has the urgency of a contemporary Grail hunt—an exhilarating but dangerous and uncertain ordeal, and as for all but the saintliest Arthurian knight a marvelous, inevitable frustration.

Star Maker also had more secular aims, to which Leo Myers was blind. Some of the advice he gave did not improve the book, and the political dimension suffered particularly. It was at Myers's urging that explicit references to Spain were dropped from the preface and replaced with generalities about politics and art. But worse than that exclusion was the dropping of a powerful image of Abyssinian resistance to Mussolini from the book's final panorama as the narrator orbits and surveys the earth on his return journey. As Africa comes into view, the manuscript reads:

> I peered further, over the earth's shoulder, and saw the mountains where the last free black men had desperately defended their homes with muskets and spears against Italian guns, Italian aircraft. Desperately, vainly, yet not in vain; for the rumour of their stand and of their slaughter spread through Africa. Camels bore it through the gritty storms of the Sahara. Negro workers by the great lakes, where wild elephants trouble the crops, whispered it to one another, with sidelong glances at their own white masters. Hunters in the gorilla-haunted jungles, and in the veldt among the great wild herds, told the same tale. Far to the south, where Dutch and English thrive on the negro millions, I heard it whispered, 'The Blacks are waking.'

In the text as published, everything in this splendid passage is flattened into three cautious sentences. The great racial awakening, the liberation of a continent becomes an ill-defined dream: "Far southward, black men slept beside the great lakes. Elephants trampled the crops. Further still, where Dutch and English profit by the Negro millions, those hosts were stirred by vague dreams of freedom."[40]

Remembering how quickly the topical first forty pages of *Last and First Men* had dated, Stapledon blunted a sharp image of a new Africa, and in the process the passage lost its political edge and visionary luminance. In the published version the elephants are more prominent and more active than the sleeping Negro millions. Elsewhere in the final panorama, similar passages were deleted from the manuscript at Myers's urging: the "fiery glow in the sky" over Madrid where Spaniards "fought for life against the power of money, equipped with bombs and lies"; a glimpse of Rome, "city of past glory, where now the great idol of the mob, empty, echoing the mob's inarticulate howls, spell-bound the young men"; across the Alps more young men, "ranked together in their thousands, exalted, possessed, saluting the flood-lit Führer;" beyond China's Great Wall "fur-coated troops, Western in equipment but Eastern in devotion, spread the Pax Japonica with machine guns." By the time he was finished revising, Stapledon had drafted and redrafted *Star Maker* nearly as many times as the Star Maker had created and re-created the Cosmos. When the book was in page proofs in April, he wrote: "At the moment I am thoroughly disgusted with it, and can't imagine why I wrote it or why anyone should read it."[41]

As he composed his preface, Spain remained on Olaf's mind. Younger authors, he wrote, were "gallantly plunging into the struggle" and taking up arms in "the great enterprise of defending (or creating) civilization." In his measured, impartial way, he genuinely admired the writers who enlisted in the International Brigade and found genuine merit in the propagandistic writing that emerged from their experiences. He, however, had chosen a different course:

> Those who are in the thick of the struggle inevitably tend to become, though in a great and just cause, partisan. They nobly forgo something of that detachment, that power of cold assessment, which is, after all, among the most valuable human capacities. In their case this is perhaps as it should be; for a desperate struggle demands less of detachment than of devotion. But some who have the cause at heart must serve by striving to maintain, along with human loyalty, a more dispassionate spirit. And perhaps the attempt to see our turbulent world against a background of stars may, after all, increase, not lessen, the significance of the present human crisis. It may also strengthen our charity toward one another.[42]

The ellipsis of thought in the last sentence's leap from the partisan struggle to human affection predicts the startling convergence of political and personal issues in this book about the stars. "You seem to get *more* necessary as time

20. Manuscript page from *Star Maker*.
Courtesy Stapledon Archive, Sydney Jones Library,
University of Liverpool.

goes on," Olaf wrote to his wife from London in early 1936. "Yes, air and water. That's what it's like. Somehow I seem to have come quite recently into a new realisation of it. Hence the opening chapter of *Star Maker*."[43] Despite what Olaf wrote to Agnes, the mood of *Star Maker*'s opening is actually distress. At midnight on pitch-dark Caldy Hill, overlooking West Kirby and the Irish Sea, the narrator has fled to be alone. He picks out the street lamps and lit windows on Grosvenor Avenue, locates his own house, recalls the homely pleasures of fifteen years of marriage, wonders at the "sudden new lives" of the children born in that house. "All this, surely, was good. Yet there was bitterness. And bitterness not only invaded us from the world; it welled up also within our own magic circle."[44] This first page of *Star Maker* deliberately echoes Dante setting out for hell. "Midway in the journey of our life I found myself in a dark wood, for the straight way was lost. Ah, how hard it is to tell what that wood was, wild, rugged, harsh; the very thought of it renews the fear! It is so bitter that death is hardly more so."[45] Stapledon and his narrator are not easily disentangled here. The locale of Caldy Hill had been central to Stapledon's life for twenty-five years. And the dark night of the soul, prompting a spiritual voyage through space and time that the narrator at first mistakes for his own death, is no mere literary conceit. All other lofty ambitions aside, *Star Maker* expresses the author's middle age.

When the children were growing up, the house at 7 Grosvenor Avenue was boisterous and Olaf was at the center of the fun. "There seemed to be a constant ripple of frivolous chat going on—banter, teasing and jokes, good, bad and indifferent, philosophically sophisticated and totally unsophisticated, amusing incidents would be remembered to tell to the rest of the family and so on. We all did it, but he was best." So his daughter recalled the early 1930s, but in 1935 both Mary and David left for boarding school, and Agnes and Olaf were alone together in a quiet house for the first time since 1920. In December 1935, Emmeline Stapledon died peacefully at the age of eighty-four, and Annery stood empty at the top of Caldy Hill. With both parents dead and both children gone, Olaf's personal life was suddenly severed from its past and its future. The grim condition of the world, a shrunken home life, and the arrival of what he called his "bad year"—1936, when he turned fifty—left him gloomy.[46]

The earliest version of the cosmos-book, the 1933 fragment known as *Nebula Maker,* contains nothing like the intensely personal first chapter of *Star Maker.* But by midsummer 1936 the story about the stars had become inextricably linked to the "prized atom of community," the "little treasure" of Olaf-and-Agnes living in "intricate symbiosis" like "two close trees whose trunks have grown upwards together as a single shaft, mutually distorting, but mutually supporting."[47] Olaf's incorporation of his wife and marriage into the fiction of *Star Maker* was hardly sentimental, though. The unhappy narrator questions the "complacent and ingrown domesticity" of his marriage and alludes vaguely to "our own not infrequent discordancy." That Agnes was uncomfortable with this shadowy portrait of her married life can be surmised from her copy of the book, in which passages that refer to herself are marked for cutting in a future edition.[48]

The often-recalled image of Agnes as the bright-eyed young visitant of 1903, his predestined lover, still held Olaf—and he retold the old story in the first chapter of *Star Maker,* though demoting the myth to a "fever of adolescence." The narrator's appraisal of his wife as she is in the present is unnervingly clinical: "Coldly I now assessed her as merely a useful, but often infuriating adjunct to my personal life. We were on the whole sensible companions. We left one another a certain freedom, and so we were able to endure our proximity."[49]

Physically, the onset of middle age had treated Agnes more harshly than her husband. Eight years younger than Olaf, she actually looked older; her sister had witnessed an awkward moment on a holiday in 1931 when a waiter mistook Agnes for Olaf's mother.[50] She was a handsome, energetic matron, but there was no pretending that she still looked like the pretty dream-child of Olaf's youth. He had sometimes joked with her early in their marriage about his wandering eye, but by the 1930s, Agnes grew nervous that his flirtations might be more than boyish gallantry. His itinerant lecturing, his regular trips south, and his new fame created many opportunities to meet other women, and in 1933 he tried writing Agnes a reassuring note from London:

> Taffy, don't worry. I know so absolutely for certain that it's you I want infinitely more than anyone else. And anyhow as far as Olive is concerned, we are just good friends that get on swimmingly as long as we don't see too much of one another. Don't let's get in a muddle any more, because there's no need. . . . Taffy, let's enjoy ourselves all we can. Time flies. We have had pretty good fun in a modest way so far, don't let us spoil it all by getting in a muddle. I feel so absolutely I am yours & you are mine whatever happens. That is the bed rock of life, and it can't possibly be affected by my taking a rather senile interest in other girls sometimes.[51]

As in politics he insisted that pacifist principles could be adjusted to accommodate uncongenial circumstances, so in his personal life Olaf wanted to affirm his marriage but leave room for other loves. In both *Last and First Men* and *Last Men in London,* he had sketched imaginary societies in which monogamy might be freely chosen, and yet for both sexes guiltlessly refreshing extramarital intimacies would be possible. In London he knew married couples like Naomi and Dick Mitchison who were forthright about their agreement that each could take other lovers, and Wells's appetites before as well as during widowerhood were legendary. New freedoms in marriage were a preoccupation of some of Olaf's friends in the Progressive League. But the mores of London were not those of West Kirby, and ideas coolly advanced in social theory or applied in futurist fiction were not harmless when introduced into his own marriage.

Agnes had no interest in finding a lover and was pained that Olaf was interested, whether or not he acted on the interest. To be in love with so preternaturally youthful and attractive a man, she was learning, might make marriage more experimental than she liked. For his part, Olaf was less liberated in fact than in fancy. He told an American reporter in 1936 that he was "emancipated

from 'Victorian' morality, but in practice thoroughly respectable and domesti-
cated."[52] Almost certainly no serious extramarital attachments underlay the first
chapter of *Star Maker*. (Those came in the last decade of his life; in this, as in
other respects, he was a late bloomer.) But the narrator's bitter feelings reflect
complicated and contradictory impulses in an author who viewed his marriage
as a "treasure" but also yearned for the erotic freedoms of a youth now unde-
niably past and of a utopia not likely to come into being in his lifetime.

The reunion of wife and husband in *Star Maker*'s epilogue, following a
shattering vision into the inhumanity of space, time, and deity, is Olaf's provisional resolution of his discontent. If love is not the motive of the universe,
as the narrator's flight to the stars teaches him, his marriage nevertheless remains "the one rock in all the welter of experience. This, not the astronomical
and hypercosmical immensity, nor even the planetary grain, this, this alone,
was the solid ground of existence." The epilogue restates one of the oldest
Stapledonian principles, first committed to print in 1914: "The beauty of the
world is less than the beauty of men and women. Their lives are more wonderful than the obedient march of the stars."[53] It is *Star Maker*'s last chapter,
not its first, that most deeply affirms Agnes's place in Olaf's life. The homage
did not work a charm over their last thirteen years together, but despite fric-
tions Olaf always maintained that his fidelity was unshakable, that loving others did not cancel or alter his faith. Four years after *Star Maker* appeared, during
a rough passage in their marriage, he told Agnes, "Anyone reading my books
can see quite well what you have done for me. Both the theoretical ones and
the fiction have your influence writ large throughout. There's so much about
loving, so much about the mutual enriching of different kinds of beings."[54]

Agnes's presence in *Star Maker* anchored a narrative that, in its imaginative leaps into the unknown and the unknowable, was always threatening to
become unmoored from real life. But Olaf built all his fantasies on the actual,
and *Star Maker*, even in its most extravagant episodes, is as much cultural history as pure imagination. While there is little direct commentary on the state
of the world in the mid-thirties, the narrator's tour of other galaxies is nonetheless full of parables on terrestrial society. In public speeches Olaf analyzed
fascism as a form of "mass neurosis"; chapter 9's "mad worlds," drawn into a
perverse United Empire and ineffectively resisted by a defensive "League" of
sane worlds, are far-flung counterparts to the Axis Powers and the impotent
League of Nations.[55] The brilliant episode of the Nautiloids—huge, intelligent
ships of flesh—in which children born on the starboard side of their mothers
are raised to be workers while those born on the port side become masters turns
the arbitrariness of social class into biting comedy. In another chapter a species of insectile beings decides to disarm unilaterally when threatened by a
bellicose neighboring species. The pacifist insects make a heroic gesture that

carries an entire galaxy from repression through martyrdom to Utopia. But just as Olaf was unsure of the power of pacifism by itself to resist fascism and its fanatical young Brownshirts and Blackshirts, so the narrator of *Star Maker* questions the applicability of this fantastic scenario: "On the Earth, though all civilized beings belong to one and the same biological species, such a happy issue of strife is impossible, simply because the capacity for community in the individual mind is still too weak. I wondered, too, whether the tyrant races of insectoids would have had greater success in imposing their culture on the invaded country if there had been a distinct generation of juvenile malleable swarms for them to educate."[56]

Star Maker's most sustained cultural criticism occurs in the long third chapter on "The Other Earth," where parallels with the terrestrial twentieth century allowed Stapledon to show off his gift for satire. The first giveaway to the chapter's mischief is a casual detail about costume. The Other Earthmen wear their trousers with the crease at the side of the leg—an eccentricity of King George V.[57] "As essentially human as Londoners," the horse-faced alternative earthlings have highly developed senses of taste and smell; their ethnic prejudices derive from regional preferences for sweet, salty, sour, or bitter flavors. Pogroms against the distasteful are a recurrent phenomenon, and some minority groups survive by purchasing an honorary "sweetening" or "salting"; since racial mixing has in fact been widespread, few people are really "purely" flavored, but deodorants and degustatants are used to disguise impurities.

The Other Earth's mass media create a passive, hedonistic society of consumers, each with a pocket receiving set, not unlike the ubiquitous stereo headphones of the 1980s and 1990s, but with features that stimulate the senses of taste and touch, making possible new refinements to pornography. Church and State turn broadcasting into a tool of indoctrination, distraction, and illusory luxury; under pressure from the churches, the head of the World Broadcasting Authority, sounding suspiciously like Sir John Reith at the BBC, requires married employees to furnish proof that they have never spent a night away from their spouses, on pain of dismissal. Religious strife on the planet turns societies upside down over fine points of doctrine about the taste of God and whether the deity should be worshipped as a person or a flavor. Near the end of his stay on the Other Earth, the narrator witnesses the bombing of a metropolis, compounded out of news reports about Abyssinia and Guernica and the cinematic images of "Everytown" in Wells's *Things to Come:*

> So great was the heat still radiated from the city's incandescent heart, that we could not penetrate beyond the first suburb. Even there, the streets were obliterated, choked with fallen buildings. Human bodies, crushed and charred, projected here and there from masses of tumbled masonry. Most of the

population was hidden under the ruins. In the open spaces many lay gassed. Salvage parties impotently wandered.[58]

To an alert contemporary, *Star Maker* would have mapped the familiar world of 1937 as intriguingly as it disclosed Pascal's terrifying immensities. But it was not easy reading. Just before it was published, Olaf told an interviewer that it was "much wilder, more remote and philosophical" than *Last and First Men* and he expected it to be his "last fantastic book."[59] By a lucky coincidence readers had a chance to make the comparison for themselves. *Last and First Men* had been selected as one of the first ten books in the new paperback series known as "Pelicans." The Pelican edition of *Last and First Men,* issued in May 1937, sold out by the time *Star Maker* appeared from Methuen on 24 June; there was an immediate reprint of the Pelican in June. It seemed a good omen for *Star Maker.*

If reviewers had the final word, rather than just the first word, on a book, *Star Maker* would have been Olaf's best seller. The *Times* claimed it must "automatically enter the small group of modern classics." At the *Daily Herald,* the reviewer reached into his journalist's index to "take out unhesitatingly that dustiest and most precious card—the one marked 'Masterpiece.'" "The most ambitious novel, if novel it can be called, that I ever read," thought L. P. Hartley. *Punch* praised Stapledon's "dauntless imagination" and recalled another vision on a hillside—the fourteenth-century *Piers Plowman.* The sole North American review (there was no separate U.S. edition) appeared in the *Christian Science Monitor,* whose reviewer gasped at the book's daring: "Beside his stupendous panorama, his vision of worlds and galaxies, of cosmos piled upon cosmos, the glimpses of the future that Mr. Wells and others have provided for us are no more than penny peepshows." The local press on Merseyside joined the chorus. The *Birkenhead News* thought the author "courageous" to make alien worlds "have a close bearing on present problems"; even the *Liverpool Post* found the fantasy ingenious, though there was a predictably stingy complaint that Stapledon's imagination lacked Swift's humor and sense of proportion.[60]

In private and in print, friends and other writers told Olaf that *Star Maker* was the best thing he had yet done, though the tenor of their praise, often highlighting the book's difficulty, intimated that it would not be popular with the ordinary reader. Cyril Joad said it was the work of "a great man" and "I should almost suppose that that is what you are." From Denmark, Marcus sent a lengthy appreciation of "the absolutely overwhelming *crescendo* in it, of scale, style, everything; the ever and ever widening out of the mental horizon till one feels as if all was going to burst." Virginia Woolf wrote a flattering note: "I don't suppose that I have understood more than a small part—all the same I have understood enough to be greatly interested, & excited too, since sometimes it seems to me that you are grasping ideas that I have tried to express, much more fumblingly, in fiction. But you have gone much further, & I can't help envying you—as one does those who reach what one has aimed at."[61]

Perhaps the most gratifying response came from one of Olaf's intellectual heroes, someone he had occasionally criticized, often learned from, always respected, but had not yet actually met. Leo Myers knew him, though, and couldn't stand him:

> I saw Bertie R. again the other day, & I wish you could meet him to see what a fool he is. . . . Anything in the nature of worship, any hint at any glory outside man's present, conscious, rationalizing mind, touches him on the raw. He is a humanitarian, & to such all that gives your books breadth & beauty, is odious, and the expression thereof clap-trap. I did not get a chance of asking him if he had read L. & F.M.[62]

But Myers let his bias carry him away. Bertrand Russell *had* read *Last and First Men,* thought Stapledon owned "a very remarkable cosmological imagination" and an instinct for tragedy, and admired his freedom from the "common imaginative defect" of utopians who trust too much in government, scientific progress, and virtue as its own reward. Russell enjoyed the "grim jest" of *Star Maker*'s political allegory and the "austere beauty" of its style. The book's spiritual inquiry—which Myers expected him to revile—engaged Russell for its "intellectual courage." He liked the notion of the Star Maker as "an artist rather than a philanthropist," and in the final meditation on the "two lights" of reason and love he found "all that is good in religion without any of the bad features of most historical creeds."[63]

In mid-July, buoyed by such responses, Olaf took a holiday from cosmology with Agnes and their young friends Norman and Margaret Cullen in the Shetland Islands. He had signed agreements for two new books, neither of them fiction, for his imagination was temporarily exhausted. In the most primitive of the British Isles, he and his party lived simply among the classless crofters, more Norse than English in culture.[64] He dipped sheep, cut peat, and fished for herring and haddock in the sheltered voes of an intricately indented shoreline. The Shetlanders were a balm: "Their country, whose very real beauty is too subtle to spring to the eye, is not likely to attract many tourists. It is remote, bleak, monotonous, and singularly devoid of amenities. But its inhabitants are human. In comparison with our specialised, robotised minds they give an unexpected impression of vitality." He worried about the fragility of the Shetland way of life as progress in communication and transport linked the islands more closely to the wider world. Any global utopia worth the trouble, he decided, would have to make room for the Shetland crofters, as for other marginal societies:

> Those who, like myself, desire a unified world-wide culture should also desire all distinctive and valuable insularities of culture to be preserved, though for their own enrichment they must also be modified by contact with the rest of the world. What we desire is a true world-community; but a community in which there was no diversity would be barren. The greater the diversity of the components, the richer their communal life.[65]

When he got back to West Kirby at the end of July, reviews of *Star Maker* were still coming in. The *Illustrated London News* was calling it the season's most notable book, and in the *Evening Standard,* Howard Spring said it was the book of the year and its author "the most deeply and widely imaginative of all our contemporaries."[66] Olaf had predicted that *Star Maker* would "raise thunder on the Left and on the Right." But some of its best reviews appeared in Conservative newspapers. One grumbler on the religious Right, C. S. Lewis, for the moment repressed his complaint that *Star Maker* ended in "sheer devil-worship," but the next year he replied in kind with a romance of his own, *Out of the Silent Planet,* which put a Christianized deity back in charge of the universe.[67] On the far Left there was one noisy response: "The trouble with these utopia-mongers is (in spite of Mr. Stapledon's apologetic preface) that they are not concerned with things that happen this year, next year or in ten years time, nothing intrigues them that is not removed from our civilisation by at least ten billion light years." Still, it was more a squall than a storm of protest, and in good spirits Olaf left for the continent in August. "On the whole I think the book is the best that I have done," he wrote that month, "and it certainly has had a good reception."[68]

After a visit to Geneva, headquarters of the League of Nations, and to the International Exposition at Paris, where he found the monumental German Pavilion and the unimaginative British one depressing, Stapledon came home less sanguine than ever about the European situation. At an educational conference at Cambridge in September, he was stunned by the cheeriness of most of the speakers, and in his address warned that the old civilizations, including the decrepit British Empire, didn't realize that "they were living at the end of their world." He debated Harold Nicolson, who thought England was stronger than the fascist states, but Stapledon feared that the democracies underestimated the spirit of pride and regeneration in Germany and Italy.[69]

In mid-October, at a protest meeting in West Kirby on the bombing of Chinese civilian populations by Japan, he restated his message. He now reluctantly supported "rearmament for collective security," but not to advance the imperialist dreams of his generation's youth. "That idea is finished to-day." What must ultimately defeat fascism was not military force alone but free thought, the dissolution of empire, a commitment to transnational ideals. In Birkenhead he told stories, passed on to him by Iris Origo, of repression in Italy. Because Mussolini was unable to jam radio signals coming out of Spain, he resorted to having people beaten in their homes and in restaurants when Blackshirts burst in and found radios tuned in to banned foreign broadcasts. "The only thing that is going to save the world in the long run is an educated public opinion," Olaf told the National Secular Society. If England manipulated information, as he feared was the government's aim in using the radio "to warm up your imperialistic emotions," it would squander the one advantage the disunited democracies retained over the highly-disciplined fascist states.[70]

On the evening of 1 November, a deputation of twenty politicians, academics, clergymen, and writers caucused at the House of Commons and then walked over to the Cabinet room at 10 Downing Street to call on the new prime minister, Neville Chamberlain. Stapledon and Virginia Woolf were to have been the two creative writers in the delegation; Woolf, however, was revising *Three Guineas* and was uncomfortable with the role. On the morning of the meeting, she vacillated: "Must I go? Cant I get out of it?"[71] That night Olaf searched for her in vain. "Virginia Woolf did not turn up," he wrote sadly, having lost what proved to be his one chance ever to meet her. He was still enough of a provincial to be dazzled by the occasion, though discouraged by its outcome. After the session at Number 10 broke up, he went to the Authors' Club in Whitehall and described it for Agnes:

> The PM & the President of the Board of Trade sat on one side of a long table, and we all sat on the other or in a row of chairs behind the other, about 20 people. [Sir John] Shute started the proceedings, then [Sir Richard] Gregory, Editor of Nature, made a very dull speech. He was followed by Sir Arthur Salter who was very good, & the P.M. kept interrupting with questions. Then the PM answered at considerable length, with interruptions by Salter. But he really wasn't having anything to do with any of the proposals, though of course he was very polite & very plausible. He kept on saying the *first* thing we must get is good will, and nothing can be done till we get it. But he had no constructive proposals.[72]

It was all "quite futile," he told Agnes. Within the week Germany, Italy, and Japan had entered a new alliance, and Chamberlain was embarked on a course of personal diplomacy that resulted not in Britain's divesting itself of its own empire but in assisting Hitler to acquire one of his own.

Barely visible as a supporting actor in the minor drama at Downing Street, Olaf would not be so deeply involved in public and international peacemaking efforts again until events a dozen years later, in the first phase of the Cold War, unexpectedly made him front-page news in London and New York. For now, feeling powerless to avert the coming war, he took a six-month sabbatical from speechmaking and returned to his study to tackle the three books, numerous reviews, and series of essays for *Scrutiny* he would complete in the next two years. None of this work would much resemble the philosophical myths on which he had staked his literary career. For all its critical acclaim, *Star Maker* did not find a wide audience. At year's end the reviewing staff for The *Bookseller* classed it with the "Cinderellas of 1937" and regretted that it "didn't reach the thousands who would have been both enchanted and instructed had it come their way."[73] The first print run of 2,500 copies sold sluggishly; eventually there was a small, cheap second printing of another 500 copies in the summer of 1938, and then a still cheaper third run in 1941. But all told, *Star Maker* sold barely 5,000 copies in Stapledon's lifetime. For several years he pursued a different line of writing. His imagination, like his pacifism, went into hibernation.

13

SAINT OLAF

1938–1939

NINETEEN THIRTY-EIGHT was the worst year of the decade. In 1914 the Great War came upon people unprepared for it, but the road to September 1939 was laid out as plain as spilt salt in 1938. In that year the Nazi Empire ingested Austria, demanded and got Czechoslovakia. Chinese cities fell to Japan, Franco launched a final assault against Catalonia, Mussolini sized up Albania as his next imperial acquisition. The terrorizing of German Jews reached a new level of deadliness on Kristallnacht, 9 November, and in December the first of many transports of refugee children, dispatched by frantic parents anticipating the sealing of borders, reached the English port of Harwich. Neville Chamberlain, confident he could negotiate peace on his own, snubbed Franklin Roosevelt's unpublicized overtures for a summit meeting; the United States sank back into isolationist indifference to Europe, and Mussolini and Hitler made a meal out of Chamberlain.

By the time 1938 ran its course, everyone felt what was coming, and in that portion of literary Britain most critical of Baldwin's timorous foreign policy and Chamberlain's eager capitulations, there was anger and depression and paralysis. The publisher Fredric Warburg was tersely scatological: "'Merde' is a word applicable to the whole of that dreadful year, 1938." The young novelist and critic Walter Allen found everything after Chamberlain's September flight to Munich a protracted anti-climax: "1938 became 1939, which I remember mainly as a period of waiting, as though life and significance were in suspense." For Naomi Mitchison, retreating to Scotland with her children, protest faded into helpless, eloquent sorrow: "It seemed unfair. Such a short time since 1918." In mid-October, Olaf despaired. "It is too late. Germany is already master of

Europe, or rather Hitler is. And no one is going to put any trust in Britain again."
That month he addressed his old colleagues from the ambulance unit at Friends'
House in London at a clouded twentieth anniversary gathering; the world was
once more in "regression from kindliness and intelligence" and in the "sinister grip of fate." He told the Quakers he could no longer say, "I am a pacifist
and will have nothing to do with war." The next day his name joined many
others on a letter to the *Times* expecting that "we were about to enter the valley of the shadow of death."[1]

H. G. Wells, a bellwether of progressive sentiment, began 1938 in a
foul mood. His allegorical novel *The Brothers,* published early in the year,
foresaw the collapse of human fraternity in the present circumstances and
announced that Utopia was indefinitely postponed. In language reminiscent
of *Star Maker* but calibrated to a deeper pessimism, one of the titular brothers prophesies an unguessably distant date "when the monstrous discrepancy between the scale of our lives and the starry intervals will cease to
be a disharmony." Fed up with ideology, the author inscribed a copy to a
fellow utopian, "To Olaf Stapledon & Damn the Left & Damn the Right.
Love, H. G. Wells." Olaf resisted facile comparisons of communism and
fascism ("I cannot agree that there is so little to choose between the extreme Left and the extreme Right"), but he too could see no imperfect, let
alone utopian, resolution to the European crisis. Fascism, he told a Cambridge audience that year, was the likeliest future for England, whether by
invasion or infection.[2] But in his one significant publication of 1938, an
essay on "Science, Art and Society," Stapledon cautioned that the communist might assume the face of the fascist:

> There is a real danger that the Left, through the effects of a desperate struggle,
> may lose sight of its fundamental aims, and slip into a kind of inverted
> Fascism, or "para-Fascism." It may gradually begin to use the methods and
> pursue the ideals which in its enemies it rightly condemns. It may, that is,
> turn to ruthlessness, herd-mindedness, the glorification of the State, the
> contempt of individuality.[3]

Although he emerged for important political occasions during 1938—a
conference on Literature and the People sponsored by Victor Gollancz's Left
Book Club; a June writers' rally against fascism; protests on behalf of Czech
freedom; the launching of a food ship to eastern Spain; local committee meetings on Jewish refugees—Olaf spent most of the year in his study. In 1937,
worn out from *Star Maker,* he had declined an appeal for a prophetic novel
about Great Britain. "My hands are full at present. Moreover, as I have just
finished writing a long fantasy about the remote future and past, I think my

imagination needs a rest."[4] The work he turned to in 1938 was not fantastic but expository. He had contracts for three books: a new Pelican on philosophy for the layperson; a study of British patriotism for Methuen; and an analysis of religion in the modern world for Heinemann's *I Believe* series. When he reviewed Christopher Caudwell's *Studies in a Dying Culture* at year's end, his last sentence served partly to justify his seclusion: "Though the Ivory Tower seduces many into sterility, it is also for some a means of strengthening intelligence and integrity against the hypnotic influence of the herd; and for some few it is a retreat where they can prepare for society a treasure which it is not yet ready to accept."[5]

Of his three new books, *Philosophy and Living* was finished first, by the middle of 1938, though much to his disgust with the "fantastically unbusinesslike" pace at Penguin Books, it was the last published, near the end of 1939. Promoting the value of abstract thought in the practical world, *Philosophy and Living* finds in "the present breakdown of civilisation" a reason to see philosophical study as the necessary complement to "revolutionary ardour."[6] It continues where *Star Maker* left off, celebrating the two lights of wisdom and love, knowing and doing, detachment and commitment. In dedicating *Philosophy and Living* to his former WEA students, Olaf signaled his intent to write not for the professional but for the curious and the uninitiated. Its two volumes fall somewhere between an introductory textbook and a popular guide, applying the technical lexicon of philosophers to homely examples of metaphysical and epistemological dilemmas. The book does not break new ground like some of his scholarly articles or his best fiction, but it more accurately reflects his principles and energies as a teacher than anything else he wrote.

As an introduction to its discipline, *Philosophy and Living* is idiosyncratic. Not many other philosophers would have chosen to frame a topical exposition of *practical* philosophy with a beginning chapter on the problem of immortality and a speculative conclusion on time and mysticism. The structure of presentation has the Stapledon signature on it, as does the repeated caveat against intellectual fads masquerading as philosophical insights. When he makes the case against the existence of any compelling body of evidence, other than human desire, for personal immortality, he also cautions against a rush to embrace mortality for inadequate reasons. The fashion for nihilism is no more philosophically rigorous than wish-fulfilling dreams of heaven, and the philosophical novice should beware of those who love dark visions and take perverse joy in human ephemerality. Stapledon writes with the metaphorical bite and passionate conviction of one who has known the temptation: "The masochist, the addict to self-torture, is apt to hug the brevity and futility of personal existence to his breast like a block of ice."[7]

Philosophy and Living is a register of the debts, doubts, and changes in
Stapledon's philosophical thinking. The long chapter on metaphysics, criticizing the major positions from Descartes through Whitehead, is particularly revealing. Although he practices a scrupulous impartiality, balancing unbiased
summary with cautious criticism of each philosophical school, his allegiances
and distastes are not hard to ferret out. Cartesian dualism, Bergson's vitalism,
and the linguistic and antimetaphysical propensities of logical positivism are
each explained patiently and unenthusiastically. But when he turns to Spinoza
there is evident affection—and identification. Spinoza, we read, has been belittled for promoting philosophical escapism, but his life refuted such charges.
In courageous action united to unshakable mental detachment, in his intuition
of cosmic beauty and his devotion to the human enterprise in the universe,
Spinoza is "the outstanding example of the true philosophic temper." It sounds
like a portrait of the philosopher Stapledon wanted to be. "The temper of our
age is out of tune with the temper of Spinoza," Olaf lamented about Spinoza,
the age, and himself.[8]

In Hegel he valued the effort to reconcile the eternal and the temporal.
"Of course he fails to give a coherent account of them. But who has succeeded?" Olaf Stapledon, perhaps? Almost. He had nursed a similar ambition
in *Star Maker,* whose climactic chapters include eloquent confessions of failure.[9] On a contemporary philosopher *Philosophy and Living* also betrays the
author's affinities. Judging Whitehead's the most brilliant, comprehensive, and
difficult of modern metaphysical systems, he depicts the process of reading
Whitehead as a remarkable adventure into dense jungles of ideas from which
the explorer "emerges upon some bare mountain-top, to be rewarded by a panorama that embraces seemingly a whole virgin continent, the home, perhaps,
of a future civilisation."[10] Like Balboa on the peak in Darien and Stapledon on
the cliffs of Anglesey, Whitehead has the commanding view of the visionary
who espies new worlds.

The twentieth century, as one reader of *Philosophy and Living* phrased it,
"shut philosophy up in an ivory tower, to live there like a harmless paranoiac
in a world of its own."[11] Stapledon wanted to unlock the door, haul the philosopher back into living, and democratize the philosophical habit. As he presented it, philosophy is not an intellectual luxury in the keeping of specialists
but an essential ingredient in the will to found a just society. Surprisingly, his
message found plenty of readers. As sixpenny paperbacks, the two volumes
of *Philosophy and Living* drew little critical notice, but the Pelican imprint attracted an audience more efficiently than a heap of reviews. Among nonspe-
cialist publications, only the *Times Literary Supplement* and a church
newspaper, the *Guardian,* gave it more than a two-sentence nod; both praised
its lucidity, and the *Guardian* thought that "in the space allotted to him the

author does wonders." The single review in a philosophical journal, not printed until 1941, advised specialists that the book was not the work of an amateur, that in breadth of reading and searching criticism it went far beyond the usual introductory bromides.[12] *Philosophy and Living* sold more copies in Stapledon's lifetime than any of his fiction—95,000 by the time it went out of print during the war.[13] He received no advance, the royalty per copy was minuscule, most academic philosophers ignored the book, but the old WEA tutor still had a knack for getting ordinary people interested in philosophy by talking about it as if it mattered.

After writing *Philosophy and Living,* Olaf with his family made a summer expedition by electric train north through Sweden, passing the line of white stones labeled "Polarcirkel" and moving on to the bleak iron mines of Kiruna and the frigid Lake Torneträsk high in the mountains. In arctic Lapland he sought again the remoteness and cultural strangeness that the Shetlands had provided the summer before. He tracked reindeer over Mount Tsasinaskatchoko, collecting their fallen antlers, observed the fabled lemmings swarming in the tundra, and learned the social arrangements of the nomadic Lapps. He holidayed as an anthropologist and a pastoral utopian, but also as an exile seeking refuge from "the horrors of the international situation."[14]

During the later months of 1938, while *Philosophy and Living* was idled in the Penguin editorial offices and Olaf was sorting out saints, revolutionaries, and sceptics for his *I Believe* book, the horrors acquired a fresh immediacy. He learned about the growing harassment of Jews in Austria since the Nazi annexation in March. A young au pair girl working for Professor T. S. Simey at Liverpool University reported what she was hearing from relatives in Vienna. The Nazis had cowed university administrators into denying Jewish students a date for their final examinations; they were being forced to leave without degrees, and they feared that these humiliations presaged a full-scale persecution. Simey, Olaf's colleague in the Liverpool Council of Social Service and on the editorial board of the *Liverpool Quarterly,* enlisted several university friends in a plan to bring Austrian Jews to Liverpool to finish their degrees.

Because the Chamberlain government would approve no scheme that might increase the number of Jewish refugees finding asylum in Britain, Simey was told that his group must put up money for each student's passage to Australia after he or she took a degree at Liverpool. Olaf incorporated a stinging denunciation of that policy into the book he was then writing, *New Hope for Britain:* "The little that [government ministers] have done has been forced on them by public opinion. Instead of welcoming this precious human treasure, they have done all they can to restrict the influx, and have insisted that all refugees who come shall be privately cared for, and shall be sent abroad as soon as

possible." In the absence of government support, Simey's group recruited
people willing to take students into their families and able to guarantee fares
to Australia.[15] So it was that an engineering student at Vienna's Technical University received a letter from Agnes Stapledon early in 1939 telling him that
she and her husband were sponsoring his emigration. Wolfgang Brueck's friend
Hertha, Simey's au pair girl, had set in motion the events that got him out of
Austria and saved his life.

On the twenty-fifth of March, the morning of Wolfgang Brueck's arrival
at Lime Street Station in Liverpool, Olaf was wrapping up a three-day conference of the Association for Education in Citizenship a few blocks away at the
university. Agnes and Hertha met the diminutive Wolfi, shy and nervously polite, at the station and took him to West Kirby to await Olaf. When they met,
Wolfi was surprised at how well informed his host was about conditions in
Nazi-controlled Central Europe. For relief from his writing in the Grosvenor
Avenue attic, Olaf often went to the garden at mid-morning or for a game of
tennis late in the afternoon, and Wolfi began joining him and practicing his
English:

> He teased me about a certain formality on my part which, I soon realized,
> was not the English approach. Any remnant of reticence I may still have felt
> was finally demolished when, not knowing the term "safety pin," I used my
> own invention "insurance needle" instead. This was greeted with an outburst
> of mirth which I have seldom experienced. Olaf just lay back on the lawn
> where we were having morning coffee and shook with laughter.[16]

The Stapledons expected Wolfi to be with them for no more than six
months until he sailed to Australia. As it turned out, Australian permits were
canceled later in 1939 and he remained a year and a half before the British
army interned him in Wales and then deported him, with other aliens, to Que-
bec in 1940. Before that happened Wolfi became part of the family, finding in
Agnes a substitute for his own mother, who had died when he was three, and
in Olaf a stimulating, unpatronizing friend. Their conversations were never literary, often political. Olaf liked to challenge Wolfi's conservatism, as when
he extenuated the sins of Stalin: "People have been killed in both Soviet Russia and Nazi Germany—in Russia out of neglect, in Germany from evil." When
they were separated during Wolfi's Canadian internment, Olaf continued to play
the gadfly by mail; to Wolfi's assertion that English democracy was superior
to Russian discipline he replied, "I am much more sympathetic to Russian Communism than you are, but certainly Russia has something to learn from us. I
am quite sure that we have a very great deal to learn from the Russians. Whatever its faults, I believe the new Russian state to be the most important achieve-

ment in the modern world."[17] At home, Wolfi noticed, Olaf always set the large globe in his dining room so that Russia, not the United States, faced the table.

Much as he admired the Russian experiment, Olaf's deepest loyalties, as he had said long ago, were not to any nation but to the human species. Early in 1939 the American Clarence Streit published his controversial book *Union Now*. Streit advocated a federation of fifteen North Atlantic democracies as the first step toward a world government and proposed a "declaration of dependence" in which all human beings would recognize their common interests.[18] This was a bandwagon Olaf was ready to board. The failure of the League of Nations, premised on power sharing by sovereign nations, had persuaded him that the idea of sovereignty had to be jettisoned. Although he disputed details of Streit's proposal (including its American focus), the idea of a planetary community fired up his cosmopolitanism, and in a letter to the *Liverpool Post,* he preached a crusade for global unity. "Men and women throughout the world, all true democrats, all true progressives, whether Liberals or Socialists, and also, I suggest, all true Conservatives, must work to create it." On the day his letter was printed, the Conservative *Post,* surprisingly, editorialized on behalf of the Federal Union and thanked Dr. Stapledon for ventilating an idea that "thoughtful men in many countries" could not lightly dismiss.[19] By the end of 1939 over a hundred local chapters of Federal Union had sprung up in Britain, and Olaf chaired the Merseyside branch. His analysis of federalism and a plea for welcoming Russia into the Union was published in a 1940 symposium on Streit's book.[20]

Early in 1939 he finished his *I Believe* volume, now titled *Saints and Revolutionaries,* and previewed its theme at a Progressive League meeting.[21] Human history was a story of dialectical oppositions among three human types whom he designated as saints, sceptics, and revolutionaries. Scepticism, the critical loyalty to intellect, he saw as the antithesis to the saint's intuition that self-cultivation and kindness to others were the central principles of life. The revolutionary represented an incomplete synthesis of the other two—with comradeship borrowed from the saint's notion of love and a passion for objectivity drawn from the sceptic. At the crossroads human history had reached in 1939 a new stage of the dialectic might be developing, with saintly pacifism in antithesis to revolutionary violence; whether a new synthesis would emerge, before the species succumbed to catastrophe, was in doubt. "The triumph of the archaic in a world that is by now structurally modern may well cause a long period of misery and mental darkness," Stapledon feared.[22]

Saints and Revolutionaries explored the notion that "the perfect man" was an amalgamation of the saintly, sceptical, and revolutionary tempers. (In the less saintly mood of *Philosophy and Living,* however, the perfect man was ridiculed as a Cartesian "monster in whom all virtues are unlimited and no vices occur.")²³ In his new book Olaf the revolutionary and Olaf the sceptic both show their faces, but his temporary pessimism about utopian change and the apparent decline of rationality on the world stage tipped the rhetorical energies of the writing to the third category. It is Saint Olaf who appears most prominently and speaks most articulately. More appealingly than in the stiff-jointed *Waking World,* he fashioned in *Saints and Revolutionaries* his spiritual self-portrait.

Stapledonian sanctity is not the same as kindheartedness or doctrinaire zeal. His saints are not those celebrated in Foxe's *Book of Martyrs* or in a sentimentalist's pantheon of immaculate worthies. In Olaf's vocabulary the effortlessly virtuous are angels, not saints; "they have never had to pass through the saint's agony of heart-searching and self-discipline." The more he wrote on this subject the more he produced an inventory of his own character: The saint must resist the fatal attraction of introspection in order to achieve sympathy with others. He is a born-again sinner whose sins are "rather of weakness than of wickedness." Politically, he is unreliable and ineffectual; partisans find the saint treacherous because he can "hold the world at arm's length" and see it "in detachment from all special human desires." But in personal relations he is intensely loyal, and to avoid hurting those he loves he will sacrifice his own yearnings. By instinct, the saint is pacific, though capable of suspending pacifism in an emergency; unlike the revolutionary, if he must countenance violence he does so "with an agony of shame and horror." Saints are deficient in "pushfulness." Vigorous and brilliant, they yet miss spectacular success because they are hampered by "lack of self-regard and by absorption in what they sometimes call the life of the spirit."²⁴ Olaf often reshaped his own experiences to fill out his fictions and animate his philosophical positions, but not until the book he wrote in his final year, *The Opening of the Eyes,* did he ever make a more relentless self-diagnosis.

The last of his three 1939 books, *New Hope for Britain,* his most radical analysis of society, could not have had a less auspicious context for publication. The product of his decade of opposition to British foreign policy, his unextinguished utopianism, and his recent campaign on behalf of Streit's Federal Union, *New Hope for Britain* tops off the critique of patriotism and the vision of a Wellsian cosmopolis he had been developing since World War I. He finished the book late in the spring, but the declaration of war eight weeks before it came out on 26 October made most British citizens rally round the Union Jack and left Stapledon without an attentive audience. The argument of *New Hope* is complex—probably too complex for most people to absorb under the circumstances, despite a one-page preface inserted in page proofs to underline the book's continuing pertinence in wartime. The passions of war, Stapledon urged, must not obscure intelligence. The end of British "demo-plutocracy" was as necessary in the long run as the defeat of Nazism. "Nothing short of abolishing, not only imperialism, but national sovereignty itself, and creating a World Federal Union of peoples, can establish peace."[25]

New Hope's survey of the failures of the existing political parties reveals the disaffection that lay behind Olaf's fervent stumping on behalf of a new socialist party, Richard Acland's Common Wealth, during the war years. The Conservatives, true believers in social stratification but deeply fearful of class warfare, tolerate democracy only as a dangerous necessity; they embody the obsolescence of the English gentleman. The other three parties stand for different grades of progressive thought. The Liberals—the party of Olaf's political inheritance from William and Emmeline—champion individualism and democratic principles, but their faith in the good works of the rich together with a distaste for "state interference" leave them with no social or economic vision adequate to the aspirations of the unprivileged classes. The Labour party, intellectually allied with Marxism and visibly linked to the trade unions, plays the role of the opposition better than it exercises power; Labour, he thought, lacked the practical imagination to lead the mass of British citizens. Finally, the Communists' understanding of economic history is a key to making social change happen, but dogma blinds them to all but the material needs of people. Playing on the Christian aphorism, "Man cannot live by bread alone," Olaf offered a thumbnail political history of the previous half-century and predicted a new synthesis:

> Liberal Democracy saw that man cannot live without "bread"; but by concentrating on the production of "bread", and neglecting (in practice) the just distribution of it, Liberal Democracy became a farce. In reaction arose Socialism and Communism, which, in revulsion from cant and hypocrisy, declared that "bread" was man's whole need, and that all spiritual values were mere Capitalist dope. Fascism and Nazism succeeded because they appealed to the newly dawning sense that after all "bread" (and butter) are not enough. But by substituting guns and the mystical race with its heroes, they have led the unhappy peoples tragically astray.
>
> The good Communist, by admitting the need for a united popular front against Fascism, has taken the first step towards recognizing that, though "bread" is necessary, "bread" alone is not enough. He has joined forces with Liberals and Christians, and is discovering that, after all, there is something in the Liberal and Christian values.[26]

New Hope for Britain, as its title intimates, was written to counteract the panicky despair of a decade of crushing unemployment, war scares, and pervasive doubt about fundamental beliefs and values. Though unforgiving of the failures of British domestic institutions and of the crimes of imperialism abroad,

New Hope identified things precious in British tradition that needed only to be cleaned up and separated out from the sinister features of sentimental patriotism. Few Britons had a deep or thoughtful sense of their own cultural past because the teaching of history in the schools was almost exclusively a roll call of military and imperial events; little of the artistic and virtually none of the social and economic history of the culture was in the curriculum. Rotten with snobbery and class hatred, its spiritual health in a state of "fatty degeneration," British national life was "an outrage to the democratic spirit." Writing directly from recent experience, Olaf remarked that his compatriots had become so used to a state of debility that only the privileged few, returning from holidays in "Scandinavia or the strangely dignified and almost classless culture of such remote regions as the Shetland Isles," could see the great gulf between Britain's reputation for democracy and the actuality.[27] Hope for the future lay in a critical provincialism that encouraged loyalty to the valuable traditions of one's own region or nation, freed from any mystical apotheosis of the state and from a braggart's pride in geographical or racial superiority. The new patriot would, paradoxically, promulgate the essential English or Welsh or Scottish spirit by working to abolish the fatherland as an entity and to create in its stead a global union.

This kind of assessment of the strengths and limitations of his nation's past was to preoccupy Olaf straight through the war and into the postwar period. In a 1941 lecture to a military audience called "Is There an English Spirit?", he denied that the "biological Englishman" had any more reality than Hitler's Aryan. But he affirmed a cultural tradition of nine hundred years' standing that England stood for a humane spirit, for conventions of forbearance toward differences, and for moral indignation in the face of brutality. The tradition had been violated often enough, but there was enough truth to it to make it worth preserving. He summarized his English inheritance in a litany he put together for an article, most of which was cut from the printed version:

> One may reasonably be proud of being English, so long as one is also ashamed. I am proud to be the fellow-countryman of Shakespeare and Newton; ashamed of the slave-traders, the industrial exploiters, the imperial adventurers. I am proud of Milton and Keats, Darwin and Kelvin, Arkwright and James Watt, Robert Owen and the Tolpuddle Martyrs; ashamed of the Black and Tans, of the Amritsar Massacre, of the treatment of the unemployed; proud of English gentleness (some call it squeamishness), and ashamed of our vile snobbery.[28]

With both *Saints and Revolutionaries* and *New Hope* at the printer's, and with Penguin's promise, soon to be broken, that *Philosophy and Living* would be out in September, Olaf, Agnes, David, Mary, and Wolfi departed for a last, carefree holiday in western Ireland in mid-August 1939. For the third summer in a row, without traveling much beyond England, Olaf managed to get as far from familiar civilization as possible. "We visited the most westerly inhabited island in Europe (the Great Blasket), and found that no one spoke English," he told Aage Marcus.[29] But the air of crisis penetrated even to that distant outpost. News came on 24 August that Parliament was being called into session to pass an Emergency Powers Act to mobilize army, navy, and air force reserves. For years Olaf had almost never written anything in his pocket diaries except the bare notations of appointments to be kept; two days before he left Ireland, however, a single sentence appeared in the blank spaces for the two holiday weeks of August: "War now seems almost inevitable."[30] When the Stapledons returned to Liverpool and West Kirby on the twenty-seventh, they were caught up in the rush of war anxieties and preparations.

On the afternoon of the twenty-ninth, Olaf addressed the Liverpool branch of an organization Agnes had recently joined, the Women's International League for Peace and Freedom. He spoke of the war as if it had already begun, urging his audience not to assume that the outcome must be simply a reinstatement of Chamberlain's or of Hitler's status quo. The world was at a turning point, and in the peace that followed war, there would be an opportunity to rebuild from the ground up—from new blueprints. "It is up to you, and to all people of goodwill, to do everything we can during that war to work, not only for federation, but for that new spirit of world unity. Everything depends on that."[31]

That night Leonard and Dorothy Martin came to 7 Grosvenor Avenue for supper. Everyone made an effort to hold the deepening gloom at bay and to focus on the literary topics that called out Leonard's conversational brilliance. Wolfi, fascinated by the university friends who came calling on the Stapledons, listened for hours, charmed and silent. A little after eleven o'clock, the telephone rang. Julza Langfelder, sounding tense and sad, was on the line from Vienna. She was Wolfi's elderly aunt, his favorite aunt who raised him after his mother's death. Before he left Austria he and Aunt Julza had arranged the code name "Aunt Mathilde" to refer to Hitler. In letters and telephone conversations, a message that Aunt Mathilde was improving meant that the situation for Jews in Vienna had eased; if Aunt Mathilde's condition was worse, danger and the likelihood of war were on the increase. On 29 August, Aunt Julza's news was brief and frightening. Aunt Mathilde was very seriously ill indeed. Wolfi, shaken, put the receiver down and came back to the drawing room to repeat the message to the Stapledons and the Martins. He did not hear Julza Langfelder's voice again. She and four other members of his family were later murdered in concentration camps.[32]

On the last day of August, the evacuation of children from English cities began; for three days Olaf drove children from the Birkenhead Town Hall to outlying towns and villages of Wirral. On 1 September, Hitler's attack on Poland began. In the blackout on the night of the second, Olaf had an accident, knocking down a woman on a darkened road, and memories of harrowing ambulance runs more than twenty years before flooded back. The next day he reported to the police office to answer questions about the mishap and returned home to hear Chamberlain announce a state of war with Germany on the radio. That night, Sunday, 3 September, he and Mary listened to the nine o'clock bulletin with its news of London's air-raid sirens going off (in a false alarm), France's declaration of war, and the torpedoing of a Cunard steamer in the Atlantic on its way to Canada. Mary shut off the radio and stepped outside with her father; the sky was clear and full of stars. "He was profoundly depressed and said, 'Look at all that up there, aeons of light years away. It makes our affairs seem totally insignificant. Yet if they matter to us that means they *do* matter.'"[33]

Within a few days Olaf became an air-raid warden with regular night duties in Caldy and West Kirby; he was, he told Aage Marcus, a very inefficient sort of warden—a self-deprecation belied by his precise and detailed Air Raid Precautions notebook, full of first-aid instructions, procedures for ticketing neighbors who ignored the blackout, and stern reminders to himself always to bring his sleeping bag and a book, to blow his whistle at the appropriate times, and never to leave his post. During the long period of the 1939–1940 "phony war," when there were few air raids, he caught up on his reading: Jung's commentary on the Taoist *Secret of the Golden Flower,* Drucker's *The End of Economic Man,* and C. S. Lewis's gorgeous extraterrestrial romance, *Out of the Silent Planet,* Olaf's ambiguous description of which ("a delightful though in some ways perverse fantasy") may mean that he resented the parody of Stapledonian agnosticism in the character of Professor Weston. Meanwhile he, David, and Wolfi began making a dugout in the Grosvenor Avenue garden; Mary went off to Oxford to work on a degree in political science and economics; and he and Agnes made room in the house for two Liverpool children, "well stocked with lice."[34] His three books were all due out within a few weeks; the presses were still running, only slightly behind schedule, but Olaf could not guess what sort of reception his books would meet. "I wonder whether anybody will want to read any of them in these terrible times," he confided to Marcus.[35]

Reviews of *Saints and Revolutionaries* were scanty. The novelist Hugh Walpole, a faithful fan of Stapledon's throughout the 1930s, gave it more lavish praise than anyone else, thinking that it showed even more "genius" than his fiction. "He is as wise as Wells," Walpole wrote, "but much more human."

The *Times Literary Supplement* was not so sure. While admiring the fire of the prose and the book's visionary conjectures, the *TLS* critic found the ideal of a sainted revolutionary more a neat intellectual formula than a psychologically credible synthesis; as for the sceptic, Stapledon's argument that, in the abstract, even torture might conceivably be justified moved the reviewer to insist that for some behaviors one must demand ethical closure.[36] A few years into the war, Olaf recanted: "In an age when a rigid conventional morality was firmly established it was healthy to be an ethical sceptic. But to-day we are rediscovering, in blood and fire, that there are fundamental moral principles which must not be betrayed. In relation to these, scepticism is an extravagance, an intellectual affectation, an insincere pose of detachment, when genuine detachment is impossible."[37]

New *Hope for Britain* was published just two weeks after *Saints and Revolutionaries,* and the *Liverpool Post* looked at them as a pair. The *Post*'s reader surmised that the Stapledon sallying forth on "his splendid high ethical horse" was, despite skeptical and revolutionary tendencies, at heart in the company of the saints; but the very sanctity of *New Hope*'s political program disqualified it from serious consideration. *New Hope,* more widely reviewed than either *Saints and Revolutionaries* or *Philosophy and Living,* was treated as a curiosity. A Quaker newspaper was one of the few able to muster much enthusiasm, but critics generally saw it as out of step with the times. "The Wellsians, the planners, the educationists, and the Federal unionists would all agree with it," wrote the *Adelphi's* critic, but the whole thing amounted to nothing more than the "old nineteenth century ideal of Progress, dressed up in biological-psychological jargon." A more approving review may have disquieted the author almost as much as the negatives. John Middleton Murry made an extended comparison of Stapledon's emphasis on spiritual politics with the return to religion being championed in T. S. Eliot's new book, The *Idea of a Christian Society;* the comparison could not have gratified Olaf, who had just made a disparaging observation on Eliot's decline after "he retired into religious orthodoxy."[38]

New Hope's publishing history is the most anomalous of all Stapledon's works. Despite little evidence of demand, the original small edition of 841 copies was supplemented by a second, cheaper issue of 530 copies in 1944 (when almost all his earlier books remained out of print). In 1948, Methuen informed Olaf that interest in the book had long ceased and that the "large number of copies on hand" would be remaindered. Nevertheless, in 1952, a year and a half after his death, a third issue of *New Hope,* in 647 copies, appeared—the only posthumous reissue of a Stapledon book by Methuen until the firm printed paperback editions of his most famous fictions in 1978.[39] In the mid-1940s, Olaf received numerous requests from readers for copies of *Odd John, Star*

Maker, and other books long out-of-print. It is ironic that during and after the war that, an editor at Cambridge University Press told Olaf in 1940, "has made that new hope quite hopeless," almost his only obtainable earlier work was the unwanted *New Hope for Britain.*[40]

The lukewarm response to *Saints and Revolutionaries* and *New Hope,* and to *Philosophy and Living* a month later, left Olaf in a miserable state. Although he continued to work at his writing regularly until a few days before his death in 1950, the autumn of 1939 marks the clearest beginning of a steady decline in his self-estimate. Early in 1940 he told Marcus how he was feeling:

> I should have sent you copies of my three new books if someone had not told me that a special permit was needed to send books abroad in war time. Evidently this was a mistake, since you are yourself receiving books. If you have still not received copies of mine, let me know, and I will send some. They have not had much of a reception,—a few good reviews but far less than I have generally had. Two of the books, I fear, I ought never to have written; but one, "Saints and Revolutionaries," seems to me good, though slight. At present I feel very despondent about my literary career, which has been on the whole not much of a success.[41]

The most engaged responses to his favorite of the three books came not from reviewers but from friends, though the criticisms of H. G. Wells and Jack Haldane would not have done much to alter his anxieties about success. When Wells read *Saints and Revolutionaries,* he mixed praise with crankiness. "I like the way your mind plays about in it," he wrote. "And I don't believe a word of it."[42] Anything that took "spiritual" or "religious" issues seriously set H. G.'s teeth on edge. A few years earlier he had written to another correspondent, "I suffer from the want of sincere religious convictions, because if I had a God I could kick him."[43] *Saints and Revolutionaries,* which he thought reminiscent of his own World War I flirtation with theism in *God the Invisible King,* gave Wells a chance to flex his aging but still restless foot: "You are a lot younger than I am & you don't know what faith is yet," he told Stapledon. "You have faith but ultimately you will realize you can do without believing." In a mixture of jaded sympathy and condescension, H. G. told his younger colleague that he had done nothing to be ashamed of in *Saints and Revolutionaries,* and if he followed the old man's advice he'd survive the mistake of giving unwitting aid and comfort to clerics. "I've been through it all. I've been no worse than you. I am still quoted from the pulpits."

In a reply that has the tone of an impatient declaration of independence, Olaf told Wells that he simply wasn't a materialist (except, with qualifications, in the Marxian sense) and perhaps in the long run he wasn't much of a Wellsian:

Of course I can do without "believing", if you mean believing in metaphysical doctrines. I like to think of myself as following in your footsteps, as you suggest, but as a matter of fact I don't think I am quite on the same track and recently I have in some ways been going badly astray, from your point of view. I have even at times been called a Christian, which is a bit disturbing, I confess. . . . But I don't really side with anybody, even with you. I have thankfully followed you a long way, but with occasional excursions hither and thither beside the track which you have made and so many have since pursued. . . . I might claim that though you have incomparably greater power and skill than I have, and a far more encyclopaedic mind, or encyclopaedic range of knowledge, yet in a horribly sketchy sort of way I do take into account aspects of experience which you are inclined to underestimate, mainly because in your early days it was *necessary* to underestimate them, whereas in my early days it became necessary to recover the essence of them without the silly wrappings. After all, great innovators like you are almost bound to do less than justice to the traditional culture.[44]

Haldane also had problems with Olaf's discussion of saints, skeptics, and revolutionaries. A card-carrying skeptical revolutionary (he was by then chief of the editorial board of the *Daily Worker*), Haldane read the book, a year after it came out, under unusual conditions. "I have recently been mortifying my flesh, e.g. lying in a *bath of ice and water* for half an hour at a time, not with a view to improving my soul, but to saving other people's lives," he wrote, alluding to his famous, self-punishing experiments, conducted on behalf of the British Admiralty and designed to discover what physiological stresses the victims of sunken submarines could withstand.[45] If not quite a saint in Olaf's sense, Haldane had the constitution and temperament of a grumpy martyr, and he took issue with Olaf's dictum, as he roughly paraphrased it, that "people should be as sensitive as possible": "This seems to me very doubtful. I do not think that Samkura Acharya or St. Benedict, John Ball or Lenin, would have agreed with you. St. John of the Cross or St. Teresa might have done so." For Haldane, the realities of the anti-Nazi crusade made sensitivity a dangerous luxury. Olaf, he suggested, was too saintly for his or anybody else's good. "In a time of war and/or revolution the highly sensitive person may be so overwhelmed with agony and horror as to be incapable of appropriate action." He concluded by asking if he couldn't "swing over a little nearer to the revolutionaries and farther from the saints."[46] In his typical fashion he told Olaf not to bother writing back but to answer him in his next book. In fact, Stapledon's next novel, *Darkness and the Light,* with alternative histories of a cruel future dominated by fascists and a kindly one organized by saintly Tibetans, sounds like a calculated reply to Haldane.

Between 1937 and the long-anticipated outbreak of war, Olaf began losing contact with the first generation of his literary friends, those who had "discovered" him through *Last and First Men* in 1930 and 1931. On visits south he still occasionally dropped in on Haldane's lab at the University of London or debated philosophy with Cyril Joad, but his regular Café Royal lunches came to an end when Gerald Heard emigrated to California in 1938 and Naomi Mitchison went off to spend the war years learning to farm her Scottish estate in Argyllshire. Olaf invited Wells to speak in Liverpool in 1939, but H. G. declined, and the two of them never met privately again after the summer of 1937, although they exchanged occasional letters for another five years. He also lost touch with two foreign friends. After the summer of 1939, the exotic Iris Origo—on a "Bird of Paradise flight through the gay world," Virginia Woolf used to think when she saw the hats with long green feathers the Marchesa liked wearing—was encaged in the Tuscan Val d'Orcia for seven years, where she worked for the Italian Red Cross and, secretly, for the anti-fascist resistance.[47] Nor could Aage Marcus leave Denmark during the war, and once the Nazis occupied the country in 1940, his letters to England stopped until 1946. In London, Olaf still dined sometimes with Leo Myers, and they corresponded at length about their fiction, but Leo's moody irritability and nitpicking arguments strained the relationship. The friends Olaf and Agnes had in common in Wirral and Liverpool—their neighbors Dorothy and Leonard Martin; their Labour party cohorts George and Nell Allen, Sidney and Mona Scholefield-Allen; their folk-dancing companions Margi and Norman Cullen, Winifred Primrose—remained constant.

But Olaf's intellectual circle, especially in London, was slowly being redrawn. He had a short-lived association with F. R. Leavis and D. W. Harding of the Cambridge group that produced *Scrutiny,* but there was no basis for friendship. Through PEN, the international writers' association, he came to know Arthur Koestler, Mulk Raj Anand, Storm Jameson, and Herman Ould. The well-connected Myers introduced him to a cousin of the Queen Mother, the poet and social worker Lilian Bowes-Lyon, who won praise for her labors in London's East End during the Blitz. At a house party for the Progressive League, he met a researcher at the Ministry of Works, Evelyn Gibson, then estranged from her husband; she was interested in literature and philosophy, began reading Olaf's books and attending his lectures, and fell in love with him. Throughout the war he traveled to RAF posts to lead discussions with young officers, hoping to train a radical cadre of England's best and brightest who would build Utopia after destroying Nazism. He himself became a footsoldier in the new political party Common Wealth, whose leader, the former Liberal M.P. Richard Acland, wanted to meld socialism and Christianity and light a fire under those middle-class progressives whom the Labour party had been unable to inspire. The 1940s dimmed the lights on Olaf as a literary celebrity, but in his personal relationships and political activities there was new growth and new conflict.

14

COMPENSATIONS

1940–1942

STAPLEDON SPENT SEPTEMBER 1939 writing a pamphlet, "The War and the Peace"; its themes were taken from his own experience in the first month of the war as an air-raid warden and from conversations with Wolfgang Brueck. On nightly patrol in Wirral, alert for signs of the Luftwaffe in the sky or for scofflaws defying the blackout, he saw democratic cooperation and social discipline at work. But while the tradition of English pluck under duress flour-ished during the war, there were less heartening evidences of failures of English character and English institutions. Recording Wolfi's shock at Liverpool's slums, unlike anything he knew in Austria, Olaf added his own thoughts on the clash of cultures underway in suburban households that had become temporary refuges for the young, once invisible, urban poor. He wondered if Britain really knew what it was fighting for:

> The recent evacuation of children from danger-zones must have opened the eyes of many comfortable middle-class people to the fact that masses of our population live in conditions which no really civilized democracy would permit. Not only the dirt, the lice, the rags of these fugitives should impress us, but also their savage and feckless, though often fundamentally well-disposed, minds. If this is what civilization does to its children, is civilization worth defending?[1]

The disruptions and displacements exposed the need for something more than the defeat of Nazism. The war effort must not be built on unreal longings for a restored Merrie England with all its hidden dry rot, but on hope for a

21. "Stapledon's Factory," Simon's Field.
Author's photograph.

new Britain in a new world culture. This was the fervent message Stapledon carried, Cassandra-like, from one end of the country to the other for the six years of the war, challenging British insularity and myopia. "Many people in this island still cling to the hope that victory will restore the old order. This is a delusion. A new order of some kind is inevitable, Hitler's or another."[2]

"The War and the Peace" disappeared into Olaf's desk drawer. "My pamphlet on the war was never published, as G. D. H. Cole produced a much better one and forestalled me," he wrote early in 1940, in his last communication with Aage Marcus until 1946. "My mind turns away from politics just now, having produced a semi-political book. Moreover I have such a lot of speaking to do on Federal Union that I want some compensation."[3] With *New Hope for Britain* and *Saints and Revolutionaries* failing to reach large audiences and his pamphlet failing even to find a publisher, Olaf sought compensation in several senses. He wanted relief from political writing and speeches, he longed to return to literature, he looked for new sources of emotional vitality, and he was worried about money.

He and Agnes had begun building a new house in Caldy, a few miles from West Kirby on a bare, windswept site they picked out in 1938. They purchased their acre of ground from a tract known as Simon's Field. "Who Simon was, and why the field was his, nobody knows," Olaf mused, like Hamlet in the churchyard. "His life is now only a fibre indistinguishable in the matted felt of the past."[4] In 1940 a boxy two-story building in the simple style of local Cheshire sandstone barns was erected. Its material was white-painted brick topped with thick Welsh slate; inside, unpainted pine woodwork, rough greenish slate for hearths and fireplaces, and made-to-order furnishings of light oak contrasted with the heavy Edwardian mahogany of the few pieces brought down from Annery. On the upper floor Olaf finally had a proper study, giving onto a tiny sun porch where he could write in luxurious nakedness, keeping a blanket handy for strategic draping when visitors showed up. Downstairs the dining room and large sitting room were separated by double folding doors that permitted nearly the whole length of the house to be opened up for dancing or political meetings. Large casement windows running all the way across the western face of the house let in a flood of sunshine on bright afternoons and gave Simon's Field a sweeping view down over golf links and a single-track railway to the gull-haunted mudflats of the Dee and, across the estuary, to the glowing ironworks and Welsh mountains in the distance.

"Stapledon's Factory," some of his friends called the house behind his back, both for the industrial look (to British eyes) of all that glass and for the plain, functional appointments of the rooms. The one striking piece of decoration was on the ceiling above the stairs and landing where, on a diamond pattern of pine boards and battens neatly spliced at the angles, there was a green-and-white painted design in which an A nestled alongside an O—Agnes and Olaf, Alpha and Omega.[5]

Stapledon loved Simon's Field for its seclusion amid open spaces and for a new freedom in his life it represented. The only house he ever lived in that he had had anything to say about, Simon's Field offered compensation and refuge, even if the expense seemed foolhardy. "It seems ironical to be building a new house in war time," Olaf wrote late in 1939. "And of course we may now find it impossible to keep it up."[6] The uncertainty of his finances—poor royalties and a dangerously high proportion of his income tied up in stocks—led Olaf to write nervously to his daughter at Lady Margaret Hall, Oxford:

I am beginning to wonder rather seriously whether we shall be able to carry on with our present way of living indefinitely. At present we are well in hand, but if dividends go fut I don't know what will happen. So you must be prepared for an untimely end to your Oxford career. However we are all right at present. If I had some trade or other, things would not be so precarious. But if you live on ill-gotten gains you can't complain if they vanish.[7]

He found more paid reviewing for the *New Statesman* and picked up the pace of his free-lance lecturing (though he continued to speak gratis for many political causes). But advances from publishers dried up, and a paper shortage began playing havoc with printing schedules. With outlets for book-length work harder to find in the forties, Olaf grew nostalgic for his old books and eager for new readers, including his own children. "I believe it is time you read my Last & First Men, and that you would like it," he urged Mary as she neared twenty and he turned fifty-four in May, 1940.[8] By then, he was thinking up a new fantasy that, in outline, sounded like a variant on his earlier histories of the future, but the unfolding war left an ugly imprint on its images.

In May and June, after a long spell of watchful waiting—the so-called phony war—that lulled people into a vague hopefulness, the Germans assaulted Scandinavia, the Low Countries were overrun, France surrendered, and British forces were hurriedly evacuated across the Channel. After months of food rationing, blackouts, and drills, England braced itself for an attack. On 10 May, Olaf's birthday, the day German paratroopers landed in Holland and Chamberlain's ministry collapsed, he urged Mary to come home to Simon's Field: "I don't want to be fussy, but Oxford is the sort of place the Nazis would smash just for spite. Not that this is a safe spot. Planes overhead always now."[9] He and Wolfi dug up the brick-hard clay behind the new house, in a place once contemplated for a tennis court, to make a not very fertile plot for potatoes and cabbages. His air raid warden's work at night grew heavier after the winter respite, and he was often too sleepy to write in the afternoons. After Churchill took power, Olaf agreed to lecture to troops and civilians for the Ministry of Information, "now that the Chamberlain Government has gone."[10] No friend to the new prime minister's social conservatism, he had such total contempt for Chamberlain that, like others on the Left, he welcomed the intelligence and grit that Churchill restored to the government.

In midsummer 1940, Olaf heard from Naomi Mitchison in Scotland. At forty-three she had been in her final pregnancy, but the baby died shortly after birth. He wrote to console her and to bring her up to date on his activities, since they hadn't seen each other in a year and a half. He told of hours spent in the pouring rain passing out "immense quantities of leaflets" in the streets of Liverpool to drum up an audience for Forward March, Sir Richard Acland's forerunner to the new Common Wealth Party. ("How I hate all political work," he complained.) Gingerly, he linked the modification of his pacifist principles since she had last seen him to his concerns about Nazi terrorism and English insularity. About his literary efforts he was glum:

> I am writing occasional articles (e.g. in Scrutiny) and a book, but it's all futile now. We must concentrate on keeping Hitler out, surely, bad as our present regime is. I think the country is learning its lesson fairly rapidly, and there may really be a chance of something better after the war, if we are not wiped out. . . . My (qualified) pacifism has been put in cold storage. But how loathsome it all is! And of course I remain fundamentally just as much pacifist as before. But at present pacifism simply won't work. I note in Gandhi's autobiography that his non-violence movement's success depended on the fact that some officials were decent folk. It would not have worked against a Nazi regime. But though so far as I can see we must keep the Nazis out, we must also keep our heads; and at present many people are losing them, particularly over refugees. Our Austrian student whom we had for 15 months has been taken away, and was very miserable about it.[11]

As the war went on, Olaf showed a different face from that of the Quaker ambulance man of twenty-five years before. He applied to join Anthony Eden's newly formed Home Guard, the poorly armed civilian militia preparing for the expected invasion; his age disqualified him and he continued his air-raid patrols. His lectures and essays displayed a new tone of militancy as he defined what England—alone against the Reich now—was fighting for. And he meant "fight." The time for passive resistance was past:

> After the last war there was, I believe, a moment for absolute pacifism and unilateral disarmament, had we and the French been capable of it. . . . Nazism has shown us the limitations of non-violence. Some hooligans may be open to conversion by non-violence; but conversion may well be impossible in the case of hooligans organized on a huge scale by perverts in a society that has been violently embittered (as Germany was) by false protestations of good will and pacific intentions on the part of well-armed conquerors.[12]

In "Under Fire," a talk given in July 1940 on the eve of the Battle of Britain, Stapledon proclaimed that this war could not be thought of as purely defensive. Nazism was triumphing because of an idea, and the opposition must be similarly possessed by a passionately felt idea. That utopian idea (summed up in his intellectual shorthand as "personality-in-community") required a political order that ensured educational and economic equity in a class-free culture and a government-sanctioned compact of individual rights and social responsibilities for all citizens. A vision of the future, he believed, must motivate the present fight. Patriots argued that the first priority was to win the war and that work for social justice would come after victory. But the old order, Olaf told his audience, couldn't inspire and wasn't worth defending. The new idea needed to be worked on in concert with the war effort. They must start, he said, by calling on the government to purge all the old appeasers left from Chamberlain's regime, to free India and the other colonies immediately, and to extend food rationing, not as a military measure but for the sake of social equity.[13]

That summer Olaf heard from Wells. He got a querulous reply to a letter that opened wide their differences over global federation and Wells's project of a universal declaration of rights. Olaf had been feeling that Wells overemphasized individual rights as against social needs, and that he too hastily rejected all gradualist cosmopolitan schemes (such as C. K. Streit's in *Union Now*). Wells replied out of the sour gloom that permeated his last years: "I must write like mud. If I cannot make *you* understand what I am saying, then what is the good of my writing?" He hectored Stapledon, accusing him of misreading or distorting his Rights of Man Declaration. "Like old Gandi [*sic*] you sigh, 'Duties first.' *The Declaration is not asking you to stand up for your own Rights* but the Rights of other people. Didn't you even get that?" But Wells's heart wasn't in the fight. Tired of the war and of arguing, he sank back into the mood of Candide. "What my dear Stapledon is the good of writing books? You go on with your garden by the Dee & grow food. People of our sort can have no say in the fate of mankind."[14]

Having fallen out with Wells, Stapledon unexpectedly found himself taken up, temporarily, by someone who was Wells's ideological opposite, though equally crusty and opinionated. He had never cracked any of the quarterlies of the literary coterie, but suddenly he had three essays accepted over the space of nine months by F. R. Leavis for *Scrutiny*. Olaf had been discouraged over his unsung 1939 books and stoic about the reviews he was writing to order; his paternal brag about this small triumph in 1940 is understandable: "If you see Scrutiny," he wrote to Mary, "read my article in the June number on Tradition and Innovation. [D. W.] Harding and Leavis (editors) liked it a lot."[15]

"Tradition and Innovation To-Day" was the third in a series of essays on politics and the arts he wrote for *Scrutiny*. It wasn't exactly his kind of journal. Leavis's notion of a "great tradition" in the English novel and his disdain for Marxism did not predispose him to favor Olaf's imaginative writings; although the twenty-year careers of *Scrutiny* and of the mature Stapledon were almost exactly parallel, none of his fantasies or novels was ever reviewed in its pages. Perhaps Leavis decided to publish the wartime essays because he remembered approvingly the role of literary studies in Stapledon's discussion of education in the Progressive League's 1934 *Manifesto;* or because he liked the maverick quality of Stapledon's reviews for the *London Mercury,* including a doubting appraisal of Haldane's *Marxist Philosophy and the Sciences;* or because he admired him for refusing, in all the essays he sent to *Scrutiny,* any crude equation of tradition with the Right and innovation with the Left.[16]

Or the explanation may be simply that Olaf profited, rarely for him, from the literary network. Leo Myers was well known in the Cambridge circle that produced *Scrutiny;* in a retrospective on the 1930s, Leavis had even claimed, in a typically monolithic judgment, that *The Root and the Flower* was the decade's only significant achievement in the novel.[17] Myers may have arranged for Leavis to read his friend's work, especially since the subject of tradition and innovation was a longstanding issue in their correspondence. "My impulse is to praise the new and disparage the orthodox," Olaf told Leo in 1940, crediting him with awakening him to the danger of being "superficially modernistic."[18]

Olaf's *Scrutiny* essays grew out of public talks he gave in 1938 and 1939 when he wrestled with the role of the artist in a time of crisis. He rejected all formulations of the writer as an apolitical being. Literature, he told an audience at London's Conway Hall in 1938, always has had two complementary functions—a quickening power to entice people with fresh visions of the world, and a propagandistic one to make them want change passionately enough to act on their visions. Vision was not a luxury when life-threatening and culture-threatening crises demanded action, because the artist keeps seeding the imagination lest the outcome of crisis be the Pyrrhic victory of "a democracy of submen."[19] Out of that talk came his second, and best, *Scrutiny* essay, "Escapism in Literature," in which he worked out his own ascending hierarchy of literary functions: escape, propaganda, release, and creation.

In 1940, Olaf worked both sides of the divide between visionary literature and propaganda. For the first time since the end of 1936, when he drove himself to finish *Star Maker,* he was writing fiction. In 1937 he had announced that *Star Maker* was his last fantasy, but now the joy of turning his imagination loose again on the blank canvas of the future helped compensate for the meager rewards of his recent nonfiction and the cheerless routines of civilian wartime. His new book, *Darkness and the Light,* reprised the prophetic mythmaking of *Last and First Men,* still his surest claim to celebrity, but on a much-diminished scale. Like his other fiction of the Forties, *Darkness and the Light* was more topical and modest in scope than his dazzling inventions of the thirties. *Star Maker,* ending one long cycle in the creative work begun in 1914 with his first draft of "In a Glass Darkly," remained Stapledon's last, best effort to fulfill a youthful dream, described to a journalist in 1942:

One book I have wanted to write ever since I was an undergraduate and have occasionally attempted in vain. I now realize that I am not the one to write it. That I did not know this long ago must have been due to fantastic conceit on my part, for it was to be the greatest book of the age. It was to be both philosophy and literature in the most exalted sense, and it was to tell the truth about the universe and man's place in it, more precisely and more feelingly than any other book.[20]

Darkness and the Light, finished sometime in the first four months of 1941, is driven by the author's anxieties about the war in progress and the kind of world that would emerge from it, but the cosmological speculations and imaginative splendors that lit up the vast spaces of *Last and First Men* and *Star Maker* are fewer. Its grandest metaphor—in an episode in which telepaths, seeking to unveil ultimate mystery, glimpse "snowflake universes" being trampled into slush by brawling titans—is muted and blurred. Dispensing with the Neptunian machinery of his early fictions of the future, *Darkness and the Light* adopts a viewpoint frankly preternatural and fantastic. The author's mind slips out of his body and peers beyond the borderline of his own death, ranging forward in time to discover a "bifurcation of history," with two divergent futures, each of which he lives through.[21]

The result is a chronicle in tandem, following two streams of time that represent possible post–World War II directions. In one scenario the forces of darkness, already gathering for their first campaign in 1940, eventually subjugate the world, thriving on torture and the malicious use of scientific knowledge to reduce the human population to mindlessness and torpor. In the alternative future, a will for light, emanating from Tibet, slowly and with many setbacks overpowers the dark tendencies and turns the planet into a global village of universal economic justice, spiritual health, and racial and regional diversity.

The dark history shows the influence of several literary dystopias of the 1930s: Huxley's *Brave New World,* John Cowper Powys's sadistic fantasy *Morwyn, or The Vengeance of God,* and, especially in the mythologizing of the Führer, the reduction of women, and the cultural neuroses leading to the end of reproduction, *Swastika Night* by Katharine Burdekin (known to Olaf as the pseudonymous "Murray Constantine").[22] The parallel story of the Light also has a philosophical and literary inheritance drawn from Wells's Samurai in *A Modern Utopia* (1905) and William Morris's "obstinate refusers" in *News from Nowhere* (1890), with echoes of Ruskinian medievalism and James Hilton's Shangri-La and large doses of the Federal Union movement. The triumph of the Light, accomplished by Tibetan mystics, realizes some of Olaf's own favorite syntheses: of tradition and innovation, saintliness and revolution, individual rights and social duties, personality and community. The closing chapter, a symbolic rendering of the collapse of Utopia, the final extinction of Light, the ultimate Darkness at the end of cosmic history, is pure Stapledon—

a recrudescence of the chilling and ecstatic apocalypses that climaxed *Last and First Men* and *Star Maker.*

Leo Myers—revealing again his disappointment with *Star Maker*—read the new book in draft and told Olaf it was his best work since *Last and First Men.* He was stunned by the ghastliness of the dark half—with its images of howling mobs assembled for the spectacle of vivisection machines dismembering political dissidents, of the excised wombs of sacrificed women preserved in chemical baths for continuous artificial reproduction, and of cryogenic warehouses where the unemployed could be refrigerated and stored until such time as the state needed to draw on its surplus of workers. "Who," Leo wondered, "wd have thought of you as a Hieronymus Bosch?"[23]

Darkness and the Light, while a return to the form that had served Olaf so well in the first flowering of his creativity, is an astringent fantasy. The weariness of the prose reflects the author's wartime mood and his uncertainty about his talent. A short preface alludes to the national paper shortage—the manuscript had languished for six months until Methuen got a sufficient stock to print it—and asks dolefully whether this kind of book is worth writing or publishing.[24] Although all his fiction leaned more to the side of literature that instructs than to the side that delights, *Darkness and the Light* proclaims its didactic intent with unusual fervor. It reads like a demonstration of the principles outlined in the *Scrutiny* essay on "Escapism in Literature," merging the literary functions of release, propaganda, and creation while ruthlessly excluding any possibility of escape from present realities.

Nearly every reviewer thought the book inventive, if often horrifying, and "ingenious" was the most commonly employed adjective, but it created little excitement. For the *Times Literary Supplement* the strategy of pairing a projected Hitlerian future with an alternative extrapolation of Utopia was too harsh for wartime: "a little too much like kicking a hungry man in the stomach as preliminary to showing him a menu of the meal his unborn grandchildren may one day consume." The most memorable, and devastating, comments on *Darkness and the Light* appeared in Rebecca West's review. "This book should be read, though it is unlikely to be read with any exhilaration," she decided. Stapledon's sensibility was too ascetic and his style flat-footed. His apocalyptic imagination had epic scope without epic phrasing, "and the effect is as if Milton had sent the completed manuscript of 'Paradise Lost' to be rewritten by the author of Bradshaw's Railway Guide." Those willing to take the book as a "caricature," as Stapledon's preface classified it, were more approving. L. A. G. Strong read it alongside C. S. Lewis' *Screwtape Letters* and worried that "our national allergy to satire and fantasy" would keep *Darkness and the Light* from finding the audience it deserved. In a pair of reviews, Cyril Joad admired how it both terrorized the reader with pictures to make the flesh creep and fortified the intellect. To give yourself to Stapledon for twenty-four hours, Joad wrote, "is a process akin to surrendering a pair of gloves to the ministrations of a glove-stretcher. You go with him as far as you can and then—I think I am speaking here for most of us—you fall back at the point at which your mind simply won't stretch any further."[25]

Olaf wrote more mind-stretching fantasies in the 1940s, two of them among his most brilliant creations, but *Darkness and the Light* was his last hurrah in the genre of the future-chronicle, a form he had pioneered. Unlike *Last and First Men*, which cut a straight path from 1930 to the year 2,000,000,000, and unlike *Star Maker,* with its dizzying multiplicity of universes that subverted the very idea of history, *Darkness and the Light* adopted a deliberately schematic Either/Or formula for the history of the future. World War II, explicitly evoked in the first chapter, was situated just before a fork in the path of human destiny, with one route leading to Utopia and the other to hell on earth. The narrator, looking down on the twentieth century from a point outside space and time, perceives humanity "on the knife-edge of choice."[26] History in *Darkness and the Light* is not arbitrary and determinate; neither single nor infinitely variable, history is choice, and human beings get the future they make. That was the point of his new myth, and it underlay Olaf's decision to rededicate himself to utopian agitation during the war, through the Federal Union project and the new party politics of the renegade Liberal M.P. from North Devon, Sir Richard Acland.

By 1939, Acland, a devout Anglican, had abandoned the Liberal party's platform of benevolent capitalism and declared his conversion to a distinctive socialism grounded in a prototype of liberation theology. He wrote pamphlets, made speeches, and founded a journal—*Common Wealth*—that advocated root-and-branch reformation, including common ownership of industries, abolition of the House of Lords, legal equality of women and men, a universal scheme of education, and the dismantling of the Empire. Both the Liberal and Labour parties shunned Acland, but his message began arousing public interest.[27] In May 1940 he came to Liverpool as head of a movement then called "Forward March," which evolved into the Common Wealth Party. Writing to Mary at Oxford, Olaf described "our great Acland meeting," for which he had helped sell tickets. Olaf watched closely, took the speaker's measure, and decided he was worth following:

> He is not an orator or a great leader, I should say, but he has the right approach, and gets hold of the middle class people. He was much impressed by the meeting, and we have to give full particulars of how we did it, so that the rest of the movement can learn the trick from us. The meeting cost £31 and the proceeds of sale of tickets and the collection were £53, so we made £22 for starting a movement on Merseyside.[28]

The rally on 2 May was Olaf's first venture on Acland's behalf. By the middle of the month, however, the war had become a much soberer affair and the campaign for socialist reconstruction developed against a backdrop of daily gloom and occasional nighttime terror from the Luftwaffe. During the war years Olaf campaigned for Acland and his candidates for parliamentary by-elections, and he and Agnes pushed back the folding doors in Simon's Field to host Common Wealth fundraisers. But his eagerness for the movement competed with occasional black moods when all political enthusiasms were swallowed up in his own sense of uselessness and irrelevance. At home he was discovering that he could not re-create a version of himself in his own son. He had sent David to his former boarding school, Abbotsholme, and he hated it. Despite the fact that his son obviously had different ambitions for himself, Olaf kept pressing him to apply to Oxford. In 1941 he planned for "Dibs," as he called him, to work at Liverpool University "till Balliol will have him." But David rebelled at the prospect and announced that the only thing he wanted to do was to write for the oboe. Finally Olaf eased off. David had time for one year of study at the Royal Academy of Music before he was called up by the navy in October 1942.[29]

Once he gave up imagining David as a reborn Olaf, Stapledon fretted that Mary might become too much like her father. When she showed an interest in WEA tutoring, he told her to choose some other path. "Extramural work leads nowhere," he advised. "I do so hope you don't have such a miserably scrappy career as I have had."[30] In a passage of autobiographical reflection addressed to Agnes, written near the end of the war and used as the endpiece for his fantasy *Death Into Life,* Olaf struggled with the inevitable fact of his son and daughter's independence:

> Throughout their minds your mothering and my fathering are a deep-written, an inerasable palimpsest; but over and over that archaic script truths not of our teaching, values not of our preaching, and maybe errors not ours, are strongly superscribed. And so, though for us the two are for ever our children, yet also they are strangers.

Even then, acceptance competed with anxiety over David and Mary's differences: "They make their alien choices, and we dread the issue for them."[31]

"I feel how depressed you are," the poet Lilian Bowes-Lyon wrote to him in 1940. Olaf made no particular effort to hide his low spirits from those who were close to him. "People like me are just futile in these days," he told Mary, linking literary self-doubt to wartime melancholy. In his last letter to get through to Aage Marcus in Copenhagen, he wrote, "At present I feel very despondent about my literary career, which has been on the whole not much of a success."[32] To middle age and a conviction of literary failure was added the ordeal he shared with other Britons on the home front. The long year from June 1940 to June 1941 when Britain was Hitler's only active adversary and when the country was repeatedly bombed was a time of psychological isolation and nerve-racking tension from which Olaf was not immune. When Hitler ordered the invasion of the Soviet Union in the summer of 1941, Olaf's mood changed. Like others on the Left, he had felt betrayed by Stalin's nonaggression pact with Germany in 1939; now he could feel solidarity with the Russians once more. Although the casualties on the Eastern Front were massive and the success of the Soviet resistance far from assured, Britons felt their own siege lighten, after a year spent rushing for shelter when the sirens went off and holding their breaths while waiting for Nazi troops to land on their coasts.

In that season of renewed hopefulness in the middle of 1941, Olaf worked on a book for Secker and Warburg's series of blue-jacketed paperbacks known as "Searchlight Books," little volumes "designed to blueprint the post-war world."[33] With a direct reference to the world's amazement at Russia's "titanic battle" against the Nazi war machine taking place as he wrote, Stapledon shone his "Searchlight" on three major changes that needed to come out of the war: an effective world government, the creation of a social welfare state, and a new ethics of human living. All three, he argued, were interdependent, but the last was fundamental. He told Mary he might simply call his book *Human Living,* but eventually it was titled *Beyond the "Isms".*[34]

Forecasting an altered world beyond the war, *Beyond the "Isms"* was another effort to harmonize saintly and revolutionary ideals. "No one can really transcend the mental climate of his age," Stapledon cautioned. "But in transitional moments, and our time is one of them, it is possible to 'feel forward' a little toward the temper of the coming age." The emergent order would have to be fundamentally socialist while addressing the two glaring deficiencies of communism: its disregard of moral principles and its treatment of citizens as social units rather than as persons. The new society needed a spiritual grounding, but the old theological and metaphysical questions didn't matter. "We can well afford agnosticism about the universe," the book concluded, "for we have our great certainty about the spirit. Our perception of the beauty and rightness of the spirit in day-to-day personal living is all that we need for inner peace and for action."[35]

"Mr. Stapledon knows all the answers," a Church of England reviewer remarked sarcastically. The nondoctrinal approach to spirituality in *Beyond the "Isms"* caused Charles Williams to see him as "called to the Way of Rejection" and the pseudonymous John O'London to complain that "to Mr. Stapledon the mere word 'spirit' seems to be a kind of abracadabra—a charm or spell against all error."[36] Even approving critics, however, passed over an intriguing aside in the preface to *Beyond the "Isms".* This was not the book his pub-

lisher had bargained for, the author stated; in its making it became "a much
more personal book than I had planned."[37] A remarkable instance of the inser-
tion of his own life into the book's argument occurs in a passage on Nazi atroci-
ties. Stapledon described a feeling "that the universe is no more than a huge
desert of matter with here and there an equally futile, and a tortured, living
dust. I, at least, have recently faced this despair. Events in my personal life
have perhaps quickened my perception of it, and forced me also to see beyond it."[38] Such autobiographical mumbling is rare in his nonfiction, but the
private difficulties he alluded to had had a uniquely disruptive effect on him.

In the first week of February 1942, a houseguest at Simon's Field provoked some gossip. "I have a mind to ask Olaf who this Mrs. Gibson is," one
of the Stapledons' university friends said to Cyril Joad, who was lecturing in
Liverpool that week. Joad, who often saw Olaf in London, became agitated.
"For God's sake, don't do that. They've been lovers for years." At the same
time Olaf was mentioning the visitor among other items of news in a letter to
his daughter. "We also have a guest here, Evelyn Gibson, whom I met at a
conference some time ago. She has been ill, has lost her job, and is convalescing here for a week or so."[39] Joad exaggerated the length of the affair, but
Olaf told something less than the complete truth. This was actually Evelyn
Wood Gibson's second stay at Simon's Field; she had been there the previous
November to meet Agnes and to reach an understanding about her relationship with Olaf. The details of the love affair with Evelyn Gibson are likely to
remain in the shadows, but in the summer and autumn of 1941—while Olaf
was composing *Beyond the "Isms"*—he and Agnes faced up to some painful
facts.

Although Olaf's restlessness in his marriage had been building for some
time, a love affair could not have been in progress "for years" by early 1942.
He first met Evelyn at a Progressive League house party hosted by Joad in
London in the autumn of 1939; not until after a second meeting a year later
did they became lovers.[40] When Agnes learned of the relationship is not clear;
the surviving evidence of difficult discussions about Evelyn goes back only to
the summer of 1941. Before that summer, when the three parties began talking openly together, the record is nearly blank. Correspondence tells a little of
the story, but letters between Olaf and Evelyn in the early 1940s no longer
exist. Forty years later, all that Agnes Stapledon would say about Evelyn was
that she used to organize weekend meetings for the Progressive League. "She
was 'a progressive individual,' Agnes commented with restrained irony, "&
gave Olaf some good books."[41] That unelaborated portrait was meant to explain the one public acknowledgment Olaf ever made of Evelyn's existence,
in the foreword to *Beyond the "Isms"* where her unfamiliar name is poised
between two standard fixtures in his prefaces: "My thanks are due to L. H.

22. Evelyn Wood Gibson, ca. 1937.
Courtesy Geoffrey Wood.

Myers for encouragement and disagreement, Evelyn Gibson helped me with stimulating criticism. Agnes Stapledon I thank once more for being both my critic and my wife."[42]

Evelyn Gibson, an intense young woman with a feline face and waved auburn hair, was separated from her husband when she met Olaf. She was twenty-nine years old, and had a degree in economics and English from the

University of London but, in the hard times of the mid-1930s, could not find work that suited her talents or ambitions. She took a secretarial course and was happy neither in the temporary jobs she was able to find nor in the stormy marriage she had entered in 1935 in defiance of her parents' objections. Joining the Progressive League, she found opportunities to indulge her penchants for argument and political satire, and distraction from her disintegrating marriage; she was also moving in a circle in which casual love affairs were taken for granted. When Olaf first met Evelyn, she was lonely and still alienated from her parents. Her new job, conducting a nutrition survey for the Ministry of Food, involved constant travel and tiresome, repetitious interviews. She hated the work and vented her frustration in sharp-edged verse parodies.[43] Strong-willed, alertly intelligent, but prone to bouts of depression, she had already had other, unhappy love affairs and longed for security, respect, and a child. Perhaps most important to Olaf, she was, unlike Agnes, well-read in philosophy and literature and eager to enter fully into discussion of his intellectual work. They met at a time when they each, for different reasons, felt the need for someone else to take them seriously.

When Evelyn came to Simon's Field in February 1942, she and Agnes and Olaf had been negotiating for six months, in letters and personal meetings, to work out an accommodation. "I am by nature polygamous," Evelyn told Agnes candidly once the affair was being discussed by the three principal parties. (Anthony Gibson, from whom Evelyn was later divorced, took no part). The discussions were not acrimonious, but Evelyn was surprised both by the discovery that this was Olaf's first extramarital liaison and by the severity of Agnes's pain. "I hadn't realised that it was so terribly new to think of his making love to someone else. He says that he isn't by nature exclusively monogamous, & so I had the idea that it had happened before."[44]

Agnes had started corresponding with Evelyn one night at 2:00 A.M. while Olaf was at his air-raid warden's post. "I am all alone in our big bed thinking of you & him & me," she wrote plaintively. She struggled to accept the affair and to articulate her grief:

I have felt awfully unkindly towards you at first. It was so new to me to think of Olaf making love to someone else. We have been married for 22 years & it seemed to strike at all my foundations. I am beginning to see now that I must have been awfully grasping & possessive. I wanted to be the only one to bear his children—even the only one to make love with him. . . . Whatever else results it has been good for him because it has liberated something in him & given him more self-confidence & it was sweet for him to get from you the sympathy & understanding of his work in which I have failed him so abominably. He wants to go on seeing you sometimes & I don't want to stop him. I would like to see you too—only you will think me so terribly middleaged & dull. I am. Olaf looks so ridiculously young for his age. But I am fat and forty seven.

As she wrote, Agnes revealed the anger just below the surface of her self-accusations. She had been required to surrender her exclusive claims on her husband, and Olaf, she knew, had already refused Evelyn's wish to have a child. In a rare burst of outspokenness about the sexual privileges of men, Agnes observed that only she and Evelyn were suffering real losses: "Do you think the situation is one which is capable of a solution that will make us all three reasonably happy people? *loving fully* & yet eating our hearts out for something we can't have? If so it means that I must give up something for you & you must give up something for me. I think Olaf is going to be the one who can have his cake & eat it—or perhaps it's the world for him where 2 & 2 make 5 or where the string has 3 ends."[45]

Evelyn was moved by a detailed journal that Agnes sent her to read, but she did not volunteer to break off the relationship:

> Olaf says that his relationship with you is unchanged—and I know that that matters most to him. It seems that you have everything already, & I don't want to spoil it. Even before I met Olaf I knew from his books that his loving you was part of him, & that he wouldn't be him without it. If I am spoiling that I mustn't go on seeing him—but he says I'm not spoiling it. It is difficult to think straight, because it is such pain to think of not seeing him again.
>
> Oh, can't it be alright? You see, I am so used to a world in which people find completely happy marriages quite compatible with love affairs as well. And it is all a bit of a shock, because my ideas about it have been—not formed—but very much confirmed & developed by his own books.[46]

To Evelyn's sorrow, Olaf drew clear boundaries around their relationship. Having a child would invest the affair with a permanency that he no more than Agnes wanted. In *Last and First Men* he had sketched the mores of the "Second Men," a future culture in which "strict monogamy was deprecated." Women and men comfortably accommodated both casual and generative sexual relations; the latter expressed a deep intimacy based on "true union of minds," and the former offered "a delightful embroidery on life" and renewed vitality with "elegance, light-hearted tenderness, banter, and of course physical inebriation."[47] But as a First Man, Olaf was finding the lighthearted, temporary refreshment he hoped for impossible, since neither his wife nor his lover could take that view of things. Evelyn, writing to Agnes from Wales, hinted at suicide if she had to give up Olaf altogether. "At present I can't *help* feeling that life wouldn't be worth living without him. And I do feel terribly unhappy sometimes at the hopelessness of it all. Whenever I crossed the river at night in

Cardiff I used to feel like jumping in it. And then I thought how remorseful he would feel, & you too—not that it would be anyone's fault but my own."[48]

Evelyn gave Olaf a poem she wrote about her fantasy of leaping into the Severn River; Olaf, in turn, handed it to his eighteen-year-old son, an aspiring composer of folk tunes, and asked him, without ever explaining the poem's significance, to set it to music. Even after fifty years John David Stapledon could still recite the haunting lyric from memory:

> When it's time for me to die
> In the river I shall lie;
> Silver water flowing over
> Shall my tired body cover.
>
> I shall know no more of needs
> Than the quiet water weeds,
> And then at last I shall be free
> From this tormenting restless me.[49]

The depth of Olaf's ambivalence about his extramarital love—his uncertainty whether to conceal it or flaunt it—is evident in his decision to bring his son partway into the secret without fully disclosing it, just as he told Mary that Evelyn Gibson was visiting Simon's Field without explaining her place in his life. With Agnes he tried to be forthright and ended up sounding tepid. He said he believed in their marriage, "whatever the minor snags," and he assured his wife that as they grew older their lives would be "filled with deeper understanding of one another & deeper though less exciting love."[50] She was not entirely reassured.

After much hesitation, in November 1941, Agnes asked him to say in writing how he actually felt about her. Olaf's long letter, written over two days, is a stiffer and less creditable performance than either of the two women's writings. Sentimentally, he rehearsed his old storybook romance with Agnes and the eternal meaning of his love, but about the present realities of his marriage he mustered only bloodless generalities. His fussiness about failures of language and mixed metaphors gives a weirdly literary cast to the letter, and the effusive rhetoric, especially by comparison with the straight talk in Agnes and Evelyn's letters, inevitably raises questions about protesting too much. That Olaf believed what he wrote need not be doubted, but the depth of his self-knowledge is harder to measure. He found the role of "cad" extremely disagreeable and sounded more anguished over the damage to his own image than over Agnes's diminished self-respect. Apologizing abjectly for what he delicately referred to as "the incident," "the trouble," "the muddle," he wrote the letter while on his way to visit Evelyn again:

Taffy dearest,

You are the only one whom I call dearest. Others may be dear, but you are the only dearest. Surely you can never doubt that, dearest, dearest Taffy. I was to write to tell you how much I love you. The trouble is that it really goes too deep for words. Think what there is between us! I seem to have known you and loved you always. Everything that I do I always want to share with you. Some things I can't share with you fully, for one reason or another, for instance philosophy, but I always *want* to share everything. Even when I fall superficially in love with someone else I automatically want to share it with you, not only to have your sympathy but to give you your share in the new experience I have gained. . . . Between us, Taffy dearest of all dears, there has been very great mutual enrichment. When you are despondent about yourself you say you don't feel that you have given me anything. If you feel that, it's because what you have given me is not anything that you yourself can be clearly conscious of. . . . You have been the window through which I have seen half the world. That is not a good way of putting it. The point is that the sunlight (I have changed the metaphor here) coming through that window (a wide-open window!) has given me an emotional and moral healthiness that I did not have before we were married. That is not a good way of putting it either. The real point is that in loving you so much all these years I have got in step with your personality, and because it is a particularly generous and wise one, I have become a much better thing than I should have been. . . .

Such a lot has happened since we first met when you were eight and I was sixteen! (The time when you came to England as a baby hardly counts!) I remember so well that meeting. You came into the room and were introduced, and you looked straight at me with wide-open blue eyes; and I felt it was like a look of recognition. I felt right away that we belonged to one another. I was very young and romantic, but that is how it felt. You were wearing a green silk frock with a white petal-like collar, as in the old photos of you. You stood by the fire and warmed your hands. England seemed cold to you. Well, ever since then, however many other people I have loved, in different ways, I have always loved you, and always shall. In the beginning, no doubt, it was largely a sentimentalization of you. I didn't really know *you* at all. Largely I was just in love with the idea of being in love. But the "you" I loved then and the "you" I love now are all of a piece. . . . Well, it has been a success, hasn't it, Taffy, best beloved? It can't all go wrong because of what has happened recently. If it did, I should break up completely. It's not only that we have a common life to go on living, and that no other life could possibly do for either of us. So far as I am concerned the bond between us gives meaning to the universe. If that breaks there's no sense in anything. It's a grim and murderous universe, but also it has this sort of thing in it, and that redeems it. But if this sort of thing can turn to dust and ashes—then *everything* is all wrong. But it *can't* turn to dust and ashes. I have hurt you horribly over Evelyn, but you have been so good and so wise about it. So far as I am concerned the incident really has made me treasure our love more than ever, partly because it has waked me up, but partly also because you have made me realize *you* more. Oh Taffy, it has been a horrible time for both of us, and all my fault. I don't really *feel* any wrongness in loving Evelyn the way I do, but I do feel the awfulness of having hurt you. That is what makes it so distressing to be going to see her again, knowing that you will be unhappy while I am away. According to my *theories* it is quite all right for me to love her a bit, but your unhappiness makes me doubt my theories, and shakes my confidence in myself. . . .

It's true that we *had* got a bit too used to one another recently. It's true that I did sometimes feel cross and critical and badly-done-to, quite unreasonably. It's true that this affair over Evelyn has waked us both up, though painfully. But the fundamental fact is that we have all along been very firmly united, grown together. It has always seemed to me that nothing could ever divide us, though it has never seemed to me impossible that either of us should have minor loves with other people. . . . Anyhow, Taffy dearest darling, what has been between us is a great good for all eternity. And what will be, apart from possible bombs or diseases or other troubles, is also a great good for all eternity. I mean, what has been and what will be are as much a part of the texture of the real universe as what is now. Oh love me always! Don't, don't any more be unhappy! . . . It's intolerable when you are unhappy. It makes me doubt whether I can ever make you happy again. It makes me feel such a horrible cad. It makes everything I have stood for seem a mockery and myself a mere self-deceiver. But above all it hurts so much to have hurt you. Oh my dearest of all, forgive me, love me happily again. And while we are away from one another, remember that I shall be thinking very much of you. And even while I am glad to see Evelyn again I shall be longing to see you again and to know that all is well in spite of the muddle. Dearest, darling Taffy.

Love!

Olaf[51]

Agnes decided to be generous and took on the burden of being the partner at fault. "I had never really believed I should be asked to share even my most precious treasure," she wrote back to him. "I feel I really am beginning to live now in your world. I don't want to go back to mine. I feel you have helped me to catch up now, and I'm not going to be left behind. So don't be sad about me, darling Olaf, while you are away. Enjoy being with Evelyn, and get all the happiness and delight that her warm love and sympathy and understanding will bring to you. And when you think about me, don't think of me as grudging you the happiness, but as being happy that I am not still bound in misery in my own old ungenerous world." With almost audible relief, Olaf replied, "You are a dear and a heroine and a brick." He assured her that things would become easier after "this time of strain and readjustment."[52]

It wasn't as easy as Olaf wanted to believe. He told Evelyn that Agnes was finding the relationship among the three of them difficult to bear, and, in the end, the major readjustment was Evelyn's. By the beginning of 1942, she was writing to Agnes, "I know he's fond of me, just as much as ever, but it *has* all changed rather & I can't help minding." When she came to Simon's Field for her week-long visit in early 1942, she was, she said, "not myself, mentally or physically."[53] Olaf, too, had to rearrange some assumptions. When *Beyond the "Isms"* was published in March, it bore the impression of the affair in its prose. The author alluded, unspecifically, to "the perennial mental torture which the instruments of the spirit inflict on one another in the intimate sphere of personal relations." More pointedly, he offered his views on "sexual energy as a factor in a genuinely human sexual personal relationship." He was unapologetic about his principles, but uncertain about his practice:

> For my part I see nothing wrong with fleeting and light-hearted sexual intercourse, so long as it neither damages a more fully "personal" union nor leads to a debilitating obsession with sex. But those trivial unions are not the best that can be. Better, whether in marriage or apart from marriage or in adultery, are those in which sexual intercourse is a symbol of developed personal love. Whether the best of all is necessarily a strict monogamy, or necessarily not a strict monogamy, I do not know.[54]

By the summer of 1942, Olaf had accepted that the affair with Evelyn must end. In July and August he was in London for meetings between the 1941 Committee, a lobby of writers and intellectuals chaired by J. B. Priestley, and Richard Acland's Forward March—the first step in the merger that led to the formation of the Common Wealth party. He steeled himself to go to Evelyn's flat in Hampstead to explain why they could not continue to be lovers. Agnes copied out part of the letter Olaf sent Evelyn to prepare her for the breakup. It was a simpler, more believable account of his feelings than what he had written the previous November, and it remains one of the more revealing self-studies he made in his older years:

> You know that in my way I do love you very much, but it has been more & more borne in upon me that I am no lover at all for you in the ordinary sense, simply because I am really so fundamentally one with Agnes. If she also had a lover, then I could be your lover without misgiving, though of course not fundamentally, since fundamentally I am always with her. But she has no "lover," never had & will never have. And so, dear Evelyn, I just cannot do anything that distresses her, even though she does nothing to prevent me. Oh I can't explain. I don't understand my own feelings anyhow, so how *could* I explain? It's not a matter of morals or even of generosity, but simply that even

if I say "To Hell with it all, I'm going to enjoy myself," I find that something in me rises up & turns the prospect of enjoying myself in this way to dust & ashes. I mean, to go deliberately from her to you to make love to you just tastes all wrong. . . . It would not seem so if *she* were doing the same kind of thing. But at 48 she is not likely to get a chance, even if she wanted it. And I at 56 have no business to be acting a much younger part. (I wish we had both done so long ago, but we didn't, & now we are old.) I think she knows now that even if I do make love to you I shall never love her less. Indeed you have quite certainly made me love her more, & she me. But—well I can't do anything any more that makes her feel at all deeply "left out." It is true, & she knows it, that you have given me something that she has never given me so fully, but on the other hand she gives me so very much always that is more fundamental for me because of our wonderful "unity in difference." . . . And there's another side to it all. Though you are quite wrong in supposing that I am overstraining myself (I am really disgustingly fit for my age) it is certainly true that the state of the world has rather got me down psychologically. I mean things are so frightful that I feel most horribly sober & old, not in body, but in mind, so that in these circumstances I live only for work (in the very diverse ways that I do work in). My work has been no great success, but with the world all in pieces, & my time running out I just feel that what really matters is to do whatever I can in my way however small to salvage things. And so—well, this is not the frame of mind for love making unless we can do it without mental conflict. . . . Don't be sad about this letter my dear because it is for the best really, for all of us— you too really. Don't be sad, oh don't.[55]

Olaf and Evelyn continued to meet as friends during and after the war, knowing, she wrote in 1947, "that the time for ardours between us is long past."[56] She was alone, often despondent, working at various ill-paid civil service jobs, and once or twice a year Olaf would drop by for a nostalgic chat. "You haven't seen my new flat yet," she wrote once. "Do come, & I will give you dinner & we can talk as we used to do." But for Evelyn those reunions usually ended tearfully. She was still in love:

We seem to have drifted rather apart & I don't want us to. It's mostly my fault, because you're busy & have lots of other things to think about, whereas I am merely living a rather hermit-like life & getting, I fear, rather stagnant.

I am, alas! getting middle-aged. But all of me is still there underneath.

You, for all you say, just don't get any older. You're the only one of my illusions that has stood up to time & change, which shows that it wasn't an illusion.[57]

Before the decade was out, Evelyn finally found work to her liking and made a more-than-modest success as a specialist in criminological statistics for the Home Office. But she minded time's toll on her looks. She lost her girlish figure and some of her youthful pertness (though not the red highlights of her hair or the sharp and stubborn mind), but like so many others who knew Olaf, she wanted to believe that he, like his Divine Boy of Patagonia in *Last and First Men*, was immune to change and age. On that score, at least, the chronicler of the mortality of species and worlds had no illusions about himself. In the spirit of a utopian story he wrote for Arthur Koestler in 1943, he remained optimistic about social regeneration but realistic about the inescapable consequences of the procession of time. He called his story "Old Man in New World." Poignantly, but with saving humor, the Divine Boy acknowledged clay feet and creaturely brevity, though he continued for the rest of the decade to search for compensatory solace in literature, in progressive politics, in adult-education work, in travel, in a new generation of admirers of his ideas, and, once more late in life, in love.

15

FANTASIES AND WOOLLY IDEALISM

1942–1944

"JAMES JOYCE DID WELL to load his work with subtle allusions to the life of a little western city that few Europeans ever visit. Dante did well to crowd the Divine Comedy with Florentine notables. For only in so doing could each give concrete and significant expression to such experience as he himself had gained." So Stapledon, celebrating the union of the cosmopolitan and the provincial in literature, told the seventeenth international congress of the PEN club in London, where, with Jacques Maritain, E. M. Forster, Mulk Raj Anand, and Thornton Wilder, he was a featured speaker in September 1941. The conference's theme, in that year in which the host country had just passed through the nine-month Blitz, when Virginia and Leonard Woolf had stockpiled poison in case the Germans landed in Sussex and when the government's opposition to Indian independence grew harder, was Writing and Freedom. Writers promoted liberty and human unity, Stapledon told his audience, not when they strained for universality but when they wrote out of their local and intimate experience.[1]

It might seem perverse for the author of *Darkness and the Light, Star Maker,* and *Last and First Men* to champion the virtues of regionalism, but his most outlandish landscapes were always glimpsed from well-traveled roads, his wildest inventions always copied from nature, his visions of the future always drawn partly from memory. The swooping "flying men" of *Last and First Men* were modeled on the seabirds of the Dee estuary, on which Olaf kept meticulous notes for many years; Panther, the Neptunian "last woman" in *Last Men in London,* is unmistakably a version of Agnes Stapledon; and the "brilliantly green peninsula" of "a maritime country in the temperate zone" on *Star*

Maker's Other Earth, where everything is "at once so strange and so familiar," is an alternative Wirral peninsula where even the urban architecture of the alien planet is a variation on the famous two-tiered shopping district of the medieval town of Chester.[2]

In 1942 a risky new work of fiction, giving full scope to his talent for creating the strange out of the familiar, delighted Olaf in the composition and frustrated him in its slow progress toward publication two years later. Near the end of 1941, he was feeling "stranded" after proofreading *Darkness and the Light* and finishing a third revision of *Beyond the "Isms"*. "I have nothing large on hand, nothing but a review and masses of letters to write."[3] A push to his beached imagination came from the embryologist C. H. Waddington, whom Olaf joined on 20 December for a broadcast on "Fantasies of the Future." Waddington was conducting experiments, written up for *Nature* the following summer, on pregnant rats injected with hormones to stimulate fetal brain growth. He was still pondering the "speculative possibility" that craniums artificially enlarged to accommodate big brains could result in dramatically smarter rats. Waddington's speculation, translated from rats to sheep dogs, shaped the most daring and moving creative work of Olaf's final years. Within two months he was well into a first draft of what many readers found his most accessible novel and what he himself considered, using a term he rarely applied to his work, "my best science fiction."[4]

"I have been writing my 'Odd Dog' novel," he informed Mary Stapledon in February 1942. "I have done about half, in the rough. It goes with a swing."[5] As his provisional title suggests, he imagined the book as more like *Odd John* than his future histories. The chemically engineered dog with a superhuman mind shares with John Wainwright both a relentless criticism of *homo sapiens* and the tragic fate of a visionary misfit, though the canine protagonist grew into a richer, more "human" character than Odd John. The book Stapledon finally called *Sirius* (after rejecting the allegorical title "The Beast and Beauty") belongs among the modern achievements in the fantastic and satirical tradition. *Gulliver*-like, it skewers the vices of "normal" human society as experienced by a cultural and physical outsider. Investigating the ethos of the scientific imagination and the psychology of an artificial being, it aligns itself with *Frankenstein*. With Wells's *Island of Dr. Moreau* and David Garnett's *Lady Into Fox*, it redraws the boundary lines between the animal and the human. One of Olaf's favorite contemporary fantasists, Karel Čapek, used animal fables in *War With the Newts* and *The Insect Play* for biting political criticism. In Viscount Samuel's *Unknown Land,* which Olaf reviewed while he was composing *Sirius,* parents in utopian Bensalem apply suction to their babies' heads to prevent the cranial sutures from closing and to let the skull and brain expand beyond the normal limits.[6]

The literary pedigree of *Sirius* helps establish its place in the history of fiction, but as with all Stapledon's work, it is deeply rooted in scientific research and in his own imaginative life. As early as January 1930, nearly a year before his first work of fiction was published, he was lecturing to the Liverpool Psychological Society on the minds of apes, and the central idea of *Sirius* was already latent in an undeveloped episode of *Last and First Men*. Olaf's friend John Gloag, "a close and acute reader" of his books, shrewdly observed the link: Stapledon's "Third Men" and "Third Women" enjoy "psychical symbiosis," including a "frankly sexual intimacy," with their hounds—specially bred from wolflike stock.[7] A message written just after the end of World War I also forecasts the issues of *Sirius*. Agnes Miller was packing up to leave Australia for her wedding when her pet dog Joey suddenly died. In a letter that reached her in Bombay, Olaf answered one of her questions:

> As for dogs' having no souls, what is a soul? I am sure I don't know. It seems to me that dogs and men are on exactly the same footing in the matter anyhow. Differences between them are only differences *in degree* of life, of aliveness, of spirit. If by "soul" you mean a spirit that lives on after death as a person with memories of its earth life, I don't know; but most surely dogs and men and trees and all living things are of the same nature, unless perhaps it be that only the most alive of them can project their lives beyond death.[8]

His uncertainties had not been resolved twenty years later. The central question of a 1942 essay, "Sketch-Map of Human Nature"—Stapledon's first scholarly article in a philosophical journal in over a decade—was: "In what respects is man identical with beast?"[9] It is the most concise abstract of the theme of *Sirius*.

By the early 1940s, Olaf had made a thorough study of the scientific literature on animal intelligence, a fact disguised by the single amateurish reference in a prefatory note to *Sirius* citing his debt to a popular book on *Sheep Dogs and Their Masters*. The chemical technique Thomas Trelone uses to fashion his super–sheep dog owes much to Waddington's experiments, but the more crucial situation in which Trelone raises the dog in his home alongside his youngest child Plaxy is derived directly from the Americans W. N. and L. A. Kellogg, who in 1930 raised a chimpanzee with their baby son for nine months. Where the Kelloggs, however, frankly made their nonhuman subject *"as anthropomorphic as possible,"* in *Sirius* all inclinations to treat the super–sheep dog as if it were a human being are fiercely resisted by the dog's-eye viewpoint on the human world. In a 1944 lecture on "The Minds of Animals," Olaf revealed that he had not only read the Kelloggs on *The Ape and the Child,* with its still-amazing photographs of baby Donald and the chimpanzee Gua, but had studied the nineteenth-century hoax of Clever Hans the horse, Pavlov's experiments on sensory discrimination and boredom in dogs, Kohler on *The Mentality of Apes,* Arnold Gesell's *Wolf Child and Human Child,* and the 1940 Penguin by H. Munro Fox, *The Personality of Animals* (his copy of which he marked up heavily).[10]

More personally, *Sirius* is not only a literary fantasia on scientific themes but a remembrance of things past. In 1947 he spoke of an "original vision" from which *Sirius* sprang. He never wrote down its details, but he had a reverie as early as 1917 when he was in the ambulance corps in France. There he imagined entering a terrier's mind "to feel the world as it is to him, and to relish all the thrilling smells that constitute his daily experience, and to explore the limits of his doggy mind." In the early 1920s he wrote as part of a prose poem:

> Under the skin I am a wolf. And the skin fits ill. It chafes me, it splits over my long jaw. None but a wolf would take me for human.[11]

The private sources of inspiration for *Sirius* go back still farther. The chief locale of the narrative—the Welsh mountain village of Festiniog—was the earliest British landscape in Olaf's memory. There he had first gone with his mother and Edith Hope Scott at the age of three, and when Emmeline took him permanently from Egypt in 1892, she bought a house in Festiniog, where she and her son spent long parts of each year alone. Later Olaf courted Agnes Miller on the moors above the Vale of Clwyd, just north of the village; in their married life they returned so often to Festiniog that in old age Agnes could still map the routes of Sirius's runs through the Welsh hills.[12] If *Sirius* is not quite the equal of *Ulysses* and the *Divine Comedy,* Olaf nevertheless drew his "fantasy of love and discord," as he subtitled the novel, from provincial soil cultivated from his earliest years.

When Naomi Mitchison asked him in 1944 how he had come to write *Sirius,* Olaf mentioned neither Swift nor Shelley, Pavlov nor Waddington, but went back in memory to a time when he was no more than six years old: "I was brought up with a rather intelligent fox-terrier in Egypt, and this book profited by that quite a lot. In fact it now seems to me a sort of distorted act of piety toward that former but never quite forgotten beloved."[13] In his 1944 talk on "The Minds of Animals," he reviewed the research on animals and speech and recalled his youthful belief that his dog Rip could understand English and Arabic words. After he was separated from his pet in 1892, Olaf used to enclose notes in tiny envelopes for "Mr. Rip" in his letters to Willie. One of his earliest letters described his last Christmas in Port Said, when Rip sat in a high chair at the breakfast table with tea and sugar on his plate.[14] In his Welsh exile, young Olaf longed to know how Port Said looked and felt and smelled to Rip,

23. Forecast of *Sirius:* Olaf and Emmeline Stapledon
with Rip at tea in Port Said.
Courtesy Mary S. Shenai.

just as later during World War I a similar fascination with canine perception
recurred with Ginger, mascot of the ambulance corps.

In naming his imaginary dog not for his actual terrier Rip or Ginger but
after the Dog Star, most brilliant star in the sky, Olaf linked an old canine love
to an old astronomical love—and to a literary relic of his younger days as well.

He owned a fine edition of Francis Thompson's devotional poem, "The Hound of Heaven," a favorite of his until his tastes in poetry changed after World War I. Once, lying out on the ground in France with his ambulance unit colleague John Smeal, he listened to the boom of distant guns as shells exploded against the background of the stars and thought of Thompson's image of God as a great dog pursuing souls.[15] In the overripe diction of late-Victorian angst, the poem dramatizes the problem of suffering in the Creation, an issue for Stapledon throughout his career. "Ah! must Thou char the wood ere Thou canst limn with it?" the speaker in "The Hound of Heaven" asks a God who tortures creatures for his mysterious ends. It is a version of the *cri de coeur* that Mary Shelley borrowed from *Paradise Lost* as epigraph to *Frankenstein* ("Did I request thee, Maker, from my clay / To mould me Man?") and of the image of the creator in *Star Maker*. Adam's alienation is echoed in Sirius's lament to the scientist who engineered him, "Why did you make only one of me? It's going to be lonely being me." Thompson's divine hound, tracking its quarry of men, became Stapledon's articulate sheep dog on the trail of an elusive divinity. "Surely the thing that I was crazily hunting must be the very thing that men called God, the dear and beautiful and dread," Sirius announces in interpreting an obsessive dream of his. "I am going to be the hound of the spirit."[16]

As *Sirius* took shape in 1942, its scientific fantasy blended into the texture of the war that transformed British civilian life. *Sirius* is full of the atmosphere of blackouts and air raids, of rationing and the mood of siege, of war research in the laboratories of Cambridge and the unprecedented conscription of women. The Battle of Britain over London and the Great Merseyside Blitz of 1941 contributed important episodes—including Sirius's harrowing flight through the Mersey Tunnel during the height of the bombardment of Liverpool. Some events depend directly on Olaf's experiences on the home front. Thomas Trelone, the scientific maker of Sirius, stands in for Olaf Stapledon, the imaginative maker of *Sirius*. Killing off Trelone with a bomb in Liverpool, the author, who had witnessed scattered bombing as an air-raid warden in Wirral and much vaster destruction across the Mersey as he bicycled from Caldy to the city, enacted the sense of mortality that grew on him during the war.[17] In a displacement of his anger over the deportation of Wolfgang Brueck and other "aliens" in England, he made Sirius the object of slanderous charges that he was a Nazi spy. Trelone's younger son Giles quietly awaits the notice calling him to active duty, as John David Stapledon was waiting in 1942. Finally, in making the narrator of *Sirius* an officer in the Royal Air Force, he drew on the World War II experience that gratified him more than any other. He wrote the novel while engaged as a lecturer to military audiences in Home Guard Units in Cheshire, at bases around the country, and at prisoner-of-war camps on the Isle of Man.

The War Office's provision for lectures, discussion groups, and short courses arose out of concern over the boredom of troops stationed for long periods of time at home bases. Much of the teaching was done by military officers through the Army Bureau of Current Affairs, but there was a demand for trained civilian tutors as well. Regional Committees for Education in H.M. Forces operated as lecture agencies, matching requests for courses or single talks with the available pool of civilian volunteers. At its busiest, the program had four thousand courses running during a six-month period in 1943, and over sixty thousand individual lectures were delivered. Many of the lecturers, like Olaf, were veterans of the Workers' Educational Association.[18] He, however, was not moved by official calls for improving morale and keeping soldiers from getting "browned off." Stapledon's utopian aim was to form a critical mass of thoughtful activists who would apply their experience in the world war to the making of a healthier postwar world. Lecturing to troops thrown together in a relatively classless camp was an experiment in democracy. For almost half a century, the WEA had been an educational laboratory for a small proportion of the population; the huge conscripted force allowed the experiment to be tried on a much larger scale. "We shall never have a real democracy," Olaf wrote of his reason for teaching in the forces, "till masses of ordinary people are educated for democratic citizenship."[19]

Rarely did audiences display an immediately visible interest in the scheme. A lecturer found that the men or women being addressed had had no say about attending, and some showed their resentment by refusing to join the discussion. Even the most polite troops typically began with the assumption that lectures were a waste of time, and the speaker would have to cajole them out of silence. Trained in the voluntary tradition of the WEA, Olaf at first found teaching soldiers forced to be students distasteful, but by the end of the war he had changed his mind. He felt there was a strong case for making education a compulsory part of military service:

No doubt from the lecturer's point of view it is much more pleasant to talk to volunteers than to educational conscripts, but he should accept the situation as a challenge to his teaching ability. It is up to him to create the right relationship with his audience, and make them glad they were compelled to come. Another reason for compulsory adult education is that only by compulsion is it possible to reach the people who need adult education most, the people who would never dream of taking the initial plunge freely.[20]

Olaf had less trouble with the educational conscripts themselves than with uncooperative base commanders. Sometimes the local commanding officer failed to provide appropriate conditions or even tried to subvert the arrangements. More than once no one turned up at the place appointed for a talk and the lecturer would be stranded for half a day with nothing to do but wait to be transported to the next location. In one egregious instance of negligent planning, Olaf was brought into a military hospital ward and told to lecture to the patients while one of them was having a tooth noisily extracted. He refused.[21]

Near the end of the war, Stapledon described one session in *Youth and Tomorrow,* and in even greater detail in an unpublished manuscript. He met with fifty young pilots-in-training, their blue air force uniforms still fresh from the maker. They had been ordered to the lecture during parade time and their aloofness was palpable. Ironically, the speaker's topic was freedom, and he thought, "How could I have the audacity to lecture to men who might so soon have to sacrifice everything?" He went ahead and analyzed how "liberty" had become a buzzword, easily manipulated and varnished with cant. Everyone needed to think about which freedoms were essential, because after the war hard choices would have to be made. They listened impassively. Hitler must be beaten, he concluded, but they had an obligation, no less important, to ensure that there would be a society worth having fought for. Then he sat down. Dead silence.

After a few moments he stood up again and paced the room. "Well, how does it strike you?" There was a determined silence before one man spoke up pointedly. "We don't want liberty, we want security." Before the lecturer could reply, a second protest was made. "Even if we come through this business, *we* can't do anything. *They* will settle it all over our heads." Olaf responded: "If you can take responsibility for flying a plane, you can take the responsibility of democratic citizenship." From the back of the room someone hooted, "Just with a bloody vote!" Someone else added, "We're trained for flying, not for political action." "Then for God's sake," Olaf said, "begin training yourselves as soon as possible." There was a sour laugh. Another pilot spoke up. "We can't. We haven't the means or the time. And the high-ups are probably trying to dope us with stuff they think is good for morale." Once the suspicion that the lecturer might be in cahoots with the authorities had been uttered, the ice was broken. The discussion became lively and focused; many of the participants talked feelingly about the future, about jobs and housing and what a decent society owed its citizens, and about what ideals could command their loyalty. When the official discussion ended, RAF pilots crowded around the speaker.[22]

Stapledon learned he must convince his audiences that he had not been muzzled by the commanding officer or a bureaucrat in the War Office. "Propaganda," in fact, became a popular topic of his discussions with troops. The content of his lectures was never censored in advance, although once—after addressing three hundred Italian sailors in a prison camp at Douglas on the

Isle of Man—he was advised to omit in future talks his account of the government's suppression of the *Daily Worker* in 1941.[23] That his audiences were frequently apathetic or hostile did not surprise Olaf. The atmosphere in the camps was tense and distracted. Discussions competed with the roar of aircraft in the background, and the speaker struggled for his audience's attention. But as Olaf told his daughter, the problem was not just acoustical: "Many of the young pilot officers are frustrated without knowing it perhaps, their minds nailed to the never-admitted realization that their lives may be cut off any day, & for the rest filled simply with the eternal wireless drivel, which is *always* on everywhere."[24]

Working the troop circuit was complicated—and trying for a man who had never taken easily to public speaking. Many bookings involved three or four lectures a day, often with a slow train journey at beginning or end, and tours to bases in the Hebrides required a lot of island hopping in fragile-looking biplanes. Olaf had to work himself up to perform, and he sometimes found the air journeys in rough weather sickening. He minded the effort to be continuously sociable, and, remembering, no doubt, how his FAU uniform marked him off from the other men in khaki during World War I, he felt awkward as the sole civilian in a sea of uniforms. When he had to stay overnight at a base, he ducked out of evening parties to retreat to his room to write. "I ought to be enjoying all this," he wrote to Agnes in 1944 from the Outer Hebrides, "and in a way I am, parts of it, but one is different from everyone else, and I find it a strain."[25]

When circumstances were right, though, the teaching was more gratifying than any since his early days in the Merseyside WEA. A group of 250 air force officers on one island enjoyed a boisterous discussion of radical social reform after the war. Elsewhere, officers were eager to talk about Marxism; an outspokenly communist corporal at Oban personally ensured a big audience for Olaf's lecture there, and one RAF doctor got away with wearing a hammer and sickle on his battle dress. Olaf felt he tapped deep feelings just below the cool surface of many of the younger men, although the authorities were less than pleased by the leftist tenor of discussions. Now and then someone in the audience would linger afterwards because he recognized the lecturer's name, usually from having read a cheap edition of *Last and First Men* or *Beyond the "Isms"*; a few days later a package might arrive for the fan, containing some hard-to-obtain Stapledon book.[26]

The relation of discipline to freedom was one of Olaf's standard topics, and he found only one sector of the forces incapable of handling the issue: the military police. He asked one group of MP's to consider the dilemma of conscientious objectors, and the reply came that the only course was to "shoot the lot." When he tried to defend conscientious objection, "they scarcely concealed their opinion that I ought to be shot too."²⁷ Olaf's toughest sell, however, was to some American army officers stationed in Wales. He was offered a huge plate of food, including more meat than English eaters were used to seeing in wartime, and coffee with "an unlimited number of doughnuts." After the meal thirty officers took to armchairs for his lecture, and their behavior confirmed the fears he had projected in 1930 in *Last and First Men* of an Americanized planet:

> They listened intently, and then got up, one after another and made speeches to the effect that America knew what Liberty was, and no one else. As for suggesting that Russia might teach America anything whatever, that was sheer nonsense. How many motors were there in Russia and how many in America? It was rather a terrifying experience, really. They claimed to be so advanced, and really they were a good 50 years behind the times. And their minds were completely closed. And they had no idea of discussion. They just orated. And some of them were quite rude to Russia.²⁸

Over the course of four years, Stapledon lectured to a great variety of military personnel, from small searchlight batteries to women's auxiliary detachments of the army and air force to antiaircraft units on the coast. But it was the RAF pilots that made the deepest impression on him. Like Wells, he romanticized the air force as the symbol of a liberated future. Both writers viewed the airplane, shrinking distances and abolishing natural barriers, as the harbinger of a world without national borders. In Wells's film, *Things to Come,* the RAF pilot John Cabal, portrayed by Raymond Massey as a clear-eyed, ramrod-straight, steel-gray visionary, heads a cosmopolitan organization of fliers calling themselves Wings Over the World who lead a ruined planet toward Utopia. Olaf also saw air force pilots as the yeast for social change once the war was over. "I very much doubt," he told Mary, "whether there will ever again be anything like a proletarian revolution. The coming people are not the proletariat but the technicians—airmen and so on. They will never go Marxist, though they may go Fascist. One can only hope that instead they will work out a new and better 'ideology' of their own."²⁹

Remembering the airmen in *Things to Come,* Olaf asked Wells to support an educational scheme being organized by flight lieutenants in the RAF Coastal Command. Known as "Freedom House," the plan called for a small library, to be set aside in every RAF unit for reading and discussion of social issues. Olaf saw the organizers as potential leaders who might eventually exercise "a really radical public influence" on postwar society. H. G. was underimpressed. He was also offended that none of the organizational brochures mentioned his Declaration of the Rights of Man instead of "that cullender of political trickery the Atlantic Charter." Suspicious of the chaplains' endorsement of

Freedom House, Wells groused, "The prospect of an England run after the war by the squire & the parson is enough to take the fight out of anyone. No I don't like your 'Freedom' House. I want Free Thought & Free Speech House."[30] Olaf was disappointed but unapologetic. He thought he understood the rising generation better than Wells, by then seventy-six, ill, and chronically disagreeable:

> I was afraid you would be suspicious of the Freedom House scheme because of the padre influence. So am I, but I am sure the young men themselves mean business, and so I am going to do whatever I can to strengthen their position. . . . There ought certainly to be a reference to The Declaration of the Rights of Man, but in my experience what the young people are most roused by today is not a claim to rights but a call to devotion. That is where the padre may side-track them. The urgent thing is to show them something really worth being devoted to.[31]

In the same month Olaf published a review, written at Wells's request, of his novel *You Can't Be Too Careful*. Again he distanced himself from the old man. The novelist had reduced essential human motives to self-interest, and the century's greatest utopian thinker was sunk in captious cynicism. "Wells's commendable determination to see man without rose-coloured glasses has led him to adopt a jaundiced pair instead."[32] H. G. lived four more years, but his association with Olaf ended in August 1942 with this exchange of correspondence and review.

By mid-1942 the brunt of the war, which had pushed Britain near to collapse the year before, was shifting to other parts of the world, but rotating duties in Caldy's Air Raid Precautions corps and the struggle to extract two tons of potatoes and more cabbage than he could tolerate from the uncongenial acre at Simon's Field continued to define the rhythm of Olaf's war. He was drawn into the fad for "brains trusts"—the combination of information and entertainment made popular in BBC broadcasts in which a question master put sometimes serious, sometimes teasing posers to a panel of amiable and articulate know-it-alls. Olaf became one of the resident brains trustees in Liverpool, where on Monday nights he fielded topics ranging from the charms of the Liverpool accent (he admitted losing his at Abbotsholme) to systematic prejudice against people of color in local housing, recreation, employment, and education. He appeared frequently in a variant on the brains trust format, "In the Witness Box." Each week a single "witness," an expert in some field of knowledge, would have questions fired at him that demanded pointed, knowledgeable, and preferably witty replies; the witness box moved all over Merseyside and Lancashire and was sometimes taken to military bases, including American camps.[33] Between such shows and his more formal lectures to troops,

between victory gardening and a renewed effort at political campaigning begun in 1942, literary work often got squeezed out of Olaf's daily routines. But
in the last quarter of 1942, *Sirius* once again clamored for attention.

"Great rush finishing the revision," he wrote in mid-September. The book
excited him more than anything he'd written since the mid-thirties, but his confidence soon suffered a shock. Leonard Martin, whose literary judgment he
had trusted since 1928, didn't care for the novel when he looked at the draft,
so Olaf tried another reader: "Dibs has read it all, and produced some very
shrewd criticisms. He found it quite readable, which encourages me."[34] Nearing nineteen, David Stapledon had left the Royal College of Music and was
having a last visit at home before joining the navy in October. He had not taken
much interest in his father's writing before, but because music played a significant part in the education and career of Sirius, Olaf had an excuse to enlist
his son as a reader, just as he had been lately urging Mary to try *Last and First
Men*. His gratitude for David's approval was short-lived. When he sent the typescript to his longtime editor at Methuen, E.V. Rieu, he was astonished to have
it rejected. Ever since he had issued a contract for *A Modern Theory of Ethics*
in 1928, Rieu had greeted each new Stapledon manuscript eagerly, but *Sirius*,
he decided, with its unblushing depiction of an erotic relationship between the
sheepdog and his human "sister" Plaxy, was obscene.[35]

The enterprising Fredric Warburg, pleased with *Beyond the "Isms"*, which
he had published in his Searchlight series, was recruiting both established and
unconventional writers for the expanding list of Secker and Warburg. He had
stolen Lewis Mumford from Routledge and Orwell from Gollancz, acquired
most of Wells's books since 1939, and discovered the revolutionary Jomo
Kenyatta, then an anthropology student at the London School of Economics,
whose *Facing Mount Kenya* appeared from his firm in 1939. Warburg offered
to pick up *Sirius* if Stapledon would sign a multibook contract. The offer led
to a tussle between Rieu and Warburg, the outcome of which was a curious
exercise in the problem of fictional genres. The author heard a slightly different version of the argument from each party. (What Olaf himself thought can
only be guessed, since his side of the correspondence was lost when German
rockets destroyed the records of both Methuen and Secker and Warburg.)

From Rieu came word that Methuen was prepared to allow Secker and
Warburg to publish *Sirius* and to have an option on Olaf's next two novels,
but negotiations then stalled on the question of how *novel* was to be defined.
Rieu's letter of 11 December 1941 has not surfaced, but on the seventeenth
he reported to Olaf on a meeting with Warburg held at the Methuen offices:

> I insisted that in your option clause with him for two further works, the
> word novel should be used, but I agreed with Warburg that to attempt in legal

phraseology a demarkation [*sic*] between your novels and your other works on the lines of my letter of December 11th would be futile. I made it quite clear to Warburg that I myself regarded as novels only those of your books in which a definite hero and heroine figure, namely "Last Men in London", "Odd John", and "Sirius". I further suggested that we were quite prepared to leave to *you* the decision in future cases whether a book was a novel or not, if he would agree to do the same. He went away to think it over.

I am sure I need not add that I am not attempting to put a spoke in your wheel with him, but only to do my best to secure for my firm future work from you of the nature and quality of "Last and First Men", "Star Maker", "Darkness and Light" etc.; indeed I seize this opportunity of wishing all success to SIRIUS in Warburg's hands.[36]

Leaving aside the touch of Pontius Pilate in Rieu's handing over of *Sirius* to Warburg, the effort at Methuen to turn Grundyism into literary criticism made a mess out of the issue of genre. Warburg decided to accept Rieu's proposal, even though he thought his rival was taking an impractical, perhaps obstructionist, position. Warburg knew that Methuen had no legal claim on work by Stapledon, but he understood that Olaf felt a moral debt to Rieu for having launched his career. When Warburg wrote to Stapledon on the eighteenth, he poked fun at Rieu's fussy distinctions between novels and "what he described as your 'fantasy' books":

I pointed out to [Rieu] the difficulty of defining what was a novel and what was a fantasy; in view of the special character of your work. Probably both types of book would be published under the general category (or rag-bag) of fiction. He suggested that books containing characters, even though they should be of a canine nature, were definitely novels, and regarded as fantasy such works as LAST AND FIRST MEN, and STAR MAKER, which have no characters, but deal with masses of people rather than individuals. . . . We recognised here the nature of your moral obligations to Methuen, but stressed the nature of our own claims, due to our agreement to publish SIRIUS, which has many risks attached to it.[37]

Because determining the subgenres of his work was left up to the author, Olaf worried over the proper pigeonholes for all the fiction he produced for the rest of his life. He subtitled each of the two books he produced for Warburg, *Sirius* and *The Flames* (1947), "A Fantasy," although according to the gentleman's agreement between the publishers, these should have been "novels." His next publication for Methuen, *Death Into Life* (1946), dutifully bore a warning label (perhaps as legal armor against Warburg): "AUTHOR'S NOTE. This fantasy is not a novel. O.S." However, to complete the farce, in 1950, Methuen published *A Man Divided,* advertised on its dust jacket as "a novel" despite

Rieu's preference for "fantasies" (but by then Warburg had rejected *A Man Divided* under the option clause in Stapledon's contract).[38] In the long run, despite the to-do over definitions, each editor simply published what he liked. In 1942, glad as he was to have acquired a book by Stapledon, Warburg was a little frightened by *Sirius*. His letter of 18 December concluded ominously, "As for the various suggestions we may have for the emendation of some of the passages in SIRIUS, we will let you have these a little later." Between low paper stocks and the censoring that became a condition of publication, it was another year and a half before Olaf saw bound copies of *Sirius*.

While *Sirius* languished throughout 1943, Olaf's writing took an unusual, and ultimately unrewarding, detour. Near the end of 1942, he was elected to the executive committee of the British PEN. Although doubtful how often he could get to London for the monthly meetings, he was persuaded by Hermon Ould, PEN's general secretary, to try. Olaf still came to London during the war for conferences and lectures, but duties as an air-raid warden, lectures to the forces, and the vagaries of the war and the growing season made the timing of his visits unpredictable. After his election he frequently had to make excuses for missing PEN sessions. "My potatoes are not all in the ground yet, and masses of peas and beans are waiting to be sown," he pleaded in the spring of 1943. "My wife and I have no help with the work, and at this time of year it is a bit of a grind."[39] Nevertheless, the organization provided him a network of other writers, an international perspective on literature highly congenial to him, and an uncloistered view of the profession of letters. In 1943, Olaf took charge of a PEN project that united his literary, political, and philosophical interests.

That year, at the annual PEN conference, organized under the theme "Coming of Age," Olaf asked whether writers, whatever their differences of nationality, ideology, and style, had any fundamental values in common. Out of that conference came a small committee, including Mulk Raj Anand, Arthur Koestler, and the children's author Eleanor Farjeon, who referred to themselves informally as "the fundamentalists." They prepared a questionnaire about the imaginative, social, and moral aims of writers. Olaf would organize the data accumulated from the survey and write a book around the responses from PEN members; the plan was for him to draft a substantial commentary on the survey and to ask Wells, if he were not too ill, to contribute an afterword. For the only time in his career, Olaf took on the job of an editor. The idea behind the book was typically Stapledonian, an attempt to reconcile diversity and unity, the absolute claims of ethics and the idiosyncrasies of art. Like other projects toward which he was fatally drawn, however, it generated more high-flown idealism and hot air than solid discussion.

A year's work on the book on fundamental values came to nothing. Of the many brief essays submitted in response to the questionnaire, Olaf himself concluded that "a lot of the stuff is fairly poor."[40] Potential publishers were even harsher. Both Macmillan and Michael Joseph turned the book down flat; at Methuen, E. V. Rieu at first got the editorial board to look favorably on the project because Stapledon was editing it, but when Olaf sent in a sample of the contributions, Rieu's tune changed at once. While used to the "mixed bag" typical of symposia, everyone at Methuen was "profoundly disappointed" in the PEN material; apart from good essays by Koestler, Storm Jameson, and F. L. Lucas, everything else was "platitudinous, pretentious, and third class." "So many people have been so scathing," Olaf wrote to Ould, that he abandoned the editorial work without ever writing his part.[41]

His pursuit of fundamental values in the literary sphere foundered, but his political work in 1943 was recharged by an unexpected triumph. Under the terms of a wartime truce within the Tory-dominated ruling coalition, the three major parties agreed not to put up rival candidates whenever a by-election had to be held to fill a vacancy in the House of Commons. Richard Acland, head of the new Common Wealth Party, refused to be bound by the truce. Common Wealth, espousing a radical agenda to the left of Labour but still right of the Communists, prepared to challenge the government in Eddisbury, a rural Cheshire constituency so conservative that Labour had never bothered to contest it.

Under Acland's leadership Common Wealth yoked Puritan zeal to utopian socialism in imagining a prosperous and unprivileged Britain. Olaf kept his distance from the doctrinal elements of Christianity. ("Faith? In the strict sense of the word I have no faith, and need none," he wrote in a volume on religion to which both he and Acland contributed.[42]) But Acland was not interested in an orthodox Christianity that made no waves. In Common Wealth's new Britain a recumbent state religion would yield to a society inspired by the political teachings of a rebellious Jesus.[43] Olaf's attraction to such a spiritually grounded politics was accentuated by the nearness of the Cheshire district to his home in Caldy and by the fact that the CW candidate, Warrant Officer John Loverseed, a handsome, energetic RAF pilot who had flown against the Luftwaffe, seemed the very embodiment of the Wellsian man of the future. When Loverseed, defying all expectations, won the by-election, Olaf and Agnes Stapledon hosted a large celebratory luncheon for him in Liverpool. Loverseed's election "offered a fresh inspiration in political life at a time when it was greatly needed," Olaf proclaimed.[44]

The possibility of a democratic uprising of workers and middle class voters spearheaded by Common Wealth led Olaf to raise money for and speak on behalf of the party throughout Merseyside from 1943 until the end of the war.

In major speeches at Wrexham in May 1943 and at St. Helens in June, he drummed up new members by alternating economic analysis of the chronic "social distress and disorder" in Tory Britain with passionate advocacy of the principles of common ownership, full representative democracy, and world unity on which Acland built his movement. Labour, Stapledon said, had gone stagnant and written off the middle class, and he welcomed Common Wealth's stand for the complete divestiture of empire and the immediate installation of William Beveridge's famous 1942 report outlining a plan for full employment, universal health care, and a national minimum income. The "Beveridge Plan" had, to Churchill's discomfort, seized the popular imagination and "Beveridge in Full Now" became the rallying cry of Common Wealth. The slogan, Olaf emphasized to the crowds at Wrexham, advertised the new party's commitment to winning the peace as well as the war.[45]

The Common Wealth crusade kept Stapledon from feeling entirely useless at a time when his literary life appeared to have atrophied. Through the spring and summer of 1943 came news from Methuen and Penguin that most of his old books were out of print with no prospect of reissues. Meanwhile *Sirius* still sat in the Secker and Warburg offices. On the day he spoke at Wrexham, he wrote sadly to his daughter "of not having really done the things I set myself to do. A spot more success would give me a new lease of life." By associating himself publicly with Acland's party, Olaf hoped to be in the vanguard of a new society, perhaps redeeming a lackluster career. Working for Common Wealth reaffirmed old convictions about striking a balance between being and doing, between the isolated life of the artist and the communal obligations of the citizen. He wanted to avoid the extremes: "The vice of the thought-respecter is barren subtlety. The vice of the action-respecter is the Hemingway pose."[46] Although Common Wealth faded dramatically as a political force in 1945, in 1943 and 1944 it represented, Olaf thought, the union of moral integrity and practical politics. Acland, thrilled by the victory in Cheshire and impressed by the evangelical energy with which Stapledon had adopted the cause, made a stunning proposal. When the war ended and a general election was called, Common Wealth wanted to be ready to contest as many seats as possible. Would Olaf agree to stand as the CW candidate for Wirral?

He was tempted and considered exchanging an unsatisfactory career in writing for a doubtful one in politics. "I am going through agonies of indecision over this problem of parliamentary candidature," he told Mary. To a Common Wealth supporter he confided that he had once before in his life agreed to stand as an independent candidate in Wirral and regretted it; he was worried that he, just like Common Wealth, had a reputation for "woolly idealism" and wondered whether the party wouldn't do better to cast against type.[47] Finally he gave Acland his decision:

> I appreciate your argument about the need for known people to come out as candidates, but it is useless their doing so if this would involve giving up work for which they are better fitted for the sake of work in which they might very well do more harm than good. In spite of what you say I am convinced that in my case candidature would involve a complete switch over to a new kind of work. Being what I am, I could not do the job *at all* without giving up everything else in a forlorn effort to make myself into a very mediocre politician. . . . CW should for the present be particularly careful to avoid having candidates like me. Rightly or wrongly the movement is sometimes criticised for being too much concerned with generalities and not enough with the detail of politics. Therefore it should strengthen itself by putting up thoroughly "practical" men.[48]

A further appeal from Acland did not sway Olaf to reconsider. He knew his limitations. Thirty years earlier he had said essentially the same things about himself, and in essentials he was unchanged: "I am over keen on broad generalizations. In haranguing people, for instance, I always get hold of one idea and run it to death, because it seems better to give people a vivid idea to carry away, even if it is grossly unqualified, rather than to qualify it and wrap it up to such an extent that they lose its general meaning."[49]

Relinquishing dreams of Westminster, Olaf redoubled his efforts to support the party both as chairman of the Merseyside branch of CW and in articles for the monthly *Common Wealth Review.* He remained a publicist, a cheerleader, a true believer. Before the war ended he produced his outline for a new social order, *Seven Pillars of Peace,* one of the sixpenny pamphlets issued by Common Wealth. But his philosophical temper, preferring the big picture to the fine details, was inimical to a life in politics, as it had kept even his best works of fiction from achieving the thickly textured human interest or the large audience they kept approaching but missing. His capacity for preaching and teaching, whether in a WEA course, on a military base, or at a protest rally, was the genuine article. He would not have made a happy politician or a scholarly professor or a very polished novelist, but he knew how to kindle enthusiasms and how to open people's eyes to a vision. Others would have to refine and channel the vivid ideas he awoke and craft institutions that could house his vision. But he was still capable of achieving a modest if not always consistent fictional art.

When Arthur Koestler asked him to write a piece for an international anthology of utopian fiction, Olaf worked up a 10,000-word fantasy that distilled his ambivalent feelings about practical politics. "Old Man in New World," set in the 1990s, thirty years after the establishment of a world state, is partly utopian dialogue, partly spectacle. It features an eighty-year-old former social activist who lived through the bad old days that culminated in the Second World War and a young pilot who flies him from the North of England to London in a sleek two-seater for a festival celebrating "the First Generation of the New World."[50] The situation duplicates many an airplane ride Olaf had been given by RAF pilots, some of them barely out of their teens, when he was on the lecture circuit. The old man both envies and resents the easeful life of the new generation of utopians who, not having known the misery of the century's earlier decades, are amused by the old revolutionary's belief in the importance of discipline. And the irreverence with which the young treat the government— including their restoration of the medieval tradition of the licensed fool, who mocks the world president's televised speeches—offends the old man's sober sense of propriety. What he sees in London is not the utopia *he* would have built, but, the story implies, the old man's fervor was the necessary catalyst for revolution even if he could not in his heart feel comfortable with the details of the new society.

When Koestler read the novella in the summer of 1943, he thought it "very moving, outstandingly good," but of the other contributions he received all but two—by Storm Jameson and Frantisek Langer—were worthless. Reluctantly he canceled the project, thinking its failure "symbolical" of the war's effect on utopian thought.[51] In October, Hermon Ould, secretary of PEN, asked to see the typescript, with a view to having it published separately. "If you think it could be used as a P.E.N. book, I shall be glad to have it off my hands," Olaf told him. Ould liked "Old Man" so much that he got in touch with Stanley Unwin, and within two weeks Olaf had a contract. "I thought the climax of your prophecy extraordinarily moving and original," Ould wrote, "and I think it is the first time I have ever seen the case for humour put so tellingly." Chagrined that reviewers so often found his work humorless, Olaf treasured Ould's appreciation of the unusual combination of witty clowning and utopian grandeur in the narrative. "I am much encouraged by your remarks about the story," he wrote, "particularly so because I sometimes wondered whether it overreached itself."[52]

The handsome chapbook Allen and Unwin issued in June 1944, with a second impression in 1945, was the best showcase Olaf ever had for any of his rare efforts at short fiction. It was overlooked by many reviewers, who concentrated on *Sirius,* which happened to appear in the same week, but the little criticism that eventually surfaced confirmed Koestler's guess that this was not an auspicious time for utopian fiction. "Big and bland and shadowless like most utopias," yawned the *New Statesman.* The *Times Literary Supplement* indulged in a playful putdown: "It can be recommended to any clergyman in want of material for a sermon out of the ordinary way." "Old Man in New World" is actually more richly shadowed and uncertain than such comments suggest, and Lilian Bowes-Lyon told Olaf it was "more important than *volumes* at present being written." The author could only sigh, "It's queer how reviewers miss my point."[53]

Sirius aroused much more attention and controversy, even though it had been censored before publication. Roger Senhouse, who edited the manuscript for Secker and Warburg, first had Olaf shorten the book by removing some geographical detail about North Wales and Wirral. If the author, recalling the textures of Joyce's Dublin, was sorry to sacrifice the local color, the further cuts demanded in the description of lovemaking between Sirius and Plaxy were more troubling. The two existing manuscript versions are not coy about either Sirius's "surging desire" or the eagerness of Plaxy, who "threw off all the restraint of conventional morality and indulged her sweet unnatural passion to the fullest extent that was possible." Plaxy tells the narrator, her future husband Robert, that "in this intercourse with a non-human creature she had passed beyond the extreme limit of tolerated acts. 'I am indeed a bitch, a bitch!'" Senhouse told Stapledon that this passage would have to be more indirect. Olaf threw a veil over the intimacy between the dog and the young woman, referring vaguely to "a manner of life which some readers may more easily condemn than understand." The narrator is left to hint at what cannot be told in full: "At a later date both Plaxy and Sirius told me much about their life together at this time; but though after our marriage she urged me to publish all the facts for the light they throw on Sirius, consideration for her feelings and respect for the conventions of contemporary society force me to be reticent."[54]

The revision tweaked the censor while leaving no doubt about the nature of the intimacy, but Senhouse accepted the alterations in mid-July 1943. The firm remained skittish about possible charges of indecency and, to Olaf's annoyance, refused him an advance. Not until a month after publication in June 1944 did he get his first check for *Sirius*.[55] While no mildly perceptive reader had trouble imagining what was implied in the narrative, one subtext of *Sirius* has remained obscure. The scandalous love affair between the superdog and the young woman successfully screened a mundane human story of misplaced love. In a hand-bound volume left for her heirs at her death in December 1989, Evelyn Gibson preserved the original pencil manuscript of *Sirius* Olaf had given her forty-five years earlier as a keepsake. Its explicit detail, she wrote, made it unpublishable. But while the unexpected existence of the first draft of *Sirius* is of great interest, Evelyn's note about the imaginative source of the novel is more remarkable: "He said that he had drawn on our tangled relationship & transmuted it, and that he had based Plaxy on me."[56] The opening phrases of

Sirius, spoken by the narrator, take on a new dimension as the "I" oscillates between narrator and author, reverberating with Olaf's troubled extramarital love in 1941 and 1942 when the book was being written. "Plaxy and I had been lovers; rather uneasy lovers."

Plaxy (like Evelyn) has large blue-green eyes and the broad face, small nose, and pointed chin of a cat. Her "ample but decisive" mouth, "auburn, faintly carroty" hair, dextrous hand movements, and cool, sparkling voice all were derived from Evelyn. Robert, the narrator of *Sirius,* uses a lover's terms of endearment to describe Plaxy, "at once cat, fawn, dryad, elf, witch."[57] And Olaf transferred some of his own intellectual attributes to Sirius: the sequence of the dog's allegiances from Browning to Hardy to the early Eliot to Wells's encyclopedic works of the twenties and thirties recapitulate the evolution of the author's tastes; Sirius, like Olaf, is a provincial, never entirely at home in the metropolis or the university precinct; the dog's waking vision of "all living things, led by man, crusading gallantly against indifferent or hostile fate, doomed in the end to absolute defeat, but learning to exult in the battle, and snatching much delight before the end" is the core of Stapledon's literary imagination. Even the bitterness of the handless Sirius, railing against humans who shun "manual" labor, including writers who can't use script properly and rely on "the cruder activity of pressing typewriter keys," reflects Olaf's contempt for the typewriter and his vanity about his own exquisite handwriting.[58]

The "strange triangle" of Plaxy-Sirius-Robert in the book's final chapters is reminiscent of—but does not duplicate—the Evelyn-Olaf-Agnes trio. It is not an exact facsimile because there is no Agnes-figure in the novel's triangle. Both Sirius and Robert are aspects of Olaf; when Sirius dies at the narrative's end, Plaxy returns to a more conventional life with Robert—but Robert represents an alternative version of Olaf himself. The marriage of Robert and Plaxy—mentioned in passing—is impossible in Olaf's actual universe, in which Agnes is the immovable center, but fictionally he accomplishes what actuality finally denied him: having his cake and eating it too. Looked at from another angle, the conclusion, in which the unsatisfactory lover, Sirius-Olaf, is removed so that Plaxy-Evelyn may settle down to a secure, loving, and "normal" marriage, was Olaf's last wishful gift to Evelyn—the permanent relationship that he himself could not offer her and that eluded her for the rest of her life.

The book's first readers did not divine a coded human love affair behind the Plaxy-Sirius connection—who could have guessed it?—but the first reviews of the bizarre story were highly favorable. Olaf was cheered by the *Times Literary Supplement*'s choice of *Sirius* as "Novel of the Week," full of gleaming vision and spiritual mystery, its critic said, and laced with social irony worthy of Montesquieu's *Persian Letters* and Goldsmith's *Citizen of the World.* Quick praise came also from the *Daily Telegraph,* the *Sunday Times* of London, the

Daily Worker, and the *Manchester Guardian.* In mid-June, Olaf wrote happily, "*Sirius* has had a lot [of reviews], all favourable, though generally with some bit of criticism. Maybe the damning is still to come."[59]

Plenty of critics soon turned up with reservations, from the gentle to the indignant to the uproarious, and there were a few loud damns. "I must confess, skilful though the story is, it makes me extremely uncomfortable," wrote Pamela Hansford Johnson. John Betjeman thought Stapledon ordinarily a "miraculous" writer, but "this time he has given himself something too difficult to do." For Robert Lynd, *Sirius* was a nightmare, "repellent as the exhibitions of freak sideshows in old fair grounds." At the *New Statesman,* Sirius's literary infatuation with Hardy and Eliot provoked "a snigger" from the incredulous Philip Toynbee. *Punch*'s critic wrote more in sorrow than anger of a novel that never rose above its technical ingenuity:

> For something, to the reader's astonishment, goes wrong, and the tale misfires; the pathos is theoretical, not real; the tragedy of *Sirius* remains a diagram drawn on the blackboard. Why a book so well-found in many ways should go down almost ignominiously is not the mystery it may seem. Detachment, which is often a virtue, is fatal here. Mr. STAPLEDON takes no sides, he tells his story logically, and to him the case of poor *Sirius* is no more than "an unfortunate situation," an ingenious hypothesis to be worked out correctly. Unfortunately he also works it out without those brilliant intellectual flights that take the place of emotion in pieces of this kind. Fantasy may be bloodless, but then it must fly.[60]

In Olaf's mind the negative reviews came to overshadow the early raves. After the war he sent a copy of *Sirius* to Aage Marcus in Copenhagen and was pleased by his old friend's warm response. "I am so glad you liked my *Sirius,* because it is one of my favourites. It had on the whole a very bad press. In fact it was reviled by nearly all the critics."[61] Two years after the novel's publication, he remembered, inaccurately, a general critical revulsion, but at the time it was Philip Toynbee's lengthy, derisive review that particularly galled him. As he told Mary, "Like several other reviewers he failed to see that it was meant to be funny in quite a lot of places. Also he got the whole aim of the book wrong, supposing that the social criticism was the main point, whereas of course the main point was to work out the implications of the original idea—a non-human yet "human" personality. I do think some of the reviewers have been obtuse."[62]

Stapledon seldom replied to his critics, but he started a correspondence with Toynbee over the review in the *New Statesman.* Toynbee brushed aside the protest that the book had been mistreated. He was disinclined to judge fiction "by any standard except its artistic quality." Acknowledging the author's contention that *Sirius* was a fantasy rather than a novel, he still maintained there was "confusion between its fantastic nature, and the use you made of the dog's eye view to make serious moral judgments on the human race." Typically, reviewers who said unkind things about *Sirius* sugared the criticism with praise for Stapledon's earlier fiction. Not Toynbee. He concluded his letter with an incidental snub to *Last and First Men,* "one of the most depressing books I've ever read."[63]

Perhaps Olaf asked for it by challenging Toynbee's review. Other, unsolicited letters treated *Sirius* royally. From Julian Huxley he heard, "It is something that I think only you could have done—or would have done!—or both. Anyhow it brings home in a unique and arresting way the uniqueness of man, and also of individual minds treading out beyond the everyday." Eleanor Farjeon found it "piercing & valuable" and wondered, like many readers since, "Why is Plaxy called Plaxy?" Jack Haldane thought the book "far more plausibly futuristic" than anything else Stapledon had written, and anticipated a day when human beings would "make animals into colleagues rather than pets, food producers, or beasts of burden." A characteristically insightful note came from Naomi Mitchison on Stapledon's narrative rhythms: "It was like you always are, sometimes jogging along like a nice reasonable scientific paper, and sometimes suddenly becoming very moving." Arthur Koestler, reserving only the scene in which Sirius sings canine tunes in an East End church, called it "almost a great book" and admired "both the courage and execution." "[I] hope with all my heart that it will find the great success it deserves and the necessary paper for a dozen reprints."[64]

A dozen was far too much to hope for, even though sales triumphed over the mixed reviews. The first printing of 4,000 copies sold out within a month, and a second printing of 2,250 was nearly gone by the autumn. In the spring of 1945, when the second printing was exhausted, Olaf made an accounting: "Sirius has brought me something over £300. There will be more if they can get more paper for a third edition." But, as had become the pattern with Stapledon's books, no further editions appeared until after his death.[65]

One of Olaf's friends did not live to see *Sirius* published. Leo Myers read a draft in 1942 and, knowing that "Methuens have funked your book," urged him to compromise by making cuts. But he and Olaf began to drift apart in 1943; others of Leo's friends also felt him withdrawing from them. Lilian Bowes-Lyon, a mutual friend, talked with Olaf about the situation, but they could find no way to get through to Leo.[66] His periodic depressions grew worse. His letters veered between crabbed attacks and abject apologies. "You are certainly as *kind* a man as ever lived," he wrote when asking Olaf to be his literary executor, an office he declined. Repeatedly, Leo praised the vigor, tact, and charm of Olaf's hundreds of letters to him, which he often reread. "Your letters are God-like. Such patience, such wisdom,—so unanswerable in their majestic rightness." Of Olaf's talks to the forces, he wrote, "If your lectures are like your letters they must do a helluva good." In horror of biographers, Myers asked all his friends to burn his letters. Olaf could not bring himself to destroy more than a handful, but when Leo, without consulting his friend's wishes, put almost all Olaf's voluminous correspondence into the furnace, it made the single greatest loss of literary and philosophical papers from Stapledon's mature years.[67] On the night of 7–8 April 1944, Myers took an overdose of sleeping pills and was found dead in the morning.

Stapledon enjoyed writing letters, and he had learned to be more concise than in the days of his epistolary courtship. He thought again, as he had at Abbotsholme and in the First World War, of compiling a volume of imaginary letters, perhaps under the stimulus of C. S. Lewis's "priceless" *Screwtape Letters,* which he savored as "both witty and wise, in spite of their Christian orthodoxy."[68] The Indian writer Mulk Raj Anand proposed over lunch that they collaborate on a collection of letters, an idea whose immediate appeal never got beyond casual brainstorming.[69] Sometime during the war Olaf began a "postal discussion" between middle age and youth in the form of an imaginary correspondence between a civilian and a soldier, named simply "Senior" and "Junior." Although "Letters to a Militiaman" was abandoned after eight installments, the junior correspondent's self-portrait of "conflicting selves," alternating between moods of savagery and enlightenment, reads like an early study for *A Man Divided.* A second epistolary experiment, also unfinished, was attempted shortly after the war. In "Letters to the Future," addressed to the author's unborn great-grandson, the aging Stapledon left a spiritual legacy inscribed "to those who will be young when we are dead." These letters came out of the same impulse to make contact with the end of the century in "Old Man in New World" and in a book originally intended as a school text, finished in 1944, but not published until 1946 as *Youth and Tomorrow.*[70]

Before 1944 ended, Olaf endured his most nerve-racking moments of the war. PEN International's annual summer conference was to celebrate the three-hundredth anniversary of Milton's tract on freedom of publication, *Areopagitica;* E. M. Forster had agreed to preside at the conference, and Olaf to chair its opening session. But in that August, Hitler unleashed the first of his secret weapons on London. Olaf's diary records with simple eloquence his arrival at the congress:

>Aug 21 London—Flying bombs!
>Aug 22 Areopagitica Conf
>2:30 EM Forster, WOS

Although not as deadly as everyone feared, the V1 "flying bombs," buzzing, sputtering, and falling day and night, gave Londoners a deeper scare than anything since the Battle of Britain three years earlier. In early August the executive committee of PEN gathered in the midst of the attack and debated canceling the congress, but Olaf believed that it was an important gesture of inner freedom not to abandon London. Later he admitted that his "few very unpleasant nights" during the VI attacks were psychologically more terrifying than any he had spent in Liverpool or relatively tranquil Wirral, or than the later assault of the V2 rockets.[71]

His fears for his own safety were less than his constant anxiety about Mary and David. His daughter, doing war work in London for the Board of Trade and as a telephone operator while studying for medical school examinations, was living in an old building, and Olaf worried about a collapse if a bomb should fall nearby. When his son, trained as a Navy radio mechanic, was granted a final leave before being shipped out in July 1943, he excused himself from a scheduled PEN meeting in London. Olaf, usually reserved in his public expressions of sentiment, was moved to write, "It's extraordinary how small and inadequate one feels when one's son blooms into gold anchors and wings."[72] As a father he wavered between paternal chest-puffing and concern over David's military service. After visiting troops in Scotland a couple of months later, he confessed to Mary his worries as well as his pride in her brother: "I do wish we could hear from Dibs. Ten days with the forces has made me feel that he (such a lone wolf) must loathe being sardined with others."[73]

By the time of the Areopagitica meeting, David had been on a destroyer in the Mediterranean for a year in the Italian campaign. Near the end of 1944 he nearly died. A most uncanny anticipation of reality occurs in *Sirius* when Elizabeth Trelone learns of a disaster involving her son, Maurice:

> It so happened that on the table there was an unopened newspaper. She picked it up and opened it. "BRITISH CRUISER SUNK," said the main headline. It was the ship on which Maurice was serving. Owing to the fact that the Germans were the first to announce the sinking, the Admiralty had been forced to break their rule and publish the information *before* the next of kin had been told of the casualties.[74]

Maurice survived. In December 1944, six months after *Sirius* appeared in print, the destroyer *Aldenham,* to which Dibs Stapledon was assigned, was torpedoed and sank off the coast of Italy; for almost an hour David swam in the wintry waters, hoping for rescue. He was among the fortunate third of the ship's crew to survive the explosion and the exposure to the cold.

About that time, Olaf began writing a fantasy about the death of a young RAF rear gunner and the six fellow crewmen of his bomber. The transference of his naval radio-mechanic son to the RAF gunner is indirectly acknowledged in the final pages of *Death Into Life* in an authorial afterword on parenthood that recalls the departure of David for the navy:

> We shall not forget his going. With untried strength he set out to face the horror that the elders had made. When his ship was sunk, and he, among the few survivors, was taken from the water, no mystic message told us. And when at last we learned of it, we went about our affairs unchanged; but when we thought of him in the water, it was with bated breath. We were awed, and vaguely shamed, by our continued good fortune in a tormented world. Where millions are struck down, those who are spared shudder.[75]

Olaf's mingled sense of luck, guilt, and mortality, an old theme for him, going back to *Latter-Day Psalms* at the dawn of the First World War, returned in force as the world staggered through its second great war.

16

GROWING OLD IN SPRINGTIME

1945–1946

AS THE WAR MOVED toward its fiery ends in Dresden and Berlin, in Auschwitz
and Hiroshima, and as people in England prepared to resume their lives and
replace their government, time and change were on Olaf's mind. Outwardly,
the passage of years seemed to have affected him little. Lean and light on his
feet, his blond hair faded to ash, his upturned nose still hinting at a never-quite-
outgrown adolescence, he continued to be mistaken by strangers for a man of
forty. An aspiring novelist who met him at the end of the war was astounded
many years later to be reminded that she was a quarter of a century younger
than Olaf. "The boyish look was more than a look. He was one of those people
who can be the age of whoever he's with. I never considered in my mind that
I was of a different generation."[1] People who knew or guessed just how old
he was began calling him "elfin," as though his age were irrelevant. But the
image he projected was not the reality he experienced. He felt his years.

"I am now 58, and decidedly older than I was at 50, but not yet seriously
broken down," he joked in 1944.[2] Privately, he looked ahead and saw not many
years left before body and mind grew unreliable. "I shall finger my memories
in public and repeat my anecdotes," he wrote of a senility he would never undergo. Looking backwards, he sought the continuities from the child to the
man, from the gallery of Victorian memory to the rubble-strewn present:

> But how I span the days, the years! Yesterday's voices, yesterday's greetings
> and disputations, echo now in my memory. Far behind these, and behind the
> bomb-blasts of our present warfare, I remember the shell-bursts of another
> war, now laid up in history. And farther still, I remember being a schoolboy

with an ink-splashed Eton collar and a passion for model boats. Did I, the
very I of to-day, wear that collar, feel that passion? Surely that was a very
different being, whose experience I have somehow inherited, like an old
photograph album full of impossible uncles and aunts, grandparents and great-
grandparents, all seemingly in fancy dress. I of to-day nurse no passion for
model boats; I am for philosophy and for mankind and all high questions.
And yet, and yet even now, with my hair grey, when boys sail their trim or
their dowdy craft on the park lake, I linger to watch them. That child lives in
me still; I was and am that child. Yes, and a still earlier child. I, and no other,
as a very little child, left a wet patch on the knee of a doting visitor in a
Victorian drawing-room. Oh yes, it was I, for I remember it.[3]

As he aged, the autobiographical urge grew in him, although he rarely sustained it beyond momentary retrospection in published and unpublished writings. A renewed interest in seeing and coming to terms with himself may have
helped overcome his reluctance to sit for a portrait in time for his sixtieth birthday. In fact, to sit for two portraits. A stiff-looking figure executed in oils early
in 1946 by G. B. H. Holland was exhibited that year, along with portraits of
other notable Liverpudlians, at the Bluecoat Chambers gallery.[4] Holland's gray
and reserved Stapledon offers no hint of the onetime Peter Pan, no glimpse of
humor or charm beneath the patrician stare; the complacency of the formal
image suggests, inaccurately, a mummified professor. After four decades in
Simon's Field, the picture now hangs in Liverpool University, where the
subject never held a permanent post, as a memorial to the city's greatest
philosopher.

A more unconventional and interesting portrait was begun in 1945, largely
at Agnes Stapledon's instigation. The opportunity came during a holiday in a
favorite spot in the Lake District that during the war replaced the foreign va-
cations she and Olaf used to enjoy. In the 1930s, Richard Hall had converted
a disused gunpowder works on Elterwater, near Kendal, at the southern gateway to the Lakes, into a holiday park with a small hotel built on stone pillars
from the old manufacturing buildings. Scattered around the grounds was an
array of simple bungalows and wood-floored tents. As it was in the 1940s,
Langdale Estate was not a fancy resort, but Hall ensured a diverse and interesting clientele with accommodations geared to a variety of incomes and tastes;
guests could have a simply furnished room in the Pillar Hotel, or rough it under canvas or in a dormitory-style lodge, or park their own mobile home in
one of the deftly concealed spaces for caravans. Even in wartime an ample
supply of butter, cream, eggs, and bacon produced on the estate's farm made
Langdale seem a gourmand's paradise to protein-hungry visitors; many returned
regularly, not only for the food and scenery but for the conversations, which
the proprietor took pains to orchestrate.[5]

Hall, a reclusive and irascible man, prided himself on a loyal group of writers and intellectuals who had discovered his informal retreat; around them and a small colony of painters and sculptors who had taken up semipermanent residence at Langdale, including the German expatriate Kurt Schwitters renowned for his *Merz* collages, Hall formed a pastoral salon in which discussions of art, politics, and ideas alternated with boating trips, rambles through the hills, and communal meals in the intimate dining room of the Pillar. Often there was an evening discussion in the drawing room chaired by one of the guests. Any visitor with a special talent shared it: a pianist was asked to play after dinner; a professor of agriculture lectured on soil preparation for the home gardener; a ballet dancer pirouetted on the lawn.

Whenever Olaf came, invariably in the autumn and sometimes in spring or summer for a few days, Hall would ask for a talk. One of the Langdale regulars, the painter Gwynneth Alban-Davis, watched Olaf leaning casually against the mantelpiece, jacket off and tie loosened from his russet shirt, holding forth on the Soviet Union on one occasion, on the spiritual evolution of humanity on another, and sometime after August 1945 on atomic power. After a while he would encourage everyone to voice an opinion, sometimes picking out an obviously shy person to draw into the debate. "It was his gift," Gwynneth wrote, "to make us feel that we were taking part in a fascinating talk among friends, though obviously it was being directed by an expert."[6]

Gwynneth was young, adventuresome, still learning her craft, and strapped for money. She had talked her way into setting up quarters in a decrepit, one-room caravan that Hall let her fix up and inhabit in exchange for designing postcards and brochures for Langdale. There she came to know one of the local artists, Hilde Goldschmidt, pupil of the Austrian expressionist Oskar Kokotschka and a refugee from the Nazi occupation. "Pimpo," as Gwynneth called Goldschmidt, was in as desperate a financial plight as the younger woman. She supported herself by sewing fur gloves and doing landscapes and portraits for tourists, and Agnes Stapledon did not hesitate to work on her husband's economic conscience to get him to agree to a portrait. Olaf, like his father Willie, could never resist an appeal of this kind and sat for Hilde Goldschmidt in January and April 1945. The portrait was completed only after a final sitting in the summer of 1948, but the result was the most distinctive of the images of Stapledon rendered by photographers and painters.[7] Bright pastel splashes suggest the combination of energy and exuberance that fooled many people into thinking him younger. But the face of Goldschmidt's Olaf, androgynous and unworldly, is not notably youthful; the eyes are wide and melancholy under brows arched in faint perplexity, the mouth firmly shut and downturned. The brilliant coloration hints at an incandescent spirit contained by the cool surface of philosophical detachment. The figure looks less like the

24. The Hilde Goldschmidt portrait, 1948.
Courtesy Abbot Hall Art Gallery, Kendal, Cumbria, U.K.

Divine Boy of his and other people's myths than like an embodiment of the aloof and wry narrative voice heard in his cosmic histories.

Not designed to flatter, the portrait is a vivid interpretation of the inner man. Olaf, his championing of the Unit One artists in 1934 notwithstanding, liked the idea of experimental technique in painting more than the actuality. On the day he first saw how Goldschmidt had viewed him, he pounded on Gwynneth Alban-Davis's door and stood, hands to hips, in a posture of mock-indignation:

> "Gwynneth! I want a direct answer to a question, yes or no!"
> "What is it?" I asked with some hesitation. Who was I to answer Olaf's questions?
> "Is my hair blue?"
> Ah, I thought, the portrait. Pimpo's portraits often upset her subjects.
> "Well," I said, considering how to put it, "it all depends on the light. It can be any colour."
> He shrugged in resignation. "I might have known the artists would stick together!"
> "Don't you like your portrait?" I asked.
> He leant forward confidentially. "If you want to know," he whispered, "I look like an old lady with a blue rinse."[8]

He laughed as he walked away, embarrassed perhaps by the matronly look Goldschmidt had given him, but she had caught something of the humane and saintly Olaf whose mind inhabited regions where tragic vision yielded up calm acceptance. Owned by the Abbot Hall Gallery in Kendal, the Goldschmidt portrait is the only image of Stapledon, apart from the nine photographic poses done by Howard Coster stored at the National Portrait Gallery, in a public museum.[9]

When he started sitting for his portraits, Olaf was writing the autobiographical fragments that became the seven Interludes and the After-Piece of the 1946 fantasy *Death Into Life*. To the seventh and most moving of the Interludes he gave the title "Growing Old in Spring-Time." He watches spring come to the vegetable garden he and Agnes tended at Simon's Field all through the war: potato-shoots running dotted lines down the beds; pea seedlings nosing their way through the soil; infant cabbages in the cold frame awaiting transplantation; lusty stalks of leafy young rhubarb grabbing for light. "Spring is painting the earth's old face young again," and the two aging gardeners stand warming themselves in the pale sun with a momentary illusion of returning youth. Then, as they stoop to work the earth, their backs stiffen, their muscles go limp, their eyes cannot get the birds in focus at the garden's edge. More troubling than physical wear and tear is the loss of mental suppleness. "Youth's gift of sudden and reshaping insight comes no more," the speaker realizes. The "dying fires of my body and the cravings of this withering ego" still clamor for attention, but no longer seem compelling. He feels a purging of desire, a curbing of power "as though in readiness for some grave impending event." The great sleep is coming, and the speaker is almost ready to welcome it.[10]

25. Growing old in springtime: Olaf and Agnes at Langdale.
Courtesy John D. Stapledon.

By the end of May 1945 he had finished *Death Into Life,* and the clang-
ing bells of V-E Day, 8 May, sound throughout the latter half of the book. Even
for Stapledon this fantasy had only the slenderest narrative line, however. The
promising first chapter details the mission of a seven-man British heavy bomber
blasted apart over Germany, its entire crew incinerated. The central consciousness, that of the nineteen-year-old rear gunner, then undergoes absorption into

the composite spirit of his six dead colleagues. The disembodied seven join still larger communal entities: they are linked to all the dead of the war, then to the dead of the previous war, to the universal "Spirit of Man," and at last to the Cosmic Spirit. "It is rather different from my other books," Olaf told Aage Marcus before *Death Into Life* was published, "and is mainly concerned with the survival or annihilation of the individual after death."[11]

The preoccupation with life after death and the flavor of the occult do represent new emphases of his older years, but the problem with *Death Into Life* is that it is not nearly different enough from his earlier fictions. As in *Last and First Men* and *Star Maker,* there is an impulse to construct myth in the form of a secular Genesis and Apocalypse, but as the narrative ascends into the stratosphere it turns stale with old images Stapledon had already worked hard in his more vigorous cosmic histories. Even its memorable description of *homo sapiens* as "a mere pterodactyl of the spirit," flapping its way awkwardly toward extinction in its second world war in twenty-five years, is a symbol invented fifteen years earlier in *Odd John.*[12] What was most new about *Death Into Life* was not its ideas but its biographical candor. Before trying it on a publisher, Olaf asked Mary and David to approve the sections concerned with them, since he had never before portrayed them directly in his work. Then, because clause 18 of his contract with Secker and Warburg specified that "I submit books with conversation in them to Secker, and others to Methuen," *Death Into Life* went off late in the spring of 1945 to his editor at Methuen, E. V. Rieu.[13]

The spring of 1945 was a time of rejuvenation, with victory in Europe declared and bright prospects for a socialist government in Britain. When a general election was called, Olaf campaigned for both Common Wealth and Labour candidates. "We know at last the kind of world we want," he said from the stump. "Every human being must have full opportunity not merely to have a good time but to be fully human: full health, worthy work, adequate leisure, broad humane education, no mental crippling." Bold new policies were required, and Britain needed to take heart from Russian economic experiments as well as to take warning from Stalin's suppression of liberty.[14] Striking an old theme, he insisted that democratic principles would remain only hollow and hypocritical assertions unless Britain moved decisively to surrender its colonial possessions. And on a new note, he urged people to look under their noses for evidence of homegrown suppression of freedoms.

As the son of a shipowner, Olaf was powerfully drawn to the issue of living conditions for people of color in Liverpool. The commercial successes of the city in the nineteenth century had been tainted, he knew, by complicity in the slave trade. The crime was an old one, and much of that wealth had evaporated, but the effects persisted into the present, as he pointed out at a brains trust on racial prejudice sponsored by the League of Coloured Peoples. People of color were ghettoized in Liverpool's South End, and their places of recreation were segregated; education for their children was even more inadequate than what was available for the poor Irish; and rates of pay for sailors continued to be scaled to ethnic and racial identity.[15] Olaf's earliest prose writings had been tinged with the racism of Anglo-Saxon manifest destiny, and although his later multiracial utopians in *Odd John* demote "the White Man's trivial superiority," there were still references to the "nigger-brown" complexion of Ng-Gunko and the unfortunately named infant Sambo.[16] But in the last five years of his life, Olaf, whose daughter had fallen in love with an Indian and his son with a Sicilian, became a cosmopolitan in more than theory. The culminating visionary passage in *Death Into Life* celebrates the "multiple flesh" of the global human community as the "spirit of Man" yearns for union with "those dark-skinned and still unfree dwellers in the great peninsula" of India and with "the darkest peoples, who now uneasily stir in their long servitude."[17] The fantasy of racial integration and the brains trust on prejudice, along with later speeches on racism in the United States and South Africa, suggest new moral concerns of Stapledon's final years.

What he could observe of cruelty and degradation at first hand in the slums of Liverpool or London was augmented by the horrific revelations at the end of the European phase of the war. With Graham White, the Liberal M.P. for Birkenhead, he viewed films of what British soldiers had encountered when they liberated the Nazi camps. Those visual images of Buchenwald were never erased until his death. In *The Opening of the Eyes* he has the Star Maker, whose artistry he had once mythologized, challenge the agnostic piety that everything that is in the universe is right:

> But if your nails were being torn back, or the nerves of your teeth drilled for sheer malice; or if you were compelled to watch this happen to your dearest, would you then imagine that such devilry was all part of cosmical poetry? Would you sit back in your royal box applauding the aesthetic rightness of her agony? Were the masters of Buchenwald my ministers? Did I, for my poetry's perfection, hunt down negroes for slaves, and pack them in the slave-ships? Did I send children into the mines, congest the slums, create the atom bomb? Is all the frustration and agony of all the worlds in all the aeons mere imagery for my poetry?[18]

The spring's paradoxes did not fade in the summer. The massive Labour victory in early July revealed the depth of disaffection from the Conservative effort to resume things as they used to be in 1939. But Common Wealth's failure to win more than a single seat (Richard Acland himself was turned out) did not presage the great radical break with traditional politics Olaf had hoped for.

Meanwhile, the defeat of Nazism in Europe still left the war against Japan un-
resolved; in May 1945 people were resigned to another year and a half of
fighting in the Pacific theater. And then another paradox. Within three months
the Japanese surrender was being unexpectedly, deliriously celebrated, but at
a terrible cost. V-E day brought the merciless era of Auschwitz and Buchenwald
into the light but to a close; V-J day brought the Atomic Age into being and
the towering clouds over Nagasaki and Hiroshima cast a dark, frightening
shadow over the peace.

Two days after the first atomic bombardment, a scientist writing for a
Sheffield newspaper recalled how two decades earlier Olaf Stapledon had "brilliantly described" the risk of global catastrophe from the misuse of atomic energy. Death by atomic war and accident was part of the varied program of
destruction in *Last and First Men,* and in the "gigantic mushroom of steam
and debris" rising over Lundy island in his fictional version of the first atomic
test he foresaw the definitive image of the nuclear era. In the days just after
the attacks on Hiroshima and Nagasaki, other columnists and correspondents
also cited the prophecies of Stapledon and Wells, though none seems to have
recalled how the doomed freaks who represented the first tentative stage in
the evolution of *homo superior* immolated themselves at the end of *Odd John*
in a blazing atomic flash.[19]

At home on the Wirral peninsula, friends and neighbors turned to Olaf
for perspective. On 6 August, Margaret and Norman Cullen were having a garden party at their house in Heswall when news of the instant cremation of a
city came over the radio. Like many who learned of the American use of atomic
weapons, the guests in Heswall were stunned and afraid. After a few minutes
of dispirited conversation, Margi finally said, "We'd better ring up Olaf and
ask him about it. He'll know what to think." Olaf was at home and had heard
the broadcast. When he picked up the phone and heard Margi's anxious questions, he was silent for a moment. "Don't feel too gloomy. This might be the
event that will finally unify the world," she recalled him saying. Unsatisfied,
she pressed him further. "Is that what you really think, Olaf?" There was a
longer pause this time before he continued: "Yes, but it may be a totalitarian
world."[20]

Ten days later in a newspaper article, he elaborated on the prospect of a
"soulless totalitarian world, in which the ordinary individual will fall hopelessly under the control of a supreme class of technicians and organisers, working through the machinery of the mighty world state." A single world
government, whose virtues he had been preaching for over a decade, might
turn out tyrannical, but it was the only recourse for a species at risk of blowing itself up. He still hoped the split atom would open new vistas in industry,
leisure, and environmental sculpting, he told an audience in Chester, but its

first use in an act of needless aggression was not a good harbinger. Within the first weeks of the Atomic Age he was warning of a Russo-American war that would be fought over Europe. Before much longer, he said, anticipating the doctrine of Mutually Assured Destruction (MAD) that came to dominate policy decisions in the arms races of the 1950s and 1960s, the current crude prototypes would be replaced by far more powerful weapons that would accomplish the "irreparable mutual destruction" of those who deployed them.[21]

At year's end he recalled his dismay and anger on 6 August at "the hideous danger of the prostitution of atomic power":

> When I heard the announcement on the radio, I was flung back into that sense of the precariousness of all good things. This time [in contrast to the Battle of Britain] the prospect was not simply the ending of the English way of life but the ending of civilisation, perhaps the final ruin of mankind. Surely this discovery of titanic might had come too soon. Man was not yet fit to be trusted with it. Moreover, the manner in which the bombs were used seemed to me shocking and irresponsible. No doubt, by hastening the end of the war, they probably reduced the total number of Allied and Enemy casualties; but how easily a demonstration of their power could have been given without dropping the very first one on a city."[22]

As the United States monopolized the techniques for making the bombs and refused to let an international authority regulate atomic energy, cranking up Russian paranoia, Olaf's disgust grew. "What on earth is the good of holding a secret when we all know that within five years it will be open to everyone?" he asked. The real issue was not maintaining secrecy—an extremely shortsighted, reckless, and aggressive policy—but establishing effective controls on the uses of the new power. In the political sphere nationalism and atomic power were on a collision course and there was little time left to plot an alternative course. Equally important, scientific development needed to be restrained by philosophical prudence; the Atomic Age required a fresh and immediate attention to ethics. "Science is like Aladdin's lamp," he cautioned, using a favorite analogy. "The genii gives whatever is demanded, whether good or bad."[23] More than ever before, moral choices were inextricably linked to survival.

"Upstart man," Olaf wrote in an unpublished fragment from this period, took over the earth at a late stage in planetary history when some of its most impressive creatures, the great reptiles, no longer existed. In recent centuries human power had accelerated dramatically and fearfully, and it reached a crisis in the explosions of 1945. Despite the promise of a millennial breakthrough glimpsed by various writers of the past century, himself included, the imminent end of the species was now a more likely consequence of the latest unlocking of "physical secrets." "It is not impossible that we, who are the first

generation of the Atomic Age, may also be the last of all the generations of
Man." Nor did he see atomic weaponry as an isolated threat. Its development
and use was a symptom of a broader range of economic, cultural, and spiritual disorders: the improvident pursuit of luxury, quick political fixes to complex problems, deluded notions of national honor, ecological obtuseness, and
the anesthetizing of the ethical sense. He foresaw fertile farmlands turned to
dusty wastes and oceans plundered by ever more efficient fisheries. "The whole
balance of nature is dislocated by man's greed. In a few decades more, unless
man sharply disciplines himself, there will be such starvation and misery as
has never before decimated our species. Either way, by war or by greed, the
slowly won tradition of humane life may be lost forever."[24]

When Olaf described his "Arms Out of Hand," a Jekyll-and-Hyde story
about a man unable to control the murderous and self-destructive reflexes of
his right arm, Hermon Ould responded, "Your theme is too terrifyingly like
mankind and its atomic bomb!"[25] The resemblance was more accidental than
intentional, since the story antedated the bombings in Japan, but Ould's remark may have moved Olaf to develop a fantastic plot he was sketching about
solar creatures loosed on the earth. The ghastly fires of Hiroshima backlit this
last fictional masterpiece, an epistolary novella "slowly de-chrysalising itself
from an intended short story." Its working title, "The Salamander," connected
it to ancient myths of fabulous creatures who lived in fire, and in *Star Maker*
he had already imagined a scientifically rationalized race of fiery organisms
nourished on stellar energy. He sent a synopsis in December 1945 to Roger
Senhouse, his editor at Secker and Warburg, explaining how an atomic war
might provide "a permanent and extensive fiery home" to alien beings who
thrive on pure energy and who were loosed on the cold earth during the
firebombings and atomic blasts of World War II. Layering the narrative with
ambiguities, he attributed the discovery of the flame creatures to a self-styled
Cassandra ("Cass") writing a letter to an old school friend; the return address
was the mental home in which Cass was a patient. In a late revision the friend's
name was changed from Charles to Thos ("Doubting Thomas") to further com-
plicate the issue of belief. Senhouse found the parable "really exciting" and
penciled in at the bottom of Stapledon's letter: "Strong appeal—topical. Atom
& regeneration espec suitable to your mind."[26]

Olaf wanted the story, renamed *The Flames,* to be read as "a fantastic symbol" of the emerging Cold War, "of the difficulty of entering into comradely
mutual trust with a mind alien to oneself in tradition and general texture, though
identical in fundamental purpose."[27] As with all his novels of ideas, however,
The Flames did not originate in a propagandistic intention but in visionary
speculation. Cass's encounter with solar beings follows a near-death experience in the Lake District. While rock climbing during a blizzard, Cass has a

momentary fantasy that he is the last man on earth. "Why am I telling you all this?" Cass asks Thos. "Frankly I don't see *how* it is relevant to my story, and yet I feel strongly that it *is* relevant."[28] But Olaf knew the relevance. Something like Cass's brush with extinction had appeared in *Last and First Men*. There the Divine Boy of Patagonia, the most autobiographical figure in Stapledon's first work of fiction, recalls his first insight into the nature of the universe:

> I have a queer love for clambering about the high mountains; and once when I was up among the snow-fields and precipices of Aconcagua, I was caught in a blizzard. . . . I fell into a snow-drift. I tried to rise, but fell again and again, till my head was buried. The thought of death enraged me, for there was still so much that I wanted to do. I struggled frantically, vainly. Then suddenly— how can I put it?—I saw the game that I was losing, and it was good. Good, no less to lose than to win. For it was the game, now, not victory, that mattered.

Completed in April 1946 and published the next year, the enigmatic and undervalued fable of *The Flames* was dismissed by its disheartened author as "not a book of any importance, just a wild little fantasy," but it is a grim emblem of the mental and moral dislocations induced by the sudden birth of the Atomic Age.[29]

The aftermath of August 1945 plunged Olaf into a dark mood observed by many of his friends. Doomsday became a recurrent theme of his conversations and his public speeches. Worried by Stalin's perversion of the revolutionary spirit in the USSR, he worried even more about a swaggering United States, unscathed in comparison to the nations of Europe and Asia, unleashing a new, possibly terminal, world war. When his West Kirby neighbor, the economist George Allen, returned from a tour of Japanese industrial facilities for the British Foreign Office, he fueled Olaf's suspicions of an untrustworthy America: "He says that Japan was really quite beaten *before* the atomic bombs were used. The American Government is evidently feeling guilty about the use of those bombs, as they have hushed up all accounts of the damage done."[30] In Liverpool seven months after V-J Day, he made a bitter prediction. "America needs these islands as a base in a conflict with Russia, and if there is another war in the next few years—or weeks—it will be goodbye Britain." The world was being twisted out of shape as the emergent superpowers muscled their way forward to eye each other across Europe. "Let us face up to the unpleasant truth that we are no longer a great Power," Olaf told his hearers. "People speak of the "three great Powers,' but there are not three, there are only two and a half. We are the half."[31] He did not mourn the shrunken old empire; he wanted, if anything, to hasten its end. Decades ahead of the ground swell for a boundary-less European community, he said, "I am convinced that if we do not get a United Europe, then I am afraid we are pretty well doomed to war."[32]

The diminishment of Britain suited Olaf's mood. The post-war springtime was pinched and austere for Europeans suffering the prolonged aftershocks of the war. Olaf thanked his old friend Aage Marcus for a Danish parcel of typing paper, cheese, and cooking fat, but English privations were nothing compared with what he discovered when he flew to Holland in September 1945 with a delegation of PEN observers led by Vera Brittain. The country had been sacked and stripped by its German occupiers; shortages of clothing were extreme; public transport had ceased to exist. Dutch commuters and shoppers made their way through the streets on bicycles with only one rubber tire, back or front according to personal preference, or none at all. An effort at sprucing up had been made with bright paint ransacked from the German stores, but there was little to eat except relief rations supplied by the army. He met a family of six living in a chicken coop, the children with scabby, stick-thin legs. Girls were selling themselves to Canadian soldiers for cigarettes. In Amsterdam people showed him how they used to bury their radios in their gardens each day after listening to forbidden broadcasts.

In rural areas families lived on the upper floors of flooded houses, as they had been doing since the Nazis blew up the dikes and ruined the arable land with salt water. Witnesses told him of being forced to watch the Gestapo's execution of twenty young boys as punishment for actions of the Dutch underground. The mood of hatred, though he understood it, appalled Olaf as he watched Dutchmen identified as collaborators being marched with shorn heads through a street. The country had been so isolated during its occupation and so demoralized after its liberation that news of the atomic bomb had had almost no impact; great numbers of the younger generation talked only of leaving Holland. After six years of enforced insularity, the British visitors came away with impressions of a martyrdom more gruesome and costly than anything they had experienced in the blitzes and a sobering example of what might have been had the feared Nazi invasion of the island ever occurred. On his return Olaf campaigned throughout England for assistance to Dutch reconstruction.[33]

After his years of lecturing to British forces, he also took an interest in veterans returning to civilian life, many having had their educations or careers disrupted for five years or more. He helped administer a fund at Liverpool University that assisted ex-servicemen trying to establish themselves as writers. The scheme paired an aspiring writer with an experienced mentor, and Olaf volunteered, somewhat uneasily, to play the role of the published author who could nurture new talent. He may have advised several young writers, but there is evidence of only one such relationship. It failed. In 1946 an M.A. candidate wrote to Olaf "with timidity," recalling having once taken tea with him in the Union as an undergraduate at Liverpool in 1938. With painful self-consciousness the applicant explained, "I mention this because it gives me the courage to hope that, since you were so urbane with the enthusiastic child, you may be tolerant of the presumptuous youth." The applicant, hoping to be a playwright, was the future literary critic Frank Kermode.[34]

For most of a year, Kermode and Stapledon met over lunch for critiques of the younger man's drafts, for advice on job applications, and for literary talk. Olaf was not in much sympathy with the Aristotelian principles favored by his pupil or the classical models on which he constructed his plays, but neither was Kermode fond of his mentor's sort of fiction. Olaf's career had been eccentric enough and the subjects and style of his fiction so far removed from the literary mainstream that it would have been an unusual novice writer who could have profited from his example. Besides, Kermode found his advisor's notions of the qualifications of a writer peculiar: "He once took my hands, examined them, & saw that they bore no mark of physical labour, which he seemed to regard as essential to good writing." After eight months Kermode decided, "with a sort of dim gratitude" to the author with whom he had been so ill-matched, to seek a teaching appointment rather than continue his writer's apprenticeship.[35]

If Olaf was too much on the margins of the literary world to be a helpful guide to writers looking for a way in, he still had the personal magnetism to draw other young people to him. He was in demand with political groups and university audiences. At a summer school for the Independent Labour party just after the war ended, he promoted his unorthodox view that Lenin was the outstanding saint of the century. "Despite its anti-religious thought, the Russian revolution was the greatest religious event of modern times," he claimed. The Oxford Socialist Club gathered an audience of several hundred to hear his analysis of the philosophical problems of Marxism; although there were scattered charges that the lecture was "reformist" and "Menshevik," most of the students applauded the directions he laid out for Marxist thought and action. Only at Manchester University, where a mostly Catholic audience turned out to hear him debate the broadcaster Father Agnellus Andrew, did he find young people openly hostile to his ideas. At the end of the debate, widely reported in the Catholic press of England and Ireland, the students voted overwhelmingly against Stapledon's position that doctrinal religion was not necessary to human progress; when he suggested that their attitude was archaic, the audience laughed at him.[36]

The appeal to the young did not take place only on the lecturer's dais. In the thirties his chief correspondents had been the famous: Wells, Haldane, Mitchison, Myers, Priestley. As the literary world withdrew from him and as he turned to cultivating the rising generation, the correspondence of his last five years was mostly with little-known men and women thirty or forty years younger than himself. Time was the commodity he could least spare, and yet he was unfailingly generous. He sat down with the thirty-year-old Wendy Hollander and, sliding salt and pepper pots back and forth on the kitchen table, patiently illustrated how she could restructure the novel she had been unable to complete. A young couple drawn to him by the analyses of love in his fiction and essays used to meet him in Liverpool for tea and advice on their courtship and planned marriage. In Sussex the manager of a small hotel and several of his young friends invited Olaf down to talk to them (which he did) about their plan for a Stapledon Society for disciples (which did not materialize). American science fiction fans wrote to him—assuming that he had a secretary to handle his correspondence—and were not bashful about asking for autographed copies of his out-of-print novels.[37]

From Vancouver during the war came a letter from an admirer of *Last and First Men* who was struggling with the questions of pacifism and the philosophical challenge to orthodox Christianity that Stapledon's cosmic panorama posed. Although Geoffrey Ashe, the future authority on the Arthurian legend, later realized that most authors "aren't generally enthusiastic about hearing of their readers' spiritual travails," in this respect Olaf was an exception. As he nearly always did, he made a sensitive reply, sending along an inscribed copy of *Beyond the "Isms"*. When Ashe came to Cambridge after the war, he met Olaf and got him to contribute a piece to a student publication about his talks to the RAF. He wrote an appreciative review of Stapledon's hopeful Baedeker for the coming generation, *Youth and Tomorrow,* and in 1948 he broadcast over the BBC's French service one of the earliest sustained commentaries on Stapledon's great scientific romances. Refusing the popular view of him as a cosmic pessimist, Ashe found evidence of a moral philosopher who was an "optimiste foncier"—and he underestimated Olaf's age by a dozen years.[38]

In 1946 attention was more muted than in the heady days when the author of *Last and First Men* and *Odd John* was lionized in newspapers and on radio. His following was smaller now but perhaps more loyal than those who had been attracted by a flashy review in 1930. His new readers were likely to have discovered him by accident or in out-of-the-way places. The physicist Freeman Dyson picked up a tattered copy of *Star Maker* from a bookstall in Paddington Station, and it led him down the path to his pioneering research in artificial biospheres. C. S. Lewis sent his followers scurrying to secondhand shops when he announced in a preface to *That Hideous Strength* (1945) his debt to Stapledon's imagination (though not to his philosophy).[39] Anyone happening into Conway Hall in London's Red Lion Square, where Olaf often spoke on politics or ethics or religion—or on some typically Stapledonian

combination of all three—heard a voice that still awakened minds. His platform manner, like his prose, was deliberate, unembellished, low-key, free from
the histrionics that broadcasting had made popular in the various tones of
Churchill, Joad, and Lord Haw Haw. Preferring a comradely air of participation, never invoking expertise or authority, he could enter gracefully and in-
structively into dialogue with the cleverest or the most naïve of listeners. He
had the charisma that only speakers who shun affectations of style earn, and
those drawn to Olaf in the postwar years felt, as Lilian Bowes-Lyon told him,
that he was "speaking to today's people—& also to people on the precipice-
edge of today, who half belong to tomorrow already."[40]

That was the audience Olaf had in mind for one of his least-known books,
Youth and Tomorrow. Conceived as a sixth-former's textbook that he expected
Nelson to publish in 1944, it was nearly another casualty of the paper shortages and altered publishers' schedules of the war. *Youth and Tomorrow* finally
appeared, lightly revised to take account of the Labour victory in the 1945 election, in a miserably printed edition from the tiny firm of St. Botolph in mid-
1946, over two years after it had been finished. It was, in fact, probably too
idiosyncratic to be marketed effectively as a school text, but its very unbookish
medley of personal anecdote, historical outline, cultural critique of the past
seventy-five years, and speculation about the immediate and more distant future gives it energy and eloquence. J. H. Blackham, in its only lengthy review,
regretted Stapledon's inordinate fondness for abstractions like "personality-in-
community," but welcomed "the outlook of a mellow genuine progressive who
has lived through the attack on the Victorian Age and the nihilism of the Twenty
Years' Crisis and has forgotten nothing and learned a great deal."[41]

Except for *Last Men in London,* nothing else he published drew so much
on childhood memories as the first third of *Youth and Tomorrow.* Wanting to
arouse a young audience to social activism, he tried to recover how the world
had felt just before the century turned—particularly in those moments when
the young Stapledon was most irreverent or bored or enraged. Some of his
memories are risible (his uncle Willie Kirkus, a Liverpool stockbroker, climbing Welsh mountains "in a morning coat and striped trousers, and a square-
topped hard black hat, a cross between a bowler and a topper"). Others are
excoriating, like his recollection of late-Victorian Liberals appeasing their social consciences by subscribing to public charities: "I have more than once
heard it seriously suggested that God had created poverty in order that the more
fortunate might have an opportunity of exercising charity."[42]

The recovery of such Victorian memories helped Olaf establish his credentials with the post-1945 young. He respected their disinclination to trust
the reliability of elderly guides into the future, and at a youth conference in
Truró in 1946 he was his usual disarming self: "I am old—what right have I

to speak on youth or on the New World. A cat may look at a king—and age at youth."[43] He was not the sort of sixty-year-old who hankered for the good old days; he ridiculed and scourged the deficiencies of the past because his allegiance was to a Utopia still to be born. He knew he was too old to inhabit it. "But not for us that promised land," he lamented on behalf of his own generation in *Youth and Tomorrow*.[44] Nevertheless, he was not too old or too compromised to help inspire it.

He did not try to relive his own youth but to empower the coming generation. He spoke on behalf of the future. The caterpillar world in which he grew up was ready to burst asunder and be remade into "some sort of winged thing." The young could make a new order, and they needed to feel not only the possibility but the adventure of creating Utopia:

> Today some strangely unimaginative people suppose that when mankind has turned the corner into a happier social order the adventure and romance will have gone from life, and the human spirit will be undermined by comfort, security and lack of purpose. But how much more likely it seems that when man's latent capacity is at last able to express itself fully, without the universal frustration that now cripples the whole race, the result will not be stagnation but the opening up of new worlds of experience and creative action, at present hidden from our damaged sight.[45]

Written in the same mood and largely at the same time as his futurist story, "Old Man in New World," *Youth and Tomorrow* belongs among several late works in which Stapledon explicitly aimed to speak to succeeding generations. While his hopes for the future were qualified by apocalyptic intimations in the political sphere and by personal doubts whether his own literary and philosophical works would survive his death, his imagination remained intact and his darker forebodings were countered, as always, by an unshaken commitment to the light.

Barely reviewed outside the left-wing press and educational newsletters, *Youth and Tomorrow* was the sort of book that had to be picked up by chance or recommended by word of mouth. The numerous typesetter's errors and almost unreadable print on the cheapest paper were additional discouragements. Ernest Martin, who at the time was finishing the first major essay on Stapledon as a philosopher, wrote angrily, "I could wish that the St Botolph people had realised that your work was worthy of a better presentation. Damn it, it was shocking!"[46] The physical condition of the book, coupled with its lack of publicity, led Olaf to write it off, even though it contained some of his finest social analysis of the decade. When an editor in the summer of 1946 offered to help arrange French translations of his works, Olaf made many suggestions about suitable texts but thought *Youth and Tomorrow* "not the sort of thing to recommend."[47]

With *Death Into Life,* published two months after *Youth and Tomorrow,* he remained pleased, although its fantasy was far less coherent than his personal tour through yesterday, today, and tomorrow. Aage Marcus and the visionary painter Fay Pomerance, both of whom shared Olaf's growing fascination with psychic phenomena and mystical experience, were enthusiastic about *Death Into Life,* but other friends tactfully limited themselves to praise of the autobiographical Interludes. Speaking as one writer to another with her customary candor, Naomi Mitchison (who hadn't seen him in six years) wrote from Scotland that Olaf should write either straight philosophy or a real novel. Ignoring the main narrative—"the latest installment of your myth," she called it—Naomi identified what remains potent in *Death Into Life.* "Actually, I was so much interested in what it told me about you and your life and how you are dealing with this awful business of getting old."[48] When he was detailing the personal toll of mutability, *Death Into Life* rang true; the more it reached for the immutable and the eternal, the more it felt like a thesis-ridden exercise. Olaf believed there was an organic connection between the Interludes and the rest of *Death Into Life:* "Art (of any sort) must feed through its roots in concrete life. And the more cosmical or universal its theme, the more of that concrete food it needs if it is to avoid being lost in abstraction. In my book the Interludes symbolize the roots."[49] But most readers found the roots more attractive than the flower.

Olaf had always been a writer alert to paradox; in *Death Into Life* he produced only a contradiction between his voice and his message. Many reviews refrained from detailed criticism, sticking to perfunctory and noncommittal summaries of its spiritual thesis, but some critics were less kindly. To Valentine Ackland it was "confused and overworded." Another reader described it as the psychical flotsam of a philosopher "communing with his own ego." The *New Statesman*'s Rayner Heppenstall found a delicate power in the articulation of symbols vitiated by leaden abstraction and narrative clumsiness. His frustration with *Death Into Life* glosses with unequaled precision the author's never-resolved uncertainties about his talent and identity: "How bitterly the artist and the thinker have struggled for the soul of Mr. Stapledon."[50]

The major public event in Olaf's life in 1946 was the eighteenth international PEN congress, held at Stockholm in the first week of June. Stapledon was one of two official representatives from England, joined by the International Secretary of PEN, Hermon Ould; the total party of British writers at Stockholm was nearly fifty. Exempt from the ravages of the war by virtue of its political neutrality, Sweden seemed unspoiled and luxurious. Its progressive welfare legislation caused European delegates to marvel at the vigor of its citizens and the absence of massive urban poverty pervasive elsewhere on the continent. Stockholm seemed the gateway to Utopia. "The wealth, prosperity, politeness, sanity and true civilization of this country is pure fairy story," Olaf told Agnes. The congress offered elegant ceremony, an unlimited supply of fish and eggs that could be ordered without coupons, nearly twenty-four hours of daylight, and a smorgasbord of special events: lunch with Prince Wilhelm for the two representatives from each country, a reception at the National Museum (where Olaf had a reunion with Aage Marcus after nearly a decade), a private tour of the royal family's art collection, performances at the Royal Opera House, a huge dinner hosted by the Swedish PEN, and an expedition for silk stockings, unprocurable in England. "Tomorrow we *may* do something worth doing," a sleepless Olaf wrote to Agnes on the third day.[51]

The business side of the congress proved unexpectedly controversial. For the first time since 1939, European writers, many of whom had lived under occupation, were able to gather for discussion of the writer's role in society. Almost all could gather. Although the USSR did not have a membership in PEN, an invitation had been sent to Russian writers; none, however, had been permitted by the Soviet Writers' Union to go to Stockholm. Olaf, inclined to sympathize with Russian suspicion of the Western democracies ever since the World War I allies launched their counterrevolutionary invasion of the Soviet Union in 1918, told the congress it was understandable that discipline in the USSR might at present have to take precedence over individual liberty. Rather than condemn the Writers' Union for keeping its members from attending, he argued that PEN should protest political repression everywhere, in Franco's Spain, in Stalin's Russia, and in the nominal democracies like Britain, but the organization must remain welcoming to all writers. He then put a motion before the congress to send a message to Russian writers, regretting their absence and inviting them to join PEN International, and urging writers from all countries to press for exchanges of visits and the free circulation of books and information. His resolution, carefully worded to avoid offending the Soviet government and thereby making things harder on Russian writers, was unanimously adopted by all members who voted, but—in a chilly gesture reflecting the ideological warfare of the superpowers—the American delegation abstained.[52]

A still pricklier political issue centered on the question of ostracism of writers who had collaborated with the Nazis. Olaf was not surprised that it was a Dutch delegate who introduced the motion to blacklist authors (many of them by then living in Switzerland, Spain, and South America) who were identified by the PEN center in their native countries as collaborationists. The U.S. delegates, confirming Olaf's belief that as the Russians always erred on the side of discipline, the Americans could be counted upon to sacramentalize individual liberty, took an absolutist position on freedom of expression and opposed the motion. The greatest support for the Dutch resolution came from delegates whose countries had been occupied, and when it became clear that the British were going to waffle, someone remarked caustically that England had only had a calling card in the form of the V1 and V2 rockets but had not known the sound of the Gestapo knocking at the door. Hermon Ould took the floor to argue vehemently against the blacklist, but Olaf reluctantly spoke on its behalf, with memories of his visit to Holland still fresh. Ostracism was a dangerous tactic to use against fellow writers, he said, mindful of the inconsistency between the inclusive nature of his own resolution on the Russian writers and the repressive implications of a blacklist. "But the right course is always dangerous," he concluded. In the end, against his advice, the divided British delegation fell back on abstention.

As Olaf wrote in a report on Stockholm for the *New Statesman,* there are times when intellectual allegiance to abstract principles must yield to emotion and experience. It was too easy for the Americans and some Britons not to want to sully literature with political considerations. "Throughout the discussions, the cleavage was mainly between those who had suffered under tyranny and those who had not. The terrific experience of inhuman oppression and heroic resistance, though to some extent it had clouded judgment, had also burnt into many minds a lesson which the more fortunate could learn only at second hand, and through the exercise of imagination." After the Society of Authors asked him to write about Stockholm, its chairman gulped over Olaf's text ("It is not quite on the lines I had expected"). In fact, he took an even harder line than in his *New Statesman* article, this time in a journal that held the writer's independence sacrosanct: "While humanity is still in the mere chrysalis stage, there will still be occasions when the "sword' has to be called in, whether in the form of state discipline or private blacklists."[53] Olaf's role in the PEN congress served as a rehearsal for the more widely publicized international peace conferences of 1948 and 1949 when he at last had his chance to meet Russian writers and musicians and sample the effects of Soviet state discipline.

By the time of Stockholm, Stapledon had begun such a binge of conferences and lecture tours that in the last four years of his life, imaginative writing was relegated to scarce odd moments. After he had *The Flames* typed in April, he wrote almost nothing for the rest of the year, except for commissioned book reviews, occasional pieces of journalism, and an allegorical story that became another occasion for autobiography. Peter Albery, whose London discussion group known as "The Four Arts League" Olaf often attended, asked him for a 5,000-word piece for the literary miscellany *Here and Now* he and his wife Sylvia Read were editing. Albery wanted writing that caught "a sense of the rhythm of life, of "the substance of things unknown.' "[54] Olaf took this open-ended invitation as an opportunity to create a parable about his own career as writer and social activist, about the uncertainties of his accomplishments and the imminence of his death. The key image in the story was one he had just tried out in a recording for the BBC's "Purple Network" for broadcast in India. Speaking on "What Philosophy Means to Me," he described how the speculative imagination plumbs the mysteries of the cosmos: "We start from the valley to climb a mountain. With many set-backs, we explore the foot-hills for the route. The nearer we approach the peak, the loftier and more for-bidding it appears. In the end, it turns out to be inaccessible; but, how superb!"[55]

What Olaf wrote for Albery, initially titled "The Journey" and in a later draft "The Peak and the Town," was a Bunyanesque pilgrim's progress that reprised his own intellectual and ethical struggles in the context of an alle-gorical history of his generation. The old oppositions between saints and revo-lutionaries, being and doing, the perspective of the slums of Toxteth and the view from Caldy Hill that had exercised him all his life were clothed in an account of life's journey, sometimes pursued in solitude and sometimes within a vast crowd of fellow travelers, in which the call of the city, squalid and full of life, alternates with the lure of the peak, whose clear, cold prospect offers both vision and death. Nearing the end of his journey, torn by the dilemma of competing obligations, the traveler is offered a solution by an old watchmaker. "It is quite simple. You want to be in two places at once, living two lives at once. Duplicate yourself." One can continue to work in the town while reserv-ing a portion of the mind for scaling the peak. "There is no satisfactory life," says the watchmaker, "but the double life." The traveler adopts "this marvel-lous duplicity," but the parable closes with him lost and weary in the foothills as darkness falls with the peak still distant. In the earlier typescript the narra-tor wonders, "Perhaps I shall never reach the high valley. Perhaps I shall die frozen and frustrated on the mountain, stifled and ineffective in the town." But later Olaf excised the gloomier notes and added a more upbeat conclusion. "Well, what matter? Perhaps some others of our party, more fortunate or more clear-headed, will find their way to the heights, will at last bring the Peak to the town and the town to the Peak. For me, the only thing is to press on. The day is not yet done. And death even here would not be wholly defeat."[56] Albery found the allegory too obscure and asked for something else.[57] In rejecting "The Peak and the Town," he failed to appreciate either the intellectual stoicism or the emotional vulnerability of one of Stapledon's most piercing self-revelations.

The metaphorical journey in "The Peak and the Town" was not merely a metaphor. As he passed sixty Olaf was constantly, increasingly on the move. The big international expeditions to Sweden in 1946, to the South of France and Poland in 1948, to New York and Paris in 1949, and again to France in 1950 are only the most visible stops in an almost unbroken succession of con-ferences on political, religious, scientific, philosophical, paranormal, but sel-dom literary topics that took a huge toll on his energy. During 1946 alone he traveled around England for a variety of one-, two-, and three-day meetings sponsored by the World Unity Movement, the World Union of Freethinkers, the Scottish Architectural Society, the India League, the Association of International Clubs, the London Personalists, the Oxford Rationalists, the Chester YMCA Army School, the Council for Education in World Citizenship, the Langdale Conference on Education, the York WEA, and the Save Europe Now Committee. One of the most significant of these smaller meetings—and in personal terms even more momentous than the PEN congress at Stockholm—was a remarkable gathering at Exeter, organized by, as an anonymous participant put it, "a small group of queer people, parsons, psychiatrists, social workers and others" to consider the present state of the human species.[58] Over two hundred people, many of them new to conference routines, showed up for a week in August for what was billed as the Present Question Conference.

The prime mover behind the conference was the Jungian psychotherapist Heinz Westmann, who enlisted the aid of two colleagues, the army psychiatrist Brigadier Alfred Torrie and Eric Graham Howe, a Fellow of the British Psychological Society, who chaired the conference and whose books Olaf came to scorn as "embroidery without any coherent tissue of cloth behind it."[59] In the summer of 1945, the three psychologists conceived of a "yeast group" who would concentrate on the evident tensions and anxieties of the postwar world and ask: What is the present question—"the growing-point of new experience"—that human beings most need to cultivate in order to reconstitute a healthy society?[60] As they invited others into the yeast group, they sought a dialectic between the opposing viewpoints of science and religion, and particularly of psychologists and churchmen. Out of those informal discussions came the idea for a meeting at Exeter University with both plenary speakers and carefully focused study groups that would explore the same "present question" from a variety of angles. Stapledon was invited by the organizers to give a talk and co-direct, with the Cambridge theologian Bishop Stephen Neill, the study group on the religious approach to the question.

Olaf was underimpressed with the first few days' "tiresome" proceedings and found excuses to escape into the town to look over the bomb-damaged cathedral that contained the tomb of his ancestor Bishop Walter de Stapeldon. Of the conferees, he told Agnes, "There are some quite nice young people here, but the older ones are what I call "sheltered minds', and I think the whole affair is rather remote from real life."[61] Among the nice young people were three women, none of whom had ever been to a conference before, none of whom had heard of Olaf Stapledon, but each of whom became an important friend and correspondent. Wendy Hollander, a struggling novelist and one of Westmann's patients, walked through the gardens of the university with Olaf one afternoon, airing her views freely with someone she assumed was a neophyte like herself; the next day she was embarrassed to discover him on the podium as one of the invited experts.[62] Wendy's sister Fay Pomerance was a painter whose early sketches for the cycle of Lucifer myths that became the major creation of her career were on display at Exeter. With an artist's observant eye and uninhibited self-assurance, she took the speaker's measure as he addressed the conference: "Olaf, though greying, had the walk and verve of a schoolboy, accentuated perhaps by a falling-forward, repeatedly, forelock, which one felt as a mother one should say, `Push your hair back from over your eyes, Olaf.' "[63]

A third woman, in her late twenties and a war widow, had been drawn unwillingly by a friend into attending the conference. She listened to Olaf's long speech on agnostic piety, full of his trademark formulas of "evolutionary humanism," "mental symbiosis," and "vessels of the spirit." With some irritation she tried to follow the shoptalk in the technical questions he put to other speakers. The young woman, N., thought to herself, "What a pompous bore!" Later, seated next to him, she found herself in conversation with a far more interesting person than she had guessed he could be.[64] Over the next three years their correspondence and meetings in London blossomed into a last great but troubled love in Olaf's life and gave a fresh turn to his autobiographical musings on growing old in springtime.

17

DOORS OUT, DOORS IN

1947–1948

OLAF DID NOT FALL IN LOVE with N. all at once, but he did write to her soon after the Present Question meeting. She had given him a chocolate bar when the conference ended to nourish him on the long trip to Liverpool in the postwar austerity when food was unavailable on trains. He asked her now about her widowhood and whether she shouldn't find a man who would make her feel worthwhile again. N., who was independent-minded enough not to identify matrimony with self-esteem, did not guess he might mean himself—and perhaps at this stage Olaf did not even realize that he was flirting. But N.'s reply mixed insouciance, candor, and imagination in a combination that delighted Olaf and prompted him to keep up a correspondence. "I felt you didn't believe me when I said I was happy—but it was really true," N. wrote:

> Only mine was the happiness of a cow in a field who doesn't concern herself with the cosmos or the ultimate slaughterhouse. . . . I am mentally very lazy, and have always tried to avoid thinking by filling my life with action. I just shut off any feelings which seemed to involve a spiritual stock-taking, because half of me refused to acknowledge that I had anything as immaterial as a spirit, and the other half was frightened that it would be shaken out of its complacency if it looked, and found what it suspected must be there.

She confessed that she had had no high philosophical motive for attending the Present Question Conference. She was a teacher in London and had gone to Exeter to oblige a well-meaning friend who thought it would do her good, but she was suspicious of the type of person she expected to find at a gathering of intellectuals. "I didn't go as a seeker after truth, but with a sketch book and the intention of caricaturing all the likely subjects I felt sure would be there." Instead, she discovered that she couldn't concentrate on drawing and the lectures she had been prepared to disdain cracked open her protective armor:

> As for the young man—you must believe me when I say that I have absolutely no urge in that direction at the moment; but neither have I a prejudice, and if one turned up and it seemed the right thing to do, no doubt I'd meet him half way. But one of the things you said struck me as being so true and right, that I shall never again be without it—and that was your theory that there is a *time* to open a new door, and a time to shut the old one. If and when it ever seems the time to open that particular door, I shall, and if it never does, I shall feel no sense of loss. I am content to live in the "now"—I always have been—but I have only just learnt to relate the immediate now to the larger one. This I must thank you for—and for everything. A bar of chocolate seems a very poor exchange for what you gave me.[1]

On visits to London, Olaf began saving time for lunches and conversations with N., but for a time neither of them was inclined to open the new door any wider. Olaf, aside from a reluctance to renew the pain he and Agnes had undergone five years earlier over Evelyn, had other competing family claims on his energies. His daughter Mary had begun medical studies at the University of London, as had the intriguing man she first met two years earlier at a Charing Cross bookshop. Shiva Shenai, full of political passion and resentments, had lived in Russia and Germany (speaking both languages) but was prevented from returning to his native India when his passport was taken away for supposed dissidence. Mary "burned with indignation on his part," and she and Shiva began to imagine setting up their joint practice in an independent India. Olaf admired his daughter's ambition but didn't take very readily to Shiva. He worried whether she was making the right decisions, but she had learned both cosmopolitanism and independence of mind from him at an early age. Olaf silenced his reservations, and by 1946 he and Agnes were making regular contributions to Shiva's medical school expenses as well as to Mary's.[2]

On the very summer day of 1946 when Olaf was giving his major speech to the Present Question conference, a new daughter-in-law arrived at Simon's Field. After John David Stapledon's ship was sunk at the end of 1944, he spent the war's last months in the mountainous regions of Sicily and the toe of Italy, setting up radio stations in a network of military shortwave links between Malta and Naples. While installing one station halfway up Mount Etna, he met Sarina Tetto, who was working at the small hotel where he was billeted. In April 1946 he and Sarina were married at the Waldensian church in Catania just a few weeks before he was sent home to England; Sarina had to remain behind. At the end of May, Olaf was preparing to go to Stockholm when his son arrived in Liverpool after an absence of three years. The boy whom he had always called David or Dibs announced that Sarina called him John. His musical education, interrupted by the war, seemed to him a pleasant and distant luxury. He wanted a practical way of supporting a family, and Olaf offered to help him get trained as a market gardener. So often disdainful of intellectuals who had no calluses on their hands or dirt under their fingernails, Olaf now found himself the perplexed father of a young stranger who insisted, proudly, that he was "a peasant." By his own account, John Stapledon was hard to get along with that summer, irritable and distracted by his wife's absence. He spent weeks negotiating the regulations that governed the immigration of servicemen's wives into England, and at the other end of the red tape, Sarina endured long delays as the trains carrying war brides wound tortuously through Italy, Austria, and France. When she reached Liverpool on 24 August, she was exhausted, frightened, unable to speak much English, and pregnant.[3] Simon's Field, which Agnes and Olaf had had to themselves since they moved in during the spring of 1940, now made room for a second couple and, in January 1947, for a grandchild.

The new configurations in his family were not without impact on Olaf's literary fortunes. Before Mary and John had so definitely embarked on new lives, and when his own time for writing was constrained by various speaking engagements, he had begun experimenting with shorter forms of fiction. A notebook contains plans for a collection of stories based on various paranormal experiences. There is a bare listing of fictional situations—"stepping into another world," "becoming a tree," "one mind in two bodies," "reluctant magician," "a visit to a dead world," "struggle for a soul"—alongside an inventory of topics, including telepathy, clairvoyance, psychokinesis, precognition, possession, poltergeists, and co-consciousness. Only three of these ideas were ever developed into full drafts: "Arms Out of Hand," "A Modern Magician" (his story of psychokinesis), and the remarkable fantasy, a version of which he had toyed with as early as World War I, "The Man Who Became a Tree." The latter two were never printed until long after his death.[4]

By the summer of 1946, however, he was turning away from short fiction in an effort to make a more substantial profit from his work. He asked Frederic Warburg, who was publishing *The Flames,* to look into the possibility of selling its film rights, and he wanted to know what Secker and Warburg had done about finding an American publisher for *Sirius.* Warburg's reply was not encouraging. He didn't see obvious cinematic possibilities in *The Flames,* and when he tried to market *Sirius* in the United States, he had been turned down by eight publishers. Roger Senhouse wrote somewhat unhelpfully in the

margin of Warburg's letter that he had spoken to a film agent about *Sirius*—
"since M.G.M. have a canine wonder-star."⁵ It is difficult to imagine Lassie in
the part of Stapledon's super–sheep dog.

Warburg insisted that he was glad to be publishing *The Flames,* "a most
distinguished performance," he told the author. "You have succeeded beyond
expectation of [*sic*] making plausible what in the hands of any other contemporary writer would appear merely ridiculous." But the publisher drove a hard
bargain. He expected *The Flames* to be "a difficult book from the sales point
of view" and, since he considered it exempt from the notorious clause 18 of
Stapledon's contract, he wanted more work out of him. "THE FLAMES hardly
seems to be covered by it since it is not strictly a full length novel but a short
novel, so we should take it as a book outside the option clause."⁶ Olaf took
the news well and promised to try to give Warburg a more marketable manuscript. "I am entirely satisfied with your firm's treatment of me throughout our
dealings, and I only wish that I had produced books that would sell more extensively, as well as the sort I have already written. I am contemplating trying
a rather more popular novel soon, as my family is demanding large sums for
its belated professional training."⁷ Economics drove him to abandon the projected collection of short stories on esoteric themes.

Throughout the summer of 1946, Olaf explored possibilities for a popular novel, including what would have been the most pronounced departure from
all his previous fiction had he written it, a novel on the ancestry of Jesus Christ.
He intended to open the book in prehistoric South America, he advised
Warburg, with later episodes set in Africa, China, and the Celtic world. Warburg
was thrilled, but he made the mistake of advising Olaf that Robert Graves might
be pursuing a similar idea and urged him to get in touch with Graves. To
Warburg's dismay, he immediately got cold feet and decided that "if Graves
is doing it, that is that." The idea died on the vine. Olaf next tried to interest
Warburg in another novel, already under way and with "conversation in it,"
as clause 18 specified. "I am now engaged on a *fairly* straight full length novel
about a queer sort of divided personality. I started it long ago, had to drop it,
and have recently taken it up again." It was to be his last completed work of
fiction, *A Man Divided,* and very definitely not the hoped-for "popular novel."⁸
His option clause was never again exercised nor did he come close to writing
his best-seller.

Olaf had always been a cloistered writer, dependent on the soundproof
attic at Grosvenor Avenue and later on the solitary study at Simon's Field. In
1947 all that changed, and he began taking long walks away from home. It
was not just that Simon's Field had become a noisier place with its young family and baby. Olaf was accustomed to being at the center of his microcosm
and the chief object of Agnes's attentions, but the presence of a grandchild

altered the equation. His friend Mulk Raj Anand wrote from Bombay, commenting on Olaf's mild complaint that "as a grandfather you have been pushed from the focus of the home into a side room. I am sure you retreated with your usual calm dignity and restraint."[9] In fact, he retreated to London. In early 1947 his trips to the metropolis grew more frequent and lasted longer, and occasional meals with N. became a refuge and solace. The atmosphere at Simon's Field was becoming tense, and Sarina, who understood more English than her in-laws realized, knew that the visits to N. were the subject of unhappy conversations. In March, Olaf reassured Agnes, the day after a supper with N., that he felt nothing more than "a rather odd sort of slightly paternal friendship."[10] For the time being that was an accurate reflection of the boundaries he and N. drew around their relationship.

But Olaf was getting restless. The previous year he and Agnes shared the platform at Conway Hall in London. Agnes read from Shakespeare's sonnets and Austen's *Northanger Abbey,* and Olaf followed with a lecture on "Personal Relations in the Family." He presented one of his typical paradoxes. Monogamy, he said, makes possible the fullest experience of love, but promiscuity adds breadth and vigor to sexual experience. Straining for sophistication, he pitched headlong into euphuism. "Perhaps the ideal is to sip a few flowers before marriage so as to have practice in the difficult art of love before attempting the masterpiece. It is also possible that the masterpiece itself would sometimes benefit from occasional side-line sketches after marriage. Such aberrations, such holidays from monogamy might in some cases revivify the marriage. But in other cases they might merely wreck it." He was careful not to claim such marital refreshment as a male prerogative; the sexes must be "on equal footing in this matter." Married women, imprisoned in their homes, were so unhealthily identified with their children that when they grow up and leave home, he said, "an important part of the mother's personality is destroyed." He proposed a national system of day-nurseries so that women would no longer be "stranded without any valuable external interests."[11]

The personal grounds for this alternately quaint and thoughtful argument for the liberation of men and women from a stifling domesticity grew stronger over the next year. During 1947, as his attraction to N. became more insistent, Olaf's public references to the advantages of provisional monogamy increased. In June he told the Oxford Socialists, in an aside to a speech on the family in society, that he personally favored monogamy "but with occasional holidays." A September article for *Common Wealth Review* argued that love "cannot be possessive, or dictatorial" and must always allow "the free and spontaneous expression of the other's personality."[12] Then, in December, he chose an unpropitious audience for his views on sexual ethics. Liverpool newspapers reported that he had caused "a first-class controversy" by telling the leaders of local boys' clubs that "there was something wrong in monogamy as we know it to-day" and the time had come for "all sorts of sanctioned and respectable experiments."[13] The more sensational London newspapers gleefully picked up the story, in one case distorting it with headlines that bore no close relation to the temperate words Stapledon had used. The *Daily Express* leered in a headline:

Two-husband women?

It may be best, says

husband-lecturer

The titillation even reached across the Atlantic a year later when *Time* magazine, reporting on his address to the British Interplanetary Society, identified the little-known Stapledon with just three details: he was sixty-two, had lived with the same wife for twenty-eight years, and believed that while monogamy wasn't for everybody, the ideal was "monogamy with well-spaced holidays."[14]

Olaf wrote sheepishly to Aage Marcus that he had "recently become notorious in the worst section of the British press for some rash remarks about marriage. A Stockholm paper has telegraphed for an article." In fact, Svante Löfgren followed up his telegram with a solid offer of £15 for a popular article on new forms of marriage for his journal *ALLT*.[15] Although Olaf may have been embarrassed by the attention he was receiving, he did write the article, printed in Swedish in spring 1948. Flippant references to "holidays" from marriage were replaced by more complex formulations that tried to do justice to his own unaltered love for Agnes and his deepening affection for N. In his handwritten draft, titled "The Varieties of Marriage," he wrote:

> It is mistaken to suppose that, because love in its fullest expression is necessarily monogamous, therefore in marriage sexual desire must henceforth be automatically directed *exclusively* toward the monogamous partner.
> . . . .
> If a married person is sexually attracted by a third party, the monogamous love is not necessarily dead, nor the marriage necessarily in ruins.
> . . . .
> In rare cases a triple union of one man and two women has been known to endure.[16]

Such pronouncements caused little stir in Scandinavia and barely kept pace with Bloomsbury and Hampstead, but if the editors of the seamier London papers had been able to read Swedish, they would undoubtedly have given the author another taste of notoriety.

Even for provincial Olaf these were not new ideas, however. Everything he wrote about love and monogamy in 1947 and 1948 was foreshadowed as early as 1930 in the fictional marital arrangements of the Eighteenth Men in *Last and First Men*. What was different for him in 1948 was a personal urgency below the surface of philosophical speculation. When Agnes traveled to London, as she did more rarely than her husband, she fell in with Olaf's hope to keep the relationship with N. open, casual, and unanxious. They made an occasional "happy trio," in Olaf's phrase, at a meal or a play, but in time he recognized that his feelings for N. went deeper than paternal friendship. He and N. continued to observe a scrupulous propriety; they shared meals, conversation, walks, an occasional hour painting together, nothing more. Still, Agnes remained unhappy over the amount of time Olaf spent in London, and he grew tense as they seemed to have reached a stalemate. In June he asked her whether she could not enter into the spirit of an experiment: "I feel we might create something valuable to all of us that way, and something original. Anyhow, Taffy dearest of all, you and I are one indissolubly, and she is only a trimming as far as I am concerned, a charming outsider to be enjoyed occasionally in small doses."[17]

But Olaf knew that wasn't a fair or complete description of his feelings, and so did Agnes. In early July, when he came back to Simon's Field after a visit to N., Agnes was in great distress, and Olaf fell into a gloomy mood that made her feel still worse. He talked of his helplessness to resolve two loves and wondered if Agnes had put him on a pedestal, expecting a standard of fidelity he could not meet. Agnes summoned up a dignified reply, but her emotions were fragile:

I don't want you to say, or think, any more about "fallen idols." It's just a wrong answer to a false question. The other night when you were feeling very low you said you ought never to have married me—& that made me feel the most frozen white-washed plaster saint that nobody could possibly love. I have never never felt on *my* account that you ought not to have married me—but I have sometimes felt on *your* account that you ought not to have done because of all the things I know I haven't got that you would have liked—some of which I know that N. has got. But I have thanked heaven, & go on doing so, that you *did* marry me & that you are helping me to understand what love really is.[18]

Olaf went off to Langdale, and Agnes's letter, received there, elicited a reply that told the truth, fudged reality, and concealed feelings behind linguistic analysis in about equal measures. The author of this letter is a smoother version of the brusque young man of 1913 who claimed his mother misinterpreted his brotherly affection for Dorothy Miller:

At present, after reading your letter again, I feel I don't want to take any notice whatever of any woman but you, ever. But no doubt I shall not stay like that. But I do feel so strongly that you really needn't seriously mind about N., because she doesn't really compete with you at all. . . . So far as anyone ever *can* belong to anyone else, I belong to you and you to me. She doesn't belong to me, or I to her. No doubt a bit of her belongs to me, and vice versa, but fundamentally we are independent. On the other hand, of course, neither you nor I *exclusively* belongs to the other. You are not really *all* mine, because some of you belongs to Mary & some to Dibs & some to [their grandson] Thomas and so on. But fundamentally and at heart you do belong to me and I to you. And yet "belong" is the wrong word. In a sense you don't belong to me *at all,* namely in the sense that I have no right whatever to *use* you. In that sense, only things can belong, not persons. . . . Oh Taffy, darling, don't worry about it! I love you so much that the rest is negligible. I love you so much, and yet I hurt you! It's terrible. I can't even honestly ask for forgiveness, because I know I shall go on loving N. unless I just stop seeing her at all. And so all I can do is to say to you I love you so much that the rest is of no account.[19]

Olaf's tone toward Agnes alternated between solicitude and exasperation, as he sometimes felt the urge to apologize for the pain he was causing and sometimes was angry that she could not help seeing his attraction to N. as a rejection of herself. In a letter from Langdale, he sought the high road: "My *loving* N. does not really need to be forgiven, for *love* is always good. But my *desiring* her does need to be forgiven I suppose. But believe me, it's second-ary and consequent on the loving. And anyhow I don't desire her as I desire you, as a constant, lifelong companion and bedfellow." He acknowledged a desire for a friendship more than paternal, but would settle for the status quo, hoping only that Agnes would not blame him for wanting more: "I just want to see her sometimes, if it can be done without having to feel guilty."

But when he didn't address Agnes directly and transmuted his feelings into fiction, his anger became more pronounced. In a 1947 monologue a fictional alter ego presented the opposite view to the one Olaf issued from Langdale:

The common "we" was wrapping me round with a web of subtle spider threads, and sucking the life out of me. I would soon be not myself anymore, but a mere part of that "we." It was a pleasant enough process, up to a point; but it was lethal to *me,* the real, hard, dynamic individual. So long as I was content to be not myself, I was happy in a drowsy, doped way. But sometimes I felt like murder; when she assumed that because I still needed a life of my own, she had failed me, and I did not love her. It was partly my work that she grudged, as something in me that she could not share. Worse, when I showed any interest in other girls, she went all tragic. But I hadn't really changed toward her. I just wanted a bit of variety and refreshment. Well, it was clear to me I must begin cutting the threads. And to my horror I found that I bled at every cut. The irrational sentimentalist in me sided with her, and shrieked with her pain and my own."[20]

Olaf's Langdale letter reached Agnes at Geneva on 11 July, where she was at a conference of the Women's International League for Peace and Freedom. She debated emergency resolutions about the situation in Palestine and voted to recommend that the United Nations Security Council impose sanctions against Arab states refusing to observe a truce with the new state of Israel. At fifty-four, she was trying to forge an identity separate from that of "author's wife." She had not been on such a distant journey without Olaf since she sailed from Australia in 1919, and she wanted to play the part of a modern spouse, accommodating her husband's wish for a creative love affair and not reprising the tearful scenes over Evelyn. "I think it is good for me to be away from you & learn to be a person on my own," she replied to him. "I am still a person that works properly—not just a stuffed image that falls over when its support is gone."[21]

Agnes knew N. well enough and was feeling confident enough of her ability to face the situation directly that she wrote to her too. In early August, N. wrote back from Florence, where she was on holiday, and the two women succeeded better than Olaf in getting straight to the point. "I think yours is the corner of the triangle which must be considered first," N. wrote. "As you must know, the last thing in the world I would ever want to do would be to come between you." She knew Agnes would have been happier if Olaf had never met her at Exeter, but that fact could not be erased. She was certain that Olaf's marriage was the central psychological fact of his experience—the bedrock of his life as an individual and as an artist. But women's and men's experience of marriage was profoundly different:

I don't think most women are able to love more than one man at a time, and so it seems impossible to them that men can do so. But they can—lots of them do—probably just because they aren't focused in the same direction. With Olaf, I'm sure that *you* are his focus, always have been and always will be. But being a man, and one who isn't afraid of recognising his feelings for what they are, he spills out over the edges occasionally. I'm not trying to minimise his feelings for me, because that wouldn't help, but I really can't believe that it lessens his love for you. I hope we can work our way through to a satisfactory solution, but if it proves impossible and we have to make an end, it would be absurd for you to be upset because it was on account of you. It would be because the two-relationship which you have both built up together is of such value and importance that no side issue can be allowed to put grit in the machinery. Grit would never be disruptive enough to wreck the machine, but it might make it run less smoothly.

N. thought if there were a reasonable solution it would be "a pity to pack up without trying to reach it," but the delicately balanced triple union proved unworkable. It was not just that Agnes found the pain impossible to ignore. N. herself was, in her own word, "a puritan." She disliked deception of any kind and had an unfeigned respect for Agnes and Olaf's marriage that she was disinclined to put into jeopardy. The thought of being a party to emotional cruelty was repugnant; she had even once objected to Olaf that making Sirius handless was "a very cruel thing" and "my heart bled for the poor creature." Her moral positions were not merely abstract or literary; she liked Agnes and could not bear playing the distasteful role of "the other woman." And N. was as good as her word. Of the three parties it was she who was most resistant to redrawing the lines of the relationship and it was she who initiated the distancing of the affair after an experimental period in 1949. Forty years after Olaf's death, she called it "a grand passion with nowhere to go and therefore very uncomfortable."[22]

Both N. and Agnes, who remained friends until Agnes died in 1984, recognized more quickly and certainly than Olaf that his wishfully neat triangle was at odds with the complexity of their actual feelings; what might make perfect sense in the vacuum of futurist fiction or philosophical theory was nearly impossible to manage by the three real people who became entangled in a profoundly stressful situation for which none of them was emotionally prepared. Even Olaf, who liked to think himself unconventional and who moved in circles in which extramarital loves were common, was the product of a Victorian respectability never entirely outgrown. How Eric Robertson or Naomi Mitchison or H. G. Wells conducted their love lives could not be a reliable guide for his own conduct, no matter how much he wanted to emulate their sexual freedoms. The "eighteenth men" of his scientific romance enjoyed holidays from monogamy without guilt or grief, but the author was inescapably a first man, and a provincial one to boot. That Olaf himself could not see this as clearly as could Agnes and N. was almost certainly exacerbated by the sense of literary failure that nagged at him in 1947 and 1948.

Olaf connected his susceptibility to a love affair to his decline in popularity as a writer. As he drew closer to N., he explored with her his tangled feelings with exceptional candor:

Old men are fatally attracted by young women, and apt to make fools of themselves. In my case the attraction was the more fatal because I found you actually cared for me, a withering old thing. And it happened that I was in need of somebody to buck me up because I had grown very disillusioned about myself and my work, and I was feeling very low.[23]

To Agnes he wrote something similar. "The attraction was intensified by my disillusionment about myself. I hoped I was going to 'contribute' in some way, and I have not brought it off. And so I felt stranded and 'out of it'. And so, quite irrationally, I found satisfaction in being cared for by a woman of thirty who was not *already* implicated with me, and she moreover a very lovable person."[24]

His sense of being stranded in the world of letters had been growing throughout the decade, and the failure of *The Flames* may have been the decisive blow. Secker and Warburg never expected a huge profit from *The Flames*, but the firm still thought of Stapledon's as a name worth having on their list. H. G. Wells had died in 1946, and there was no other contender for the honorific title of Eminent Scientific Prophet than Olaf Stapledon. When *The Flames* came out late in the summer of 1947, it was duly hailed as the work of "the greatest living writer of scientific romances." One reviewer rhapsodized, "Contemporary literature's most ingenious master of macabre fantasy has excelled himself." But such praise from the *Johannesburg Star* and the *Daily Worker* did not sell many copies in London. *The Flames* got scant attention from the mainstream press. *John O'London's Weekly* applauded a brilliant application of fantasy to contemporary fanaticism, but John Betjeman in the *Daily Herald* found it all "a strain on the mind." The most revealing critical comment may have been P. H. Newby's intimation of a change in public taste. *The Flames,* he wrote, is "a parable for the times, ingeniously and colourfully worked out. But either you like this sort of thing or you don't and that is all there is to say."[25] Papers that had routinely reviewed Stapledon's earlier fiction—the *Times,* the *Times Literary Supplement,* the *New Statesman,* the *Liverpool Post,* the *Manchester Guardian,* the *Scotsman*—had not a word for *The Flames.*

Olaf's editor, Roger Senhouse, was disappointed at the poor sales. Hoping for a boost at the Christmas season, he prevailed on the author to go to Manchester in October for an exhibition of autumn books. The plan was for Olaf to promote *The Flames* by giving a talk on the history of the scientific romance, including a retrospective of his own career in applying the scientific imagination to the forms of fiction. There is no evidence that the speech accomplished its aim—Secker and Warburg's ledgers show a loss, with only 1,692 sales from a print run of 5,000 before the book was remaindered in 1952— but it prompted Olaf to his most extensive and learned assessment of the literary tradition in which he made his name, and for the first time in his career he adopted the term "science fiction" to describe his masterpieces.[26] Ironically, he was also making his exit as a writer of scientific romances, for *The Flames* was his final effort.

The Manchester talk on "Science and Fiction" came at a point in his life when Olaf was inclined to be self-conscious about the genre he had most often chosen since 1930. He made up his mind that *Star Maker,* though never as popular as some of his others, was the book he was happiest to have written. " 'Last and First Men' is easier reading, I am told. But it has not so much meat in it."[27] In 1946 he told his friend John Gloag, who was collecting his own short fantasies into an omnibus volume, "All this modish playing about with time and space, which you and I have so often indulged in, is of course symptomatic of our period. It opens up new worlds for the writer of fantastic fiction, or at any rate it gives him a new and exciting game to play." The fantastic writer must keep adjusting to new rules imposed by the unfolding disclosures of scientific research, but the pleasure of creation, he wrote to Gloag, resides in the artist's freedom to go beyond what is known so long as plausibility is not violated.[28] In a more doubtful mood at the end of 1946, Olaf wrote in the past tense of his fiction-making, "Sometimes looking back on my own work, I feel I had the power of conception, but not adequately the power of execution." He continued his letter to the painter Fay Pomerance with pointed reflections on "the tragedy of the sincere artist who nevertheless fails":

> I find that this game of creating myths and symbols, in whatever medium, is in a way rather frightening. One gets completely absorbed, and rides triumphantly on the irresistable [*sic*] wave of imagination; and then when the thing is finished one wonders whether one was at all inspired or merely rather mad; and again, whether, although to oneself it may seem magnificent, to others it may seem just silly. And sometimes one looks back on things done years earlier and sees so clearly the difference between the parts that are 'inspired' and those that are not.[29]

The themes introduced privately to his fellow artists Gloag and Pomerance—the conventions of fantastic writing, the scientific romance as a sign of the times, mythic and symbolic functions of science fiction, the sources of imagination, the impulse to look backwards in satisfaction and judgment— were all folded into Olaf's lecture at Manchester. All artful fiction, he said, uses symbolic situations to quicken the mind and the feelings to fresh awareness. What he called "the straight novel" does it by putting personal relations at the center and exploring the effects of person on person. The historical novel focuses on time and place, as the imagination recreates a human society from the past. The propaganda novel—of which he took *Pilgrim's Progress* to be the prototype—makes ideas central, and the author aims to convert the reader. But science fiction was widely regarded as "barbarous," he argued, because critics had turned literary convention into a tyranny by demanding novels "strict as sonnets." The science-fictional imagination, he said with only slight exaggeration of his own practice, bodies forth "no people, no heroine, no love, no talk." While the usual norms for the novel were inapplicable, the speculative fictions of science did not constitute a literature without standards. Stapledon distinguished, as he had in the past, "serious science fiction" from the "sheer marvels" of what he scornfully called "the science fiction mags"—"often scientifically poor & humanly atrocious."

He surveyed the precursors of science fiction—the *Divine Comedy, Paradise Lost, Gulliver's Travels,* in each of which science was peripheral to some other central concern—but took the genre as a distinctively modern one, tracing it back no farther than Verne and Wells. There was less real science fiction in the twentieth century than one might guess, he told his audience. Many books grouped with science fiction—and he listed such favorites of his own as C. S. Lewis's space novels and *Screwtape Letters,* David Lindsay's *Voyage to Arcturus,* T. H. White's *Sword in the Stone,* and Katharine Burdekin's *Proud Man* and *Swastika Night*—were "fantasies not primarily scientific." Aside from Wells and Verne, the modern "masters" were Karel Čapek, Regis Messac, M. P. Shiel, John Gloag, and, purely on the basis of his speculative essays, J. B. S. Haldane. He included no American author, and, discreetly, he did not list his own name, but the remainder of his lecture was a detailed examination of the creative aims of his major scientific romances.

In working out scientifically plausible inventions and possible futures, Olaf said at Manchester, he wanted to create "modern myths" and to "relate science to religion." Typically, there were two stages to his writing. Over the first he had no control: an image or vision came to him and seized his imagination. Then "the artificer" got to work: consulting scientific friends, researching the intellectual background that would make the vision plausible, and structuring the episodes through which the vision would be prosecuted. In all his fiction, mind and spirit were the paramount issues, and he hazarded the opinion that while *Star Maker* was the most ambitious canvas he had ever attempted, *Sirius* was likely to be judged his best science fiction. Although "Science and Fiction" was probably the most scholarly anatomy of the subject presented in England until C. S. Lewis's celebrated lecture "On Science Fiction" at the Cambridge English Club in 1955, Olaf never turned his notes into an essay.

Had *The Flames* been successful and had there been a call for Stapledon's views on the scientific romance, he might well have been able to advance the thoughtful discussion of science fiction, which did not begin to take place until almost twenty years after his death. But, as he told Fay Pomerance, *The Flames* "is not the sort of thing to be popular," and a taste for his sort of philosophical fiction was becoming rarer. In the postwar literary marketplace, science fiction grew in popularity, but the genre—like much else in popular culture—was increasingly Americanized, and the distinctive British tradition of the scientific romance, in which fictional invention served as a pretext for philosophical, political, and scientific speculation, began yielding to the determinedly lowbrow style of the space operas and what C. S. Lewis caustically termed "engineers' stories" that dominated the American pulp magazines.[30] Olaf acquired some new American readers in the 1940s who were discovering the rich imagination of his work, but an author in his sixties could not sustain his reputation on the enthusiasms of a few fans in another country reading him in scarce secondhand copies.

As English readers' tastes were moving away from the scientific romance, Olaf's own intellectual and imaginative interests were also in a ferment signaled by the emphasis in *The Flames* not only on the physics of the split atom but on the questionable science of parapsychology. His planned series of short stories on paranormal phenomena shows a similar fascination with what he once would have called pseudoscience. The interest was not brand new; even before World War I, he joked with Agnes, during their long-distance courtship, about the slowness of the mails. "I should like some method of wireless telepathy. If Marconi and Mrs. Eddy and Brahms were to get into partnership they might discover the thing."[31]

The chief attraction of paranormal phenomena for Stapledon was that, if their reality could ever be demonstrated, the insufficiency of a purely materialist philosophy would be inescapable. He was uncomfortable, however, with the fanatics who clustered around parapsychologists, and his curiosity was tempered by a determined skepticism. "Heaven preserve us from table-rapping" had been his caveat to all speculation about spiritual afterlives for thirty years.[32] His imagination mapped alternative states of being, while his intellect stood watch against fraud and self-delusion. Both *Last and First Men* and *Last Men in London* were premised on telepathic communication between the future and the present, and the utopians in *Odd John* flaunted a host of psychic powers. But in the 1930s, Olaf still considered parapsychology more fantastic than scientific, despite the proselytizing of Gerald Heard and such heralded books as J. W. Dunne's *Experiment with Time* and J. B. Rhine's *Extra-Sensory Perception*. A passage cut from the draft preface to *Last and First Men* calls its use of telepathy the most "grossly extravagant" of fictional devices, and the annotated reading list appended to *Philosophy and Living* warns that the few books on "super-normal powers" worth consulting remain "intellectually disreputable."[33]

The Flames takes a different tack from his writings of the 1930s. Instead of asking readers to suspend disbelief, the narrative aggressively challenges complacent skepticism. Stapledon turned the question whether Cass is in direct mental communication with solar beings or whether he is insane into the central interpretative problem in *The Flames;* in begging his friend Thos to publish his long letter about the "salamanders" who inhabit the sun, Cass admits that unless his account is presented as fiction, editors will refuse to publish it. Those readers with "sufficient imaginative insight" will, he trusts, realize that *The Flames* is not "*mere* fiction." And Stapledon left his readers with precisely that problem of discriminating the truth in the tale from the craziness of the teller. The teasing design of *The Flames* reflected the author's more probing study of the evidence of parapsychological research as well as his continuing hesitations about the conclusions to be drawn from the research.

Psychic power was a Stapledonian issue of long standing, going back to his 1908 Oxford paper on Joan of Arc's voices, but his heightened and studious interest in the subject after the war was not peculiar to him. Investigators of the paranormal (and a variety of quack hypnotists and mediums) seemed at large everywhere. The Progressive League, with which Olaf had continued an intermittent association since the mid-1930s, made inquiry into the paranormal one of its principal occupations after the war, culminating in a national symposium at Brighton in February 1949—the first large-scale conference on the topic in England in twenty-five years. Through the League and London's venerable Society for Psychical Research, founded in 1882, Olaf met G. N. M. Tyrrell, H. H. Price, and other scholarly researchers on telepathy, precognition, and psychokinesis, as well as more dubious figures like Lawrence Hyde and Graham Howe. The lure of parapsychology drew in incautious and sometimes unstable devotees, and psychical experimentation became so fashionable a topic that Heinz Westmann's Present Question group chose it as the focus for its second conference, at Birmingham in the summer of 1947. Although papers by Herbert Read and G. Wilson Knight gave the PQ sessions a respectable sheen, Olaf was put off by a "high proportion of cranks—astrologers, numerologists, and so on." The general run of speeches, "beating the air, scrabbling after something sure to hold on to," disappointed him. His agnostic-skeptic side found the effort to get "the lowdown on the Whole" to be "both impious and comic."[34]

Just after the war, while Olaf was reading all the pamphlets of the Society for Psychical Research he could find, his art-historian friend Aage Marcus was making the rounds of séances in Copenhagen. The Marcus-Stapledon correspondence in 1947 and 1948 is dominated by exchanges of information about parapsychology, which Olaf now considered "the growing point of thought in our day." He confessed to Marcus that he and Agnes made up occasional private experiments in telepathy "because she does sometimes seem to be a bit 'spooky.'" (Some letters Olaf wrote back in 1943 when he was in the Hebrides on his RAF lecture tour included charts, organized by time and topic, of their efforts to send and receive images.) By the end of 1947, he had contracted to do a pair of articles for a new journal, *Enquiry*, devoted to research in the paranormal. "I feel rather anxious about my intrusion into these fields," he told Marcus, "as I have no experience."[35]

Marcus's experiences, on the other hand, were dumbfounding. During a series of séances in the winters of 1946–1947 and 1947–1948, he claimed to have observed psychokinetic episodes, twenty instances of levitation, and rappings and knockings of "colossal intensity." He was satisfied—as were the Danish novelist Jacob Paludan and several doctors also present—that no chicanery was used. A professional photographer filmed one levitation; when the film was broken down by frames, there was a sequence of images of the medium sitting quietly at the table succeeded by shots of him in the air, with his clothing falling away piece by piece until he was stark naked. Marcus told Olaf he had witnessed this event and saw the medium ascend instantaneously to the ceiling. On the promise that Olaf would return them without reproducing them, Marcus sent a selection of still photographs of the levitation and of chairs flying through the room, with the understated commentary, "It is a queer time to live in at present."

When the photos arrived in Caldy, Olaf happened to be dining with Leonard and Dorothy Martin and their guest E. M. Forster, who gave a full account of his own psychic episodes. He showed the Danish pictures to an ardent Forster, but Olaf tried to keep some detachment. On returning the pictures, he told Marcus that he still thought "one should not pledge oneself absolutely to belief in them as wholly valid until they have stood the fire of public criticism, after publication." Wishing he could have seen the events with his own eyes, Olaf nevertheless wrote, "I move at a bound from grave scepticism about 'physical' paranormal phenomena to a state of cautious acceptance, coupled with bewilderment and excitement."[36]

For Olaf, who at that very time was saying in print that "we should always be as sceptical as possible before accepting any theory," such a statement was tantamount to conversion. As a "recent recruit" to psychic research, as he labeled himself in an interview, he prudently avoided both controversy over the technical issues of evidence and the sensational claims of the lunatic fringe. He awaited the conclusive proof that "will knock the bottom out of scientific materialism. We seem to be discovering a vast universe beyond the confines of physical science. What we have to do now is reflect on these discoveries; to interpret them correctly."[37] That is, there was a place for the speculative philosopher just outside the door being opened by psychic research;

as the shape of the mental universe changed, and as people tried to enter and map what Olaf called the "dark continent" espied through the portal, guidance would be needed in asking new ethical and metaphysical questions. Data were accumulating that might require serious analysis even of such possibilities as communication with the dead—the sort of spiritist highjinks he would once have ridiculed. Everything was open for reconsideration:

> The situation is rather like that which confronted the physicists just before the establishment of the physical theory of relativity. Physicists were perplexed by a number of queer little facts which no ingenuity could harmonize with the classical theory. Einstein produced a new theory, which successfully coped with the awkward facts, but at the cost of a seemingly nonsensical attitude to space and time. But the ideas of physicists as to what was nonsensical were gradually transformed. They learned to think thoughts that were formerly quite unthinkable.

Retaining a modest sense of his lack of expertise and resisting a rush into uncritical advocacy, Olaf preferred the role of doorkeeper rather than explorer of the realms being disclosed by parapsychology, recalling, in a metaphor drawn from his sailor-forebears, that what explorers sometimes believe is land turns out to be cloudbanks on the horizon.[38]

When the big Brighton Conference on Psychical Research was held in 1949, Olaf was asked to be commentator, making the final summation of the conflicting views that had been advanced by the leading British researchers. He did not commit himself on the substantive theories of any of the speakers. Instead, he reminded the audience that no matter what emerged from study in this field, certain "perennial principles" of human behavior would not be altered. And the issue of life beyond death, which had most intrigued the conference, was to be approached with special caution. Whether consciousness survived destruction of the body—and the evidence seemed to him less strong than some claimed—made no fundamental ethical difference. The big metaphysical questions would always fascinate, but they might bear little on how people conducted their daily lives. "We should not derive our values from the ideas of survival or of a divine personality. The values of love, wisdom, and creative action did not depend on anything except ordinary experience."[39] The medium and the telepath would never render the philosophical temper obsolete.

Although his fiction roamed space, time, and the ultimate mysteries, Olaf himself was always more expansive, confident, and definite when his focus was mundane. Metaphysical speculation, he took mischievous pleasure in saying, "*is* just a pastime."[40] The serious business of teaching people how to cope with the actual world and make it better—the utopian inclination—was, for him, never just a pastime. After 1945 he believed that more urgently than ever before. An unusual opportunity for Olaf to do some educating came early in 1948 when the Centre de Connaissance Internationale in Montpellier asked him to make a three-week lecture tour through southern France. The Centre promoted international understanding by inviting foreign speakers to travel from town to town, addressing invited audiences of no more than 150 on one day and then leading a number of small-group discussions the following day. The pedagogy was not unlike what Olaf had perfected in his WEA teaching, although this audience would be largely middle-class and professional: academics, scientists, teachers, doctors, social workers, local politicians, housewives, priests, nuns. Olaf and Agnes accepted the invitation jointly, he ready with two long lectures (one on art and society, the other on the making of a European community) to use with various audiences, she prepared to speak on women in postwar Britain.[41]

After a welcoming dinner in Paris on 19 February 1948 with Emmanuel Mounier, editor of *Esprit* and leader of the Personalist movement in philosophy, Olaf and Agnes began their circuit of Avignon, Nimes, Montpellier, Marseilles, Carcassonne, Toulouse, and Pau before winding up with a series of discussions in Paris. Aside from family holidays in the isolation of Lake Annecy near the Swiss border in the 1930s, Olaf had had no French experience since 1919, when the Friends' Ambulance Unit was disbanded. He found himself sorting through those thirty-year-old memories in an effort to understand the French character. He recalled the friendly simplicity and obsessive nationalism of the infantrymen—"les poilus"—with whom the ambulance drivers spent the most time, and he revered the name of the "noble priest" Abbé Saglio, the army chaplain with whom he had shared countless hours talking religion and philosophy before he died of a gangrenous wound. But the French character also had to accommodate the officers who hid ammunition in the ambulances going to the front, in willful defiance of the Quakers' ground rules, and the unforgettable spectacle of poilus viciously kicking wounded German prisoners as they were carried away on stretchers. "I am no Francophile," Olaf told his colleagues at the London PEN.

For all the long-standing English bias against things French, to which Olaf was not immune, the antiquated notion of the French as Britain's "natural enemy" had to be replaced by a conviction that they are "our natural friends, with whom we must combine for the resuscitation of Western Europe and the reassertion and development of the European tradition. This reawakening of Europe is urgent not only for Europe's sake but for the world's." If Europeans failed to set aside their local prejudices to forge a new unity, "those two great adolescent peoples," the Russians and the Americans, might be left to start a "Third World War, the first atomic war, and the ruin of civilization, if not the end of Man." That was the central theme of Olaf's lecture on "Mankind at the Crossroads."

The European countries had had both a long enough time to mature their cultures and sufficiently strong doses of war in the twentieth-century mode to appreciate the need to synthesize the Russian virtues of solidarity and discipline with the American devotion to individual liberty and personal comfort. His message to France was to seek its future neither in the Gaullist siren song of past glories nor in an adoption of the "wickedness" of Stalin's violation of liberty in the name of revolution; a livable future lay in the creation of "a liberal communism" in partnership with the forward-looking Labour movement in England. On his return to London, the message he delivered was: "The plight of Man is desperate, and time flies." Look across the Channel, extricate yourselves from a dangerous dependence on America, and throw in your lot with Europe. To both France and England he asserted that Germany remained part of Europe. Germany was the "neurotic neighbor" who had landed himself in prison, could someday be rehabilitated and released, and needed to be lived with.

Overestimating the average Briton's loyalty to the new socialist government, underestimating the appeal of de Gaulle to the demoralized French, and misjudging the time it would take to heal Germany internally, Stapledon's call for the first steps toward a united Europe were forty years ahead of the time. In a letter to an imaginary great-grandson living at the end of the century, he expressed the hope that the categories of "Frenchman" and "German" would have been rendered obsolete: "Or is your Europe still mad with multiple personality?"[42] His prediction of imminent atomic war if Europe failed to unite was (just barely) too pessimistic. But he knew which was the door in, even though for the time being it wouldn't budge. And he was establishing his personal agenda for the last years of his life. It was not to be a literary agenda. Olaf's French tour in February and March 1948 previewed his strenuous and controversial peace embassies of 1948 and 1949 when he received far more public attention and many more inches of newspaper space than his published works had been allotted.

18

PILGRIM'S PROGRESS

1948–1949

IN THE SPRING AND SUMMER OF 1948, Stapledon struggled to finish a novel begun in 1946. When Fredric Warburg promptly rejected it, Stapledon decided he had "quite lost interest" in *A Man Divided*. Not finally published until 1950, *A Man Divided* was his last effort as a writer of fiction. When Aage Marcus asked him late in 1948 what his new project was, he admitted, "Agnes and I are always busy rushing from meeting to meeting. I have got into a bad habit of giving innumerable talks to local and other societies, frittering away far too much time."[1] The defining event of 1948 for Olaf, one that thrust him into a political rather than a literary spotlight for the rest of his life, had come in August when he accepted an invitation to a "World Congress of Intellectuals in Defense of Peace" in Poland.

Under the joint chairmanship of the biologist and director of UNESCO Julian Huxley, the French Nobelist Irène Joliot-Curie, and the Russian novelist Alexander Fadeyev, the congress at Wroclaw was the largest assembly of artists and scholars since the war. The British delegates included J. B. S. Haldane, J. D. Bernal, and C. H. Waddington among the scientists, the historians A. J. P. Taylor and Christopher Hill, the novelist Louis Golding and the journalist Kingsley Martin, and assorted architects, painters, and musicians. Unlike PEN's Stockholm gathering two years earlier, this congress was not a creature of Western Europe and North America. Besides twenty-three delegates from the Soviet Union and contingents from the Eastern European satellite nations, there were West Africans, Algerians, Iraqis, Brazilians, Vietnamese, Mexicans, Israelis, Uruguayans, and Chinese. The Polish government supplied air travel, lodging, and food, and Hermon Ould of PEN naïvely exclaimed that

Poland would "not only pay our expenses but even give us pocket money!"[2] It was a generosity Stapledon later regretted.

On 25 August, Olaf arrived at the Gothic town hall in bombed-out Wroclaw, known as Breslau when it was under German rule. The five hundred delegates were crowded together, refectory-style, at long tables separated by narrow aisles. At a perpendicularly placed head table sat the several international presidents and vice-presidents, a ruling "presidium" of elected delegates, and the day's speakers. Four speeches setting the conference's agenda were scheduled for the opening session—twenty minutes each for a Russian, a Briton, a Frenchman, and a Pole. Though inexperienced at international political gatherings, Olaf was assigned the keynote address for Great Britain.

First up was the husky, blond, bland-faced president of the Soviet Writers' Union, Alexander Fadeyev, a strict ideologue with a voice that scraped the skin off language. His twenty-minute talk stretched to forty minutes, then to sixty, and finally to an hour-and-a-half harangue punctuated by clockwork applause from the Communist delegations. As Madame Joliot-Curie in the chair made no move to cut him off, the Western delegates, heads shaking beneath the earphones they wore for simultaneous translation, became agitated. Fadeyev's paean to the Red Army's liberation of eastern Europe slid into a relentless and inclusive assault on American culture, from Hollywood's glorified gangsters to the biased reporting of *Life* and *Reader's Digest* to the provocation of Voice of America broadcasts to the "disgusting filth" and "convulsion" of popular dance fads. When he turned to literature, the English and French were not spared. He heaped scorn on "British decadence" and condemned the works of Eliot, Henry Miller, O'Neill, Dos Passos, Malraux, and Sartre. In the conference's most often quoted words he shouted, "If hyenas could type and jackals could use a fountain pen they would write such things." The Eastern bloc clapped noisily and Madame Joliot-Curie called a recess. The American delegates were paralyzed, silent, acquiescent. Some of the Britons murmured that Fadeyev had been "savage" and rendered the business of the congress impossible.[3]

Juliette Huxley, in a private memorandum written just after the event, said the English and American delegates "crawled out to lunch," feeling belittled and betrayed. She and Julian Huxley, J. D. Bernal, the writer Ella Winter, the American sculptor Jo Davidson, and Olaf gathered over sandwiches to plan strategy. Olaf was due to speak when the proceedings resumed, and he wanted to throw out his speech and take on Fadeyev. He was feeling perverse, telling Agnes the next morning, "The total atmosphere is very Left, which makes me go rather Right."[4] His luncheon companions, however, persuaded him to refrain from attacking at length or in kind and instead to register a dignified protest, recover a more moderate tone for the oratory, and go on with his prepared text. As he ate, Olaf scribbled pencil notes at the top of his typed speech for his extemporaneous reply to Fadeyev.[5]

At the microphone Olaf did not raise his voice beyond his customary level tones. He had not come to Poland to praise his own country, he said, nor was he interested in ritual praise of other nations. If the congress was to succeed in promoting peace, each delegate must enter sympathetically into the point of view of others. No ideology could claim the whole truth, and no nation was blameless in abusing its artists. Taking up Fadeyev's blacklist, Stapledon defended just one writer to represent the whole. He chose someone whose politics he loathed, but the poems of T. S. Eliot, he asserted, should be prized by everyone at Wroclaw as the work of one of the century's great imaginations. Then he shifted into his prepared talk: an analysis of the meanings of "culture," a vision of a united but pluralist world, and an appeal for understanding between East and West in the atomic age. "Ours is indeed a great and a very strange moment of man's career, a moment big with tragedy and hope," he concluded. "And our responsibility is great. How those future men will smile at our crude theories and our adolescent passions! But also they will recognize in our tortuous antics the first, confused, tentative, ludicrous gestures of a new-born humanity."[6]

The response of his own delegation and of various observers was mixed. Juliette Huxley claimed that few delegates welcomed the defense of Eliot and that she alone of the forty Britons clapped. Her husband Julian thought the speech right in tone and moving, but too vague to do much good.[7] To a Czech journalist Stapledon was "a typical individualist and idealist who overlooks the real nature of the conflicts." Kingsley Martin, no friend to Stapledon, missed the speech but got a secondhand report; he patronized him in the *New Statesman* as "a mild but sturdy character" who had contented himself with a homily on the value of tolerance.[8] Three members of the U.S. foreign service doing surveillance for the State Department were shocked by Fadeyev's virulence and wanted a pugnacious rebuttal. Instead, they wrote in a confidential memo, "Stapledon of Great Britain droned through a prepared paper suitable to a polite academic gathering." The American ambassador to Poland was more sanguine and advised Secretary of State Dean Acheson that the plea for cooperation had caused Stapledon to be labeled an American sympathizer in the Polish press. The paper trail from Wroclaw to Washington describes a temperate, modest, and harmless Stapledon, and it helped script the drama six months later when he applied for a visa to the United States.[9]

As the conference continued, so did the fireworks. In a short, sharp speech the Oxford historian Alan Taylor gave Fadeyev the tongue-lashing he felt Stapledon should have administered, and a typically long-winded performance by the Russian writer Ilya Ehrenburg generated another indictment of

Euro-American culture, full of "brilliant demagogics and venom," said Juliette Huxley. It was apparent that if anything was going to happen at Wroclaw, delegates had to get out of the Great Hall with its set speeches, competitive posing, and claques. Serious conferees moved into the corridors and hotel lounges for informal talk and formed committees to work on resolutions to put before the congress on its final day. Olaf took the lead in arranging a midnight supper for the British and the Russians at the end of the second day. Over a buffet of smoked salmon, fruit, and cake, helped out with vodka and cigarettes in plenty, they worked until four in the morning to find common ground. Stapledon's defense of Eliot prompted one Russian to ask whether the poet was not, in fact, a fascist. One British delegate, attempting to be helpful, said that Eliot was simply a traditionalist and a monarchist. "You mean he is only a little reactionary?" the Russian persisted. "But is he a big or a little poet?" The Englishman walked right into the trap, affirming that Eliot was indeed a very big poet. "Then he must be a big reactionary!" Despite the awkwardness of jokes and conversations brokered through interpreters, Olaf was relieved at last "to meet Russians face to face beyond the 'iron curtain.' "[10]

Julian Huxley tried to craft a final resolution whose wording the Eastern and Western blocs and the colonized countries of Africa and Asia could all accept. The job proved immensely difficult, as Soviet and Polish participants in the drafting committee dug in and demanded a text that rebuked American warmongering and deleted anti-Stalinist references to the open circulation of ideas. Huxley was as determined to have a clause on freedom of expression and research as he was to avoid insulting particular countries. "The Drafting Committee was terrible," he wrote of the belligerence and delaying tactics that drove him to a state of silent fury. When he finally got what he thought was a usable text, he showed it to the Polish writer Jerzy Borejsza, the congress's general secretary and a reputed secret police agent. He was told to start over. "You could have passed this in 1903, and in 1913, and in 1933—it means nothing," Borejsza snapped.[11] By then Huxley was exhausted and his heart was racing; a doctor examined him, gave him some medicine, and told him not to go back to the committee. He left Poland a day early, before the final votes. Without Huxley, the committee descended into chaos and the British representative, John Boyd Orr, walked out. At that point Stapledon was brought in to try to rescue the situation.

He engineered a compromise between Huxley's draft, with its liberal emphasis on freedom and its political reticence, and a Polish-Russian text that took a hard line on the U.S. Two much-amended and patched-together drafts were sent off to typists for a fresh copy of what Olaf called "a very imperfect amalgamation." What came back—and almost went to the floor of the congress—was a version that omitted several of the most hard-won verbal concessions from the Eastern bloc. When the errors were discovered, the committee nearly broke up. In Stapledon's account:

> I happened to be the one to spot the omission of vital clauses. Though at first I suspected dishonesty, later I realized that such a trick would have been merely childish, as it could not possibly escape detection when we came to read the final typescript. The committee met again to revise the product of the typists, and we had to argue the whole thing through again phrase by phrase because no one seemed to know precisely what had been agreed. At one point the French (communist) member banged his fist on the table and declared with passion that too many concessions were being made, and that the resolution would be rejected by his delegation. The Russian was equally sore, but I must emphasize that he showed a real will to understand our objections, and that he accepted a number of important concessions. The communists wanted a straight declaration that the whole source of danger was in the U.S.A. From their point of view the resolution was very badly watered down.[12]

Olaf's patience produced a text that most British delegates and all the Russians felt they could sign. There was a syntactic problem, however, that even Huxley had missed in earlier drafts. A clause on World War II read: "The culture of mankind was saved at the price of unheard-of sacrifices and privations by the rallying to the full of all democratic forces—of the Soviet Union, of the peoples of Great Britain and of the United States, and of the heroic popular Resistance movements in countries invaded by fascism."[13] While the government and people of the USSR were treated as one, only the British and American people, not their regimes, were democratic forces. The syntax enraged Alan Taylor, one of three Britons to vote against the resolution on the floor. Taylor, whose anti-Fadeyev speech had been snubbed by his colleagues, painted Olaf as the goat in what he saw as the ultimate failure of the congress. In a note to the absent Huxley, Taylor grumbled that "Stapledon really made a mess of all you had done on the drafting committee."[14] Not content to keep his opinion private, Taylor threw a public punch. The Russians, he claimed in the *New Statesman,* pretended to endorse the principle of freedom but tried to "swindle" it out of the resolution as it was typed, while a "befogged" Stapledon thanked the clever communists for purported concessions that were in fact propaganda triumphs.[15]

For his part, Olaf was disappointed with the outcome at Wroclaw. He ended up signing, with nine other Britons on the noncommunist Left, a minority report deploring the conference's parochialism and the time wasted on rehearsing tired ideological formulas. "The first duty of intellectuals is to be intelligent and the duty of this Congress should have been to examine impartially the germs of a future war," the minority wrote. To Agnes, Olaf confided that he had learned little from the debate; "mostly it could be got out of the *Daily Worker.*"[16] A lot of energy went to "mere blowing off steam," he told one newspaper. The resolution stated "the more important half of the truth, namely that the danger lies in American capitalism. It ignored the complementary truth that Russia has recently behaved very provocatively." The Soviet tirades, he wrote in an essay for a Polish journal, diluted the emotional center of the congress in "the long sequence of indictments made by the representatives of the oppressed coloured peoples"—the delegates from Madagascar, Algeria, Vietnam, the West Indies, French Equatorial Africa, and India, and a black American from New York.[17]

At the close of the conference, Olaf stayed on briefly for a tour of shattered Warsaw, the pink brickwork of its ruined buildings reminding him oddly of Toulouse and the police armed with tommy guns casting a pall over the tributes to the new democracy delivered at Wroclaw. Nevertheless, he was not yet cynical about congresses of peaceable intellectuals, and he was determined to keep up the effort to make common cause with his counterparts in the Communist and Third worlds. In Poland he accepted election to the newly forming British Cultural Committee for Peace. He was set up to become something like a professional pilgrim for the peace movement over the next eight months, speaking at a mini-congress in London in December 1948 as well as at the major events held in New York and Paris in March and April of 1949.

Stapledon resented insinuations that he was pliable material for propagandists, but he decided against battling Taylor and other critics in the press. Privately, he fumed that he knew well enough that Stalin had "poisoned" life in the USSR, but he would stick by the peace movement, no matter who sponsored its meetings. "The whole business disgusts me, and I wish I could decently shrug my shoulders and get on with other matters. But I'm damned if I'm going to join the silly witch hunt."[18] Convinced that America posed the greater risk for a third global war, he was still worried about the Russians. "Psychologically, their whole attitude is pathetically and dangerously adolescent. They see everything as black or white. They indulge in schoolboy vituperation. They blow the nationalist trumpet unashamedly." Given American Russophobia, Olaf concluded that "the relatively adult mentality of Western Europe is the most precious thing in the world at the moment."[19]

Between local peace rallies and planning for the big international conferences of 1949, Stapledon had little time left over for imaginative work. Among his papers for this period there are false starts, abortive manuscripts, projects sketched but not drafted, and occasional bits accumulated for an untitled "prose-poem" intended to sum up his fully evolved philosophy. The one notable excursion of 1948 into his well-trodden territory where literary, philosophical, and futurist imaginings converge was a lecture. It dealt with pilgrimages on a vaster scale than the ones he was making, and it was the most famous and often-reprinted talk he ever gave. "Interplanetary Man?" originated from the invitation of a young man who would shortly become the best-known English science fiction writer of the second half of the century.

As a boy Arthur C. Clarke had memorized the shelf of his local library where Stapledon's fiction was kept, and the prophetic grandeur of *Last and First Men* made a permanent impact on him. When he was nineteen he became secretary to a group of engineers and aerospace enthusiasts known as the British Interplanetary Society. Fittingly, the organization devoted to the practical problems of space travel had been founded in Wallasey, Stapledon's birthplace, in 1933. When Olaf joined, just after the BIS opened a London headquarters in 1936, some of his Wirral neighbors snickered. Writing fables about the stars was one thing; joining a *society* of rocketeers seemed daft. But Olaf was perfectly serious. He liked to read the BIS journal, although he had never attended its meetings. By 1948 the society had over five hundred members and the thirty-one-year-old Clarke was in charge of the speakers' program. He had never met Stapledon but saw his boyhood idol's name on a membership list and decided to ask if he would address the society on "anything you might care to say on the general subject of interplanetary travel." At first hesitant to speak to a group whose technical knowledge greatly surpassed his own, Olaf accepted Clarke's assurances that BIS engineers needed a humanist's views and questions about their enterprise.[20]

He took great care over this lecture. After a nine-page outline and two heavily revised longhand drafts, he produced a forty-one-page typescript with numerous inked emendations in his meticulous penmanship. All his oldest themes got folded into the talk—the cosmic scale against which humanity and its planet were dwarfed, the rich variety of physiologies intelligence might inhabit, the techniques by which human explorers could make inhospitable worlds livable, the dangers of scientific experimentation when divorced from philosophical restraints, the long view of a commonwealth of worlds and the pooling of the spiritual wealth of all minded beings.

As he sketched thrilling possible futures, he spoke also to the present. Speculating about the immensities, dreaming of other worlds, and devising the means to get there were fundamentally human activities, but such fantasies became escapist if the BIS did not realize that its first concern must be with the here and now. Stapledon recited a "law of nature" he attributed to J. B. S. Haldane: that any species that harnessed atomic power before achieving world unity was bound to destroy itself. Before "conquering" Venus or Mars, his audience had better figure out how to reconcile Russia and America. Failure could doom the species and make dreams of a future Republic of Worlds irrelevant.

Moreover, space travel raised ethical and ecological issues. Humanity needed a better justification for exploring the solar system than a replication of the rape of the earth. "I conclude that if the fruit of all the devotion of the British Interplanetary Society is to be merely the debauching of mankind with the riches of other worlds, you had better all stop paying your subscriptions."[21] Expeditions to the stars, it was clear, would require a resident moral philosopher.

For two and a half hours, in the formal lecture and in a discussion moderated by Clarke, the Interplanetarians who gathered at the Charing Cross Road Art School on Saturday evening, 9 October, heard the quintessential Stapledon. "Interplanetary Man?"—Olaf's typical question mark was usually omitted when his title was cited—received extensive coverage in the world press, but journalists seized on exotic details that could be readily lampooned. A London cartoonist had fun visualizing "homo jovianus," a man reengineered for life on Jupiter as a low-slung quadruped with its head pushed back along the spine, protruding eyes, and a long proboscis ending in sets of fingers. *Time* magazine chortled over the "altitude record" for "high-flying thought" in the prescriptions for colonizing alien planets. A colorful piece in a London review emphasized Stapledon's "romantic glamour" and "whoosh of the imagination," but found his assumptions about the future "mostly morbid."[22]

Most reporters missed or chose not to hear the political subtext of "Interplanetary Man?" The language of science fiction needed only minor adjustment to become the language of the Cold War's peace pilgrim; speaking of alien worlds, Olaf recapitulated his appeal to the U.S. and USSR at Wroclaw. "If any of them is inhabited by intelligent beings, then clearly man should do his utmost to adopt a relationship of genuine community with those non-human intelligences, seeking earnestly to enter into their point of view and to co-operate with them for mutual enrichment, both economic and spiritual." The difficulty he had getting a hearing for either his philosophical or political ideas is neatly epitomized by the American correspondent who ended his dispatch by quoting this very passage with a snide put-down: "The rest of his address was also right out of this world."[23]

What no journalist seeking a clever angle on a philosopher's talk to a group of amateur scientists could guess is how very much down-to-earth Olaf's daily routines were. On every visit to London, he spent a morning, sometimes the better part of a day, in a hospital room with Lilian Bowes-Lyon as she read poetry, talked through her depression, and prepared to die. The day before his BIS lecture that was what he was doing. Lilian, like Naomi Mitchison, was a rarity among his women friends. Most of the men he knew well were his contemporaries—academics or established writers or professionals with good left-wing credentials and a club membership. The women he befriended tended to be a generation younger than himself, not well connected, bright and bohemian,

without a public identity. Sad-eyed, her dark hair pulled back tight to expose
an oval, unglamorous face, Lilian Bowes-Lyon was born rich, a cousin to the
Queen Mother. She was a friend of Cecil Day-Lewis and a poet herself, but
she was best known for her social work. During the war she helped Anna Freud
care for bomb-shocked children at the Hampstead war nurseries, and from her
flat in the East End she ran a mobile canteen at the docks, pulled bodies out
from under the ruins of blitzed tenements, and provided relief for the home-
less by dunning her friends for contributions. Journalists liked to call her "the
Queen of the Slums"; her Cockney neighbors thought of her as a latter-day
Florence Nightingale.[24]

Lilian had never married nor had a satisfying love affair. She got a collected edition of her poetry published, but it drew little attention. Now, in 1948
in her early fifties, her life was an excruciation. In an unsuccessful effort to
arrest the degenerative arthritis that was diagnosed after the war, both her legs
had been amputated. Her pain was unremitting. When Olaf saw her in her final
months, crippled and weeping in her wheelchair, she seemed to be passing
through a fiery ordeal that, after a morning by her side, left him feeling
"scorched."[25] Not since World War I, when he carried the broken bodies of
screaming men in his ambulance, had he confronted anyone who so insistently
challenged his philosophical piety toward the universe.

Many of his hours in her sickroom were given over to a private drama he
and Lilian enacted. She raged against a God who inflicted more suffering than
she could take and longed to end her life. As an agnostic Olaf could offer no
consoling phrases about compensation in another world. But he improvised
dialogues in which he spoke as "God's prophet"; through his mouthpiece, Olaf,
a hypothetical divine spirit issued counsels against despair. Stapledon had
played that game brilliantly twenty years before in *Last and First Men,* ratio-
nalizing the annihilation of whole species, whole planets by invoking a universal "music" in which tragic experience was subsumed. But the words came
less easily in front of a living amputee wandering in and out of lucidity and
worn out with pain. As he reshaped Lilian's last weeks of life in his book of
meditations called *The Opening of the Eyes,* Olaf recalled how his oracular
voice could produce only the lamest message: "You must not, must not, wish
for death. You must keep alive and alert and very sensitive. For much is still
required of you. Death will come to you at the right moment, but do not yearn
for it." Lilian responded through tears:

> Oh, God, you are too great and terrible for me. Your cruel music is breaking
> your poor little instrument. And I am so very lonely. The whole world is
> slipping away from me. Everything is going except pain, and that keeps
> growing, growing. No one can know what it is like to be as I am. Your
> prophet, here, does not really know.[26]

The protracted dying of Lilian Bowes-Lyon, completed at last in July 1949, exposed the weak joints in Olaf's mental armor. The faith that "whatever is, is right" was easy to sustain in the abstract but seemed obscene in the face of the hell he witnessed in Lilian's hospital room. He reexamined his life and in his notebook recorded a shamed sense of contrast between his luck and her misery. His optimism, his security, the uncompromising choices of which he was proud were the conditioned products of a life of relative luxury:

> I have always been favoured. My body a sturdy nag, mettlesome but seldom unruly, has served the rider well. I have watched others, their mounts less hardy, collapse into life-long sickness. Shuddering, I have not experienced that seemingly eternal damnation. Liberty, liberty has been my treasure, perhaps my undoing. The freedom of health, the freedom from a tyrannical wage, the freedom to serve as seemed best to myself and not in bondage, the freedom of mind that scorns the security of any cult, the great freedom of spirit that flowers from a deep-rooted, many-summered and many-wintered love.[27]

Before she lapsed into the delirium that preceded her death, Lilian often distracted herself from her own fears and sufferings by involving herself in those of others. Olaf, who rarely sought advice from anyone on intimate matters, had told Lilian of his growing love for N. and his worry that an affair might endanger his marriage. As in his youth he had used Dorothy Miller as a sisterly confidante to whom he could turn for advice about his infatuation with Agnes, now in his sixties he found himself confessing to Lilian the conflict between his loyalty to Agnes and an unappeasable desire for N. "Diffidently," according to Olaf, she took up his perplexity, "always urging that love should have its way."[28]

Olaf kept none of his conflict a secret from Agnes. In the summer of 1948, he told her of his "impulse to go all the way in love-making" with N., but he resisted the impulse and at that time believed there was "no question of its being done."[29] To N. he wrote passionately of his unconsummated love, of his wish for the freedom and energy of youth, and of a mitotic fantasy:

> I "click" with you in so many ways, your delight in visual experience, your habit of collecting interesting objects, your jackdaw habit. Of course the 30 year gap is an added attraction. If you were (say) 60, I should not have fallen in love with you. I am in love with Agnes at 54, but for falling in love the vital attraction must be the physical freshness which by then has faded. . . . Oh how I wish there were two of me, so that one of me, if you would have me, could be all that you want and need of a man, all that you began to have with your husband and have lost. But it would have to be a different me, at least 20 years younger.[30]

By early 1949 he had resolved to stop living a life divided between fantasy and fidelity. Olaf told Agnes he had reached a crossroads. He was determined to ask N. to be his lover. Lilian, acting as mediator, asked Agnes to accept and even encourage the idea of a trial open marriage. Agnes, dreading a reopening of the scar tissue from the affair with Evelyn Gibson, nevertheless implored N. to cooperate in the experiment in the hope that her husband would get it over with. N. herself, under siege now by both Olaf and Agnes, proved far more difficult to persuade.

Finally, in "an awfully queer letter to write," N. told Agnes that she was reluctantly consenting to let Olaf stay with her on his next visit to London. It was a decision she felt little confidence in. "I am not repudiating all that I have said and felt about this before, but I too feel that to drift on any longer is a strain that I can no longer bear," she explained to Agnes. She did not know whether a state of being might pain Agnes less or more than constant anxiety about a possible state of being, but she hoped for clarification, if nothing else. N. believed that the alternative solution—to break off altogether—would not change Olaf's feelings or relieve Agnes's mind. Caught between Olaf's "state of real distress" and her ability to imagine the suffering Agnes would undergo if she put an end to his distress, N. was desperate for a resolution. In mid-February, with everyone's feelings in a knot, N. and Olaf became lovers.[31]

Agnes rode the train from London to West Kirby the night Olaf stayed behind with N. Lilian had urged her to write a poem as a way of cauterizing the wound, but Agnes followed a more familiar routine for probing her feelings: she wrote a letter. She addressed it to Olaf but may not have given it to him. "Perhaps," she said, "I am just writing it for myself." In her long letter, begun, as she noted precisely, between 11:30 and midnight on the train, she imagined herself a mother-to-be, growing a new person inside herself—not for nine months but for two and a half years, the length of time since Olaf had first met N. at Exeter. In other cases, she realized, a night like this would mark the end of one marriage and a movement toward another. Could theirs, she asked, really be an exception? She tried to take to heart Lilian's suggestion that "I would be helping to make a little more love come about in this world," and ended her letter with a brave toast: "I drank our health all three in gin and orange. And now good night & a good night. 2.25 a.m." The next morning she resumed the letter, without the last night's forced cheer and protesting Olaf's old myth about seeing her when she was nine years old. "I do want to be loved for what I am *now*—just as you spontaneously love N. for what she is *now*—not because you remember me as a little girl with blue eyes & an expression like a new laid egg. . . . Can you really tell me that there is enough of me apart from all the old roots to make you *choose* to be with me?"[32]

Lilian was urging Olaf to say exactly that to Agnes. His wife's sacrifice, Lilian told him, would "enlarge the liberty of your love with her."[33] But Olaf's pursuit of an extramarital love that he wanted to enjoy without concealment and without risk to his marriage came with a price tag. Agnes was willing to make the sacrifice but unwilling to disguise the fact that it *was* a sacrifice; his liberty, she reminded him, was being purchased at the expense of her diminishment. On the way to Sheffield for a lecture after a tearful parting at Caldy Station, Olaf wrote pleadingly, "Don't grieve because I am still capable of wild oats. Just laugh at me. Despise, if you must, but *don't* be brokenhearted. I can't bear it." When Agnes could not adopt a mood of lighthearted acceptance, he became distraught. "My mind is going all jittery under the emotional strain," he said, and he predicted what would be the ultimate resolution of his and Agnes's and N.'s mutual unhappiness in the "triple union" of his fantasies. Perhaps, he recognized just one week after he and N. became lovers, nothing short of breaking off the affair would do. "But it would be a defeat, and I seem defeated all round."[34]

As it happened, Evelyn Gibson ran into Olaf and Agnes in London just as the new phase in the relationship with N. was beginning. The chance encounter prompted Evelyn to write of her continuing "special feeling" for him and her refusal to regret their affair. "I feel that if I added something to your life & your work, then it makes my having lived worth while." But she noticed—without realizing the reason—that Olaf looked tired and depressed, and she wondered if he were ill.[35] A tenuous second love, undertaken at sixty-two but not sustainable, revived feelings Olaf had indulged earlier in the decade about his "miserably scrappy career," and once again his professional errors in judgment were linked to serious miscalculations about the most intimate and durable relationship in his life.

While struggling with the dilemma of his loves for Agnes and for N., Olaf prepared for a second international peace conference, a sequel to Wroclaw. He was unsure whether he was up to the rigors and intrigues of another meeting like that one, but the chairman of the conference, Harlow Shapley of Harvard, was an astronomer whose work he had long admired, and the location was to be New York. Olaf had often written of American values and the American character—notably in *Darkness and the Light* and in a long section on the "Americanization" of the planet in *Last and First Men*. But he had never crossed the Atlantic except in imagination. On 8 March 1949 he stopped in at the American consulate to make, as he thought, a routine application for a visa. Two days later Secretary of State Acheson asked his ambassador in London for a prompt report on four Britons invited to New York, among them Stapledon. He wanted to know the "line" they were likely to take at the conference; on that basis a decision would be made about visas.[36] Acheson's telegram was the first step in the two-week drama that culminated in Olaf's lone interview at La Guardia Field.

Stapledon had no way of knowing that by the time he requested a visa the hysteria that would engulf the Cultural and Scientific Congress for World Peace in the last days of March was already being whipped up. The first American press reports on the planned meeting at the Waldorf-Astoria appeared on 21 February. In a radio broadcast on the twenty-seventh, Walter Winchell announced the prospective visit of Dmitri Shostakovich and denounced his supposed allegiance to a "system which has produced the most terrible sound in 2,000 years—the sound of millions of clenched fists beating helplessly against the barb-wire fence." Winchell rallied his listeners to keep such men out of the country by making a massive letter-writing protest to their congressmen.[37]

Anticommunists inside and outside the government dreamed up scenarios for subverting Shapley's congress. The most Byzantine plot came from an "outside kibitzer," the journalist Dorothy Thompson. If "this whole schemozzle" of a peace conference can't be prevented, she told Acheson, "we should have *some* fun out of it all." Sneering at Shostakovich for "repeatedly bowing the knee to the Russian Gestapo," she wanted the State Department to get Toscanini and the Metropolitan Opera to stage *Lady Macbeth of Mtsensk,* denounced and banned by Stalin, while the composer was in New York. Then, she advised the secretary of state, get Shostakovich an invitation to the White House. Her plan, she thought, would certainly enrage Stalin, might trap Shostakovich by making him afraid to go home, and could "blow up the whole conference."[38] By the time Thompson hatched her cruel scheme, Acheson had already decided on a less outlandish deception. With President Truman's indulgence, he would manipulate the granting of visas to create a public impression of the conference as a propaganda tool of communist governments.

Oblivious to these political shenanigans and the degree of paranoia that American officials and journalists would expend on the Peace Congress, Olaf spent most of February and March 1949 going about his usual business of freelance lecturing, addressing architects in Glasgow, philosophers in London, and miners in Swansea. At a memorable party after a talk in Sheffield, he boggled minds during a long debate with a tipsy Shakespearean professor, John Danby, over the question, "If you can't kill your father and then eat him, how can you ever become a father yourself?"[39] In early March Olaf began writing a talk for a panel on religion and ethics, which he expected to be his chief venue at the three-day meeting in New York. Preoccupied with his personal life, he wanted to give New York as little thought as possible, but by the second week of March he was complaining mildly about the "official fussations" that were consuming huge portions of his days, along with the nuisance of repeated trips to the consulate to inquire about his visa.[40] Still, he did not anticipate the storm of controversy about to overtake him. Having booked his flight to New York, he calmly went about keeping long-standing commitments, including a talk on "Man Today and Tomorrow" at Hull on 22 March, the night before he was to leave England.

On 22 March, the dramatic day when blanket revocations of visas were announced at American embassies in London, Paris, and Rome, Olaf was, characteristically, not at center stage but in the provinces, inaccessible. The afternoon papers gave full play to the story, including ripe political quotations from some of the British delegates. A reporter finally reached Stapledon by telephone at his hotel in Scarborough. Unclear about the status of his own visa and assuming that delegates were being punished for having gone to Wroclaw the previous summer, Stapledon said, "It is scandalous that because people attended a conference for peace in Poland they are to be barred from going to a similar conference in America. It shows a rather sinister light on the present set-up in America."[41]

Stapledon remained out of view for much of the twenty-third, when he learned that his visa had been reissued. He was not easy to locate because he was spending much of his last afternoon in London with N., but the press tracked down Agnes at Simon's Field, and she reported that her husband had phoned her to say that he doubted he'd ever get on the plane that evening.[42] When he arrived at the airport, Patricia Burke, J. D. Bernal, and J. G. Crowther were waiting to make a joint condemnation of infringements on freedom of travel and speech. They handed Olaf a recording of their greetings to America, which he would play on several occasions, and then waved their colleague on to the Pan Am Clipper. Over the next eleven days, an unlikely star, Olaf would make several major addresses, learn to handle a press conference, endure heckling and a bruising television debate with an American philosopher, share the limelight with Shostakovich at Madison Square Garden, tour the East Coast, and savor a flattering introduction to a women's caucus: "We are sorry not to have Glamour Girl Patricia Burke, but we are glad to have Glamour Boy Olaf Stapledon instead."[43]

As the sole Western European admitted to the conference, he was not only in constant demand for interviews but had been asked to help open the proceedings with a speech at a black-tie dinner in the Waldorf's grand ballroom. A packed itinerary left him little time to take in what was happening, but the luxury of his surroundings amused and disgusted him. The hotel was "full of extravagantly wealthy people," Olaf told Agnes, and a microcosm of the whole "air-conditioned civilization" of America. The contrast with England, where wartime food rationing persisted, was inescapable. "A *huge* hunk of meat is presented to one at every meal. Everyone leaves some of it, I leave more than half. Waste! Cream is very lavish, and if I don't hold back a bit I shall probably be sick."[44]

American extravagance was on full display on 25 March at the opening night of the conference. The delegates dined on roast turkey, strawberries melba, and baked Alaska, and the featured speakers sat dwarfed beneath an enormous mural, commissioned for the occasion, by the socialist artist William Gropper. The image of a fallen man and horse, their armor shattered by a lightning bolt, allegorized a revolutionary and sternly retributive Peace smiting down War; a crowd of newly liberated workers looked on amid skulls, crosses, aircraft, guns, and gallows in the background. Olaf sat alongside Shostakovich, Lillian Hellman, the former vice-president Henry Wallace, the editor of the *Saturday Review* Norman Cousins, and his old nemesis from Wroclaw, Alexander Fadeyev, who was practicing a more mellow style than he had used the previous summer.

Introduced to the two thousand delegates and guests by Harlow Shapley, Stapledon admitted his nervousness at the responsibility of being the only speaker from Western Europe. But he was not fazed by hostile newsmen's descriptions of the conference as "pro-Communist." To an attentive audience that frequently applauded him he insisted that the average British worker still admired "the new Russia," for all its faults. The war had determined Britons to repair their "bad social record at home" and they could teach Americans to do the same. "We used to think of America as being in many ways far ahead of us. Today we don't," he said. "We are convinced that America is 50 or 100 years behind us in social consciousness." Laying aside his prepared text, he retold his horror riding into Manhattan when the taxi driver flatly asserted that a third world war was coming. Britons, Stapledon admonished his host country, would not be bullied into a new war. Having begun to outgrow their own imperialism, they were not about to embrace American imperial fantasies in the new atomic era. He spoke warmly of the American effort against Hitler but warned that Europeans would resist letting postwar economic assistance turn them into client states. "We are not anxious to sell our souls to America."[45]

Some American liberals, attending the conference in order to write it up for *Partisan Review, Commentary,* and *Horizon,* were unimpressed by the rhetoric or the celebrities. For Irving Howe there were too many Broadway dilettantes, and most of the speakers were "intellectual flyweights." The philosopher William Barrett carped that contemporary philosophy was represented only by "William Olaf Stapledon, a run-of-the-mill pedagogue of very little reputation." And Dwight Macdonald, surveying "all the old familiar Stalinoid names" on the program along with others he considered "political illiterates," gave short shrift to the credentials of "W. O. Stapledon, billed as 'professor' but innocent of any academic experience."[46] Macdonald's dismissal was not merely snobbish (although all three liberal journalists enjoyed guying those they thought intellectually unworthy). He believed the event was "a manoeuvre of our native Communists" to weaken America in the Cold War, and he had already proposed a counterconference to impugn the political standing of the conference, its delegates, and its organizers, above all Harlow Shapley, "an old hand at staging such carnivals."[47]

Those who called themselves Americans for Intellectual Freedom first assembled in Macdonald's Manhattan apartment, but the group's leader was Barrett's New York University colleague, Sidney Hook, who had a lively sense of personal grievance. He had proposed to deliver a paper at the peace conference on the absence of "class truths" in science; it would repudiate the infamous anti-Mendelian ideas of class-based genetic inheritance advanced by Trofim Lysenko under Stalin's patronage. The proposal had been turned down. Told by a disaffected member of the program committee that the committee had never formally met, Hook concluded that Shapley himself, whom he continued for the rest of his life to call a Communist collaborator, had personally rejected the paper in a mixture of spite and censorship.[48]

That Shapley was responsible for Hook's exclusion seems certain, that his motives were those ascribed to him by Hook far less so. Ten days before the conference opened, Shapley told a correspondent that Hook could not be trusted and wanted to sabotage the proceedings by speaking at a plenary session where he could publicly denounce the event.[49] An intellectual bully with a voracious ego, Hook aroused strong feelings in the victims of his often histrionic attacks. He was not above staging confrontational scenes for public consumption, as when, accompanied by a reporter from the *New York Herald Tribune,* he gate-crashed a cocktail party at Shapley's fourth-floor suite in the Waldorf and, by his account, "plumped down" letters supporting his paper proposal and demanded an explanation of its rejection. Shapley, to Hook's satisfaction, called hotel security and had him thrown out in front of the *Trib* reporter.[50] Shapley never succeeded in containing Hook and AIF, who contributed an atmosphere of often sophomoric guerilla theater to the proceedings in New York. During the three days of the conference, some newspapers gave nearly as much space to Hook's sideshow as to the main events. Once Olaf was awakened after midnight by a distressed voice on the phone asking him to come at once to a room in the hotel to help resolve an emergency that could only be discussed in person; when he arrived, he discovered to his embarrassment that he had been called to the bedroom of one of the women secretaries to the conference.[51]

Unprepared for the tactics that made Hook notorious among the American Left, Stapledon had not been in New York long before he realized that Sidney Hook was not to be taken lightly. He wrote to Agnes on 28 March that he was scheduled for "a very ticklish" live televised debate with "a rabid enemy of the Conference." But he decided not to worry the matter, and looked forward to the $25 fee he would collect from CBS to apply to the purchase of nylons for his several "lady friends": wife, daughter, daughter-in-law, and N. But after the debate was broadcast the next day, a demoralized Olaf went straight to his hotel room and described the experience to Agnes:

> I have just had a frightful television wrangle, with the rabid Sydney Hook. I felt I put up a very bad show, but the broadcasting staff, young men & women, *seemed* to think I was fine. Anyhow it was obvious that they were all on my side. But it was a horrid experience. He was very voluble and savage, and when he did give me a chance under pressure I had forgotten what I wanted to say.[52]

The CBS producer tried to tell Olaf after the show something about the popular mood in America and the constraints on outspokenness he should observe as the era of McCarthyism took hold:

> If you unwittingly allow yourself to be tarred and feathered with the Communist brush in this country, you will not be able to reach the people to whom your message must be addressed—the true liberals here. . . . In England, where the audience knows your background, there is not so much danger of your being mis-understood. In this country it is necessary to state that you are neither a Communist, nor an apologist for Communism.[53]

Olaf did not find it easy to trim his language to suit the American context. More surprisingly, he failed to gauge the power of the American mass media. Although in *Star Maker* he had brilliantly satirized cultural indoctrination through a manipulative broadcasting system, in New York he underestimated how words and pictures would shape public perception of the peace movement. "The Conference has been a fantastic success, whatever the papers say," he told Agnes. Reporters were nicknaming the Waldorf the "Little Kremlin" ("Comic!" he crowed) and they inflated the numbers of anticommunist pickets into the thousands. "Actually the highest number was 400, and they were the miserablest creatures. They caused us no trouble at all." Yet those journalistic distortions constituted what most Americans took for the reality. Stapledon thought Shapley's conference would change American opinion, but public opinion was crystallized in *Life* magazine's photographic imagery: Czech immigrants kneeling in prayerful protest outside the hotel, the single British delegate flanked by grim-faced Russians, and a two-page gallery of fifty "Dupes and Fellow Travelers" (Einstein, Chaplin, Leonard Bernstein, Langston Hughes, and Dorothy Parker among them) whom readers were invited to scorn. It was not until he got home and assembled the clippings furnished by his press agency

26. The New York Peace Conference:
left to right: Olaf Stapledon, Dmitri Shostakovich,
Alexander Fadeyev, Harlow Shapley, R. E. G. Armattoe.
*Courtesy Harry Ransom Humanities Research Center,
the University of Texas at Austin: New York* Journal American *morgue.*

that Olaf grasped the magnitude and effectiveness of the "lies" generated by the press.[54]

The long weekend was a continuous whirl of activity for Stapledon. The speech he had originally thought would be his main contribution to the conference—a paper on ideology and religious warfare for a panel on religion and ethics—had less impact than any of his other activities. His patented agnostic piety was ill-fitted to the American scene. None of the Protestant bishops, rabbis, and Catholic theologians with whom he sat seemed to know what to make of his kind of "religion." And the panel did not draw the large audiences and lively discussion that percolated through the sessions on natural science, where the leader of the American Left, Henry Wallace, spoke on atomic weapons; on the fine arts, where attendees could listen to Aaron Copland and gawk at Shostakovich; and on writing and publishing, where Fadeyev, W. E. B. Du Bois,

F. O. Matthiessen, and Norman Mailer held forth and a feisty audience, including Mary McCarthy, Robert Lowell, and Dwight Macdonald, answered back.

The conference came to a spectacular close on Sunday night, 27 March, before eighteen thousand people who purchased general admission tickets to Madison Square Garden. Loudspeakers in the dimly lit hall broadcast the distress call of a radio operator. "Calling London, calling London . . ." Silence. "Calling Rome, calling Rome . . ." Again, silence. Unanswered calls went out to Calcutta, Paris, Mexico City—all cities in which American embassies had denied visas to potential delegates. When the lights came up, three prominent foreign delegates took curtain calls. Stapledon was one of them. Speaking without a text, he responded to the effective melodrama of the radio simulation by chastising a U.S. government fearful of criticism. He was cheered when he said, "I did not want to come—thank God, I came! For heaven's sake, remember that you are a great country of free speech, and don't keep out decent citizens." Catching the mood of his audience, he declared that Americans were "losing their heads," and he raised his voice in defiance as the cheering grew: "I am no Communist, but I am not afraid of working with Communists when they happen to be right." The *Manchester Guardian*'s New York correspondent, Alistair Cooke, was derisive: the final session of the Cultural and Scientific Congress for World Peace was "as peaceful as Madison Square Garden is on championship nights, as scientific as the jungle, and as cultural as a swarm of bacteria."

The most dramatic moment came when the Garden was darkened once more and Shostakovich appeared in a spotlight at a piano. Throughout the conference he had often been glimpsed, looking tense and expressionless, chain-smoking and with his long legs wrapped tightly together beneath his chair. He had seldom spoken, and then always in Russian from scripts translated by the delegation's interpreter. Betraying no emotion, he sat and played a keyboard transcription of the second movement of his Fifth Symphony—the 1937 masterpiece he had been obliged to subtitle, "A Soviet Artist's Reply to Just Criticism." When he finished the seven-minute performance, the crowd yelled for an encore, but Shostakovich disappeared and Shapley came forward to say that he was too exhausted to play any more. Later, a biographer wrote that the composer feared internal exile or death on his return to the Soviet Union and was in severe depression, thinking he might be making his final public appearance in such alien and unreal surroundings.[55]

Shapley had planned a cross-country tour of lectures and performances after the conference; but the State Department moved to scotch that plan on 28 March, the day after the finale at Madison Square Garden. Shostakovich, who had in hand an invitation from Serge Koussevitzky to guest-conduct the

27. Speaking for the future:
the rally at the Mosque Theater, Newark, New Jersey.
Courtesy Queens Library, New York: Herald Tribune *morgue.*

Boston Symphony Orchestra, was due first to cross the river into New Jersey on Tuesday the twenty-ninth with Stapledon, the West African anthropologist R. E. G. Armattoe, and the three-member Cuban delegation for a rally in Newark. The Russian was the drawing card, and tickets were selling briskly in Newark for a chance to hear the composer play some of his own work. The government's strategy of portraying Shapley's conference as a Communist-front meeting supported only by left-wing New Yorkers had worked in the short term but might fall apart once the conference became mobile and the allure of Shostakovich began to be felt around the country. Secretary of State Acheson ruled that the visas of delegates from the Soviet Union and the Eastern bloc limited their stay to New York City and to the dates of the conference at the Waldorf. Over Shapley's protests, the Russians and Eastern Europeans were told to pack their bags; by midweek they were flying home.[56]

On Tuesday night in Newark, an announcement was made at the Mosque Theater that Shostakovich was not being allowed to attend. A spotlight was shone on an empty piano while the disgruntled audience murmured. Those who stayed for their money's worth got an evening of attacks on the State Department, charges that the Catholic hierarchy had engineered the picketing at the Waldorf, speeches in Spanish from the Cubans, a lengthy fundraising pitch, and entertainment from local folk dance clubs. For the better part of two hours, a shock of gray hair was the only evidence of Stapledon, seated behind the bulky speakers' lectern. By the time he rose to speak, the audience had shrunk. He walked stiffly to the front of the stage and announced that he didn't enjoy traveling, cities, or political meetings but was doing what had to be done. Adopting, although only imperfectly, the advice given him at CBS, he framed his political views with a disclaimer and a prophecy: "I am not a Communist. I am not a Christian. I am just me. I am, however, a socialist, as are the majority of my countrymen. It doesn't matter anyway. You'll all be socialists in one form or another in the next fifty years."[57] He urged Americans to persuade their leaders to think globally and learn how to work with the Soviets. But his words had little of the punch or conviction of his grand windup at Madison Square Garden two nights before. He was tired and disheartened by the State Department's decision to kick the Russians out. Shapley was pressing him to stay in the United States an extra ten days to help salvage the tour to the Midwest and West Coast, but Olaf decided to limit his travels to the Northeast and return to England on 4 April, as planned.

Before leaving the New York area for Baltimore and Boston, he had two off-duty days when he could set issues of war and peace to one side and talk about literature. On 30 March, Clifford Odets brought Olaf to a small dinner party at a Romanian-Jewish restaurant. Conversation ranged from such Stapledonian favorites as the mentality of apes to what Olaf called "a furious battle" over the relative merits of two current Broadway plays—Odets's own *Big Knife* and Arthur Miller's *Death of a Salesman*. Olaf liked Odets so much that he wanted to see *The Big Knife*, but arrangements had already been made for him to go to the new Miller play. In fact, *Death of a Salesman* made a powerful enough impression that, when he returned to England, he wrote about its dissection of "the American myth of the go-getting individual."[58]

Stapledon's other diversion from public oratory arose from a conversation with Theodore Sturgeon. The young author of "Thunder and Roses," a brilliant science-fiction story about atomic war and the American character, phoned the Waldorf and asked if he could spare time for a social evening with some New York fans of his fiction. Stapledon had reason to make room in his schedule for Sturgeon and his friends. Several science-fiction writers had learned that his funds were frozen when he entered the United States and that he had appealed, unsuccessfully, to an American publisher for pocket money. Frederick Pohl immediately wrote to Stapledon with an offer of help and asked in return only that he try to meet with some of his American colleagues while he was in New York. On 31 March, Stapledon showed up at the West Side apartment of Fletcher Pratt, who was hosting the Hydra Club, a science-fiction discussion group that included two of the most important American editors of the genre—John W. Campbell and Donald Wollheim. A night of handshaking, autographing, and discussion of *Last and First Men, Odd John,* and *Sirius* with an author who was a legendary figure for American science-fiction readers provided the solitary and wholly unpublicized moment when Olaf's literary accomplishment was recognized during his American journey. Sturgeon, soon to prove himself the most venturesome of postwar American science-fiction writers, gave Stapledon his new collection of stories called *Without Sorcery* to thank him for being "what this country and the world so urgently needs— a dynamic and directive liberal." And more:

> I feel a real gratitude for the experience of having read SIRIUS; for having been able to share, through his beautiful detachment, your affectionate objectiveness toward mankind. . . . I was impressed, not only on meeting you, but before, over the telephone, by a quality I can only call gentleness. That word is inaccurate if it seems to take an iota from the consistency of your demonstrated convictions, but that gentleness is a pleasure to encounter in this nation of antiquarians, which persists in the preservation of its original rawness.[59]

The magnetism of Olaf's personality lost nothing in the translation across the ocean. Within three years Sturgeon was writing *More Than Human,* his fiction of *homo gestalt,* in part a homage to Stapledon's invention of *homo superior* in *Odd John.*

Stapledon arrived in Baltimore on 2 April. The Maryland Council of the Arts, Sciences, and Professions set up a press conference at Johns Hopkins University and rented the Lyric Theater downtown for a road-show version of the rally at Madison Square Garden. At Hopkins, in the aftermath of the expulsion of the Russians, Stapledon took a different tack on his political affiliations, about which reporters were always curious. "I am not a Communist, but coming to this country makes me wish I could say I was." He also made one of his sternest public statements on Americans' blithe acceptance of the possibility of another war, contrasting their ignorance with the experience of Europeans whose countries had been bombed or occupied.

At the theater the turnout was disappointing, and not all the five hundred paying customers came in good faith. Of the four speakers, R. E. G. Armattoe got the most attention in the local press. Born in the Gold Coast, he was an anthropologist working in Northern Ireland and the first black person ever to appear on the stage of the Lyric. Armattoe's speech was received politely by the mostly white audience (thirty-five black Americans sat in the balcony), but when Stapledon and the American novelist Howard Fast spoke, booing and shouting erupted in the theater.

Olaf played his recording of Bernal, Burke, and Crowther denouncing the loss of their visas, and the audience's anger escalated. "Would you allow a thief in your home?" someone yelled. Stapledon tried to challenge the heckler: "It is up to us in Britain now to show you what real liberty is." Another man burst out, "We are feeding you now!" In a rare show of temper, Stapledon shouted back, "I think that we know more of liberty than you do." A young naval officer and his girlfriend walked out. Around the theater others got out of their seats; some stalked toward the stage and taunted the speaker, "Good night, good night." More people headed nervously for the doors. A young woman screamed at him, "Go back to Britain." Appalled but undeterred, Olaf went on stubbornly: "The Russian revolution is the greatest event of this age, an expression of the will for comradeship and brotherhood." A woman in the front row began jumping up and down, saying loudly over and over, "Mr. Chairman! I want to ask a question." A still louder voice from the back, responding to the woman and her unasked question, boomed out, "Shut up." Olaf at last gave up and stood silent. A pianist eventually calmed the crowd with a Shostakovich prelude, but when Howard Fast came forward, the heckling started up again. Fast, used to taking this kind of heat from American anti-Communist audiences, was unflustered by a voice raised in accusation, "I think this place is full of traitors." He responded smoothly, "Shrill voices and anonymous slander don't require courage."[60] It was the most unpleasant of Olaf's American experiences, and he was glad at last to board the night train to Boston.

The third of April, Olaf's last full day in the United States, put him back in the care of Harlow Shapley. His ostensible purpose for coming north was to address the New England branch of the National Council of the Arts, Sciences, and Professions. From well-worn notes on "The Plight and Hope of Man," a favorite subject of his talks in England, he described the human species as a "pterodactyl of the spirit," wanting to rise to a new plane of living but inadequately equipped for the task. He evoked, as he did throughout his American tour, the specter of atomic destruction, but this time examined the Cold War through another lens. He sounded his old theme of "agnostic worship"— the need for a new religion that would meld Eastern mysticism with Western activism, a spiritual attitude toward the cosmos with utopian world building. The talk was different in mood and manner from his other American speeches, nonideological, almost professorial. In Boston there were no pickets, but there was also little interest in the speech. The peace conference had ceased to be news. The day's highlight was an afternoon at the Harvard Observatory with Shapley; the astronomer and the scientific romancer talked politics and physics in equal measure, and Olaf found in his host a kindred spirit—"a great stargazer whose feet walk surely and boldly on the earth."[61]

When Olaf got back to England everyone wanted to know what had really happened in New York. He gave an impromptu report at a National Peace Council meeting at Oxford, and Kingsley Martin asked him to write up the conference for the *New Statesman,* but the long arm of journalistic anticommunism had reached from Manhattan to Holborn. Stapledon wrote an article praising Shapley's principled liberalism and his fearless facing down of Washington demagoguery. Martin refused to run it. "It really is not possible for an article in the *New Statesman* to suggest that the New York Conference was anything but Communist in its inspiration." He offered a check for Stapledon's services and space in the letters column. Stapledon wrote back with unusual, icy sarcasm: "Well, well! If you have *knowledge* that the New York Conference was in fact Communist-inspired, organized and financed, you ought to publish your facts." He insisted that while the 1948 meeting in Wroclaw was "obviously" the instrument of a Communist agenda, the American organizers of the New York conference acted independently. ("However," he added, as he customarily did to Red-baiters, "what matter if it *was* in origin Communist?") He abbreviated his article to fit the letters column, but told Martin, "In the circumstances, please don't send the cheque."[62] The letter retained an account of his loss of temper on television when the "seemingly psychopathic" Sidney Hook accused him of defending Russia because his passage had been paid by Communists. Omitted was his article's hopeful closing, "These much-reviled conferences are a small but not a forlorn beginning." But Olaf continued to smart from Martin's suggestion that his analysis was not impartial or sophisticated and from Hook's innuendo, augmented by a whispering campaign in England, that his opinions had been bought in exchange for an airline ticket. "In future," he told friends, "I shall always pay myself for any conference I go to."[63]

There was little time to look backwards. Even before his letter appeared at the end of April in the *New Statesman,* Olaf was in Paris for the World

Congress of Partisans of Peace. Secretary of State Acheson had telegraphed the American ambassador there to suggest how he might "discreetly" advise the French government to discredit the Paris congress. Abusive press attacks and picketing outside the hotel had created some sympathy for the New York conference; Acheson wanted the French to try different tactics. "Lofty scorn for and ridicule of those who assume man [is] infinitely and eternally gullible seem better weapons than violence, physical or moral, directed against those who would obviously welcome martyrdom."[64]

Sidney Hook, who knew little about discretion, transported his counterconference to Paris, but Olaf steered clear of it. By one American's account, Hook's Paris mission flopped. Audiences often walked out, and the show played to nearly empty rooms, nor did French newsmen cooperate as readily as the New York press had in feeding Hook's ego.[65] The third of the great peace gatherings was not dominated by a single figure, as the Waldorf had been by Shostakovich. Picasso, W. E. B. Du Bois, Paul Robeson, and Pablo Neruda were all objects of curiosity in Paris, along with some of the by-then standard figures on the peace circuit: the chairman Frédéric Joliot-Curie, Howard Fast from the United States, J. D. Bernal from England, and the ubiquitous Russian Fadeyev. Olaf himself had become something of a fixture, but his speech in Paris took a new turn and he did not stay for the entire congress.

At Paris, Stapledon was a grimmer presence than in New York. The ideological hysteria he had witnessed in America put him in a mood to preach: "We are here together on the same planet. We must learn to live and let live." He worried about the fate of Shapley and others who had antagonized the witch-hunters. "Like all who speak for peace in America," he said of Shapley, "he is now being called a Communist or a dupe of the Communists. And to be a Communist is now regarded in America as being equivalent to a traitor. Those who worked for the Conference are now steeling themselves to face a campaign of bitter persecution." Having said that, he then made his toughest analysis of Stalin's regime. The USSR could win and keep friends only by renouncing the police state, restoring respect for the human person, tolerating dissent, and creating a political ethic that required its leaders to tell the truth to its own people. Most British socialists, he said reversing his emphases in New York, "believe that Russia, in spite of its magnificent economic achievement, is in some ways a very sick society." The Russian government talked peace more than it practiced it; now it must prove that the hostility being marshaled against it in Europe and North America was unwarranted.[66]

Olaf had concluded that, although American arrogance accounted for the most immediate danger of an apocalyptic war, Russia was being let off the hook at the peace conferences. Too little, he told a group in Britain, was being said about "Russian intransigence and ruthlessness" and the imbalance played into the hands of those who wanted to depict the peace movement as a Communist ploy.[67] He may also have wanted to demonstrate his independence by showing that he was not beholden to anybody and could depart from the "script" that journalists like Kingsley Martin thought he was expected to follow. Olaf told a correspondent that the Paris meeting was "a much more Communist and violent affair" than the others.[68] In leftist Warsaw he had tilted to the right, just as he had adopted a defiant leftishness in right-wing Baltimore. So a heavy dose of Soviet rhetoric at Paris triggered him, typically, to weigh in with an opposite view. The reaction was as much temperamental as principled.

After a day and a half in Paris, he had had enough. When he got back to Simon's Field, he felt exhausted and intellectually spent. "I am sick of politics, and no good at it anyhow. I only do these things through a feeling that one must *try* to do something to stop the threatened war."[69] The pilgrimage from London to Wroclaw to Manhattan to Paris had stalled in its later stages, and its goals grew more elusive. He continued to write about global peace and the pacific temper, but the path got steeper and harder to travel. He wasn't young anymore, the effort took a lot out of him, and he craved rest and company and reassurance.

"For a long while I climbed alone in the mist, until at last it was borne in on me that I was lost. And here I am, lost and very tired. And darkness is coming." So Olaf wrote in a little allegory about peace of mind and peace on earth he called "The Journey." The speaker in that luminous spiritual autobiography, modeled in genre and mood on Bunyan's *Pilgrim's Progress,* knows that death is not far off, but he is still unable to see the "high valley" that he has long been seeking and from which he hopes to see at last the universe as it truly is. Though feeling "stifled and ineffective," though grieved that his "work with the comrades is confused and suspect," the speaker refuses to despair. Others will finish the journey even if he cannot. "For me, the only thing is to press on. The day is not yet done. And death even here would not be wholly defeat."[70]

19

To the Riverside

1949–1950

IN THE SUMMER OF 1949, Stapledon put the experiment of mass peace meetings behind him. His travels had yielded few tangible results and left him, as he told Aage Marcus after coming home from the Paris peace conference, disgusted with "the whole atmosphere of mutual distrust and recrimination."[1] He was still smarting from criticism that he had been manipulated by Communist organizers of the peace movement, and, like others on the noncommunist Left, he felt compromised whichever way he turned. Naomi Mitchison captured the dilemma exactly:

> A non-communist mixing with communists is told by many otherwise sensible bodies of persons he is a "dupe"! He is always assumed to be fundamentally silly and unable to keep his position or integrity. . . . The communist or near-communist working sincerely in a non-communist peace movement (and this certainly does happen, especially in our own Great Britain, mother of paradoxes) is of course accused of "infiltrating".[2]

In the last year of his life, Stapledon avoided close ties with any specific ideological group. More and more, he began marking the numerous letters he received inviting him to make political addresses with a large NO in green pencil. When he was offered the presidency of the Merseyside branch of the British Peace Committee, he declined. "I am more effective for peace if I work independently." Russian refusals to admit their own complicity in the Cold War discouraged him: "At the three great International Conferences (Wroclaw, New York, Paris) I felt increasingly distressed by the one-sidedness, though fully

384

in sympathy with the charges levelled against the West."[3] He began telling English audiences that they must be "very critical of both the USA and the USSR."
Sharing a platform with the vice-chairman of the British Communist Party,
he took sharp exception to R. Palme-Dutt's defense of Stalin. Many Britons,
he said, now identified communism with the police state and were haunted by
stories of ruthless suppression of dissent. "If these stories are mythical, ex-
plode them; if true, explain them."[4]

In the summer of 1949, another experiment came to an end, another myth
was exploded. Olaf and Agnes and N. concluded that the open marriage they
were trying to sustain was wrecking both love and friendship. N., haunted by
the specter of a third party always standing at the foot of her bed, told Agnes
that she was "emotionally exhausted. I seem to have no feelings left at all—
they are suspended." Regretfully, Olaf accepted reality. In June he wrote to
Agnes, who was at a meeting of the Women's International League for Peace
and Freedom in Lübeck. By the time she came home, he promised, he and N.
would no longer be lovers:

> The 17th is the end. After that, we shall be just friends. . . . I am sad about
> N., because the end of the chapter hits her much worse than me, since I have
> you. I can see that she feels it. And so I feel horrible about both of you. And
> yet I *cannot* help feeling deep down that the total upshot is going to be life-
> giving for all of us in the long run. I am still very fond of N., in a special
> sort of way, and that is that. But oh believe me when I say (again and again)
> that what I have felt for you is of a different order and not harmed at all,
> except by the horrible knowledge that I have given you pain. But let the pain
> be all past now, Taffy darling. Come home soon, and help me to get on with
> real life in the next chapter.[5]

The next chapter had just fifteen months to run. Olaf would have liked to
inhabit Utopia, not just glimpse it from afar, in his lifetime. But in the personal as in the social sphere he was denied the role of "Old Man in New World"
he had imagined in his 1944 story. He would at least assume the part of the
grandfatherly elder—above partisanship, superior to the temptations of the
flesh, calmly preparing a last philosophical testament. He wanted time for playing and birdwatching with his grandson Thomas in the garden at Simon's Field.
As for the impulse to make love to N., he told Agnes later in the summer of
1949, it did not go away, but restraint was coming more easily.[6] He turned
away from international congresses and back to the local meetings and lectures where he had had his start. Although one newspaper in the first month
of 1950 listed him, along with Stravinsky, Einstein, and Diego Rivera, among
ten people who would still be discussed in a hundred years, his name was

seldom uttered in literary circles. The steep plunge into obscurity that followed his death had begun.[7]

With *A Man Divided* in press at Methuen, he revealed, in a rare interview, that he was writing his definitive philosophical work, an old man's book designed to sum up his career. At a lunch he told E. V. Rieu about the book, with a sense of assurance and content that his longtime editor had rarely seen in him. "He had reached the goal of his thinking," Rieu recalled Olaf saying serenely. To his daughter he said simply that with that book, titled by Agnes after his death *The Opening of the Eyes,* he would be finished with writing.[8]

The title fits. Quiet and withdrawn as his final year was, Stapledon was seeking new insights while consolidating the visionary legacy he wanted to leave behind. Eyes became a persistent theme, and not always a solemn one. He told Fay Pomerance that, though he had long been nearsighted, he seldom wore glasses in public because when he saw his fellow human beings too clearly he didn't like them half so much. In a lecture given several times in 1949, he championed the artist as the eye of society—"the organ through which the upper unconscious creates new awareness" in all spheres from the personal through the cosmic. But when he looked at Fay's painting of an unfallen angel with lidless eyes, he felt anxiety rather than celestial peace. The unblinking gaze, like 20/20 vision, was a doubtful gift.[9] The episode that opens *A Man Divided* depicts Victor Smith suddenly raising his droopy lids and staring with wide blue eyes into the face of his bride at the altar and announcing to her and the startled congregation, "I've just waked up, and I see quite clearly that I am not the one for you." And in the never-quite-completed *Opening of the Eyes* he revised himself into "the ageing man, who with new eyes sees his small triumphs as failures."[10]

In his last months Olaf took a fresh look at one issue he had misapprehended in the past. As a youthful and bookish imperialist, he had assumed without question Anglo-Saxon superiority. But ever since World War I, when he encountered the Senegalese and Thai soldiers of the French army and the Negro units of the American expeditionary force, his eyes had been gradually opening a little wider. In the thirties he took up the cause of Ethiopia, and in the forties he agitated for Indian independence in newspapers and at meetings of the India League. "For the advancement of empire," he wrote in *New Hope for Britain,* "natives in India and Africa were tricked and terrorized."[11] At Wroclaw, New York, and Paris he was part of a multiracial peace movement and discovered how uninformed he still was about the nonwhite world. His commitments to freedom broadened into study of the African liberation movements and of racial injustice in the United States.

As he left New York in April 1949, Helen Rosen asked him to call on Paul Robeson in Paris and fill him in on what happened at Shapley's confer-

28. "Hungry Asia and Martyred Africa":
addressing the India League.
Courtesy Mary S. Shenai.

ence. Olaf had seen Robeson as Othello in London, and he had been collecting his recordings since the late twenties. Now, in the spring of 1949, he found
himself talking with Robeson at the Paris peace conference, joining the official greeting party at Lime Street Station when he came to Liverpool in May
of that year, and chairing a huge gathering at St. George's Hall, where Robeson
sang and spoke about the struggle of black Americans for their civil rights.
The speech moved Stapledon to start a file on a 1948 Trenton murder case in
which six black men, convicted on dubious evidence and with confessions that
may have been elicited under drugs, were sentenced to death in the slaying of
a white New Jersey shopkeeper. Meanwhile he had begun writing in *The Opening of the Eyes* of "hungry Asia and martyred Africa," whose oppressions could
no longer be ignored.[12]

Early in 1950, galvanized by the charismatic Anglican priest Michael Scott,
Olaf joined the fledgling antiapartheid campaign in England. The last national
conference at which he spoke, in June 1950, was devoted to "The Human Crisis
in Africa" and the newly formalized color ban imposed by the Afrikaner Nationalist party in South Africa. Both English and black African speakers told

of the new government's aim to incorporate other parts of southern Africa into its white supremacist "Union." Scott's homemade film of life in the black quarters of Johannesburg provided graphic evidence of the misery and degradation in a key member-state of the British Commonwealth. At the end of the three-day conference, Olaf gave the closing address to 350 delegates, calling modestly for "an act of wider selfishness" by Europeans responsible for the colonization and oppression of millions of Africans. Not just the indigenous peoples but the whole world, Stapledon insisted, would profit from a liberated Africa. New forms of democracy struggling for life in Africa were the birth pangs of the future.[13]

Racial politics, the abolition of atomic weapons, the continued building of the British welfare state, protests against the execution of Greek Communists and the persecutions of the House Un-American Activities Committee, and reform of the divorce laws occupied Olaf's attention from the middle of 1949 through the late summer of 1950, but spiritual questions took primacy over everything else. In a lecture to the New Renascence School in London, he reiterated the central paradox of his own spiritual life: "Agnosticism, far from destroying religion, is the gateway to live religion. For only when we have been stripped of all our frail theories, can we realize that religion is concerned not with theories but with direct experience, feeling, action in this actual world."[14] Never drawn to orthodox theology or doctrinal religion of any kind, Stapledon had maintained a profound interest since the pre–World War I days in what he liked to call simply "the Spirit." As he grew older and as his parapsychological interests were given fresh stimulus, the spirit became an issue both intimate and urgent. Spirit, he wrote in his last professional philosophical article, is best understood as a way of life, as "Tao." It is experienced by the young mind in love "when it first becomes aware of 'I' and 'you' and 'we,' and finds that participation in a 'we' is for it the way of life."[15]

In a 1949 anthology on religion, Olaf gave simple, precise expression to a problem he had wrestled with all his life: the emotional inadequacy of atheism and the intellectual unacceptability of theism. Spirit, for him, meant a character of aspiration, not a substance attributed to souls or deities. Imagining personality as a set of concentric rings surrounding a central point of possibility, he worked outward from body to self to community to the outermost sphere of spiritual experience. Ultimately, spirit could be imaged in this way and exemplified more readily than it could be defined:

> Since the kind of experience signified by the word "spirit" is only possible when we are at our highest pitch of lucidity, we cannot say much about it without slipping into nonsense. We have as yet no language adequate to it, for all languages were developed in relation to inner circles, and they cannot

be used to describe the outermost circle of experience, save in a very metaphorical way.[16]

Because metaphor worked better than exposition, Stapledon was more successful at capturing the nature of spirit not in essays but in fiction and in the confessional meditations and dramatic monologues he was accumulating for *The Opening of the Eyes*. He never outdid *Star Maker's* fictional brilliance, where he pushed both invention and language to their limits in exploring the nature of spirituality and creativity. His last narrative work, *A Man Divided*, a far more modest and mundane venture, nevertheless worked some of the same ground as *Star Maker*. In form his most realistic novel, *A Man Divided* explores the fitful lucidity of a personality torn between competing impulses of self-indulgence and self-discovery, between a life of suspended animation in which all spiritual questions are ignored or suppressed and those "rare and precarious moments of full consciousness" when a person lives a fully human existence.[17]

The divided man, Victor Smith, has enough similarities to Olaf to have misled some readers into taking the novel as straightforward autobiography, even treating it as if it were a clinical study of the author's schizophrenia.[18] But Victor is a far more slippery autobiographical figure than even Paul had been in *Last Men in London*. Where Paul was created out of memories of the Olaf who once was, the new novel combined reminiscence with fantasy by projecting an Olaf who might have been, had history forked differently. Victor, like Olaf, once worked in a shipping office, volunteered at a boys' club, taught for the WEA and for the army during the Second World War, but unlike the young Olaf, he continued his business career—nearly marrying the boss's daughter—and served in the army in World War I. Victor's unpredictable bouts of nastiness, violent headaches, and drunken binges correspond to nothing in the author's life. Of Maggie, the unusual woman he eventually marries, Victor speaks in Olavian fashion of his visions of her as a little girl who haunted his dreams, but Maggie, a red-headed waitress and Shetland Islander, is no simple Agnes-substitute. The complex relationship of the narrative to autobiographical experience is clearest in a painful analysis of Maggie's grief over her husband's extramarital affairs, in which the narrator, Harry Tomlinson, disputes Victor's self-exculpation:

> Victor assured her that his inveterate habit of falling in love with any girl that was specially attractive to him could not lessen his feeling for her. But inevitably she felt insecure; and jealous, in spite of her modern theories. She was tormented by the fear that from one of these light-hearted relations with other women some serious attachment would arise. It seemed to her

that they must arise from some inadequacy in herself. Evidently she could not permanently satisfy her husband. This idea Victor vehemently rejected. He said (so Maggie told me) "For me you are, and always will be, the dearest, in fact the very best of all possible mates. But, damn it, I won't blind myself to other women! And you must not blind yourself to other men. Of course, of course, monogamy, the single life-long partnership, is the only way to fullness of love; but don't you see, don't you feel, that if monogamy excludes every other attraction, if it turns—well, *monastic,* it may miss fullness of love after all." Then he added, garbling a famous quotation, "Besides, I could not love thee, dear, so much, loved I not other girls quite a lot."

Honesty compels me to record that Victor's behaviour in this matter seemed to me rather heartless and irresponsible. Even if he did know that his attachment to Maggie was unshakable, she had every reason to be distressed; and surely it was cruel and selfish to let her suffer. When I said this to Victor, he replied emphatically that for both their sakes he was justified in these occasional loves. For himself, he was justified because they quickened him (so he said) spiritually for his work, and because they did actually deepen his love for his wife. And on Maggie's account too he was justified because (he insisted) only in such experience, however painfully, could she learn the truth about him, and about herself, and about love.

Well, this all sounded to me rather specious. Yet I find I have to reserve judgment. I have no illusion that Victor was perfect, even in his most lucid state; but so often he has proved himself far more sensitive than my very commonplace self! As for Maggie, she claims that she now entirely approves of Victor's conduct. But then, she was always too forgiving.[19]

The relationship of invented to actual persons in Stapledon's fiction was always problematic, even when it seems most transparent. As this tortuous passage indicates, the narrator of *A Man Divided* has as much in common as its protagonist with the author. Harry often judges Victor much as Olaf judged himself. Both Harry and Olaf were North Country provincials who read history at Oxford, worked as schoolmasters for a time, were devoted to astronomy and theories of heredity, and were ardent Wellsians. Harry is near his sixtieth birthday when he sets down the narrative of Victor Smith, as Olaf was when he began writing *A Man Divided* at the end of World War II. If Olaf Stapledon was really "a man divided," he was not a self-destructive split personality like Victor Smith but someone who was drawn both to Harry's conscientiousness and Victor's extravagance. Harry is the Stapledonian plain man, an ideal-ization of the unpretentious common sense Olaf prized, while Victor—"a young snob without a mind"—is a potential Olaf poised between the squandered talent of a somnolent dilettante and the awakened insight of a visionary. In the Jekyll-and-Hyde formulas of the novel, the awakened Victor idealizes Stapledon as he would have liked to be, while the somnolent Victor is a kind of extrapolation of the long-dead Julian Grenfell into the contours of an adult Stapledon.

Olaf liked to call himself a jackdaw, a scavenger bird with a keen eye for usable debris. His most personal fiction was always less likely to be an autobiographical transcript than an ingenious nest of odds and ends shaped into a serviceable and highly idiosyncratic construction. He built a novel the way he constructed a boat from driftwood, or patched up a handbag out of stray pieces of leather and Duro-fix, or made a domestic gadget out of whatever came to hand. In *A Man Divided,* Maggie, even more than Victor, typifies the Stapledonian style of creation.

While Maggie is an homage to Agnes Stapledon, there are pronounced differences. As Victor's nursemaid, therapist, and spiritual caretaker, Maggie performs services that go well beyond any ministrations Mrs. Stapledon provided for a sometimes moody but basically healthy husband. With her coarse features, ungainliness, hippopotamus face, and eye-patch, Maggie little resembles Agnes but is a lot like the wife of an RAF physician Olaf met on his wartime lecture tour through the Hebrides. He wrote about her in a 1943 letter: "My young doctor's wife, who had been with him on the island for some months, was one of the most strikingly beautiful people I have ever seen. By conventional standards she was almost ugly in a way, but the more I looked at her the more I was spell-bound. She had a face like a young horse in perfect condition, and inside the horse was a frank, friendly, humorous spirit."[20] Yet in many respects, Maggie *was* Agnes. The loyalty under stress, the long-suffering fidelity, the confidence in her husband were traits Olaf knew intimately. But by dedicating *A Man Divided* to "A in gratitude to her for being T" he intimated that his wife was a woman divided between Agnes and Taffy. The relationship of fiction to fact could not be simple when the factual itself divided and shifted.

When *A Man Divided* was published in the spring of 1950, most reviewers pronounced it artless and lifeless: "a psychologist's case-book," "indigestible," a modern *Dr. Jekyll and Mr. Hyde* with all the apparatus showing.[21] *John O'London's* critic was unusual in finding it a successful philosophical novel that continued Stapledon's characteristic exploration of Reason and Imagination. Reviewing the author's twenty-year career, he observed shrewdly: "He works, so far as I can judge, down in the very mine of his own personality, hewing out the ore and smelting it with an agony of labour. Thus, his few books are all of a piece, variations upon a single theme, that theme of the sea-captain who watched the thinking stars and said, 'There's something going on there!' "[22] When Naomi Mitchison read *A Man Divided,* though, she felt it tapped into something bigger than the author's idiosyncrasies. "I suppose it's really about all of us, at least that was how it seemed to me, and we're getting old and less and less 'awake'. We are all of us sometimes the awake Victor and the times when we know we are get rarer and rarer and we are awfully afraid they won't come back. Is that how you are?"[23]

That was how Olaf was, much of the time, in 1950. He was recording the feeling, "with strenuous even painful honesty" as a friend of his marveled, in a "prose-poem" that became *The Opening of the Eyes:*

> When I was young I promised myself that beauty should spring from my hands and truth from my brain.
> . . . .
> But my high ventures one by one have stalled. Spiritually false, they yield no gold for the payment of my fabulous debt. And now, in old age, the reckoning![24]

At other times, though, as he told Gwynneth Davis, "I keep on forgetting I am old."[25] He turned with renewed vigor to his youthful interests in watercolors, taking art instruction in London and reveling in the joy of expression without the worry that invariably attended verbal creation. There he could surrender the need to make a professional reckoning and become a schoolboy again. "This time we had to do a composition, the subject being 'Industry.' I did a dock scene of ships, buildings, people. It is extraordinarily interesting working it all out, and struggling with the paints. The final effect is rather like 'child art'! Generally I go to art class and draw lovely naked ladies or gents!"[26] Assigned to paint a cityscape without any preliminary sketches, he did King's Cross railway terminal in a gouache rich in color and energy. In his last letter to Naomi Mitchison, he wrote of a new landscape he was working on, "It's an exciting and impossible picture, and I call it 'Nowhere on Earth.' Of course I don't really paint pictures, but Agnes gave me some poster paints, and I have decided I ought to have been one of the world's great artists!"[27]

His pictures disclosed the bright side of what he called the "dark-bright" world he was exploring in the fifty-four meditations of *The Opening of the Eyes*. As Olaf by day painted almost effortlessly, in the darkness he struggled for language adequate to the last odyssey he was undertaking in prose. "All the words!" he cried out. "The brave, the significant, the misused words, that men have spoken and written about the unseen reality, the ineffable, the eternal, the beatific! And all of them so manacled together in chain-gangs for forced labour, that the upshot is mere high-sounding, meaningless noise."[28] He was revisiting familiar landmarks in his intellectual, artistic, and spiritual development—dismayed to realize that the thorniest questions of his immature years remained just as difficult, and answers just as elusive and contradictory, in old age. Freedom and uncertainty were still twinned in him, at once the engines of a restless imagination and nemesis of a mind longing for truth. He had long ago outgrown the Victorian God of his mother's religion but had not been able to throw off the emotional claims of antique faith. "Is this perhaps hell's most exquisite refinement," he asked in one of the most piercing questions in *The Opening of the Eyes,* "that one should be haunted by the ever-present ghost of a disbelieved-in God?"[29]

In the thirty-second meditation, titled "The Heavens declare—Nothing," Stapledon recapitulated his first and his greatest artistic works, *Latter-Day Psalms* and *Star Maker.* Section 32 begins with the speaker walking onto Caldy Hill on a starry night, with the lights of West Kirby spread out below him and the dark, flat Irish sea in the distance, just as the modern psalmist of "The Heavens Declare" had done in 1914 and the narrator of *Star Maker* in the mid-thirties. In the intimate and lyrical style he had chosen for *The Opening of the Eyes,* Olaf once again indulged in cosmological speculation. As his eyes, cleansed of the inherited pieties of his early poetry and the fantastic inventions of scientific romance, roamed the starlit darkness, he was most intensely aware of absences and negations, of his century's incapacity for responding to the spectacle of the night sky or for placing the human species in any meaningful relationship to the vastness:

> Gone for ever is the East's great elephant that supports the world and is supported by a greater tortoise. Gone for ever are the celestial spheres, that box of boxes, which Dante described, Hell-centred, God-surrounded. Gone too the sun-centred universe within the sphere of the fixed stars. Gone the uniqueness of the sun's system, the uniqueness of our earth, the uniqueness of man."[30]

The Opening of the Eyes grew literally into a Book of Revelations, an Apocalypse that peeled back the veils of illusion obscuring the heart of reality. The lack of a satisfactory resolution to this incomplete book may have been inevitable no matter how long the author lived.

While the reflections recorded in *The Opening of the Eyes* were stark and apocalyptic, full of shadows cast by the concentration camps, the eighteenth-century slave ships, and the atomic bomb, the child in Olaf could resurface at a moment's notice. At Simon's Field he danced to country tunes for exercise and fun, though with little adult grace, and in London he sought out ballet for the enchantment of its fantastical movement. To his friends and family the frivolous, whimsical Olaf—descendant of the gleeful Old Abbotsholmian, irreverent Balliol Man, fabricator of the "John Stories," and satiric inventor of *Star Maker*'s "Other Earth"—was on frequent display. He kept an envelope of favorite jokes in his desk at Simon's Field to be brought out for company, and he wrote a set of sparkling "Notes on being in the Chair" for the would-be chairman or chairwoman who needed a tip from a mischievous professional. "If there are several official speakers, see that each knows how long a speech he is to make; and if there are many speeches and not much time, tell them (when they go on too long) that you are afraid you must ask them to stop. And if they still go on, drag them down by the seat of the pants." His advice was humane and easeful, and bespoke his own kindliness:

> Always err on the side of too little formality
>
> rather than too much.
>
> Don't speechify, just prattle.
>
> A bit of flippancy may help.
>
> Be friendly.[31]

If he seemed as preternaturally boyish as ever, the signs of age were growing. With friends he openly admitted being tired, and on his Lake District holidays he chose less strenuous walks than he had undertaken even two or three years earlier. Visiting his daughter in London, he rolled up his shirt-sleeve and said, "Feel this and tell me what you think." He was pointing to the hard, bulging brachial artery in his upper arm. Mary was alarmed at the evidence of arteriosclerosis but, given the prominence of blood vessels in people as thin as her father, was unsure just how worried to be.[32] Early in August 1950 he met Wolfgang Brueck for the last time at a small restaurant near Victoria Station. He told Wolfi that he and Agnes were about to leave for France for two weeks and then tour Yugoslavia for the National Peace Council; the Tito government had appealed for outside inspectors to come and refute Stalin's accusation that the Yugoslavs were readying an invasion of their Balkan neighbors.[33] In one of her last letters to Olaf, N. worried that his "social conscience" was ravaging him. "*Don't* overwork yourself and kill yourself with fatigue," she wrote, "even to save world peace." The trip would have marked Olaf's reentry, after a fifteen-month hiatus, into the international peace circuit, but after a week's lecturing and a short holiday in France he had had enough travel. Uncharacteristically, he withdrew from the Yugoslavian venture to go home and relax.

Back at Simon's Field at the end of August, Olaf worked steadily at *The Opening of the Eyes*. With his typical mixture of confidence and self-deprecation, he had told Naomi in June that it was going to be his "only really worthwhile book" on the subject of religion. "It's semi-poetry, very short, and of course profound. But when it is in print I shall discover that it's not profound at all, but just a stepping stone."[34] Even though he had not found a conclusion for the book, in the first week of September he began making a fair copy of the entire manuscript—his usual procedure before sending a new book to his typist. When he wasn't working on the manuscript, he returned to his easel. In France he had begun a nude of Agnes, but September in Caldy was too chilly for Agnes to pose comfortably. He turned to other subjects, and Agnes later remembered how "he seemed to be painting almost feverishly during his last week as if he knew he would not have much more time."[35]

On 5 September, as the cool weather continued, he gathered wood for a fire and began chopping it into usable pieces. But the effort wearied him, and he spent the afternoon on the divan in his study. That day he wrote a long letter to Gwynneth Davis at Langdale, who had been asking why he objected so strongly to organized religions and what he meant by "real religion." He explained that the religious spirit was antithetical to systems and sects, and that the genuinely religious person had to engage in a constant struggle between doctrine and poetry, between institutional authority and spiritual life. The founders of churches usually began as poets and satirists, "with their tongues perpetually in their cheeks" and their sights on the truths obscured by orthodoxy. "But very soon after the new organization has found its feet it loses its soul. That, surely, is what has happened to the whole lot of religious movements, including even the Quakers, who in their prime really were a religious body with a live 'soul.' " The real difficulty with religion was that although the churches had failed, spirituality was only fully satisfying when experienced as part of a group. As he had before, Olaf distanced himself from the religion of the hermit or the mystic or the fakir:

> I don't deny for a moment that religion is essentially *communal*. "Salvation" and "worship" are not really for the lone individual but for the group. And so, of course some minimum of organization is desirable. But it is desperately dangerous. And in a transitional time like ours, people who are really sensitive to the need for religion simply won't find a group anywhere. The real religious community today is not any Church but a widespread "peppering" of bewildered groping people in all sorts of odd places, inside & outside all sorts of other groups, political, cultural, vocational.
>
> You challenge me to say what I mean by "real religion." The nearest I can get to it in a few words is this. It is an attitude of the *whole* person to the *whole* of the universe in so far as he experiences it; and it is a consequent pattern of behaviour which he feels bound to *try* to put in practice in relation to his universe.[36]

After he posted the letter to Gwynneth the next morning, 6 September, Olaf spent the day home alone. Agnes, accompanied by her visiting eighty-four-year-old mother, Margaret Miller, went off to Heswall to see her grandson

Thomas and didn't return to Simon's Field until it was time for the evening meal. Dinner was simple and uneventful. Olaf's appetite was off, but he was merry and attentive to his mother-in-law. According to his custom, he cleared the table while Agnes and her mother continued to talk. He carried the tray of dirty dishes and silver into the kitchen and set it down next to the sink. Then Agnes heard a loud smacking sound and called out to her husband. When he failed to reply, she rushed into the room. Olaf lay on the stone floor of the kitchen, blood soaking the hair where his head had struck hard against the counter as he fell. A massive thrombosis that had been building up for days killed him almost at once.

Every sudden death is shocking; only hindsight discloses its inevitability. In Olaf's case an almost uncanny appearance of physical freshness belied his sixty-four years, and his reputation as a vigorous climber and swimmer left mourning friends mystified. For most of his years, he himself had worried more about the prospect of aging and senility than premature death. At forty he wrote of "the dumb scream of our dying youth" and the terrifying "first gray hair / encountered on the morning after love's night."[37] In one of the notebooks for *The Opening of the Eyes,* he boasted of "my body, a sturdy nag, mettlesome but seldom unruly." But in the summer of 1950 he knew he had not been feeling right. In a late passage in *The Opening of the Eyes,* he portrayed himself as "already rather old and tired, and soon perhaps to die."[38] He worked determinedly, as if by adherence to a literal internal deadline, to bring the book into final form. As congestion in his chest and shortness of breath tired him in his last weeks, did he find himself remembering earlier intimations of coronary trouble? A diary entry from 1907, when he underwent a physical examination by the college physician before a rowing match at Oxford, provokes the question: "I went to Dr. Collier at 10.15. After a lengthy examination he said I was a border case. I have not a weak heart or anything but he does not know if my heart's strong enough for racing."[39] If there was some weakness, generated perhaps by a bout of scarlet fever among his long succession of childhood illnesses, it may have been compensated by his passion for exercise, but a lifelong weakness for cream, butter, eggs, and tobacco undoubtedly took a toll.

Olaf lived zestfully and had not been afraid of dying. He measured individual lives against a cosmic scale, insisted on placing the flickering light of human consciousness in the context of the cold, remote, and impersonal light of the stars. Worried as he was about the cataclysm of atomic war, he went on hoping that human beings would see the back of the moon "in a few decades." His last article, published a month after he died, foresaw new horizons opening out so long as people worked to "get round these dangerous corners." And astronomical speculation provided cold solace for the otherwise unthinkable alternative: "If we blow this world to pieces it will be sad after all these centuries of human adventure, but I find a certain comfort in the thought that there are millions of worlds like ours."[40] He accepted his own mortality calmly. For him the extinction of species and of cosmoses was more profoundly tragic than any individual death. In a chapter written sometime in his last two years and designed for an unwritten book on humanism, he imagined the finale of London:

> The London streets will not always be crowded. Sooner or later the tide of human life will recede from them. An atom bomb, or bacteria, or sheer starvation, or causes still inconceivable, will some day destroy this ant's nest. What ruins will remain, weed-possessed or sterile from radiation? Or if by some freak of history this city is to be inconceivably long-lived, what unimaginable ruins will in the end be snow-blanketed in the final glaciation of the planet, or blown into space in the planet's shattering death agony? In one way or another there will surely be an end to this daily thronging. And even if man escapes to other worlds, to other stars, he will not escape the ultimate freezing out of all life in the cosmos. This, not individual death but universal death, is for the awakened mind the probability to be reckoned with.[41]

The obituaries celebrated Stapledon as the creator of the superman Odd John, a maker of Wellsian fantasies of the future, a teacher and a zealous speaker, a "longtime one-worlder," and inevitably (according to the ideology of the newspaper) a hero or a dupe of the international peace movement. But the eulogists who knew him personally could not refrain from remembering what his friend Leonard Martin called "the human kindness which pervaded all his dealings with his fellow man." Ritchie Calder, who had joined him in the antiapartheid campaign, called him simply "one of the nicest men I have met," and a colleague from the Progressive League wrote, "Above all things he was a good man."[42]

Agnes arranged the funeral that preceded his cremation in Birkenhead on 12 September. For several days Olaf's body was laid out in the study at Simon's Field, dressed in a white robe with a bright red scarf at the neck. At the Landican Crematorium the vice-chancellor of Liverpool University delivered the eulogy, but Agnes chose the words from *Pilgrim's Progress* that introduced the memorial program. It is the epitaph for the character whom Bunyan called Valiant-for-Truth:

> When the day that he must go hence was come, many accompanied him to the River-side, into which as he went he said, *Death, where is thy Sting?* And as he went down deeper he said, *Grave, where is thy Victory?* So he passed over, and all the Trumpets sounded for him on the other side.[43]

Agnes wanted Olaf's remains brought down to the side of the river he loved, the Dee. But there was a long delay. To everyone's grief his daughter Mary could not be located in time for the funeral. She and her husband Shiva had gone off for a long camping trip in Spain, and after fruitless efforts to find them, Agnes reluctantly went forward with the cremation and wrote to her daughter's London flat. When Mary returned home on 24 September, she learned that her father had been dead for nearly three weeks.

Mary came to Simon's Field and found Agnes still tending her frail mother, who had been distraught and unable to return to her home since the night of Olaf's death. They cried and talked and waited for John to arrive from his market garden in Heswall. Then the three Stapledons made an ending. Reluctantly, Agnes told her mother where they were going and what they must do. Leaving Margaret Miller in tears in the sitting room, Agnes, Mary, and John took the box of ashes and went out the back door and through the garden to the curving bridge over the railway track. They walked quickly across the golf links to the sandy cliffs overlooking the Dee estuary. There, where for fifty years Olaf had stood to watch the little steamers and fishing boats coming in from and going out to the Irish Sea and where he had rejoiced in the flight of the peninsula's birds wheeling over the water, his wife and daughter and son, without words or ceremony, poured his ashes on the cliff-top.

NOTES

A Note on Sources and Abbreviations

ITEMS IDENTIFIED IN THE NOTES as SA are in the largest public collection of Olaf Stapledon's papers, the Stapledon Archive at the Sydney Jones Library, University of Liverpool. Founded by Agnes Stapledon in 1970 with a donation of seventeen manuscripts, it was greatly expanded in 1983 by the loan of thousands of additional manuscripts, proofs, letters, diaries, notebooks, lecture notes, press cuttings, and annotated books. The library has printed a two-volume guide to the archive; items not easily located in the guide are identified in my notes with the full catalogue number.

Many documents remain with the Stapledon heirs. All items identified as SFP are in the Stapledon Family papers.

Items in other private hands are identified with a P.

Public archives frequently cited are abbreviated as follows:

PEN PEN Archive, Humanities Research Center, University of Texas
LU   Liverpool University Archives, Harold Cohen Library
NLS National Library of Scotland

The following abbreviations are used for personal names:

AM Agnes Miller
AS   Agnes (Miller) Stapledon
EM Emmeline Miller
ES   Emmeline (Miller) Stapledon
OS Olaf Stapledon
WS William Stapledon

The books of Olaf Stapledon are quoted from first editions, using these abbreviations:

BI   *Beyond the "Isms"* (London: Secker and Warburg [Searchlight Books no. 16], 1942)
DATL *Darkness and the Light* (London: Methuen, 1942)
DIL   *Death Into Life* (London: Methuen, 1946)

FE	*Four Encounters* in *Nebula Maker and Four Encounters* (New York: Dodd, Mead, 1983)
FFC	*Far Future Calling: Uncollected Science Fiction and Fantasies of Olaf Stapledon,* edited by Sam Moskowitz (Philadelphia: Oswald Train, 1979)
FL	*The Flames: A Fantasy* (London: Secker and Warburg, 1947)
LFM	*Last and First Men: A Story of the Near and Far Future* (London: Methuen, 1930)
LMIL	*Last Men in London* (London: Methuen, 1932)
LDP	*Latter-Day Psalms* (Liverpool: Henry Young, 1914)
MD	*A Man Divided* (London: Methuen, 1950)
MTE	*A Modern Theory of Ethics: A Study of the Relations of Ethics and Psychology* (London: Methuen, 1929)
NHB	*New Hope for Britain* (London: Methuen, 1939)
NM	*Nebula Maker* in *Nebula Maker and Four Encounters* (New York: Dodd, Mead, 1983)
OE	*The Opening of the Eyes,* edited by Agnes Z. Stapledon (London: Methuen, 1954)
OJ	*Odd John: A Story Between Jest and Earnest* (London: Methuen, 1935)
OMNW	*Old Man in New World* (London: Allen and Unwin [PEN Books], 1944)
PL	*Philosophy and Living,* 2 Vols. (Harmondsworth, U.K.: Penguin, 1939)
SI	*Sirius: A Fantasy of Love and Discord* (London: Secker and Warburg, 1944)
SM	*Star Maker* (London: Methuen, 1937)
SPP	*Seven Pillars of Peace* (London: Common Wealth, 1944)
SR	*Saints and Revolutionaries* [*I Believe,* No. 10] (London: Heinemann, 1939)
TATW	*Talking Across the World: The Love Letters of Olaf Stapledon and Agnes Miller, 1913–1919,* edited by Robert Crossley (Hanover, N.H.: Univ. Press of New England, 1987)
WW	*Waking World* (London: Methuen, 1934)
YT	*Youth and Tomorrow* (London: St. Botolph, 1946)

Except as noted, information on Stapledon's publishing history depends on the essential work of Harvey J. Satty and Curtis C. Smith's *Olaf Stapledon: A Bibliography* (Westport, Conn., and London: Greenwood, 1984), abbreviated in the notes as Satty-Smith *Bibliography.*

Boiling the Bones: Biography and the "Minor" Writer

1. The only printed reference to these photographs is in Terence Pepper's exhibition catalogue for a 1985 show, *Howard Coster's Celebrity Portraits* (New York: Dover, 1985), 111. The OS portraits were not displayed.

2. Brian Aldiss, "In Orbit With the Star Maker," *Times Literary Supplement,* 23 Sept. 1983, 1007–8.

3. *LMIL,* 85.

4. OS, "Letters to the Future," ed. Robert Crossley, in *The Legacy of Olaf Stapledon,* ed. Patrick A. McCarthy et al. (New York: Greenwood, 1989), 107.

5. H. G. Wells to OS, 7 Apr. 1936, "The Letters of Olaf Stapledon and H. G. Wells, 1931–1942," ed. Robert Crossley, in *Science Fiction Dialogues,* ed. Gary Wolfe (Chicago: Academy Chicago, 1982), 39.

6. OS, "Letters to the Future," 107.

7. G. H. Bantock, writing a biography of Myers in the late 1940s, asked OS for information. Stating his misgivings, OS nevertheless sent all the letters Myers had earlier asked him to burn (AS, interview with author, 15 June 1982).

8. *LFM,* 104.

9. Arthur Koestler to OS, 14 June 1944 (SA).

10. Michael Fletcher, note to author.

11. Iris Origo, *Images and Shadows: Part of a Life* (New York: Harcourt, 1970), 4.

12. Sometime in 1896, OS mailed his collection of Shakespeare extracts to his father in Egypt, with a note saying that the quotation from *Hamlet* was "the one I like best" (SFP).

13. OS to H. G. Wells, 16 Oct. 1934, "Letters of OS and HGW," 36–37.

14. Leslie A. Fiedler, *Olaf Stapledon: A Man Divided* (New York: Oxford Univ. Press, 1983).

15. Sam Moskowitz, "Peace and Olaf Stapledon," in *Far Future Calling: Uncollected Science Fiction and Fantasies of Olaf Stapledon,* ed. Sam Moskowitz (Philadelphia: Oswald Train, 1979), 267. His biographical essay, "Olaf Stapledon: The Man Behind the Works," appears in the same volume, 15–69.

1. Last Things First: La Guardia Field, 24 March 1949

1. Telegrams from Ambassador Lewis Douglas to Dean Acheson, Secretary of State, 17 Mar. and 18 Mar. 1949; National Archives, Washington, D.C., doc. # XR 811.42700(R) and XR 811.111 Non-Immigrant. Like most other government documents cited in this chapter, these were classified as secret.

2. "No Visas for a New York 'Peace' Conference," *Manchester Guardian,* 23 Mar. 1949, p. 5.

3. Memorandum, "For the President from Secretary Acheson," 14 Mar. 1949; handwritten annotation and approval, initialed HST. National Archives, Washington, D.C., doc. #800.00B/3-1849.

4. OS's self-description prepared for the 1946 Present Question Conference in Exeter (SA, STAP B.70[2]); Alfred Kazin, "As a Superman Sees the World," *New York Herald Tribune,* 19 July 1936, sec. II, p. 2.

5. My chief documentary source is the sworn statement of William Olaf Stapledon made before Immigrant Inspector Joseph R. McHugh, La Guardia Field, 24 Mar. 1949. The "releasable portions" were furnished by the Immigration and Naturalization Service of the U.S. Department of Justice.

6. "Dr. Stapledon Questioned," *Daily Telegraph,* 25 Mar. 1949, p. 1; "Stapledon Grilled for Two Hours," *Daily Worker,* 25 Mar. 1949, p. 1; "Dr. Olaf Grilled for 3 Hours," *Daily Herald,* 25 Mar. 1949, p. 1; "Five Page Story Opens the Door," *Daily Express,* 25 Mar. 1949, p. 2. In a letter to her husband on 27 Mar. 1949, AS reported, "Your interview grew in length according to the sensationalism of the paper" (SFP).

7. "Questioning of Dr. Stapledon," *Manchester Guardian,* 25 Mar. 1949, p. 5.

8. Charles Grutzner, " 'Culturists' Evade Queries of Press," *New York Times,* 26 Mar. 1949, p. 3; "18,000 Join Final 'Peace' Session," *Liverpool Echo,* 28 Mar. 1949, p. 3. A secret intelligence report on delegates admitted to the country (U.S. Department of State doc. 100-356137-523) stated that OS had "no known political activities."

9. Memorandum from the American Embassy in Warsaw to the Department of State, National Archives, Washington, D.C., doc. #800.00B/9-148; memorandum from J. Edgar Hoover to Immigration and Naturalization Service, 18 Mar. 1949, FBI doc. #100-356137-364x. Speculation that OS's speech at Wroclaw in August 1948 facilitated his visa appeared in "London Unruffled by U.S. Visa Bar," *Christian Science Monitor,* 24 Mar. 1949, p. 10.

10. "U.S. Revokes Visas of Four Britons," *Daily Telegraph,* 23 Mar. 1949, p. 1.

11. "Dr. Stapledon Not Turned Back," *Liverpool Post,* 25 Mar. 1949, p. 1; OS, "Peace and War in New York," *New Statesman,* 30 Apr. 1949, p. 432.

12. *OJ,* 107.

13. Joseph P. Lash, "Weekend at the Waldorf," *New Republic,* 18 Apr. 1949, p. 11; "Red Visitors Cause Rumpus," *Life,* 4 Apr. 1949, p. 40.

14. OS to Naomi Mitchison, 10 July 1940 (NLS).

15. OS to AS, 24 Mar. 1949 (SFP).

16. Sam Moskowitz heard OS introduced this way in Newark. "Peace and Olaf Stapledon" in *FFC,* 266.

17. *LFM,* 57, 54, and 43–91, passim.

18. OS to AS, 24 Mar. 1949 (SFP).

19. *SM,* 332.

2. Bondage in Egypt, 1886–1901

1. Edith Hope Scott, *Autobiography of an Unknown Author* (SFP).

2. On Holt's early steam liners, see R. H. Thornton, *British Shipping,* 2nd ed. (Cambridge: Cambridge Univ. Press, 1959), 57–58, and George Chandler, *Liverpool Shipping: A Short History* (London: Phoenix House, 1960), 212–16.

3. See M. M. Oppenheim, *The Maritime History of Devon* (Exeter: Univ. of Exeter Press, 1968).

4. From the manuscript "Fields Within Fields" (SA). OS first read the Captain's journal, now in SFP, in the 1930s; in "Fields Within Fields" he wrote: "When I first came into possession of this heirloom I regarded it only with superficial curiosity. . . . There is nothing outstandingly remarkable in it, but it has come alive in my hands, as though after long hibernation, the warmth of human contact had awakened it. Somehow, I feel, it has a special message for me, as though my young grandfather had written it with a deep unconscious purpose of communicating something to his aging grandson in another world."

5. Kipling based *Stalky and Co.* (1899) on his student days from 1878 to 1882 at United Services College in Northam, just down the road from the Stapledon house; OS used the setting in *LFM,* 34–37.

6. For this and other details about Captain Stapledon, I draw on a talk with Mariel Stapledon of North Devon, 15 Oct. 1989.

7. Margaret Barnard Miller, "Memoir of the Barnard Family and Their Friends," written in 1949 (SFP). A Yorkshire Quaker, she met Frank Miller (whom she later married) at a dinner party when her family came to Liverpool in 1882.

8. WS to ES, 11 Oct. 1891; ES to WS, 21 Oct. 1891 (SFP). The Liverpool–North Devon visits led to another alliance between the families when Ernest Miller and Thomazena Stapledon married in 1880.

9. WS to EM, 11 Apr. 1883 (SFP).

10. Draft of a letter from WS to Mary Stapledon, enclosed in his letter to EM, 11 Apr. 1883 (SFP).

11. WS to EM, 30 Mar. 1884 (SFP). Just before their wedding, WS wrote: "I am glad you *enjoyed* the Ruskin meeting, although—well never mind—I am glad you enjoyed it." He believed she might have married sooner were it not that the Ruskin Society "did you a great deal of harm" (11 Sept. 1884). The Society's naïveté may be guessed from Edith Hope Scott's memory of its founding: "Curiously enough we had not heard of the other people who, full of ideas and idealism, were forming Fabian Societies and Toynbee Halls. We rather thought we were alone in our new discoveries, and set to work at once to reform the world" (*Autobiography of an Unknown Author* [SFP]).

12. Letters of John Ruskin to EM, 19 Feb. and 10 Mar. 1883, printed in Edith Hope Scott, *Ruskin's Guild of St. George* (London: Methuen, 1931), 73–75.

13. WS, commonplace book, Apr. 1883 (SFP).

14. Paper marked, "W.C.S. *Private*. 24th December 1884"; Coventry Patmore: WS to EM, 9 Sept. 1884 (SFP).

15. ES to WS, 31 Aug. 1891 (SFP).

16. *YT*, 44.

17. ES to WS, 3 Jan. 1900 (SFP).

18. André Chevrillon, *Dans l'Inde*, as quoted and translated by D. A. Farnie, *East and West of Suez: The Suez Canal in History 1854–1956* (Oxford: Clarendon, 1969), 401. I owe a general debt to Farnie's monumental study, especially to chap. 22, "The Rise of Port Said, 1887–1914."

19. G. W. Steevens, *Egypt in 1898* (New York: Dodd, Mead, 1899), 22, 27.

20. Rudyard Kipling, *The Light That Failed* (New York: Doubleday, 1925), 29–30.

21. Thomas Carlyle, *The Early Kings of Norway* and *An Essay on the Portraits of John Knox* (London: Chapman and Hall, 1875), 175–76.

22. Writing to WS on 3 May and 5 May 1886, ES longed for her husband in the "nervous fever" of advanced pregnancy, but still in "about the eighth month," she felt she could "count on a couple of weeks more with some confidence."

23. WS to OS, 18 Nov. 1894 (SFP). OS's birth certificate lists the place of birth as 49 Falkland Road, Poolton cum Seacombe, Wallasey. The baptismal registration is blank.

24. In *Twentieth-Century Authors*, ed. Stanley J. Kunitz (New York: H. W. Wilson, 1942), 1325–26, OS said he considered the Suez Canal "my home." But his daughter recalled that he always gravitated toward Switzerland, the Lake District, and Scandinavia rather than southern England and Mediterranean Europe (Mary Shenai, interview with author, 15 Oct. 1989).

25. According to Mary Shenai, WS also worried about erecting workers' housing near the business complex because of the risk of infection (interview with author, 2 Oct. 1989).

26. All from a letter of OS to AM, 3 Nov. 1913 (SFP).

27. Manuscript, "Fields Within Fields," SA; for the child's belief that "there was something in the blood" of the English that authorized them to rule "backward races," see *YT*, 39.

28. OS, "What Philosophy Means to Me," typescript of a talk broadcast 5 June 1946 by the BBC, in SA (STAP D.I. 2). He included some of this incident in the account of Paul's childhood in his novel *LMIL*, 72.

29. Incidents in OS's scientific education come from "Fields Within Fields" (SA). He commented on his asymmetrical eyes in a letter to AM, 18 Jan. 1917 (NLS).

30. *SM*, 227.

31. *LMIL*, 84–85.

32. *YT*, 7. Of WS's physics lesson (adapted to fiction), the narrator of *LMIL* observes: "It was his father who first pointed out to him the crossing wave-trains of a mountain tarn, and by eloquent description made him feel that the whole physical world was in some manner a lake rippled by myriads of such crossing waves." For discussion of this episode see John Kinnaird, *Olaf Stapledon* (Mercer Island, Wash.: Starmont, 1986), 14–15.

33. WS to ES, 15 Oct. 1888 (SFP).

34. WS to ES, 6 Aug. 1891 (SFP).

35. WS to ES, 24 Aug. 1891 (SFP).

36. WS to OS, 14 June 1891 and 22 July 1894 (SFP).

37. *LMIL*, 85; *OJ*, 191.

38. OS to Naomi Mitchison, 10 June 1944 (SFP).

39. Notes for "Science and Fiction," 1947 (SA); *LMIL*, 86–87

40. ES to WS, 21 Oct. 1891 (SFP).

41. ES to WS, 20 Aug. 1891; WS to ES, 26 Aug. 1891 (SFP). When WS proposed visiting for Christmas in North Wales or at her sister Louisa's Liverpool home, she said there wasn't enough room and that "we should both commit suicide before the winter was over if we were cooped up in lodgings" (15 Oct. 1891 [SFP]).

42. WS to ES, 30 Nov. 1891 (SFP).

43. On 2 Aug. 1891, ES told WS of attacks so severe that she could not walk; her doctor felt the condition "had gone on too long now & would never be cured. He thinks it is the ulceration which causes the frightful depression & irritation of the nerves" (SFP). OS's daughter, a physician, believes that gynecological problems, misdiagnosed or ineffectively treated, kept Emmeline from having more children, underlay her morbidity, and exacerbated her hypochondria (Mary Shenai, interview with author, 17 Oct. 1989).

44. ES to WS, 20 Aug. 1891 (SFP). In this letter she blames Port Said ("a *deadly* place for me") as much as her physical ailments for the severity of her depression.

45. *YT,* 42.

46. ES to WS, 21 Oct. and 1 Nov. 1891 (SFP).

47. ES to WS, 5 Apr. 1892 (SFP).

48. The Articles of Partnership for Messrs. William Stapledon and Sons, dated 17 Nov. 1892, are in SFP.

49. ES to WS, 25 Oct. 1894 (SFP).

50. ES to WS, 25 Nov. 1894 (SFP).

51. WS to ES, 5 Jan. 1892 (SFP).

52. ES to WS, 12 Dec. 1897 (SFP).

53. ES to WS, 19 Dec. 1897 (SFP).

54. ES to WS, 12 Dec. 1897 (SFP).

55. OS recorded this anecdote in *YT,* 46.

56. ES to WS, 1 Oct. 1891 (SFP).

57. *YT,* 45.

58. Manuscript, "Fields Within Fields" (SA). In the diary he began keeping in 1900, OS recorded the Captain's death with typically uncertain spelling: "My dear old Grandfather *died* this morning, after being practically unconscious for $4^1/_2$ years (parallysis)" (OS, diary, 14 May 1902; SA). The portrait of Captain Stapledon is now held by John Stapledon.

59. OS to WS, undated, but certainly among the very earliest surviving letters (SFP).

60. WS to OS, 14 June 1891; 9 Sept. 1894; one undated (SFP).

61. ES to WS, 8 May 1898 (SFP).

62. ES to WS, Easter Sunday 1896 (SFP).

63. ES to WS, 25 Oct. 1894 (SFP).

64. ES to WS, 8 June 1898; 24 Nov. 1899 (SFP).

65. ES to WS, 14 Jan. 1900 (SFP). On the childhood copying of proverbs see OS, "The Pen and the Sword," *The Author* 57 (Autumn 1946), 4.

66. ES to WS, 8 Aug. 1894; Edith Hope Scott, *Autobiography* (SFP).

67. *YT,* 20.

68. ES to WS, 5 June 1898 (SFP).

69. ES to WS, 17 Nov. 1899 (SFP).

70. *YT,* 42; Liverpool College, *Upper School Magazine,* 22 July 1901, p. 3. For the school's history and personnel, I rely upon David Wainwright, *Liverpool Gentlemen: A History of Liverpool College, an independent day school, from 1840* (London: Faber, 1960).

71. According to a letter to WS on 18 Jan. 1900, ES wrote to Dyson protesting OS's promotion because he didn't really understand the work (SFP).

72. Information on OS's spelling and history is from a letter of ES to WS, 18 Jan. 1895; on Latin, from letters of WS to ES, 25 Apr. 1896 and of OS to WS, 16 Dec. 1900 (SFP). Prize lists, including a commendation from the Royal Drawing Society, are in Liverpool College's *Upper School Magazine*, 22 July 1901, p. 4, and 16 July 1902, p. 3. In *YT*, OS recalled Latin lessons from "an Anglican parson, who, by the way, was already embarking on the process of drinking himself to death" (23).

73. Lecture notes for "The Use and Danger of Youth Movements," given near the outbreak of World War II (SA).

74. ES to WS, 16 Nov. 1899 (SFP).

75. ES to WS, 24 Nov. 1899. OS's suspicion of a parental conspiracy was not altogether imaginary. Among arguments for sending him to board, WS included a hope that ES might come back with him to Port Said, but, she told him on 3 Jan. 1900, in Egypt she would still see little of her busy husband, and without her son her loneliness there would be intolerable (SFP).

76. ES to WS, 23 Jan. 1900 (SFP).

77. *YT*, 46.

78. Francis E. Hyde, *Blue Funnel: A History of Alfred Holt and Co. of Liverpool, 1865–1914* (Liverpool: Liverpool Univ. Press, 1957), 80–81.

79. The early records of the Holt company were destroyed in the Liverpool blitz of 1941. When Crompton died in Paris in 1908, OS was at Oxford and wrote in his diary: "It would appear to be he that did most to get Father into the OSSCo at L'pool" (OS, diary, 30 Sept. 1908 [SA]). Crompton and WS had known each other for nearly twenty years as members of the Positivist Church of Humanity in Liverpool.

80. OS diary, 1901–03 (SA).

3. An Educational Laboratory, 1902–1905

1. Edith Hope Scott, *Autobiography of an Unknown Author* (SFP); interview with Scott's niece, Holda Fowler, 9 Oct. 1989. The Abbotsholme scheme appeared in the *Pioneer*, April 1889, signed by Cecil Reddie, Robert Muirhead, Edward Carpenter, and William Cassels. Newspapers often noted the school's "Ruskinian" cast; see *Abbotsholme an Educational Laboratory: Press Opinions*, 3rd ed. (Derby and London: Bemrose and Sons, 1912). WS devised the reading plan in a letter to ES, 28 Nov. 1888 (SFP).

2. Scott, *Autobiography*. His parents' trip to Abbotsholme was noted in OS's diary, 18 Mar. 1902 (SA); fifty-eight pocket diaries, used in his younger years for irregular journal entries, survive.

3. C. R. Reddie, *An Educational Atlas* (London: George Allen, 1900), 3.

4. OS to WS, 31 May 1902 (SFP).

5. The chairs and an extraordinary Ashbee oak cabinet painted with verses from Blake's *Auguries of Innocence* remain at Abbotsholme; the cabinet appears in plate 105 of Elizabeth Aslin's *Nineteenth Century English Furniture* (London: Faber, 1962). On Ashbee's relation to Ruskin, Morris and the New School movement, see Alan Crawford, *C. R. Ashbee: Architect, Designer and Romantic Socialist* (New Haven: Yale Univ. Press, 1985).

6. Carpenter's role at Abbotsholme is assessed by Reddie's early partner, R. F. Muirhead, "Memories of Edward Carpenter," in *Edward Carpenter: In Appreciation*, ed. Gilbert Beith (London: Allen and Unwin, 1931), 155–57. The best biography of Reddie is a Dutch dissertation, published in English, by J. H. G. I. Giesbers, *Cecil Reddie and Abbotsholme: A Forgotten Pioneer and His Creation* (Nijmegen, Netherlands: Centrale Drukkerij, 1970). It supersedes B. M. Ward's pious *Reddie of Abbotsholme* (London: Allen and Unwin, 1934).

7. Jan Marsh discusses Abbotsholme and late-Victorian agrarian and arts-and-crafts movements in *Back to the Land: The Pastoral Impulse in England, from 1880 to 1914* (London: Quartet Books, 1982), 204–14.

8. Edmond Demolins, *Anglo-Saxon Superiority: To What It Is Due*, trans. Louis B. Lavigne (London: Leadenhall, 1899), 52.

9. Cecil Reddie, "How Shall We Educate Our Directing Classes?", *Abbotsholmian* 3 (1908–09), 13; originally delivered to the Authors' Club, London, 5 July 1909.

10. Reddie printed a sample application form in *An Educational Atlas*, 15.

11. Examples of Abbotsholme pedagogy are cited in the OS diary, 7 Mar. 1904 (SA), and by Colin A. Scott, a Boston educator, who described Abbotsholme in *Social Education* (Boston: Ginn, 1908), 43–55. Less friendly views are in F. B. H. Ellis, "Teaching at Abbotsholme in 1895" in *Fifty Years of Abbotsholme, 1889–1939*, anonymously edited (London: Unwin, 1939), 23.

12. Cecil Reddie, *Abbotsholme* (London: George Allen, 1900), 637. Students also kept meteorological records; one of OS's first tasks on arriving at Abbotsholme was to devise a "Formula for the Weather" (diary, 8 May 1902 [SA]).

13. "Essentially Reddie continued to see himself as a Senior Prefect—'on the side' of the pupils, or at least of their higher selves, against those who strove to destroy and pervert the splendour and purity of 'Boy Nature.' " Robert Skidelsky, *English Progressive Schools* (Harmondsworth, U.K.: Penguin, 1969), 104.

14. "The Ceremony for Going Up into the Senior School," in the anonymously edited *Abbotsholme School Prayer Book* (Plaistow, U.K.: Curwen, 1935), 87.

15. OS, notes for a lecture, "The Use and Danger of Youth Movements," given during World War II (SA).

16. C. R. Reddie, "Is Abbotsholme an Experiment?", *Abbotsholmian* 2 (July 1908), 4–5. The lecture was originally written in Oct. 1902.

17. The following incident is recorded in Preston W. Search's account of a one-day visit with Reddie, "The Abbotsholme," *Century Magazine* (June 1908), 238.

18. Sir Stanley Unwin, *The Truth About a Publisher: An Autobiographical Record* (New York: Macmillan, 1960), 47–55.

19. C. R. Reddie, preface to *From the Abbotsholme Liturgy* (Derbyshire: Abbotsholme Press, 1910), 7.

20. OS diary, 6 May 1904 (SA).

21. Reddie, *An Educational Atlas*, 2.

22. OS to WS, 4 May 1902 (SFP).

23. Cecil R. Reddie, "How Is the Life in Dormitory Organised?" *Abbotsholmian* 4 (1909–10), 15; a reprint of a monograph Reddie had most recently revised in Sept. 1903.

24. Patrick Geddes, "A Pioneer School," *Saint George* 8 (Jan. 1905), 46; Scott, *Social Education*, 47. The sermon is quoted by Giesbers in *Cecil Reddie and Abbotsholme*, 121.

25. The above excerpts come from Reddie, "How Is the Life in Dormitory Organised?", 13–19; see Michael Holroyd, *Lytton Strachey: A Biography* (1967–68; rev. 1971; rpt. New York: Holt, 1980), 83–84, 737.

26. "What Are the Educative Merits of Bathing?" was revised for the fourth time by Reddie on 20 May 1903 and printed at the Abbotsholme Press as No. 6 in a series of school monographs. It was reprinted in the *Abbotsholmian* 4 (1909–10), 27–31.

27. The examples are from three of Reddie's broadsheets: "What Are the General Aims as to Clothing, Etc.?" (revised 24 Oct. 1903), "What Are the Rules for the Boys Regarding Clothes, Etc.?" (revised 1 Oct. 1903), and "What Are the Good Points in the Abbotsholme Suit?" (composed 16 Nov. 1909). All printed first by the Abbotsholme Press, they were republished in the *Abbotsholmian* 4 (1909–10), 19–22, 23–27, 28–31.

28. OS diary, endleaf to 1902 volume (SA).

29. Preston Search ("The Abbotsholme," 235–36) quotes Reddie on the school's "protest against the luxuriance of British education, against the abandonment of the country for the artificial life of the city, against the kid-gloved aristocracy which fails to recognize the nobility of labor." Another observer thought the manual work light; the roughest tasks on the Abbotsholme estate were done by hired help. See Wilbur S. Jackman, "Notes on Foreign Schools," *Educational Review* 21 (Mar. 1901), 225.

30. The detail is in a letter of AS to her parents Frank and Margaret Miller, written on her honeymoon, 5 Aug. 1919 (SFP).

31. Patrick Geddes in "A Pioneer School" (51) wrote in amazed detail of his observation of a "boy-surgeon" at work.

32. OS to WS, 29 Sept. 1902 (SFP).

33. OS diary, 21 Nov. 1902 (SA). Allusions to Abbott's *Flatland* occur in OS's first two published fictions, *LFM*, 136 and *LMIL*, 227.

34. OS diary, 3 Dec. 1903 (SA).

35. OS to WS, 26 Sept. 1902 (SFP).

36. OS diary, 24 Nov. 1904; 9 Mar. 1905 (SA).

37. OS diary, 13 Mar. 1904 (SA). Copies of the *Book of Illustrations* are in the Abbotsholme School library.

38. Skidelsky, *English Progressive Schools*, 72–74. See also Paul Delany's view of Reddie as someone who "never really developed beyond puberty" in *The Neo-Pagans: Rupert Brooke and the Ordeal of Youth* (New York: Free Press, 1987), 11–13. The virginal Reddie moved uneasily around the edges of Edward Carpenter's homosexual circle; he revealed his own identification with what he called "the homogenic temperament" only in his posthumously published memoir, *Edward Carpenter* (London: British Sexological Society, 1932), 6–7.

39. OS diary, 23 June 1905 (SA).

40. Reddie, "What is the Educative Value of Life in Dormitory?", *Abbotsholmian* 4 (1909–10), 12; originally composed Dec. 1903. Colin Scott admired Reddie's rejection of the typical boarding-school horror of homosexuality: "In class work one boy is set against another. Close friendships among the boys are carefully watched and broken up in the fear of unmentionable evils. Such watchfulness against vice becomes so marked at times that it actually suggests its commission" (*Social Education*, 46).

41. Cecil Reddie, "Presidential Address" [delivered to the Old Boys Club at Abbotsholme, 30 Mar. 1902], *Old Abbotsholmian* 1 (1903), 55.

42. "The Abbotsholme School Song" in the *Abbotsholme School Prayer Book*, xii. Excerpts from *Leaves of Grass* were often used in the chapel liturgy. On Whitman's impact on Edward Carpenter's cult of comradeship and on the "New School" movement, see Fiona MacCarthy, *The Simple Life: C. R. Ashbee in the Cotswolds* (Berkeley: Univ. of California Press, 1981), 82–83.

43. ES to WS, 24 Sept. 1904 (SFP).

44. OS diary, 8 May and 12 May 1905 (SA).

45. OS diary, 30 Mar. 1908; he began reading the *Vita Nuova* in Italian on 20 Oct. 1907 (SA).

46. OS diary, 10 Apr. 1903 (SA).

47. OS to WS, 22 Sept. 1904 (SFP).

48. OS to WS, 20 Oct. 1903 (SFP). Stevenson was one of OS's favorite authors, and *Dr. Jekyll* lies behind his 1950 novel about a dual personality, *MD*.

49. OS diary, 25 June; 7 July 1905 (SA).

50. H. C. Maxwell Lyte, *A History of the University of Oxford from the Earliest Times to the Year 1530* (London: Macmillan, 1886), 137–41.

51. OS to WS, 23 Sept. 1903 (SFP).
52. ES to WS, 25 Sept. 1904; WS to ES, 25 Sept. 1904 (SFP).
53. WS to ES, 28 Sept.; 30 Sept. 1904 (SFP).
54. OS to WS, 15 and 20 Nov. 1904 (SFP).
55. OS to WS, 26 Jan. 1905 (SFP); OS diary, 24 Mar. 1905 (SA).
56. OS to WS, 18 Feb. 1905 (SFP).
57. OS diary, 14 June 1905 (SA).
58. *Old Abbotsholmian* 2 (1907), 183–84.
59. G. H. Dixon witnessed bouts of shouting and caning, tirades against women and England, insults to parents, and "reigns of terror" during World War I when Reddie's notions of Teutonic superiority were shattered. See "During the War: The Decline Begins (1912–1917)," in *Fifty Years of Abbotsholme*, 36–39.
60. OS to WS, 19 Dec. 1916 (SFP).
61. Apparently the photographs, with many other letters and personal papers connected with his years at Abbotsholme, were destroyed after Reddie's death in 1932.
62. *From the Abbotsholme Liturgy*, 122.
63. OS diary, 27 July 1905 (SA).

4. Mediocria Firma, 1905–1909

1. Leslie A. Fiedler's disingenuous labeling of the Stapledon marriage as "not-quite-incestuous" is an extrapolation from OS's fiction; see *Olaf Stapledon: A Man Divided* (New York: Oxford Univ. Press, 1983), 12, 18, 110.
2. OS diary, 3 Oct. 1905 (SA).
3. OS diary, 6 Oct. 1905 (SA).
4. On Ezra Hancock and details of life at the college before World War I, see John Jones, *Balliol College: A History 1263–1939* (Oxford: Oxford Univ. Press, 1988), 225–44, 254–56.
5. OS diary, 20 July 1908 (SA).
6. In 1915, OS rehearsed for AM his friendship with Kermack (*TATW*, 87). The poem, "Fidèle" (SFP), was written about 1911; when AM reread it in 1917, she guessed, "I always took that to be written of two men—a David and Jonathan" (AM to OS, 26 Mar. 1917). Perhaps embarrassed, he denied her interpretation of his "funny little old verses" (11 July 1917) [SFP]. OS revised "Fidèle," retitling it "The Misfits," for a hand-bound manuscript collection, "Verse by WOS" in the mid-1920s (SA).
7. Writing to Naomi Mitchison, OS called himself "a provincial" (undated, c. 1931, NLS), and he defended provincialism in "Liverpool and Britain," *Liverpolitan* 11 (Jan. 1946), 8–9.
8. H. W. Carless Davis, *A History of Balliol College*, revised by R. H. C. Davis and Richard Hunt and supplemented by Harold Hartley et al. (Oxford: Basil Blackwell, 1963), 223–24.
9. OS diary, 16 Oct. 1905 (SA).
10. On Smith's teaching style see Davis, *A History of Balliol*, 238–44. V. H. Galbraith said of him, "Had A. L. given to personal research what he gave to young men he could, one felt, have been an outstanding historian" (quoted in Davis, 242).
11. L. E. Jones, *An Edwardian Youth* (London: Macmillan, 1956), 20; on Maitland's teaching of history, see Norman F. Cantor, *Inventing the Middle Ages* (New York: William Morrow, 1991), 55–56.
12. OS diary, 13 Jan. 1906 (SA).
13. OS diary, 19 Jan. 1906 (SA).

14. OS diary, 6 Mar. 1906 (SA). The Arnold Society's records for 1 May 1906 read, "Mr Stapledon's appeal to the members against his fine was sustained" (Balliol College Archives).

15. OS diary, 23 Sept. 1906 (SA).

16. OS diary, 21 Nov. 1908 (SA).

17. The manuscript "Verse by WOS" (SA) dates the poem to 1916 in France. "Sin" appears with one minor alteration in *LMIL*, 91.

18. Draft of "Manners," 14 Feb. 1906 (SFP).

19. OS diary, 15 Mar. 1907 (SA).

20. OS diary, 12 Feb., 15 Mar., 11 Apr. 1907 (SA). The Garden Cities movement was favored both at Abbotsholme and in ES's Ruskinian circles. On the link between Ruskin's St. George's Farm and planned workers' villages, see Jan Marsh, *Back to the Land: The Pastoral Impulse in England, from 1880 to 1914* (London: Quartet Books, 1982), 93–99; 220–44.

21. Jones, *An Edwardian Youth*, 70; the OS diary records cycle rides on 14 and 17 Oct. 1905, and then on 18 Oct.: "Rowed for the first time. . . . There is evidently a lot to learn in rowing" (SA). Jones was OS's coach.

22. OS diary, 24 Nov. 1905 (SA).

23. OS diary, 29 Nov. 1905 (SA).

24. Reported in Jones, *An Edwardian Youth*, 80; "Athletics," *Oxford Magazine*, 6 Mar. 1907, pp. 259–60.

25. *Balliol Boat Club Records, 1902–1927*, entries on Torpids 1907 and Torpids 1908, presumably in the hand of Laurence Jones (Balliol College Archives).

26. OS to WS, 2 May 1909 (SFP).

27. OS to Mary Stapledon, 15 May 1943 (SFP).

28. Rev. Ronald Knox, "Eton and Balliol, 1905–6" in Charles Lister, *Letters and Recollections*, ed. Lord Ribblesdale (New York: Scribner's, 1917), 241; Hastings, Duke of Bedford, *The Years of Transition* (London: Dakers, 1949), 73.

29. *MD*, 15.

30. OS diary, 30 Mar. 1908 (SA).

31. OS to AM, 6 Apr. 1918 (SFP).

32. OS diary, 9 Apr. 1908 (SA).

33. OS diary, 4 Apr. 1908 (SA).

34. OS diary, 2 Apr. and 6 May 1908 (SA).

35. OS diary, 6 May 1908 (SA).

36. OS diary, 28 May 1908 (SA).

37. Retold ten years later, OS to AM, 6 Apr. 1918 (SFP); a full account of the boat ride is in OS's manuscript poem, "A History, 1903–11" (SFP).

38. OS diary, 28 May 1908 (SA).

39. OS diary, 30 May 1908 (SA).

40. OS diary, 31 July 1908 (SA).

41. On Balliol's celibate tutors see J. Jones, *Balliol College*, 235–36. Rupert Brooke's "emotional apprenticeship" at Cambridge, where being in love mattered more than making love and "friendship gained what sexual love renounced," sounds like OS's regimen. See Paul Delany, *The Neo-Pagans: Rupert Brooke and the Ordeal of Youth* (New York: Free Press, 1987), xvi.

42. Cyril Bailey, *A Short History of the Balliol Boys' Club 1907–1950* (Oxford: Oxford Univ. Press, 1950), 6.

43. Hubert Secretan, quoted in Bailey, *Short History*, 9.

44. Jones, *An Edwardian Youth*, 155.

45. OS diary, 1 Nov. 1908 (SA).

46. *LMIL*, 115.

47. Hartley's supplement to Davis, *History of Balliol*, 244.
48. Hartley's supplement, 245.
49. OS diary, 25 Jan., 2 Feb. 1908 (SA).
50. OS to WS, 2 May 1909 (SFP).
51. OS, "The Most Splendid Race," *Old Abbotsholmian* 2, no. 7 (1907), 159–61.
52. OS, "The Splendid Race," *Old Abbotsholmian* 2, no. 8 (1908), 212. The similar titles of this essay and his 1907 piece for the magazine derive from a line of the Abbotsholme school song, "We will make the most splendid race the sun ever shone upon."
53. OS diary, 8 Mar. 1908 (SA).
54. OS, "The Splendid Race," 214–15.
55. OS diary, 23 Oct. 1908 (SA); OS, "Jeanne d'Arc," p. 1 (Arnold Society Archives, Balliol College Library).
56. OS diary, 23 Oct. 1908 (SA).
57. OS diary, 4 Dec. 1908 (SA).
58. OS diary, 7 Apr. 1909 (SA).
59. OS diary, 22 and 24 May 1909 (SA).
60. OS diary, 30 May 1909 (SA).
61. OS diary, 29 July 1909 (SA).
62. OS, "The Splendid Race," 215.

5. Lifting the Curtain, 1909–1912

1. Manchester Grammar School song, printed in J. Rivers, "J. L. Paton and the School, 1903–1924" in *The Manchester Grammar School 1515–1965*, ed. J. A. Graham and B. A. Phythian (Manchester: Univ. of Manchester Press, 1965), 93.
2. OS diary, 16 Sept. 1909 (SA).
3. OS diary, 10 Sept. 1909 (SA).
4. OS diary, 21 and 29 Sept. 1909 (SA).
5. OS to AM, 17 Sept. 1913 (SFP).
6. *LMIL*, 122, 123.
7. OS to AM, 25 Oct. 1916 (SFP).
8. J. Lewis Paton, "Schoolboys as Navvies," *Saint George* [Ruskin Society of Birmingham] 7 (Jan. 1904), 55.
9. J. Lewis Paton, "Shakespeare's Boys," *Saint George* 9 (Apr. 1906), 77.
10. J. Lewis Paton, "The Feelings as a Factor in School Training," *Saint George* 8 (Jan. 1905), 13.
11. J. L. Paton, "The Place of Manual Training in the School Curriculum," *Journal of Education* 40 (Aug. 1908), 562.
12. OS, "The Novice Schoolmaster," *Old Abbotsholmian* 3, no. 1 (1910), 17.
13. Harold Laski to OS, 1 July 1943 (SA).
14. OS, "Novice Schoolmaster," 16.
15. OS diary, 18 May 1910 (SA).
16. OS diary, 4 Mar. 1910 (SA). Drake, whose place in Devon maritime history attracted OS, was an agreeable heroic figure for Edwardian social reformers; Paton liked to quote Drake's assertion, "I will have the gentlemen to haul and draw with the mariners" ("Schoolboys as Navvies," 58). When OS read Alfred Noyes's 1908 poem on Drake, he gave up his projected epic; a decade later he recalled how he used "to enthuse over" Noyes's *Drake* (OS to AM, 22 Dec. 1918 [SFP]).
17. OS diary, 27 and 28 Dec. 1909 (SA).

18. OS diary, 31 Dec. 1909; 3, 4, 7, 10 Jan. 1910 (SA). The diary bolsters John Kinnaird's guess that the "daughter of Man" emerging from the ocean in chap. 3 of *LFM* is modeled on Botticelli's Venus; see *Olaf Stapledon* (Mercer Island, Wash.: Starmont, 1986), 41.

19. OS to AM, 31 Dec. 1909–1 Jan. 1910 (SFP). A page of this illustrated letter is reproduced in *TATW*, xv. OS saved many earlier letters from AM, going back to 1904.

20. OS diary, 7 Dec. 1909 (SA).

21. OS diary, 16 July, 13 May, 27 July 1910 (SA).

22. OS, "Novice Schoolmaster," 17–18.

23. OS diary, 29 Aug. 1910 (SA).

24. OS to AM, 30 Oct. 1910 (SFP).

25. OS diary, 18, 22 Sept. 1911 (SA).

26. *OJ*, 139–41.

27. OS, "Problems and Solutions, or the Future" in Naomi Mitchison's encyclopedia *An Outline for Boys and Girls and Their Parents* (London: Gollancz, 1932), 693. The bishop's role in establishing Exeter College and endowing its scholarships had no bearing on the political events that led to his death.

28. OS diary, 1 Nov. 1910 (SA).

29. OS diary, 19 Apr., 3 May, 14 June, 3 July 1911 (SA).

30. OS to AM, 10 May 1911 (SFP).

31. "Hyperion is the most splendid of unfinished poems. It is so firm, & so gorgeous. It makes you feel like a god. . . . It is finer than Milton, & far finer than anything else Keats ever wrote, except 'La Belle Dame' " (OS to AM, 10 May 1911, SFP).

32. OS diary, 31 Dec. 1911 (SA).

33. Pencil manuscript, "A History, 1903–11" (SFP). OS began the poem on 30 Mar. 1911, the eighth anniversary of his first meeting with Agnes (diary, SA).

34. *SM*, 4; *DIL*, 105.

35. OS to AM, 26 Feb. 1911 (SFP). For many years he used letters to AM as a forum for literary experiments.

36. OS diary, 10 Feb. 1911 (SA).

37. OS diary, 14–25 Aug. 1911 (SA); D. E. Baines and R. Bean, "The General Strike on Merseyside, 1926" in *Liverpool and Merseyside: Essays in the Economic and Social History of the Port and Its Hinterland*, ed. J. R. Harris (New York: Augustus M. Kelley, 1969), 242–44.

38. OS to AM, 13 Nov. 1911 (SFP).

39. OS to AM, 4 Dec. 1911 (SFP).

40. From a notebook headed "The Literary Aspects of Carlyle's Past and Present" in SA, STAP. D.I.39(1). He addressed the NHRU on 9 Nov. 1911.

41. "In firms like Alfred Holt's there was obviously an expectation that senior managers would take on civic responsibility . . . but this was not normal elsewhere." Tony Lane, *Liverpool: Gateway of Empire* (London: Lawrence and Wishart, 1987), 82.

42. OS, manuscript, "Fields Within Fields" (SA).

43. OS, manuscript, "Fields Within Fields" (SA). In *WW*, OS acknowledged the incongruity of living on "dividends and other ill-gotten gains" (11) while writing utopian proposals for dismantling a class-ridden society.

44. OS to AM, 7 Jan. 1912 (SFP).

45. OS to AM, 3 Nov. 1913 (SFP).

46. OS diary, 10 Sept., 19 Nov. 1913 (SA). The Egyptian sketches have not survived.

47. From nine manuscript pages headed "Captain James Walker," enclosed in several 1912 letters from OS to ES (SFP).

48. OS diary, 15 Mar. 1912 (SA).

49. "Captain James Walker" manuscript (SFP).
50. OS diary, 22 Mar. 1912 (SA).
51. OS to ES, 29 Mar. 1912 (SFP).
52. OS to ES, 1 Apr. 1912 (SFP).
53. *OJ*, 191.
54. OS to WS and ES, 8 May 1912 [misdated 1910] (SFP).
55. OS made a lexicon of his shorthand symbols in the endpapers of his 1912 diary (SA).
56. OS to AM, 22 July 1912; OS to ES, 21 June, 5 July 1912 (SFP).
57. OS diary, 30 June, 2 July, 3 July, 5 July 1912 (SA).
58. OS diary, 8–9 July 1912 (SA).
59. A shorthand draft of the epic's invocation survives in the 1912 diary (SA).
60. OS diary, 17 Aug. 1912 (SA).
61. I have found two published poems from this period: "The Builder" in the *Old Abbotsholmian* 3, no. 11 (1912), 169, and "A Prayer" in the *Highway* 5 (Oct. 1912), 5. Other poems may have appeared in provincial newspapers. Of the prose pieces, only the last exists in finished form: "The People, Self Educator," *Old Abbotsholmian* 3, no. 12 (1913), 203–207. OS's interest in eugenics dates to his Oxford years; he published an encomium on Francis Galton's proposals for the "Improvement of the Human Breed" in "The Splendid Race," *Old Abbotsholmian* 2, no. 8 (1908), 212–16.
62. OS to ES, 23 Jan. 1913 (SFP). His diary entry for the same date (SA) indicates he knew that he and Dot were responsible for his mother's "flight."
63. OS to ES, dated "Thursday night"—probably 23 Jan. 1913 (SFP).
64. OS diary, 12 and 18 Jan. 1913 (SA).
65. OS to ES, 12 Feb. 1913 (SFP). Letters from ES to her husband in the 1890s express a wish for more children.
66. OS, manuscript, "Letters to a Militiaman" (SA).
67. OS, from a self-portrait written for the dust jacket of *PL*.

6. Poetry and the Worker, 1913–1914

1. OS diary, 24 Feb. 1913 (SA). Comparisons of AM with women in myth and literature, often gently ironic, are scattered throughout OS's letters to her. He called her small, thin mouth "very unlike that of a Rossetti maiden" (27 Mar. 1915; SFP).
2. OS to AM, 10 May 1911 (SFP).
3. OS to AM, 5 Feb. 1912 (SFP).
4. OS to AM, 30 Mar. 1913; *TATW,* 5.
5. Ruth ("Pete") Fletcher, interview with author, 1 Oct. 1989.
6. OS diary, 19 Apr. 1913 (SA).
7. AM to OS, 4 Apr. 1913; *TATW,* 9.
8. In his diary, 3 May 1913 (SA), OS recorded Frank Miller's blunt response to his proposal of marriage to Agnes: "He objects strongly to cousinship." During the war he added OS's pacifism to his objections.
9. OS to AM, 15 Nov. 1915; 4 June 1914 (SFP).
10. OS to WS, 28 Oct. 1912 (SFP).
11. In a note in the *Old Abbotsholmian* 3, no. 11 (1912), 194, OS called the Carlyle circle his "most interesting and instructive" work since returning from Egypt. The same issue contains OS's first published poem, "The Builder" (169), a psychological study of the royal architect of a "great world wonder"—perhaps meant to be Cheops' great pyramid at Gizeh.

12. OS to Margaret Miller, 13 July 1913 (SFP). His application to the WEA (dated 1 May 1913) and an approved course syllabus are in the Liverpool University Extension Board Report Book #2 (LU); his three winter courses in industrial history were announced in the *Highway* 6 (Nov. 1913), 28; Thomas Kelly's *History of Adult Education in Great Britain,* 2nd ed. (Liverpool: Liverpool Univ. Press, 1970), esp. 238–65, surveys organizations relevant to OS's early career.

13. For histories of the David Lewis Club and the NHRU see, respectively, Constance M. and Harold King, *"The Two Nations" : The Life and Work of Liverpool University Settlement and Its Associated Institutions 1906–1937* (Liverpool: Liverpool Univ. Press, 1938), 68–88, and George Radford, *The Faculty of Reading: The Coming of Age of the National Home Reading Union* (Cambridge: Cambridge Univ. Press, 1910). On the David Lewis Club's place in Liverpool working-class life, see F. J. Marquis and S. E. F. Ogden, "The Recreation of the Poorest," *Town Planning Review* 3 (Jan. 1913), 250–52.

14. OS's organization of Merseyside study circles "on a considerable scale" was reported in the *Highway* 5 (July 1913), 198. An account of "Study Circles for Working Men and Women," signed W.O.S., tells how the circles grew out of his talks at the David Lewis Club; Liverpool University Settlement *Report for Years 1911 and 1912* (Liverpool, 1913), 11, Sydney Jones Library, University of Liverpool.

15. OS to AM, 10 Nov. 1913 (SFP). *Being and Doing* never got beyond the planning stage; its title—a favorite formula of the Ruskin-inspired National Home Reading Union—embraces OS's lifelong theme of relating self-cultivation to social action. The outline is in a letter to AM, 17 Sept. 1913 (SFP).

16. OS diary, 5 Jan. 1914 (SA); interview with John D. Stapledon, 30 July 1984. Of his remarkably juvenile face, OS told AM, "I am a proverb" (22 Oct. 1913; SFP).

17. Minutes of the Liverpool University Settlement Council, 8 July and 24 Sept. 1913 (LU).

18. Liverpool University Settlement, *Report for Years 1911 and 1912,* 5.

19. OS to AM, 26 Sept., 10 Oct. 1913 (SFP). He outlined a typical working night in winter, 1914–15 when he had four WEA courses and a weekly lecture on poetry for teachers: "I got here at 5 pm, had a meal, lectured from 6.15 to 7.15, discussed till 7.30, then lectured till 8.30, discussed till 9.30, and walked the streets discussing the universe till 10.40, and all on top of a six hour railway journey" (OS to AM, 20 Jan. 1915; SFP).

20. OS to ES, 7 Feb. 1913; OS to AM, 25 Oct. 1913 (SFP).

21. OS to AM, 17 Feb. 1914 (SFP).

22. OS to AM, 9 Feb. 1914 (SFP). Mottram was later astonished that OS had been "scared" of him at the Settlement because of Mottram's habit of psychoanalyzing his colleagues' behavior. V. H. Mottram to OS, 22 May 1943 (SA). On the controversial Burt see L. S. Hearnshaw's biography, *Cyril Burt: Psychologist* (Ithaca, N.Y.: Cornell Univ. Press, 1979).

23. [Frederick J. Marquis], *The Memoirs of the Rt. Hon. The Earl of Woolton* (London: Cassell, 1959), 26.

24. WS became treasurer of the Settlement's finance committee (Minute Book of the University Settlement Council, 18 Nov. 1915; LU). Letters from WS (16 Feb. 1919) and C. Sydney Jones to Marquis (1 Mar. 1919) show a postwar deficit of £283.18.1, all but fifty pounds of which WS quietly paid to cancel the debt (Marquis papers, Bodleian Library, Oxford, MS Woolton 30).

25. *YT,* 21–22.

26. OS to AM, 3 Oct. 1913 (SFP).

27. "The City," *LDP,* 1–2.

28. "Men," *LDP,* 10. The cover reprint of "Men" in the *Highway* 7 (Mar. 1915) is accompanied by an editorial endorsement of *LDP.*

29. OS to AM, 8 Mar. 1914 (SFP).

30. OS to AM, 29 Mar., 22 Apr. 1914 (SFP). The first untitled psalm he sent on 29 Mar., opening with "In the beginning was Love," was heavily annotated by OS but not used in the final collection. On 8 Apr. he sent "more sham psalms." The earliest manuscript of any poem in *LDP* is a version of "The City," dated 3 Apr. 1914 (SFP).

31. *LDP*, 18.

32. OS to WS, 11 May 1914 (SFP).

33. OS diary, 14 and 16 May 1914 (SA).

34. OS to AM, 16 June 1914; *LDP* manuscript (SFP). "Buddha" was retitled "Brahma" in *LDP*. A letter to AM on 22 June (SFP) provides a key to the poems' intended allegories: Artemis is "the pure ideal that lures and is never seized"; Jaweh, the "stern law" governing atoms, stars, and souls; Buddha, "conscious self-denial"; Christ, "unconscious self-forgetfulness in pure love"; Satan, "fortitude even in despair" and "courageous individualism"; and Our Lady is "Christ feminine," the embodiment of maternity. Psalms on Apollo and Athena were written later, but those figures are already schematized in June as, respectively, the "divine fire" of inspiration and "sweet reasonableness."

35. OS to AM, 16 June 1914 (SFP).

36. *LDP*, 23.

37. OS to AM, 22 June 1914 (SFP).

38. *LDP*, 28–29.

39. OS to AM, 10 June 1914 (SFP).

40. Untitled manuscript, dated 8 June 1914; an enlargement is incorporated into a 93-page manuscript written between Oct. 1914 and Feb. 1915, a medley of prose and poetry on reason, beauty, and the spiritual factor in human culture (SFP).

41. OS to AM, 25 Oct. 1914 (SFP).

42. OS to AM, 8 Nov. 1914 (SFP).

43. *LDP*, 32.

44. OS to AM, 15 Nov. 1914 (SFP).

45. OS to AM, 28 Jan. 1914 (SFP).

46. AM to OS, 6 Aug. 1914 (SFP).

47. OS to AM, 17 Nov. 1914 (SFP).

48. *LDP*, 49–50. Discussing the *Psalms* in 1915, John Dover Wilson told OS that "War" was his favorite; by then, however, the author feared the poem would encourage belief in a holy war (OS to AM, 7 Mar. 1915; SFP).

49. OS to AM, 9 Jan. 1915 (SFP).

50. *LMIL*, 116. The narrator illustrates the failure of Paul's verse by quoting some of "Men," but in a form somewhat altered from the text in *LDP*.

51. In the month he began *LDP*, he recalled Abbotsholme boys singing psalms in unison to Gregorian chant morning and night (OS to AM, 18 Mar. 1914; SFP). *YT* tells how his mother had him put himself to sleep at night by reciting psalms from memory (19).

52. *LDP*, 20. Cf. the indictment of priests and kings "Who make up a heaven of our misery" in Blake's "The Chimney Sweeper." Patrick A. McCarthy also observes Blake's influence on the poem "Satan" (*Olaf Stapledon* [Boston: Twayne, 1982], 19).

53. Leslie A. Fiedler, *Olaf Stapledon: A Man Divided* (New York: Oxford Univ. Press, 1983), 90; McCarthy, *Olaf Stapledon*, 18; AM to OS, 20 June 1914 (SFP), noting the borrowed image of "ships passing in the night" from part 1 of *Tales of a Wayside Inn*.

54. OS to AM, 17 Nov. 1914; *TATW*, 62.

55. OS to Hannah Maria (Nina) Barnard, 22 Dec. 1914 (P; courtesy of Arthur C. Clarke). Three weeks later OS acknowledged a few small, kind notices in the press, "but not enough to be of any use" (OS to AM, 9 Jan. 1915; SFP).

56. OS to AM, 3 Oct. 1913; to Margaret Miller, 13 July 1913 (SFP). Two unsigned articles for the Warrington *Examiner* can be identified from clippings OS sent to AM in 1913: "The Spirit of Education," 1 Nov. 1913, and "The Tutorial Class," 15 Nov. 1913. A third *Examiner* article on "Study Circles" (6 Dec. 1913) is probably also his. A search of *Public Opinion* has not located among its anonymous contributions a likely candidate for OS's two guineas. His diary, however, records many efforts at journalism in 1913 and 1914.

57. OS, "The People, Self Educator," *Old Abbotsholmian* 3, no. 12 (1913), 203–207; he read the paper to the Ruskin Society on 17 Mar. 1913.

58. OS to AM, 21 July 1913 (SFP).

59. OS, "Poetry and the Worker," *Highway* 6 (Oct. 1913), 4.

60. OS, "Poetry and the Worker. Wordsworth," *Highway* 6 (Dec. 1913), 51.

61. OS, "Poetry and the Worker.—Browning," *Highway* 6 (Apr. 1914), 125.

62. OS to AM, 9 Feb. 1914 (SFP).

63. Letter of James George to the editor, *Highway* 6 (July 1914), 200.

64. University Extension Board Report Book #2 (LU).

65. Albert Mansbridge, *University Tutorial Classes: A Study in the Development of Higher Education Among Working Men and Women* (London: Longmans, Green, 1913), 118.

66. OS to AM, 9 Feb. 1914 (SFP); OS diary, 8 Feb. 1914 (SA).

67. OS to AM, 3 Feb. 1914 (SFP); the likely inspector was E. J. Hookway. After the war the WEA gave more arts and humanities courses; see Thomas Kelly, *Adult Education in Liverpool: A Narrative of Two Hundred Years* (Liverpool: Univ. of Liverpool Department of Extra-Mural Studies, 1960), 43.

68. Quoted in "Summer Classes. 1913," *Highway* 6 (Oct. 1913), 13–14. OS often had passionate arguments over theology or poetry with Sam Whittall after his 1914 and 1915 Barrow WEA classes. Whittall "stirs up one's brains" and is "a staunch agnostic and a sentimental cynic touched with transcendentalism" (OS to AM, 2 and 25 Oct. 1914; SFP).

69. OS to AM, 7 Aug. 1913 (SFP).

70. OS to AM, 7 Aug. 1913; *TATW*, 17.

71. AM to OS, 16 Aug. 1914; *TATW*, 50–51.

72. OS to AM, 1 Aug. 1914 (SFP).

73. OS diary, 2 Aug. 1914 (SA).

74. OS to AM, 3 and 6 Aug. 1914 (SFP).

7. Thoroughly Bewildered, 1914–1918

1. OS diary, 24 July 1914 (SA).

2. OS, "Experiences in the Friends' Ambulance Unit," in *We Did Not Fight: 1914–18 Experiences of War Resisters*, ed. Julian Bell (London: Cobden-Sanderson, 1935), 359.

3. OS to AM, 1 Dec. 1914; *TATW*, 64.

4. *LMIL*, 58–61.

5. OS diary, 1 Jan. 1915 (SA); in a letter to AM, 27 Dec. 1914, he worried about the eye examination (SFP).

6. Leslie Fiedler, *Olaf Stapledon: A Man Divided* (New York: Oxford Univ. Press, 1983), 17; OS, "Experiences in the FAU," 360.

7. The decision to invest the group with the name Friends' Ambulance Unit was made at a meeting of 26 Nov. 1914 (FAU Committee Minute Book, Friends' House, London).

8. The FAU's early work was covered in the weekly column, "The Peace Service of the Society of Friends" in the *Friend*, 30 Oct. 1914, p. 796; 6 Nov. 1914, pp. 813–14; 13 Nov. 1914,

pp. 832–33; 27 Nov. 1914, pp. 866–68; and in Henry W. Nevinson's article, "The Work of the Anglo-Belgian Ambulance Corps," 13 Nov. 1914, pp. 827–28. This chapter relies on many reports in the *Friend* from Aug. 1914 through May 1919, supplemented by Meaburn Tatham and James E. Miles, *The Friends' Ambulance Unit 1914–1919: A Record* (London: Swarthmore Press, 1920). More on the Unit's history is in the introduction to *TATW*, xxvi–xxxii.

9. OS to Hannah Maria Barnard, 22 Dec. 1914 (P; courtesy of Arthur C. Clarke); OS had met the Fryers in May when he visited Agnes in Paris.

10. *Friend*, 5 Mar. 1915, p. 183; 19 Mar. 1915, p. 218. Entries for 10 Feb. 1915 and 11 Mar. 1915, FAU Committee Minute Book, Friends' House, London.

11. In Brian Gardner, ed., *Up the Line to Death: The War Poets 1914–1918*, 2nd ed. (London: Methuen, 1986), 111.

12. OS to AM, 28 Oct. 1914; *TATW*, 59.

13. OS to AM, 15 Nov. 1914; 30 Nov. 1914 (*TATW*, 64–65). Of pacifism and conscription he later wrote to her, "I can never forget that it was my WEA classes that first made me think about these matters" (12 Jan. 1918; SFP).

14. On the effect of Lord Derby's speech of 28 Aug. 1914, see John Stevenson, *British Society 1914–45* (Harmondsworth, U.K.: Penguin, 1984), 50–52.

15. OS to ES, undated 1914 (SFP). Cf. OS to AM, 14 Dec. 1914; *TATW*, 66.

16. OS to AM, 14 and 21 Dec. 1914 (SFP).

17. OS to AM, 9 Nov. 1915 (SFP); *LMIL*, 197; *MD*, 51.

18. *LMIL*, 196–97.

19. OS to AM, 2 Feb. 1915 (SFP).

20. John Stapledon, interview with author, 15 June 1982; OS to Naomi Mitchison, 10 July 1940, printed in her *You May Well Ask: A Memoir 1920–1940* (London: Gollancz, 1979), 142. On the difference between OS's "anti-war sentiments" and pacifism, see Thomas C. Kennedy, Review of *TATW* in *Quaker History* 78 (Fall 1989), 115–16.

21. OS, "Experiences in the FAU," 361. On Wilson and the League, see a letter to AM, 25 May 1917 (*TATW*, 227).

22. OS to AM, 20 Jan. 1918; *TATW*, 274.

23. *LMIL*, 204. The lunch with Herbert Sharpe is recorded in a letter to AM, 19 Oct. 1916; *TATW*, 179–80.

24. OS to AM, 21 Feb. 1916, 24 Sept. 1918; *TATW*, 132, 325.

25. OS to AM, 10 Feb. 1915 (*TATW*, 72). See Modris Eksteins, *Rites of Spring: The Great War and the Birth of the Modern Age* (Boston: Houghton Mifflin, 1989).

26. OS to AM, 27 Mar. 1915 (SFP).

27. On leave in 1916, OS told John Dover Wilson, "I confess I envy you in being able to keep to educational work through it all. I am sure it is more useful than most of what is being done in France, far more useful than driving a car!" (letter of 27 Oct. 1916, Dover Wilson Papers, NLS).

28. A typical night is described by OS's commanding officer, L. B. Maxwell, in "The Ambulance Driver," *Friend* (1 Oct. 1915), 745–46; other details are from OS, "Experiences in the FAU."

29. AM to OS, 6 Nov. 1915, *TATW*, p. 108.

30. OS to AM, 26 July 1917 (SFP). See a letter of 10 Mar. 1915 in *John Masefield's Letters from the Front, 1915–1917*, ed. Peter Vansittart (New York: Franklin Watts, 1985), 62–63. OS often lampooned the clichés of war talk while avoiding clinical description, a syndrome analyzed by Paul Fussell in *The Great War and Modern Memory* (New York: Oxford Univ. Press, 1975), 155–90. John Stapledon, interview with author, 10 Oct. 1989; Mary Shenai, interview with author, 16 Oct. 1989.

31. *LMIL*, 208–209; the authorial self-reference is on p. 200.

32. OS to AM, 1 Apr. 1917 (SFP).

33. Tatham and Miles, *Friends' Ambulance Unit*, 184.

34. OS to AM, 6 Feb. 1916 (SFP) and 29 Oct. 1918 (*TATW*, 334).

35. *LMIL*, 199.

36. The story of "old Tory" Marshall and the lurid radical is in OS's letter to WS, 14 Oct. 1916; Robertson is described in a letter to AM, 26 July 1917 (SFP). He discussed other FAU members in many letters to Agnes (some in SFP and some in *TATW*). Oliver Ashford reports OS's reputation in SSA 13 in *Prophet or Professor? The Life and Work of Lewis Fry Richardson* (Bristol, U.K.: Adam Hilger, 1985), 57–59.

37. OS to AM, 11 Mar. 1916; 26 June 1917; on 9 May 1916 he told how his notebook was always handy for impromptu writing (SFP). The cartoon illustrates a page of verse beginning "The Stymie is so very small" in E. A. Frith and R. W. Smeal, *The Little Grey Book* (undated, privately printed); copies at Friends' House, London and in SA. An Eric Robertson drawing of OS writing is printed in *TATW*, 271.

38. OS to ES, 7 Jan. 1915 (SFP).

39. Untitled manuscript of 1914–15 (SFP).

40. OS to AM, 25 Nov. 1915 (SFP). He dismissed *LDP*: "Those old psalm things were not so bad as an experiment, but they are crude & vague" (OS to AM, 20 June 1917 [SFP]).

41. OS to AM, 22 Jan. 1916 (SFP). Notations of hunts with Uncle James and disgust at the kill are in his diary (21 July 1909; 18, 22 Sept. 1911 [SA]); he recalled stag-hunting on Exmoor in a letter to AM, 18 Feb. 1917 (SFP).

42. OS to AM, 10 Feb. 1918 (SFP). His story "A World of Sound" appeared in *Hotch-Potch*, ed. John Brophy (Liverpool: Royal Liverpool Children's Hospital, 1936), 243–51.

43. All these scenes are included in letters printed in *TATW*, 193–94; 266, 275, 337.

44. Some "snapshots" (his term in a letter to AM, 18 Sept. 1916; *TATW*, 173) survive in verse and prose pieces sent to her: "A man is God's eye and God's heart" (1 Oct. 1916), "Leave me, leave me, oh Thou" (7 Dec. 1916), "Tommy's Discovery" (21 Oct. 1916), and "A man with a pack and a rifle" (27 Nov. 1916) [SFP].

45. The novel is described in various letters to AM from 13 Jan. through 23 Aug. 1916; he discussed *Ann Veronica* on 13 Feb. 1916 and the booklet on 13 June and 12 Aug. 1917 (SFP). No drafts of the novel or pamphlet survive. A vanished essay, "Back from Leave," was submitted to the *Hibbert Journal* (OS to WS, 3 Feb. 1917) [SFP]. "Unsaleable madness": OS to AM, 23 Aug. 1916 (SFP).

46. OS to AM, 13 Nov. 1917 (SFP).

47. SA has a 250-page carbon typescript (STAP.D.I.19) of an 11-chapter book lacking its title page and first two chapters. Internal evidence suggests a date in the early 1920s; this is probably the book OS called "The Sleeping Beauty" (letter to AM, 6 Feb. 1919 [SFP]), the new title for "In a Glass Darkly."

48. OS to AM, 20 Jan. 1918; *TATW*, 274.

49. AM to OS, 16 Oct. 1915. On 1 Oct. 1916 he wrote: "By the way, those old story-things I wrote before coming to the war are appearing in the Friends' Quarterly Examiner. Sir George Newman himself (who is editor) provided a title for them, & a good one: 'The Seed and the Flower.' I wish they were better" (SFP). See *Friends' Quarterly Examiner* 50 (Oct. 1916), 464–75.

50. "The Road to the Aide Post," *F.A.U. Monthly Magazine* 1 (Jan. 1916), 13. The article is unsigned, but OS initialed ES's copy (SA [STAP.J.IV.R62]); he told AM about it on 3 Dec. 1915 (SFP). Only two numbers of the journal were published.

51. "Road to the Aide Post," 14. As reprinted in *Friends' Quarterly Examiner* 50 (Jan. 1916), 125–28, the story's final question and some sentences criticizing pacifism and defining war as "love gone mad" were cut. Stripped of queries about the sufficiency of Quakerly values, the *FQE*

text is more pious than the prickly original. Despite the Friends' tradition of open debate, OS was censored once he moved from the isolation of a handmade journal circulated at the front lines to an official publication of the Society.

52. "The Reflections of an Ambulance Orderly," *Friend* (14 Apr. 1916), 246; AM identifies the piece as OS's in a letter of 15 June 1916; *TATW*, 155.

53. Tatham and Miles, *Friends' Ambulance Unit*, 188.

54. T. Corder Catchpool, one of the original forty-three FAU volunteers, described his decision to leave and his prison ordeal in *On Two Fronts* (London: Headley Bros., 1918). OS to AM, 12 Jan. 1917 (SFP).

55. My account combines information from several sources: OS, "Experiences in the FAU," 368–70; letters to AM of 5 Apr. 1917 (SFP) and of 20 Apr., 29 Apr., 25 May 1917 (*TATW*, 220–23, 225–26); a letter to WS and ES, 5 May 1917 (SFP); and an eyewitness account by an unnamed driver from SSA 13 in Tatham and Miles, *Friends' Ambulance Unit*, 104–106.

56. Tatham and Miles, *Friends' Ambulance Unit*, 185; OS, "Experiences in the FAU," 361–62. He told AM of his hope to do stretcher-bearing (20 June 1917; *TATW*, 232) and of the failure of the proposal (27 Oct. 1917; SFP).

57. On OS's injury see *TATW*, 255–56; this was, according to his FAU service records (Friends' House, London), the only time he missed for sickness or injury during the war.

58. Quoted by John Kemplay in the exhibition catalogue for a show of Eric Robertson's paintings at the City of Edinburgh Art Centre, 5–27 Oct. 1974.

59. OS diary 20 Mar., 21 Mar., 26 Mar., 2 Apr., 10 Apr. 1918 (SA). Censorship was tightened at this time, and few details of the springtime offensive got into letters to AM.

60. OS to AM, 5 May and 16 May 1918 (SFP). On 14 Feb. 1919 he sent her "Swallows at Maffrécourt," with stresses marked to show an "intentional irregularity of the metre"; a simplified revision appeared in S. Fowler Wright's anthology *Voices on the Wind*, Second Series (London: Merton, 1924), 165.

61. OS diary, 13 and 26 Apr. 1918 (SA); letters to AM, 6 Apr. 1918 (*TATW*, 293), 29 Apr. 1918 (SFP); "Experiences in the FAU," 366.

62. OS to AM, 23 Mar. 1916 (SFP).

63. OS to AM, 14 Dec. 1917 and 2 June 1918 (SFP).

64. OS diary, 15 July 1918 (SA). He wrote about this incident many times: to AM, 21 July 1918 and 8 Nov. 1918 (*TATW*, 314–15, 340); *LMIL*, 205; "Experiences in the FAU," 372.

65. OS to AM, 22 Nov. 1918 (SFP).

66. OS to AM, 8 and 18 Nov. 1918 (*TATW*, 339, 343).

67. Fiedler's *Olaf Stapledon*, 16–17, assumes guilt and shame as OS's primary reactions to his war experiences, but Patrick A. McCarthy, in *Olaf Stapledon* (Boston: Twayne, 1982), p. 22, catches exactly the mixture of embarrassment and pleasure in his response to the Croix de Guerre and other war decorations.

68. OS to AM, 31 Dec. 1918 (*TATW*, 350).

8. The Sleeper Awakes, 1919–1924

1. AS to Frank and Margaret Miller, 26 Aug. 1919; *TATW*, 372.

2. OS to AM, 21 July 1916 (SFP).

3. OS to AM, 18 Mar. 1919; AM to Margaret Miller, 7 May 1919 (SFP).

4. OS to AM, 11 May 1919 (*TATW*, 362); AM to Margaret Miller, 1 June 1919 (SFP).

5. Taffimai Metallumai ("Small-person-without-any-manners-who-ought-to-be-spanked") appears in two of Kipling's *Just So Stories* (1902), "How the First Letter Was Written" and "How the Alphabet Was Made."

6. *MD*, 2.

7. OS to AM, 8 Nov. 1918 (SFP).

8. OS to AM, 25 Nov. 1915 (SFP).

9. "The heroic days": Thomas Kelly, *A History of Adult Education in Great Britain*, 2nd ed. (Liverpool: Liverpool Univ. Press, 1970), 254. Statistics on tutors in the 1914–15 term come from *The University Tutorial Class Movement* (London: World Association for Adult Education, 1919), 16.

10. OS to AM, 5 Oct. 1918 (SFP). Throughout the war he taught classes to the ambulance men, struggled to keep up his scholarly reading, and anticipated a return to WEA work: "I often plan out imaginary subjects to myself" (OS to John Dover Wilson, 27 Oct. 1916; Dover Wilson Papers, NLS).

11. OS to AM, 20 Jan. 1918 (SFP). WS chaired Beechcroft's finance committee during the war and was, according to the *Fourth Annual Report 1917–1918*, the largest contributor to its building fund. Horace Fleming wrote a history, *Beechcroft: The Story of Birkenhead Settlement 1914–1924: An Experiment in Adult Education* (London: Education Settlements Association, 1938).

12. OS to AM, 18 Mar. 1919 (SFP).

13. WS's analysis of his assets is on a single, handwritten sheet, signed W.C.S. and dated 3 Apr. 1919 (SFP).

14. On recommendations to improve the situation of WEA tutors, see *University Tutorial Class Movement*, 15–16, 25.

15. OS to AM, 25 Mar. and 11 May 1919; AS to Frank and Margaret Miller, 5 Aug. and 17 Sept. 1919 (SFP). Letters to AM of 25 Mar. and 11 May 1919 referring to an unnamed job paying £400 plus an extra £120 for two courses suggest that OS sought a WEA inspectorship; if so, the application failed.

16. OS to AM, 8 Dec. 1918 (SFP).

17. AS to Frank and Margaret Miller, 30 Sept. 1919 (SFP).

18. AS to Margaret Miller, 7 Oct. 1919 (SFP). Unable to stretch his budget, OS soon resorted to loans: "Our finances are tragic. I have just had to borrow another £50 from Father—£200 in all" (diary, 26 Apr. 1921 [SA]).

19. OS to AS, 15 Jan. 1923 (SFP). On Reddie's last years at Abbotsholme and his forced resignation, see J. H. G. I. Giesbers, *Cecil Reddie and Abbotsholme* (Nijmegen, Netherlands: Centrale Drukkerij, 1970), 40–44.

20. Carbon typescript of an unpublished book (SA, STAP D.I.19), incomplete and untitled but probably the 1922 version of "The Sleeping Beauty," chap. 8, p. 21.

21. Albert Mansbridge, *University Tutorial Classes: A Study in the Development of Higher Education Among Working Men and Women* (London: Longmans, Green, 1913), 58; *University Tutorial Class Movement*, 12. On the founding women of the WEA, see Mansbridge, *An Adventure in Working-Class Education, Being the Story of the Workers' Educational Association 1903–1915* (London: Longmans, Green, 1920), 18.

22. OS to AS, 12 and 18 Feb. 1920 (SFP).

23. *MD*, 66.

24. OS, lecture notes for "Why Teach?" delivered at Beechcroft Settlement, 9 Oct. 1923 (SA).

25. OS to WS, 24 Nov. 1920, 1 May 1921 (SFP).

26. *MD*, 59.

27. OS to Mary Stapledon, 18 June 1942 (SFP).

28. OS diary, 1 Jan., 10 May 1921 (SA).

29. OS, typescript prepared for *PL,* SA (STAP B.71); these sentences were cut from the printed dust-jacket blurb.

30. OS diary, 21 Apr. 1921 (SA).

31. The words are OS's in a letter apologizing to AS, 24 Apr. 1922 (SFP).

32. OS diary, 2–3 May, 25 May, 9 June, 29 June, 21 Aug., 25 Aug. 1921 (SA).

33. Chap. 4, p. 31, and chap. 5, pp. 5–8, of the typescript [SA, STAP D.I.19] that I take to be the last version of "The Sleeping Beauty." The eleven-chapter script lacks the title page and first two chapters; marginal notes not in OS's hand may be Mair's. A reference to AS and her baby daughter (chap. 7, pp. 28–29) makes a date between 1920 and 1923 probable.

34. SA, STAP D.I.19, chap. 9, p. 16.

35. "The First Men," a tantalizing anticipation of the name of OS's first major work of fiction, is the title of a subsection of chap. 11: "A Myth of God and Spirit."

36. "Author's Late Development," [London] *Evening Standard,* 5 Oct. 1935, p. 6.

37. Registration form for William Olaf Stapledon, University of Liverpool, Faculty of Arts, 26 Oct. 1921 (LU).

38. OS's diary (SA) records many visits with Chang, who finished his M.A. thesis, "The Philosophy of Moh Tih," in 1926.

39. OS diary, 4 Nov. and 9 Dec. 1921 (SA).

40. OS diary, 2–6 Jan. 1922 (SA). A ring binder contains voluminous notes on these texts and on Freud's *Introductory Lectures on Psychoanalysis,* which he read in the Picton Library, Liverpool (SA, STAP D.III.8).

41. OS to AS, 13 Feb. 1922 (SFP). OS wrote in the Suggestion Book of the Club (LU) on 1 Feb. 1932 "that some foreign papers should be taken in place of some of the numerous English ones." Notes on meetings with Dr. Wilkinson, 11 and 16 May 1922, are in OS's psychology notebook (SA, STAP D.III.8).

42. OS to AS, 15 and 20 Feb. 1922 (SFP).

43. OS to AS, 15 Jan. 1923 (SFP).

44. OS to AS, 18 Feb. 1922; his Esperanto lessons enraged his cousin Edith Hope Scott, who feared it "would damage her precious nationalism" (OS to AS, 27 Apr. 1924) [SFP].

45. SA, STAP D.I.19, chap 7, p. 30.

46. The poem exists in two drafts and several trial titles ("Post-War," "Parenthood," "Outgrown") in the manuscript "Verse by WOS" (SA).

47. By 1925 sixty new poems had accumulated in "Verse by WOS"; ten poems (all dated 1924) were revisions of old pieces from *LDP.* OS may have been planning a collection of his best poems—but he had evidently decided that most of *LDP* no longer interested him.

48. "Al Fresco" in "Verse by WOS," dated 1923 (SA). OS named it his "Shocking Poem" in a letter to AS, 29 Apr. 1924 (SFP).

49. Interview with AS, June 1982.

50. OS to AS, 5 May 1924 (SFP). The poem appears in "Verse by WOS" under the title "At First Sight" (SA). On Primrose Morgan see Grace Wyndham Goldie, *The Liverpool Repertory Theatre, 1911–1934* (Liverpool: Liverpool Univ. Press, 1935), 147, 154.

51. OS to WS, 30 July 1925; OS to AS, 3 May 1924 (SFP).

52. OS to AS, 12 Feb. 1920 (SFP).

53. Arthur Quiller-Couch and G. K. Chesterton presided over the conservative Empire Poetry League in the 1920s, but Fowler Wright was its secretary and chief workhorse. From 1923 to 1926, OS published ten poems in *Poetry* (later called *Poetry and the Play*) and eleven in Fowler Wright's anthologies *Poets of Merseyside* (London: Merton, 1923) and *Voices on*

the Wind, Second Series (London: Merton, 1924). Abercrombie lectured at Beechcroft and read OS's work in 1920 (AS to OS, 8 Aug. 1920 [SFP]). OS's diary shows a meeting with Eliot in London on 30 Aug. 1927; Eliot recalled the event in a letter to OS, 17 Feb. 1937 (SA).

54. *Poets of Merseyside*, no page.

55. *Poets of Merseyside*, 95; also in *Voices on the Wind, Second Series*, 166–67. A note in "Verse by WOS" indicates it was broadcast on 31 July 1924 (SA). On the Empire Poetry League's radio readings, see S. Fowler Wright, "The British Broadcasting Co., Ltd.: A Study in Monopoly," *Poetry and the Play* 8 (Dec.–Jan. 1925–26), 376–83.

56. "Timber" and the 1921 poem "The Cosmic Egg" appeared in *Poetry* 6 (June 1923), 147. Revised—and with the homiletic final line cut—"Timber" became one of Paul's World War I poems in *LMIL*, 201. The letter to Fowler Wright was excerpted in the editor's column of *Poetry* 6 (June 1923), 144.

57. OS, "Rhyme, Assonance and Vowel Contrast," *Poetry* 7 (Aug.–Sept. 1924), 194–96. The rhymes are in "Ephemera," composed in 1923 and preserved in "Verse by WOS" (SA).

58. Arthur O'Shaughnessy, "Ode," *Music and Moonlight* (1874). To AM on 20 Jan. 1914, OS wrote complacently of his Preston WEA class: "I recited 'We are the music makers' to them, and the big man said, 'There's more in that than in all the history of trade unionism' " (*TATW*, 28).

59. OS, lecture notes for "On Poetry," delivered at Beechcroft Settlement, 14 Nov. 1922 (SA).

60. OS, lecture notes for "New Aims in Verse," given at Beechcroft Settlement, 22 Oct. 1924 (SA).

61. OS, "Smoke," *New Age* 36 (29 Jan. 1925), 160.

62. S[ydney] F[owler] W[right], "Editorial," *Poetry* 8 (Sept. 1925), 253; Preface to *Voices on the Wind, Second Series*, no page.

63. S. Fowler Wright, "Studies in Contemporary Poetry (VI): C. A. Dawson Scott," *Poetry* 6 (Aug. 1923), 207. In *Poetry* 7 (Oct. 1924), he asked rhetorically, "Through what medium has the highly experimental work of Mr. Olaf Stapledon won a hearing?" (203). The preface printed in each of the thirteen volumes of his *County Series of Contemporary Poetry* (London: Merton, 1925–28) cites OS's poems as examples of acceptable *vers libre*.

64. "Of Poems" in "Verse by WOS" (SA). See the analysis, centered on OS's prose, in Patrick A. McCarthy's "Stapledon and Literary Modernism," in *The Legacy of Olaf Stapledon: Critical Essays and an Unpublished Manuscript*, ed. McCarthy et al. (New York: Greenwood, 1989), 39–51.

65. OS, "Two Chinese Poems," *Poetry of To-day: A Quarterly "Extra" of The Poetry Review*, no. 3 (Winter 1925), 18. He published four other poems in the same number.

9. Philosopher and Provincial, 1925–1929

1. Unpublished typescript, "Philosophy and the Public" (SA), marked "Liverpool Daily Post" in OS's hand. On the British (later Royal) Institute of Philosophical Studies, see I. D. MacKillop, *The British Ethical Societies* (Cambridge: Cambridge Univ. Press, 1986), 97. OS was featured speaker at the Liverpool BIPS on 12 Dec. 1927 (diary, SA).

2. Untitled poem beginning "Whoever gropes" in "Verse by WOS" (SA). Undated, it appears with other poems of early 1925.

3. The thesis was refereed by A. D. Lindsay, a moral philosopher, a vocal supporter of Labour, and a champion of the WEA. He was an ideally sympathetic external examiner for some-

one of OS's convictions. See Drusilla Scott, *A. D. Lindsay: A Biography* (Oxford: Basil Blackwell, 1971), esp. 104–31.

4. Notes for "Democracy as an Ideal," given at the Anno Domini Club at Beechcroft, Mar. 1925 (SA); letters of OS to WS, 3 and 18 Feb. 1925 (SFP).

5. OS, "Meaning" (Ph.D. diss., University of Liverpool, 1925), 3. On deposit at the Sydney Jones Library, University of Liverpool.

6. "Meaning," 28, 111–12, 276.

7. Alexander Mair, letter of reference for Dr. W. O. Stapledon, dated 1 July 1926, for a lectureship in moral philosophy at Queen's University, Belfast (SFP); the neglect of OS as philosopher was the subject of the 1985 inaugural lecture of Stephen R. L. Clark as Professor of Philosophy at Liverpool.

8. *LMIL*, 228.

9. OS to AS, 10 Feb. 1922. In a less confident mood he wrote on 19 Jan. 1923: "I am wondering if it would have been better if I had never been allowed to choose a career at all but had been just tied down to some simple job long ago. There's no doubt this is the work I want to do, but heavens it seems pretty hopeless just now. I'm not clever enough, that's about it" (SFP).

10. OS to WS, 3 Feb. 1925 (SFP). "The Problem of Universals," derived from chap. 9 of "Meaning," was published in the *Monist* 34 (Oct. 1924), 574–98.

11. OS, "Mr. Bertrand Russell's Ethical Beliefs," *International Journal of Ethics* 37 (July 1927), 391, 400.

12. OS to WS, 30 July 1925 (SFP).

13. "The Theory of the Rational Good" and "Ethics and Teleological Activity," *International Journal of Ethics* 36 (July 1926), 357–63; and 38 (Apr. 1928), 241–57. Another trial chapter of *MTE*, "The Need for Ethics," was printed in the University of Chicago's *Open Court* 41 (Apr. 1927), 206–19.

14. OS to WS, 28 May 1927 (SFP); the former tutor was A. E. Heath. OS's terse record of his first job hunt is in his Country Life Diary, 19 July 1926: "To Swansea by hired car for interview. Failed to get the post" (SA, STAP A.I.).

15. The paper was published as "The Location of Physical Objects," *Journal of Philosophical Studies* 4 (Jan. 1929), 64–75; the Seminar's Minute Books are in LU.

16. AS described nervous changes in OS's voice in a letter to her parents, 22 Sept. 1919 (SFP). Details of his demeanor in the Seminar come from letters to AS (2 May 1924; 22 Jan. 1926 [SFP]) and from my conversation in Sept. 1986 with Arnold Nash, a colleague of OS's in the Seminar. An ongoing forum of the Liverpool philosophy department, the Seminar was renamed in the mid-1980s the Stapledon Society.

17. *LFM*, 102, 104.

18. OS to AS, 22 Jan. 1926 (SFP). He had heard Carr-Saunders's inaugural lecture as Professor of Sociology on the topic of eugenics (OS diary, 29 May 1925 [SA]).

19. Thomas Kelly profiles staff members in *For Advancement of Learning: The University of Liverpool 1881–1981* (Liverpool: Liverpool Univ. Press, 1981). Martin, considered languid and "frail" (Kelly, 222), read OS's manuscripts eagerly and in 1944 wrote a satiric, Stapledonian piece of science fiction, "You and Your English Education by Investigator XD 54"; the typescript is at the Sydney Jones Library, University of Liverpool.

20. OS diary, 22 Aug. 1928 (SA); OS to WS, 19 Nov. 1928 (SFP).

21. "Modern Ethics," *Times Literary Supplement*, 7 Mar. 1929, p. 176; C. D. Burns, *International Journal of Ethics* 40 (Oct. 1929), 134; Laurence Sears, *Journal of Philosophy* 26 (15 Aug. 1929), 470–73.

22. Two 1929 letters by OS from the correspondence with Lloyd Morgan survive in the University of Bristol Library.

23. *MTE*, 273. In "Two Faces of Philosophy," his 1985 inaugural address at Liverpool University, Stephen Clark guessed that an aversion to "the dry and technical unraveling of academic puzzles" did OS no good: "At a time when those professional philosophers who had a public name were busily refusing to look beyond the boundaries of the minnow's pond, Stapledon tried to cope with Pascal's terrifying immensities by facing up to them." I thank Professor Clark for a transcript of his lecture.

24. Review signed W.W. in the Philadelphia *Public Ledger,* 31 Aug. 1929, p. 6. A similar reservation about the technical knowledge required to follow the argument was made in the *Saturday Review,* 7 Sept. 1929, p. 120.

25. *MTE*, 248. OS told AM how an ambulance driver's "queer position" let him observe horror from within a calm center. "The great need after the war will be for these very two qualities—detached sympathy and a faith in beauty and goodness that is strong enough to afford to realise evil" (18 May 1918; *TATW,* 300–301).

26. C. S. Lewis, never friendly to Stapledonian philosophy, charged him with "sheer devil worship" (Roger Lancelyn Green and Walter Hooper, *C. S. Lewis: A Biography* [New York: Harcourt, 1966], 173).

27. E. W. Martin, "Between the Devil and the Deep Sea: The Philosophy of Olaf Stapledon" in *The Pleasure Ground: A Miscellany of English Writing,* ed. Malcolm Elwin (London: MacDonald, 1947), 204–16; Crane Brinton, ed., *The Fate of Man* (New York: George Braziller, 1961), 171–78; Robert Shelton, "The Moral Philosophy of Olaf Stapledon," in *The Legacy of Olaf Stapledon,* ed. Patrick A. McCarthy et al. (New York: Greenwood, 1989), 5–22; Leslie A. Fiedler, *Olaf Stapledon: A Man Divided* (New York: Oxford Univ. Press, 1983), 48.

28. AS's "devastating sanity": preface to *LFM,* viii. She described her editorial advice in interviews with me on 15 and 19 June 1982. Of his difficulty working she said: "Poor Olaf, he suffered from the noise of the children very much and had to enlarge that room under the roof to make his study. It wasn't quite so noisy one floor further up."

29. The "John Stories" were the forerunners to *OJ.* Mary Shenai, interview with author, 2 Oct. 1989. Other information in this section comes from an informal memoir by Mary Shenai written for the late Professor Claude Fournier.

30. Winifred Primrose, interview with author, 19 June 1982.

31. OS to AM, 24 July 1915; *TATW,* 92. Ruth "Pete" Fletcher and Mary Shenai, interviews with author, 1 Oct. 1989.

32. Edwin Faulkner, "Merseyside Poetry (1)," *Poetry* 6 (Feb. 1923), 42.

33. Grace Wyndham Goldie, *The Liverpool Repertory Theatre, 1911–1934* (Liverpool: Liverpool Univ. Press, 1935). OS's diaries contain numerous entries for the films, plays, and public lectures he attended.

34. OS diary, 27 May 1921; lecture notes for two "Talks on Psychology" (SA).

35. OS to AS, 26 Jan. 1926 (SFP).

36. Joan Walker, letter to the author, 7 June 1988.

37. OS to WS, c. 1896 (SFP). Frye's words, from *The Educated Imagination* (1963), were applied to OS by Susan Glicksohn, "A City of Which the Stars Are Suburbs," in *SF: The Other Side of Realism: Essays on Modern Fantasy and Science Fiction,* ed. Thomas D. Clareson (Bowling Green, Ohio: Bowling Green Univ. Popular Press, 1971), 334–47.

38. Mary Shenai memoir.

39. OS, "Star Worship," *Poetry and the Play* 9 (July-Sept. 1926), 527.

40. *LMIL*, 246.

41. "Sir Richard Gregory," *New York Times,* 20 Nov. 1938, p. E8.

42. J. B. S. Haldane, "How to Write a Popular Scientific Article" in *A Banned Broadcast and Other Essays* (London: Chatto and Windus, 1946), 6.

43. James Jeans, "Recent Developments of Cosmical Physics," *Nature* 118 [Supplement] (4 Dec. 1926), 38.

44. The typescript and carbon, each with handwritten corrections, are in a packet in SA that includes, with Jeans on "Cosmical Physics," three other cuttings: Jeans, "The Wider Aspects of Cosmogony," *Nature,* 29 Mar. 1928; Harlow Shapley, "The Centre of the Galaxy," *Nature,* 29 Sept. 1928; and Richard Paget, "Human Speech," *Nature,* 23 Feb. 1929. Subsequent quotations from *Metaphysical Posters* are from the script in this packet.

45. Jeans, "Recent Developments," 40.

46. With altered wording the poem appears in *LMIL,* 239.

47. Manuscript, "The Nether Worlds," SA, STAP D.II.3. Another copy, entitled "The Seven Spheres" (STAP D.II.2), includes notes for *LMIL,* presumably drafted when OS decided to adapt material from the aborted *Metaphysical Posters.*

48. The passage from Bede is in b. 2, chap. 13 of *Ecclesiastical History of the English People.*

49. OS to AM, 9 Jan. 1915 (SFP); OS reevaluated Carlyle in a talk at Beechcroft on "Sartor Resartus," 19 Mar. 1923 (SA).

50. "Introduction by One of the Last Men," *LFM,* 4.

51. J. B. S. Haldane, "Possible Worlds," *Possible Worlds and Other Essays* (London: Chatto and Windus, 1927), 286. OS's annotated copy is in SA.

10. The Future Speaks, 1930–1932

1. OS diary, 28–31 July 1926 (SA); two sets of diaries, one reserved for appointments and the other for nature observation, exist for 1922–1928.

2. OS diary, 21 Aug.–3 Sept. 1928 (SA).

3. W. H. G[illings]., "The Philosopher of Fantasy," *British Scientifiction Fantasy Review* 1, no. 3 (June 1937), 8.

4. OS, lecture notes for "Science and Fiction," 1947 (SA).

5. OS to AS, 18 Feb. 1920 (SFP).

6. OS to Fay Pomerance, 23 Dec. 1946 (P).

7. Manuscript of *LFM* (SA).

8. AS, interview with author, 18 June 1982.

9. AS's version of OS's vision is in John Kinnaird, *Olaf Stapledon* (Mercer Island, Wash.: Starmont, 1986), 39.

10. *OE,* 29.

11. *LFM,* 275. My claim in "Olaf Stapledon and the Idea of Science Fiction" (*Modern Fiction Studies* 32 [Spring 1986], 38) that seals inspired *LFM* but had no role in the narrative is wrong. I thank Arthur C. Clarke for correcting me.

12. "The Future Speaks," containing outlines, notes, and some rough drafts of episodes in *LFM,* is in SA [STAP B.7(1)].

13. Joan Walker, letter to author, 7 June 1988; Mrs. Ruth Fletcher, interview with author, 2 Oct. 1989.

14. P. G. H. Boswell, "A Narrative": autobiographical typescript in LU (D.4/1, p. 165). Unpublished interviews between Harvey J. Satty and Sidney Scholefield-Allen and Leonard Martin, 1972; transcripts courtesy of Harvey Satty.

15. The term "open conspiracy" in "The Future Speaks" indicates OS's awareness of Wells's program for global revolution, first developed in *The World of William Clissold* (1926) and distilled in *The Open Conspiracy* (1928).

16. Colored time charts for *LFM*, SA (STAP I.1); the five monochrome charts printed in *LFM* are much less detailed. The memorandum is opposite diary entries for 20–26 Oct. 1929 (SA).

17. OS to WS, 23 Jan. 1930 (SFP).

18. The copy OS gave his typist is full of changes driven by the need to cut, and the preface is unfinished. The final draft and printer's typed copy, both in SA, have been studied by Curtis C. Smith in "The Manuscript of *Last and First Men*: Towards a Variorum," *Science-Fiction Studies* 9 (Nov. 1982), 265–73.

19. The first quoted phrase is from the published preface to *LFM*, vi; the second, from the final manuscript (SA), is a cut passage intended for the preface.

20. According to an unidentified cutting in OS's scrapbook [SA, STAP I.9], presumably from a local Wirral newspaper, Martin assigned the book for discussion shortly after its publication to his WEA literature class in West Kirby.

21. For further analysis see Patrick A. McCarthy, "*Last and First Men* as Miltonic Epic," *Science-Fiction Studies* 11 (Nov. 1984), 244–52.

22. Proctor, *Other Worlds Than Ours* (London: Longmans, Green, 1893), 305–306. At age seventeen OS "was very interested" in it (diary, 14 Nov. 1903, SA); he borrowed Reade's book from Sam Whittall, the WEA student "whose bible it is" (OS to AM, 21 Feb. 1915, SFP).

23. Bertrand Russell, "A Free Man's Worship" in *Mysticism and Logic and Other Essays* (London: Longmans, Green, 1918), 48; OS's annotated copy is in SA.

24. "The Last Judgment" appeared in Haldane's *Possible Worlds* (London: Chatto and Windus, 1927); OS's copy (SA) was the 1928 printing. Sam Moskowitz discusses its relevance to *LFM* in "Olaf Stapledon: The Man Behind the Works" in *FFC*, 35–37. Of *The Ascent of Humanity* (1929), OS told Naomi Mitchison it was "helpful, though there is much in it that seems to me unjustified. I feel very doubtful about his theory of 'co-consciousness,' and about spiritualism" (20 Jan. 1931; NLS). In *PL*, vol. 2, pp. 457–58, he criticized the presentation of evolution in the *Ascent*.

25. Katharine Burdekin's novels were originally published under the pseudonym Murray Constantine. Daphne Patai compares the narrative strategies of Burdekin and OS in her foreword to a reprint of *Proud Man* (New York: Feminist Press, 1993), xiii–xvi. On *LFM* and W. Warren Wagar's *Short History of the Future*, see Robert Crossley, "Fiction and the Future," *College English* 55 (Dec. 1993).

26. These responses are in a special file on *LFM*, assembled by OS, now in SA. Mitchison's was written to her godfather, the philosopher Samuel Alexander, who enclosed it in a note to OS. In a letter of 28 Jan. 1931 (SA), Heard took credit for reviews he contributed to the *Listener* (24 Dec. 1930) and the *Week-End Review* (10 Jan. 1931), for persuading the *Spectator*'s book editor to assign it to him, and for getting Harold Nicolson to review for the *Daily Express* (8 Jan. 1931). He "made" Roger Fry read *LFM* with a view to French translation and recommended an agent who might get OS a bigger advance for his next book.

27. Geoffrey Dennis, *English Review* 53 (June 1931), 116.

28. *Times Literary Supplement*, 18 Dec. 1930, p. 1086; Bennett, "Books and Persons," London *Standard*, 23 Oct. 1930, p. 11; Priestley, *Book Society News* [seen only in OS scrapbook, SA].

29. Fred T. Marsh, "Gordelpus!" *Saturday Review*, 25 Apr. 1931, p. 774; John Carter, "The Next Two Billions Years or So," *New York Times Book Review*, 19 Apr. 1931, p. 2; J. K. Atkins, "Beyond Man," *New York Herald Tribune* (21 June 1931), sec. II, p. 15.

30. "A Brilliant Fantasy," *Observer*, 23 Nov. 1930, p. 6; review, *Oxford Magazine*, 30 Oct. 1930, p. 110. For a sample of comments on the Martians, see Ralph Straus, "New Fiction," [London] *Sunday Times*, 2 Nov. 1930, p. 7; "The New Books at a Glance," *John O'London's Weekly*,

15 Nov. 1930, p. 264; Proteus [Hamish Miles], "New Novels," *New Statesman*, 22 Nov. 1930, p. 207; and the *Times Literary Supplement* review.

31. "The Book Taster: 'On the Table,' " *Liverpool Post*, 22 Oct. 1930, p. 4; C. V. C., "A Mythic History of Man," *Liverpool Post*, 19 Nov. 1930, p. 4.

32. J. B. Priestley, "These Literary Leg-Pulls," *Clarion* I (2 June 1934), 11; Arthur C. Clarke, Introduction to OS, *NM and FE* (New York: Dodd, Mead, 1983), vii; Brian Aldiss, "In Orbit with the Star Maker," *Times Literary Supplement*, 23 Sept. 1983, p. 1007; Doris Lessing, Afterword to *LFM* (Los Angeles: Tarcher, 1988), 305.

33. OS, "Squire to Knight," *The Two Houses* [Beechcroft Settlement Magazine] I (Oct. 1927), 11.

34. From notes of a conversation between Curtis C. Smith and Mona and Sidney Scholefield-Allen; courtesy of Smith.

35. The gossip about the Hawthornden prize is in "Literary Notes" in the *English Review* 53 (July 1931), 240.

36. OS to Naomi Mitchison, 1931 (NLS).

37. "If We Were Angels," [Liverpool] *Evening Express*, 1 Oct. 1931, p. 5. The diner's comments appear in the Rotary newsletter, a cutting from which is in OS's scrapbook (SA).

38. Mary Adams for the BBC to OS, 19 Mar. 1931. Adams's seven letters, with a contract for the broadcast, are in the *LFM* correspondence file (SA).

39. "Our Critic Listens In," *Catholic Times* [London], 24 Apr. 1931, p. 17. The transcript of "The Remaking of Man" was published in the *Listener*, 8 Apr. 1931, pp. 575–76.

40. "Far Future Calling" was privately printed by Harvey Satty, who discovered the script in 1975, and reprinted in *FFC*, 171–207.

41. OS was a signatory with Wells, Mitchison, A. S. Neill, Vera Brittain, and others of a letter, published in newspapers around Britain on 28 Nov. 1935, protesting this policy.

42. *LFM*, 177.

43. OS, "Broadcasting and World Unity," *World-Radio* 14 (1 Apr. 1932), 632, 634.

44. Robert Crossley, ed., "The Letters of Olaf Stapledon and H. G. Wells, 1931–1942" in *Science Fiction Dialogues*, ed. Gary Wolfe (Chicago: Academy Chicago, 1982), 35.

45. H. G. Wells to OS, 30 Oct. 1931. Seven letters from Wells to OS survive in SA; all but this first letter are in *Science Fiction Dialogues*, 27–57. The letter of 30 Oct. appeared in the *Wellsian*, n.s. 7 (Summer 1984), 38–39. See also Crossley, "Famous Mythical Beasts: Olaf Stapledon and H. G. Wells," *Georgia Review* 36 (Fall 1982), 619–35. The best literary comparison is Robert Shelton's "The Mars-Begotten Men of Olaf Stapledon and H. G. Wells," *Science-Fiction Studies* 11 (Mar. 1984), 1–14.

46. For AS's memory of the demand for a sequel, see Kinnaird, *Olaf Stapledon*, 51. A 22-page gap in the *LFM* manuscript represents the unused material that OS appropriated for *LMIL*. On the manuscript of *LFM* and *LMIL*, see Curtis Smith's introduction to a reprint of *LMIL* (Boston: Gregg, 1976), v–xiv.

47. *LMIL*, 200, 280.

48. *LMIL*, 8, 5, 10.

49. *LMIL*, 303, 304.

50. H. G. Wells, *Experiment in Autobiography: Discoveries and Conclusions of a Very Ordinary Brain (Since 1866)* (New York: Macmillan, 1934), 12.

51. Kinnaird, *Olaf Stapledon*, 52.

52. *LFM* manuscript (SA).

53. Lewis Richards, "Let's Look at the Books," [Birmingham] *Sunday Mercury*, 30 Oct. 1932, p. 8; "Novels of the Day," *Guardian: The Church Newspaper*, 16 Dec. 1932, p. 985; W. Lyon

Blease, "Books of the Week," *Liverpool Post,* 4 Jan. 1933, p. 4; John Brophy, "Writers of Merseyside: W. Olaf Stapledon," *Liverpolitan* 2 (Jan. 1933), 20.

54. *LMIL,* v. "New Novels," *Times Literary Supplement,* 15 Dec. 1932, p. 960; "From the Future," [Wellington] *Dominion,* 10 Dec. 1932, p. 19.

55. Naomi Mitchison, *You May Well Ask: A Memoir 1920–1940* (London: Gollancz, 1979), 36. For a survey of her remarkable career, see Jill Benton, *Naomi Mitchison: A Century of Experiment in Life and Letters* (London: Pandora, 1990).

56. OS to AS, 20 June 1933 (SFP).

57. Quoted in "Storm Over Book," *Edinburgh Evening Dispatch,* 6 Oct. 1932, p. 3.

58. Arnold Lunn, "The Scandal of the Outline," *English Review* 55 (Nov. 1932), 471–84; Mitchison, *You May Well Ask,* 170. Mitchison's belief, however, that Lunn unleashed the torrent of churchmen's criticism is unfounded; his article appeared after most of the negative criticism was already in print.

59. Excerpts from OS, "Problems and Solutions, or The Future" in *An Outline for Boys and Girls and Their Parents,* ed. Naomi Mitchison (London: Gollancz, 1932), 691–749.

60. "The Abbotsholme School Song," *Abbotsholme School Prayer Book* (Plaistow, U.K.: Curwen, 1935), xii.

61. OS to Naomi Mitchison, 21 July 1932 (NLS).

62. *LMIL,* 84.

63. OS to Naomi Mitchison, 21 July 1932 (NLS). He first reported his father's being "taken seriously ill" in a letter to L. H. Myers, 24 Feb. 1932 (SA).

64. *LMIL,* 86.

11. Mapping Utopia, 1933–1935

1. The sketches are in SA (STAP I.2.B).

2. "Temporary Marriages: Views on Earl's Ideas About Students," *Liverpool Echo,* 20 Sept. 1932, p. 8.

3. L. H. Myers to OS, 8 Nov. 1932 (SA).

4. OS's letter of 11 Nov. is quoted from Myers's letter to OS, 19 Nov. 1932 (SA). OS replaced Prof. Alan Dorward, who was struck by a tram in 1942.

5. Report of a talk to a Unitarian Men's League, "Science Can Make a Utopia," *Birkenhead Advertiser,* 9 Dec. 1933, p. 4; notes for "Ourselves and the Future" (SA).

6. OS to Aage Marcus, 22 Nov. 1934 (SA); he spoke over the BBC at 11 AM, 3 Dec. 1934.

7. OS to AS, 27 Apr. 1924 (SFP). Eight minutes of the twenty-minute talk were recoverable when the Stapledons transferred the disk to audiotape; I thank Thomas Stapledon for a copy. The complete script is in the BBC Written Archives Centre, Reading.

8. *WW,* 7.

9. OS often cited "Murray Constantine" in his talks on contemporary literature, but he did not know the author's identity; the *Manchester Guardian*'s review of *Proud Man* (1 June 1934, p. 7) actually suspected OS to be "Murray Constantine." In the 1980s, Daphne Patai solved the mystery; see her editions of Katharine Burdekin's *Swastika Night* (New York: Feminist Press, 1986) and *The End of This Day's Business* (New York: Feminist Press, 1990).

10. Contributors to *Manifesto: Being the Book of the Federation of Progressive Societies and Individuals,* ed. C. E. M. Joad (London: Allen and Unwin, 1934) included OS and Wells. Reviews: John Strachey, "The Intelligentsia Adrift," *Daily Worker,* 20 June 1934, p. 4; "Getting Together," *Life and Letters* 10 (Aug. 1934), 624–26.

11. OS diary, 14 Apr. 1933 (SA).

12. OS, "Education and World Citizenship," *Manifesto,* 147–48. Notes for "The Aims of World Planning," delivered 14 Apr. 1933, are in SA.

13. F. R. L[eavis]., "Comments and Reviews," *Scrutiny* 3 (Sept. 1934), 215–17.

14. Unsigned obituary of OS, *Plan* 18 (Oct. 1950), 2. Brief histories of the Progressive League are in Jack Coates, *A Common Faith or Synthesis* (London: Allen and Unwin, 1942), 118–21; 143–46, and in "What Is the Progressive League?" *Plan* 22 (May 1953), unpaged addendum.

15. H. G. Wells Society, *Monthly Bulletin,* no. 1 (June 1934), 1. Quotations and paraphrases of OS's speech are from this source.

16. Gertrude Mack, "H. G. Wells Society," *Sydney Morning Herald,* 4 Aug. 1934, p. 19.

17. OS to Aage Marcus, 22 Nov. 1934 (SA). In "The Open Conspiracy and the Labour Party," Wells Society *Monthly Bulletin,* no. 7 (Jan. 1935), p. 2, OS criticized the Society for failing to make a class analysis of the problem of world unity or to enlist workers' participation in the open conspiracy.

18. H. G. Wells to Mr. Thompson, 13 Dec. 1934 (H. G. Wells Collection, Mugar Library, Boston University).

19. Mary Longe to H. G. Wells, annotated by Wells, 2 July 1943 (Wells Archive, Univ. of Illinois). The Wells Society of the 1930s was the second of three incarnations. The first, prompted by Wells's *Modern Utopia* (1905), called itself "The Lesser Rule," was headed by J. H. Skilton in 1906–08, and set up the Samurai Press; relevant documents are at Illinois. The third, begun in London in 1960, remains an active scholarly association devoted to the study and promotion of Wells's work.

20. OS to H. G. Wells, 25 Nov. 1931, 15 Sept. 1937; printed in "The Letters of Olaf Stapledon and H. G. Wells, 1931–1942," ed. Robert Crossley, in *Science Fiction Dialogues,* ed. Gary Wolfe (Chicago: Academy Chicago, 1982), 35–37, 43. The inscribed copy of *Things to Come* is in SA.

21. OS diary, 7 June 1932 (SA).

22. Naomi Mitchison to OS, undated (SA); *WW,* v. The advertisement (seen only in the OS scrapbook) calls "It Is Up to You" an inspiration to teenagers to do "revolutionary work" in a new spirit, which, "at cost of misunderstanding, may be most conveniently called religious" (SA [STAP I.9]). The manuscript was last seen by Harvey Satty at OS's house in the mid-1970s.

23. *WW,* 10.

24. H. G. Wells, *The Work, Wealth and Happiness of Mankind* (New York: Doubleday, 1931), 892–93; OS, "Sleepers Wake!" *Listener,* 24 Jan. 1932, supplement p. iv.

25. *WW,* 130.

26. OS to Wells, 16 Oct. 1934; "Letters of OS and HGW," 36–37.

27. "Waking World," *Times Literary Supplement,* 13 Dec. 1934, p. 893.

28. J. D. Bernal, "New Wine in Old Bottles," *Listener,* 7 Nov. 1934, p. 794; OS to Naomi Mitchison, 4 Jan. 1935 (NLS).

29. Amabel Williams-Ellis, "Reverence for Machinery," *Left Review* 1 (Feb. 1935), 190; W. Lyon Blease, "Little Man, What Now?" *Liverpool Daily Post,* 13 Feb. 1935, p. 7; C. R. Morris, "Reviews," *Adult Education* 7 (Apr. 1935), 248–49.

30. OS to Aage Marcus, 22 Nov. 1934 (SA).

31. *WW,* 244. The book was judged unfavorably in this light by Bernal, cited above; Basil de Selincourt gave the opposing view in "The World-To-Be," [London] *Observer,* 4 Nov. 1934, p. 5. OS told Aage Marcus (22 Nov. 1934) that these two were the only reviews "of much consequence" (SA).

32. *WW,* 249.

33. A detailed ledger of the value of the probated will is in SFP.

34. Lecture notes for "Why I Am a Socialist," SA.

35. *WW,* 11.

36. OS to Aage Marcus, 31 Aug. 1937 (SA). Mitchison to Wells, undated (Wells Archive, Univ. of Illinois). Mary Stapledon Shenai recalled a children's party at River Court when she was dazzled by Naomi's elegance, so different from AS's tastes in dress (interview with author, July 1986).

37. *WW,* 37.

38. OS characterized David in a letter to Naomi Mitchison, 4 Jan. 1935 (NLS); other details from John David Stapledon, interview with author, 7 Oct. 1989; and Mary Shenai memoir (SFP).

39. Report of OS's address to the Hope St. Social Problems Circle, "Propoganda and Education," *Liverpool Post,* 15 Nov. 1934, p. 13; George Eustance, interview with author, 7 Oct. 1989.

40. *WW,* 266.

41. OS, "Thoughts on the Modern Spirit," undated typescript, 14, 18; SA. See also Patrick A. McCarthy, "Stapledon and Literary Modernism" in *The Legacy of Olaf Stapledon,* ed. Patrick A. McCarthy et al. (New York: Greenwood, 1989), 39–51.

42. *WW,* 92.

43. Quoted in Herbert Read's introduction to *Unit 1: The Modern Movement in English Arthitecture, Painting and Sculpture* (London: Cassell, 1934), 10.

44. The Post Man, "Day to Day in Liverpool: Unit 1," *Liverpool Post,* 19 Apr. 1934, p. 6. *Unit One: Spirit of the 30's,* a catalogue of the half-century retrospective of Unit One at the Mayor Gallery, London, May 1984, recounts the original exhibit.

45. "Unit One," *Liverpool Evening Express,* 15 May 1934, p. 3.

46. "The Art of 'Unit One,' " *Liverpool Post,* 14 May 1934, p. 6.

47. OS, "The Art of 'Unit One,' " *Liverpool Post,* 28 May 1934, p. 4. The annotation of this letter in the Satty-Smith *Bibliography,* Item C30, accurately reflects OS's usual misgivings about Freudian psychology but misrepresents his generally positive response to Unit One, especially to John Armstrong's paintings.

48. "Sedition Bill Protest," *Liverpool Post,* 26 June 1934, p. 10.

49. *OJ,* 199–200.

50. Mary Shenai memoir (SFP).

51. *LMIL,* 290, 302.

52. The rejected chapter, "The Story of John," is at the back of the holograph manuscript of *LMIL,* SA.

53. OS to Aage Marcus, 17 Oct. 1935 (SA); AS, interview with author, June 1982; Lyon Blease, "An Odd John," *Liverpool Post,* 30 Oct. 1935, p. 7.

54. OS to AM, 4 July 1916; *TATW,* 160.

55. *OJ,* 127. Two OS diary entries on stag hunts in Devon in 1911 read: "I fired several shots at long range, & brought down a calf by mistake. What a brutal business" (18 Sept.); "Stags were poor, but I fired, wounded, reloaded, fired at wrong one, wounded. I had to finish off both & did it badly. Horrible business" (22 Sept.) [SA]. For other references, see ch. 7, n. 41 above.

56. *OJ,* 186, 113–14.

57. *OJ,* 276. In a letter to Aage Marcus of 17 Oct. 1935 (SA), OS tells how SM had already been started "several times" but that the drafts so far left him "dissatisfied."

58. *OJ,* 273.

59. *OJ,* 166.

60. *OJ,* 282.

61. *OJ,* 3, 22.

62. Doris Lessing, *The Fifth Child* (New York: Knopf, 1988), 133.

63. OS to AM, 12 Jan. 1918; *TATW,* 273. On Nietzsche and *OJ* see John Kinnaird, *Olaf Stapledon* (Mercer Island, Wash.: Starmont, 1986), 55–56; Leslie A. Fiedler, *Olaf Stapledon: A Man Divided* (New York: Oxford Univ. Press, 1983), 98–100; and Patrick A. McCarthy, *Olaf Stapledon* (Boston: Twayne, 1982), 54–55, 72–73.

64. J. B. S. Haldane to OS, undated (SA).

65. W. E. Hayter Preston, [London] *Referee,* 13 Oct. 1935, p. 6; V. S. Pritchett, "Fantastic Speculation," *Christian Science Monitor,* 6 Nov. 1935, sec. 6, p. 13; Peter Quennell, "New Novels," *New Statesman,* 5 Oct. 1935, p. 454. Tom Lincoln made a political critique of *OJ*'s defeatism in *The Left Review* 2 (Nov. 1935), 90; M. D. Cole argued against its morality in *Life and Letters* 14 (Spring 1936), 192–93.

66. Howard Spring, "Evening Standard Book of the Month," [London] *Evening Standard,* 3 Oct. 1935, p. 11; L. A. G. Strong, "Heroes Who Think for Themselves," *Yorkshire Post,* 9 Oct. 1935, p. 6; M. R., "A Colony of Superhumans," *World Jewry,* 4 Oct. 1935, p. 22; C. E. M. Joad, "The Coming of the Superman," *Spectator,* 18 Oct. 1935, pp. 624–25. Joad's other review, "The Super-men of Tomorrow," appeared in *John O'London's Weekly,* 19 Oct. 1935, pp. 105–106.

67. "Super-Human," *Davenport* [Iowa] *Sunday Democrat,* sec. 3, p. 22; Charles Hanson Towne, "Books," *Buffalo Evening News,* 15 July 1936, p. 23; Elmer Davis, "The Superman and the Human Spider," *Saturday Review,* 18 July 1936, p. 6.

68. Alfred Kazin, "As a Superman Sees the World," *New York Herald Tribune,* 19 July 1936, sec. 11, p. 2; Lucy Tompkins, "A Fabulous Fantasy That Makes Sense," *New York Times Book Review,* 19 July 1936, p. 7; G. Killan Hyde, "Philosopher's Fable," *Brooklyn Citizen,* 11 Aug. 1936, the last seen only in OS's scrapbook (SA).

69. I except the Penguin *Philosophy and Living,* printed in England and made available in the U.S. in 1940, and the 1949 omnibus volume *Worlds of Wonder* (Los Angeles: Fantasy Publishing Co., 1949) which collected *OMNW, DIL,* and *FL.*

70. "Olaf Stapledon Again," [Glasgow] *Forward,* 12 Oct. 1935, p. 5.

71. As quoted by Carolyn Marx, *New York World Telegram,* 16 July 1936, p. 19.

12. But Today the Struggle, 1936–1937

1. *LMIL,* 85.

2. OS to AM, 7 Jan. 1912 (SFP).

3. H. G. Wells to OS, 22 June 1937, "The Letters of Olaf Stapledon and H. G. Wells, 1931–1942," ed. Robert Crossley, in *Science Fiction Dialogues,* ed. Gary Wolfe (Chicago: Academy Chicago, 1982), 41.

4. OS to Aage Marcus, 17 Oct. 1935; Marcus to OS, 13 Dec. 1935 (SA).

5. Naomi Mitchison to OS, undated [but probably summer 1933] (SA); Mitchison, letter to author, 27 Feb. 1985. *NM,* first printed in England in 1976, appeared in the U.S. with another incomplete manuscript as *Nebula Maker and Four Encounters* (New York: Dodd, Mead, 1983). The 100-page, handwritten discarded manuscript is in SA.

6. J. B. S. Haldane to OS, undated [1935]; Marcus sent the Bernal book with a letter of 29 Feb. 1936 (SA).

7. Leo Myers to OS, 9 Apr. [1934?]; 24 and 25 Dec. [1936] (SA). Iris Origo to OS, 6 Aug. 1936 [filed with Myers's letters in SA, STAP H.IIA.21(29)].

8. Drawn for the London *Evening Standard,* Low's cartoon was reprinted in *The Tragedy of Abyssinia: What Britain Feels and Thinks and Wants* (London: League of Nations Union, 1936), 94. Wells and OS met on 20 April 1936; Wells sent a copy of the screenplay of *Things to Come* as a memento of the visit.

9. OS diary, 8, 10, and 17 May 1936 (SA). Reports of his speeches: "Mussolini 'Drunk With Success,' " *Liverpool Post,* 9 May 1936, p. 5; " 'Drunk with Victory': Hoylake Speaker and Mussolini," *Birkenhead News,* 9 May 1936, p. 9; "Our London Letter: Letting Mr. Baldwin Know,"

Liverpool Post, 12 May 1936, p. 8; "Manifesto Against Raising Sanctions Unconditionally," *Manchester Guardian,* 1 July 1936, p. 14; and "Gregism in Italy and Germany: Dr. O. Stapledon on an 'Appalling Tragedy,' " *Liverpool Post,* 18 May 1936, p. 6.

10. OS to Aage Marcus, 27 Apr. 1937 (SA).

11. L. H. Myers to OS, 21 Mar. [no year]; SA, STAP H.IIA.21(54).

12. OS, "Religion and Science—the Conflict," *London Mercury* 33 (Feb. 1936), 444–45; "Mr. Wells Calls in the Martians," *London Mercury* 36 (July 1937), 295–96; "Mr. Aldous Huxley's Conversion," *London Mercury* 37 (Dec. 1937), 228–29.

13. OS, "A World of Sound," *Hotch-Potch,* ed. John Brophy (Liverpool: Council of the Royal Liverpool Children's Hospital, 1936), 243–51. He told Aage Marcus (22 Nov. 1934) that he sent "East Is West" to *Life and Letters,* which lost the typescript; on 8 Jan. 1936 he told Marcus he had given up on the story (SA). Both "East Is West" and "A World of Sound" were printed posthumously in *FFC.*

14. The "Ignotus" episode began with a press report on OS's views on Ethiopia, after which OS wrote to the editor urging economic sanctions against Italy and Britain's unilateral disarmament. Two days later "Ignotus" opened an epistolary debate that went on intermittently for a year. See *Liverpool Post:* "Pacifism and the League," 26 Oct. 1935, p. 10; OS, "International Law-Breaking," 29 Oct. 1935, p. 4; Ignotus, "International Law-Breaking," 31 Oct. 1935, p. 4. Curtis C. Smith analyzes the controversy in "Diabolical Intelligence and (Approximately) Divine Innocence" in *The Legacy of Olaf Stapledon,* ed. Patrick A. McCarthy et al. (New York: Greenwood, 1989), 87–98.

15. OS to Aage Marcus, 26 June 1936 (SA).

16. OS, "Alleged Communist Peace Racket," *Birkenhead News,* 20 June 1936, p. 7.

17. Ignotus, "Militant Pacifism," *Liverpool Post,* 2 Oct. 1936, p. 4; Radix, "Constructive Idea Wanted," *Liverpool Post,* 5 Oct. 1936, p. 4.

18. "International Law and Order," *Liverpool Post,* 3 Nov. 1936, p. 4.

19. "International Law and Order," *Liverpool Post,* 3 Nov. 1936, p. 4.

20. OS, "The International Crisis," *Liverpool Post,* 23 Mar. 1936, p. 4. Dorward's letters to the *Liverpool Post* (20 Mar. 1936, p. 4; 27 Mar. 1936, p. 4) have also been noticed by Curtis Smith, "Diabolical Intelligence" (p. 90) as "worthy of Ignotus."

21. Charles L. Mowat, *Britain Between the Wars: 1918–1940* (Chicago: Univ. of Chicago Press, 1955), 538.

22. From a broadsheet, "Peace Letter. To All the Peoples of the Earth" pasted in the flyleaf of OS's scrapbook, SA (STAP I.9[2]). Printed in newspapers and posted in bookshops and public places, the broadsheet urged supporters to send postcards to OS.

23. Letters to OS from Viscount Cecil, 2 Apr. 1936; Lord Allen, 14 Mar. 1936 and six letters thereafter; John Strachey, 2 June 1936; Aldous Huxley, 2 Apr. 1936 (SA).

24. OS to Wells, 27 Mar. 1936; Wells to OS, 4 Apr. 1936; OS to Wells, 6 Apr. 1936, in "Letters of OS and HGW," 37–39.

25. OS, lecture notes labeled "IPC" (SA, STAP F.77); the talk was given in London to the International Writers Association, 22 June 1936 (diary); OS told Aage Marcus on 20 July 1936 that he had lately been "much occupied with work for the International Peace Campaign" (SA). "Mausoleum": "Council Chairman Leads Protest," *Hoylake Advertiser,* 15 Oct. 1937, p. 4.

26. OS to Aage Marcus, 6 Sept. 1936 (SA).

27. Text of Peace Letter in OS scrapbook (SA). Dudley Wightwick, "Idealism and Peace," *John O'London's Weekly,* 23 Oct. 1936, pp. 179–80; OS replied in the issue of 13 Nov. 1936, p. 301.

28. OS to AS, 23 June 1936 (SFP).

29. "Peace Week in Liverpool," *Liverpool Post,* 29 Sept. 1936, p. 6.

30. On these political shifts see Mowat, *Britain Between the Wars,* 577–78.

31. Ignotus, "Militant Pacifism," *Liverpool Post,* 2 Oct. 1936, p. 4; OS, "A Programme for Peace," *Liverpool Post,* 6 Oct. 1936, p. 4.

32. OS diary, 14, 16, 21, and 22 March; 4 Apr. 1937 (SA). From the *Liverpool Post:* OS et al., "Sufferings in Madrid," 10 Dec. 1936, p. 4; "Charge Against a Crew," 26 Apr. 1937, p. 5; "Merseyside and Spain," 15 Mar. 1937, p. 11; "Five Empty Chairs," 5 Apr. 1937, p. 9. OS, notes for a speech, "International Brigade" (SA, STAP F.45).

33. OS diary, 1 July; 26 Sept. 1937 (SA). *Authors Take Sides on the Spanish War* (London: Left Review, 1937), 25. Leslie Fiedler's claims in *Olaf Stapledon: A Man Divided* (New York: Oxford Univ. Press, 1983), 32–34, that OS was "neutral" on the war, could not confront it, pretended it didn't exist, and never discussed it in print until 1946, are all incorrect.

34. OS, "But To-day the Struggle," *London Mercury* 39 (Jan 1939), 348–49.

35. "Fascism Is Madness," *Birkenhead Advertiser,* 30 Jan. 1937, p. 3.

36. L. H. Myers to OS, 24 and 25 Dec. [1936] (SA).

37. L. H. Myers to OS, 9 Aug. [1934] (SA).

38. L. H. Myers to OS, undated [1937; STAP H.IIA.21(114)]. Iris Origo, however, with first-hand experience of Italian fascism, urged OS on 27 Feb. 1937 (STAP H.IIA.21[115]) not to mute the political perspectives. See G. H. Bantock's extended analysis of *The Root and the Flower* in *L. H. Myers: A Critical Study* (Leicester: University College, 1956), 39–88.

39. *PL,* vol. 2, p. 460. *The Idea of the Holy* is on a list of books read at the back of OS's 1933–34 diary (SA). On the impact of Dante on *Star Maker,* see Robert Scholes, *Structural Fabulation: An Essay on Fiction of the Future* (Notre Dame, Ind: Notre Dame Univ. Press, 1975), 64–66, and chap. 4, "Divine Tragedy," of Patrick A. McCarthy's *Olaf Stapledon* (Boston: Twayne, 1982).

40. *SM,* 331; manuscript of *SM* (SA).

41. OS to Aage Marcus, 27 Apr. 1937 (SA).

42. *SM,* vi–vii.

43. OS to AS, 21 Feb. 1936 (SFP).

44. *SM,* 1.

45. *Inferno,* trans. Charles Singleton (Princeton, N.J.: Princeton Univ. Press, 1970), 3.

46. Mary Shenai memoir (SFP).

47. *SM,* 4, 328.

48. AS's copy of *SM* (SFP); there was no second edition of *SM.*

49. *SM,* 4.

50. Ruth "Pete" Fletcher, interview with author, 2 Oct. 1989.

51. OS to AS, undated; the envelope is postmarked 20 June 1933 (SFP). OS's diary indicates at least two other meetings with Olive Bowe-Carter, on 17 Apr. and 26 July 1933 (SA).

52. Carolyn Marx, "New Books," *New York World Telegram,* 16 July 1936, p. 19.

53. *SM,* 328; OS, "Poetry and the Worker.—Browning," *Highway* 6 (Apr. 1914), 125.

54. OS to AS, 18–19 Nov. 1941 (SFP).

55. OS's speech on mass neurosis is reported in "Fascism Is Madness," *Birkenhead Advertiser,* 30 Jan. 1937, p. 3.

56. *SM,* 148.

57. On George V's habits of dress, see Roger Fulford, *Hanover to Windsor* (1960; rpt. London: Fontana, 1966), 175.

58. *SM,* 59.

59. Walter H. Gillings, "The Philosopher of Fantasy," *British Scientifiction Fantasy Review* 1 (June 1937), 9.

60. "New Novels: Stars and Islands," [London] *Times*, 25 June 1937, p. 10; Roger Pippett, "Galactic Utopia," *London Daily Herald*, 24 June 1937, p. 14; L. P. Hartley, "The Literary Lounger," *Sketch*, 7 July 1937, 44; "A Reading of the Universe," *Punch* 192 (30 June 1937), 728–29; E. F. B., "A Cosmic Utopia," *Christian Science Monitor*, 25 Aug. 1937, p. 10; "Local Author's Brilliant Fantasy," *Birkenhead News*, 24 July 1937, p. 4; W. Lyon Blease, "A Cosmological Fantasy," *Liverpool Post*, 4 Aug. 1937, p. 5.

61. C. E. M. Joad to OS, 21 July 1937; Aage Marcus to OS, 17 July 1937; Virginia Woolf to OS, 8 July 1937 (SA). OS replied immediately, "I have recently read 'The Years' with delight, and also with despair at the thought of the contrast between your art and my own pedestrian method" (15 July 1937; Woolf Collection, University of Sussex Library). Woolf had volunteered her admiration of his earlier books in a note of 7 Mar. 1937 (SA).

62. L. H. Myers to OS, 25 Nov. 1932 (SA). On Myers and Russell see Bantock, *L. H. Myers*, 146–49.

63. Bertrand Russell, "War in the Heavens," *London Mercury* 36 (July 1937), 297–98.

64. Norman and Margaret Cullen, interview with author, 11 Oct. 1989. At Leo Myers's suggestion, R. Ellis Roberts commissioned OS's *Saints and Revolutionaries* for his *I Believe* series (Ellis Roberts to OS, 6 Dec. 1936; SA); later OS signed to do the Pelican *Philosophy and Living* (OS to V. K. Krishna Menon, 4 Mar. 1937; Penguin Archives, University of Bristol Library).

65. OS, "Personal View," *Manchester Evening News*, 20 Aug. 1937, p. 8.

66. *Illustrated London News*, 31 July 1937, p. 218; Howard Spring, "The Year's Best Book," *Evening Standard*, 30 July 1937, p. 22.

67. *SM*, viii; Roger Lancelyn Green and Walter Hooper, *C. S. Lewis: A Biography* (New York: Harcourt, 1966), 173.

68. Simon Blumenfeld, "Prize Novelists and Others," *Left Review* 3 (Aug. 1937), 437; OS to Aage Marcus, 31 Aug. 1937 (SA).

69. "Adult Education: The Cambridge Conference," *Times Educational Supplement*, 25 Sept. 1937, p. 341.

70. "Council Chairman Leads Protest," *Hoylake Advertiser*, 15 Oct. 1937, p. 4; "Educated Public Opinion," *Birkenhead Advertiser*, 20 Oct. 1937, p. 5.

71. *The Diary of Virginia Woolf*, vol. 5, ed. Anne Olivier Bell (New York: Harcourt, 1984), 118; entry for 1 Nov. 1937. The next day's papers reported inaccurately that she was present for the meeting.

72. OS to AS, 2 Nov. 1937 (SFP). Reports of the meeting: "Economic Appeasement," [London] *Times*, 2 Nov. 1937, p. 11; "Unrest Among Nations," *Liverpool Post*, 2 Nov. 1937, p. 9.

73. P. S. et al., "Cinderellas of 1937," *Bookseller*, 3 Feb. 1938, p. 107.

13. Saint Olaf, 1938–1939

1. Fredric Warburg, *An Occupation for Gentlemen* (Boston: Houghton Mifflin, 1960), 239; Walter Allen, *As I Walked Down New Grub Street: Memories of a Writing Life* (Chicago: Univ. of Chicago Press, 1981), 114; Naomi Mitchison, *You May Well Ask: A Memoir 1920–1940* (London: Gollancz, 1979), 222; OS to Aage Marcus, 18 Oct. 1938 (SA); "The Ambulance Unit Reunion," *Friend*, 28 Oct. 1938, pp. 938–40; OS, notes for "FAU Reunion" (SA); "Moral Rearmament," [London] *Times*, 29 Oct. 1938, p. 8.

2. OS's inscribed copy of *The Brothers* (SA). OS to Wells, 3 Apr. 1938, "The Letters of Olaf Stapledon and H. G. Wells, 1930–1941," ed. Robert Crossley, in *Science Fiction Dialogues*,

ed. Gary Wolfe (Chicago: Academy Chicago, 1982), 44; "The Democratic Front," *Cambridge Review* 59 (25 Feb. 1938), 287.

3. OS, "Science, Art and Society," *London Mercury* 38 (Oct. 1938), 528. Cf. the comments on "recurrent shootings" under Stalin and the possible degeneration of Russian communism into reactionary tyranny in *PL*, vol. 2, pp. 436, 439.

4. OS to Col. A. H. Bell, 16 Feb. 1937; Bell Archive, University of Reading; two weeks later he agreed to write *PL* (OS to V. K. Krishna Menon, 4 Mar. 1937; Penguin Archives, University of Bristol Library).

5. OS, "But To-Day the Struggle," *London Mercury* 39 (Jan. 1939), 349.

6. *PL*, vol. 1, p. 17. OS corrected proofs in autumn 1938 (OS to Richard Lane, 8 Jan. 1939; Penguin Archives, University of Bristol Library); he told Aage Marcus (18 Oct. 1938) that he expected the book out in Feb. 1939 "after shocking delay on the part of the Penguin people" (SA). The delay proved much longer; *PL* was published in the second week of November.

7. *PL*, vol. 1, p. 51.

8. *PL*, vol. 2, pp. 345–46.

9. *PL*, vol 2, p. 359. Cf. *SM:* "Inevitably I face the task with a sense of abysmal incompetence. The greatest minds of the human race through all the ages of human history have failed to describe their moments of deepest insight. Then how dare I attempt this task? And yet I must" (282).

10. *PL*, vol. 2, p. 389.

11. "Freedom Will Survive," *Times Literary Supplement*, 15 June 1940, p. 291.

12. "Religion and Philosophy," *Times Literary Supplement*, 15 June 1940, p. 288; "Living More Wisely," [London] *Guardian*, 27 June 1941, p. 304; J. O. Wisdom, "New Books," *Philosophy* 16 (Jan. 1941), 83–84.

13. The figure comes from a letter of OS to Mary Stapledon, 21 Aug. 1943 (SFP).

14. OS to Aage Marcus, 18 Oct. 1938; details of the journey to Lapland are in the manuscript "Fields Within Fields" (SA).

15. *NHB*, 105; Mona Scholefield-Allen, interview with author, 19 Oct. 1989. On government regulations see A. J. Sherman, *Island Refuge: Britain and Refugees from the Third Reich, 1938–1939* (Berkeley: Univ of California Press, 1973), 91–92.

16. Here and elsewhere I rely on Wolfgang Brueck's memoir, "A Diary of 1939" (P), and my interview with him on 24 Mar. 1990.

17. OS to Wolfgang Brueck, 18 May 1943 (P).

18. Clarence K. Streit, *Union Now: A Proposal for a Federal Union of the Democracies of the North Atlantic* (New York and London: Harper, 1939), 208–209.

19. OS, "Federal Union: Old Idea; New Vision," *Liverpool Post*, 11 July 1939, p. 4; leader, "Federal Union," *Liverpool Post*, 11 July 1939, p. 6. OS's first endorsement of Streit's book was in a collective letter to the *New Statesman*, 25 Mar. 1939, p. 461. In Manchester he criticized Streit's idea of "imposing on the world the constitution of the United States" ("Federal Union," *Manchester Guardian*, 27 Sept. 1939, p. 12.).

20. Oscar L. Turner, "The European Federation Idea," *Liverpool Post*, 4 Jan. 1940, p. 6; OS, "Federalism and Socialism," *Federal Union: A Symposium*, ed. Melville Chaning-Pearce (London: Cape, 1940), 115–29.

21. OS's talk (22 Feb. 1939) was reported by "A. C. R." extensively in the Progressive League's journal, *Plan* 6 (May 1939), 8–12.

22. *SR*, 9.

23. *SR*, 60; *PL*, vol. 2, p. 337.

24. *SR*, 34, 37, 55, 45, 100, 27.

25. *NHB*, vi.

26. *NHB*, 159–60.

27. *NHB*, 101–103.

28. OS, notes for "Is There an English Spirit?"; manuscript, "Britain's Part in This New World" (SA). The latter was published under the same title but with alterations in *Common Wealth Review* 3 (Feb. 1946), 10.

29. OS to Aage Marcus, 4 Oct. 1939 (SA).

30. OS diary, 24 Aug. 1939 (SA).

31. "Looking Beyond the Present Crisis," *Birkenhead News,* 30 Aug. 1939, p. 13.

32. Brueck, "Diary of 1939" (P); interview with author, 24 Mar. 1990.

33. OS diary, 31 Aug.–3 Sept. 1939 (SA); Mary Shenai memoir (SFP).

34. OS to Aage Marcus, 4 Oct. 1939 (SA). The ARP notebook is in SA, STAP A.II.3. In "Reply to Professor Haldane" Lewis admitted the intention to satirize the "scientism" of Shaw, OS, and Haldane. See Lewis, *Of Other Worlds: Essays and Stories,* ed. Walter Hooper (1966; rpt. New York: Harcourt, 1975), 77.

35. OS to Aage Marcus, 4 Oct. 1939 (SA).

36. Hugh Walpole, "Courage Counts," [London] *Daily Sketch,* 17 Oct. 1939, p. 9; "Religion and Philosophy," *Times Literary Supplement,* 21 Oct. 1939, p. 604. The passage on torture is in *SR,* 102.

37. OS, "The Great Certainty," *In Search of Faith: A Symposium,* ed. E. W. Martin (London: Lindsay Drummond, 1943), 51–52.

38. K., "Books of the Day: A Moralist's Faith," *Liverpool Post,* 24 Nov. 1939, p. 6; F. E. Pollard, "The Book Window," *Friend,* 29 Dec. 1939, p. 1041; J. H. J., "Up, the Progressives!" *Adelphi* 16 (Feb. 1940), 223–24; "A New Patriotism," *Times Literary Supplement,* 4 Nov. 1939, p. 638. The unsigned *Times Literary Supplement* review is identified in Goerge Lilley's *Bibliography of John Middleton Murry* (London: Dawsons, 1974), 153; OS criticized Eliot in his foreword to John Pride, *Life: A Poem* (Liverpool: Daily Post Printers, 1939), 3.

39. Methuen to OS, 15 June 1948 (SA, STAP H.VIIA.15[B]). For other data on the publication history of *NHB,* I rely on the Satty-Smith *Bibliography.*

40. Frank Kendon to OS, 31 Dec. 1940 (SA).

41. OS to Aage Marcus, 6 Jan. 1940 (SA).

42. Wells to OS, 13 Nov. 1939, "Letters of OS and HGW," 45.

43. H. G. Wells to Mr. Tilsley, 29 July 1933; Wells Collection, Mugar Library, Boston University.

44. OS to Wells, 16 Nov. 1939; "Letters of OS and HGW," 45–46.

45. Ronald Clark makes a detailed narrative of these experiments in *J. B. S.: The Life and Work of J. B. S. Haldane* (1968; rpt. Oxford Univ. Press, 1984), 138–51.

46. J. B. S. Haldane to OS, Sept. 1940 (SA).

47. *The Diary of Virginia Woolf,* vol. 5, ed. Anne Olivier Bell (New York: Harcourt, 1984), 8. Iris Origo's moving diary of 1943 and 1944 was published as *War in Val D'Orcia* (London: Cape, 1947).

14. Compensations, 1940–1942

1. OS manuscript, "The War and the Peace" (SA).

2. OS, "War Between Two Faiths," [Newport] *South Wales Argus,* 5 Sept. 1940, p. 5.

3. OS to Aage Marcus, 6 Jan. 1940 (SA).

4. OS manuscript, "Fields Within Fields, " SA.

5. My observations of Simon's Field, no longer owned by the Stapledons, are supplemented by a letter from Mary Shenai, 15 Apr. 1991, and Winifred M. Primrose's memoir *From the Scottish Manse to the Wide World* (Chester, U.K.: Hunter House, 1986), 52.

6. OS to Aage Marcus, 4 Oct. 1939 (SA).

7. OS to Mary Stapledon, 27 May 1940 (SFP).

8. OS to Mary Stapledon, 10 May 1940 (SFP).

9. OS to Mary Stapledon, 10 May 1940 (SFP).

10. OS to Mary Stapledon, 10 June 1940 (SFP).

11. OS to Naomi Mitchison, 10 July 1940 (NLS).

12. *SPP*, 6–7.

13. OS, notes for "Under Fire," given at Bootle Free Church (SA).

14. Wells to OS, 26 July 1940, in Robert Crossley, ed., "The Letters of Olaf Stapledon and H. G. Wells, 1931–1942," in *Science Fiction Dialogues,* ed. Gary Wolfe (Chicago: Academy Chicago, 1982), 46–47. Gandhi's opinion that a universal Declaration of Human Duties would secure human rights automatically was often cited by critics of Wells, e.g., J. B. Coates in *A Common Faith or Synthesis* (London: Allen and Unwin, 1942), 71.

15. OS to Mary Stapledon, 8 May 1940 (SFP).

16. OS, "The Dialectic of Science," *London Mercury* 39 (Feb. 1939), 454–55. His essays for Leavis were "Writers and Politics," *Scrutiny* 8 (Sept. 1939), 151–56; "Escapism in Literature," *Scrutiny* 8 (Dec. 1939), 298–308; and "Tradition and Innovation To-Day," *Scrutiny* 9 (June 1940), 33–45. On their relevance to OS's literary practice see Robert Crossley, "Politics and the Artist: The Aesthetic of *Darkness and the Light," Science-Fiction Studies* 9 (Nov. 1982), 294–305.

17. F. R. L[eavis]., "Retrospect of a Decade," Scrutiny 9 (June 1942), 71.

18. OS to L. H. Myers, 9 Oct. 1940 (SA). In an exchange of letters in July 1940, they debated the content of the "Tradition and Innovation" article in *Scrutiny.*

19. OS, notes for "Literature and the People," delivered 20 May 1938 (SA).

20. Vincent Brome, "The Books They Never Wrote," *John O'London's Weekly,* 8 May 1942, p. 1.

21. *DATL,* 32.

22. OS often cited these books in such talks on contemporary fiction as "Science and Literature" (1937 and 1938), "The Novelist in Society" (undated), and "Science and Fiction" (1947); lecture notes (SA). He reviewed *Morwyn* in "Descent Into Hell," *London Mercury* 37 (Nov. 1937), 78.

23. L. H. Myers to OS, undated (SA STAP IIA.21[79]).

24. *DATL,* v. OS sent the manuscript to Methuen in spring 1941 but was told in May and again in June that they had no paper (OS to Mary Stapledon, 14 May, 19 June 1941 [SFP]). Fifteen hundred copies were finally issued on 12 February 1942.

25. "Visions of Catastrophe," *Times Literary Supplement,* 18 Apr. 1942, p. 194; Rebecca West, "The Universal Struggle," [London] *Sunday Times,* 19 Apr. 1942, p. 3; L. A. G. Strong, "Light and Shadow," *Observer,* 22 Feb. 1942, p. 3; C. E. M. Joad, "The Future," *New Statesman,* 28 Mar. 1942, pp. 210–11; Joad, "Power Without Wisdom," *Britain To-Day,* no. 71 (Mar. 1942), 26.

26. *DATL,* 3.

27. For Acland's relation to the existing political parties, see G. D. H. Cole, *A History of the Labour Party from 1914* (1949; rpt. New York: Augustus M. Kelley, 1969), 409–10.

28. OS to Mary Stapledon, 8 May 1940 (SFP).

29. OS to Mary Stapledon, 19 June 1941 (SFP); John David Stapledon, interview with author, 10 Oct. 1989.

30. OS to Mary Stapledon, 18 June 1942 (SFP).

31. *DIL,* 159.

32. Lilian Bowes-Lyon to OS, 9 Feb. 1940 (SA); OS to Mary Stapledon, 10 May 1940 (SFP); OS to Aage Marcus, 6 Jan. 1940 (SA).

33. Fredric Warburg, *An Occupation for Gentlemen* (Boston: Houghton Mifflin, 1960), p. 260; George Orwell's *Lion and the Unicorn* (1940) was the first Secker and Warburg "Searchlight."

34. *BI,* 12; OS to Mary Stapledon, 15 Nov. 1941 (SFP).

35. *BI,* 35, 58, 128.

36. "An Ism of One's Own," *Church Times,* 24 Apr. 1942, p. 245; Charles Williams, "Men and Books," *Time and Tide,* 23 May 1942, p. 436; John O'London, "Letters to Gog and Magog: Tomorrow," *John O'London's Weekly,* 25 Sept. 1942, p. 251.

37. *BI,* 5.

38. *BI,* 69–70.

39. Norman Cullen, interview with author, 20 June 1982; OS to Mary Stapledon, 6 Feb. 1942 (SFP).

40. Geoffrey Wood, letter to author, 15 Aug. 1990. Mr. Wood based his timetable on conversation with his sister's friend Paul Fetterlein, a member of the Progressive League, who recalled how OS and Evelyn met and the beginning of the affair.

41. AS, letter to author, 12 Sept. 1982.

42. *BI,* 6.

43. Two of Evelyn Gibson's poems appeared in the journal of the Progressive League: a political squib modeled on Lewis Carroll, titled "Invitation to the Waltz," co-written with Norman Yates-Fish, in *Plan* 9 (Sept. 1942), 5, and "The Ministry," *Plan* 10 (Sept. 1943), 8. For details of her personal history, I am indebted to her brother, Geoffrey Wood.

44. Evelyn Gibson to AS, 4 Nov. 1941; 9 Oct. 1941 (SFP).

45. AS to Evelyn Gibson, 3 Oct. 1941 (SFP).

46. Evelyn Gibson to AS, 27 Oct. 1941 (SFP).

47. *LFM,* 150–51.

48. Evelyn Gibson to AS, 4 Nov. 1941 (SFP).

49. Recitation by John Stapledon, 14 Jan. 1991; the only text is his pencil draft, faded nearly to illegibility, in the flyleaf of his copy of *OJ* (SFP).

50. OS to AS, 10 Sept. 1941 (SFP).

51. OS to AS, 18–19 Nov. 1941 (SFP).

52. AS to OS, 19 Nov. 1941; OS to AS, 20 Nov. 1941 (SFP).

53. Evelyn Gibson to AS, 5 Jan. 1942; 4 Feb. 1942 (SFP).

54. *BI,* 80.

55. OS to Evelyn Gibson, 28 July 1942 (SFP); the copy has a notation in AS's hand that the letter was written at OS's air-raid warden's post in Caldy.

56. Evelyn Gibson to OS, 7 Nov. 1947 (SA).

57. Evelyn Gibson to OS, undated (SA).

15. Fantasies and Woolly Idealism, 1942–1944

1. OS, "Literature and the Unity of Man," *Writers in Freedom: A Symposium,* ed. Hermon Ould (London: Hutchinson, 1942), 113–19.

2. *SM,* 27, 34. Harvey Satty convinced me that the "special elevated tracks slung beside the first-storey windows" of shops on the Other Earth (35) are modeled on Chester's Rows.

3. OS to Mary Stapledon, 29 Nov. 1941 (SFP).

4. OS diary, 20 Dec. 1941 (SA); C. H. Waddington, "Some Biological Discoveries of Practical Importance," *Nature* 150 (29 Aug. 1942), 260. OS's query on *SI*—"My best sc. fictn?"—is in notes for a 1947 lecture "Science and Fiction" (SA).

5. OS to Mary Stapledon, 20 Feb. 1942 (SFP).

6. On *SI* and *Frankenstein* see Eric S. Rabkin, "The Composite Fiction of Olaf Stapledon," *Science-Fiction Studies* 9 (Nov. 1982), 238–40. Leslie A. Fiedler compares it with *Moreau* in *Olaf Stapledon: A Man Divided* (New York: Oxford Univ., Press, 1983), 186–87. In an undated letter Leo Myers noticed resemblances to Garnett's fable (SA). OS saw London productions of Čapek's *The Power and the Glory* and *The Insect Play* in 1938 (diary, 21 May and 9 June 1938 [SA]); just before beginning *SI* he recommended "a fine imaginative satire," *War with the Newts*, to his daughter (OS to Mary Stapledon, 29 Nov. 1941 [SFP]). He reviewed Samuel's *Unknown Land* in *Tribune*, 6 Nov. 1942.

7. OS, lecture notes for "Koehler [*sic*]: Mentality of Apes" (SA). John Gloag to OS, 10 June 1944 (SA); *LFM*, 200.

8. OS to AM, 14 Feb. 1919 (SFP).

9. OS, "Sketch-Map of Human Nature," *Philosophy* 17 (July 1942), 211.

10. W. N. and L. A. Kellogg, *The Ape and the Child: A Study of Environmental Influence Upon Early Behavior* (New York and London: McGraw-Hill, 1933), 326. OS, lecture notes for "The Minds of Animals," delivered 26 July 1944 (SA); annotated copies of Kohler and Fox are in SA.

11. OS, lecture notes for "Science and Fiction," 1947 (SA); *TATW*, 251; "The Wolf Nature" in "Verse by WOS" (SA).

12. AS, letter to author, 27 Apr. 1982.

13. OS to Naomi Mitchison, 10 June 1944 (NLS).

14. OS to WS, undated (SFP).

15. OS to AM, 18 Aug. 1917 (SFP).

16. Francis Thompson, "The Hound of Heaven" (1893), l. 135; *SI*, 55, 118–19.

17. OS said he feared both age and bombs because he had not yet finished his work (two undated letters [c. 1941–42] from Leo Myers to OS, SA). After the war he told Aage Marcus about his scary bicycle journeys into Liverpool (3 Mar. 1946 [SA]).

18. Angus Calder, *The People's War: Britain 1939–45* (London: Cape, 1969), 249–52; Harold C. Shearman, *Adult Education for Democracy* (London: WEA, 1944), 50.

19. Unpublished typescript, "Education in the Force" (SA).

20. OS, "Adult Education in Industry," *Highway* 37 (Apr. 1946), 87.

21. OS diary, 4 Sept. 1943; typescript, "Education in the Force" (SA).

22. *YT*, 69–70; typescript, "Education in the Force" (SA).

23. OS to AS, 25 Mar. 1941 (SFP).

24. OS to Mary Stapledon, 13 Aug. 1943 (SFP).

25. OS to AS, 22 Oct. 1944 (SFP).

26. OS to AS, 10 Sept. 1943; OS to Mary Stapledon, 13 Sept. 1943 (SFP). A pilot, thanking the author for a copy of *OJ*, told how he had been sketched by a fellow RAF man, reading *BI* on base (John Badger to OS, 1 Oct. 1945; SA).

27. OS, "Planning and Liberty: Talks with the Troops," *World Affairs* 11 (Oct. 1945), 245–46.

28. OS to Mary Stapledon, 16 Feb. 1944; misdated 1942 (SFP); a briefer version of the story is in "Planning and Liberty," 250.

29. OS to Mary Stapledon, 14 May 1941 (SFP).

30. OS to Wells, 3 Aug. 1942; Wells to OS, 7 Aug. 1942, "The Letters of Olaf Stapledon and H. G. Wells, 1931–1942," ed. Robert Crossley, in *Science Fiction Dialogues*, ed. Gary Wolfe (Chicago: Academy Chicago, 1982), 48–49.

31. OS to H. G. Wells, 11 Aug. 1942, "Letters of OS and HGW," 50.

32. OS, "Some Thoughts on H. G. Wells's 'You Can't Be Too Careful,' " *Plan* 9 (Aug. 1942), 2. Wells's request that OS review the novel was conveyed in a note from his daughter-in-law Marjorie Wells, 3 June 1942 ("Letters of OS and HGW, 48).

33. Some of OS's brains trust performances were described in the *Liverpool Post:* " 'Brains Trust' in Liverpool," 10 July 1942, p. 2; "A One-Man Brains Trust," 11 Jan. 1945, p. 3. " 'South End' Complex: Tenancy Ban on Coloured Races," 13 Feb. 1945, p. 3.

34. OS to Mary Stapledon, 12 Sept. 1942 (SPF).

35. OS wrote Naomi Mitchison, 10 June 1944, that Methuen had judged *SI* obscene (NLS); in a 1950 eulogy she claimed that both *OJ* and *SI* had been censored. Mitchison, "Human Personalities: Olaf Stapledon," *Humanity Now* 9 (Winter 1950), 14.

36. E. V. Rieu to OS, 17 Dec. 1942; SA, STAP H.II.B.6(9).

37. Fredric Warburg to OS, 18 Dec. 1942; SA, STAP H.II.B.6(12).

38. In writing the contract for *MD,* Rieu was glad to end the period of competition with Warburg: "By the way, I rather imagine that Secker and Warburg's refusal releases you from the obligation to give them the first offer of future novels." E. V. Rieu to OS, 1 Dec. 1948; SA, STAP H.VII.A.15(16).

39. OS to Hermon Ould, 28 Apr. 1943 (PEN).

40. OS to Hermon Ould, 12 Jan. 1944 (PEN).

41. E. V. Rieu to OS, 2 May 1944 (SA); OS to Hermon Ould, 6 May 1944 (PEN).

42. OS, "The Great Certainty," *In Search of Faith: A Symposium,* ed. Ernest W. Martin (London: Lindsay Drummond, 1943), 37. Acland wrote "It Must Be Christianity" (96–115).

43. See William Harrington and Peter Young, *The 1945 Revolution* (London: Davis-Poynter, 1978), 132; the major study of Common Wealth is Angus Calder's unpublished Ph.D. diss., "The Common Wealth Party 1942–45" (University of Sussex, 1968),

44. "Bitterness Left in Eddisbury," *Liverpool Post,* 20 Apr. 1943, p. 2.

45. OS, notes for "Aims and Policy of Common Wealth [revised]"; SA.

46. OS to Mary Stapledon, 15 May 1943 (SFP).

47. OS to Mary Stapledon, 21 Sept. 1943 (SFP); incomplete draft of a letter from OS to Mr. Brunton, 5 Oct. 1943 (SA, STAP H.III.4). I have found no other evidence of an earlier campaign for a parliamentary seat.

48. OS to Dick Acland, 22 Sept. 1943; Sir Richard Acland Papers, University of Sussex.

49. OS to AM, 10 Oct. 1913 (SFP).

50. *OMNW,* 9.

51. Arthur Koestler to OS, 22 June 1943; in a second undated letter, later that year, he canceled the anthology (SA).

52. OS to Hermon Ould, 13 and 28 Oct. 1943; Ould to OS, 26 Oct. 1943 (PEN).

53. G. W. Stonier, "Crystal-Gazing," *New Statesman,* 22 July 1944, p. 61; "Sociology," *Times Literary Supplement,* 12 Aug. 1944, p. 395. Lilian Bowes-Lyon to OS, 26 June 1944 (SA); OS to Hermon Ould, 25 July 1944 (PEN).

54. From the earliest text of *SI,* a pencil manuscript (P), and a more detailed draft, the basis for the typescript read at Methuen and at Secker and Warburg (SA). Cf. *SI,* 179–80.

55. Roger Senhouse to OS, 12 July 1943 (SA STAP H.VIIA.15); OS to Mary Stapledon, 4 July 1944 (SFP).

56. Note by Evelyn Gibson with the *SI* manuscript, dated 2 Oct. 1979, owned by Geoffrey Wood. Her copy of the novel, published two years after she and OS had ceased being lovers, is inscribed, "Evelyn, With thanks for your part, from Olaf" (P).

57. *SI,* 7, 8, 9, 52.

58. *SI,* 76, 104.

59. "Symbolical Dog," *Times Literary Supplement,* 17 June 1944, p. 293; *"Sirius," Daily Telegraph* [London], 9 June 1944, p. 3; Ralph Straus, "New Novels," *Sunday Times* [London], 11 June 1944, p. 3; Allen Hutt, "Stranger Than Fiction," *Daily Worker,* 14 June 1944, p. 2; Charles Marriott, "Books of the Day," *Manchester Guardian,* 16 June 1944, p. 3; OS to Mary Stapledon, 17 June 1944 (SFP).

60. Pamela Hansford Johnson, "A Dog as Hero," *John O'London's Weekly,* 16 June 1944, p. 112; John Betjeman, "New Books," *Daily Herald* [London], 8 June 1944, p. 2; Robert Lynd, "Books," *News Chronicle* [London], 29 June 1944, p. 2; Philip Toynbee, "New Novels," *New Statesman,* 1 July 1944, pp. 12–13; J. S., "Dog Story," *Punch,* 26 July 1944, p. 83.

61. OS to Aage Marcus, 3 Mar. 1946 (SA).

62. OS to Mary Stapledon, 4 July 1944 (SFP).

63. Philip Toynbee to OS, 25 Apr. 1945 (SA).

64. Julian Huxley to OS, 4 June 1944; Eleanor Farjeon to OS, 10 June 1944; J. B. S. Haldane to OS, Sept. 1944; Naomi Mitchison to OS, undated; Arthur Koestler to OS, 14 June 1944 (SA). The mystery of Plaxy's name continues to resist solution.

65. OS to Mary Stapledon, 4 Apr. 1945 (SFP). Publication data in the Secker and Warburg ledgers (University of Reading) contradict the Satty-Smith *Bibliography,* which lists 2,209 copies in the first printing and 3,927 in the second. OS reported the first edition out of print to Mary Stapledon, 4 July 1944 (SFP).

66. OS to AS, 6 Aug. 1942 (SFP).

67. Various letters, undated but all in the 1940s, from L. H. Myers to OS (SA). Four of OS's letters to Myers survive in SA.

68. OS to Mary Stapledon, 12 Sept. 1942 (SFP).

69. OS to AS, 20 Mar. 1944 (SFP).

70. "Letters to a Militiaman" is in SA. The four surviving "Letters to the Future," ed. Robert Crossley, appear in *The Legacy of Olaf Stapledon,* ed. Patrick A. McCarthy et al. (New York: Greenwood, 1989), 99–120. OS announced the completion of *YT* to Mary Stapledon, 27 Apr. 1944 (SFP).

71. OS to Aage Marcus, 3 Mar. 1946 (SA).

72. OS to Hermon Ould, 17 June 1943; 6 July 1943 (PEN).

73. OS to Mary Stapledon, 13 Sept. 1943 (SFP).

74. *SI,* 169.

75. *DIL,* 158–59.

16. Growing Old in Springtime, 1945–1946

1. Gwenda Hollander, interview with author, 3 Oct. 1989.

2. OS to Wolfgang Brueck, 13 May 1944 (P).

3. *DIL,* 146; "The Core," *Windmill* 1 (July 1945), 112.

4. The exhibition was reviewed by George Whitfield, "Cheery Art Show," *Liverpool Echo,* 5 Apr. 1946, p. 2.

5. I thank George Eustance of Kendal for a tour of the site of old Langdale, now a condominium resort. Gwynneth Alban-Davis, a resident during the 1940s, provided an otherwise unobtainable brochure about Langdale, illustrated by her, and access to the manuscript of her unpublished memoir, "Dark-Bright Valley."

6. Alban-Davis, "Dark-Bright Valley," 35.

7. Sittings are noted in OS's diary (30 Jan. and 16–17 Apr. 1945; SA) and in a letter from OS to AS, 14 July 1948 (SFP).

8. Alban-Davis, "Dark-Bright Valley," 71.

9. The catalogue *Hilde Goldschmidt: Paintings, Pastels and Monotypes 1935–1971*, introduced by J. P. Hodin for a 1973 retrospective at Abbot Hall, included a monochrome reproduction of the OS portrait.

10. *DIL*, 145–147.

11. OS to Aage Marcus, 3 Mar. 1946 (SA).

12. *DIL*, 87; cf. *OJ*, 110. OS frequently used the image in lectures in the forties and coyly had an alien fire-creature quote this phrase of "one of your writers" in *FL*, 53.

13. OS to D. Kilham Roberts, 19 July 1946; Society of Authors Papers, British Library. OS always worked without a literary agent, but in 1946 he joined the Society of Authors and got advice on how to handle his contract with Secker and Warburg.

14. Notes for "Election 1945"; SA, STAP F.10.6.

15. OS diary, 12 Feb. 1945 (SA); " 'South End' Complex: Tenancy Ban on Coloured Races," *Liverpool Post*, 13 Feb. 1945, p. 3.

16. *OJ*, 222, 235.

17. *DIL*, 156.

18. *OE*, 8.

19. *LFM*, 37. T. S. Douglass, "To the Moon by Atomic Power," *Sheffield Telegraph*, 8 Aug. 1945, p. 2; R. L. Mégroz, "The Atomic Age," *Time and Tide*, 18 Aug. 1945, p. 688; T. R. F., "The Prophecies of 'Scientifiction,' " [London] *Tribune*, 24 Aug. 1945, p. 12. OS's "After the Bomb: Our Stupendous Future," [London] *Leader*, 18 Aug. 1945, pp. 9, 22, was accompanied by a boxed inset on the destruction of Lundy in *LFM*.

20. Margaret and Norman Cullen, interview with author, 20 June 1982.

21. OS, "Our Stupendous Future," 9; OS diary, 30 Aug. 1945 (SA); lecture notes, "Atomic Power" (SA).

22. OS, "Social Implications of Atomic Power," *Norseman* 3 (Nov.–Dec. 1945), 390.

23. "Social Implications of Atomic Power," 390, 391.

24. OS manuscript, "In the London Streets," SA.

25. Hermon Ould to OS, 3 Sept. 1945 (PEN). "Arms Out of Hand," similar in theme to *MD*, was the only one of his experimental short stories of the later 1940s OS was able to publish—in *Transformation Four*, ed. Stefan Schimanski and Henry Treece (London: Lindsay Drummond, 1947), 289–305.

26. OS to Roger Senhouse, 15 Dec. 1945; Senhouse to OS, 4 Jan. 1946 (Secker and Warburg Archives, University of Reading).

27. OS, "Biographical Note" about *FL* written for the Secker and Warburg publicity department; SA, STAP B.70(3). Slightly reworded, the note appears on the rear flap of the dust jacket.

28. *FL*, 9.

29. *LFM*, 105–106; OS to Fay Pomerance, 2 Sept. 1947 (P).

30. Norman Cullen, interview with author, 11 Oct. 1989; OS to Wolfgang Brueck, 27 Dec. 1945 (P).

31. "Britain 'No Longer Great Power': Author's View," *Liverpool Post*, 14 Mar. 1946, p. 3.

32. "War or Peace?" *Wallasey News*, 24 Jan. 1948, p. 4.

33. OS, "Reconstruction in Holland," *Contemporary Review* 169 (Feb. 1946), 71–76. Further details are in lecture notes for "Holland and P.E.N." (SA). One of many talks he gave between Oct. 1945 and Jan. 1946 was covered in "The Plight of Holland," *Halifax Daily Courier*, 15 Nov. 1945, p. 3.

34. Frank Kermode to OS, 30 Aug. 1946; seven letters from Kermode in 1946 and 1947 are in SA.

35. Frank Kermode to author, 3 May 1983; Kermode to OS, 8 Apr. 1947 (SA).

36. "Socialist Thought Is Changing," *New Leader*, 2 Sept. 1945, p. 8; "Marx Made Mistakes," [Oxford] *Isis*, 8 May 1946, p. 6; "Doctrinal Religion 'Essential,' " *Manchester Guardian*, 21 May 1947, p. 8; "Agnostic Lost the Day in Debate on Religion," *Catholic Times*, 30 May 1947, p. 2.

37. Gwenda Hollander, letter to author, 18 Feb. 1988. The couple, Pamela Bird and John Holden, wrote seven letters to OS (SA). The proposal for a Stapledon Society was made by H. Austin Treliving, 29 Dec. 1947, one of ten letters he sent to OS in 1947 and 1948 (SA). A sampling of fan mail from science-fiction readers is in a special file (SA, STAP H.IIA.33).

38. Geoffrey Ashe to author, 25 May 1990; his letters to OS, starting 2 May 1943, are in SA. "Discussion With the Forces" appeared in the student newsletter, *Cambridge University Labour Review*, Oct. 1946 [seen only in OS's scrapbook, SA]; Ashe reviewed *YT* for *Tribune*, 26 July 1946, p. 18. I thank Mr. Ashe for a text of his broadcast of 9 Dec. 1948.

39. Freeman Dyson, *Disturbing the Universe* (New York: Harper, 1979), 211; C. S. Lewis, *That Hideous Strength* (1945; rpt. New York: Macmillan, 1965), 7.

40. Lilian Bowes-Lyon to OS, 9 June 1947 (SA); Norman Cullen, interview with author, 11 Oct. 1989.

41. J. H. Blackham, "Youth and Tomorrow," *Plan* 13 (Aug. 1946), 8.

42. *YT*, 42, 21.

43. OS, notes for "Youth and the New World" (SA).

44. *YT*, 71.

45. *YT*, 15.

46. E. W. Martin to OS, 4 Nov. 1946; SA. Martin's essay "Between the Devil and the Deep Sea: The Philosophy of Olaf Stapledon" appeared in *The Pleasure Ground: A Miscellany of English Writing*, ed. Malcolm Elwin (London: MacDonald, 1947), 204–16.

47. OS to Miron Grindea, 8 July 1946; *Adam International* Archive, King's College, London.

48. Naomi Mitchison to OS, undated (SA).

49. OS to Fay Pomerance, 23 Dec. 1946 (P).

50. Valentine Ackland, "Books," *Our Time* 6 (Nov. 1946), 89; "Man's Blind Search," *Times Literary Supplement*, 14 Sept. 1946, p. 437; Rayner Heppenstall, "New Novels," *New Statesman*, 14 Sept. 1946, p. 192.

51. OS to AS, 3 June 1946 (STP).

52. I depend on several accounts of the congress's business sessions: Henry Baerlein, "The P.E.N. Congress in Sweden," *Manchester Guardian*, 13 June 1946, p. 8; "Notes on the P.E.N. Congress," *Time and Tide*, 22 June 1946, p. 583; and three articles by OS: "Writers Confer at Stockholm," *New Statesman*, 22 June 1946, pp. 447–48; "The P.E.N. Congress at Stockholm," *Adam International Review* (June–July 1946), p. 11, and "The Pen and the Sword," *Author* 57 (Autumn 1946), 4–6. His handwritten notes labeled "Stockholm" (SA, STAP D.I.22D) contain a draft of his Russian resolution, not printed in any newspaper account.

53. OS, "Writers Confer," 447–48; "Pen and Sword," 6.

54. Peter Albery to OS, 30 May 1946 (SA).

55. OS, "What Philosophy Means to Me," recorded 2 May 1946 for broadcast on 5 June in the series "The Kingdom of the Mind," BBC Eastern Service Purple Network; transcript in BBC Written Archives Centre, Caversham Park, Reading.

56. Quotations from "The Peak and the Town" follow the version first printed in the Satty-Smith *Bibliography*, xxxvi, xxxvii, xxxviii. Other unpublished drafts, including the typescript labeled "The Journey," are in SA, STAP D.I.21(1–3).

57. Peter Albery to OS, 5 Nov. 1946 (SA).

58. A Correspondent, "The Present Question Conference," [London] *Record,* 30 Aug. 1946, p. 497.

59. OS to Fay Pomerance, 2 Sept. 1947 (P).

60. H. Westmann, "Introduction," *The Present Question* (London: Chapman and Hall, 1947), 2.

61. OS to AS, 21 Aug. 1946 (SFP).

62. Gwenda Hollander, interview with author, 3 Oct. 1989.

63. Fay Pomerance, letter to author, 17 Feb. 1988.

64. Interviews with author, 23 Aug. 1983, 16 Oct. 1989. The person designated here and hereafter as N. does not wish to be identified.

17. Doors Out, Doors In, 1947–1948

1. N. to OS, 18 Sept. 1946. For reasons of confidentiality, locations of the few surviving letters from N. to OS and to AS are not given. Nearly all OS's letters to N. have been destroyed; much in this chapter is based on interviews with N. and with members of the Stapledon family.

2. Mary Shenai, interview with author, 17 Oct. 1989; Mary Shenai, letter to author, 15 Apr. 1991.

3. OS to D. Kilham Roberts, 15 May 1946; Society of Authors Papers, British Library. John and Sarina Stapledon, interview with author, 9 Oct. 1989.

4. The notebook, which also contains early sketches for *OE,* is in SA, STAP B.16(4). "A Modern Magician" and "The Man Who Became a Tree" appeared in *FFC.*

5. Fredric Warburg to OS, 26 July 1946; Secker and Warburg Archives, University of Reading.

6. Fredric Warburg to OS, 17 July 1946 (Reading).

7. OS to Fredric Warburg, 28 July 1946 (Reading).

8. OS to Fredric Warburg, 20 July, 24 July, 28 July, and 1 Aug. 1946 (Reading).

9. Mulk Raj Anand to OS, 14 Apr. 1947 (SA).

10. Sarina Stapledon, interview with author, 8 Oct. 1989. OS to AS, 27 Mar. 1947 (SFP).

11. OS, "Personal Relations in the Family," *Monthly Record of the South Place Ethical Society* 51 (May 1946), 10–11. The lecture was given 7 Apr.

12. "Panacea for Parents," [Oxford] *Isis,* 11 June 1947, p. 11; OS, "Beyond Christian Morality?" *Common Wealth Review* 4 (Sept. 1947), 4.

13. "Experiments in Marriage," *Liverpool Echo,* 16 Dec. 1947, p. 4; the *Liverpool Post* and the *Liverpool Evening Express* both editorialized against OS's speech the next day.

14. [London] *Daily Express,* 17 Dec. 1947, p. 3; "Science," *Time,* 18 Oct. 1948, p. 70.

15. OS to Aage Marcus, 26 Dec. 1947 (SA). The telegram and three letters from *ALLT* are in SA, STAP H.V.A4.

16. Two drafts, labeled "The Varieties of Marriage" and "Marriage (Swedish article)", are in SA, STAP D.III.5. The published version is "Är Otroheten Befogad?" *ALLT* (March–April 1948); seen only in the OS scrapbook (SA).

17. OS to AS, 24 June 1948 (SFP).

18. AS to OS, 5 July 1948 (SFP).

19. OS to AS, 8 July 1948 (SFP).

20. OS to AS, 8 July 1948 (SFP). "A Scientist" in *FE,* 184–85. The "Four Encounters," written in 1947 and published posthumously, were the only sections drafted for a planned book of imaginary conversations.

21. AS to OS, 11 July 1948 (SFP).

22. N., interview with author, Jan. 1991.

23. Draft of a 1948 letter of OS to N. The shorthand draft is in SFP; the letter actually sent, like the others to N., no longer exists.

24. OS to AS, 5 July 1948 (SFP).

25. "Earth Invaded from Sun," *Johannesburg Star,* 15 Sept. 1947, p. 6; "The Flames," *Daily Worker,* 21 Aug. 1947, p. 4; N. N., "Fit for Flames," *John O'London's Weekly,* 19 Sept. 1947, p. 609; John Betjeman, "The Flames," *Daily Herald,* 26 Aug. 1947, p. 2; P. H. Newby, "New Novels," *Listener,* 16 Oct. 1947, p. 693.

26. Secker and Warburg ledgers, University of Reading. Notes for the Manchester talk on "Science and Fiction" are in SA. See also Robert Crossley, "Olaf Stapledon and the Idea of Science Fiction," *Modern Fiction Studies* 32 (Spring 1986), 21–42.

27. OS to Fay Pomerance, 4 Mar. 1947 (P).

28. OS to John Gloag, as quoted in Gloag's preface to *The First One and Twenty* (London: Allen and Unwin, 1946), vii.

29. OS to Fay Pomerance, 23 Dec. 1946 (P).

30. OS to Fay Pomerance, 1 Oct. 1947 (P). C. S. Lewis, "On Science Fiction" in *Of Other Worlds: Essays and Stories,* ed. Walter Hooper (1966; rpt. New York: Harcourt, 1975), 62–63. Brian Stableford takes 1950 as the terminal date for the British tradition; see his *Scientific Romance in Britain 1890–1950* (London: Fourth Estate, 1985), 321–31.

31. OS to AM, 28 Oct. 1913; *TATW,* xxxvii.

32. OS to AM, 4 Feb. 1919 (SFP).

33. *LFM* manuscript, SA; *PL,* vol. 2, pp. 456–57.

34. OS to Fay Pomerance, 2 Sept. 1947 (P).

35. OS to Aage Marcus, 21 Aug. and 24 Dec. 1947 (SA). OS to AS, 2, 4, and 5 Sept. 1943 (SFP).

36. Aage Marcus to OS, 12 Aug. 1947, 23 Jan. 1948; OS to Aage Marcus, 6 Feb. 1948 (SA).

37. OS, "Scepticism and the Modern World," *World Review,* Feb. 1948, p. 55. Norman Colgan's interview of OS appeared as "Science Finds a New Universe," *Prediction* 15 (Aug. 1949), 14–16.

38. The case for taking the paranormal seriously is made in OS's two articles, "Data for a World View: 1. The Human Situation and Natural Science," *Enquiry* 1, no. 1 (Apr. 1948), 13–18, and "Data for a World View: 2. Paranormal Experience," *Enquiry* 1, no. 2 (July 1948), 13–18. He discussed the sociological and moral consequences of unleashed psychic power in "Man's Future," *Prediction* 14 (Apr. 1949), 4–6.

39. A. C. R., "The Brighton Conference," *Plan* 17 (Apr. 1949), 12.

40. Colgan, "Science Finds a New Universe," 16.

41. Details of the French tour come from three typescripts ("Mankind at the Crossroads," "Comments on French Tour," and "Thoughts After Visiting France"; SA, STAP D.I.10) and several sets of lecture notes in SA (three versions of "Art and Society" and a dinner-talk for the London PEN, "France and Britain and the Rebirth of Europe"). A file of correspondence relevant to the tour is in SA, STAP H.VI.C.5.

42. OS, "Letters to the Future," ed. Robert Crossley, in *The Legacy of Olaf Stapledon,* ed. Patrick A. McCarthy et al. (New York: Greenwood, 1989), 118.

18. Pilgrim's Progress, 1948–1949

1. OS to Aage Marcus, 9 Nov. 1948 (SA).

2. Hermon Ould to OS, 29 July 1948 (SA).

3. Public sources on the Wroclaw Congress include: Ivor Montagu's highly partisan *What Happened at Wroclaw* (London: British Cultural Committee for Peace, 1948); "Intellectuals' Con-

ference," [London] *Times* , 26 Aug. 1948, p. 3; "Intellectuals of the World, Unite!" *Daily Express,* 26 Aug. 1948, p. 3; "Russian Attack on U.S.," *New York Herald Tribune* [Paris edition], 26 Aug. 1948, p. 2; Kingsley Martin, "Hyenas and Other Reptiles," *New Statesman,* 4 Sept. 1948, 187–88; "Congress of Intellectuals, Wroclaw, August 1948: A Forum," *Our Time* 7 (Oct. 1948), 336–41 [including a piece by OS on p. 340]; and OS, "The Wroclaw Congress," *Common Wealth Review* 6 (Nov. 1948) 10.

4. OS to AS, 26 Aug. 1948 (SFP). Juliette Huxley's four-page typescript is in the Julian Huxley Papers (106:4) at Rice University.

5. OS's speech, "Address on Peace and Culture" with handwritten notes on Fadeyev, is in SA, STAP D.I.22(15). He recalled events in notes for a talk, "East & West, and Wroclaw" (SA).

6. OS typescript, "Address on Peace and Culture," SA (STAP D.I.22 [15]).

7. Juliette Huxley, typescript; Julian Huxley, memorandum on "Breslau Congress"; Julian Huxley Papers (106:6), Rice University.

8. Kingsley Martin, "Hyenas and Other Reptiles," 187. The Czech response is quoted in a letter to the *New Statesman* from J. W. Bruegel, 11 Sept. 1948, p. 216. Of Kingsley Martin, OS had said to Hermon Ould, "Between you and me I don't think he has much of an opinion of my work" (OS to Ould, 17 May 1946, PEN).

9. Confidential communications from the American Embassy, Warsaw, to the U.S. Department of State, 27 Aug. and 1 Sept. 1948, National Archives, Washington, D.C. (doc. 800.00B/8-2448 and 800.00B/9-148). Richard T. Davies, one of the Foreign Service observers, recalled events at Wroclaw in "The View from Poland" in *Witnesses to the Origins of the Cold War,* ed. Thomas T. Hammond (Seattle: Univ. of Washington Press, 1982), 267–70.

10. OS, "A New Unity is Born," in the *Our Time* forum, 340; Montagu, *What Happened at Wroclaw,* 12.

11. Julian Huxley, typescript of "Breslau Congress"; Julian Huxley Papers (106:6), Rice University.

12. "Wroclaw Congress," unpublished letter of OS, 20 Sept. 1948, to the editor of the *New Statesman* (SA). There had been ongoing correspondence in the *New Statesman* about Wroclaw, but Kingsley Martin apparently decided to end it.

13. The text of the resolution is in Montagu, *What Happened at Wroclaw,* 26–27.

14. Alan Taylor to Julian Huxley, 1 Sept. 1948; Julian Huxley Papers (17:10), Rice University.

15. A. J. P. Taylor, "Correspondence," *New Statesman,* 18 Sept. 1948, p. 239.

16. The minority report is printed by the artist Feliks Topolski in his *Confessions of a Congress Delegate* (London: Gallery Editions, 1949), 22; OS to AS, 27 Aug. 1948 (SFP).

17. OS, "A New Unity," 340. A pencil note on his typescript "The Wroclaw Congress" (SA, STAP D.I.22B) indicates it was prepared for *New Poland,* but there is no evidence of publication.

18. OS to Hermon Ould, 27 Dec. 1948, PEN.

19. OS to Aage Marcus, 9 Nov. 1948 (SA).

20. Arthur C. Clarke to OS, 19 and 26 Apr. 1948; SA, STAP H.VI.A; Winifred Primrose, interview with author, 15 June 1982.

21. A text of "Interplanetary Man?" appeared in *Journal of the British Interplanetary Society* 7 (Nov. 1948), 213–33; reprinted, *FFC,* 209–52. My summary depends on the printed version and notes for the platform version (SA, STAP F.51).

22. The cartoon accompanies "By Jupiter, What a Prospect," [London] *News Chronicle,* 11 Oct. 1948, p. 3; "Science," *Time,* 18 Oct. 1948, 69–70; "Emigrants to Mars," *News Review,* 14 Oct. 1948 (the last seen only in OS scrapbook, SA).

23. "A New War to Worry About—Invasion from Other Planets," *New York Herald Tribune* [Paris edition], 12 Oct. 1948, p. 3.

24. A brief biography of Lilian Bowes-Lyon is included in James Wentworth Day's *The Queen Mother's Family Story* (London: Robert Hale, 1967), 119–29.

25. *OE,* 11. The unnamed "friend" who appears in sec. 8–11 of *OE* is Lilian Bowes-Lyon.

26. *OE,* 14–15.

27. From one of many drafts out of which *OE* was constructed, SA STAP B.16(15). The passage is not in *OE* as published.

28. From another of the *OE* notebooks, SA STAP B.16(10).

29. Shorthand draft of a letter from OS to AS, 5 July 1948 (SFP).

30. Draft of a letter from OS to N. (SFP).

31. N. to AS, 5 Feb. 1949.

32. AS to OS, 15 and 16 Feb. 1949 (SFP).

33. Lilian Bowes-Lyon to OS, 26 Feb. 1949 (SFP).

34. OS to AS, 21 Feb. 1949 (SFP).

35. Evelyn Gibson to OS, 17 Feb. 1949 (SFP).

36. Telegram from U.S. Department of State to U.S. Embassy, London; National Archives, doc. 800.00B/3-1049.

37. A transcript of the Walter Winchell broadcast is in a secret file assembled by the State Department on 21 Feb. 1949 on the National Council of the Arts, Societies and Professions; National Archives, Diplomatic Branch, doc. 811.42761/2-2149.

38. Dorothy Thompson to Dean Acheson, 18 Mar. 1949; National Archives, Diplomatic Branch, doc. 800.00B/3-1849.

39. Reported by the hostess, Fay Pomerance, in a letter to me, 2 May 1988.

40. OS to Fay Pomerance, 8 Mar. 1949 (P).

41. "U.S.A. Bans Three Britons, But Lets Russians In" [London] *Evening Standard,* 22 Mar. 1949, p. 1.

42. "Laughter by the Russians," *Liverpool Echo,* 23 Mar. 1949, p. 5.

43. OS to AS, 28 Mar. 1949 (SFP).

44. OS to AS, 28 Mar. 1949 (SFP).

45. Seymour Freidin, " 'Peace' Rally Opens at Waldorf," *New York Herald Tribune,* 26 Mar. 1949, p. 1; "N.Y. Peace Rally Gets Under Way," *Montreal Star,* 26 Mar. 1949, p. 1; FBI report on the Waldorf speech, FBI doc. #NY100-93553. Two versions of the dinner speech, "Education for Peace in Britain," are in SA: one done by OS's typist in England and amended in his hand for delivery, the other for press release done by a typist in New York. Both typescripts differ from the text of "From England," printed in the conference proceedings, *Speaking of Peace,* ed. Daniel S. Gillmor (New York: Cultural and Scientific Conference for World Peace, 1949), 130–31.

46. Irving Howe, "The Culture Conference," *Partisan Review* 16 (May 1949), 507; William Barrett, "Culture Conference at the Waldorf," *Commentary* 8 (May 1949), 491; Dwight Macdonald, "The Waldorf Conference," *Horizon* [London] 19 (May 1949), 313, 326.

47. Dwight Macdonald, "Communist Peace Conferences and Pacifism," [London] *Peace News,* 14 Apr. 1949, p. 4.

48. Sidney Hook, *Out of Step: An Unquiet Life in the 20th Century* (New York: Harper, 1987), 382–96.

49. Harlow Shapley to Dorothy Canfield Fisher, 15 Mar. 1949; Shapley Papers, Pusey Library, Harvard University, HUG 4773.10, Box 10C.

50. For two versions of this episode, see Hook, *Out of Step,* 391–92, and Mac R. Johnson, "Hook Invades Shapley's Room," *New York Herald Tribune,* 26 Mar. 1949, pp. 1–2.

51. From OS's unpublished typescript of "Peace and War in New York," SA; whether this practical joke was Hook's idea is a matter of speculation, but OS had no doubt that it was the product of the organized opposition to the conference.

52. OS to AS, 28–29 Mar. 1949 (SFP).

53. Dorothy Doan to OS, 29 Mar. 1949 (SA).

54. OS to AS, 28 Mar. 1949 (SFP). "Red Visitors Cause Rumpus," *Life,* 4 Apr. 1949, pp. 39–43. "*Press* lies": Notes for a talk on "Peace and Recent Conferences," 1949 (SA).

55. "Global Unity Call," *New York Times,* 28 Mar. 1949, p. 1; Price Day, " 'Peace' Rally Condemns All Military Alliances," *Baltimore Sun,* 28 Mar. 1949, p. 7; Alistair Cooke, " 'Intellectuals' At a Mass Meeting," *Manchester Guardian,* 29 Mar. 1949, p. 5; "Cultural Congress Climax," *Oxford Mail,* 28 Mar. 1949, p. 1; "18,000 Join Final 'Peace' Session," *Liverpool Echo,* 28 Mar. 1949, p. 3; *Testimony: The Memoirs of Dmitri Shostakovich,* as related to and edited by Solomon Volkov, trans. Antonina W. Bouis (New York: Harper, 1979), 148.

56. No official response to the protest came until 14 April, when Assistant Secretary of State George V. Allen wrote to Shapley. The State Department, maintaining that the Russians and East Europeans came to New York as "officials of foreign governments," stated that none of those governments requested travel outside Manhattan. Incredibly, Allen scolded Shapley and the Council of Arts, Sciences, and Professions for meddling in Soviet affairs: "Private organizations should not presume to speak on behalf of foreign governments in matters of this kind." National Archives, Diplomatic Branch, doc. FW 800.00B/32950.

57. Sam Moskowitz, "Peace and Olaf Stapledon," *FFC,* 267–68. Newark newspapers made no mention of OS's speech, and Moskowitz' detailed but politically unsympathetic narrative is the chief record; I have also used the account "Communists Tour of U.S. Called Off," *Worcester Telegram,* 30 Mar. 1949.

58. OS discussed Miller's play in a talk on "The Conflict of Values" given to the National Peace Council, London, July 1949; in revised form it appeared in *Two Worlds in Focus: Studies of the Cold War* (London: National Peace Council, 1950), 44–60.

59. Theodore Sturgeon to OS, 1 Apr. 1949; Frederick Pohl to OS, 23 Mar. 1949. Forrest Ackerman learned of OS's appeal for a $25 advance from the Fantasy Publishing Co. of Los Angeles—which was bringing out an omnibus edition of *OMNW, DIL,* and *FL*—and put up the $25 himself, while alerting other writers to OS's plight (Ackerman to OS, 21 Mar. 1949). All these letters are in a special file of correspondence from science-fiction writers in SA (H.II.A.33) For a brief account of the club by a member who recalls the night OS came, see Harry Harrison, "The Beginning of the Affair" in *Hell's Cartographers: Some Personal Histories of Science Fiction Writers,* ed. Harry Harrison and Brian W. Aldiss (New York: Harper, 1975), 80.

60. Events at the Lyric Theater were reported in the Sunday *Baltimore Sun,* 3 Apr. 1949, pp. 30, 22. Details on OS's press conference come from an April report (exact date illegible) prepared by an FBI agent in Baltimore; FBI doc. #100-356137-446. See also, "Plea for Peace Made by Ewe Tribe Prince," *Baltimore Evening Sun,* 4 Apr. 1949, p. 26.

61. OS, typed text for a cable, "Greetings to Dr. Harlow Shapley," SA (STAP H.III).

62. Kingsley Martin to OS, 21 Apr. 1949, SA (STAP H.VI.4); OS to Martin, 24 Apr. 1949, *New Statesman* Archive (Univ. of Sussex).

63. OS, "Peace and War in New York," *New Statesman,* 30 Apr. 1949, p. 433; "Peace and War" typescript (SA); Mona Scholefield-Allen, interview with author, 19 Oct. 1989.

64. Telegram from Dean Acheson to American Embassy, Paris, 29 Mar. 1949; National Archives, Washington, D.C.; Diplomatic Branch, doc. 800.00B/3-2949.

65. Ella Winter wrote to OS on 4 May 1949 to tell him what had happened after he left Paris and reported the failure of "your psychopathic professor" to rouse much attention (SA). A recent account of the Paris meeting is in Howard Fast's memoir, *Being Red* (Boston: Houghton Mifflin, 1990), 212–221.

66. OS, typescript headed "Olaf Stapledon, England" for delivery at Paris Peace Conference, 20 Apr. 1949 (SA).

67. OS, typescript, "Peace Conferences in New York and Paris" (SA).

68. OS to Aage Marcus, 27 Apr. 1949 (SA).

69. OS to Aage Marcus, 27 Apr. 1949 (SA).
70. "The Journey" (SA STAP D.I.21) was published posthumously as "The Peak and the Town" in Harvey J. Satty and Curtis C. Smith, *Olaf Stapledon: A Bibliography* (Westport: Greenwood, 1984), xxvii–xxxviii.

19. To the Riverside, 1949–1950

1. OS to Aage Marcus, 27 Apr. 1949 (SA).
2. Quoted in Jill Benton, *Naomi Mitchison: A Century of Experiment in Life and Letters* (London: Pandora, 1990), 141.
3. OS to Rev. C. C. J. Butlin, 26 Apr. 1950 (photocopy, SA, STAP H.I.B.31).
4. OS, "Americans Look to Us for Peace," *Peace News,* 8 July 1949, p. 6; "National Peace Council Conference," *Peace News,* 31 Mar. 1950, p. 6.
5. OS to AS, 7 June 1949 (SFP); N., interview with author, Jan. 1991.
6. OS to AS, 25 July 1949 (SFP).
7. N. H. Partridge, "History Is Theirs—5" [London] *News Chronicle,* 24 Jan. 1950, p. 2.
8. Norman Colgan, "Science Finds a New Universe," *Prediction* 15 (Aug. 1949), 16; E. V. Rieu, preface to *OE,* viii; Mary Shenai, interview with author, 1 Oct. 1989.
9. OS to Fay Pomerance, 8 Mar. 1949 (P); lecture notes for "Art and Society" (SA).
10. *MD,* 2; *OE,* 4.
11. *NHB,* 111; on the same page he also observes that "it was the Great War which undermined the old patriotism." On Ethiopia see also OS, "Abyssinia's Plight: Four Suggested Policies," *Liverpool Daily Post,* 18 May 1936, p. 4; on India see his letter "India and Britain," *Manchester Guardian,* 13 Mar. 1941, p. 10.
12. OS diary, 5 Apr., 8 May 1949 (SA); *OE,* 68. A carbon typescript labeled "The Trenton New Jersey Case" is in a miscellaneous file in SA (H.VIII.B.15[2]).
13. "The Human Crisis in Africa," *Peace News,* 16 June 1950, pp. 1, 8; "The Human Crisis in Africa," *One World* 3 (June–July 1950), 151–54.
14. OS, "Power Through Philosophy," *Humanity Now* 9 (Spring 1950), 12. The lecture on which the printed article was based was given on 3 Nov. 1949 (diary, SA).
15. OS, "Personality and Liberty," *Philosophy* 24 (Apr. 1949), 4.
16. OS, "The Meaning of 'Spirit,' " *Here and Now: Miscellany No. 5,* ed. Peter Albery and Sylvia Read (London: Falcon, 1949), 72, 79. The *Spectator's* review of this "banal" and "grey" miscellany (17 Feb. 1950, p. 226) hailed OS as a "sage" demeaned by the company he was required to keep.
17. *MD,* 179.
18. In *Olaf Stapledon: A Man Divided* (New York: Oxford Univ. Press, 1983) Leslie Fiedler follows this route to disastrous results. He reads the novel as a psychoanalytical map of the novelist's supposed pathology, but when events do not match the author's life, Fiedler complains of an "odd commingling" of fact and fiction, "as if deliberately to confuse us" (pp. 206–207).
19. *MD,* 132–33.
20. OS to Mary Stapledon, 13 May 1943 (SFP). AS understood Maggie to be partly modeled on herself; see Patrick A. McCarthy, *Olaf Stapledon* (Boston: Twayne, 1982), 119.
21. For a sample of negative views see "Original," *Daily Worker,* 25 May 1950, p. 1; "Portraits of Personality," *Glasgow Bulletin,* 6 May 1950, p. 5; David Bateman, "A Saint in Paris," [Cardiff] *Western Mail,* 17 May 1950, p. 3; J. Betjeman, "If This Is Your Sort of Book," [London] *Daily Herald,* 17 May 1950, p. 6; A. M. Atkinson, "A Modern Jekyll and Hyde," *Liverpool Post,* 23 May 1950, p. 3.

22. Richard Church, "A Man Named Smith," *John O'London's Weekly*, 9 June 1950, p. 349.

23. Naomi Mitchison to OS, 13 June [1950] (SA).

24. *OE*, 4; comments on the manuscript are in letters from Arthur Davenport to OS, 19 and 23 Jan. 1950 (SA).

25. OS to Gwynneth Alban-Davis, 3 Aug. 1950 (P).

26. OS to Wolfgang Brueck, 25 May 1950 (P).

27. OS's June 1950 letter to Naomi Mitchison has disappeared, but she quoted portions in an obituary she wrote for *Humanity Now* 9 (Winter 1950), 15. The painting "Nowhere on Earth" has not surfaced. Three of OS's late paintings can be accounted for: the dock scene and a painting of Simon's Field are with the Stapledon heirs; the King's Cross picture was given to me by its former owner.

28. *OE*, 19–20.

29. *OE*, 23.

30. *OE*, 49.

31. OS, "Notes on Being in the Chair" (P).

32. Mary Shenai, interview with author, 19 Jan. 1991.

33. Wolfgang Brueck, interview with author, 17 Mar. 1989; "Cominform Charges of Aggression," [London] *Times*, 18 July 1950, p. 5; Kenneth Ingram, *Fifty Years of the National Peace Council, 1908–1958* (London: National Peace Council, 1958), p. 20.

34. OS to Naomi Mitchison, June 1950, as cited in *Humanity Now*, 15.

35. AS to George Allen, 8 Oct. 1950; Allen Papers, University College, London.

36. OS to Gwynneth Alban-Davis, 5 Sept. 1950 (P).

37. OS, "Our Common Shame," from a manuscript dated Jan. 1925 in the unpublished "Verse by WOS" (SA).

38. *OE* manuscript (SA STAP B.16[15]); *OE*, 83.

39. OS diary, 20 Jan. 1907 (SA).

40. OS, "Power Through Philosophy," 12; OS, "Some Comments on the Ways of Peace," *One World* 3 (Oct.–Nov. 1950), 185.

41. OS, manuscript, "In the London Streets" (SA).

42. Ritchie Calder, "Olaf Stapledon: Father of the Super Man," [London] *News Chronicle*, 8 Sept. 1950, p. 2; "The Quest for Truth," [London] *Times*, 8 Sept. 1950, p. 6; *Time*, 18 Sept. 1950, p. 102; "Olaf Stapledon, Fighter for Peace Is Dead," *Daily Worker*, 8 Sept. 1950, p. 1; [Leonard Martin] "Dr. William Olaf Stapledon," *Manchester Guardian*, 8 Sept. 1950, p. 5; "Olaf Stapledon," *Plan* 18 (Oct. 1950), 2.

43. Memorial program (SFP).

SELECTED BIBLIOGRAPHY

Primary Sources

A nearly complete record of Stapledon's published works, including posthumous publications, translations, and reprints, is available in Harvey J. Satty and Curtis C. Smith's indispensable *Olaf Stapledon: A Bibliography* (Westport, Conn. and London: Greenwood, 1984). The most significant and representative works of his career are listed here.

Fiction

"The Seed and the Flower." *Friends' Quarterly Examiner* 50 (Oct. 1916): 464–75.
Last and First Men: A Story of the Near and Far Future. London: Methuen, 1930.
Last Men in London. London: Methuen, 1932.
Odd John: A Story Between Jest and Earnest. London: Methuen, 1935.
Star Maker. London: Methuen, 1937.
Darkness and the Light. London: Methuen, 1942.
Old Man in New World. London: Allen and Unwin [PEN Books], 1944.
Sirius: A Fantasy of Love and Discord. London: Secker and Warburg, 1944.
Death Into Life. London: Methuen, 1946.
The Flames: A Fantasy. London: Secker and Warburg, 1947.
A Man Divided. London: Methuen, 1950.
Far Future Calling: Uncollected Science Fiction and Fantasies of Olaf Stapledon, edited by Sam Moskowitz. Philadelphia: Oswald Train, 1979. [Includes five short stories and the script for an unproduced radio play based on *Last and First Men*.]
Nebula Maker introduced by Arthur C. Clarke, and *Four Encounters*, introduced by Brian W. Aldiss. New York: Dodd, Mead, 1983.
"The Peak and the Town." In *Olaf Stapledon: A Bibliography*, edited by Harvey J. Satty and Curtis C. Smith, xxvii–xxxviii. Westport, Conn.: Greenwood, 1984.

Memoirs and Letters

"The Novice Schoolmaster." *Old Abbotsholmian* 3, no. 1 (1910): 14–18.
"The Road to the Aide Post." *F[riends] A[mbulance] U[nit] Monthly Magazine* 1 (Jan. 1916): 11–14.
"Experiences in the Friends' Ambulance Unit." In *We Did Not Fight: 1914–1918 Experiences of War Resisters,* edited by Julian Bell, 359–74. London: Cobden-Sanderson, 1935.
"The Letters of Olaf Stapledon and H. G. Wells, 1931–1942," edited by Robert Crossley. In *Science Fiction Dialogues,* edited by Gary Wolfe, 27–57. Chicago: Academy Chicago, 1982.
Talking Across the World: The Love Letters of Olaf Stapledon and Agnes Miller, 1913–1919, edited by Robert Crossley. Hanover, N.H.: Univ. Press of New England, 1987.
"Letters to the Future," edited by Robert Crossley. In *The Legacy of Olaf Stapledon: Critical Essays and an Unpublished Manuscript,* edited by Patrick A. McCarthy, Charles Elkins, and Martin Harry Greenberg, 99–120. New York and London: Greenwood, 1989.

Other Nonfiction Prose

"The Most Splendid Race." *Old Abbotsholmian* 2, no. 7 (1907): 159–61.
"The Splendid Race." *Old Abbotsholmian* 2, no. 8 (1908): 212–16.
"The People, Self Educator." *Old Abbotsholmian* 3, no. 12 (1913): 203–207.
"Poetry and the Worker." *Highway* 6 (Oct. 1913): 4–6.
"The Reflections of an Ambulance Orderly." *Friend,* 14 Apr. 1916, 246.
"Rhyme, Assonance and Vowel Contrast." *Poetry* 7 (Aug.–Sept. 1924): 194–96.
"Problem of Universals." *Monist* 34 (Oct. 1924): 574–98.
"Mr. Bertrand Russell's Ethical Beliefs." *International Journal of Ethics* 37 (July 1927): 390–402.
"Theory of the Unconscious." *Monist* 37 (Oct. 1927): 422–44.
"The Location of Physical Objects." *Journal of Philosophical Studies* 4 (Jan. 1929): 64–75.
A Modern Theory of Ethics: A Study of the Relations of Ethics and Psychology. London: Methuen, 1929.
"The Remaking of Man." *Listener,* 8 Apr. 1931, 575–76.
"Problems and Solutions, or the Future." In *An Outline for Boys and Girls and Their Parents,* edited by Naomi Mitchison, 691–749. London: Gollancz, 1932.
Waking World. London: Methuen, 1934.
"Education and World Citizenship." In *Manifesto: Being the Book of the Federation of Progressive Societies and Individuals,* edited by C. E. M. Joad, 142–63. London: Allen and Unwin, 1934.
"Science, Art and Society." *London Mercury* 38 (Oct. 1938): 521–28.
Philosophy and Living 2 vols. Harmondsworth, U.K.: Penguin, 1939.

Saints and Revolutionaries [*I Believe*, no. 10]. London: Heinemann, 1939.

New Hope for Britain. London: Methuen, 1939.

"Writers and Politics." *Scrutiny* 8 (Sept. 1939): 151–56.

"Escapism in Literature." *Scrutiny* 8 (Dec. 1939): 298–308.

"Federalism and Socialism." In *Federal Union: A Symposium,* edited by M. Chaning-Pearce, 115–29. London: Cape, 1940.

"Tradition and Innovation To-Day." *Scrutiny* 9 (June 1940): 33–45.

Beyond the "Isms" [Searchlight Books no. 16]. London: Secker and Warburg, 1942.

"Literature and the Unity of Man." In *Writers in Freedom: A Symposium,* edited by Hermon Ould, 113–19. London: Hutchinson, 1942.

"Sketch-Map of Human Nature." *Philosophy* 17 (July 1942): 210–30.

"Morality, Scepticism and Theism." *Proceedings of the Aristotelian Society,* n. s. 44 (1943–44): 15-42.

"The Great Certainty." In *In Search of Faith: A Symposium,* edited by Ernest W. Martin, 37–59. London: Lindsay Drummond, 1944.

Seven Pillars of Peace. London: Common Wealth, 1944.

"What *Are* 'Spiritual' Values?" In *Freedom of Expression: A Symposium,* edited by Hermon Ould, 16–26. London: Hutchinson, 1945.

"Planning and Liberty: Talks With the Troops." *London Quarterly of World Affairs* 11 (Oct. 1945): 245–53.

"Social Implications of Atomic Power." *Norseman* 3 (Nov.–Dec. 1945): 390–93.

Youth and Tomorrow. London: St. Botolph, 1946.

"Reconstruction in Holland." *Contemporary Review* 169 (Feb. 1946): 71–76.

"Education for Personality-in-Community." *New Era in Home and School* 27 (Mar. 1946): 63–67.

"Writers Confer at Stockholm." *New Statesman,* 22 June 1946, 447–48.

"Liberty and Discipline." *Modern Education* 1 (Apr. 1947): 109–11.

"Data for a World View: 1. The Human Situation and Natural Science." *Enquiry* 1 (Apr. 1948): 13–18.

"Data for a World View: 2. Paranormal Experiences." *Enquiry* 1 (July 1948): 13–18.

"The Wroclaw Congress." *Common Wealth Review* 6 (Nov. 1948): 10.

"Interplanetary Man?" *Journal of the British Interplanetary Society* 7 (Nov. 1948): 212–33.

"Ethical Values Common to East and West" and "From England." In *Speaking of Peace,* edited by Daniel Gillmor, 119–21, 130–31. New York: National Council of the Arts, Sciences and Professions, 1949.

"Peace and War in New York." *New Statesman,* 30 Apr. 1949, 432–33.

"The Peaceful Temper." *One World* 3 (June–July 1949): 54–57.

"The Meaning of 'Spirit.' " In *Here and Now: Miscellany No. 5,* edited by Peter Albery and Sylvia Read, 72–82. London: Falcon, 1950.

"A Plain Man Talks About Values." *Rider's Review* 76 (Spring 1950): 22–28.

"The Conflict of Values—The Bridge Between." In *Two Worlds in Focus: Studies of the Cold War,* 44–60. London: National Peace Council, 1950.

The Opening of the Eyes, edited by Agnes Z. Stapledon. London: Methuen, 1954.

Poems

"The Builder." *Old Abbotsholmian* 3, no. 11 (1912): 169.
"A Prayer." *Highway* 5 (Oct. 1912): 5.
Latter-Day Psalms. Liverpool: Henry Young, 1914.
Poets of Merseyside: An Anthology of Present-Day Liverpool Poetry, edited by S. Fowler
    Wright. London: Merton, 1923. [Contains eight poems by Stapledon: "God the
    Artist," "Creator Creatus," "A Prophet's Tragedy," "The Good," "Revolt Against
    Death," "The Unknown," "Futility," "The Relativity of Beauty," 93–100.]
Voices on the Wind, Second Series, edited by S. Fowler Wright. London: Merton, 1924.
    [Contains five poems by Stapledon: "Pain," "Swallows at Maffrecourt,"
    "Moriturus," "A Prophet's Tragedy," "God the Artist," 165–67.]
"Two Chinese Poems." *Poetry of To-Day: A Quarterly "Extra" of the Poetry Review*,
    no. 3 (Winter 1925): 18.
"Star Worship." *Poetry and the Play* 9 (July–Sept. 1926): 527.
"Squire to Knight." *The Two Houses* [Beechcroft Settlement Magazine] 1 (Oct. 1927): 11.
"Be Absolute." *Adelphi* 15 (Sept. 1939): 571.
"Paradox." *Adelphi* 16 (Mar. 1940): 247.

Secondary Sources

A secondary bibliography is being compiled by Harvey Satty and Curtis C. Smith, but
no full-scale bibliography of works about Stapledon has yet been published. Some of
the most significant studies of the past sixty years are listed below.

Aldiss, Brian W. "In Orbit With the Star Maker." *Times Literary Supplement*, 23 Sept.
    1983, 1007–8.
———. *The Pale Shadow of Science*, 51–60. Seattle: Serconia, 1985.
———. Foreword to *Star Maker: 50th Anniversary Edition*, ix–xiv. Los Angeles:
    Tarcher, 1987.
Aldiss, Brian W., with David Wingrove. "In the Clutches of the Zeitgeist." Chapter 8
    in *Trillion Year Spree: The History of Science Fiction*. New York: Atheneum, 1986.
Bailey, K. V. "A Prized Harmony: Myth, Symbol and Dialectic in the Novels of Olaf
    Stapledon." *Foundation* 15 (Jan. 1979): 53–66.
———. "Time Scales and Culture Cycles in Olaf Stapledon." *Foundation* 46 (Autumn
    1989): 27–39.
Bengels, Barbara. "Olaf Stapledon's 'Odd John' and 'Sirius': Ascent into Bestiality."
    Foundation 9 (Nov. 1975): 57–61.
Borges, Jorge Luis. Introduction to *Createur d'Etoiles*, 13–15. Paris: Editions Planete,
    1966.
Branham, Robert. "Stapledon's 'Agnostic Mysticism.'" *Science-Fiction Studies* 9 (Nov.
    1982): 249–56.
Brophy, John. "Writers of Merseyside: W. Olaf Stapledon." *Liverpolitan* 2 (Jan. 1933):
    20.

Casillo, Robert. "Olaf Stapledon and John Ruskin." *Science-Fiction Studies* 9 (Nov. 1982): 306–21.

Clark, Stephen R. L. "Olaf Stapledon: Philosopher and Fabulist." *Chronicles* 10 (Dec. 1986): 14–18.

Clarke, Arthur C. Introduction to Olaf Stapledon, *Nebula Maker and Four Encounters*, vii–x. New York: Dodd, Mead, 1983.

Coates, J. B. "Olaf Stapledon." In *Ten Modern Prophets*. London: Frederick Muller, 1946.

Crossley, Robert. "Famous Mythical Beasts: Olaf Stapledon and H. G. Wells." *Georgia Review* 36 (Fall 1982): 619–39.

———. "Politics and the Artist: The Aesthetic of *Darkness and the Light*." *Science-Fiction Studies* 9 (Nov. 1982): 294–305.

———. "Olaf Stapledon and the Idea of Science Fiction." *Modern Fiction Studies* 32 (Spring 1986): 21–42.

———. "Censorship, Disguise, and Transfiguration: The Making and Revising of Stapledon's *Sirius*." *Science-Fiction Studies* 20 (Mar. 1993): 1–14.

Davenport, Basil. Introduction to *To The End of Time: The Best of Olaf Stapledon*, vii–xix. New York: Funk and Wagnalls, 1953.

Elkins, Charles. "The Worlds of Olaf Stapledon: Myth or Fiction?" *Mosaic* 13 (Spring/ Summer 1980): 145–52.

———. " 'Seeing It Whole': Olaf Stapledon and the Issue of Totality." In *The Legacy of Olaf Stapledon: Critical Essays and an Unpublished Manuscript*, edited by Patrick A. McCarthy, Charles Elkins, and Martin Harry Greenberg, 53–66. New York: Greenwood, 1989.

Fiedler, Leslie A. *Olaf Stapledon: A Man Divided*. New York: Oxford Univ. Press, 1983.

Gillings, W. H. "The Philosopher of Fantasy." *The British Scientifiction Fantasy Review* 1, no. 3 (June 1937): 8–10.

Glicksohn, Susan. "A City of Which the Stars Are Suburbs." In *SF: The Other Side of Realism*, edited by Thomas D. Clareson, 334–47. Bowling Green, Ohio: Bowling Green Univ. Popular Press, 1971.

Goodheart, Eugene. "Olaf Stapledon's *Last and First Men*." In *No Place Else: Explorations in Utopian and Dystopian Fiction*, edited by Eric S. Rabkin, Martin H. Greenberg, and Joseph D. Olander, 78–93. Carbondale: Southern Illinois Univ. Press, 1983.

Herr, Cheryl. "Convention and Spirit in Stapledon's Fiction." In *The Legacy of Olaf Stapledon: Critical Essays and an Unpublished Manuscript*, edited by Patrick A. McCarthy, Charles Elkins, and Martin Harry Greenberg, 23–38. New York: Greenwood, 1989.

Huntington, John. "Olaf Stapledon and the Novel About the Future." *Contemporary Literature* 22 (Summer 1981): 349–65.

——— "Remembrance of Things to Come: Narrative Technique in *Last and First Men*." *Science-Fiction Studies* 9 (Nov. 1982): 257–64.

Kinnaird, John. *Olaf Stapledon*. Mercer Island, Wash.: Starmont, 1986.

Lem, Stanislaw. "On Stapledon's *Last and First Men*." Translated by Istvan Csicsery-Ronay, Jr. *Science-Fiction Studies* 13 (Nov. 1986): 272–91.

————. "On Stapledon's *Star Maker.*" Translated by Istvan Csicsery-Ronay, Jr. *Science-Fiction Studies* 14 (Mar. 1987): 1–8.

Lessing, Doris. Afterword to *Last and First Men,* 305–307. Los Angeles: Tarcher, 1988.

Martin, E. W. "Between the Devil and the Deep Sea: The Philosophy of Olaf Stapledon." In *The Pleasure Ground: A Miscellany of English Writing,* edited by Malcolm Elwin, 204–16. London: MacDonald, 1947.

McCarthy, Patrick A. *Olaf Stapledon.* Boston: Twayne, 1982.

————. "*Last and First Men* as Miltonic Epic." *Science-Fiction Studies* 11 (Nov. 1984): 244–52.

————. "Stapledon and Literary Modernism." In *The Legacy of Olaf Stapledon: Critical Essays and an Unpublished Manuscript,* edited by Patrick A. McCarthy, Charles Elkins, and Martin Harry Greenberg, 39–52. New York: Greenwood, 1989.

McCarthy, Patrick A., Charles Elkins, and Martin Harry Greenberg, eds. *The Legacy of Olaf Stapledon: Critical Essays and an Unpublished Manuscript.* New York: Greenwood, 1989.

Mitchison, Naomi. "Human Personalities: Olaf Stapledon." *Humanity Now* 9 (Winter 1950): 13–15.

————. *You May Well Ask: A Memoir 1920–1940,* 138–42. London: Gollancz, 1979.

Moskowitz, Sam. "Olaf Stapledon: Cosmic Philosopher." In *Explorers of the Infinite: Shapers of Science Fiction.* New York: World, 1963.

————. "Olaf Stapledon: The Man Behind the Works" and "Peace and Olaf Stapledon." In *Far Future Calling: Uncollected Science Fiction and Fantasies of Olaf Stapledon,* 15–69, 253–75. Philadelphia: Oswald Train, 1979.

Rabkin, Eric. "The Composite Fiction of Olaf Stapledon." *Science-Fiction Studies* 9 (Nov. 1982): 238–48.

"Red Visitors Cause Rumpus." *Life,* 4 Apr. 1949, 39–43.

Russell, Bertrand. "War in the Heavens." *London Mercury* 36 (July 1937): 297–98.

Rutledge, Amelia A. "*Star Maker:* The Agnostic Quest." *Science-Fiction Studies* 9 (Nov. 1982): 274–83.

Satty, Harvey J., and Curtis C. Smith. Introduction to *Last Men in London,* v–xiv. Boston: G. K. Hall, 1975.

Scholes, Robert. *Structural Fabulation: An Essay on Fiction of the Future,* 62–67. Notre Dame, Ind.: Notre Dame Univ. Press, 1975.

Shelton, Robert. "The Mars-Begotten Men of Olaf Stapledon." *Science-Fiction Studies* 11 (Mar. 1984): 1–14.

————. "The Moral Philosophy of Olaf Stapledon." In *The Legacy of Olaf Stapledon: Critical Essays and an Unpublished Manuscript,* edited by Patrick A. McCarthy, Charles Elkins, and Martin Harry Greenberg, 5–22. New York: Greenwood, 1989.

Smith, Curtis C. "Olaf Stapledon: Saint and Revolutionary." *Extrapolation* 13 (1971): 5–15.

————. "Olaf Stapledon's Dispassionate Objectivity." In *Voices for the Future,* edited by Thomas D. Clareson, 44–63. Bowling Green, Ohio: Bowling Green Univ. Popular Press, 1976.

————. "The Manuscript of *Last and First Men:* Toward a Variorum." *Science-Fiction Studies* 9 (Nov. 1982): 265–73.

———. "Horror vs. Tragedy: Mary Shelley's *Frankenstein* and Olaf Stapledon's *Sirius.*" *Extrapolation* 26 (Spring 1985): 66–73.

———. "Olaf Stapledon and the Immortal Spirit." In *Death and the Serpent: Immortality in Science Fiction and Fantasy,* edited by Carl B. Yoke and Donald M. Hassler, 103–13. Westport, Conn.: Greenwood, 1985.

———. "Diabolical Intelligence and (Approximately) Divine Innocence." In *The Legacy of Olaf Stapledon: Critical Essays and an Unpublished Manuscript,* edited by Patrick A. McCarthy, Charles Elkins, and Martin Harry Greenberg, 87–98. New York: Greenwood, 1989.

Stableford, Brian. "The Major Writers Between the Wars" and "After the Holocaust." In *Scientific Romance in Britain, 1890–1950,* 198–216; 277–81. London: Fourth Estate, 1985.

Swanson, Roy Arthur. "The Spiritual Factor in *Odd John* and *Sirius.*" *Science-Fiction Studies* 9 (Nov. 1982): 284–93.

Tremaine, Louis. "Olaf Stapledon's Note on Magnitude." *Extrapolation* 23 (Nov. 1982): 243–53.

———. "Historical Consciousness in Stapledon and Malraux." *Science-Fiction Studies* 11 (July 1984): 130–38.

———. "Ritual Experience in *Odd John* and *Sirius.*" In *The Legacy of Olaf Stapledon: Critical Essays and an Unpublished Manuscript,* edited by Patrick A. McCarthy, Charles Elkins, and Martin Harry Greenberg, 67–86. New York: Greenwood, 1989.

INDEX